DIGITAL SYSTEMS:
Hardware Organization and Design

DIGITAL SYSTEMS: Hardware Organization and Design

Fredrick J. Hill
Professor of Electrical Engineering
University of Arizona

Gerald R. Peterson
Professor of Electrical Engineering
University of Arizona

John Wiley & Sons, Inc. New York London Sydney Toronto

Library of Congress Cataloging in Publication Data:

Hill, Fredrick J.
Digital systems: hardware organization and design.

Includes bibliographical references.
1. Electronic digital computers—Design and construction.
I. Peterson, Gerald R., joint author. II. Title.

TK7888.3.H5 621.3819 58 2 72-6418

Printed in the United States of America

10 9 8 7 6

Preface

The need for a book on digital computer hardware design that is really an engineering textbook has been evident for some time. Traditionally, engineering texts are concerned with imparting a skill, with teaching the student how to do something. By contrast, most books on computer design are little more than descriptive surveys of existing computer hardware. In reading such books the student is an observer rather than a participant.

In this book it is our intent to involve the student in the design process rather than just describe the end product. The principal vehicle for this involvement is a register-transfer and control-sequence design language. Various such languages have been proposed, but none have met with any general acceptance. We have chosen to use a version of APL (A Programming Language), which we consider to be an unusually powerful and flexible language. Its flexibility is amply illustrated by the fact that it has achieved wide success as an interactive programming language even though it was originally developed as a means of describing computer organization. Also, its basic structural similarity to other high-level programming languages makes it accessible to a wider class of students than would be the case with a more specialized hardware language. Using this language we have attempted to explore the design of a wide variety of digital hardware systems. We have presented concrete design examples as liberally as possible throughout the book.

This book has been written for the computer scientist and systems programmer, as well as the electrical engineer. Undoubtedly, many users of this book will never be responsible for actual hardware design, but the design point of view is a fascinating one even for the student whose primary objective is to gain familiarity with hardware organization and system architecture. The authors have used the text in classes divided almost equally between computer science students with no engineering background and electrical engineering students with prior courses in switching theory and electronics. The response from both groups has been positive and most gratifying.

PREFACE

The only topics specifically prerequisite to the book are programming in some high-level language, the binary number system, Boolean algebra, and Karnaugh maps. Appendices covering the latter three topics were originally planned, but have fallen victim to the need to keep the size of the book within reasonable bounds. We assume that the instructor will have no trouble presenting a brief introduction to these topics if necessary. The material covered in Chapters 2, 4, and 6 of our book on switching theory* would be ample for this purpose. With the addition of this material, the only prerequisites for a course based on this book would be programming experience, a certain degree of intellectual maturity, and a serious interest in computers.

The electrical engineer who hopes to design digital hardware should master switching theory and sequential circuits, as well as the material presented in this book. For such students a prior course covering material similar in scope to the first thirteen chapters of our switching theory book is highly desirable. The engineer on his first job is far more likely to be confronted with the logical design of a small system of sequential circuits than with the design of a complete computer.

Chapters 4 through 8 of this book are critical. The principal example in these chapters is a small computer, the basic description and assembly language of which are presented in Chapter 2.

Once through Chapter 8, the instructor has some freedom in selecting the order of presentation of the remaining chapters. The three chapters on computer arithmetic are somewhat interrelated. Chapter 10 and some topics in Chapter 14 require the conventions established in Chapter 9. Chapter 15 contains some interesting design examples, which the instructor may wish to use in conjunction with or closely following Chapters 7 and 8. Between ten and thirteen chapters can be covered in a one-semester course. Most of the book could be covered in a two-quarter course. For a two-semester course, the authors recommend supplementing the book with a comparison of the characteristics of some existing machines. A variety of computer reference manuals would be helpful in this regard.

We hope that this book introduces system into the design process. In no sense does it reduce this process to a cookbook procedure. A premium is placed on the imagination of the designer. This will be immediately evident in the problem sets of Chapter 6 and subsequent chapters. A variety of problems is essential to any meaningful course, and the authors have attempted to include a broad selection. Problem solution, however, has not been reduced to the formalism of switching theory. For many problems a variety of correct solutions are possible.

* F. J. Hill and G. R. Peterson, *Introduction to Switching Theory and Logical Design*, Wiley, New York, 1968.

We have defined a very close correspondence between our version of APL and particular digital circuits. The criticism might be made that APL was devised as hardware-independent language. If used that way, it would permit the use of powerful hardware translation programs. However, our purpose is to teach the design process for digital systems. A program for automatic translation of the APL description to hardware can be (and has been) written, but this must be regarded as secondary. Only after the design process is understood should one be concerned with trying to automate it.

Tucson, Arizona

FREDRICK J. HILL
GERALD R. PETERSON

Contents

1

Introduction

1.1. OBJECTIVES OF THE BOOK

The proper approach to teaching digital hardware systems has been the subject of considerable debate. That the debaters have been unsure of their respective positions is evidenced by the scarcity of textbooks on this subject. Those books which are intended to cover the subject fall into one of three categories: (1) largely software, (2) primarily switching theory, (3) descriptive material only. It is the authors' contention that the first two categories describe subjects really quite distinct from, although related to, digital hardware. Books in the third category fail because they do not involve the reader in the design process. They don't give him "anything to do."

Our primary resolve in writing this book has been to avoid merely describing computer hardware. We have chosen the *control sequence* as the vehicle by which the reader will participate in the design experience. We have borrowed a technique from software in that we shall write control sequences in higher language form. The control sequences are easily translated into control unit hardware. Once this is accomplished, the *digital system*, except for electronic circuit details, is designed.

We have used the term digital system without providing a definition. In the broadest sense, *digital* simply means that information is represented by signals that take on a limited number of discrete values and is processed by devices that normally function only in a limited number of discrete states. Further, the lack of practical devices capable of functioning reliably in more than two discrete states has resulted in the vast majority of digital devices being binary, i.e., having signals and states limited to two discrete values. Any structure of physical devices assembled to process or transmit digital information may be termed a digital system. This includes, e.g., teletypes, dial telephone switching exchanges, telemetering systems, tape transports and other peripheral equipments, and, of course, computers. Often the word *system* is thought of as implying a large or complex system. For the present our definition will be the broader one just presented. In later chapters *large* or *complex* may find its way into our meaning of *system* as we seek to distinguish a complete computing facility from its various components, such as a memory unit.

The characteristics of digital systems vary, and the approach to their design sometimes varies as well. Consider the very general model of a digital system shown in Fig. 1.1. Although in practice the distinction may not

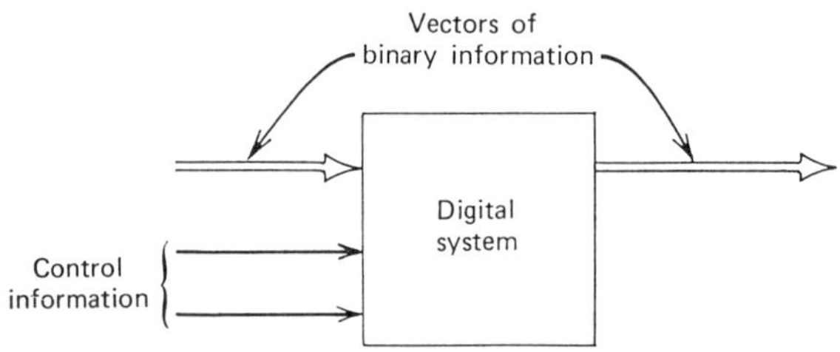

FIGURE 1.1. Types of digital information

always be apparent, we shall arbitrarily separate the information which enters and leaves a digital system into two categories: (1) information to be processed or transmitted and (2) control information. Information in the first category usually occurs in the form of a time sequence of information vectors. A vector might be a *byte*, eight binary bits; it might be a word of 16–64 bits; or it might be several words. In any case a large number of wires are required to handle a vector in a physical system. Usually the bits of a vector are treated within the system in some uniform manner, rather than each bit in a completely separate way.

The second category, control information, usually occurs in smaller quantities, involving physically one to a very small number of wires. Control information is self-defining. It is information which guides the digital system in performing its function. Sometimes control information is received only. In other cases control pulses are sent out to control the function of some other equipment.

Certain digital systems handle only control information. The controller for an elevator is a good example. Systems of this type may be designed as *sequential circuits*. The procedures for sequential circuit design are well defined and are discussed in a number of introductory textbooks. See, for example, References [3] and [4]. Classical sequential circuit techniques have not proven satisfactory for designing systems to process vectors of information. Consequently computers have never been designed that way.

The control portion of a more general digital system is a sequential circuit and may be treated as such. For more complex systems, particularly computers, the portion which may be treated effectively as a classical sequential circuit is a relatively small part of the whole. Even certain kinds of control information can be assembled into vectors and transmitted and stored as such. Our approach has been to restrict control hardware to a few standard forms, which may be analyzed once and used repeatedly. We are then in a position to investigate and develop design procedures for most any form of equipment for processing information vectors.

Digital computers certainly form the most important class of digital systems. Virtually every day we are reminded of the ways in which computers have basically altered our society, and the case for their importance can hardly be overstated. In this book we shall be primarily concerned with digital computers and their peripheral equipments for two reasons. First, computers are the most important type of digital system. Second, virtually every aspect of digital design is encountered in computer design, so that the person well-versed in computer design should be capable of designing any type of digital system.

For the computer scientist, whose primary interest is software, this book may stand alone as an engaging (we hope) introduction to the philosophy of hardware design. With more imaginative use of microprogramming, the overlap of hardware and software functions becomes increasingly apparent. A familiarity with hardware at the level of detail presented herein will be increasingly required of individuals going into the area of systems programming.

For the electrical engineer it is certainly not our intention to minimize the importance of a companion course in switching theory and sequential circuits. As contrasted with the computer scientist, the electrical engineer has the responsibility of making the hardware work. Particular circuit technologies generate intricate fundamental-mode problems in situations which have been idealized in this volume. Interface (connection between digital equipments) design will continue to occupy ever-increasing amounts of engineering effort. This area will always overlap system techniques (see Chapters 9 and 10), sequential circuits, and even circuit design. The computer engineer should have coursework background in all three of these areas.

1.2. EVOLUTION OF THE COMPUTER

Various definitions, more or less formal, have been put forth for the computer. The following six criteria, which will be interpreted as a block diagram in the next section, describe most of the important features of a computer:

1. It must have an *input* medium, by means of which an essentially unlimited number of operands or instructions may be entered.
2. It must have a *store*, from which operands or instructions may be obtained, and into which results may be entered, *in any desired order.*
3. It must have a *calculating* section, capable of carrying out arithmetic or logical operations on any operands taken from the store.
4. It must have an *output* medium, by means of which an essentially unlimited number of results may be delivered to the user.
5. It must have a *decision* capability, by means of which it may choose between alternate courses of action on the basis of computed results.
6. Data and instructions shall be stored in the same form, in the same memory, equally accessible to the calculating elements of the machine, so that the machine may treat instructions as data and thereby modify its own instructions.

The first five of the listed features were set forth by Charles Babbage in 1830 as the description of a machine which he called the Analytical Engine.

Babbage, an eccentric English mathematician, was one of the most fascinating characters in the history of science. He was concerned with improving the methods of computing mathematical tables. Until the advent of the digital computers, mathematical tables were computed by teams of mathematicians, grinding away endlessly at desk calculators, performing the same calculations over and over to produce the thousands of entries in tables of logarithms, trigonometric functions, etc. Babbage was working on some improved log tables, and so despaired at ever getting the job done that he resolved to build a machine to do it.

The result of his first efforts was the Difference Engine, the first description of which he published in 1822. The difference engine was funded by the British government and was partially completed before Babbage observed the need for features 3 and 5 in the list above. Storage as well as input was to utilize punched cards, which had been invented by Jacquard in 1801. This also provided the decision capability, since the machine could decide which instruction card was next to be brought into control on the basis of computed results.

Babbage first started work on the Analytical Engine about 1830; and the remainder of his life (he died in 1871) was spent in a fruitless effort to get the machine built. His ideas were a hundred years ahead of technology. The mechanical technology of the day was inadequate to meet the requirements of his designs. Indeed, it is doubtful if the Analytical Engine could be realized by mechanical means even today. The realization of Charles Babbage's dreams had to await the development of electronics.

In 1937, Howard Aiken, of Harvard University, proposed the Automatic Sequence Controlled Calculator, based on a combination of Babbage's ideas and the technology of the electromechanical calculators then being produced by IBM. Construction of this machine, more generally known as Mark I, was started in 1939, sponsored jointly by Harvard and IBM. The completed machine was dedicated August 7, 1944, a date considered by many to mark the start of the computer era.

Mark I was primarily electromechanical, being constructed mostly of switches and relays, a factor which severely limited its speed. Scientists at the Aberdeen Proving Ground, concerned with the development of ballistic tables for new weapons systems, recognized the need for a faster computer than Mark I. As a result, a contract was awarded in 1943 to the University of Pennsylvania to develop a digital computer using vacuum tubes instead of relays. The result was ENIAC, the world's first electronic digital computer. The same group that developed ENIAC, directed by J. P. Eckert and J. W. Mauchly, later developed the first commercially-produced computer, UNIVAC I, the first unit of which was delivered in 1951.

The sixth feature in the list presented at the beginning of this section is a suggestion made by John Von Neumann, of Princeton, in 1947. This feature is included in UNIVAC I and virtually all subsequent machines. Actually modifying the instructions is a far more powerful capability than simply being able to choose between alternate instructions.

In the succeeding years, the power and speed of computers has increased by many orders of magnitude; and computers now exercise a pervasive influence on modern society. But the improvements in computers have been due chiefly to improved devices and technology. The basic organization of most computers still conforms closely to the criteria laid down by Babbage and Von Neumann.

1.3. BASIC ORGANIZATION OF DIGITAL COMPUTERS

Any computer meeting the criteria set forth in the previous section will be basically organized as shown in Fig. 1.2. The exact nature of the components making up the five basic sections of the computer may vary widely, and the sections may overlap or share components; but the five functions associated with the five sections may be clearly identified in any digital computer.

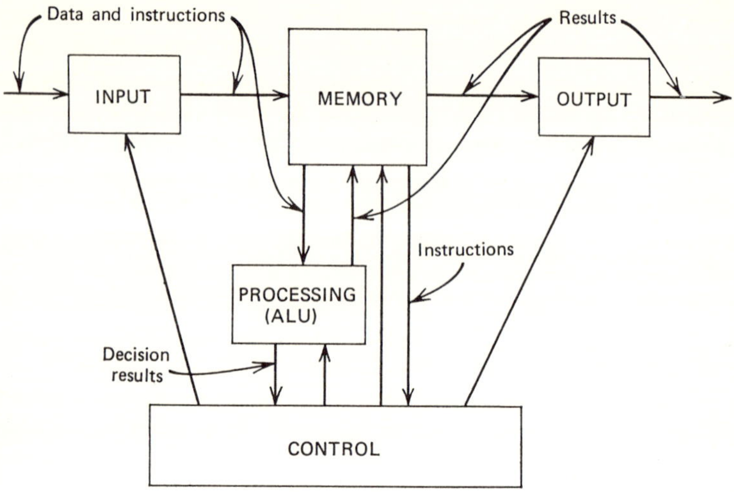

FIGURE 1.2. Basic computer organization.

The memory is the central element of the computer, in the sense that it is the source or destination of all information flowing to or from the other four sections of the computer. The memory may be regarded as a collection of storage locations for information; with each location is associated an *address*, by means of which that location may be accessed by the other sections of the computer. The amount of information that can be stored in an individually addressable location, expressed in terms of the number of bits (binary digits), is known as the *word length* of the memory. Nomenclature here is sometimes confusing, and you will hear such terms as *byte-organized* and *variable word length* applied to memory. Whatever the type of organization, we use *memory word* to signify the smallest amount of information that can be individually accessed, or addressed, in memory. Word lengths in various modern computers typically range from about eight bits to sixty-four bits.

A great variety of devices is used for memory, ranging from fast, low-capacity devices with a high cost per bit, to slow, high-capacity devices with a low cost per bit. A single computer may employ a whole hierarchy of memory devices of varying speed/capacity ratios. The main memory, i.e., that portion of memory in most direct communication with the control and processing sections, is usually a high-speed random access memory with a capacity in the range of about 4000 to a million or more words. This may be backed up by any number of slower devices, such as disk or tape, which may make bulk transfers of large numbers of words to or from main memory.

The basic functions of the input and output sections are quite obvious; but they have two subsidiary functions, buffering and data conversion, which are not quite so obvious. The buffering function provides the interface between the very fast processing section and the comparatively slow "outside world." For example, a human operator may punch data onto cards at a rate of a few characters per second. A stack of these cards may be read onto tape at a rate of a thousand characters per second. The tape may then be read into main memory at a rate of 100,000 characters per second, and main memory can communicate with the processing unit at the rate of a million words per second.

The data conversion can be illustrated in the same example. When the operator punches written information onto cards, it is converted into the Hollerith code. While the Hollerith code is fine for punched cards, it is not particularly suitable for magnetic tape; so the characters are translated to another code as they are transferred to tape. While tapes are character-organized, main memory is word-organized, with a word generally made up of several characters. So the characters are grouped into words as the tape is read into memory. The reverse operations take place on output.

The processing section, which we shall refer to as the arithmetic-logical unit (ALU), implements the various arithmetic and logical operations on operands obtained from memory. ALU's vary considerably in the number of different operations implemented. The minimum possible set of operations for a general purpose computer is a subject of some theoretical interest; as few as two may be sufficient, but most ALU's have a repertory in the range of 16 to 64 commands.

The control section receives instruction words from memory, decodes them, and issues the appropriate control signals to the other sections to cause the desired operations to take place. It also receives the results of various tests on data made by the ALU, on the basis of which it may choose between alternate courses of action. Von Neumann's criterion is satisfied since the ALU can process any word it receives from memory, and the control unit can cause any word in memory, data or instruction, to be sent to the ALU. The combination of the ALU and the control unit is often referred to as the *central processing unit* (CPU).

1.4. INSTRUCTION FORMATS

We can get an idea of what information must be included in an instruction word by considering how we might give instructions to a person who is to do some computing for us. We could provide him with a ledger sheet of data and a sheet of instructions. Then a typical instruction might read, "Take a number from column 1, add it to a number in column 2, enter the sum in 3, and proceed to line 4 of the instruction sheet for the next step." In computer terms, this is a *four-address* instruction.

An instruction word, which is simply a string of 0's and 1's, is divided up into several sections, each of which is interpreted to have some specific significance by the control unit. The format of a four-address instruction is shown in Fig. 1.3a. The *op code* is the numeric code, typically four to six bits, indicating the operation—add, subtract, shift, etc.—to be performed. The remainder of the word provides the four addresses in memory required for the two operands, the result, and the next instruction.

The main problem with the four-address instruction is the amount of space required to accommodate four addresses. Since accessing instructions takes

(a)

Op code	Operand address	Operand address	Result address	Instruction address

(b)

Op code	Operand address	Operand address	Result or instruction address

(c)

Op code	Operand address	Operand or instruction address

(d)

Op code	Operand or instruction address

FIGURE 1.3. Typical instruction formats.

time, it is highly desirable that only one memory access be required to obtain an instruction. Thus the pressure is strong to limit the complexity of the instructions so they may fit into a single memory word. The size of an address is determined by the size of the memory; the more locations in memory, the more bits will be required to specify an address. For example, a 32,000-word memory—a typical size—requires 15-bit addresses; so a four-address instruction will require sixty bits just for addresses. Only the very largest machines have memory words this long.

The number of addresses in the instruction word can be reduced by letting some of the information be "understood." Computer programs usually proceed in a fixed sequence most of the time, branching to an alternate path only occasionally. We therefore specify that the instructions shall be stored in sequentially numbered locations; and the next instruction will be taken from the next sequential location, unless otherwise specified. This concept leads to the three-address instruction (Fig. 1.3b), which will typically have the meaning,

"Take the operands from the first two addresses, store the result at the third address, and take the next instruction from the next sequential location." Deviation from the fixed sequence requires a *branch* instruction, which could have the meaning, "Compare the operands taken from the first two addresses: if they are equal, take the next instruction from the third address; if not, take the next instruction from the next sequential location."

The number of required addresses can be further reduced by allowing the destination of the result to be "understood." The two-address instruction (Fig. 1.3c) takes on two standard forms.

The *replacement* instruction typically has the meaning, "Take the operands from the two addresses, store the result at the second address (replacing the second operand), and take the next instruction from the next sequential location." This type of instruction is inconvenient if both operands need to be preserved for further operations. The problem can be avoided by specifying a standard register in the ALU, usually known as the *accumulator*, as the destination for results. Then a typical two-address instruction will have the meaning, "Take the operands from the two addresses, place the result in the accumulator, and take the next instruction from the next sequential location." With this form we must also have a *store* instruction, of the form, "Store the contents of the accumulator in one of the two specified addresses." In either case, the branch instruction might take the form, "Compare the contents of the first address with the contents of the accumulator: if they are equal, take the next instruction from the second address; if not, take the next instruction from the next sequential location."

Finally, there is the single-address format (Fig. 1.3d), which allows the source of the second operand to be "understood." Now the typical instruction will have the meaning, "Take the first operand from the addressed location, the second from the accumulator, place the result in the accumulator, and take the next instruction from the next sequential location." A typical branch instruction might take the form, "Test the contents of the accumulator: if they are zero, take the instruction from the addressed location; if not, continue in sequence." Most machines also have an unconditional branch which causes the next instruction to be taken from the addressed location regardless of the contents of the accumulator.

The choice of an instruction format is a difficult one, requiring the balancing of a number of conflicting factors. The single-address is obviously most efficient in terms of the amount of memory space required for each instruction. However, a program written in single-address instructions will certainly have more instructions than a corresponding one written in multiple-address instructions. Obviously, the more information we can put in each instruction, the fewer instructions we require to accomplish a given task. But even this is not a simple relationship, since there are some types of instructions for which more than one address is not needed. The *store* instruction discussed earlier is an example. Another is the *shift* instruction, causing the contents of the accumulator to be shifted left or right a specified number of places. In this case, the "address" portion of the instruction is not an address at all, but may be interpreted as a binary number, indicating the number of places to be shifted.

In the class of small machines generally known as minicomputers, the word length is usually 16 to 20 bits, making the single-address format really the only practical choice. As we increase the word length, we obviously increase our options. In some large computers with long memory words, two or more single-address instructions may be packed into a single word, thus reducing the number of memory accesses required for fetching instructions. Other large machines use two-address instructions. Still others do both, placing two single-address or one two-address instruction in each word. This makes the control unit more complex, but gives the programmer more flexibility.

Three-address instructions are seldom, if ever, used for addressing memory directly. Several machines use shorter addresses to select the operands and destination from eight or more operating registers. Thus a three-address instruction can specify two operand registers and one result register, using only nine bits. This approach also requires a two-address format for transferring information between memory and the operating registers. We know of no machines using the four-address format.

The number of combinations and variations on these formats is practically unlimited, and virtually any combination or variation you might think of has probably been tried by somebody. However, the single-address format is used in more different models of computers than any other; and, except in the chapters on large computers, it is the format we shall use in this book.

1.5. SOFTWARE

Programs written in the form of instructions discussed in the previous section, strings of binary 1's and 0's, are known as *machine language* programs. All programs must be ultimately placed in this form, since these are the only kind of instructions the control unit can interpret. Writing programs in this form is incredibly difficult. First, binary strings are cumbersome, inconvenient, and downright unnatural to humans. Second, the programmer must assign binary addresses to all the data and instructions, and, even worse, keep track of all these addresses.

In the early days of computers, programmers had to work in machine language; and many despaired of computers ever being of much use because it was virtually impossible to get a really useful program running. As we know, the problem was solved by writing programs to get the computers to do most of the drudgery of programming. The class of "programs to process programs" is known collectively as software. Software is so important to successful operation of a computer that the success of a particular model is often determined more by the quality of the software than by the quality of the hardware, i.e., the machine itself. Many of the developments in computer organization have come about in response to the need for efficient processing of the software.

Software initially developed in a fairly natural and straightforward manner, but has recently become quite complex. As we noted, binary strings are inconvenient, if only because they are so long. It was thus a natural first step to convert instructions to octal form, treating each group of three bits as a binary number, and replacing each group with the equivalent octal digit. And it was a simple matter to equip the input section with the capability of converting each octal digit to the equivalent binary form.

Once we recognize that the computer can convert from one form to another, it is quite natural to replace the numeric op codes with mnemonic names, such as ADD, MULT, DIV, etc., and write a program to enable the computer to convert these names to the equivalent codes. Next, as we assign variables to memory locations, we make up a table giving the addresses corresponding to the variable names. In the address portion of the instructions we simply write the variable name, instead of the actual address. When we feed the program into the computer, we also feed in the address table, and let the computer replace variable names with the appropriate addresses.

Next we note that assigning addresses is a routine bookkeeping job, just as well given to the computer. Now our programs need contain little more than instructions consisting only of operation names and variable names. At this point, we have an *assembly language*. The program which assigns the addresses and converts the instructions to machine language form is known as an *assembler*.

Assembly language is an immense improvement over machine language, but there are still many problems. The main problem is that an assembly language is computer-oriented. Each assembly language statement corresponds to one machine language statement, so that the programmer must be familiar with the instructions and internal organization of the particular computer. Knowledge of how to program one computer will be of little value in programming any other computer. We would prefer a language in which we could write programs that could be run on virtually any computer. This leads us to the concept of *problem oriented* or *high-level* languages, such as FORTRAN, ALGOL, COBOL, PL/I, APL, etc.

Problem-oriented languages (POL) permit us to write programs in forms as close as possible to the natural, "human-oriented" languages that might be appropriate to the particular problems. Thus, a mathematical formula such as

$$s = (-b + \sqrt{b^2 - 4ac})/2a$$

may be evaluated by a single, closely analogous program statement in FORTRAN.

The evaluation of a formula such as the above will obviously require many machine language instructions. There are two distinct methods for converting POL programs into machine language programs. In one method, as the program is executed, each POL statement is converted into a corresponding set of machine language instructions, which are immediately executed, before proceeding to the next POL statement. A system functioning in this manner is known as an *interpreter.*

Interpreters are inefficient for programs with repetitive loops. For example, in FORTRAN we use DO loops to apply the same set of instructions over and over to a whole set of data. An interpreter has to translate the instructions in the DO loop on every pass through the loop, which is clearly inefficient since the translation is the same on every pass. This fault is corrected by *compilers*, which translate the complete POL program into a complete machine language program that is executed only after the complete program has been compiled.

Since interpreters and compilers translate into the machine language, they must be written separately for each computer. However, the compiler or interpreter for a given language may be written for any machine having adequate memory capacity to hold the software. Thus, a programmer writing in a popular language, such as FORTRAN, can run his program on practically any computer.

Another important class of software is the control program. In the early days of computers, each program run had to be initiated and terminated by an operator. With modern computers capable of executing a complete program in a fraction of a second, such human intervention is obviously impractical. So we have *executive* routines and *monitors*, which control the actual running of the computer. For example, a card reader may be loaded with large stacks of cards, representing hundreds of programs. The executive or monitor will separate the programs, assign them to tapes, schedule compilation and execution, assign memory, schedule printing, etc., all automatically. Except for dealing with emergencies, about all the operators have to do is load the cards and tear off the printer sheets.

There are many specialized types of software that we have not discussed. Although the hardware and software of a computer make up an integral and inseparable whole, software represents a complete area of study in itself. In this book we are concerned with software only to the extent that some understanding of software is essential to good hardware design. A knowledge of programming, at least in a problem-oriented language, is a prerequisite to this book; and any person seriously interested in computer design must also study software design.

1.6. SUMMARY AND OUTLOOK

In the past four sections, the organization of a computer may have come to seem fixed almost by divine revelation. Indeed some designers lament the lack of tolerance for variety in computer design. The accusation has been made that computers are designed out of habit. There may be truth in the charge, although the present state of affairs was probably forced by practical necessity. No other engineering creation requires of its users anything approximating the level of creative effort continually demanded of the computer programmer. Pressure will always be strong to resist innovations that tend to make obsolete the background and past efforts of programmers. This is especially the case in the context of the *general-purpose* computer. By general-purpose we shall refer to a machine designed to work with nearly equal efficiency on a variety of problems in a variety of high-level languages.

The engineer has more freedom in the design of a *special-purpose computer*. This is a machine which is designed to perform particularly well at one or a few specific tasks. A special-purpose computer is nonetheless a computer, as it will include all six features listed in Section 1.2. Output information might not be the familiar hard-copy printout, and the calculating section must be interpreted broadly; but both will be there. The range of special-purpose computers will vary from a fuzzy overlap with the general-purpose to a one-of-a-kind machine for a single job, with its own higher language (if one is used at all). The designer will, of course, have complete freedom in the design of the latter type machine.

The following is a list of the classes of digital systems which we have discussed thus far in this chapter:

1. General-purpose digital computer.
2. Special-purpose digital computer.
3. Vector-handling digital system (but not 1 or 2).
4. Sequential circuit (but not 1, 2, or 3).

The last two entries on the list are not computers. A magnetic tape unit, which falls into category 3, for example, is not a digital computer because its memory does not store instructions for controlling its internal operations.*

* The concept of microprogramming will force us to modify our concepts slightly, but we defer this topic until Chapter 8.

As mentioned earlier, the design techniques to be presented in this book may be applied to digital systems in any of the first three categories.

Our approach in Chapters 2, 6, and 7 will be to treat one design example in all its facets. In subsequent chapters and in the problems, many other examples will be treated more rapidly or in part. There are few arguments for choosing other than a general-purpose digital computer as the primary example. We have chosen a minicomputer with an 18-bit wordlength. A prerequisite of the design process is a detailed description of the system to be designed. For our minicomputer this description will consume all of Chapter 2. Background, definitions, and a language for the design process are presented in Chapters 3, 4, and 5. With the exception of the input and output facilities, the minicomputer is designed in Chapters 6 and 7.

REFERENCES

1. Morrison, P., and Morrison, E., editors, *Charles Babbage and His Calculating Engines*, Dover Publications, New York, 1961.
2. Bowden, B. V., *Faster than Thought*, Putnam, London, 1953.
3. Hill, F. J., and Peterson, G. R., *Introduction to Switching Theory and Logical Design*, Wiley, New York, 1968.
4. McClusky, E. J., *Introduction to the Theory of Switching Circuits*, McGraw-Hill, New York, 1965.
5. Aiken, H. H., "Proposed Automatic Calculating Machine," *IEEE Spectrum*, Vol. 1, August 1964, pp. 62–69.
6. Serrell, R., et al., "The Evolution of Computing Machines and Systems," *Proc. I.R.E.*, Vol. 50, May 1962, pp. 1040–1058.
7. Dill, F. Y., "Battle of the Giant Brains," *Popular Electronics*, Vol. 34, April 1971, pp. 39–43.

2

Organization and Programming of a Small Computer

2.1. INTRODUCTION

This chapter contains a discussion of the organization and assembly language programming of a minicomputer. At the risk of seeming trite we shall label this computer SIC for *Small Instructional Computer*. A name will prove convenient since frequent references to the machine will be necessary.

The previous background of readers in assembly language programming will vary greatly. For the reader whose only programming experience has been in FORTRAN, COBOL, or some other high-level language, this chapter is intended to serve two purposes. First, it will serve as a first introduction to assembly language programming. Second, it provides a description of a minicomputer sufficiently complete to serve as a basis for hardware design. The reader who is already familiar with assembly language programming should be able to move rapidly through the chapter. All readers must learn the organization and instruction codes of SIC so they can follow the design of the SIC control unit in Chapters 6 and 7.

Historically the development and use of computing machines preceded the invention of high-level languages. The development of these languages was heavily influenced by the already existing machine languages. FORTRAN, for example, is really a marriage of the notation of ordinary algebra with the control features of machine language. In this chapter we shall proceed in reverse to uncover the machine language counterparts of the basic FORTRAN operations. We shall not attempt to illustrate all of the procedures involved in machine language programming. Armed with an understanding of the relation between FORTRAN and machine language, the reader should be able to expound the list of machine language programming techniques to be presented. Some of the examples may resemble elementary compiler techniques. Our purpose is only to take maximum advantage of the reader's experience in a high-level language; compilers as such will not be treated in this book.

SIC is typical of several existing minicomputers. Left out of this machine are many of the sophistications found in computers intended for high-speed, maximum throughput batch-processing applications. All of the essential features which serve to identify a digital system as a general-purpose computer are included. We shall stay with this machine through the end of Chapter 7. In this way we hope to provide the reader with the basic tools of computer design without inundating him with details at the outset.

2.2. REMARKS ON NUMBER SYSTEMS

We assume that most readers will have had some previous experience with non-decimal number systems. One topic of the binary number system, namely that of handling negative numbers in two's-complement form, will appear several times in this chapter. We will, therefore, review it briefly in this section.

The most straightforward way to store in memory a binary number, which may be positive or negative, is in sign and magnitude form. If a memory location is capable of storing n binary bits, one of these bits must be used to store the sign; so only $n - 1$ bits are available to store the magnitude. The disadvantage of sign and magnitude form is that signs must be checked separately prior to every addition or subtraction operation.

This difficulty is avoided by storing all numbers in memory in two's-complement form. If a number is positive, the two's-complement of that number is merely the number itself. If a number, x, is negative, the two's-complement of x is given by Eq. 2.1:

$$\text{Two's-complement } (x) = 2^n - |x| \qquad (x < 0) \tag{2.1}$$

In this chapter n will be the number of bits in a storage location. In order to distinguish positive and negative numbers we require that $|x| < 2^{n-1}$. If this restriction is satisfied, the left-most bit of a positive number will always be 0.

Suppose $n = 6$. Then the number -25 (decimal) may be expressed in two's-complement form as follows. First, 25 expressed in six binary bits is 011001. Thus, using Eq. 2.1 we obtain

$$\begin{array}{r} 1000000 \\ -011001 \\ \hline 100111 \end{array} = \text{Two's-complement } (-25).$$

Notice that the left-most bit is a 1. This will always be the case for a negative x, where $|x| < 2^{n-1}$. That is,

$$2^n - |x| > 2^n - 2^{n-1} = 2^{n-1}. \tag{2.2}$$

We note that 2^{n-1} expressed as n binary bits has a 1 in the left-most bit and 0 in the other bits. From Eq. 2.2 we conclude that the left-most bit of $2^n - |x|$ must be 1 also.

The advantage of the two's-complement approach is that two's-complement addition is the same as the addition of two positive arguments. Suppose, for example, that a negative number, x, in two's-complement form is added to a positive number, y, of smaller magnitude as given in Eq. 2.3. The result is, as it should be,

$$(2^n - |x|) + y = 2^n - (|x| - y) \tag{2.3}$$

a negative number in two's-complement form. Whether the arguments are positive or negative, the result of an addition will always be the correct two's-complement form if the magnitude of the result remains $<2^{n-1}$. The four possible cases are illustrated in Fig. 2.1. Notice that in two of the

$(-25) + 15$	$25 + (-15)$	$(-15) + (-14)$	$15 + 14$
100111	011001	110001	001111
001111	110001	110010	001110
110110	1 001010	1 100011	011101

FIGURE 2.1. Examples of two's-complement addition.

examples of Fig. 2.1 a one appears in the seventh-bit position. Physically, two's-complement addition will be modulo-2^n. That is, the $(n + 1)$st bit will not fit in the accumulator and will not be considered part of the result. The reader can verify that the right-most six bits are the correct result in all cases.

Before leaving this section we remark that the binary and octal number system will be used almost interchangeably in this book. Octal numbers will be used to represent binary numbers for convenience. For example, an 18-bit binary number may be expressed much more compactly as a 6-digit octal number. The familiar method of determining the octal equivalent of a binary number by arranging bits into groups of three and replacing each by an octal digit is illustrated as follows.

001	010	011	100	101	110
1	2	3	4	5	6

The binary and octal numbers shown are equal. Justification of this method is left as a problem for the reader.

2.3. LAYOUT OF A SMALL INSTRUCTIONAL COMPUTER (SIC)

In Chapter 1 it was established that every computer includes a memory for storing instructions and data in binary form. Associated with each memory location is an address. The method by which an address is used electronically to obtain the contents of a memory location will be discussed in the next chapter. SIC has $2^{13} = 8192$ memory locations whose addresses are numbered from 0 to $2^{13} - 1$. These addresses will be referred to as binary numbers or octal numbers. In octal, the range of addresses is from 0 to 17777. Each item stored in memory, whether data or instruction, has the form of an *18-bit* binary number.

The large number of memory locations required indicates that the memory must be realized physically by a set of relatively inexpensive memory elements. The speed at which a machine can execute instructions is dependent on the time required to electronically select a location and acquire or replace its contents. A memory in which any location can be accessed in the same short time interval is called a random access memory (RAM). One example of a reasonably inexpensive random access memory is a magnetic core memory.

The control unit shown in Fig. 1.2 must be capable of storing some information in order to execute instructions. The binary representation of the instruction being executed is stored in an instruction register. The address of the next instruction in memory is stored in the program counter. An accumulator for storing the results of computations is included in the arithmetic section as suggested in Chapter 1. Two additional registers called index registers are included. Two registers which need not concern us until Chapter 6 are a memory address register and a memory data register. All of these registers consist of electronic storage elements which function at the highest possible speeds. A discussion of the purpose of these registers follows.

A. Program Counter

The machine language instructions making up a program must all reside in the random access memory of the machine in order for the program to be executed.* In any machine it is possible to load a short program into memory utilizing switches on the control console. Usually programs are loaded into memory from a card reader or a magnetic tape by a program called a *loader*, which might be part of the computer's software operating system. The *program counter* is a register which stores the address of the next instruction to be executed by the computer. At some point during the execution of most instructions the number in the program counter is increased by 1. Thus instructions are executed in the order of their locations in memory. The only exceptions occur in the event of machine language branch instructions analogous to the IF and GO TO statements. The program counter is a 13-bit register, in order that an instruction may be obtained from any of the 2^{13} memory locations.

B. Accumulator

The accumulator is utilized as temporary storage for the results of a computation. In some cases it may store one of the arguments as well. For example, addition is accomplished by adding a word from the random access memory to the contents of the accumulator and leaving the result in the accumulator. A 19th bit called the *link* is placed at left of the accumulator to facilitate various arithmetic operations.

C. Instruction Register

In order for an instruction to be executed it must be *read* from memory and placed in the *instruction register*. In this position the binary bits of the instruction are decoded to generate control signals, which are active throughout the period of execution. The instruction to be placed in the instruction register is determined by the contents of the program counter. The instruction register must store 18 bits.

D. Index Registers

Two index registers are included in the machine. We shall label these *Index Register A* and *Index Register B*. The contents of these registers may be added to the address portion of an instruction to permit repetition of that instruction on an array of data words. Special instructions are provided for incrementing the index registers following each pass through some sequence of instructions.

* The exception to this rule is memory overlays. However, it is not possible to jump directly from one overlay to an instruction in another overlay.

In effect this permits convenient execution of DO loops in FORTRAN. The mechanism of indexing will become clear in the next two sections. Index registers are 13-bit registers.

2.4. SIC INSTRUCTIONS

All 18 bits of an instruction word are necessary to completely define an instruction. Any 18-bit word placed in the instruction register will cause some sort of instruction to be executed. The computer cannot distinguish between

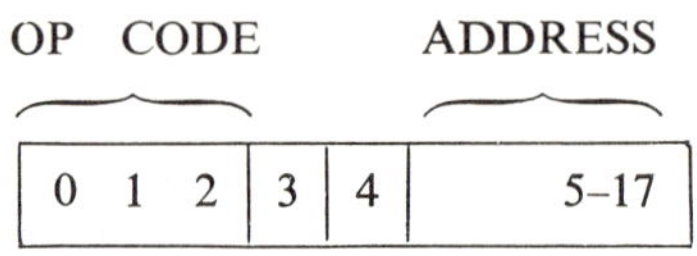

(a)

Bits 012	Octal	Mnemonic	Description
000	0	ISZ	Increment and skip if zero
001	1	LAC	Load accumulator
010	2	AND	Logical and
011	3	TAD	Two's-complement add
100	4	JMS	Jump to subroutine
101	5	DAC	Deposit accumulator
110	6	JMP	Jump (GO TO)
111	7	Operate or input/output instructions	

(b)

FIGURE 2.2. SIC memory reference instructions.

an instruction word and a data word. If a programmer error causes a data word to be executed, the subsequent results become meaningless.

As illustrated in Fig. 2.2, with one exception the first three bits of a SIC instruction identify the instruction. That exception is code 111, which indicates only that the instruction is one of many possible input/output (I/O) or operate instructions. The first seven instructions of Fig. 2.2b are *memory reference instructions*. Memory reference instructions may be distinguished from both input/output and operate instructions in that they always address an operand in the random access memory. Thus bits 5–17 are required to indicate the address of the operand in a memory reference instruction. Clearly SIC is a single-address machine. Where two arguments are used and a result is computed as in TAD, for example, one of the arguments is found in the accumulator and the result is placed in the accumulator.

No address need be specified for input/output or operate instructions. Bits 5–17 (also 3 and 4) may be used to further specify these instructions. Thus a very large number of input/output and operate instructions are possible. A list of important operate instructions will be presented later in this section. We shall defer the problem of input/output completely until Chapter 10. We are confident that the reader's experience with FORTRAN programming has left him generally familiar with the input/output process. Consideration of all of the sample programs in this chapter will be terminated with the results still in memory. In Chapter 10 we shall consider topics such as I/O busing, interrupts, and I/O software.

In order to facilitate our discussion we refer to binary instruction words by their octal equivalents. For example, the instruction

LAC		ADDRESS	
001,	00	0, 000, 000, 001, 011	(2.4)

which specifies "Load the accumulator with the contents of location 1011" and leave the contents of 1011 unchanged,* will be written

$$100013 \tag{2.5}$$

For the time being, we are assuming that bits 3 and 4 are both zero so that the second octal digit from the left will always be zero or one. Still more convenient is the form

$$\text{LAC } 13 \tag{2.6}$$

Throughout our discussion, LAC 13 shall have the same meaning as expressions 2.4 and 2.5. Clearly it is necessary for LAC 13 to be translated to numerical form before it can be stored in memory. This is part of the function of a program called an assembler.

The remaining memory reference instructions in Fig. 2.2b are explained in more detail as follows:

ISZ 13 means add 1 to (increment) the contents of memory location 13 (octal) and skip the next instruction if the result is zero.

AND 13 calls for "anding" each bit of the word in location 13 with the corresponding bits in the accumulator. The resulting word is left in the accumulator.

TAD 13 causes the number in location 13 to be added to the number in the

* This is the case with all instructions which place the contents of one register including memory locations in another register. The information remains in the first register as well. This is consistent with the nature of FORTRAN replacement statements.

accumulator. A carry bit from the left-most column of addition is exclusive OR'ed with the bit in the link. The 18-bit addition will be correct if both arguments are in two's-complement form.

JMS 13 (jump to subroutine) causes the contents of the program counter to be incremented and placed in memory location 13. The next instruction to be executed is taken from memory location 14.

DAC 13 deposits the contents of the accumulator in memory location 13.

JMP 13 causes the next instruction to be taken from memory location 13.

Example 2.1

The execution of a TAD instruction is illustrated in Fig. 2.3. The memory locations

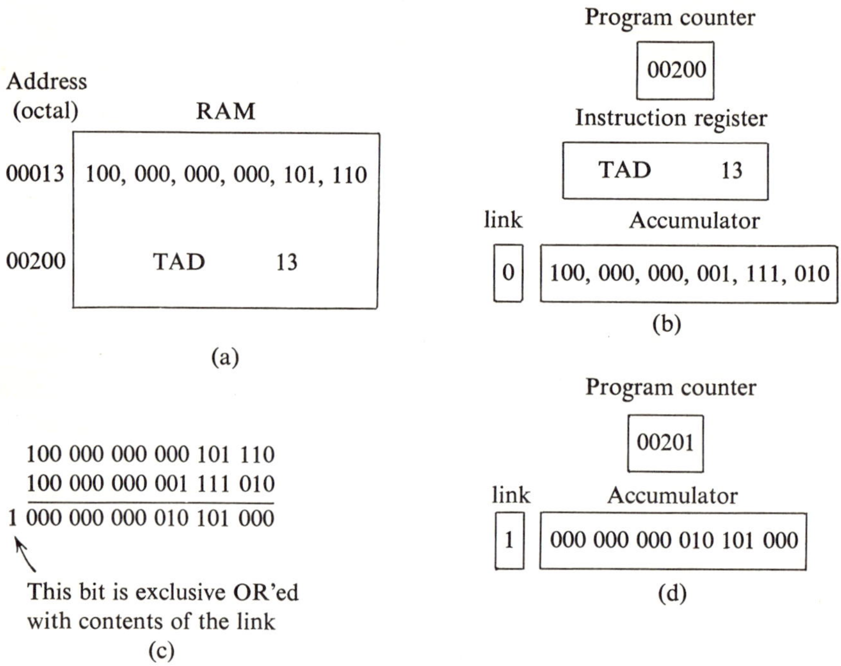

FIGURE 2.3. Execution of TAD 13.

of interest are shown in Fig. 2.3a. For convenience, only the actual arguments of the addition are shown in binary. In reality, of course, the contents of location 200 would also be stored in binary form. The contents of the program counter and the accumulator prior to execution of the instruction are shown in Fig. 2.3b. The number in the program counter is given in octal form. The operation begins by reading the contents of memory location 200 (as specified by the program counter) from memory and placing them in the instruction register. The symbolic form of the binary contents of the instruction register is shown in Fig. 2.3b. Next, the address portion of the instruction (00013 octal) is used to obtain a binary argument from memory. The actual addition of this number to the contents of the accumulator is displayed in Fig. 2.3c. Notice that the result is 19 bits long. The left-most bit is exclusive OR'ed with the contents of the link, with the result placed in the link. The presence of the link as a 19th bit of storage for the results of arithmetic and certain other operations will prove quite convenient. The result of the operation is shown in the link and accumulator in Fig. 2.3d. Also shown are the new contents of the program counter after it has been incremented to prepare for fetching the next instruction from memory. ▮

It is possible to manipulate the contents of the accumulator and exercise certain control functions without referencing the random access memory. This is accomplished by the *operate* instructions, several of which are listed in Fig. 2.4. Because of the great number of these instructions we shall identify them here in mnemonic form only. In Chapter 6, the bit codes for various operate instructions will become clear as we discuss their hardware implementation. We shall assume that the descriptions in Fig. 2.4 are self-explanatory. The use of all of the various instructions should be further clarified as we discuss programming.

HLT	Halt
NOP	No operation
CLA	Clear accumulator to zero
STA	Set accumulator to 777777
CMA	Complement bits of accumulator
CLL	Clear link to zero
STL	Set link to one
SKP	Skip next instruction if accumulator ≥ 0
SKZ	Skip next instruction if accumulator $= 0$
SZL	Skip next instruction if link $= 0$
RAR	Rotate accumulator right
RAL	Rotate accumulator left
DTA	Deposit contents of accumulator in index register *A*
DTB	Deposit contents of accumulator in index register *B*
DFA	Deposit contents of index register *A* in accumulator
DFB	Deposit contents of index register *B* in accumulator
INA	Increment index register *A*
INB	Increment index register *B*

FIGURE 2.4. Operate instructions. (In RAR and RAL the link is included in the rotation operations. For RAR the link is rotated into bit zero of the accumulator, and bit 17 is placed in the link).

2.5. PROGRAMMING

In order to avoid the presentation of an excessive number of programming examples we shall illustrate how the basic FORTRAN operations could be accomplished in machine language. Thus the reader will be able to generate his own examples by drawing on his FORTRAN programming experience. In this section we only illustrate how the reader can use his ingenuity to replace FORTRAN routines with sequences of matching assembly language instructions. This falls significantly short of defining a compiler or a set of rules for accomplishing this task automatically.

Let us consider first a version of FORTRAN consisting of replacement statements ("IXX="), GO TO statements, numerical IF statements, DO statements, arithmetic expressions, and subroutine CALLS. The reader will recognize that any program can be written, although not necessarily conveniently, using only these statements.

The replacement statement can be accomplished using only the instruction DAC. Suppose the quantity to replace the variable IXX, which we shall assume has been assigned to memory location 100, has been calculated and placed in the accumulator. Then the instruction DAC 100 causes IXX to take on its new value.

The control statements IF and GO TO are implemented easily in machine language. The statement JMP 100 could mean identically GO TO 100 if the first statement of FORTRAN instruction 100 were stored in memory location 100.

Assume now that FORTRAN instructions 100, 110, and 120 begin in the respective SIC memory locations, and IXX is assigned to location 1000. Then we may implement the FORTRAN instruction

```
IF(IXX)   100, 110, 120        (2.7)
```

as follows:

```
LAC 1000
SKP
JMP 100
SKZ
JMP 120
JMP 110
```

Notice that the argument of the IF statement is immediately placed in the accumulator. The instruction SKP causes the next instruction to be skipped if IXX ≥ 0. If JMP 100 is not skipped, then the next instruction is taken from location 100. If JMP 100 is skipped, the next instruction is SKZ. Thus control jumps to location 110 if the accumulator is zero, and to 120 if the accumulator is greater than zero.

The only instruction which is obviously intended to accomplish arithmetic is TAD. However, any arithmetic expression can be accomplished using this instruction together with LAC and the various operate instructions. Consider, for example,

$$N = M1 + ABS(M2) - M3 \tag{2.8}$$

The sequence of instructions in Fig. 2.5 can be used to compute the arithmetic expression on the right. Assume M1 is assigned to 1001, M2 to 1002, and M3 to 1003, and that the number 001 is stored in 2000. Since we shall wish to follow the program through several jump instructions, it is necessary to indicate the location in memory at the left of each instruction.

The first instruction in Fig. 2.5 loads the argument, M2. If M2 is negative,

```
100  LAC   1002          200  CMA
101  SKP                 201  TAD   2000
102  JMP    200          202  JMP    103
103  TAD   1001          203  XXXXXX
                          .
104  DAC    203           .
                          .
105  LAC   1003         1001
106  CMA                1002
107  TAD   2000         1003
110  TAD    203         2000  000001
```

FIGURE 2.5

the program jumps to location 200. The instruction CMA takes the one's-complement of M2. Adding +1 as is specified by instruction 201 leaves the two's-complement of M2 in the accumulator. Then the program jumps back to location 103. If M2 is positive, the instruction in location 102 is skipped. In either case the absolute value of M2 is in the accumulator just prior to the execution of instruction 103. Next, M1 is added to M2 and the result is temporarily stored in location 203. The instructions 105 to 107 leave the two's-complement of M3 in the accumulator. Adding the contents of 203 completes the generation of the right side of Eq. 2.8. Including the replacement statement DAC 1004 would complete the instruction in Eq. 2.8 by placing the new value of N in location 1004.

In our example of an arithmetic expression we have avoided floating point as well as the more complicated operations of multiplication, division, and exponentiation. All of these can be accomplished in terms of sequences of SIC instructions. At this point we leave these tasks to the reader. Of course, large machines contain hardware for the implementation of multiplication, division, and floating point. The reader may surmise that avoiding software routines for these operations results in a considerable improvement in a machine's overall capability. These topics are discussed in detail in Chapters 12 and 13.

Example 2.2

An interesting example of the use of the link is found in the short routine for double precision arithmetic shown in Fig. 2.6a. As 18 bits are equivalent in precision to approximately five decimal digits, it is not surprising that greater accuracy is required on occasion. Memory locations 1000 and 1001 contain a 36-bit binary

```
100   CLL                  300    000,000,000,000,000,001
101   LAC   1000            .
102   TAD   1002            .
                            .
103   DAC   1004            .
                            .
104   LAC   1001           1000   100,000,000,000,101,110
105   SZL                  1001   000,000,000,000,000,100
106   TAD    300           1002   100,000,000,001,111,010
107   TAD   1003           1003   000,000,000,000,100,110
110   DAC   1005           1004   000,000,000,010,101,000
 .
 .                         1005   000,000,000,000,101,011
 .
```

(a)

```
   100 000 000 000 101 110      000 000 000 000 000 100
   100 000 000 001 111 010      000 000 000 000 100 110
   -----------------------      -----------------------
 1 000 000 000 010 101 000      000 000 000 000 101 010
 |
 └→Temporarily stored in link ─────────────────────→ +1
                                -----------------------
                                000 000 000 000 101 011
            (b)                           (c)
```

FIGURE 2.6. Double precision addition.

number, which will serve as one of the arguments of addition. The least significant 18 bits are in location 1000. Locations 1002 and 1003 similarly store the other 36-bit argument. The 36-bit result will be placed in locations 1004 and 1005.

The first instruction clears the link to prepare for a possible carry from the least significant 18 bits. These portions of the two arguments are added by instructions 101 and 102. The result is stored in location 1004. As illustrated in Fig. 2.6b for the particular example, a carry propagates into the link, where it remains after a new argument is placed in the accumulator. The addition of the most significant 18 bits of the arguments is accomplished by instructions 104 to 107, as illustrated in Fig. 2.6c. If the link contains a 1, one is added to this result. For the example shown, the link is 1, representing a carry from the least significant 18 bits to the most significant 18 bits. The addition of this carry is shown in Fig. 2.6c. If the link contains a 0, instruction 106 is skipped; and the most significant 18 bits of the result are placed in location 1005. ∎

2.6. INDEXING AND INDIRECT ADDRESSING

In this section we shall see that DO loops can be implemented by a sequence of instructions which use indexing or indirect addressing or both. Both of these techniques may be used for other purposes. Indirect addressing, in particular, is useful in information retrieval and various types of simulations.

The reader will recall that bits 3 and 4 of the instruction have yet to be discussed. The meanings of these bits, which apply only in the case of memory reference instructions, may be found in Fig. 2.7. If bit 3 is 0 and bit 4 is 1, then

Bits 3	4	Meaning
0	0	No indexing or indirect addressing
0	1	Indirect addressing
1	0	Add index register *A* to address
1	1	Add index register *B* to address

FIGURE 2.7. Interpretation of bits 3 and 4.

the address specified in the instruction does not contain the actual argument of the operation. Instead, the instruction specifies the address of a memory location containing a word whose last 13 bits are the address of the argument. This technique is called indirect addressing. Consider, for example, a set of memory locations specified as in Fig. 2.8. Notice that the instruction in location 200 is LAC. Since bit 4 is a 1, indirect addressing is specified. Thus location 600 contains the address of the argument. This address is 700; and finally the number 000005 is loaded into the accumulator from that location.

200	120600	600	000700
		·	
		·	
		·	
		·	
		700	000005

FIGURE 2.8

In order to utilize our mnemonic notation without confusion, we indicate indirect addressing with an **I**. For example, the instruction in Fig. 2.8 could be represented by

LAC I 600

We will refer to indexing in mnemonic fashion as well. The letters A and B will be used to indicate the addition of the respective index registers. For example, 140600 and LAC A 600 would both call for loading the accumulator with the word located at the address given by Eq. 2.9.

$$\text{Address} = 600 + \text{contents of } A \tag{2.9}$$

Consider now the following DO loop:

```
    K = 0
    DO 90 J = 1, 6
    K = M(J) + K
    N(J) = K
90  Continue
```

This set of instructions computes a sequence of partial sums of the elements in array M, and leaves the result in array N. This can be accomplished by the

```
200  LAC       (-6          776   777772  (-6)
201  DAC        776        1000   000007 ⎫
202  CLA                   1001   000011 ⎪
203  DTA                   1002   000001 ⎬ M
204  TAD   A   1000        1003   000021 ⎪
205  DAC   A   1010        1004   000005 ⎪
206  INA                   1005   000006 ⎭
207  ISZ        776
210  JMP        204
```

(a)

```
1010   000007 ⎫
1011   000020 ⎪
1012   000021 ⎬ N
1013   000042 ⎪
1014   000047 ⎪
1015   000055 ⎭
```

(b)

FIGURE 2.9. Implementation of a DO loop.

SIC routine given in Fig. 2.9a. The instruction sequence of interest is stored in locations 200 to 210. The array M is stored in 1000–1005 and, the array, N, is stored in 1010–1015. The partial sums, which will be stored in these latter locations after execution of the routine, are shown there in Fig. 2.9b. Instructions 200 and 201 place in 776 the number -6 expressed in two's-complement form. All numbers are given in octal form for brevity.

Instruction 202 establishes $K = 0$. Instruction 203 prepares for the DO loop by storing $J = 0$ in index register A, and by clearing the accumulator in preparation for forming the sum. The first execution of TAD A 1000 causes the contents of location 1000 to be added to the accumulator. The contents of the accumulator are then deposited in location 1010 as the first partial sum by the instruction DAC A 1010. Now the contents of index register A are increased by 1 by the operate instruction INA. The function of ISZ 776 is to determine when six executions of the DO loop have been completed. This is done by incrementing the contents of 776 each time and then checking to see if the result is zero. If the result is still less than zero, the computer will jump back to the instruction in 204 to go through the loop again.

Since the contents of location 776 are initially -6, this quantity will be incremented six times. Each time through the loop the contents of index register A will also be increased by one. Thus the instruction TAD A 1000 will successively call out the contents of 1000, 1001, down to 1005; and DAC A 1010 will effect storage in 1010 through 1015. After the sixth time through the loop, ISZ will cause JMP 204 to be skipped; and the next instruction following the DO loop will be executed.

Not all machines have index registers. It is possible to perform the function of a DO loop utilizing indirect addressing with a location in core memory substituting for an index register. The sequence of instructions given in Fig. 2.10 will perform the same function as those in Fig. 2.9. The reader should verify this fact. The data registers may be assumed to be the same as those given in Fig. 2.10, with the exception that locations 774 and 775 are now used to store addresses. Initially these registers contain 1000 and 1010, respectively. Notice that the instruction ISZ is used to merely add one to an address. Since the address is a large positive number, a skip will never occur.

The disadvantage of the routine in Fig. 2.10 with respect to Fig. 2.9 is that the ISZ instruction is a memory reference instruction requiring longer to complete than the operate instruction INA. Thus more time is required each pass through the loop. In addition, the initial addresses in 774 and 775 are destroyed, making it impossible to repeat the DO loop of Fig. 2.10. It is possible to accomplish the function of a DO loop without using indexing or indirect addressing, by performing arithmetic on the instructions themselves. The index register method is clearly preferable, however, and repetitive loops

200	CLA			210	ISZ	776	
201	DAC		777	211	JMP	202	
202	LAC		777				
203	TAD	I	774				
204	DAC		777	774	001000		
205	DAC	I	775	775	001010		
206	ISZ		774	776	777772		(−6)
207	ISZ		775	777			

FIGURE 2.10. Implementation of a DO loop with indirect addressing.

of the sort discussed account for the inclusion of index registers in computers. Nested DO loops may be handled by the use of more than one index register. This case usually calls for the addition of a number other than one to the contents of an index register. This must be accomplished by first transferring the index to the accumulator, adding the number, and then transferring the result back to the index register.

501	LAC		506			
502	TAD		507	1001	JMP	100
503	DAC		505	1002	JMP	200
504	JMP	I	505	1003	JMP	300
505				1004	JMP	400
506	M					
507	001000					

FIGURE 2.11. SIC Equivalent of ASSIGNED GO TO.

Indirect addressing can be used to accomplish some of the more complicated control functions such as the computed GO TO. For example the instruction

GO TO (100, 200, 300, 400) M

can be accomplished by the SIC routine given in Fig. 2.11. For simplicity we assume that the beginning of FORTRAN instructions 100, 200, 300, and 400 are stored in SIC locations 100, 200, 300, and 400, respectively. The integer, M, which ranges between 1 and 4, is stored at location 506. The reader will note that the number 1000 + M is placed in location 505. The instruction JMP I 505 causes the next instruction to be a jump to 100, 200, 300, or 400, depending on M.

2.7. USING THE JMS INSTRUCTION

The use of the JMS instruction is illustrated in Fig. 2.12. The subroutine which begins at location 1000 takes advantage of DeMorgan's Theorem to compute the OR function as given by Eq. 2.10.

$$A \vee B = \overline{\bar{A} \wedge \bar{B}} \qquad (2.10)$$

```
200  LAC   300           1001  LAC     1012
201  DAC  1012           1002  CMA
202  LAC   301           1003  DAC     1012
203  DAC  1013           1004  LAC     1013
204  JMS  1000           1005  CMA
205  LAC  1012           1006  AND     1012
206  DAC   302           1007  CMA
 .                       1010  DAC     1012
 .                       1011  JMP   I 1000
 .                       1012
1000 (will contain 205)  1013
```

FIGURE 2.12. Use of the JMS instruction.

The main routine obtains the arguments from locations 300 and 301 and places them in locations 1012 and 1013, which store arguments for the subroutine. The instruction in location 204 causes the contents of the program counter (204) plus one to be stored in location 1000. Then 1001 is placed in the program counter, and the next instruction is taken from that location. The next-to-last instruction of the subroutine places the result in location 1012. Then JMP I 1000 takes the contents of location 1000, which in this case is 205, and takes the next instruction from that location in the main routine. Jumping indirectly to its first location is the standard technique for exiting a subroutine.

2.8. ASSEMBLY LANGUAGE

So far, relatively few memory locations have been required and the assignment of numbers to these locations has not been difficult. In writing programs in assembly language the task of allocating memory locations for data storage and program storage in advance is not pleasant. Should a routine require more storage or use more constants than envisioned at first it may become necessary to reassign an entire region of storage.

For most machines the assembler provides a way around this problem. As well as translating mnemonic instructions to a binary code, this program will assign actual storage locations. The programmer need only specify a string of characters representing a variable, and the assembler will assign a memory location. It may be desired to jump to an instruction whose numerical memory location is not known precisely. It is possible to label any statement by a string of characters, AAA, for example, and then write the statement JMP AAA, which will cause a jump to the instruction in AAA. The programmer is usually allowed to label a statement with a specific (numbered) memory location, or symbolically with a character string, or omit the label. If there are no contradictions between memory locations specified by number, the assembler will fit it all together in memory.

	(a)			(b)	
501/	LAC	506	LOCl,	LAC	LOCl + 5
	TAD	1000		TAD	1000
	DAC	505		DAC	LOCl + 4
	JMP	I 505		JMP	I LOCl + 4
				O	
				M	

FIGURE 2.13. Program list in assembly language.

To make the assembly process as efficient as possible most assemblers require distinct characters to separate a fixed location from its contents and a variable location from its contents. We shall use the convention that a number followed by a slash, "/", represents a fixed memory location. A string of characters beginning with a letter will indicate a location to be assigned by the assembler and will be separated from the contents of the location by a comma. Thus

200/ LAC AAA (2.11)

causes LAC AAA to be stored in location 200 while

AAA, 0 (2.12)

lets the assembler assign a location to AAA in which a zero is stored. Once the location corresponding to AAA has been assigned, the assembler must replace AAA with the number of the assigned memory location in all instructions such as LAC AAA.

In writing a program it is not necessary to precede each program line with either a fixed or variable location. Lines following locations specified as in either Eq. 2.11 or 2.12 will be assigned, in order, to succeeding memory locations. For example, the four instructions in Fig. 2.11 could be listed by the programmer in the two distinct forms given in Fig. 2.13. In the case of Fig. 2.13b the assembler will assign LOC1 to a memory location and will place the LAC instruction in that location. TAD 1000 will be placed in the next location, and so on. Notice that it has been possible to avoid labeling the two data locations at the end of the routine. Since these will be stored in the 4th and 5th locations after LOC1, the assembler allows them to be referred to as LOC1 + 4 and LOC1 + 5. This technique is convenient when handling arrays of data.

One more convenient feature is found in most assemblers. If the programmer finds it necessary to use a particular constant, he need not consider the storage of that constant. Expression 2.13 is an example of the special notation for this situation which we shall assume to be understandable by the assembler:

LAC (−6 (2.13)

The parenthesis indicates that the number which follows is a constant. The assembler assigns a location and stores the two's-complement of 6 in that location. Suppose, for example, that this location is 763. Then LAC 763 is substituted for LAC (−6 when the program is loaded in the computer.

We conclude this section with a longer programming example, which would be very tedious to write without assembly language techniques.

Example 2.3

Write a program which will accomplish the multiplication of two 18-bit numbers in SIC. Assume that these numbers are stored in two's-complement form.

Solution. The multiplication routine as presented in Fig. 2.14 assumes that the

```
1          LAC  (-18
           DAC  INDEX
           CLA
           DAC  PROD1
           DAC  PROD2
           DAC  SIGN
2          LAC  MLTR
           SKP
           JMP  COMP1
           JMP  LOC1
  COMP1,   CMA
           TAD  (1
           DAC  MLTR
           LAC  SIGN
           CMA
           DAC  SIGN
  LOC1,    LAC  MLTD
           SKP
           JMP  COMP2
           JMP  LOC2
  COMP2,   CMA
           TAD  (1
           DAC  MLTD
           LAC  SIGN
           CMA
           DAC  SIGN
3 LOC2,    LAC  MLTR
           RAR
           DAC  MLTR
           SZL
           JMP  LOC3
           JMP  LOC4
  LOC3,    LAC  PROD1
           TAD  MLTD
           DAC  PROD1
  LOC4,    CLL
           LAC  PROD1
           RAR
           DAC  PROD1
             :
           LAC  PROD2
           RAR
           DAC  PROD2
           ISZ  INDEX
           JMP  LOC2
4          LAC  SIGN
           SKP
           JMP  LOC5
           HLT
  LOC5,    LAC  PROD1
           CMA
           DAC  PROD1
           LAC  PROD2
           CMA
           CLL
           TAD  (1
           DAC  PROD2
           LAC  PROD1
           SZL
           TAD  (1
           DAC  PROD1
           HLT
```

FIGURE 2.14. Multiplication.

multiplier and multiplicand are stored in MLTR and MLTD, respectively. Thirty-six bits must be allowed for storage of the product. The most significant 18 bits will be found in PROD1 and the least significant bits in PROD2. For purposes of explanation the program has been separated by brackets into four sections. The first section merely provides for initializing the index and setting the product initially to zero.

The second section takes the absolute value of both MLTR and MLTD and stores the sign of the final product in SIGN. The actual multiplication is accomplished in the third section of the program. The method used is similar to the usual pencil and paper method. The multiplier is first rotated right, placing the least significant bit in the link. If the contents of the link are 1, the multiplicand is added to PROD1. Whether or not an addition is performed, PROD2 and PROD1 are then shifted right. The right-most bit of PROD1 is temporarily stored in the link before being rotated into the left-most bit of PROD2. Seventeen more repetitions of this process leave the final product stored as described above in PROD1 and PROD2.

The fourth section is included solely to establish the final sign of the product. If SIGN contains 777777(−1), the 36-bit product is replaced by its two's-complement. This operation utilizes the link to store a possible overflow from the two's-complementing of PROD2.

With only slight modification, the program in Fig. 2.14 could take the form of a subroutine. When called, the subroutine would develop a product as described above. It would then be the function of the main program to use as many of the 36 bits in the fixed point product as required. ∎

PROBLEMS

2.1. Prove that adding the two's-complement forms of two negative numbers will give the proper two's-complement result if the sum of the magnitudes is less than 2^{n-1}. Note that the addition is physically addition modulo 2^n

2.2 Suppose that indexing were eliminated from SIC so that 14 memory reference instructions could be permitted. List some additional memory reference instructions which you think would be of value.

2.3 Suppose that a computer is to be designed with the same memory reference instructions as SIC but with eight index registers. How could indirect addressing be employed so that 8192 words of random access memory could still be used? Suggest a bit layout for the instruction in such a machine.

2.4 Suppose that the number of I/O instructions and operate instructions in SIC are the same. In this case what would be the maximum number of distinct operate instructions which could be specified?

2.5 Write in SIC assembly language the equivalent of a FORTRAN logical IF statement.

2.6 Devise a sequence of SIC instructions which will accomplish the equivalent of the DO loop in Fig. 2.9 without using either indexing or indirect addressing.

2.7 Write in SIC assembly language a program for adding the rows of a 10 × 10 matrix. Use index registers insofar as possible to imitate a nested DO loop approach.

2.8 Suggest a routine which depends on indirect addressing to perform a search of a list.

2.9 Write a short sequence of instructions, utilizing any SIC instructions except ISZ, which will accomplish the same function as an ISZ instruction.

2.10 Write a sequence of SIC instructions which will reorder the bits of a word in memory as follows:

9 10 11	0 1 2	15 16 17	6 7 8	3 4 5	12 13 14

(*Hint*: Use the instruction AND to accomplish masking and use rotate instructions.)

2.11 Suppose two floating-point numbers are stored with 18-bit characteristics located immediately following 18-bit mantissas in memory. Assume that the binary point is between bit-0 and bit-1 for both mantissas. The characteristics need not be equal. Write a sequence of SIC instructions which will accomplish addition of the two floating-point numbers.

2.12 Write a sequence of instructions which will accomplish multiplication of two floating-point numbers, such as discussed in Problem 2.11.

2.13 Write a SIC assembly language version of a FORTRAN subroutine call. Include the mechanism for the transfer of arguments. Write routines which could tolerate separate compilations of the main routine and the subroutine.

2.14 Write a sequence of instructions which will call a subroutine without using the JMS instruction. Assume that no transfer of arguments is required.

2.15 Write in SIC assembly language a sequence of instructions which will illustrate the accomplishment of a simple FORTRAN function subroutine.

2.16 Write in SIC assembly language a sequence of instructions which will accomplish division of two 18-bit fixed-point numbers.

2.17 Write in SIC assembly language routines which will perform bit by bit the following Boolean operations on two 18-bit words.
a) OR
b) exclusive-OR
Set the operations up as subroutines which will use the accumulator and one word of memory as arguments.

2.18 Justify the method of converting a binary number to octal form given in Section 2.2.

3

System Components

3.1. INTRODUCTION

In this chapter we will present a brief and rather general discussion of some of the basic types of logic and memory devices used in digital computers. The actual design of these devices is not the concern of the system designer, who generally regards them as "black boxes" with certain known characteristics. On the other hand, intelligent selection and application of these devices does require some understanding of their operation and an appreciation of their limitations. In addition, without some physical interpretation of registers, memory, etc., much of the material in following chapters may seem too abstract to many readers. Readers who are already familiar with digital hardware may skip the majority of the topics in this chapter without loss of continuity.

Logic circuits are implemented in a tremendous variety of technologies. There is diode-transistor logic (DTL), transistor-transistor logic (TTL), MOS logic, emitter-coupled logic (ECL), etc. These various types differ in matters of speed, cost, power consumption, physical dimensions, immunity to environmental influences, etc.; but they all accomplish the same basic purpose, and from the point of view of this book, the differences are of little importance. All of them accept input signals in which the voltage levels represent the values of certain logical (binary) variables, and produce output signals in which the voltage levels correspond to logical functions of the input variables. Until recently, single logic circuits usually implemented very simple functions, such as AND, OR, and NOT. With the advent of integrated circuits, more complex functions are available in single circuit packages.

The purpose of logic circuits, then, is to process signals and produce outputs which are functions of the inputs. The outputs are available only during the duration of the input signals. The purpose of memory devices is to store information for later use, generally returning it without alteration, in the same form as it was originally stored. The definition of memory is elusive. We shall simply settle for the intuitive idea that a memory device is any device which we place in a specific, identifiable physical state for the specific purpose of preserving information, without alteration, until a later time.

Memory devices may be classified in a number of different ways. First, most may be classified as being either magnetic or electronic. Magnetic devices utilize ferromagnetic materials, which can be placed in a specific magnetic state by the passage of electric currents through them or near them, and which then maintain these states indefinitely, until interrogated. The chief types of magnetic memory are tape, disk, drum, and core. Electronic memory devices are primarily transistor and diode circuits in which the outputs can be set to certain voltage levels by the application of certain input signals, and will be maintained even when the input signals are removed. The chief electronic memory device is the flip-flop, which can in turn be used to construct *register memories* (RM).

Memories may also be classified by the type of access to the stored information. In *random access memories* (RAM), all stored information is equally accessible, in the sense that any given piece of information may be retrieved in exactly the same length of time as any other piece of information. Core memory and slower semiconductor memories are usually classified as RAM. Tape, by contrast, is a *sequential memory* (SM), in which information can be retrieved only in the same order it was stored. When you want a particular piece of information off tape, you simply start running the tape until the desired information comes into position to be read. The access time is thus dependent on where the desired information is located relative to the starting point.

Between these two categories are disk and drum, which are *semi-random access memories* (SRAM). In these devices, any given area, or sector, of memory can be accessed in the same time as any other area; but within a given area, you must wait for a given piece of information to move into position to be read.

A final special category, which resembles logic as well as memory, is the *read-only memory* (ROM). The stored information is actually built into the structure of the device. The stored information can then be read out electronically, but can be altered only by mechanical alteration of the structure of the device.

The above classification and listing is quite broad and general and is not intended to be complete. There are many other specialized memory devices, some fitting into the above categories, some not really fitting into any category.

3.2. DIODE LOGIC

The simplest type of electronic logic is diode logic. A diode is a device which can conduct current in only one direction. The schematic symbol for a diode is shown in Fig. 3.1a. Ideally, a diode offers zero resistance to the flow of

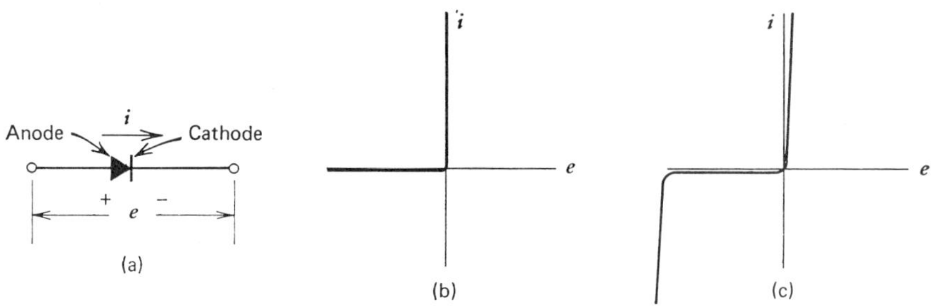

FIGURE 3.1. Diode symbol and characteristics.

current from anode to cathode (forward direction) and infinite resistance to current flow from cathode to anode (reverse direction). The ideal current-voltage characteristic would thus be that shown in Fig. 3.1b. A typical characteristic for an actual semiconductor diode is shown in Fig. 3.1c. When the diode is conducting in the forward direction, there is a small, nearly constant, positive voltage across the diode. When the voltage across the diode goes negative, a very small reverse current flows. When the voltage goes sufficiently negative, a phenomenon known as the *Zener* breakdown* occurs, and the reverse current increases sharply. In normal switching circuit applications, diodes are never operated in the Zener range. For purposes of analyzing diode circuits it is simplest just to remember that the anode cannot be more positive than the cathode. Consider the diode symbol as an arrowhead and remember that if the anode attempts to go positive, current will flow in the arrow direction until there is essentially zero voltage across the diode.

* There are actually two types of breakdown, *Zener* and *avalanche*, which are due to quite different physical phenomena. From an external point of view, however, there is no important difference.

Logical values are usually represented in digital circuits in the form of voltage levels. There is more than one possible way to define the relation between logical values and voltage levels. In order to minimize the possibility of confusion assume that a positive voltage, usually 1 to 10 volts, represents logical 1 while a voltage very near zero volts represents logical 0. This convention, which is an example of *positive logic*, will be used throughout this chapter. The opposite situation in which the more negative voltage represents

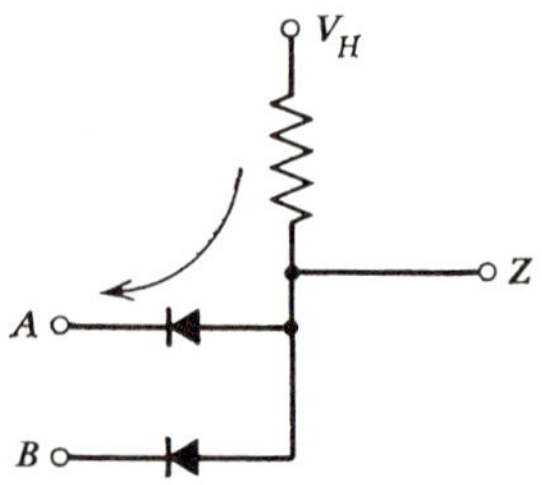

(a)

e_1	e_2	e_o
0	0	0
0	V_+	0
V_+	0	0
V_+	V_+	V_+

(b)

A	B	Z
0	0	0
0	1	0
1	0	0
1	1	1

(c)

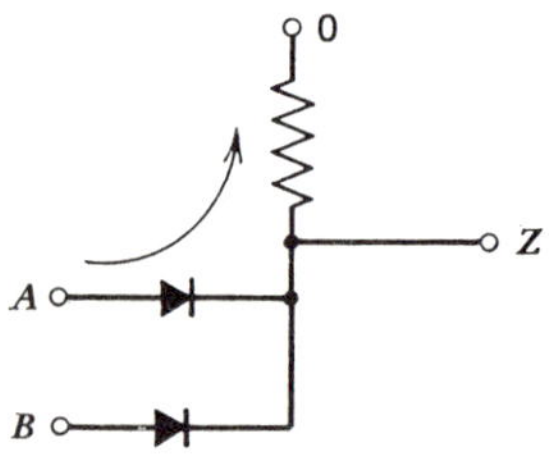

(d)

e_1	e_2	e_o
0	0	0
0	V_+	V_+
V_+	0	V_+
V_+	V_+	V_+

(e)

A	B	Z
0	0	0
0	1	1
1	0	1
1	1	1

(f)

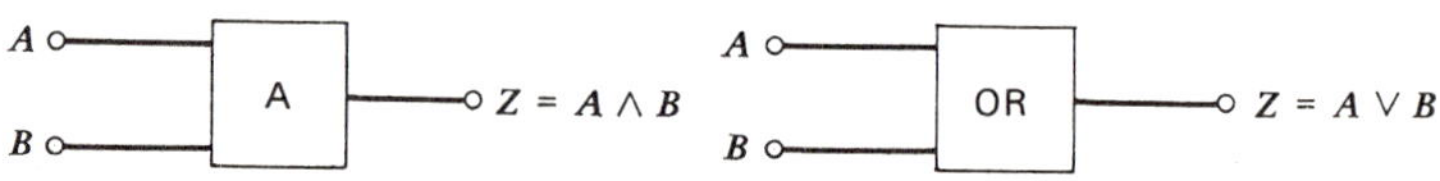

(g) (h)

FIGURE 3.2

logical 1 and the more positive voltage represents logical 0 (negative logic) may also be encountered in practice.

The circuits for the two basic forms of diode gates are shown in Fig. 3.2. The supply voltage, V_H, is positive and slightly greater than V_+, which represents logical 1. The voltage inputs to the circuit are e_1 and e_2 representing logical variables A and B, respectively. The output voltage, e_o, represents logical variable Z. First consider the circuit of Fig. 3.2a. With the diodes connected in this direction, e_o cannot be more positive than the smaller of e_1

and e_2. First assume that both e_1 and e_2 are equal to V_+. V_H is more positive than V_+, enough current will flow, in the direction shown, through the resistor R and the diodes to set up a voltage drop across R equal to $V_H - V_+$; so $e_o = V_+$. Now assume either e_1 or e_2, or both, goes to 0 (approximately zero). Then the current flow through R will increase until the drop is equal to V_H, and $e_o = 0$. This behavior is summarized in Fig. 3.2b.

In the circuit of Fig. 3.2d, the direction of the diodes is reversed, and the voltage connected to R is changed to 0. Thus, some current will always flow through R in the direction indicated. With the diode connected in this manner, neither signal voltage, e_1 or e_2, can be more positive than e_o; so e_o must be equal to the larger of e_1 or e_2. This behavior is summarized in Fig. 3.2e.

The corresponding values for Z as a function of A and B are shown in Fig. 3.2c and f. We recognize the AND* operation in Fig. 3.2c. Thus we identify the circuit of Fig. 3.2a as an AND gate. Throughout the text we shall use the symbol of Fig. 3.2g for the AND gate. Similarly, we see that the circuit of Fig. 3.2d realizes the OR operation. This will be symbolized as in Fig. 3.2h.

We have shown only two inputs on the gates of Fig. 3.2. This is not a necessary limitation. For example, in the gate of Fig. 3.2a, if we connect more diodes, in parallel to the two shown and in the same direction, the circuit will still have an output $e_o = V_+$ only if *all* inputs are at the V_+ level. For positive logic this would correspond to an ANDing of all the inputs.

Diode gates can be connected together to implement more complex logic functions, as shown in Fig. 3.3. For positive logic we have two AND gates driving an OR gate, and the function realized is

$$Z = (A \wedge B) \vee (C \wedge D).$$

If the diodes were ideal, there would be no limit on the number of inputs on a single gate (fan-in), or on the number of other gates a single gate could drive (fan-out), or on the number of gates that could be connected in series, one after another (levels of gating). However, the voltage across conducting diodes and the finite reverse current of non-conducting diodes result in continual degradation of signal level as the circuit complexity increases. For example, even in a single gate the output voltage will always be slightly different from the input voltages because of the drops across the conducting diodes. Because of the loading problems, diode logic is rarely used. It has been introduced here as a preliminary to the discussion of a more practical type of logic, diode-transistor logic.

* The reader not familiar with these logical operations and with Boolean algebra and Karnaugh maps should digress at this point to study a suitable reference, such as Hill [1].

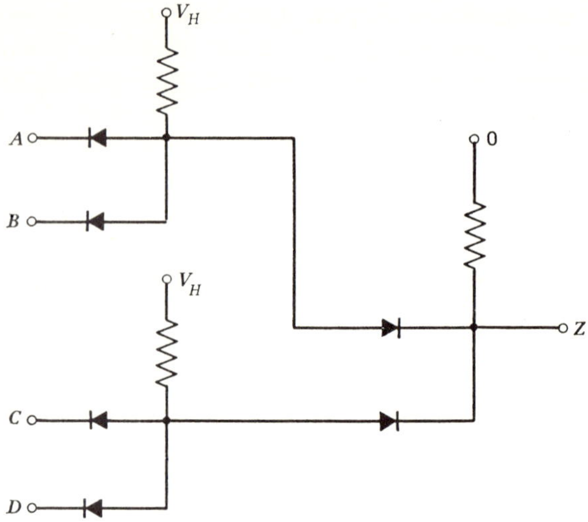

FIGURE 3.3

3.3. DIODE-TRANSISTOR LOGIC (DTL)

The signal degradation problem associated with diode logic may be alleviated by introducing amplification at appropriate points, most frequently through the use of transistors. The symbols for the two basic types of transistors, PNP and NPN, are shown in Fig. 3.4. The NPN transistor is most commonly used in computer logic circuits.

The transistors are used as switches in logic circuits. In the NPN transistor, if the base is driven slightly negative with respect to the emitter, the transistor

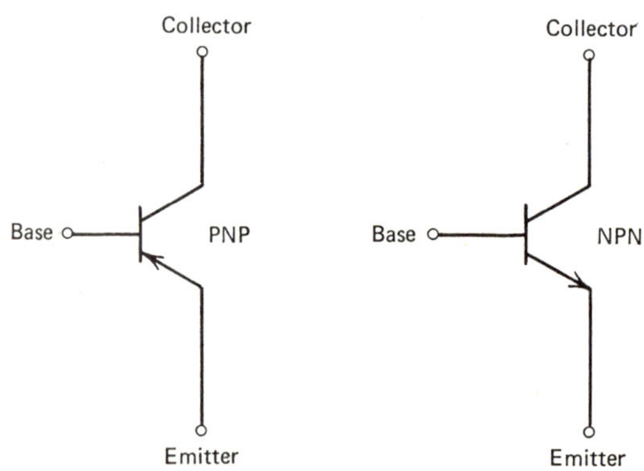

FIGURE 3.4. PNP and NPN transistors.

will be *cut off*, thus acting as an open circuit to current flow from collector to emitter. If the base is driven slightly positive with respect to the emitter, the transistor will be *saturated*, thus acting essentially as a short circuit to current flow from collector to emitter. There will be a small voltage drop from emitter to collector in saturation, but this drop will be essentially independent of the magnitude of the collector-to-emitter current.

Transistors exhibit both voltage and current gain. Figure 3.5 shows an NPN transistor connected in the standard "grounded emitter" configuration. When the transistor is cut off, the collector will be at the collector supply level, V_+. When it is saturated, the collector will be typically at about 0.1 volt.

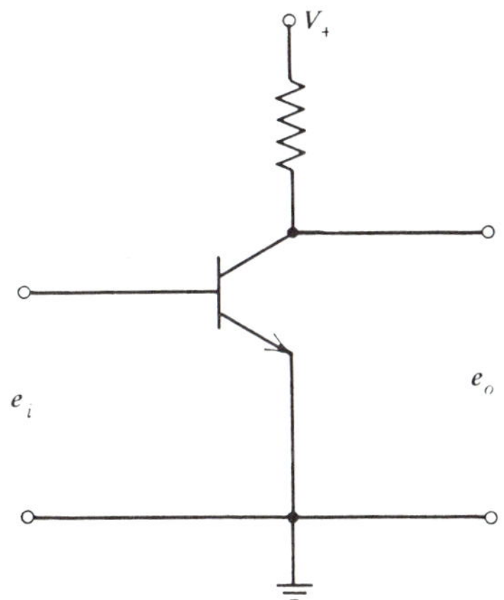

FIGURE 3.5. Transistor in grounded-emitter circuit.

This collector voltage swing will be in the range of 3 to 20 volts for typical transistors. The base voltage swing necessary to take the transistor from cutoff to saturation will be in the range of 0.1 to 0.5 volt. In addition, the current flowing in the base circuit will typically be on the order of one-hundredth of the current in the collector and emitter circuits.

Consider the NPN inverter of Fig. 3.6a. When $e_i = 0$, the voltage at the base will be negative; so the transistor will be cut off, and $e_o = V_+$. The values of R_b and R_{bb} are so chosen that when $e_i = V_+$, the voltage at the base will be positive. The transistor will thus be conducting, so that $e_o = 0$, neglecting the small drop across the transistor in saturation. This behavior is summarized in the table of Fig. 3.6b. For positive logic, this will result in the truth table of Fig. 3.6c. There are two ways of showing inversion on logic diagrams. We may use a separate symbol, as shown in Fig. 3.6d, or a small circle at the input or output of another gate, as shown in Fig. 3.6e.

In order to correct the loading deficiencies of the diode gates, we may simply let the output of each gate drive an inverter, as shown in Fig. 3.7.

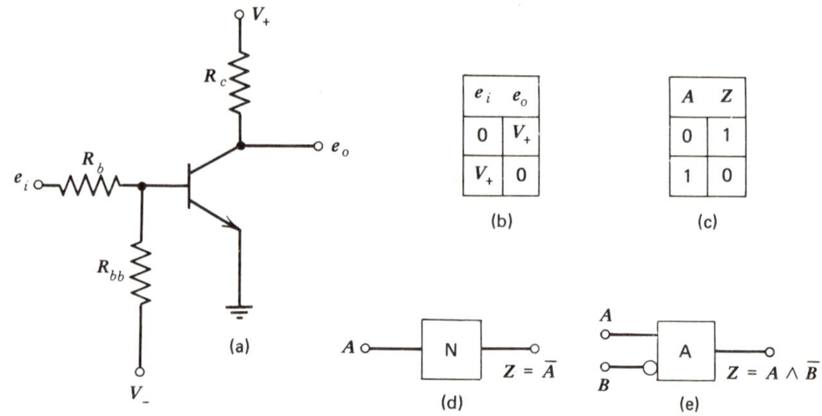

FIGURE 3.6. Inverters.

Consider the circuit of Fig. 3.7a, which consists of a diode AND gate driving a NPN inverter. If one or more inputs are at 0, e_g will also be at 0, and the voltage at the base will be negative with respect to the emitter. The transistor will be cut off, so $e_o = V_+$. If both inputs are at V_+, the voltage at e_g, which will depend on the circuit parameters in the base circuit, will be such as to drive the base positive with resnect to the emitter. The transistor will

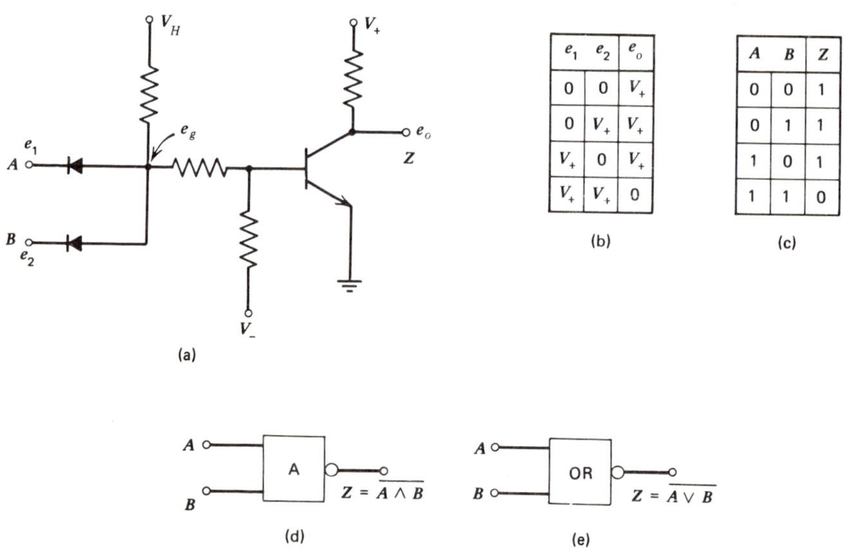

FIGURE 3.7. Diode-transistor gate.

conduct, and $e_o = 0$. This behavior is summarized in the table of Fig. 3.7b. For positive logic, this results in the truth table of Fig. 3.7c, which is seen to be the table for NOT-AND, or NAND. In a similar fashion, the diode OR gate connected to an inverter will provide NOR for positive logic. The logic symbols for NAND and NOR are shown in Figs. 3.7d and 3.7e.

The addition of the transistor inverters considerably alleviates the loading problems associated with diode logic, but it does not entirely eliminate them. For example, the assumption that the transistor output voltage is at the collector supply level in cutoff is based on the assumption that no current flows from the output terminal. Obviously, any gates connected to the output will draw some current. However, as noted earlier, the amount of current required to drive the base of a transistor is quite small. Thus a single inverter can drive a number of gates before the current required becomes large enough to have any significant effect on the inverter output voltage. In this manner the fan-out restrictions are considerably relaxed.

The fan-in can also be considerably increased over that possible with diode logic. The finite back resistance of the diodes will still cause deterioration in signal level at the gate output, but now the gate voltage, e_g, need only have enough swing to provide reliable control of the transistor. As long as we observe the fan-in and fan-out restrictions, there will be no deterioration of signal level through successive levels of diode-transistor gating.

DTL is a popular type of logic, but it is certainly not the only type used. Among other popular types, particularly in integrated circuits, are emitter-coupled logic (ECL) and transistor-transistor logic (TTL). The internal functioning of these types is somewhat more complex than DTL, but they implement the same logical functions; and the difference between them, in such matters as speed and cost, need not concern us here.

The logical inversion noted in DTL occurs in most types of electronic logic, so that NAND and NOR are often cheaper and more convenient to realize than AND and OR. This might seem to be something of a problem, since the standard techniques of switching theory, such as Karnaugh maps and Quine-McCluskey minimization do not conveniently lead to NAND or NOR forms. However, it turns out that AND-OR and OR-AND, which are "natural" forms, can be very conveniently realized in terms of NAND or NOR logic.

Consider the simple logical circuit of Fig. 3.8a, which consists of three NAND gates driving another NAND gate. From De Morgan's law,

$$\overline{X \wedge Y \wedge Z} = \bar{X} \vee \bar{Y} \vee \bar{Z}$$

we see that the final NAND gate can be replaced by an OR gate with inversion on the inputs (Fig. 3.8b). Next,

$$\bar{\bar{X}} = X$$

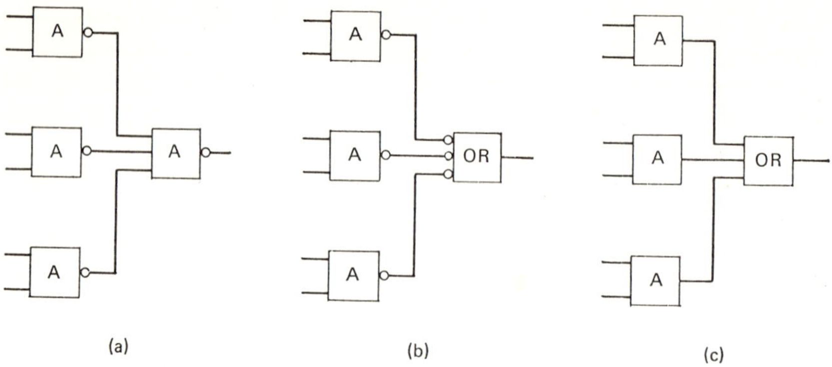

FIGURE 3.8. Conversion of NAND-NAND to AND-OR circuit.

so that the two successive inversions on the lines between the input and output gates cancel, giving the circuit of Fig. 3.8c. Thus we see that a two-level NAND circuit is equivalent to a two-level AND-OR circuit. In a similar fashion, we can show that a two-level NOR circuit is equivalent to a two-level OR-AND circuit.

3.4. SPEED AND DELAY IN LOGIC CIRCUITS

Faster operation generally means greater computing power, so there is a continual search for faster and faster logic circuits. The development of faster circuits is the province of the electronic circuit designer, but the systems designer must have some understanding of the delays in logic circuits, since they profoundly affect the operation of the entire system.

Figure 3.9 shows a grounded-emitter inverter and the response to a positive

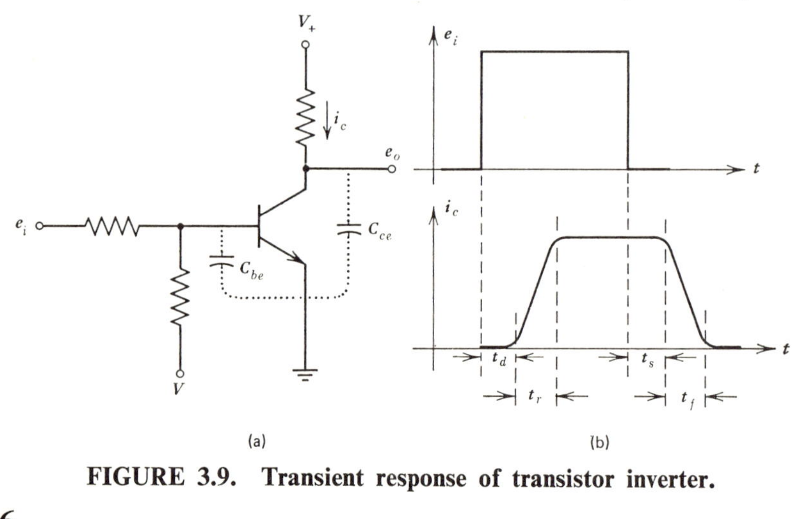

FIGURE 3.9. Transient response of transistor inverter.

pulse at the base, taking the transistor from cutoff to saturation and back. There are a number of complex physical factors entering into the determination of this response, of which we can consider only a few. First, from the time of the start of the base pulse, there is a delay time, t_d, before the collector current starts to rise. This delay is primarily caused by the effective base-to-emitter capacitance of the transistor (shown dotted in Fig. 3.9a). This capacitance must be charged to a positive level before the transistor starts to turn on. After the transistor starts to conduct, there is a finite rise time, t_r, primarily controlled by the collector capacitance. On the trailing edge of the base pulse, there is again a delay, t_s, before the collector current starts to drop. This delay is due to the base-to-emitter capacitance, as well as the storage of charge in the base region during saturation. The delay due to the storage effect t_s is longer than t_d. Finally, there is a finite fall time, t_f, again due to the collector capacitance.

There are many techniques for speeding up the response of transistor circuits. For our purposes it will suffice to note that it is possible to make the rise and fall times negligible compared to the delay times (t_d and t_s), so that it is appropriate to characterize the transistor inverter as purely a delay element, for purposes of systems design. Since we do not wish to worry about whether a given logical transition calls for the transistor to turn on or off, we take the worst case, and assume the delay to be equal to the "turn-off" time, $t_s + t_f$. The delay in NAND and NOR circuits is very similar to that in inverters.

3.5. FLIP-FLOPS AND REGISTER MEMORY (RM)

As we have seen, memory, the ability to store information, is essential in a digital system. The most common type of electronic memory device is the *flip-flop.** Figure 3.10 shows the circuit for a flip-flop constructed from two NOR gates, and the timing diagram for a typical operating sequence. We have also repeated the truth table for NOR for convenience in explaining the operation.

At the start, both inputs are at 0, the Y output is at 0, and the X output at 1. Since the outputs are fed back to the inputs of the gates, we must check to see that the assumed conditions are consistent. Gate 1 has inputs of $C = 0$ and $X = 1$, giving an output $Y = 0$, which checks. Similarly, at gate 2 we have $S = 0$ and $Y = 0$, giving $X = 1$. At time t_1, input S goes to 1. The inputs of gate 2 are thus changing from 00 to 01. After a delay (as discussed in the last section), X changes from 1 to 0 at time t_2. This changes the inputs of gate 1 from 01 to 00, so Y changes from 0 to 1 at t_3. This changes the inputs of gate 2

* The more formal name is *bistable multivibrator*. The origin of the name flip-flop is uncertain, but it has become standard.

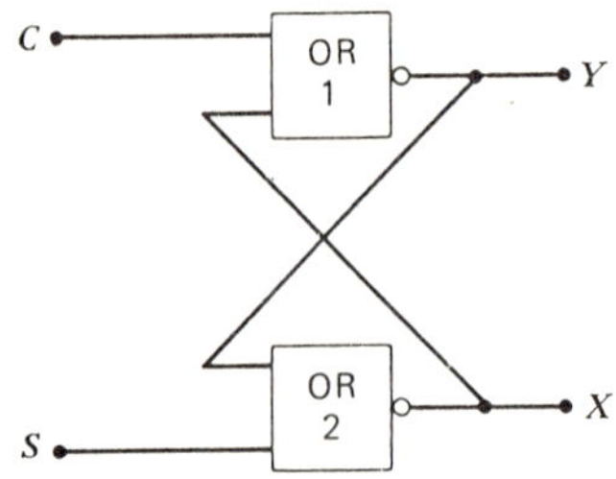

A	B	NOR
0	0	1
0	1	0
1	0	0
1	1	0

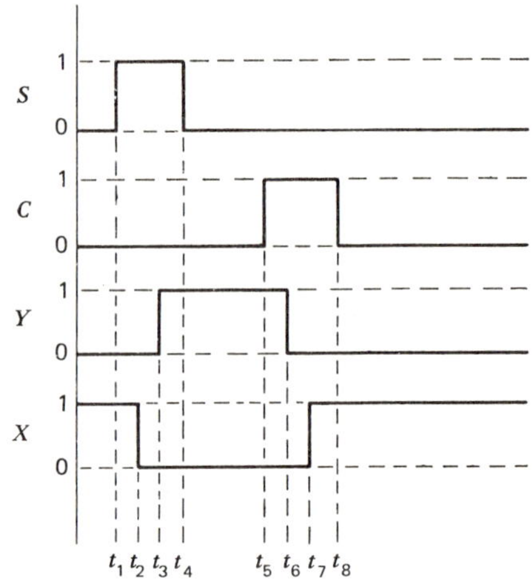

FIGURE 3.10. Operation of flip-flop.

from 01 to 11, but has no effect on the outputs. Similarly, the change of S from 1 to 0 at t_4 has no effect. When C goes to 1, Y goes to 0, driving X to 1, thus "locking-in" Y, so that the return of C to 0 has no further effect.

Note that it is the change of an input (S or C) from 0 to 1 that initiates the change of state of the flip-flop. The return of the signal to 0 has no effect; so it could occur at any time after the output change has stabilized. In Fig. 3.10, if S returned to 0 before time t_3, the input to OR-2 would again be 00, tending to cause X to return to 1. In this situation the operation of the circuit would be unpredictable.

In short, the timing of signals controlling flip-flops is quite critical; and it is usual practice to use specially timed pulses, called *clock pulses*, to control the setting of flip-flops in computer systems. A *pulse* is simply a signal which normally remains at one level (usually zero) and goes to the other level only for a very short duration. By contrast, a *level* signal is one which may remain at either the 1 or 0 level for indefinite periods of time, and which changes values only at intervals long compared to the pulse duration. Just what is meant by "very short" depends on the speed of the circuits, but is normally about the same as the delay time of the flip-flops.*

* For a more thorough discussion of timing problems in flip-flops, refer to Chapter 10 of Reference 1.

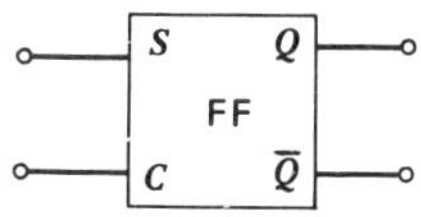

S^ν	C^ν	Y^ν	$Y^{\nu+1}$
0	0	0	0
0	0	1	1
0	1	0	0
0	1	1	0
1	0	0	1
1	0	1	1
1	1	0	X
1	1	1	X

FIGURE 3.11. ***S-C* Flip-flop.**

A flip-flop operating in the above fashion is known as a Set-Clear, or *S-C*, flip-flop,* and has the block diagram symbol shown in Fig. 3.11. The S and C inputs correspond to those in Fig. 3.10a and the Q and $\bar{Q}$ outputs correspond to the Y and X outputs, respectively. A pulse on the S input will "Set" the flip-flop, that is, drive the Q-output to the 1-level and the $\bar{Q}$-output to the 0-level. A pulse on the C line will "Clear" (reset) the flip-flop, that is, drive the Q-output to the 0-level and the $\bar{Q}$-output to the 1-level. This behavior is summarized in tabular form in Fig. 3.11. Here y represents the signal at the Q-output. S^ν, C^ν, and y^ν indicate the values of the inputs and output at some arbitrary time t_ν; and $y^{\nu+1}$ indicates the value to which the output will go as a result of an input at t_ν. The reader should satisfy himself that this table can be represented by the equation

$$y^{\nu+1} = S^\nu \vee (y^\nu \wedge \overline{C^\nu}).$$

The "don't care" entries for $y^{\nu+1}$ in the last two rows reflect the fact that the operation is indeterminate if both inputs are pulsed at the same time, and that this input condition should, therefore, not be permitted to occur. The *S-C* flip-flop may be considered a memory device because the state of the outputs indicates which input was last pulsed.

Another important type is the *J-K* flip-flop, which is the same as the *S-C* flip-flop except that simultaneous inputs on both input lines are allowed and cause the flip-flop to change state. A third type of flip-flop, the T flip-flop, has

* This type of flip-flop is more commonly known as the *R-S* (Reset-Set) flip-flop. However, the IEEE standards (ASA Y32.14-1962) specify *Clear* (*C*) as preferable to *Reset* (*R*).

only one input. If a pulse occurs on the *T* input, the output always changes, from 0 to 1 or from 1 to 0, as the case may be.

Flip-flops may be used individually to store single bits, in which case they are often referred to as *indicators*, or they may be used to construct *registers*. A register is simply a set of *n* flip-flops, used to store *n*-bit words, where *n* may range from 2 to 100 or more. For example, in SIC, the accumulator is an 18-bit register, the program counter is a 13-bit register, etc. Registers may be constructed with any type of flip-flop; we will use *S-C* flip-flops in this book. The nomenclature here is not completely standard. Some manufacturers use the word *register* to signify any storage location permanently assigned to the processing unit for some specific purpose and not addressable in the same sense as ordinary memory locations. Thus, they may speak of a computer as having several hundred registers, when, in fact, these "registers" are simply reserved locations in magnetic-core memory. There is nothing wrong with this practice, and it may reflect a tendency for the functions of memory and processing to merge in some designs. However, we shall use the term register memory (RM) exclusively to denote flip-flop memory.

3.6. RANDOM ACCESS MEMORY (RAM)

Flip-flop registers are the fastest memory devices available. Until about 1970 the cost of semiconductor memories was appreciably greater than the slower magnetic core memories to be discussed first in this section. More recently, with the continued improvement of large-scale integrated circuits (LSI), the cost of certain semiconductor memory configurations has been reduced dramatically. Still the cost of such memories varies directly with their speed. The performance of core memories remains approximately competitive with semiconductor memories of equal cost. Magnetic memories enjoy a special advantage of non-volatility. Further, the vast number of core memories in already installed systems guarantees our interest in them for some time to come. When we talk of the *main* memory of a computer, we generally refer to a relatively large store in which we can place entire programs or operating systems. Also, the main memory should feature *random access*, i.e., the access time to any given location in memory should be the same as to any other location. If access is not random, then the programmer must carefully specify storage locations for data and instructions so as to minimize access times, a requirement which makes programming much more difficult. The magnetic core memory is an example of a random access memory.

The manner in which information can be stored in a magnetic core is illustrated in Fig. 3.12. The core is a small toroid (on the order of 0.015″ to 0.030″ diameter) of ferromagnetic material with a high degree of magnetic

FIGURE 3.12. Storage in a magnetic core.

remanence (permanent magnetism). When a current is passed along a wire threading through the core, as in Fig. 3.12a, a magnetic flux (ϕ) will be set up in the core in the direction shown. Because of the high remanence, this flux will remain even after the current stops flowing. If we pass the current in the opposite direction, the flux will be set up in the opposite direction, as shown in Fig. 3.12b. If we let one direction of flux, say that shown in Fig. 3.12a, correspond to a 0, and the other direction to a 1, we have a storage device.

However, it is a useful storage device only if there is some way of finding out what is stored. In a flip-flop, there is a voltage continuously available to indicate what is stored; but there is no such continuous voltage available from a core. The means of interrogating a core is shown in Fig. 3.13. In addition to the original wire (the *drive* winding), a second wire (the *sense* winding) is included. To read the core, a current is passed along the drive winding in the

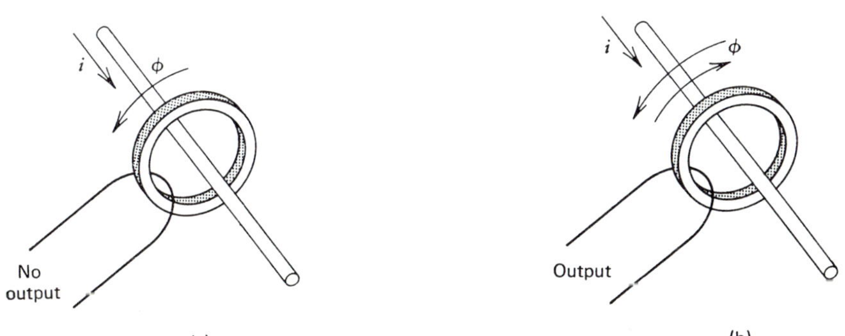

FIGURE 3.13. Reading a core.

same direction required to store a 0. If a 1 was stored, the flux will reverse; and in accordance with Faraday's law,

$$e = N\frac{d\phi}{dt},$$

there will be a voltage pulse induced in the sense winding, as shown in Fig. 3.13b. If there is already a 0 stored, there is no change of flux and no voltage induced (Fig. 3.13a).

We note one problem here, that the read operation destroys the information stored; so if we wish to preserve it, we must write it back in. However, we shall see that this is easy enough to arrange. An advantage of core storage is that it is *non-volatile*, i.e., loss of power does not affect the information stored. We have not talked about circuit details, but flip-flops require the continuous application of DC power to operate. If the power is lost, the flip-flop lapses into a passive state and the information stored is permanently lost, i.e., the storage is *volatile*. Cores (and other types of magnetic memory as well) require power only when it is desired to read or write information. Thus, loss of power to the computer (a not uncommon occurrence) will not affect information stored in core memory.

Consider Fig. 3.14, which shows a typical hysteresis loop for a magnetic core. This is a plot of the flux density (ϕ) in the core as a function of the total current (I) on any wires threaded through the core. The two points labeled 0 and 1 on the zero-current axis correspond to the two values of stored information. When a core changes from one of these states to the other, we will say that the core has *switched*. The key to the operation of the core is that unless enough current is applied to move it past the "knee" of the curve, at point a or point c, it will return to the original state when the current is removed.

Assume the core is in the 0-state and a pulse of *half-write* current, $I_w/2$, is applied. The core will move out to point a, but will return to the 0-state when the pulse ends. Similarly, a pulse of read current, I_r or $I_r/2$, will move the core toward point d, but it will return to the 0-state when the pulse ends. However, if a *full-write* current pulse, I_w, is applied, the core will move through point a to point b. As the current returns to zero, the flux follows the curve to the 1-state. Thus, a 1 is now stored in the core. Similarly, when the core is in the 1-state, write current pulses or a pulse of half-read current, $I_r/2$, will shuttle the core along the upper section of the curve, but will not switch it. A pulse of *full-read* current, I_r, will switch the core through point c to point d and thence to the 0-state.

Now let us consider how one can take advantage of these peculiar characteristics. The simplest type of core memory is the *linear select* (2-D) memory, shown in Fig. 3.15. The cores are arranged in an $m \times n$ array consisting of m words of n bits each. (For simplicity we have shown six 4-bit words. In

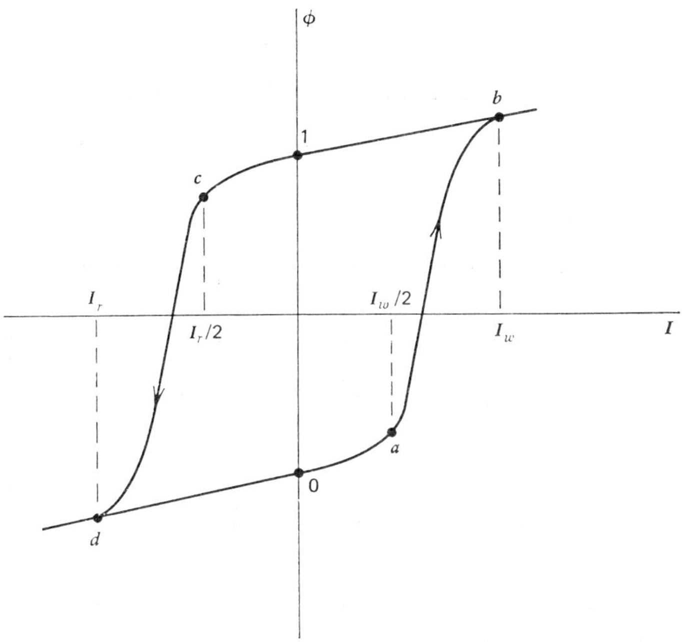

FIGURE 3.14. Hysteresis loop of a magnetic core.

practice the number of bits might be anywhere from 12 to a 100, the number of words anywhere from several hundred to several thousand.) If we wish to store information, we must provide the memory with two pieces of information: the *address* (the number of the word) where we want the data stored, and the data to be stored. We load the address into the *memory address register*, ***MAR***, and the data into the *memory data register*, ***MDR***.

As an example, assume we wish to store 0101 into word 2. We load the address (010 in binary) into ***MAR*** and 0101 into ***MDR***. The word decoder is simply a logic circuit which converts the binary address into a 1-out-of-*m* signal to select the word driver for the desired word line.* Similarly, 1's in the ***MDR*** will select the corresponding bit drivers. Before new data can be written in memory all cores in the word must first be cleared to the 0-state. Therefore, as the first step in a write cycle, the selected word driver will apply a full-read pulse, I_r, to the selected word line (word line 2 in Fig. 3.15). Next, the selected word driver and bit drivers apply half write pulses, $I_w/2$, to the selected word line and selected bit lines.

* A decoder may be magnetic or electronic. A systematic representation of electronic decoding logic will be presented in Chapter 7.

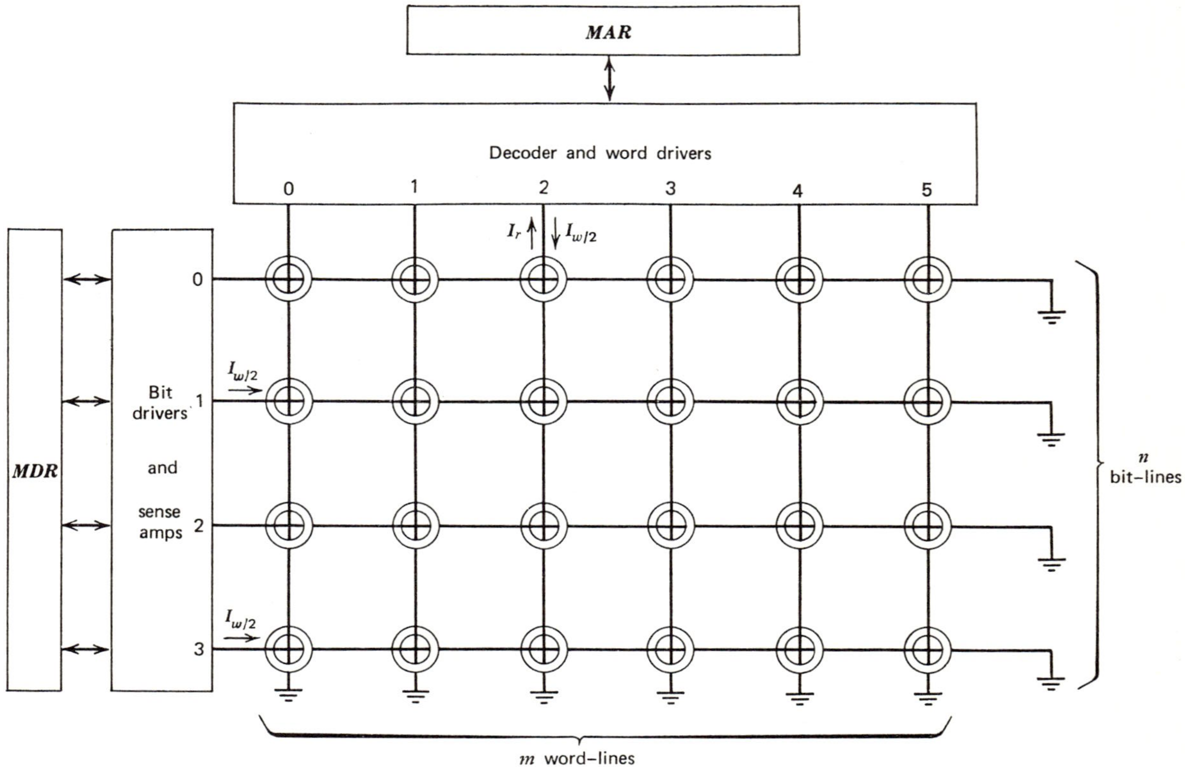

FIGURE 3.15. Linar select memory.

Note that the half-write currents on the word and bit lines pass through the cores in the same direction (from "front-to-back") and are therefore additive. Thus the cores at the intersections of the selected lines (bits 1 and 3 of word 2 in Fig. 3.15) receive full-write current and switch, storing 1's. All other cores in the matrix receive either half-write current or no current at all, so their states are not changed. Thus the data 0101 is now stored in word 2, and all other words remain as they were before the write cycle.

For a read operation, the address of the desired word is entered into ***MAR***. The selected word driver then applies a full-read pulse to the corresponding word line. The bit lines now act as sense windings. Where 1's are stored, the switching of the cores generates voltages on the corresponding bit lines. These voltages are detected by the sense amplifiers and amplified to set the corresponding positions of ***MDR***. Thus the stored word is entered into ***MDR***, from whence it can be transferred to the processing section. Recalling that the read operation is destructive, we let the just-read word in the ***MDR*** select bit drivers and rewrite the data into the selected word.

The main problem with the linear select memory is the amount of external electronics required. Suppose that we have a memory of 2048* words. Then we require enough decoding logic to select 1-out-of-2048 lines and enough drivers for 2048 lines. Without going into details, one can see that this would require a very considerable amount of electronics. An alternate organization, which requires less electronics, is the coincident current, or 3-D, memory, which is illustrated in Fig. 3.16. We have shown only the form of the array itself. The ***MAR*** and ***MDR*** registers, the decoders, drivers, and amplifiers are still required; but their basic function is the same as in the linear select memory, so we have omitted them for simplicity.

The memory consists of n bit-planes, each of which is a square array of m cores. The drive lines are divided into two groups, the X-lines, and the Y-lines, which run through all n bit-planes. To select a word, we select one X-line and one Y-line. The cores at the intersections of the selected lines, one core in each of the n bit-planes, represent the n bits of the selected word. In addition, there is a sense/inhibit winding on each plane, which passes through all the cores on that plane.

For reading, each sense/inhibit line is connected to a sense amplifier, which in turn drives a corresponding bit-position of the ***MDR***. To select a word, we pass half-read currents along one X-line and one Y-line, so that the cores of the selected word, at the intersection of the selected lines, receive a full-read current. Where a 1 has been stored, the core will switch and induce a voltage on the sense line for that plane, thus setting the corresponding position of the

* Note that the number of words in a memory is usually a power of two, simply because the address is a binary number. Thus a "2k" memory (where "k" stands for *kilo*, or 1000) actually contains 2048 words; a "4k" memory, 4096 words; etc.

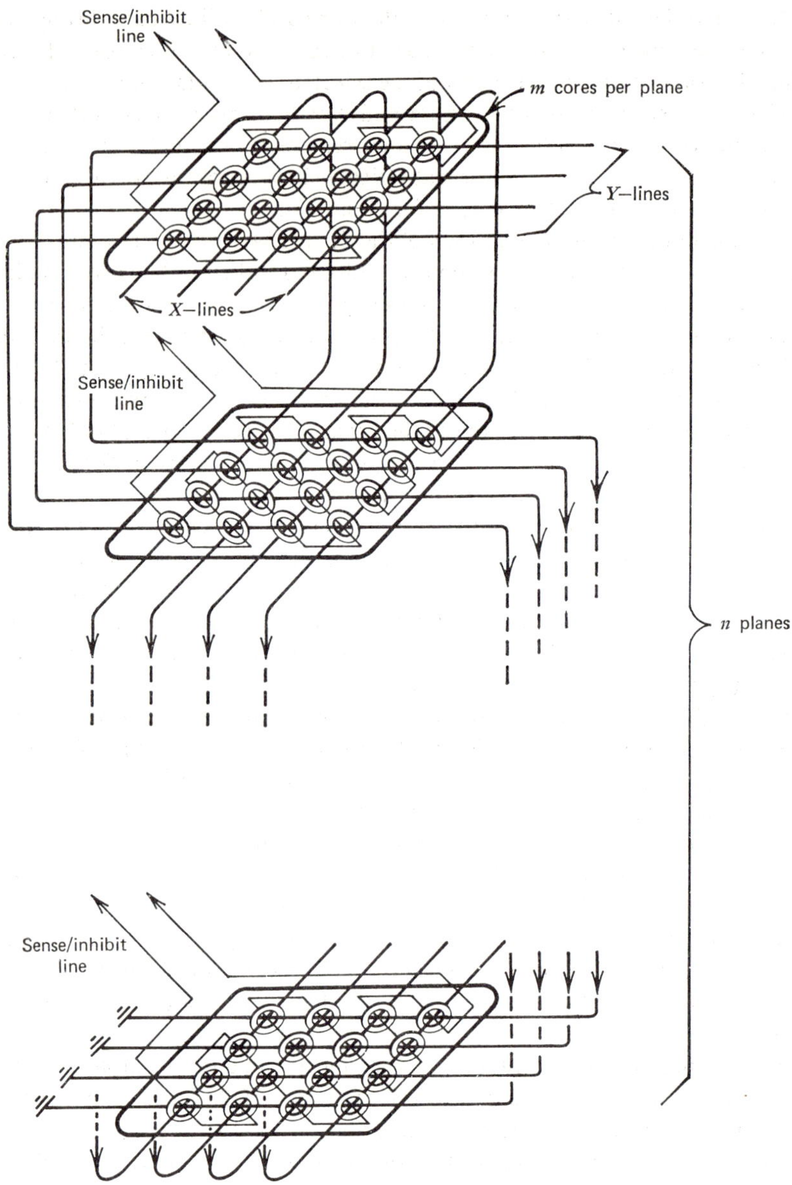

FIGURE 3.16. Coincident-current (3-D) memory.

MDR. To write, we pass half-write currents through the selected drive lines. The selected cores would thus see a net full-write current and switch. Where a 0 is to be written, we pass an *inhibit* current (equal to half-read) through the sense/inhibit line for that plane. This results in a net half-write current for the selected core in that plane, so it does not switch. All other cores in a plane subject to an inhibit current see a net drive of zero or half-read, neither of which changes the setting of any core.

This 3-D organization results in a very considerable saving in electronics relative to the 2-D form. For example, if we use 64 × 64 arrays (possibly the most common size), to select one word out of 4096 we need make only two selections of one-out-of-64, and need only enough drivers for 128 drive lines.

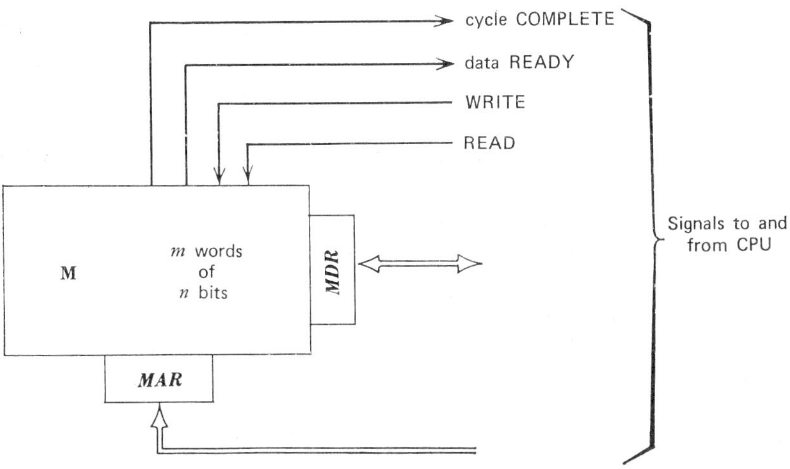

FIGURE 3.17. General model of RAM.

As is usually the case, there is a speed/cost trade-off, as the 3-D memory, for various complex technical reasons, is considerably slower than the 2-D memory. To further complicate the situation, there is a compromise between these two designs: the $2\frac{1}{2}$-D memory, which in certain sizes is cheaper than 2-D and faster than 3-D. The systems designer is generally not concerned with these details, however, regarding the memory as a total system to be selected on the basis of cost-per-bit for a given speed.

From the point of view of the system designer it is desirable to have a general model of the memory, emphasizing the flow of information to and from the memory, and essentially independent of internal details. Such a model for the random access memory is shown in Fig. 3.17. The functions of the ***MAR*** and ***MDR*** have already been discussed. For a read operation, the central processor will load the address of the desired word into ***MAR*** and request a READ operation by placing a pulse on the READ line. As soon as the requested data has been read into ***MDR***, the memory will emit a DATA READY pulse. The memory will then rewrite the data and issue a CYCLE COMPLETE signal when finished and ready to accept a new request. For a WRITE operation, the CPU will load the address into ***MAR***, the data to be stored into ***MDR***, and request a WRITE operation by a pulse on the WRITE line. The memory will execute a READ cycle to clear the desired location, then will WRITE the contents of ***MDR*** into the addressed location, and emit a cycle complete signal.

The READY and COMPLETE signals are required because a core memory is much slower than the logic of the CPU, and its timing is usually independent of the CPU timing. The standard procedure is for the CPU to request a memory operation and then either wait or proceed with other operations until a READY or COMPLETE signal is received. This same general model can also be used for other types of RAM. With the advent of large-scale integrated circuits, all-electronic RAM's, consisting simply of large arrays of registers, are becoming economically feasible. Electronic memories will be designed to operate at a variety of speeds (and costs). Slower electronic memories will be considered RAM's and the model of Fig. 3.17 will apply. Faster memories will be synchronized with the computer clock source, and data ready and cycle complete signals will not be required.

Many different types of electronic RAM's are possible. One basic logical structure is shown in Fig. 3.18, where we have an enlarged view of the connections to one cell. Each cell consists of a flip-flop and required input and output gating. To select a word, a level signal is placed on the word line, enabling the input and output gates. This gates the output of the flip-flops in the selected word onto the bit lines; note that there is a 1-line and a 0-line for each bit. For a READ operation the contents of the bit lines are simply gated into the ***MDR*** by a READ pulse. For a WRITE operation the contents of ***MDR*** are gated onto the bit lines by a WRITE pulse and thence into the flip-flops of the selected word. During the write operation both the WRITE line and the addressed word select line will be 1 simultaneously. From Fig. 3.18 it would appear that conflicting information could be gated onto the bit lines from the ***MDR*** and from the selected memory register. This is avoided electronically. We assume that the output AND gates of ***MDR*** are circuits of significantly lower impedance than their counterparts on the memory registers. Thus when the WRITE pulse is one, the bit lines will assume the values gated out of the memory data register, regardless of the contents of the addressed memory register.

The major advantages of electronic RAM's relative to core are their inherent compatibility in speed and signal levels with the logic circuits, and the fact that the readout is non-destructive. A disadvantage is the volatility.

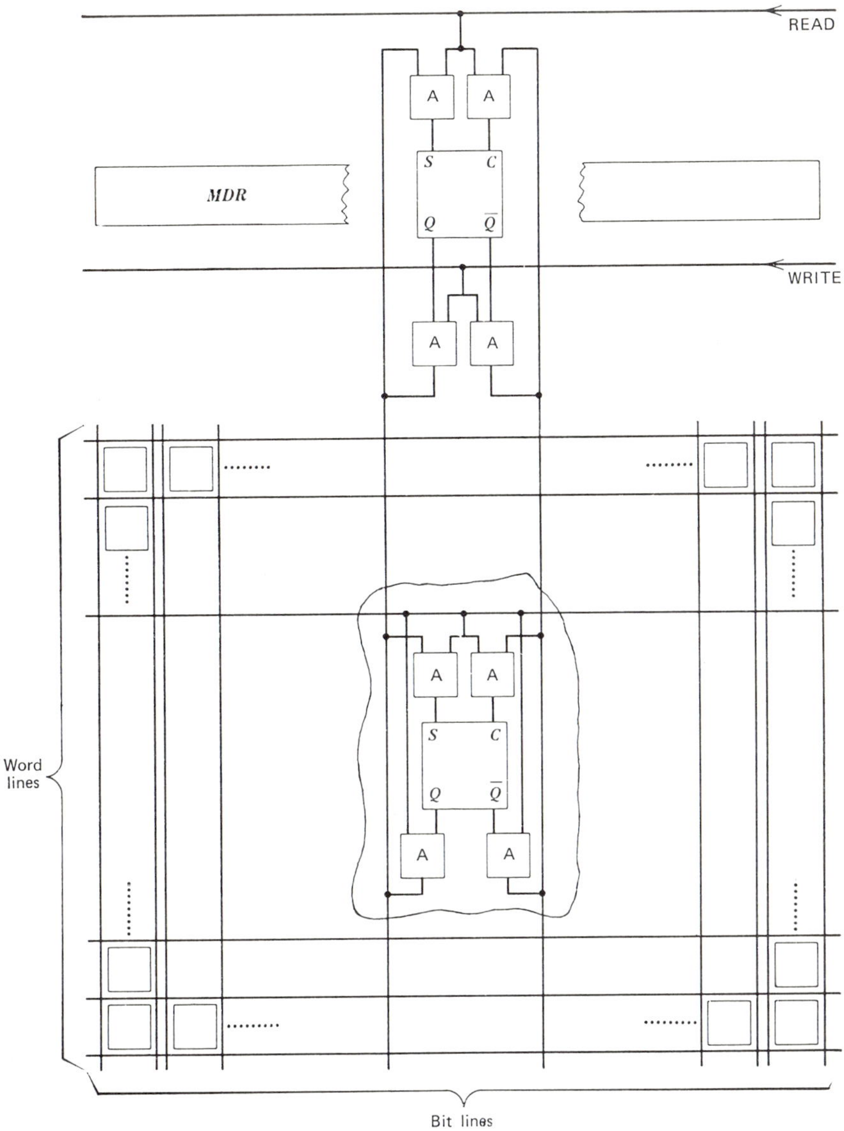

FIGURE 3.18. Basic form of an electronic RAM.

Although the economic picture is constantly changing, only slower electronic memories have become cost competitive to core except in small sizes. As a result, the popular application of faster electronic RAM's has been as *scratch-pad* memories: small, high-speed memories acting as buffers between the relatively slow core memory and the very fast logic circuits.

Finally, we might note that the rewrite cycle in core memory is not always automatic. In some computers, the memory stops after the DATA READY signal and awaits further instructions. The CPU can cause a rewrite by issuing a WRITE request without altering the contents of ***MDR***, or new data can be loaded into ***MDR*** and stored in the location just read. This arrangement may provide some additional flexibility, but this is off-set because the provision of its required rewrite control signals increases the complexity of the control unit. The automatic rewrite system is the most common, and is the arrangement we will assume.

3.7. SEMI-RANDOM ACCESS MEMORY (SRAM)

In many computer systems there is a requirement for very large capacity memory at lower cost than random access memories. *Disk* memories and *drum* memories, which we shall classify as *semi-random access*,* are widely used to meet this requirement. Disk and drum memories are based the same physical phenomena; and their external characteristics, as seen by the system designer, are essentially the same. They differ primarily in mechanical structure.

The basic structure of a small disk memory is shown in Fig. 3.19. A metal disk coated with a ferromagnetic material rotates under one or more read/

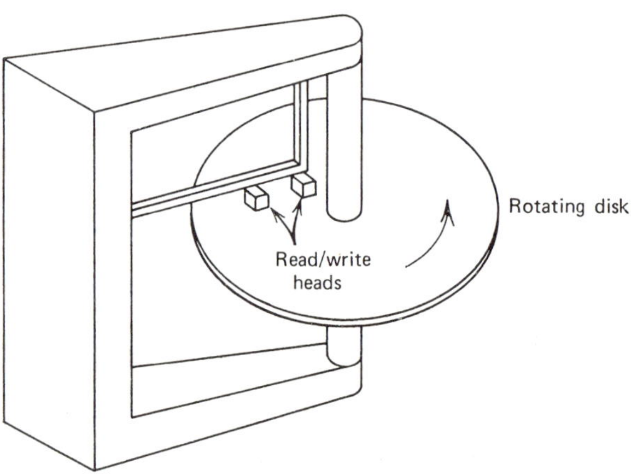

FIGURE 3.19. Basic structure of disk memory.

* MOS shift registers and delay lines also exhibit all of the external characteristics of semi-random access memories.

write heads. The speed of rotation is typically 1800 or 3600 rpm. The manner in which information is stored or recovered is indicated in Fig. 3.20, in which we show a cross section of a read/write head and the disk passing under it. To write information, we pass a current through the coil of the read/write head, which in turn sets up a magnetic flux in the armature (Fig. 3.20a). When the flux crosses the gap in the armature, it passes through the magnetic coating of the disk, thus magnetizing a small area on the disk. The size of the magnetized area depends on the speed of the disk and the duration of the write current. Bit density on disks runs from several hundred to several thousand bits per inch. For reading, the coil is used as a sense winding. As the magnetized area passes under the head, the motion of the flux field relative to the head causes a flux change ($d\phi/dt$) in the gap, which induces a voltage in the sense winding (Fig. 3.20b). This voltage is detected by a sense amplifier and used to set a

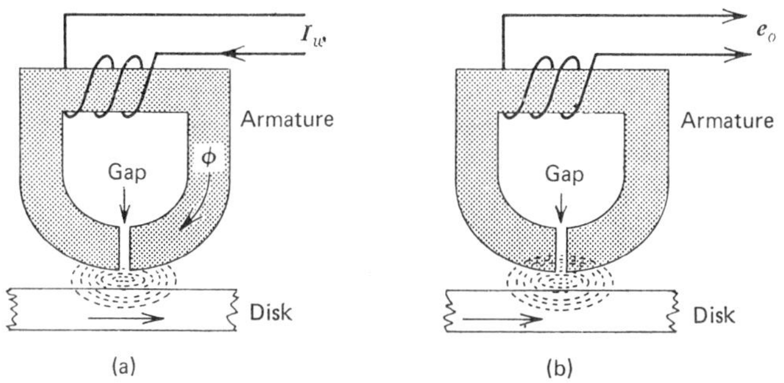

FIGURE 3.20. Write and read operations on a magnetic disk.

register. This reading process is non-destructive since there is no current flowing to alter the stored flux pattern. There are a number of different ways of coding the information on the disk. Different directions of magnetization may be used for 0's and 1's, or 1's may be indicated by a change of flux direction and 0's by no change of flux, etc. The reader is referred to the literature for details on recording processes.

There are several ways of arranging the heads. There may be a large number of heads mounted in fixed positions distributed radially across the surfaces (both sides are used) of the disk. This is known as a one-head-per-track system, where a *track* is simply the circular pattern recorded by a single head. This system is most widely used in single-disk systems. Multi-disk systems have a number of disks arranged in a stack. The heads are mounted on the arms of a *comb* which moves in or out radially to position the heads over selected tracks (Fig. 3.21). Both sides of the disks are used, but we have shown heads on only one side for clarity.

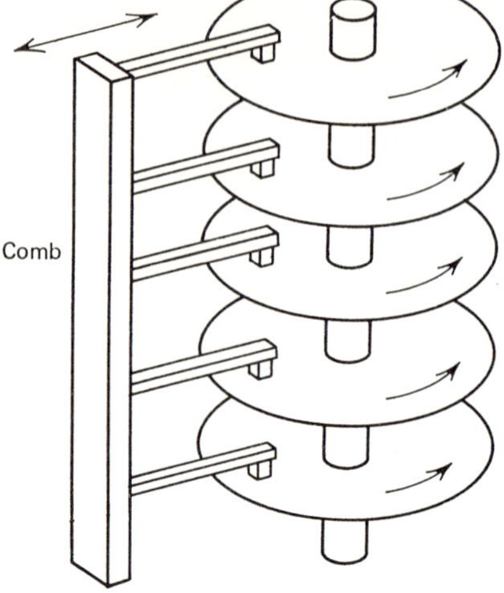

FIGURE 3.21. Basic structure of multi-disk memory.

All data transfer in disk memories is sequential in the sense that data move in or out sequentially as the disks move by the heads, but individual words may be transferred either in serial or parallel. In a one-head-per-track system, we may select a single head, in which case words are transferred serially, one bit at a time. Or, we may select n heads, one for each bit position, in which case words are transferred in parallel, each bit in a separate track. In a multi-disk system, a given track is selected by mechanically positioning the heads. Once the track has been selected, a single head may be selected, providing serial transfer, or parallel transfer can be obtained by taking one bit from each head, i.e., storing each bit on a different disk.

The access to a disk memory is termed *semi-random*, indicating that the access time to a selected word is partially, but not wholly, dependent on its location. A head, or group of heads, can be selected electronically in one clock time; but once the track is selected, it is necessary to wait for the desired location to rotate into position under the head. The average waiting time is known as the *latency* time. With one set of heads, the latency time is the time for half a revolution, $16\frac{2}{3}$ msec for an 1800 rpm disk. Some disks will have several sets of heads spaced around the disk to reduce latency time. If the heads have to be moved to select a track, this adds to the access time; and this added time is a function of the relative locations of the desired track and the current track.

There are probably as many different ways of arranging data on a disk as there are different models of disk memories, but a typical arrangement is that shown in Fig. 3.22. The timing gap is used to reset the timing and addressing circuits once each revolution. The timing track, usually engraved during manufacturing, provides the clock pulses used for synchronizing all read and write operations. If we assume serial data transfer, then each word occupies an n-bit sector in a single track. The start of each n-bit word location is indicated by the word marks, also typically permanently engraved in a special track. Specific word locations are identified simply by counting word marks from the timing gap. For example, if we want the 15th word in a given track, we load the binary address, 01111, into an address register and compare this with another register which counts the word marks; when the two agree, the desired word has been located.

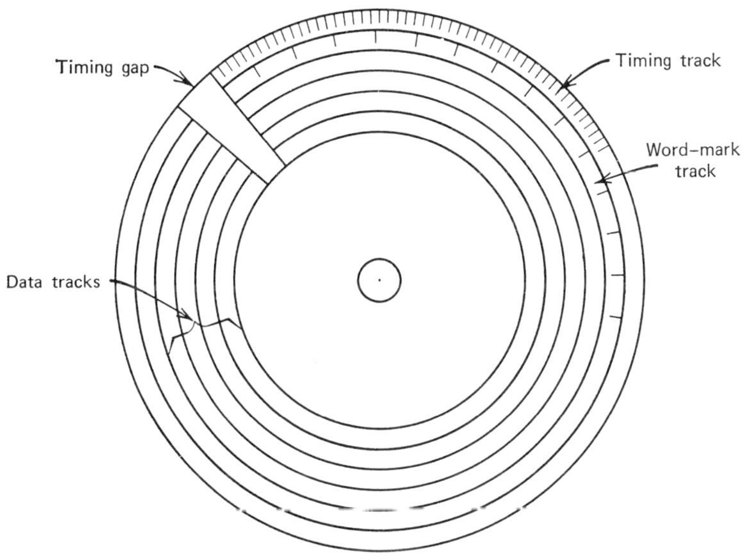

FIGURE 3.22. Typical arrangement of data on disk memory.

For parallel data transfer, where each bit is in a different track, a single word occupies only a single bit-position in a circumferential direction. In this case it is usual to address a group of words rather than a single word. The word marks will thus signify the start of a group of m words, rather than a single word. Note that the circumference of a track obviously depends on its radial location. If we record at maximum bit density on the innermost track, the outer tracks will be recorded at lower densities, thus "wasting" space. This problem can be alleviated by dividing the disk radially into zones, each zone having its own timing and word mark tracks, with the number of words per track decreasing as we move toward the center of the disk.

The other popular type of SRAM is the *drum* memory, the general structure of which is shown in Fig. 3.23. Here we have a rotating metal cylinder, or drum, which is coated with the same type of magnetic material as a disk. The read/write heads are mounted in a fixed position above the rotating surface, and information is written and read in exactly the same manner as in the disk memory. The mechanical structure of the drum is more rigid than that of the disk, making possible higher speeds (up to 24,000 rpm), and thus reduced latency time and higher data rates. Also, since all tracks have the same circumference, all can be recorded uniformly at the maximum density, with minimal timing problems. Words may be read serially from a single head or in parallel from a group of heads.

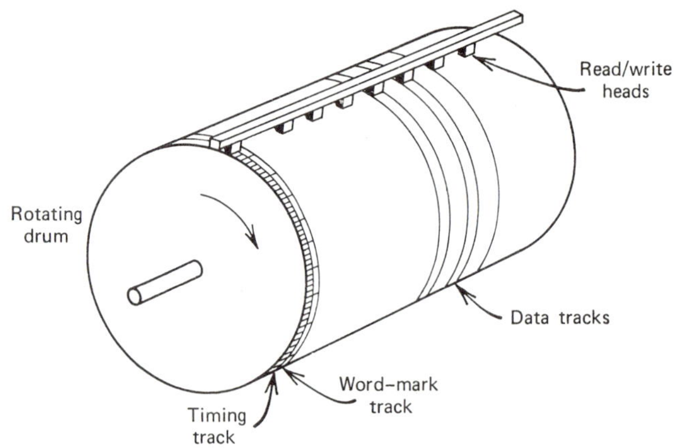

FIGURE 3.23. Typical structure of drum memory.

Single-disk and drum memories offer capacities in the range of 1000,000 to 10,000,000 bits, at roughly comparable costs, and the choice between them is far from clear. The drums are usually somewhat faster, but many disk memories have removable disks that can be changed, much like phonograph records. Multi-disk memories have capacities in the range of 10 million to one billion bits and much lower costs than drum or single-disk memories. However, they are about an order-of-magnitude slower because of the head-positioning time, typically 50 to 250 msec.

Because of the long access time, data are nearly always transferred in and out of SRAM in large blocks of hundreds or thousands of words, which will be stored in sequential locations. Thus it may take anywhere from 5 to 250 msec to access a particular location; but once accessed, and providing no further head movement is required, data can be transferred at rates of 1 to

100 μsec per word. A general model of the SRAM, shown in Fig. 3.24, is based on the assumption that data will be transferred in large blocks.

The CPU will load the address of the block (or the first word in the block) into the ***MAR*** and request a READ or WRITE operation by placing a level signal on the appropriate control line. The SRAM will then proceed to access the desired location. For a READ operation, the SRAM will issue a READY signal when the first word is available in the ***MDR***. The CPU will then transfer this word to its own registers, or into core memory, and issue a RESUME signal, indicating that it is ready for another word. The SRAM will load the next word into ***MDR*** and issue a READY signal, etc. The process will continue in this manner until the CPU has received the desired number of words, at which time it ends the READ signal, thus terminating the transfer. The WRITE process will proceed in a similar fashion, except that READY will indicate that the SRAM is ready to have a word loaded into ***MDR*** for

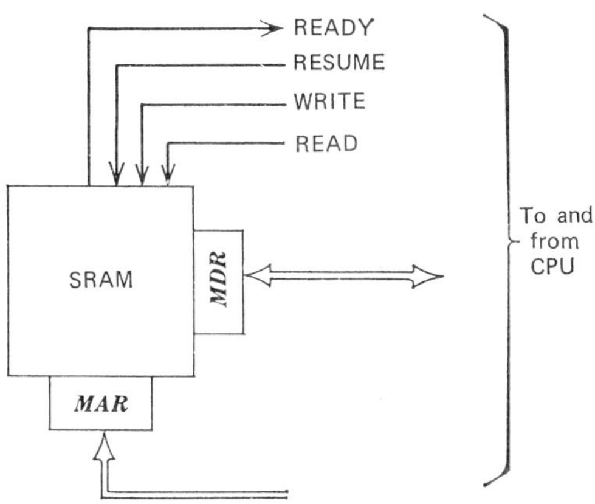

FIGURE 3.24. General model of SRAM.

storage, and the RESUME signal will indicate that the requested word has been loaded into ***MDR*** from the CPU.

Note that data transfer proceeds at a fixed rate determined by the speed of the disk or drum and independent of the clock rate of the CPU. It is thus vital that the control of the CPU be such that there is no possibility of failing to respond to a READY signal by clearing or loading the ***MDR*** before the next location moves into position. One method of handling this problem is to provide a controller, or synchronizer, between the SRAM and the CPU, which will have a small *buffer* memory of its own that can temporarily store a small block of words, thus giving the CPU more time to respond. Also, drum or disk transfer instructions may include the number of words to be transferred, and the controller may be used to keep track of this. However, such refinements may be regarded as extensions of the CPU operations, so that the above general model will still apply.

3.8. SEQUENTIAL MEMORY (SM)

Sequential memories, of which magnetic tape is the most common type, fill the need for very large capacity memory of very low cost. Digital magnetic recording tape is plastic tape coated with a magnetic surface, identical except in size and quality to the tape used for home recording. The tape is wound on reels and passes from one reel to another past a read/write head (Fig. 3.25).

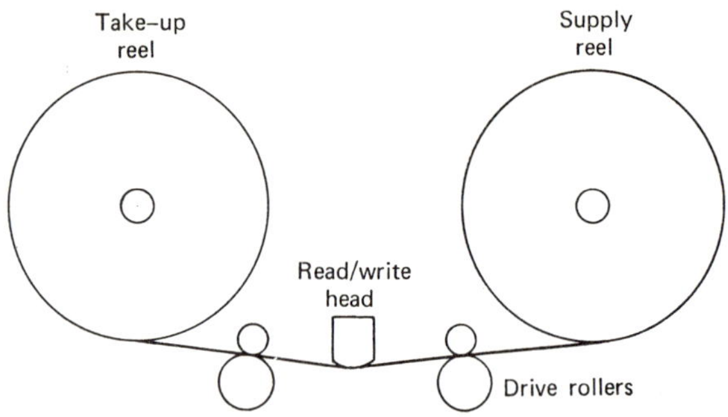

FIGURE 3.25. Basic structure of tape transport.

Digital tape transports are similar in principle to home tape recorders, but provide for much faster and more precise control of tape movement. The method of reading and writing is identical to that used in drum and disk memories.

The general arrangement of data on a tape is shown in Fig. 3.26. Data is recorded laterally in groups of seven to thirteen bits, known as *characters*, arranged laterally across the tape. One of the bits is normally a *parity* bit,

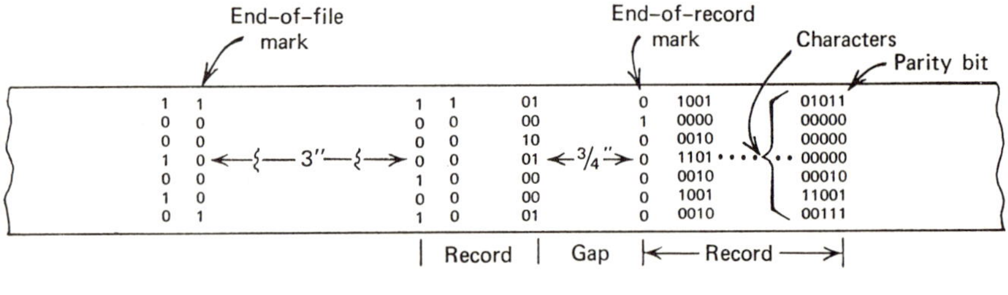

FIGURE 3.26. Typical data format on magnetic tape.

selected to be 1 or 0 so that the total number of 1's in a character will be odd. This is used as a means of detecting errors, which are primarily caused by imperfections in the tape surface. When the data are read, if the total number of 1's in a character is not odd, an error is known to have occurred.

When tape is written, consecutive characters will continue to be written at uniform intervals as long as data continue to be made available. All the characters written in a single WRITE operation will constitute a *record.* When the WRITE operation ends, an *end-of-record mark* will be generated to establish longitudinal parity over each bit position in the record; and the tape will come to a stop. When another WRITE operation is initiated, the tape will come up to speed and this process will be repeated. Because it takes time to

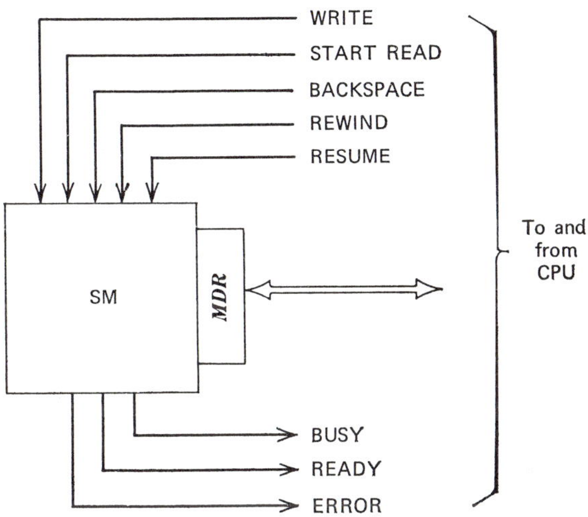

FIGURE 3.27. General model of sequential memory (SM).

stop and start the tape, there will be a blank interval (usually $\frac{3}{4}''$) between records, known as the *interrecord gap.* In addition, most systems provide for a special one-character record known as the *end-of-file mark,* where a *file* is simply a set of records which have some logical connection. Thus all the payroll records of a firm might be one file, all the sales records another file, etc. The end-of-file mark is usually placed three inches after the end of the last record in the file; and since it is considered a one-character record, it has its own end-of-record mark associated with it.

The general model for a sequential memory is shown in Fig. 3.27. The ***MDR*** may handle a single character, or a word made up of several characters. If the latter, then the SM unit must include logic for disassembling the word into characters for WRITE and assembling characters into words for READ. The CPU will initiate a WRITE operation with a level signal on the WRITE line, and the SM will respond with a BUSY signal and start the tape moving. When the tape is up to speed, the SM will request data by emitting a READY signal. The CPU will transmit data to the ***MDR*** and reply with a RESUME signal. The SM will store the data and request more by emitting another READY signal, etc., the operation continuing in this manner until the desired amount of data has been stored. The CPU will terminate the operation by ending the WRITE signal. The SM will generate the end-of-record mark, stop the tape, and end the BUSY signal, indicating that it is now available for further operations.

The CPU will initiate a READ operation by emitting a START READ pulse. The SM will respond with a BUSY signal and start the tape moving. When the first character or word is available in ***MDR***, the SM will issue a READY signal. The CPU will transfer the data into its own registers or memory and reply with a RESUME signal. This process will continue until the entire record has been read. When the SM senses the end-of-record gap, it stops the tape and turns off the BUSY signal. Note that the CPU has no control over how much is read; when a READ operation is initiated, the SM will read to the end of the record and stop, whatever the length of the record. The CPU instructions which the programmer writes to control tape operations will usually include the number of words to be read, so that an appropriate amount of memory may be set aside to receive the data. If the number of the words in the record is not what was expected, this will be indicated by the BUSY signal ending before or after the expected number of words has been received. The programmer may provide for detection of this condition, known as *length error*, if he wishes. Means for detecting length errors is sometimes provided in the tape unit, but we will consider it a function of the CPU and not include it in our general model.

However, there are a number of error conditions, such as parity errors, attempts to write past the end of the tape, etc., which can only be detected by the tape unit. Therefore we indicate an ERROR output on our general model, with the understanding that in any particular model there may be a number of error lines, depending on the number of error conditions defined by the designer.

Note that there is no means of addressing locations on tape. READ and WRITE operations start wherever the tape happens to be. We can move forward or backward on the tape a desired number of records. If we want to skip a record, for example, we simply issue a START READ command but ignore the data being read. The BACKSPACE command will move the tape back to the immediately preceding inter-record gap, i.e., one record back. We can provide for locating specific records by writing identification characters at the beginning of the record. We can then search the tape by looking for the correct identification. The REWIND command rewinds the entire tape onto the supply reel.

The recording density on magnetic tape ranges from 200 to 1000 characters per inch. The number of characters on a tape will depend on the number of records or files, since the gaps take up space. A standard $10\frac{1}{2}''$ reel of tape holds 2400 feet, providing a maximum capacity of about one-half to two-and-one-half million characters. Since the tape reels can be removed and stored, the total capacity of a tape system is unlimited. Also, because tapes can be removed, it is a matter of opinion as to whether tapes should be regarded as memory devices or input-output devices; but it doesn't much matter how they are classified as long as their characteristics are understood.

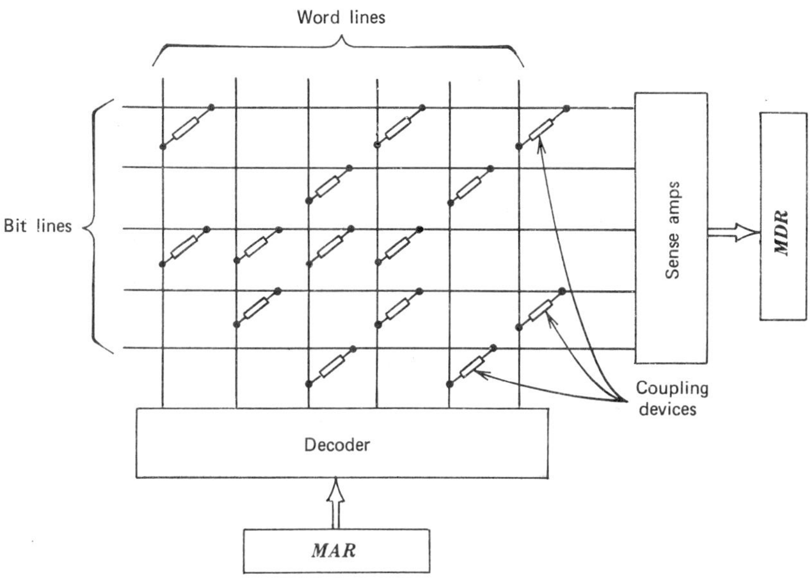

FIGURE 3.28. Basic structure of read-only memory.

3.9. READ-ONLY MEMORY (ROM)

The read-only memory is a device in which the stored information either is permanently fixed during fabrication or can be altered only by mechanical changes in the device structure. The basic form of the typical read-only memory is shown in Fig. 3.28. The address in the ***MAR*** is decoded to select one word line, in the same general manner as in the 2-D core memory. A voltage is applied to the selected word line, which in turn is coupled through to a bit line wherever a coupling element is connected. Wherever a coupling device is connected, a 1 is considered to be stored; wherever there is no connection, a 0 is considered to be stored. The coupling device may be connected during fabrication, in which case the information storage is permanent. Alternately, coupling devices may be placed at each intersection but not connected, with means provided for the user to establish connections where he wishes 1's to be stored. One common system is to use a version of a punched card, with holes punched where connections are to be made. Thus, by changing cards, the user can change the stored information.

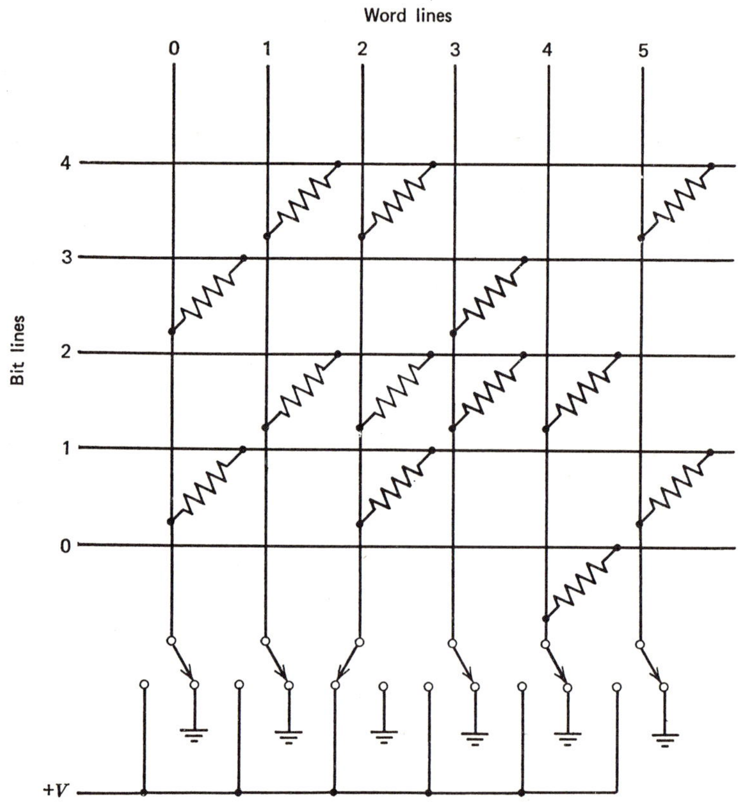

FIGURE 3.29. Resistive ROM.

Various types of ROM's differ chiefly in the type of coupling device used. The simplest possible coupling device is a resistor, but there are severe attenuation problems with resistive arrays. Suppose the selection is by switches that switch from ground to a fixed voltage when a word is selected, as shown in Fig. 3.29, where we have shown word 2 selected. Note that bit 4 is 1 for word 2, and also for two other words, 1 and 5. The current flowing through the coupling resistor from word 2 to bit 4 will flow through the other two coupling resistors to ground on word lines 1 and 5. Assuming all resistors equal, only one-third of the applied voltage will appear on the bit line. This is not too bad; but if there are several hundred words with, on the average, half of them coupled to any bit line, only a very small fraction of the applied voltage will appear on the bit line. In addition, the electronic switches that must be used for adequate speed are not ideal, and the unselected word lines will have a finite impedance to ground. Signals will thus be cross-coupled onto unselected lines and thence onto all bit lines, making it even more difficult to distinguish legitimate signals from noise. For these reasons, resistive arrays are limited to relatively small size and are relatively slow.

Another simple type of coupling device is the capacitor. In the capacitor-coupled ROM the drive signals are pulses, and for a variety of technical

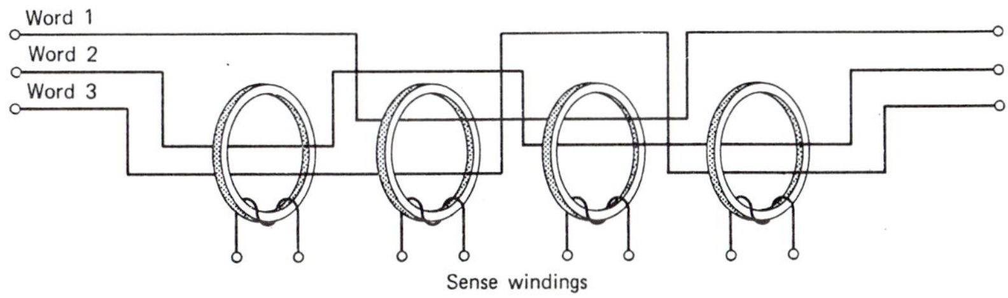

FIGURE 3.30. Transformer-coupled ROM.

reasons the attenuation and crosstalk problems are much less severe than in the resistor-coupled memory. Capacitor-coupled ROM's have been used in several models of the IBM Systems 360 and 370 with various models having capacities of 2k to 8k words and cycle times in the range of 80 nsec to 1.0 μsec.

A very popular type of ROM is the transformer-coupled ROM, shown in Fig. 3.30. Rather than using a coupling device at each line and bit intersection, there is just one magnetic core per bit. These cores are like the cores used in core memory except much larger. Each core has a sense winding. There is one line for each word: where a bit is to be 1, the word line passes through the core; where it is to be 0, it does not pass through the core. To read a word we pass a pulse of current down the word line. Where it passes through a core, the magnetic coupling results in a voltage being induced in the sense winding. There is very little crosstalk because the unselected lines are open-circuited so that no current can flow on them. As a result, the drive pulses can be quite large, producing large output pulses and relative freedom from noise problems. However, the magnetic cores limit the speed, 500 nsec being about the fastest access time obtainable. This type of ROM has been used in many computers, in virtually every size range. The final type of ROM we shall consider is the transistor-coupled, or semiconductor, ROM, shown in Fig. 3.31. At each point where a 1 is to be stored a transistor is connected, the emitter to the bit line, the base to the word line. All collectors are connected to a common supply voltage. All word lines are normally held at a sufficiently negative level to cut off all the transistors, so that the bit lines are at 0 volts. When a word

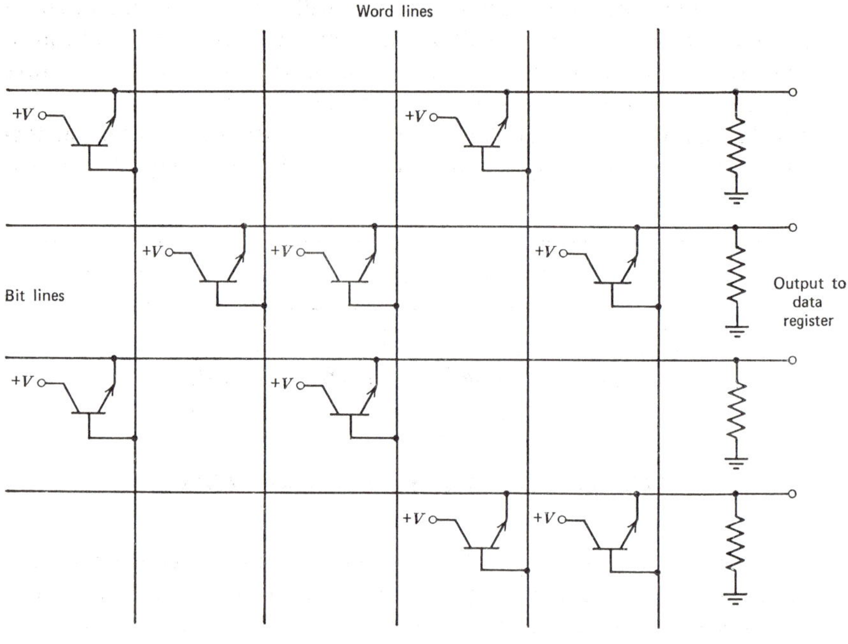

FIGURE 3.31. Transistor-coupled ROM.

line is selected, it is raised to a sufficiently positive level to switch the transistors on, thus raising the bit lines where a transistor is connected to a positive level. Please note that we have described here only the basic principles involved; the precise details of the technology vary widely.

This type of ROM has been technically possible for some years, but it is only with the advent of integrated circuits that it has become economically attractive. Integrated circuit ROM's are available in both bipolar and MOS types, with capacities up to several hundred words, including address decoding logic, in a single IC package. Depending on type, MOS or bipolar, access times range from about 1 μsec to less than 50 nsec. The direct compatibility, both in speed and logic levels, with the logic circuits is an obvious advantage. A disadvantage for some applications is that they are not alterable. The manufacturing process generally involves connecting a transistor at each intersection and then disconnecting the emitter where a 0 is to be stored, by a chemical etch or some other permanent method. However, as costs decrease and capacity and speed increase with continuing developments in integrated circuit technology, it is likely that this type of ROM will become the dominant type.

3.10. SUMMARY AND PERSPECTIVE

As we stated at the beginning of the chapter, this is not intended to be an exhaustive survey. There is at least one whole category of memory that we have not treated: mass memory to handle the problems of very large stores, such as census or tax records. At present, magnetic tape is the dominant medium for such applications. Its capacity is unlimited, but it has the disadvantage of requiring manual handling of the tapes. A mass memory in which the computer could have access to any part of the store without human intervention would have obvious advantages. Most research in this area has centered on optical and photographic techniques. A few systems have been developed, but this is basically an area with many difficult problems and few solutions.

Even with better access, the problems of searching very large files are formidable, and there has been much interest in the *associative*, or *content-addressable*, memory. As an example, in a hit-run investigation it might be desired to search the license plate files for all owners of cars of a certain make, year, and color. But these files would be indexed under license number or owner's name, so that a complete search of the entire file would be required. In an associative memory we would simply input the desired identifying characteristics, and all records with matching characteristics would be immediately identified, without exhaustive search. Many techniques for implementing this type of memory have been suggested, but none have even approached the low cost required for very large files. The associative memory which seems so inviting as a means of handling large files may also be used as a high-speed buffer memory. This application will be discussed in the next-to-last chapter of this text.

Even within the categories we have discussed, we have treated only those types which seem to have the greatest present and continuing importance. However, continued technical developments will undoubtedly produce new devices and change the relative importance of existing devices. Rather than attempt to prophesy the future (with our very cloudy crystal ball), we will try to give the reader some perspective on the cost-speed relationships among the various categories of memory. These relationships are, hopefully, somewhat independent of exact form of implementation and may, therefore, have some continuing validity.

In Fig. 3.32 we show a logarithmic plot of memory speed vs. cost per bit. The four main types of memory—register, random access, semi-random access, and sequential—are represented by dark areas on the graph, since there are wide variations in speed and cost in each category. Even with these variations, however, it is notable that there are distinct intervals between the

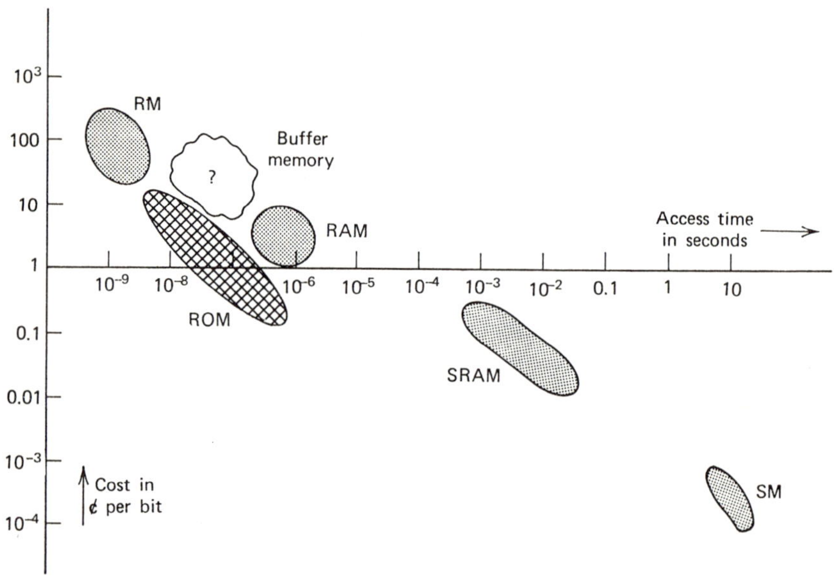

FIGURE 3.32. Cost/speed relationships of memory.

four categories, a fact which presumably accounts for the continuing importance of all four types over the past 15 to 20 years. Over these years, the graph as a whole has shifted downward and to the left, i.e., toward cheaper and faster; but the relative position of the four types has not changed significantly.

Further, it seems likely that this relationship will remain valid for some years to come, with one exception. The scratch-pad or high-speed buffer memory falls into the interval between register memory and RAM. As developments in integrated circuits continue to improve the cost/speed factor for electronic memory, the register and random-access areas will probably merge. As a result, electronic memory will increasingly replace core memory.

In time, core will probably be limited to very large memories and to applications where its non-volatility is important. (The relative importance of volatility in memories is a subject of spirited debate among computer designers). Where the speed of the core memory is inadequate but non-volatility is important, the plated-wire memory may find considerable application. A plated-wire memory is a 2-D memory in which the individual cores are replaced by a magnetic film plated onto the bit lines, and the word lines are wrapped around the plated bit lines. The operation is basically similar to the 2-D core memory except that the readout is non-destructive, resulting in shorter cycle times. These memories offer cycle times as low as 200 nsec at costs roughly comparable to core memory.

In the area of semi-random access, integrated circuit manufacturers are offering MOS shift registers as possible replacements for the drum memory in the smaller size ranges. They offer faster speed and greater logical flexibility, but their volatility may be a problem. Advocates of semiconductor RAM have suggested that loss of volatile main memory in case of power failure may be avoided by providing sufficient standby battery power to unload the volatile memory onto disc or drum. This option is obviously ruled out if the disc or drum are replaced by volatile memory types. Whatever the future of MOS shift registers, it is unlikely that they will significantly change the cost/speed position of SRAM.

There appears to be nothing in prospect to replace tape; and magnetic tape may very likely prove to be the most durable of all memory types.

A cross-hatched area covering most of the read-only memory technologies, discussed in the previous section, is shown in Fig. 3.32. Notice that the ROM is cheaper than read-write memories with the same access time.

We noted earlier that it is a matter of choice as to whether magnetic tape should be regarded as a storage medium or an input/output medium. Similarly, ROM could equally well be regarded as stored logic, and electronic RAM is just a special case of register memory. It is important that the designer recognize these multiple points of view and remain flexible in his attitudes about the possible applications of specific devices. Rigid classification of devices leads to rigid thinking and stereotyped design.

REFERENCES

1. Hill, F. J., and Peterson, G. R., *Introduction to Switching Theory and Logical Design*, Wiley, New York, 1968.

2. Gschwind, H. W., *Design of Digital Computers*, Springer-Verlag, New York, 1967.

3. French, M., "Rotating Discs and Drums Set Peripheral Memories Spinning," *Electronics*, Vol. 42, No. 11, May 26, 1969, pp. 96–101.

4. Burroughs Corp., *Digital Computer Principles*, 2nd Ed., McGraw-Hill, New York, 1969.

5. Husson, S. S., *Microprogramming*, Prentice-Hall, Englewood Cliffs, N.J., 1970.

6. Fedde, G., "Plated-Wire Memories," *Electronics*, Vol. 40, No. 10, May 15, 1967, pp. 101–109.

7. de Atley, E., "The Big Memory Battle: Semis Take On Cores," *Electronic Design*, Vol. 18, No. 15, July 19, 1970, pp. 70–77, 113–114.

8. Talbert, C. D., "Simplify Random-Access Memory Selection," *Electronic Design*, Vol. 18, No. 17, Aug. 16, 1970, pp. 70–74.

9. Joseph, E. C., "Memory Hierarchy: Computer System Considerations," *Computer Design*, Vol. 8, No. 11, Nov. 1969, pp. 165–169.

10. Mrazek, D., "Shrink Delay Line Costs with MOS," *Electronic Design*, Vol. 17, No. 5, March 1, 1969, pp. 50–57.

11. Taren, W., "Semiconductor Memory Systems: How Much Do They Really Cost?," *Electronics*, Vol. 43, No. 21, Oct. 12, 1970, pp. 94–97.

12. Bremer, J. W., "A Survey of Mainframe Semiconductor Memories," *Computer Design*, Vol. 9, No. 5, May 1970, pp. 63–73.

13. Hoff, M. E., "MOS Memory and Its Application," *Computer Design*, Vol. 9, No. 6, June 1970, pp. 83–87.

14. Bryant, R. W., et al., "A High-Performance LSI Memory System," *Computer Design*, Vol. 9, No. 7, July 1970, pp. 71–77.

15. Bonn, T. H., "Mass Storage: A Broad Review," *Proc. IEEE*, Vol. 54, No. 12, Dec. 1966, pp. 1861–1869.

16. McAteer, J. E., et al., "Associative Memory System Implementation and Characteristics," *1964 Fall Joint Computer Conf., AFIPS Proc*, Vol. 26, Pt. 1, pp. 81–94.

4

Design Conventions

4.1. INTRODUCTION

The procedure which we shall propose for computer design will be based on a high-level language. Most of this language will be presented in the next chapter. The purpose of this chapter is to interpret certain of the more basic conventions in terms of hardware. Enough of the language will be presented to permit the design of a simple vector-processing digital system. The need for a more sophisticated notation will become evident in the process. The reader will find that the language of Chapter 5 will satisfy this need.

4.2. REGISTER TRANSFERS

Much of the activity of a vector-handling digital system consists of transferring vectors of information from one register to another. A computation consists of placing some Boolean function of the contents of argument registers into a destination register. It is quite possible to view a digital computer simply as a collection of registers among which data may be transferred, with logical manipulations taking place during the transfers. As we shall see, a major part of the description of a computer will consist of a schedule, or listing, of data transfers. All this being the case, it is essential that the designer have a thorough understanding of the ways in which data may be transferred in a computer.

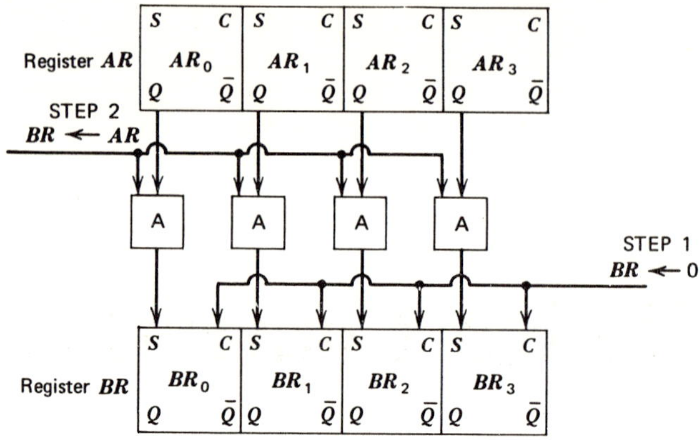

(a) Clear and set transfer

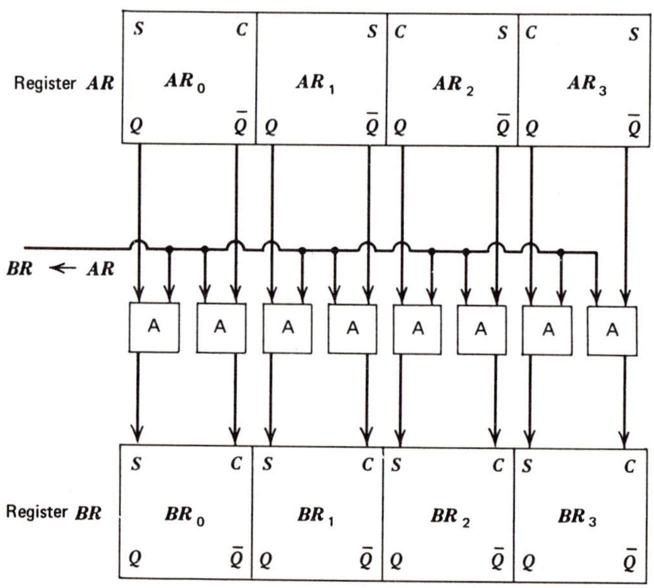

(b) Jam transfer

FIGURE 4.1. Transfer hardware.

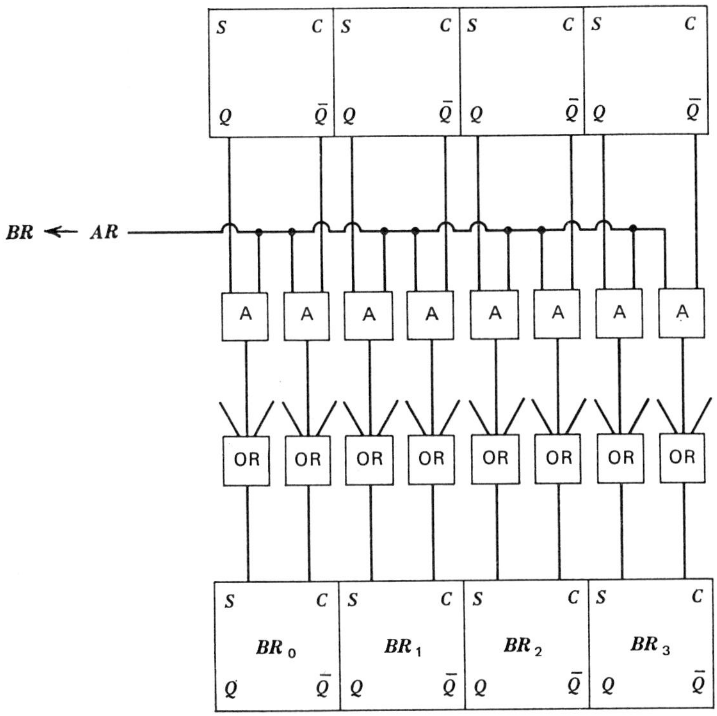

(c) Jam transfer allowing other inputs to *BR*

FIGURE 4.1. *(Continued)*

As we discuss register transfers, we shall need a system of notation. The notation we shall develop is part of a formal design language, the details and formal definition of which will be the subject of the next chapter. Registers will be noted by strings of italic capitals, such as ***MA***, ***PC***, ***AC***, etc. Transfer of the contents of one register into another is indicated by an arrow, e.g.,

$$AC \leftarrow MD$$

signifies that the contents of ***MD*** are transferred to ***AC***. The contents of the source register, i.e., ***MD*** in the above example, are not affected by the transfer; but any previous information in ***AC*** is, of course, destroyed. The notation

$$AC \leftarrow 0$$

will indicate that all the flip-flops in ***AC*** are cleared, while

$$AC \leftarrow 1$$

will indicate that all the flip-flops in ***AC*** are set.

There are two basic methods by which a register transfer may be accomplished: *clear-and-set* transfer and *jam* transfer. The typical configuration for a clear-and-set transfer is shown in Fig. 4.1a. (For simplicity, we shall assume 4-bit registers for the examples in this section.) We wish to transfer the contents of register ***AR*** to register ***BR***. We first clear ***BR***,

$$BR \leftarrow 0$$

by placing a pulse on the line so labeled, which clears all the flip-flops in ***BR***. We then transfer ***AR*** to ***BR***,

$$BR \leftarrow AR$$

by placing a pulse on the line so labeled. In each bit-position, this pulse is ANDed with the Q-output of the ***AR*** register. Where there is a 1 stored (Q-output = 1), the corresponding flip-flop in the ***BR*** register will be set, i.e., a 1 will be stored. Where there is a 0 stored (Q-output = 0), the ***BR*** flip-flop will remain cleared, i.e., a 0 will be stored.

A typical jam transfer configuration is shown in Fig. 4.1b. To transfer data a pulse is applied to the line labeled

$$BR \leftarrow AR.$$

In those positions where a 1 is stored in ***AR***, the corresponding ***BR*** flip-flop is set; where a 0 is stored, the ***BR*** flip-flop is cleared. The clear-and-set method uses less hardware; the jam transfer is faster. Both are used; the choice is a matter of speed vs. cost. For the remainder of this book we shall use the jam transfer exclusively.

Note carefully that a statement such as

$$BR \leftarrow AR$$

not only specifies a data transfer, but also has a specific hardware implication. It implies the existence of AND gating to control the transfer and the generation of a pulse to cause the transfer to take place. This is the basic philosophy behind the design procedure developed in this book: A description of what is to take place in the computer directly implies a corresponding hardware configuration. Fig. 4.1c is identical to Fig. 4.1b except that OR gates have been added at the input to each flip-flop in ***BR***. This provides for transfering information to ***BR*** from other registers in addition to ***AR***. We shall always assume these OR gates to be available, if needed.

The statement

$$BR \leftarrow \overline{AR}$$

specifies the transfer of the logical complement of the data in ***AR*** to ***BR***.

This is accomplished by a circuit of the same form as Fig. 4.1b, except that the Q-outputs of the $\boldsymbol{AR}$ flip-flops are gated to the clear inputs of the corresponding $\boldsymbol{BR}$ flip-flops, and vice versa. This is the first example of processing, or logical manipulation, during transfer.

In the above cases we have assumed that the two registers are the same size and that all bits are being transferred. When this is not the case, the bit-position involved in the transfer must be clearly indicated. As shown in Fig. 4.1, the bit-positions of an n-bit register are numbered from left-to-right from 0 to $n - 1$, and are denoted by the subscripted register name, e.g., $\boldsymbol{AR}_0$, $\boldsymbol{AR}_1$, $\boldsymbol{AR}_2$, $\boldsymbol{AR}_3$. With this notation we can specify the transfer of individual bits or small groups of bits; for example,

$$\boldsymbol{BR}_2 \leftarrow \boldsymbol{AR}_1$$

In some cases it is necessary to specify the transfer of a large group of bits, in which case listing all the bits to be transferred would be cumbersome. For this reason we use the notation

$$\alpha^j/\boldsymbol{AR}$$

to indicate the first (left-most) j bits of the indicated register, and the notation

$$\omega^j/\boldsymbol{AR}$$

to indicate the last (right-most) j bits. For example, in SIC, suppose the address portion of an instruction in the last thirteen bits of the instruction register, $\boldsymbol{IR}$, is to be transferred to the 13-bit memory address register, $\boldsymbol{MA}$. This transfer is indicated by

$$\boldsymbol{MA} \leftarrow \omega^{13}/\boldsymbol{IR}.$$

These transfers imply the same kind of gating shown in Fig. 4.1b, except that only the specified bits are gated.

4.3. THE SYNCHRONOUS SYSTEM

Before considering further approaches to register transfers, we pause to include a section of background material primarily for the non-electrical engineer. The terms *voltage level* and *voltage pulse* have already been used without precise definition. The only physical difference between the two terms is the duration of their existence. In Chapter 3 we chose the convention that logical 0 will be represented by zero volts and that logical 1 will be represented by some positive voltage. To facilitate the discussion of this section we shall use +5 volts. A voltage pulse, then, will refer to a brief transition of the voltage from zero to +5 volts and back to zero. The precise duration of a pulse will vary with the type of devices used in the system. A

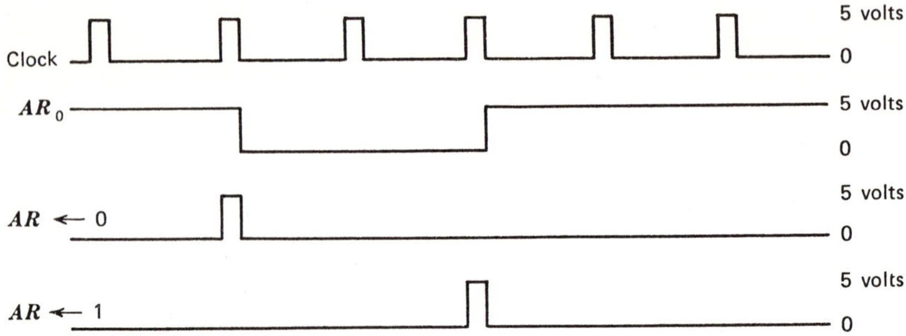

FIGURE 4.2. Pulses and levels.

voltage level will be of longer duration, at least as long as the interval in time between two consecutive clock pulses. As will become apparent, the system application of levels and pulses will be quite different. Information vectors will be represented in the form of a set of voltage levels, while control signals will be pulses.

The basis of the control of a clock mode, or synchronous, digital system is a periodic sequence of clock pulses, as illustrated in the timing diagram of Fig. 4.2. Every transfer pulse occurring within a system is of the same duration as a clock pulse and approximately coincides in time with a clock pulse. Two transfer pulses are also shown in Fig. 4.2. Both of these pulses in some way transfer information into a register ***AR***. The effect of these transfers on one particular flip-flop, $\boldsymbol{AR}_0$, is shown. Although the origin of the 0 is not specified, the first pulse places a 0 in $\boldsymbol{AR}_0$. This is illustrated on the timing diagram, as the voltage at the 1-output of $\boldsymbol{AR}_0$ falls from 5 volts to zero immediately following the transfer pulse. The output of $\boldsymbol{AR}_0$ returns to 5 volts two clock periods later, following a transfer pulse which is denoted as placing a 1 in this flip-flop.

The output of $\boldsymbol{AR}_0$, or of any flip-flop, is a *logic level.* Logic levels may change following any clock pulse but remain at a fixed value in the interval between clock pulses. The output of any Boolean logic network whose inputs are all levels will also be a level. The following example is concerned with the interaction of levels and pulses within a logic network.

Example 4.1

Consider the logic network of Fig. 4.3a, in which initially a and b are set and c is cleared. At some point in time a tranfer pulse enters the network on a line labeled $c \leftarrow a \wedge b$, as shown in Fig. 4.3b. This line serves as one of the inputs to AND-gates 2 and 3. The other input to A2 is the line $a \wedge b$, which is initially at a 5-volt level since a and b are both 5 volts. During the pulse input, both inputs to A2 are logical 1, so that the output of A2 (labeled P_1) will be 5 volts for the

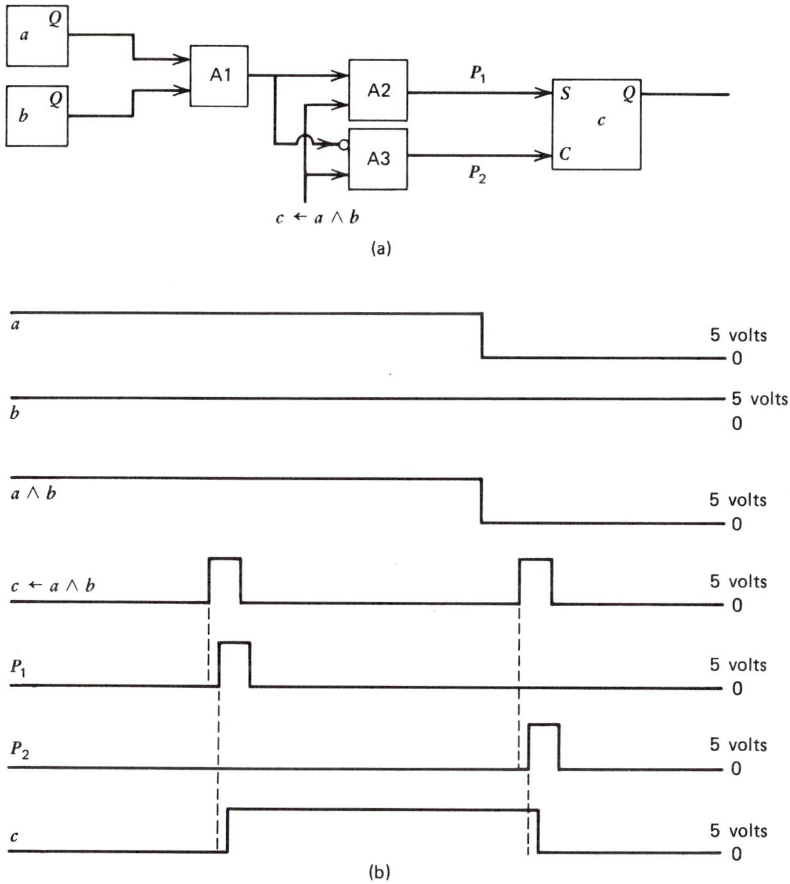

FIGURE 4.3. Propagation of levels and pulses.

duration of the input pulse. Notice in Fig. 4.3b that the pulse on P_1 is a slightly delayed version of the input pulse. As pointed out in Chapters 3, delay is characteristic of all logic. Colloquially, we say the pulse propagated through the gate A2.

At this same time the level input to A3, $a \wedge b$, is at the O-level, so the pulse does not propagate through A3. Thus, only the S input to flip-flop c is pulsed, so that c goes to 5 volts, again after a short propagation delay.

Notice that a second pulse appears on the line $c \leftarrow a \wedge b$ at a later time, as shown in Fig. 4.3b. By this time, flip-flop a has been cleared *to* O by a transfer pulse not shown, so that $a \wedge b$ is not O and $a \wedge b$ is logical 1. This second pulse therefore propagates through gate A3, clearing flip-flop c to O.

The reader with some previous experience in logical design may wonder at the advisability of transmitting data in the form of pulses. From the previous discussion in this section it would appear that we are committed to this approach. This may not necessarily be the best approach in practice. In very high-speed systems noise problems and problems of pulse skew sometimes make it desirable to minimize the number of lines that will carry pulses.

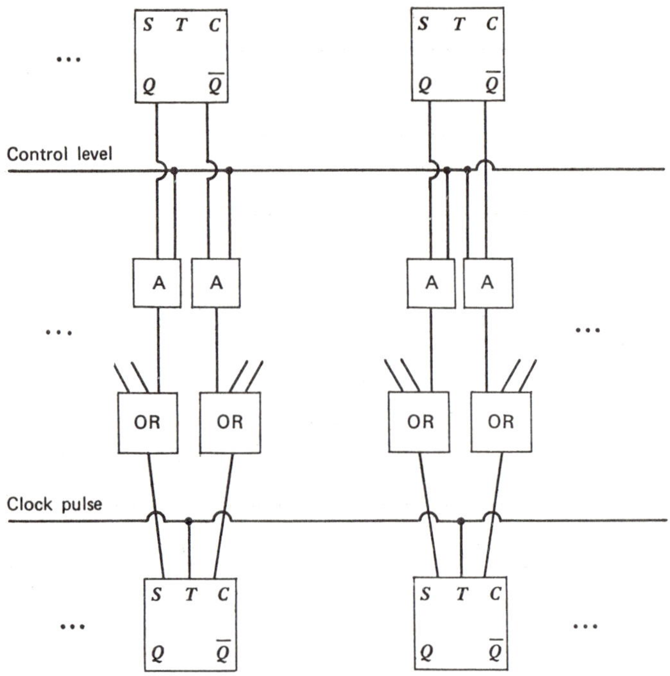

FIGURE 4.4. Partial register transfer using clocked flip-flops.

Many commercially available memory elements have a third input line, as do those shown in Fig. 4.4. This input is designed to accommodate a pulse which triggers the change of state of the flip-flop. In this case the set and clear signals are levels, both of which may not be 1 simultaneously. If $S = 1$ when a pulse appears at the T input, the flip-flop will be set to 1. If $C = 1$, when a pulse appears at T, the flip-flop will be cleared to 0. These are the types of memory elements that are usually assumed in a treatment of clock mode sequential circuits.

Where this type of memory element is used, the control unit must provide control levels to route the flow of data for register transfers. Either clock pulses or specific control pulses may be used to trigger the data into the destination register. Various approaches are possible, and these imply various constraints on the design of the control unit. Where noise is a problem, there is an advantage in triggering the input of data to all registers by way of a clock pulse of a single low-impedance line. Many different data transfer schemes with corresponding control unit designs are in use. It is not our purpose to consider them all. The scheme which we shall use consistently throughout the book makes liberal use of pulses. It may not be the most satisfactory electronically, but it will work under ordinary circumstances. It has the advantage of clarity and can be adapted in a straightforward manner to handle all control situations which will arise throughout the book. For completeness, level-oriented control will be treated briefly in Section 7.10.

4.4. BUSING

In the examples of Section 4.3 we considered only the gating between a single pair of registers. Many times we must provide for the gating of any one of several registers into any one of several other registers. For example, suppose we have two registers, ***AR*** and ***BR***, both of which we must be able to gate to either of two other registers, ***CR*** or ***DR***. The direct extension of the method of Fig. 4.1b to this requirement is shown in Fig. 4.5a. For each transfer desired there must be a set of AND gates to combine the register outputs and the transfer pulses, and there must be a set of OR gates at the input of each receiving register.

As the number of registers increases, the above method gets very expensive. For example, with four registers to be gated to any one of four other registers, 16 sets of AND gates will be required; and the OR gates must all have four inputs. An alternate method which is generally less expensive is the use of an interconnection *bus*, as shown in Fig. 4.5b. The reader will note that the bus wire is merely a network of OR gates. A hardware saving is achieved by not realizing the complement lines of the bus separately. The AND gates at the complement ($\bar{Q}$) output of each flip flop in ***AR*** and ***BR*** have been omitted. Instead the complement lines of the bus are formed by routing the uncomplemented bus lines through a set of NOT gates. In some cases depending on the electrical characteristics of the AND gates, the OR gates may be replaced by direct connection on bus wires.

The notation for a bus will be the same as for a register, i.e., italic capitals, except that the name of a bus will always end in the word "***BUS***." For

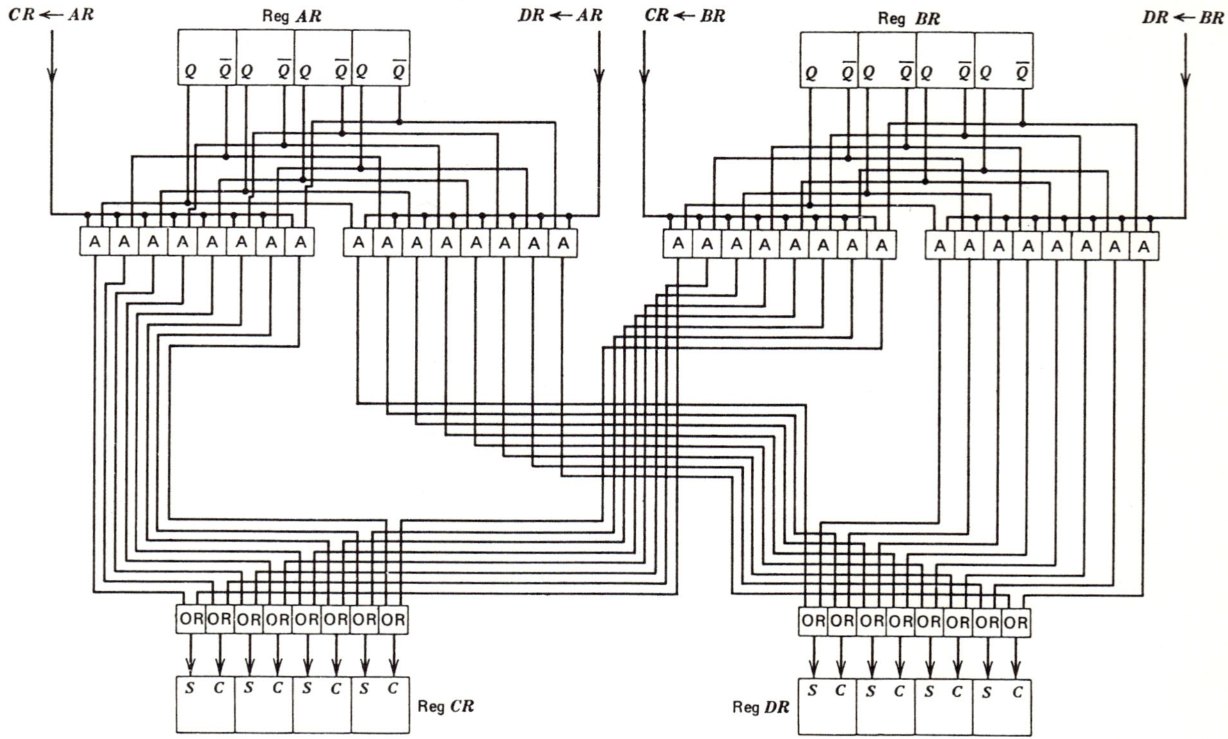

FIGURE 4.5a. Transfer among a group of registers.

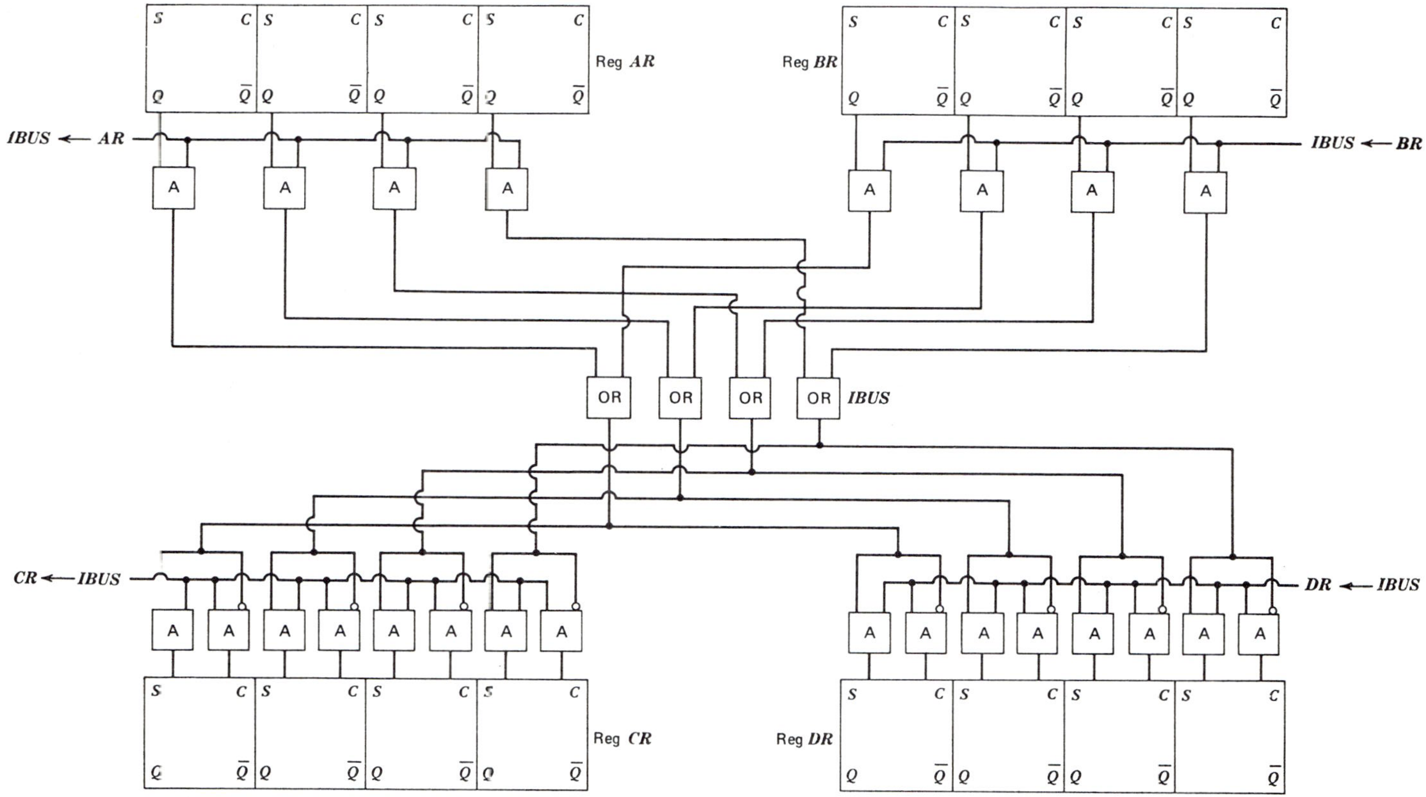

FIGURE 4.5b. Bus connection of registers.

example, the bus in Fig. 4.5b will be referred to as the ***IBUS***. This notational similarity will not prove inconvenient as a bus exhibits many of the characteristics of a register. Transfer of data through a bus is a two-step process. The first step will require generating a logical 1 level on one of the input control lines. In Fig. 4.5b these control lines are designated

$$IBUS \leftarrow AR \qquad \text{and} \qquad IBUS \leftarrow BR$$

Establishing a level signal on a control line will require setting a flip-flop. This requires one clock period just as does transferring a new information vector into a register. The second step consists of generating a control pulse on one of the output control lines to transfer the contents of the bus into a destination register. This last operation does not differ from transferring the contents of a register to a destination register. These control lines are designated

$$CR \leftarrow IBUS \qquad \text{and} \qquad DR \leftarrow IBUS$$

in Fig. 4.5b. The distinction between a bus and a register is the limitation that the information vector stored on a bus must always be identical with the information vector currently stored in some register.

Theoretically, both the output signals gating onto the bus and the input signals gating from the bus could be pulses. However, this would require careful synchronization. Wherever possible, we should avoid the necessity of synchronizing pulses. In this book, all transfers having a bus as destination will be assumed to be gated by level signals; all transfers to a register will be assumed to be gated by pulse signals.

The actual physical realization of a bus may be something far more complex than simply a set of gates, as implied by Fig. 4.5b. The exact form will depend on the type of input and output gates used, the number of registers connected, and a variety of other factors. The result of gating more than one register onto the bus at a time will depend on the exact form of the bus. In some cases the result may be a logical OR'ing of the data; in others the result may be unpredictable. In this book we shall assume that only one register may be gated onto the bus at a time. It is acceptable to pulse the data on a bus *into* any number of registers simultaneously.

Both methods of register interconnection, separate gating and busing, are used. The use of a bus will increase the time required (unless transfers can be overlapped) by a register transfer from one clock period to two. To suggest the possible hardware saving achieved through the use of a bus, suppose that it is desired that a path be made available for the transfer of information *from any one of n registers to any other of the same n registers.* Let us neglect the cost of the bus and the cost of the OR gates at the register inputs (see Fig. 4.5a). These may be required whether busing is employed or not. *If busing is not used, n^2 banks of AND gates are required. If busing is*

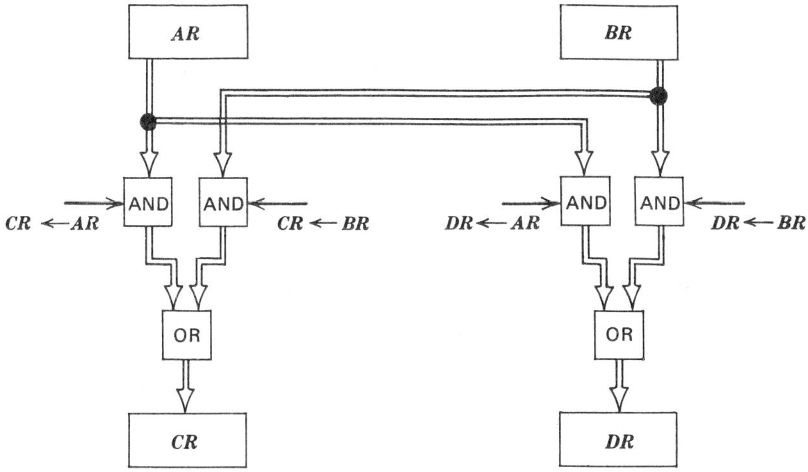

(a) Simplified equivalent of Fig. 4.5a

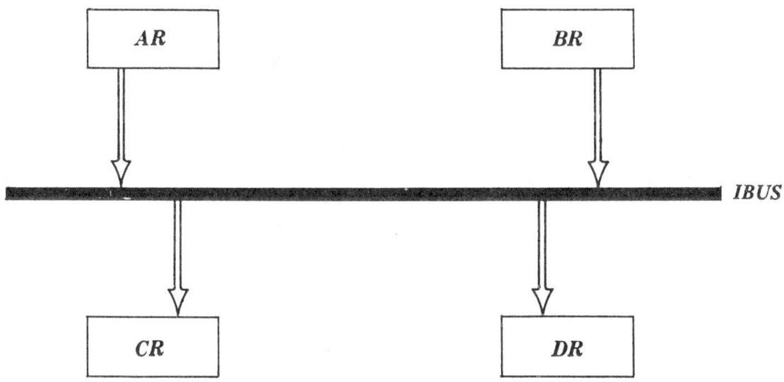

(b) Simplified equivalent of Fig. 4.5b

FIGURE 4.6

used, only 2n banks of AND gates will be needed. Thus where interconnections between three or more registers are required, the use of busing will permit a savings in hardware. Where not all possible paths between registers are needed, the situation is more complicated; but the analysis is similar.

Before proceeding, it will be necessary to have a simplified diagrammatic form for representing these interconnections; diagrams showing all the individual lines, as in Figs. 4.5a and 4.5b, are obviously impractical. The simplified equivalents to these figures are shown in Fig. 4.6. Single lines indicate individual data or control lines, double lines indicate sets of lines, and solid lines indicate buses. Where the inputs to gates are sets of lines, the gate symbol is understood to indicate the appropriate set of gates. In the case of direct connections, the control gates may be shown, as in Fig. 4.6a, or they may be omitted for clarity since their use is generally clearly implied by the very existence of the interconnections. For bus systems, Fig. 4.6b, the control gates will not be shown since the use of a bus always requires the input and output gating, as shown in Fig. 4.5b.

4.5. MORE COMPLEX TRANSFERS

In the transfer of the complement we saw an example of processing data simply by altering the destination. There are several other operations that may be accomplished in a similar fashion. For example

$$BR_1,BR_2,BR_3,BR_0 \leftarrow AR_0,AR_1,AR_2,AR_3$$

indicates right rotation of ***AR*** into ***BR***, i.e., each bit is shifted one position to the right, except for the right-most bit which "rotates around" to the left-most position. As this is an awkward notation, we shall use

$$BR \leftarrow \downarrow AR \qquad \text{and} \qquad BR \leftarrow \uparrow AR$$

for right and left rotation, respectively. A very similar operation is shifting, identical to rotation except that the bit shifted out at one end is lost and a 0 is entered into the vacated position at the other end. We shall use

$$BR \leftarrow \overset{0}{\downarrow} AR \qquad \text{and} \qquad BR \leftarrow \underset{0}{\uparrow} AR$$

for right and left shift, respectively.

On block diagrams these "processing transfers" will be indicated by separate transfer paths, with the appropriate symbol written next to the path. For example, in Fig. 4.7, in addition to the direct transfers to or from

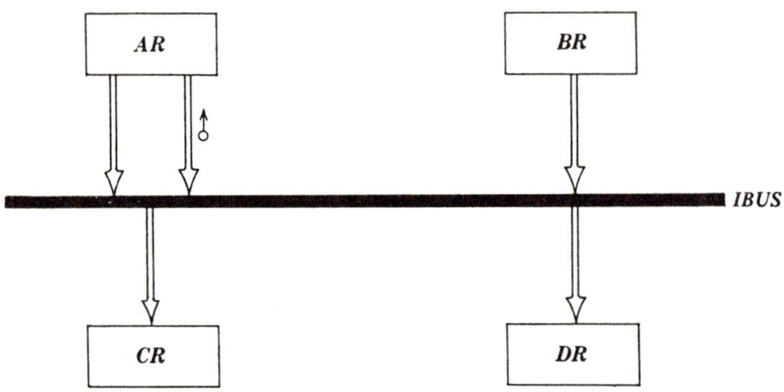

FIGURE 4.7. Processing transfer paths.

the bus, we also indicate a path for

$$IBUS \leftarrow \underset{\circ}{\uparrow} AR$$

Obviously, it is not possible to accomplish all processing operations simply by "redirecting" data transfers. However, a discussion of logic circuits and interconnections for more complex operations will be deferred to later chapters.

4.6. MASTER-SLAVE FLIP-FLOPS

In the previous section all transfers were from one register to another, but sometimes the same register may be both source and destination. For example, left shift within a single register might be accomplished by the circuit shown in Fig. 4.8. Note that the inputs to each flip-flop are controlled by the flip-flop immediately to the right, except for AR_3, which is cleared. Thus when the shift pulse is applied, the contents of each flip-flop should be transferred to the flip-flop immediately to the left. While this type of circuit, known as a *shift register*, is entirely practical, there are some special timing problems.

Assume that in the course of a particular shift operation the contents of AR_2 are to change from 0 to 1. When the shift pulse is applied, a signal will be applied to the clear input of AR_1 and the set input of AR_2. After a certain delay, the outputs will change. If the shift signal is still present when the output of AR_2 changes to 1, the result will be a signal at the set input of AR_1, causing it to change again. The control pulse must be short enough to ensure that it is gone before the outputs change; but if it is too short, it may fail to

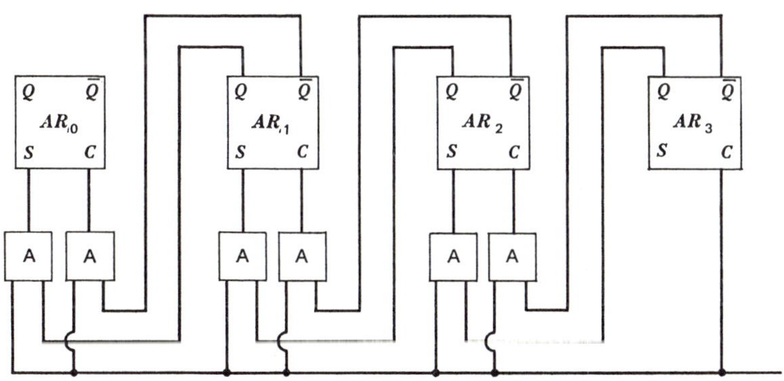

$AR \leftarrow \underset{\circ}{\uparrow} AR$

FIGURE 4.8. Shift register.

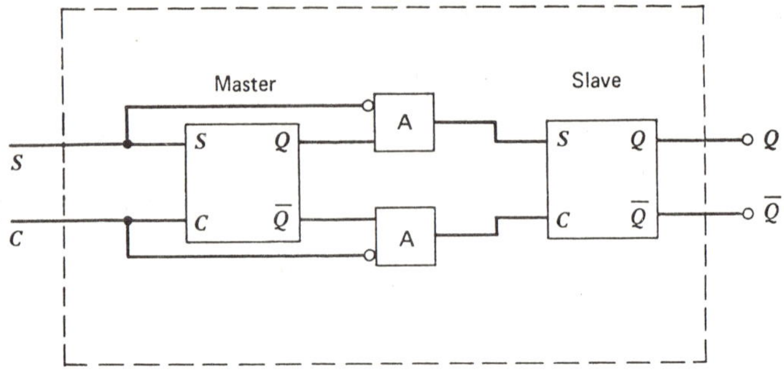

FIGURE 4.9. Master-slave *S-C* flip-flop.

trigger a transition. It is quite possible to design flip-flops such that the delay in output transition is longer than the minimum pulse duration required for reliable triggering, but the allowable tolerance on pulse duration becomes very small as speed increases.

There are a number of ways of solving this timing problem, but one of the most popular is the use of the *master-slave* flip-flop. A master-slave flip-flop may be either *S-C* or *J-K*; in either case it simply consists of a tandem connection of two flip-flops, as shown in Fig. 4.9. We might note that there are many different circuit configurations for master-slave flip-flops, but Fig. 4.9 illustrates the basic logical character of any of them. In the absence of input pulses, both master and slave sections are in the same state, SET or CLEAR. Let us assume the flip-flop is in the CLEAR state and a SET pulse is applied. This pulse is applied to the *S*-input of the master flip-flop and is inverted and applied to the upper AND-gate, thus blocking any possible input to the *S*-input of the slave flip-flop. (There is a signal at the *C*-input of the slave flip-flop; but since it is in the CLEAR state, this has no effect.)

The SET pulse triggers a transition in the master flip-flop, causing the *Q*-output to go to 1, the $\bar{Q}$-output to 0. This removes the signal from the *C*-input of the slave flip-flop; but because of the inhibiting effect of the inverted pulse, no signal is applied to the *S*-input. When the input pulse ends, the inhibiting signal is removed; and the 1-output of the master flip-flop passes through the upper AND-gate to trigger the slave flip-flop to the SET state.

Note that this sequence guarantees correct operation even if the input is a function of the output, since the output cannot change until the input has properly triggered the master flip-flop; and the change in the output, taken from the slave, cannot affect the master until the time of the next pulse.

In system block diagrams we will not use any special symbol for master-slave flip-flops, since *logically* they are the same as ordinary flip-flops. From a logical point of view, a master-slave *S-C* flip-flop is simply a flip-flop so constructed that the output cannot possibly change until after the input pulse has ended, regardless of how long the input pulse may be. This characteristic relieves the system designer of many timing problems, but does not change the logical character of the system. Further, master-slave flip-flops are obviously more expensive than ordinary ones, and should not be used unless their conservative timing characteristics are really needed.

4.7. CLOCKING AND CONTROL

In previous sections we have seen the need for pulse signals to control the gating of information into registers. This obviously raises the question of the origin of these pulses. In the majority of digital systems, and virtually all computers, these pulses are ultimately derived from a pulse generator or oscillator known as the *clock*. The clock emits a continuous string of pulses, with very accurately controlled frequency (repetition rate) and duration. The main function of the control unit is to gate these pulses to the appropriate places at the appropriate times. There are many different techniques for distributing these pulses, and a detailed study of two methods will be the main topic of Chapters 7 and 8.

One popular technique uses what is sometimes referred to as a *multiphase* clock. The output of the clock oscillator is applied to a *commutator* circuit, consisting of a ring counter or a binary counter with decoder, which successively gates clock pulses, one at a time, onto a set of lines, as shown in Fig. 4.10. For an eight-phase clock, these signals might be denoted $\boldsymbol{CLK_0}$, $\boldsymbol{CLK_1}$, $\boldsymbol{CLK_2}$, . . . , $\boldsymbol{CLK_7}$. This set of clock lines is applied to a control logic section, along with the op code of the instruction being executed and, possibly, some status signals from various parts of the computer. The outputs of this control logic section are the lines carrying the control signals to the other sections of the computer (Fig. 4.11). For example, a pulse on one line might cause transfer of the accumulator, ***AC***, to the memory data register, ***MD***. Another clock pulse might initiate the writing of the contents of ***MD*** in

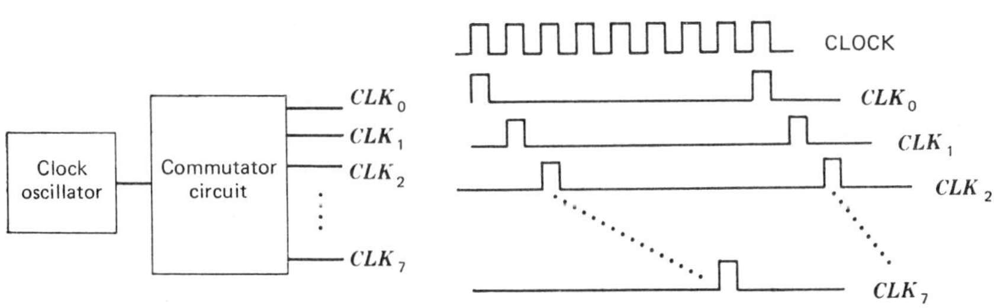

FIGURE 4.10. Multi-phase clock.

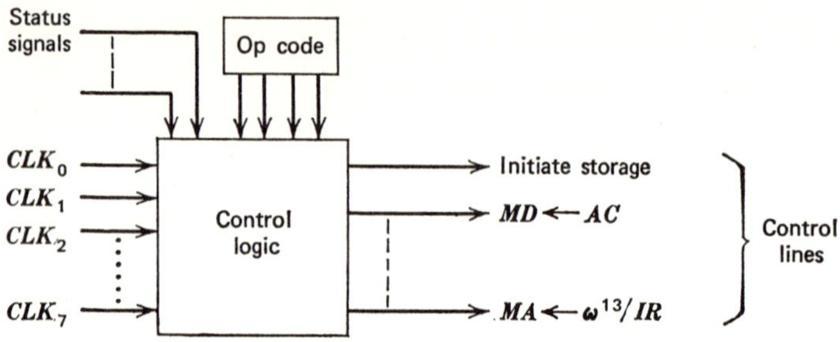

FIGURE 4.11. Control section with multi-phase clock.

memory, etc. Thus, in the execution of the DAC (Deposit Accumulator) command, for example, the control logic might use a CLK_0 pulse to place an address in the memory address register MA. This is symbolized by

$$MA \leftarrow \omega^{13}/IR$$

These would be followed by a CLK_1 pulse, triggering

$$MD \leftarrow AC$$

and then a CLK_2 pulse on the INITIATE STORAGE line.

The above procedure would allow for a maximum of eight steps in a control sequence. If more are needed for some commands, the op code may be stored in a special counter. The CLK_7 pulse may then be used to step this counter to a new value, which will initiate a new set of steps. The counter may be designed to provide a sequence of any length which is a multiple of eight. This last point is the weakness of this method. All sequences must have a fixed starting point, usually with CLK_0; so if all eight steps are not needed, time is wasted waiting for the next CLK_0 pulse.

An alternative approach which makes it simpler to vary the number of steps in a sequence is shown in Fig. 4.12. Here the clock drives an arbitrary sequence counter, the outputs of which directly drive the control lines. By means of appropriate input and feedback logic a counter can be made to generate any output sequence. See Reference [3]. Here the op code and various status signals are used to control the counter logic in such a manner as to produce the desired sequence of control signals.

The outputs from the counter will be level signals, which may be used to gate clock pulses when pulse signals are required. Timing problems may be avoided by the use of a two-phase clock, which is particularly convenient for bus transfers, as shown in Fig. 4.12. When a CLK_0 pulse moves the counter into the appropriate state, a level signal will be generated, say

$$IBUS \leftarrow MD$$

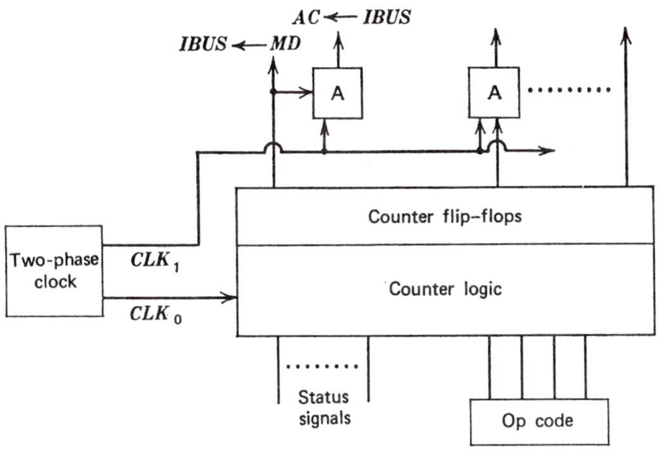

FIGURE 4.12. Control with arbitrary sequence counter.

and this same signal will gate a CLK_1 pulse to generate

$$AC \leftarrow IBUS$$

The next CLK_0 pulse will move the counter to a new state, ending the input gating to the bus. This method also makes it convenient to vary the time allotted to various steps. For example, INITIATE STORAGE can be followed by a sequence of several steps with no outputs, to allow time for the memory reference. The main drawback to this method is that the counter tends to be extremely complex and difficult to design.

Both of the above methods are handicapped by lack of flexibility, although the first method is perhaps the most economical approach to the design of a hardwired control unit. As we shall see in Chapter 6, the optimal control sequence very much resembles a computer program with branching permitted anywhere within the sequence. The above methods necessarily limit the flexibility of this branching. The method which will receive primary consideration in this book does not suffer from this drawback. In fact it will take the form of a physical realization of an arbitrary control sequence flow chart. Rather than risk confusion with an abbreviated treatment of this method of control unit design here, we shall wait to present the method in detail in Chapter 7.

Our primary reason for concentrating on the method of Chapter 7 is pedagogical. It will greatly assist us in keeping evident the close correspondence between the design language version of the machine and the actual hardware. In certain actual design situations economics may dictate the use of some variation of one of the methods discussed above.

Finally, we might note that the concept of clocking is closely related to the concepts of synchronous and asynchronous operation. Indeed, *synchronous* and *clocked* may be used synonomously on occasion, and *asynchronous* may mean *unclocked*; but this is not usually the case. In general, *synchronous* is taken to mean that all operations in the computer—register transfers, memory references, logical operations—are allotted certain fixed periods of time for completion. All of the methods discussed above are synchronous. Different types of operations may be allotted different periods of time, e.g., memory references will be allotted more time than register transfers; but the time allotment for any given type will never vary.

By contrast, asynchronous operation generally signifies that the control unit issues a signal to initiate some operation and then waits for a *completion signal* from the device carrying out the operation before continuing. For example, core memory is often controlled by its own clock, completely independent of the control unit; and the usual procedure is to make a memory request and then wait for a completion signal to be returned. The method of Chapter 7 will include a mechanism for handling asynchronous operations.

Most computers use a combination of synchronous and asynchronous operation. The central processor is usually synchronous; but the memory and various input/output devices may be under the control of independent clocks, and are thus asynchronous *with respect to the CPU.* It is theoretically possible to build a computer without a clock, with each device generating completion signals to initiate the next step; but there seems to be little or no advantage to such an arrangement. By contrast, a clock provides accurate control of pulse duration and interval, both critical factors in the very fast circuits used in modern computers.

4.8. A SIMPLIFIED DESIGN EXAMPLE

To illustrate the basic approach of this book we shall develop the sequence of register transfers to be performed by the particular digital system illustrated in Fig. 4.13. We have deliberately stripped this system of a number of complicating factors, which will be discussed in subsequent chapters. The function of digital system *B* (to be designed) is to facilitate the transfer of information from system *A* to system *C*. System *A* might be a computer, and system *C* might be some sort of peripheral memory such as a magnetic tape unit. In that case, system *B* will perform part of the function of a magnetic tape controller.

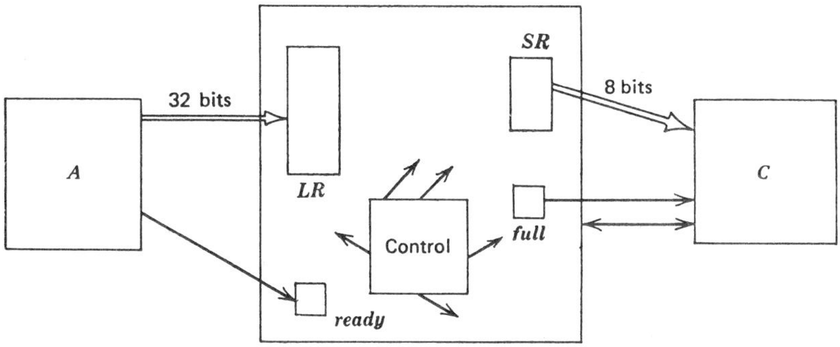

FIGURE 4.13. Word disassembler.

The output from system *A* will be a 32-bit vector, which we shall refer to as a word. System *C* will accept only 8-bit vectors or bytes as input. System *B* then must sequentially disassemble the 32-bit word into four 8-bit bytes. The principal hardware elements in system *B* are a 32-bit register ***LR*** and an 8-bit register ***SR***. Also included are a single flip-flop labeled ***ready***, associated with ***LR***, and a single flip-flop labeled ***full***, associated with ***SR***.

We assume that the clock source is provided by system *C* so that systems *B* and *C* are synchronized. During any clock period for which the flip-flop ***full*** is 1, system *C* will read a byte from register ***SR***. In the clock period immediately after it places a byte in ***SR***, system *B* will set ***full*** to 1. During the next clock period, system *C* will utilize the byte in ***SR*** and simultaneously clear ***full*** to 0. System *B* may place another byte in ***SR*** during this same clock period. Since systems *B* and *C* are synchronized, it is possible to reliably read from ***SR*** and place a new byte in ***SR*** during the same clock period. The flip-flops in ***SR*** must be master-slave for this scheme to work. In effect we have assumed that system *C* can react in one clock period to simplify the design of system *B*, our first design example.

Whenever a word is placed in ***LR***, the flip-flop ***ready*** will be set to 1 by system *A*. After the fourth byte has been read from ***LR***, system *B* will clear ***ready*** to 0.

The following is a sequence of register transfers which describe the function of system *B*. The illustrated control unit must supply the proper control pulses in the proper order to cause the sequence of transfers to be executed. Notice the use of some notational devices from FORTRAN. The first two steps constitute a waiting loop. When a 1 appears in the flip-flop ***ready***, the control unit issues a sequence of transfer pulses beginning at step 3. A discussion of how the waiting loop of steps 1 and 2 might be accomplished by hardware must wait until Chapter 7.

1. If (***ready*** = 1), GO TO 3
2. GOTO 1
3. $SR \leftarrow \alpha^{8}/LR$
4. $full \leftarrow 1$
5. $SR \leftarrow \omega^{8}/(\alpha^{16}/LR)$
6. $full \leftarrow 1$
7. $SR \leftarrow \omega^{8}/(\alpha^{24}/LR)$
8. $full \leftarrow 1$
9. $SR \leftarrow \omega^{8}/LR$
10. $full \leftarrow 1$
11. $ready \leftarrow 0$
12. GO TO 1

Step 3 places the first eight bits of ***LR*** in ***SR***. Step 4 represents a pulse which sets ***full*** to 1 to alert system *C* to the presence of the word in ***SR***. This pair of steps is repeated three more times for the remaining three bytes of ***LR***. The notation on the right-hand side of step 5, for example, refers to the last eight of the first sixteen bits in ***LR***. This, of course, is the second byte.

Once all of the information has been read from ***LR***, the ***ready*** flip-flop is cleared to 0 by the transfer pulse corresponding to step 11. Step 12 returns control to step 1 to await a new word in ***LR***.

Because of the limited notation developed thus far, the example discussed above has necessarily been a very simple one. A magnetic tape controller, for example, must provide several operations in addition to the one described above. This the reader can verify by a quick reference back to Chapter 3. As evidenced by our recourse to familiar FORTRAN conventions, the notation developed thus far is not even sufficient for this example. Our next major step would seem to be to expand and strengthen this notation. We shall do this in Chapter 5 by presenting a language sufficiently complete to represent all hardware operations which may take place in a computer.

4.9. ECONOMICS OF DIGITAL SYSTEM DESIGN

Most tasks which are accomplished by vector-handling digital systems are sufficiently complex that a variety of approaches are possible. The costs (both production and design) are likely to vary with the approach chosen. So will the amount of time required by the digital system to perform a given task.

In many cases the digital system must interact with some very slow system, either physical or biological. Two examples might be desk calculators or a controller for a chemical process. For such cases the speed of the digital system is not important. The most economical approach consistent with adequate reliability should be chosen.

Occasionally a digital system must interact with a very fast system. In such cases, if indeed any available approach is suitable, only the fastest may be satisfactory.

The above are the two extreme examples of what may be called *real time* digital systems. In general, the speed at which a real time digital system must operate is dictated by some other system with which it must interact. The appropriate design approach is the most economical one which will operate at the required speed.

The situation is quite different for *non-real-time* systems, of which the general purpose computer is the most common example. Such systems can operate at various *levels of performance*. In batch processing, for example, performance might be measured in terms of the dollar value of jobs executable per hour. Dollar values can be estimated when there is a past history of other digital systems performing the same type of job.

In designing a digital system, many of the choices which affect cost and speed are choices of whether to perform sets of similar operations simultaneously or sequentially. The choices range from handling bits in a word serially or in parallel to the possibility of processing more than one job at a time by the computer. Simultaneous or *parallel* operations almost always imply larger numbers of components and, therefore, greater overall cost. In addition, choices must be made between component technologies on the basis of speed and cost.

There are a finite number of essentially different combinations of choices which might be made in the design of a particular digital system. It is possible to analyze all of these alternatives in sufficient detail to estimate their cost and speed. The effort which one would actually devote to this would depend on the number of copies of the system to be constructed, as well as the cost of this effort in relation to the overall design cost. If such an analysis were made, the result might appear in the form of Fig. 4.14.

Each cross on the figure represents a design based on some set of choices. The solid line on the figure is not a minimal mean square error fit of the data points but is rather a smooth curve approximately joining points with the lowest cost/speed ratios. The two points which are circled on the figure represent design choices, which need not be considered seriously. There are higher-speed-lower-cost alternatives available.

Notice that the dashed tangent line passes through the point on the curve which has the optimum cost/speed ratio. If cost/speed ratio were the only criterion, then the design point nearest this tangent point might be chosen. Where system performance must be matched to some other system, it may be necessary to move in one direction or the other from the optimum. As mentioned, this is common in the case of real time systems. If the designs of several subsystems of a larger system are projected to depart significantly

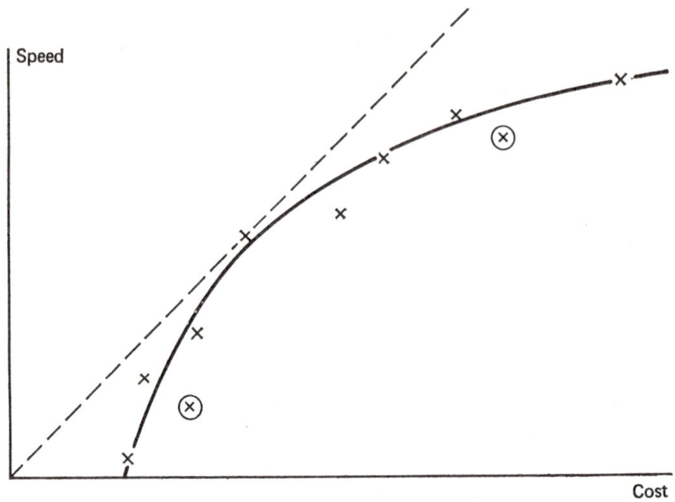

FIGURE 4.14. Cost/speed relation.

from the economic optimum, a reconfiguration of overall system *architecture* may be in order.

Vector-handling systems, which are not computers, are more likely to be described by Fig. 4.14. In a complete computer, storage capacity as well as data handling speed is a factor in overall system performance. For some jobs there is a trade-off between speed and memory capacity. The analysis of overall computer performance in terms of cost/speed characteristics and storage capacities of subsystems in an interesting but difficult problem. In many cases it is not possible to complete as accurate an analysis as might be desired. We postpone further discussion of this topic until Chapter 14.

PROBLEMS

4.1. The detailed logic block diagram of one form of a master-slave flip-flop is given in Fig. P4.1. Suppose initially $a = z = 1$ with $S = C = 0$. Determine the initial values of points b, d, e, and f. Now assume that a pulse appears at point C. Construct a timing diagram showing the effect of this pulse at points a, b, d, e, z, and f. Assume that the delay in each gate is approximately 20% of the width of the pulse applied at point C.

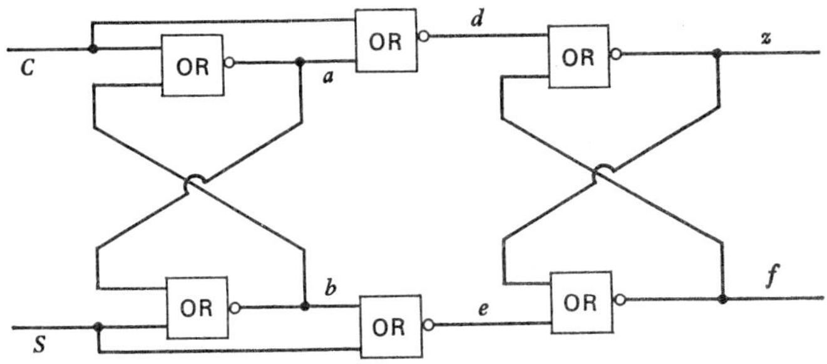

FIGURE P4.1

4.2. Let AR be a 4-bit register. Construct a detailed logic block diagram of the hardware necessary to accomplish the transfer

$$AR \leftarrow \uparrow (\uparrow AR)$$

The master-slave flip-flops may be represented by single blocks.

4.3. Let AR, BR, CR, and DR all be 8-bit registers which form part of a digital system. Included at various points in the control sequence for the system are the following transfers:

$$\begin{array}{ll} BR \leftarrow AR & AR \leftarrow BR \\ CR \leftarrow AR & CR \leftarrow \uparrow BR \\ DR \leftarrow \uparrow AR & AR \leftarrow DR \\ BR \leftarrow \overline{AR} & BR \leftarrow DR \end{array}$$

Construct a busing diagram of the form of Fig. 4.7 showing paths for all listed transfers. Determine the total number of AND gates required to provide paths for these transfers, (a) using busing and (b) not using busing.

4.4. Figure P4.4 shows the logic diagram of a clocked S-C master-slave flip-flop. Assume that initially $C = h = 0$, $S = z = 1$, and CLOCK = 0. Determine the initial values at all points identified by a letter. Then

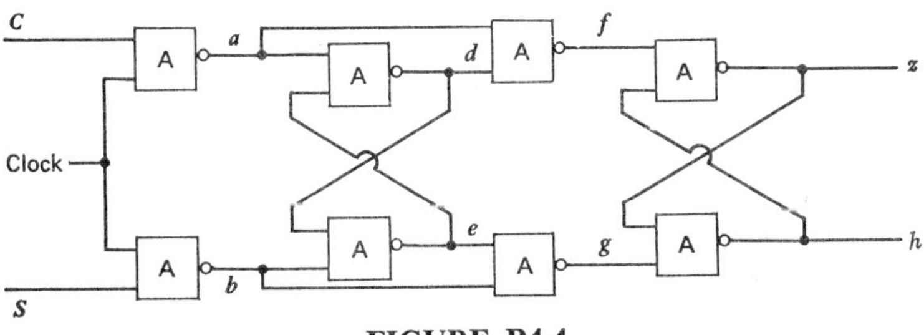

FIGURE P4.4

show in a timing diagram the effect on all points of a CLOCK pulse. Assume the delay through a gate equals 20% of the duration of the pulse.

4.5. Repeat Problem 4.4 for the circuit shown in Fig. P4.5, except assume initially $J = K = 1$, $z = 0$, and $h = 1$.

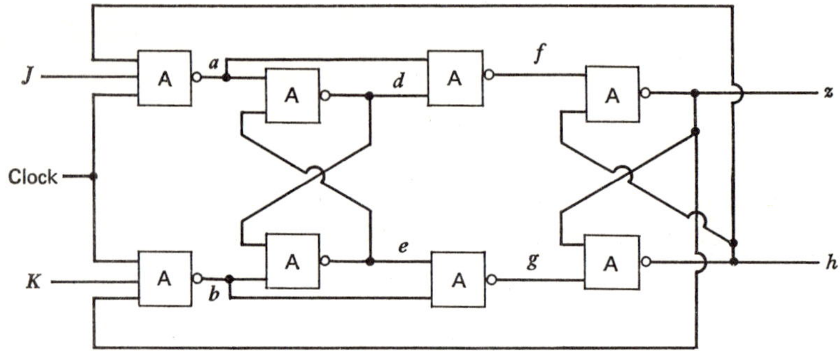

FIGURE P4.5

REFERENCES

1. Hill, F. J., and Peterson, G. R., *Introduction to Switching Theory and Logic Design*, Wiley, New York, 1968.
2. Hellerman, Herbert, *Digital Computer System Principles*, McGraw-Hill, New York, 1967.
3. Golomb, S. W., *Shift Register Sequences*, Holden-Day, San Francisco, 1967.

5

Introduction to A Hardware Programming Language (AHPL)

5.1. INTRODUCTION

A digital computer is a very complex device, and a complete description of a computer is going to be correspondingly complicated. We have already seen in Chapter 2 that it can take a lot of words to describe even a few of the operations of a very simple computer. Certainly something better than the English language is going to be needed if we are to achieve efficient and concise descriptions of the design and functioning of digital computers.

There are many levels at which computers can be described: block diagrams, wiring tables, etc. We are concerned here with a description of what the computer does in terms of the sequencing of operations and the flow of information from one point to another in the computer. Developing this description is the fundamental job of the designer. Once this description has been completed, the development of logic diagrams, schematics, wiring tables, etc. becomes largely a mechanical procedure, subject to considerable automation, as we shall discuss in later chapters.

A program is a list of statements, or instructions, which are to be executed in a certain sequence. *Specification* statements specify new values for some quantities (operands) in terms of finite operations on already specified operands. Specification statements are executed in the order listed, unless a *branch* statement causes a change in the order of execution. The concept of specification, or replacement, is very important. In FORTRAN we can write the statement

$$N = N + 1$$

even though we do not mean conventional algebraic equality. To avoid any possible confusion, we shall use the symbol ($\leftarrow$) to signify specification; thus the statement

$$N \leftarrow N + 1$$

signifies that the new value of the variable N is specified as being equal to the old value of N plus one.

In Chapter 4 we saw that hardware register transfers could be represented by a programming language of this form. The example of Section 4.8 suggested that branch statements as well would be useful in the representation of control sequences. Assuming that it is possible to represent all hardware functions in language form, the question arises as to what language to use. The choice of a language is very important. This language must permit sufficient detail to describe even bit-by-bit operations, and must at the same time have sufficient power to permit concise descriptions of complex operations. The language which we feel best meets our requirements was developed by K. E. Iverson, and is known simply as *A Programming Language* or *APL* [1]. Although APL is now primarily used for interactive programming, hardware description was one of the applications originally envisioned by Iverson. APL has subsequently been implemented with various modifications on several computer systems, the most widely known version being APL/360, which is available on several IBM computer systems.

A skeletal version of APL will be presented. Only part of this version of APL is directly translatable to hardware operations. To avoid confusion we shall refer to that portion of APL which is translatable into hardware as *A Hardware Programming Language* or *AHPL*. In later chapters a few conventions which are not part of APL will be added to AHPL. In Section 5.9 we shall point out restrictions which must be made on APL to form AHPL.

Alternatively we might have introduced only concepts from the AHPL portion of APL at various points as they were first required in the discussion of hardware. We feel that this procedure would have been much less satisfactory for the reader in the long run. Most of the APL operations will appear in some form throughout the book. Trying to learn APL operations while struggling with a design concept can only interfere with the reader's mastery of the latter. We do *not* expect the reader's experience in learning APL to be unpleasant. The reader is already familiar with one or more programming languages such as FORTRAN, COBOL, PL/I, etc. Learning APL will be a much less difficult task than learning a first language.

First, APL is, more than any other programming language, just an extension and systematization of conventional mathematical notation. Second, if you have already learned to program, in whatever language, you have already mastered the basic *concepts* of programming, concepts which apply equally to APL. Third, we will not be concerned in this book with actually writing ready-to-run computer programs, so many of the troublesome details associated with actually running a program can be neglected. This is not to say that having mastered APL the reader may not wish to try his hand at actual APL programming. APL has many advantages over the more commonly used programming languages. But mastery of APL computer programming as such is not the objective of this book, nor is it necessary.

All books on computer systems have some system of notation which must be mastered by their readers. Often this amounts to fragments of several notational systems, the use of which varies from topic to topic and chapter to chapter. It has long been recognized that the control section of a computer is essentially a hard-wired program for the execution of the machine's instrution set. (In fact, this concept leads directly to *microprogramming*, which will be treated in Chapter 8.) We believe, therefore, that a programming language is the natural way to describe a digital computer. And the power of APL is such that we can completely describe a digital computer in one consistent, concise language, without resorting to awkward special conventions to handle special cases.

5.2. OPERAND CONVENTIONS

In any programming system there are a number of different types of operands, and some system must be used to distinguish between them. In FORTRAN, for example, the different types of variables must be declared. In print, however, it is more convenient to use different typographic conventions for different kinds of operands. The conventions to be used in APL and AHPL are shown in the table in Fig. 5.1.

For handwritten or typed material where italics are unavailable or inconvenient, our convention has been to underline lower-case strings for

Type of Operand	Printed Representation
Literal	
Numeric	Standard numerals
Alphanumeric	Standard letters or numerals set off by apostrophes
Variables	
Scalar	Bold lower-case italic letters
Vector	Bold upper-case italic letters
Matrix	Bold upper-case Roman

FIGURE 5.1. Typographic conventions for APL and AHPL.

scalars, underline upper-case strings for vectors, and double underline upper-case strings for matrices.

The distinction between variables and literals is very important. In conventional programming systems, a variable is a *name* by which we refer to operands; a literal is an actual value for an operand. Thus in FORTRAN we write

$$X = Y + 1$$

meaning "The new *value* of X is to be equal to the *value* of Y plus one," i.e., Y is a variable and 1 is a literal. *In AHPL a variable is the name of a register*, the *contents* of which are referred to in a program statement; and a *literal* is the actual data to be placed in a register. For example

$$\boldsymbol{MA} \leftarrow \boldsymbol{PC}$$

means to transfer the *contents* of $\boldsymbol{PC}$ to $\boldsymbol{MA}$, while

$$\boldsymbol{MA} \leftarrow 0,1,0,1,0,0,0,0,1,1,1,1,0$$

means to store the string of bits shown in $\boldsymbol{MA}$. In APL, as illustrated, letters or strings of letters indicate variables while numerals indicate literals. For this reason, as in FORTRAN, operators must not be omitted. Thus, $\boldsymbol{MA}$ is the name of a single variable, and should in no case be interpreted as $M \times A$.

A *vector* is simply a collection of operands arranged in a one-dimensional array. The number of elements (operands) in a vector is known as the *dimension* of the vector and will be denoted by ρ. Registers of more than one bit are considered to be vectors since they consist of a number of bit positions,

$$\begin{bmatrix} M_0^0 & M_1^0 & M_2^0 & \cdots & M_{\rho_1-1}^0 \\ M_0^1 & M_1^1 & \cdots\cdots & & M_{\rho_1-1}^1 \\ \cdot & & & & \cdot \\ \cdot & & & & \cdot \\ \cdot & & & & \cdot \\ M_0^{\rho_2-1} & \cdots\cdots\cdots & & & M_{\rho_1-1}^{\rho_2-1} \end{bmatrix}$$

FIGURE 5.2. Matrix.

the contents of which are generally independent of one another. Thus if the ***PC*** register has 18 bits, then $\rho PC = 18$; and the individual bit positions are denoted $(PC_0, PC_1, PC_2 \cdots PC_{17})$, with PC_i denoting the bit in the ith position. Note that the first position of the vector is denoted PC_0, a procedure which is known as 0-origin indexing. In some programming systems, such as FORTRAN, 1-origin indexing is used. In this book, 0-origin indexing will always be assumed unless otherwise specifically stated.

A matrix is a two-dimensional array of operands as illustrated in Fig. 5.2. The vector $(\mathbf{M}_0^i, \mathbf{M}_1^i \cdots \mathbf{M}_{\rho_1-1}^i)$ is known as the ith row vector of **M**, denoted by $\mathbf{M}^i$. Its dimension $\rho_1\mathbf{M}$ is known as the row dimension of the matrix. The vector $(\mathbf{M}_j^0, \mathbf{M}_j^1, \ldots \mathbf{M}_j^{\rho_2-1})$ is known as the jth column vector of **M**, denoted by $\mathbf{M}_j$. Its dimension $\rho_2\mathbf{M}$ is known as the column dimension of **M**. The operand $\mathbf{M}_j^i$ is known as the (i, j)th element of **M**.

The matrix most commonly encountered in AHPL is the memory matrix, **M**, which is considered to have ρ_2 words, each of ρ_1 bits length. Thus, for a memory of 4096 18-bit words, $\rho_2\mathbf{M} = 4096$ and $\rho_1\mathbf{M} = 18$. Note that in this convention each word is a row of the matrix, so that $\mathbf{M}^i$ denotes the ith word in memory. In a similar manner, a stack of registers could be considered a matrix.

5.3. APL PRIMITIVE OPERATORS

The primitive operators are those which are primarily defined in terms of scalars (i.e., operands which are single numbers) although they all may be extended to vectors and matrices. The primitive operators are listed in the table of Fig. 5.3. Notice that some operators (unary) operate on only one argument while other (binary) relate two arguments. In a complete version of APL [1] [2], most symbols have both unary and binary meanings. In some cases these meanings are unrelated. Fortunately we have managed to avoid this possible source of confusion. All of the operations extend to vectors on an element-by-element basis.

A set of examples which illustrate the use of the operators in Fig. 5.3

Operation	Name	Meaning
$z \leftarrow x + y$	Addition	z = algebraic sum of x and y
$z \leftarrow x - y$	Subtraction	Algebraic difference
$z \leftarrow x \times y$	Multiplication	Algebraic product
$z \leftarrow x \div y$	Division	$z = x$ divided by y
$z \leftarrow \mid x$	Absolute value	z = absolute value of x
$z \leftarrow x \lceil y$	Maximum	z = most positive of x and y
$z \leftarrow x \lfloor y$	Minimum	z = most negative of x and y
$z \leftarrow \bar{x}$	NOT	If $x = 0$, then $z = 1$ If $x = 1$, then $z = 0$
$z \leftarrow x \wedge y$	AND	If $x = 1$ and $y = 1$, then $z = 1$, otherwise $z = 0$
$z \leftarrow x \vee y$	OR	If either $x = 1$ or $y = 1$, then $z = 1$, otherwise $z = 0$

FIGURE 5.3. Primitive operators in APL.

follow. The reader will note that the literals in these examples are represented in decimal form and may take on all real values. *In AHPL every literal element in a register transfer statement must be either* 1 *or 0*. Only these two values can be stored in a flip-flop, which is the hardware counterpart of a scalar variable. In the following examples, let $x = 1$, $y = -5$, $W = (3, 5, -1, 4)$, $U = (1, 0, -1, -1)$.

Statement	Meaning
$z \leftarrow x + y$	$z = -4$
$z \leftarrow \bar{x}$	$z = 0$
$Z \leftarrow W + U$	$Z = (4, 5, -2, 3)$
$z \leftarrow x \div y$	$z = -0.2$
$Z \leftarrow U \lceil W$	$Z = (3, 5, -1, 4)$
$Z \leftarrow W \times U$	$Z = (3, 0, 1, -4)$
$Z \leftarrow U \div W$	$Z = (0.333, 0, 1, -0.25)$

The operators extend to matrices in an analogous fashion. When both operands are vectors or matrices, the dimensions must conform, as shown in the above examples. However, it is permissible to mix scalars and vectors or matrices. For example,

$$Z \leftarrow x + W$$

signifies that x is to be added to each element of W, and

$$Z \leftarrow x \times W$$

signifies that each element of W is to be multiplied by x.

When more than one operator occurs in a single statement, it is desirable to have a convention in regard to the order in which operations are performed. The rule in APL is this: *In the absence of parentheses, operations are performed in a right-to-left order.* Parentheses take precedence in the usual manner and must be removed by starting with the innermost set and working outward, the above rule applying within any set. The examples below should clarify these rules.

Statement	Equivalent
$z \leftarrow w + x \div y$	$z \leftarrow w + (x \div y)$
$z \leftarrow (-w) + x \div y$	$z \leftarrow (-w) + (x \div y)$
$z \leftarrow w + x \times y + 1 \div y$	$z \leftarrow w + (x \times (y + (1 \div y)))$

Unlike FORTRAN, there is normally no precedence of one operator type over another.

It should be obvious to the reader that precedence defined over so large a number of operators would be chaotic. Later, in AHPL expressions in which only the operators NOT, $\wedge$, $\vee$, $\times$, and $+$ can appear, this order of precedence will be assumed. This convention will be used only in the interest of clarifying statements which would otherwise be very awkward.

The logical operators AND, OR, and NOT differ from the other primitive operators in that they are defined only in terms of logical variables, i.e., variables which take on only the values 0 or 1. In operating versions of APL, such as APL/360, an attempt to apply a logical operator to a variable having a value other than 0 or 1 will result in a *domain error*. On the other hand, there is no distinction made between logical and arithmetic variables with regard to the arithmetic operators. When an arithmetic operator is applied to a variable which takes on the value 0 or 1, it is treated as a numeric 0 or 1, whatever the programmer's intent as to the meaning of the variable may have been. In the following examples, $U = (1, 0, 0, 1, 0, 1)$ and $V = (0, 1, 1, 1, 0, 1)$.

Statement	Result
$Z \leftarrow \overline{U}$	$Z = (0, 1, 1, 0, 1, 0)$
$Z \leftarrow U \wedge V$	$Z = (0, 0, 0, 1, 0, 1)$
$Z \leftarrow U \vee V$	$Z = (1, 1, 1, 1, 0, 1)$
$Z \leftarrow U + V$	$Z = (1, 1, 1, 2, 0, 2)$

5.4. RELATIONAL OPERATORS

A special form of primitive operator is the *relational* operator, which appears in statements in the general form

$$z \leftarrow (x \mathscr{R} y)$$

where $\mathscr{R}$ stands for the relational operator. If the relationship between x and y is satisfied, $z = 1$; if not, $z = 0$. For example, the statement

$$z \leftarrow (x > y)$$

specifies $z = 1$ if $x > y$, but $z = 0$ if $x \leq y$. The relational operators are summarized in the table of Fig. 5.4.

The relational operators extend to vectors and matrices in the usual manner. The relational operators may apply to either arithmetic or logical operands, with logical 1 being considered "greater than" logical 0 for this purpose. The relationals may also appear in more complex statements, in which case the complete relational

$$(x \mathscr{R} y)$$

is considered as a logical variable taking on the value specified in Fig. 5.4. For example, the statement

$$z \leftarrow (x > 0) \wedge (x < 2)$$

specifies that $z = 1$ only if x is between 0 and 2.

Notation	Meaning
$z \leftarrow (x < y)$	$z = 1$ if x is less than y, $z = 0$ otherwise
$z \leftarrow (x \leq y)$	$z = 1$ if x is less than or equal to y, $z = 0$ otherwise
$z \leftarrow (x = y)$	$z = 1$ if x equals y, $z = 0$ otherwise
$z \leftarrow (x > y)$	$z = 1$ if x is greater than y, $z = 0$ otherwise
$z \leftarrow (x \geq y)$	$z = 1$ is x is greater than or equal to y, $z = 0$ otherwise
$z \leftarrow (x \neq y)$	$z = 1$ if x is not equal to y, $z = 0$ otherwise

FIGURE 5.4. Relational operators in APL.

5.5. SPECIAL VECTORS

Certain vectors occur so frequently in AHPL programs that it is convenient to assign special symbols to them. These are summarized in Fig. 5.5. The following examples should clarify these definitions. Note that in the unit

Notation	Name	Meaning
$\epsilon^j(n)$	Unit vector	A vector of all 0's, except for a 1 in the jth position
$\epsilon(n)$	Full vector	A vector of n 1's
$\alpha^j(n)$	Prefix vector	A vector of n elements, the leftmost j are 1's, the rest 0's
$\omega^j(n)$	Suffix vector	A vector of n elements, the rightmost j are 1's, the rest 0's

FIGURE 5.5. Special vectors in APL.

vector, the 1 goes in the ϵ_j position; since 0-origin indexing is used, this is *not* the jth position from the left. These special vectors normally operate on

$\epsilon^2(6)$	(0, 0, 1, 0, 0, 0)
$\epsilon(6)$	(1, 1, 1, 1, 1, 1)
$\overline{\epsilon}(6)$	(0, 0, 0, 0, 0, 0)
$\alpha^2(6)$	(1, 1, 0, 0, 0, 0)
$\omega^2(6)$	(0, 0, 0, 0, 1, 1)

other vectors, and the dimension n will generally be omitted and dimensional conformity assumed. For example, in the statement

$$A \leftarrow \omega^{13} \wedge B$$

we assume that ω has the same dimensions as B.

5.6. MIXED OPERATORS

Much of the special power of APL derives from the mixed operators, which operate on various combinations of scalars, vectors, and matrices. There are a great many of these in APL, some of considerable complexity. A few of the simpler ones are listed in Fig. 5.6.

The CATENATE operator simply joins vectors together to form larger vectors. Thus, if $X = (1,2,3)$ and $Y = (4,5,6)$, then

$$Z \leftarrow X,Y$$

Notation	Name	Meaning
$Z \leftarrow X,Y$	CATENATE	$Z = X_0, X_1, \ldots, X_{\rho X-1}, Y_0, \ldots, Y_{\rho Y-1}$
$Z \leftarrow n \rho x$	RESHAPE	Reshape x into n-element vector
$Z \leftarrow k \uparrow X$	LEFT ROTATE	Circular left (right) shift of X by k places
$Z \leftarrow k \downarrow X$	RIGHT ROTATE	
$\mathbf{M} \leftarrow \Uparrow \mathbf{N}$	ROTATE UP	Circular shift up (down) of **N** by one row
$\mathbf{M} \leftarrow \Downarrow \mathbf{N}$	ROTATE DOWN	
$Z \leftarrow k \underset{\circ}{\uparrow} X$	LEFT SHIFT	Left (right) shift of x by k places, bringing zeros into vacated positions
$Z \leftarrow k \overset{\circ}{\downarrow} X$	RIGHT SHIFT	
$z \leftarrow j \perp X$	DECODE	z is the base-j value of the vector
$X \leftarrow j(n) \top z$	ENCODE	X is the n-element vector corresponding to the base-j representation of the number z
$z \leftarrow \odot / X$	REDUCE	$z = X_0 \odot X_1 \odot X_2 \odot \cdots \odot X_{\rho X-1}$
$X \leftarrow \odot / \mathbf{M}$	ROW REDUCE	$X_i = \odot / \mathbf{M}^i$
$X \leftarrow \odot // \mathbf{M}$	COLUMN REDUCE	$X_i = \odot / \mathbf{M}_i$
$Z \leftarrow U / X$	COMPRESS	Z obtained from X by suppressing each X_i for which $U_i = 0$
$\mathbf{A} \leftarrow U / \mathbf{M}$	ROW COMPRESS	$\mathbf{A}^i = U / \mathbf{M}^i$
$\mathbf{A} \leftarrow U // \mathbf{M}$	COLUMN COMPRESS	$\mathbf{A}_j = U / \mathbf{M}_j$

FIGURE 5.6. Mixed operators in APL.

specifies that $Z = (1,2,3,4,5,6)$. We also permit use of the CATENATE operation on the left side of a statement. For example, in a computer with double-precision arithmetic, it is common to use two registers catenated together for each operand. Then a register transfer might take the form

$$M,Q \leftarrow AC,D$$

In FORTRAN, when we use arrays we must set aside enough storage space for them with the DIMENSION statement. There is no exact equivalent of the DIMENSION statement in APL. The first time a vector or matrix is used in an APL program its dimension is set by specifying values for all its elements. For example,

$$X \leftarrow (1,2,3,4)$$

specifies X as a four-element vector with the values given. Later operations on X may change any or all of the values, but it will remain a 4-element vector unless it is completely redefined.

In some cases it is necessary to compute values for individual elements of a vector as the program progresses. Some APL interpreters require that in this case the number of elements in the vector be called out in advance. This can conveniently be done with the RESHAPE operator in a statement of the form

$$X \leftarrow 20\rho 0$$

which specifies X as a 20-element vector, with all elements initially set to zero.

The meaning of the ROTATE and SHIFT operators will be clarified by the following examples, in which $\boldsymbol{PC} = (1, 2, 3, 4, 5)$. Note, as in the last example, that k may be omitted for a one-place rotate or shift.

Statement	Result
$\boldsymbol{MA} \leftarrow 2\uparrow \boldsymbol{PC}$	$\boldsymbol{MA} = (3,4,5,1,2)$
$\boldsymbol{MA} \leftarrow 2\downarrow \boldsymbol{PC}$	$\boldsymbol{MA} = (4,5,1,2,3)$
$\boldsymbol{MA} \leftarrow 2\underset{\circ}{\uparrow} \boldsymbol{PC}$	$\boldsymbol{MA} = (3,4,5,0,0)$
$\boldsymbol{MA} \leftarrow \overset{\circ}{\downarrow} \boldsymbol{PC}$	$\boldsymbol{MA} = (0,1,2,3,4)$

The decode and encode operators are a bit more complex, but simple enough to use once you get the idea. The natural numbers may be regarded as *concepts*, derived primarily from counting, that are independent of the system of *representation* used. The most common systems of representation, such as the decimal and binary systems, are *radix*, or base systems.

Vectors are also strings of digits; and the decode operator specifies the conversion of this string of digits into the natural number corresponding to the interpretation of this vector string as a base-j number. The encode operation is the reverse, the conversion of a natural number to a vector string representing the number in base j. A problem here is that we have to represent the natural number itself in some manner. We shall use the ordinary decimal representation to represent the natural number. On this basis the following examples will clarify the decode and encode operators. As shown, conversions to and from base 2 are so frequent that the 2 may be deleted, in which case base 2 is assumed. For $\top$, if the number of bits is also omitted, the minimum number of bits are used.

<table>
<tr><th>Statement</th><th>Result</th></tr>
<tr><td>$z \leftarrow 10\perp(1,4,7)$</td><td>$z = 147$</td></tr>
<tr><td>$z \leftarrow 5\perp(1,4,3)$</td><td>$z = 48$</td></tr>
<tr><td>$z \leftarrow 2\perp(1,1,0,1)$</td><td rowspan="2">$z = 13$</td></tr>
<tr><td>$z \leftarrow \perp(1,1,0,1)$</td></tr>
<tr><td>$\boldsymbol{MA} \leftarrow 10(4)\top 147$</td><td>$\boldsymbol{MA} = (0,1,4,7)$</td></tr>
<tr><td>$\boldsymbol{MA} \leftarrow 5(4)\top 147$</td><td>$\boldsymbol{MA} = (1,0,4,2)$</td></tr>
<tr><td>$\boldsymbol{MA} \leftarrow 2(5)\top 13$</td><td rowspan="2">$\boldsymbol{MA} = (0,1,1,0,1)$</td></tr>
<tr><td>$\boldsymbol{MA} \leftarrow (5)\top 13$</td></tr>
</table>

An operation which is applied to all elements of a vector or matrix to produce a simpler structure is called a *reduction*. The reduction of a vector is denoted by

$$z \leftarrow \odot /X$$

where $\odot$ may be any binary operator, and signifies that

$$z = (\cdots((X_0 \odot X_1) \odot X_2)\cdots) \odot X_{\rho-1}).$$

For example,

$$z \leftarrow +/X$$

is equivalent to

$$z = \sum_{i=0}^{\rho-1} X_i$$

Reduction is a very powerful operation and can be used in many ingenious ways. For example, if V is a logical vector,

$$z \leftarrow +/V$$

will give a count of the 1's in V,

$$z \leftarrow \vee/V$$

will be 0 if and only if every element of V is 0, and

$$z \leftarrow \wedge/V$$

will be 1 if and only if every element of V is 1. Suppose that a vector, V, has no elements. (While it may seem absurd, this case will arise in later chapters.) Consider, for example,

$$\wedge/\boldsymbol{\omega}^i/Y$$

where $i = 0$. Looking carefully at the above definition we reason that, if a vector has no elements, all of the elements which it does have are 1. Therefore,

$$\wedge/\boldsymbol{\omega}^0/Y = \wedge/\boldsymbol{\alpha}^0/Y = 1 \tag{5.1}$$

If you prefer, consider Eq. 5.1 to be a definition. By a similar argument we have Eq. 5.2:

$$\vee/\boldsymbol{\omega}^0/Y = \vee/\boldsymbol{\alpha}^0/Y = 0 \tag{5.2}$$

Reduction is extended to matrices in two ways. *Row reduction* is denoted

$$X \leftarrow \odot/\mathbf{M}$$

and signifies that each row is reduced individually, producing a vector of dimension $\rho_2 M$. Column reduction is denoted

$$X \leftarrow \odot//\mathbf{M}$$

and signifies that each column is reduced individually, resulting in a vector of dimension $\rho_1\mathbf{M}$. For example, if

$$\mathbf{M} = \begin{vmatrix} 1 & 1 & 0 & 1 \\ 1 & 0 & 0 & 1 \\ 0 & 1 & 0 & 0 \end{vmatrix}$$

then $+/\mathbf{M} = (3,2,1)$, $+//\mathbf{M} = (2,2,0,2)$, and $+/(+//\mathbf{M}) = 6$.

Effective use of vectors and matrices depends not only on operators for handling them, but also on the ability to select specific elements from them. Single elements can be selected through the use of indices, as in PC_i, $\mathbf{M}^i$, $\mathbf{M}_j$, or $\mathbf{M}_j^i$, but often we need to select a group of elements. For this purpose we define the *compression* operator, denoted by

$$Z \leftarrow U/X$$

where U is a logical vector. The vector Z is obtained by suppressing from the vector X each element X_i for which $U_i = 0$. For example, if $U = (1,0,0,1,0,1)$ and $X = (1,2,3,4,5,6)$, then

$$Z \leftarrow U/X$$

results in $Z = (1,4,6)$.

As an example of the use of the compression operator in AHPL, recall that in SIC the instruction word is loaded into the IR register, and that the address portion of the instruction is in the last (right-most) 13 bits of the instruction. Then the moving of the address from IR to the MA register would be specified by

$$MA \leftarrow \omega^{13}/IR$$

The compression operator also extends to matrices on a row or column basis.

5.7. BRANCHING AND SEQUENCE CONTROL

The steps in a program are normally executed in the order listed, unless a branch command of some sort changes the sequence. In FORTRAN the commands used for this purpose are the IF and GO TO forms. There are analogous forms in APL. To illustrate some of them, consider a simple program to compute the sum of the absolute values of the ten elements of a vector, X. The program in Fig. 5.7 is a FORTRAN program for this calculation. The programs in Fig. 5.8 are equivalent APL programs. The program in Fig. 5.8a is in a pictorial or "semi-block-diagram" form which is often useful in planning the structure of a program, while Fig. 5.8b contains a formal listing.

```
      S = 0
      I = 1
2     IF (X(I).LT.0) GO TO 7
3     S = S + X(I)
      I = I + 1
      IF (I - 10) 2, 2, 6
6     STOP
7     X(I) = -X(I)
      GO TO 3
```

FIGURE 5.7. FORTRAN program for sum of absolute values.

In these programs you will note equivalents of the logical and arithmetic IF and the unconditional GO TO. The APL equivalent to the COMPUTED GO TO of FORTRAN is

$$\rightarrow(n_0, n_1, n_2, \ldots)_i,$$

which has the meaning "If $i = 0$, go to statement n_0; if $i = 1$, go to statement n_1; if $i = 2$, go to statement n_2, etc." This is identical to the COMPUTED GO TO in FORTRAN, except that FORTRAN uses 1-origin indexing. In APL, i may be a single variable or any arithmetic expression which, when computed, will give a suitable integer value.

Another form suitable for multiple branches is

$$\rightarrow \text{(EXP)}$$

where EXP is any expression which, when computed, will give a suitable statement number as a value. As an example, consider expression 5.3:

$$\rightarrow (\overline{IR}_3 \times 10) + (IR_3 \times 20) \tag{5.3}$$

This type of expression will be common in AHPL. If IR_3 is 0, control branches

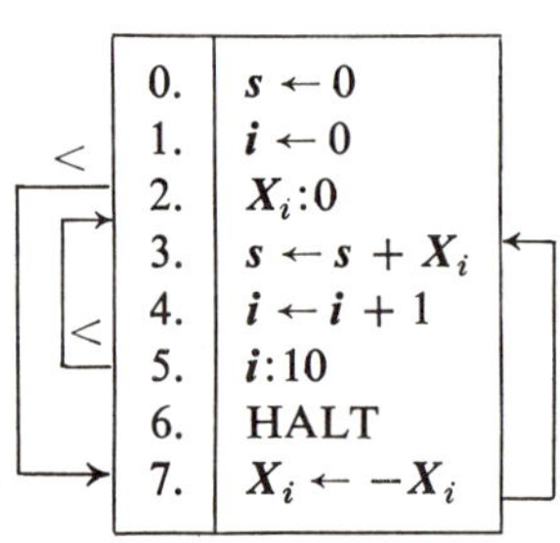

(a)

0.	$s \leftarrow 0$
1.	$i \leftarrow 0$
2.	$X_i{:}0, (<, \geq) \rightarrow (7,3)$
3.	$s \leftarrow s + X_i$
4.	$i \leftarrow i + 1$
5.	$i{:}10, (<, \geq) \rightarrow (2,6)$
6.	HALT
7.	$X_i \leftarrow -X_i, \rightarrow (3)$

(b)

FIGURE 5.8. APL equivalents of Fig. 5.7.

Notation	Meaning
$\rightarrow(10)$	Branch to statement 10 unconditionally
$\rightarrow(3,7,12)_i$	Branch to statement 3, 7, or 12 as the value of i is 0, 1, or 2, respectively
$z \leftarrow x + y, \rightarrow(7)$	The specified operation is to be carried out, the program then branches to statement 7 unconditionally
x:4, $(<,=,>) \rightarrow (3,7,9)$	x is to be compared to 4, the program to branch to statement 3, 7, or 9 as x is $<$, $=$, or $>$ than 4, respectively
$\rightarrow((\overline{IR_3} \times 4) + (IR_3 \times 7))$	Branch to statement 4 if $IR_3 = 0$, to statement 7 if $IR_3 = 1$.

FIGURE 5.9. Examples of branch notation.

to step 10; and if IR_3 is 1, control branches to step 20. Note that we are mixing logical and arithmetic operations and assuming precedence for logical operations. For convenient reference, examples of all the various forms of branch commands are listed in Fig. 5.9.

5.8. APL PROGRAMS*

Although our primary interest in APL is for hardware description, we feel that most students, having mastered the conventions already presented, will wish to see some programming examples. First, it is interesting to note that the mixed operators of Section 5.6 are not essential. In effect they replace subroutines of more elementary operations with single transfer statements. We also note that the program of Fig. 5.8, which computes the sum of the absolute values of elements in $\boldsymbol{X}$, may be replaced by the single reduction step

$$s \leftarrow +/|X$$

As a similar example we see that the following program accomplishes the compression U/X.

1. $j \leftarrow 0$
2. $i \leftarrow 0$
3. U_i:0, $(=, \neq) \rightarrow (6,4)$
4. $Z_j \leftarrow X_i$
5. $j \leftarrow j + 1$
6. $i \leftarrow i + 1$
7. i: ρX, $(<, \geq) \rightarrow (3,8)$

* This section may be omitted without loss of continuity.

List-searching and matrix-operations are two types of programs which can be expressed very concisely in terms of APL. Both are involved in the following example.

Example 5.1

Write an APL program which will search a list of words in memory for words, the left-most 3 bits of which are all ones. These words should be assembled into a separate list.

Solution. Let the list of words be represented by the matrix, N, whose elements are all ones and zeros. We assume an 18-bit memory, so $\rho_1\mathbf{N} = 18$. We let $\rho_2\mathbf{N}$, the number of words, be some unspecified large number. The following short program will accomplish the search:

1. $U \leftarrow (\rho_2\mathbf{N})\rho 0$
2. $i \leftarrow 0$
3. $(\wedge/\alpha^3(18)/\mathbf{N}^i):1, (=, \neq) \rightarrow (4, 5)$
4. $U_i \leftarrow 1$
5. $i \leftarrow i + 1$
6. $i:\rho_2\mathbf{N}, (<, \geq) \rightarrow (3, 7)$
7. $\mathbf{Z} \leftarrow U//\mathbf{N}$

A vector U is created with an element corresponding to each row of N. A one is stored in each element of U, which corresponds to a word in N whose first three bits are one. All other elements of U remain zero. The inspection of words in N is carried out at step 3. At step 7, U is used to select the desired list Z.

The power and flexibility of APL becomes even more apparent as the reader recognizes that the following shorter program will accomplish this same job:

$$\mathbf{Z} \leftarrow (\wedge/\alpha^3(18)/\mathbf{N})//\mathbf{N} \quad \blacksquare$$

There exists in APL a convention providing for relating two vectors or two matrices with two binary operations. This permits a further abbreviation of various complex operations. In particular, matrix multiplication may be expressed this way. A thorough explanation and illustration of the usefulness of this convention would take us too far from the subject at hand. The reader is referred to Iverson [1] or Hellerman [2]. Chapter 2 of Hellerman is particularly recommended for its detailed treatment of several APL programming examples.

The reader might wonder how a compiler or interpreter would handle a logical matrix of the type discussed in the above example. Hopefully it would store rows of the matrix in single computer words. Processing individual bits then becomes a time consuming task in most computers. There is no guarantee that an APL compiler or interpreter will handle all of the myriad of bit-by-bit manipulations efficiently. Quite likely the opposite will be true. When used as a super-high-level language, APL leaves more to the compiler or interpreter than a common language such as FORTRAN. The resultant inefficiency makes APL an unlikely choice for a large program.

5.9. AHPL IN PERSPECTIVE

Only those APL operations which satisfy the constraints imposed by available hardware are included in AHPL. We wish to make this point in the strongest possible way. Every AHPL step written down by the designer will represent some action on some already-specified hardware elements. The designer will always have a mental picture of the hardware involved prior to writing a AHPL step. Developing the precise correspondence between AHPL and its hardware realization is the topic of the remainder of this chapter and of Chapters 6 and 7.

As we shall see in Chapter 7, some AHPL transfer statements fall short of uniquely defining a hardware realization. In a few cases a comment must be appended to the transfer statement. These comments will be in ordinary English and will be self-explanatory. In all there will be about five possible comments.

With the exception of comments, all features of AHPL may be described using the notation provided by APL. It is not possible to completely define AHPL in advance and then proceed to apply it to a sampling of applications. The structure of AHPL operations must necessarily reflect the yet to be discussed structure of the hardware which they purport to describe. AHPL will be assembled gradually as the fundamental hardware configurations are examined. This assembly will take place using the material of APL.

There are several aspects of AHPL which must be investigated in detail in light of possible need for new definitions or restrictions. Several of the items have been partially treated already. Most of these topics will be considered in the next few pages. A few conventions of AHPL must await formulation in Chapters 7 and 9.

Of the two types of routines, the *control sequence routine* is by far the most important. It contains the list of register transfers and branch statements which specify the function of the digital system. A translation of this routine will result in a logic block diagram for system hardware. Often the logic functions which must appear in transfer statements become very complex, and therefore impossible to write on a single line. Significant portions of these functions may be replaced by reference to a *combinational logic subroutine*. A combinational logic subroutine is a sequence of APL program steps which efficiently define a combinational logic network. The rules for writing combinational logic subroutines will be presented in Chapter 7.

Of the five types of statements which will appear in control sequence routines, branch and transfer statements are of most interest. Any of the five

- I. Control sequence routine
  - A. Branch statements
  - B. Transfer statements
    - 1. Left side
      - a. Fixed destination
      - b. Conditional destination
    - 2. Right side: as a function of registers, flip-flops, and buses
    - 3. Conditional transfer
    - 4. Simultaneous transfers
  - C. Register declaration
  - D. Bus logic declaration
  - E. Bus load
- II. Combinational logic subroutine

FIGURE 5.10. Outline of AHPL.

forms of branch statements listed may be used. We shall see that the form of expression 5.3 will be preferred because of its more natural translation to hardware.

There are several considerations involved in the definition of a valid transfer statement. The *left side* of the statement identifies the flip-flop or set of flip-flops, or register or set of registers, into which new information is to be placed. A single transfer may involve a matrix whose rows are registers. A fixed transfer designation may use catenation, constant subscripts, constant superscripts, and compression operations. For example, expression 5.4 is a valid transfer statement where both A and B are 4-bit registers:

$$A_3, \omega^2/\alpha^3/B, a \leftarrow A \tag{5.4}$$

This type of statement causes no particular problems as it quite specifically identifies the memory elements which must be connected to the corresponding control line. The principal criterion which must be satisfied is that the same number of bits must be specified on each side of the transfer statement.

A technique which is not used in software but is conveniently implemented in hardware is that of allowing the destination of a transfer to be a function of other stored information. Consider expression 5.5 as an example:

$$(A * a) \vee (B * \bar{a}) \leftarrow \bar{A} \tag{5.5}$$

If the flip-flop, a, contains a 1, the register A is complemented. If $a = 0$, $\bar{A}$ is placed in the register B. We shall call the flip-flop a a control flip-flop. The left side of such a *conditional destination* statement must yield a register of the same length for all combinations of control flip-flop values. The hardware realization of expression 5.5 is illustrated in Fig. 5.11. The conditional destination transfer is really a special case of the *conditional transfer* to be developed in chapter 7.

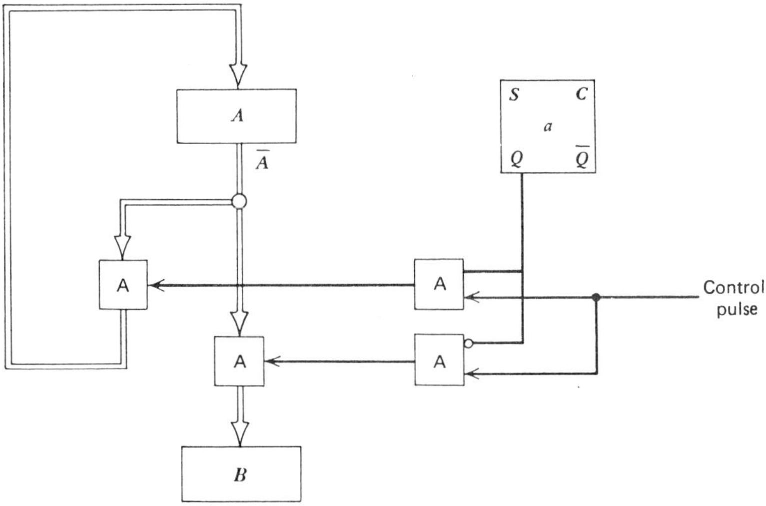

FIGURE 5.11. Hardware realization of statement 5.5.

Variable destination statements will not be widely used. A few very important special cases will appear repeatedly, however. One of these is the *deposit in memory statement*, as given by statement 5.6:

$$\mathbf{M}^{\perp MA} \leftarrow MD \tag{5.6}$$

This statement calls for depositing the contents of the memory data register in the memory location specified by the number stored in the memory address register. Actually $\mathbf{M}^{\perp MA}$ is an abbreviation which stands for a massive combinational logic decoding network which will select a single location in memory. In Chapter 7 we shall see that this abbreviation may be expressed in the form of a combinational logic subroutine.

The *right side* of a transfer statement may be any APL expression whose arguments are flip-flops, registers, or buses expressed in terms of no *primitive operations other than* ∧, ∨, *and NOT*. Constant subscripts, constant superscripts, the mixed operators of Fig. 5.6, and logical constant vectors specified in APL are also allowed. These conventions serve to simplify the expressions which remain Boolean in form. The number of bits computed on the right of a transfer statement *must always be the same* as the number of bits specified on the left. The reason for eliminating other primitive operators is that simple physical realizations are available only for ∧, ∨, and NOT.* In

* NOR and NAND operations are not needed as they duplicate the capability of ∧, ∨, and NOT. In practice NOR or NAND circuits are most likely to be used, but this should present no conceptual difficulty.

certain cases simple abbreviations for Boolean expressions such as Exclusive-or and symmetric functions will be allowed. The right side of transfer statements will quite commonly be complex. Often it will be convenient to represent Boolean expressions by combinational logic subroutines.

The mixed operator $\perp$ (decode) will not be allowed on the right side of AHPL transfer statements. The one exception is the abbreviation for reading and writing in memory, discussed above. All other mixed operators are allowed with only two restrictions. The use of the encode operation, $(n)\top a$, is restricted to the case where a is a constant and the result is a vector of ones and zeros. Used in this way, $\top$ presents a compact method of specifying constant vectors. Similarly the compression operation $\boldsymbol{U}/\boldsymbol{Z}$ may be used only where $\boldsymbol{U}$ is a means of selecting flip-flops from a register as was illustrated in expression 5.4.

Example 5.2

Many combinations of APL operations, while unambiguous and possible to realize in hardware form, would result in grossly impractical logic networks. Suppose, for example, that it is necessary to determine if there is at least one word in the computer memory, **M**, which contains all 1's. Assume that the memory consists of 2^{16} 32-bit words.

A perfectly valid APL solution to this problem is given by the following statement:

$$z \leftarrow \vee/\wedge/\mathbf{M}$$

Indeed this would be allowable in AHPL, if a semiconductor memory were used with the output of all flip-flops available. The translation to a realization of a simple Boolean sum-of-products expression is evident. A closer examination, however, reveals that this expression calls for more than 64,000 AND gates together with a 64,000-input OR gate. Moreover, this hardware would very likely be usable only in this one operation. Clearly this approach is unacceptable.

A more reasonable approach would be to read each word from memory, one at a time, and test for all 1's using $\wedge/\boldsymbol{MD}$ while the word is in the memory data register. As soon as a vector of ones is identified by this sequential search, the flip-flop z is set to 1 and control proceeds to the next operation. These contrasting approaches illustrate the common situation in which a parallel approach will require considerable special hardware whereas a sequential approach can share hardware used in other functions. ▮

Situations like Example 5.2 are the primary reason we cannot at this stage present a concise list of acceptable AHPL procedures. Instead we must be content to illustrate good digital system design practice in terms of examples. Many such examples will appear as we develop a control sequence for SIC in Chapter 6.

In order to speed up the functioning of a digital system, it is often convenient to specify the *simultaneous execution* of completely separate register transfers. This may be done quite naturally by catenating both sides of the statement, as in expression 5.7:

$$\boldsymbol{A,B} \leftarrow \boldsymbol{C,D} \tag{5.7}$$

In some cases we shall find it convenient to denote the registers separately. We shall assume that separate transfers, listed on the same line but separated by a semicolon, will be executed simultaneously

$$\boldsymbol{A} \leftarrow \boldsymbol{C};\ \boldsymbol{B} \leftarrow \boldsymbol{D} \tag{5.8}$$

Expression 5.8 assumes that $\boldsymbol{A}$ and $\boldsymbol{C}$ as well as $\boldsymbol{B}$ and $\boldsymbol{D}$ have the same number of bits. If this is true in expression 5.7, then the two expressions are equivalent.

Transfer statements which require only one clock period for execution may be specified without any additional notation. Some transfers require a longer time, while others are asynchronous. Control unit design is somewhat complicated by these cases. In order to completely specify the design for such cases, it is necessary to append comments to transfer statements. Similarly, comments will be required to indicate sequences of transfers which take place in parallel and to provide for pulse communications between systems. All of these situations may be lumped under the heading of *timing*. Further consideration of timing must wait until Chapters 7 and 9.

It is possible to write a program which will automatically translate AHPL programs into logic block diagrams. The generation of hardware by such a program is quite closely analogous to generation of assembly language programs from programs written in a high-level language. For this reason such a program might be called a *hardware compiler*. Hardware compilers have been written [3, 4], including one for AHPL [5]. Programs of this type show some promise of becoming practical for the generation of pattern masks for LSI circuits.

The reason for including register declaration and *bus logic declaration* statements in the outline of Fig. 5.10 is to satisfy the requirements of a possible hardware compiler. The existence of registers appearing in the control sequence should be listed in advance. Similarly, buses should be defined and the corresponding logic networks specified in advance. Automatic hardware translation is not our primary interest in this volume. We are interested in providing the reader with sufficient understanding that he can accomplish this translation process whenever he desires. Consequently we shall rarely bother to list register declaration statements, and bus declaration will usually be accomplished in the discussion.

Before designing SIC in the next chapter, it is desirable to present a less involved example of digital system design at this point. So far we are prepared to handle any control sequence in which all transfers are synchronous and which does not require pulse communications with other systems. Unfortunately this eliminates some interesting peripheral equipment design problems. The following example is somewhat more involved than the final example in Chapter 4.

Example 5.3

A simple machine tool controller is to be designed using a read-only memory to store sequences of tool positions. Eighteen-bit numbers are used to specify the tool position in three dimensions in a way which need not concern us here. There are four possible sequences, any of which may be requested by an operator at any time. Each sequence is 256 words long. The system hardware must include an 18-bit register, ***PR***, for storing the current tool position. The tool electronics continually monitor this register through three digital-to analog converters. Communications with the operator is provided using a start-stop flip-flop, *ss*, and a two-bit register, ***SQR***, which specifies the desired sequence. The bit combinations 00, 01, 10, and 11 in ***SQR*** indicate that the sequence presently being utilized (if any) is *A*, *B*, *C*, or *D*, respectively. Setting the flip-flop *ss* to 1 will cause the controller to begin reading out the sequence specified by ***SQR***. If the operator causes the flip-flop *ss* to be reset to 0, the controller responds by terminating the sequence in progress and storing a vector of 18 zeros in ***PR***. Upon completing a sequence, the controller must reset *ss* and store zeros in ***PR***. A synchronizing* mechanism has been provided so that the contents of *ss* and ***SQR*** will never change during a controller clock pulse.

Solution. The only required storage registers in addition to those described above are a 10-bit address register for the read-only memory and the read-only memory itself. These devices may be represented by the vector ***AR*** and the matrix **ROM**, respectively. The complete register configuration is given in Fig. 5.12. The read-only memory (**ROM**) contains 1024 18-bit words in all. Sequence *A* is stored in locations 0–255 (decimal). In decimal, the first addresses of sequences *B*, *C*, and *D* are 256, 512, and 768, respectively.

The frequency of the clock source has been established compatible with the

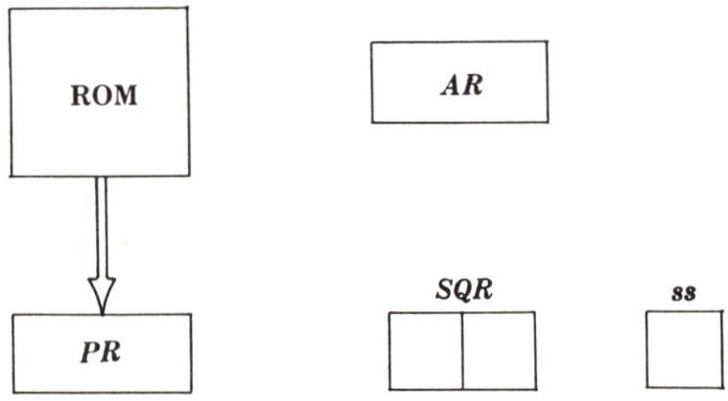

FIGURE 5.12. Controller registers.

* A detailed discussion of synchronization will be provided in Chapter 9.

required data rate of the tool, and therefore is slower than the **ROM**. Thus, a word can be read from **ROM** into ***PR*** in one clock period. The following is a control sequence for the machine tool controller. The first two steps form a waiting loop similar to the FORTRAN loop in the example of Section 4.8. Whenever *ss* goes to 1, control goes to step 3 to place the first address of the appropriate sequence in ***AR***.

1. $ss:1, (=, \neq) \rightarrow (3, 2)$
2. $\rightarrow(1)$
3. $\boldsymbol{AR} \leftarrow (\overline{\epsilon(10)} \wedge (\overline{\boldsymbol{SQR}_0} \wedge \overline{\boldsymbol{SQR}_1})) \vee [(\top 256) \wedge (\overline{\boldsymbol{SQR}_0} \wedge \boldsymbol{SQR}_1)]$
   $\vee [(\boldsymbol{SQR}_0 \wedge \overline{\boldsymbol{SQR}_1}) \wedge (\top 512)] \vee [(\top 768) \wedge (\boldsymbol{SQR}_0 \wedge \boldsymbol{SQR}_1)]$
4. $\boldsymbol{PR} \leftarrow \mathbf{ROM}^{\perp \boldsymbol{AR}}$
5. $\boldsymbol{AR} \leftarrow \text{INC}(\boldsymbol{AR})$
6. $\vee/\omega^8/\boldsymbol{AR}:1, (=, \neq) \rightarrow (7, 8)$
7. $ss:0, (\neq, =) \rightarrow (4, 9)$
8. $ss \leftarrow 0$
9. $\boldsymbol{PR} \leftarrow \overline{\epsilon(18)}$
10. $\rightarrow(1)$

Depending on the two bits in ***SQR***, the right side of step 3 will reduce to one of the four 10-bit vectors, $\overline{\epsilon(10)}$, $(10)\top 256$, $\top 512$, or $\top 768$, which indicate whether the desired sequence is *A*, *B*, *C*, or *D*. For example,

$$\top 768 = 1,1,0,0,0,0,0,0,0,0.$$

Physically, each bit of $\top 768$ is connected to a fixed voltage source. Thus if $\boldsymbol{SQR}_0 = \boldsymbol{SQR}_1 = 1$, the set-inputs to flip-flops $\boldsymbol{AR}_0$ and $\boldsymbol{AR}_1$ will be pulsed, and the clear-inputs of the remaining eight flip-flops in ***AR*** are pulsed. Note the different forms, $\overline{\epsilon(10)}$ and $\top(512)$. In general, we shall allow a fairly liberal use of APL for denoting constant vectors. Constants are isolated within a statement and are easily translated to vectors of 1's and 0's.

Step 4 is an example of what will become a familiar *read-from-memory* notation. The contents of the address in **ROM** specified by ***AR*** are placed in ***PR***. $\mathbf{ROM}^{\perp \boldsymbol{AR}}$ will be recognized as another example of the abbreviation given in expression 5.6. This will be the only allowed abbreviation which does not follow combinational logic subroutine format.

Step 5 is our first encounter with combinational logic subroutine notation. This step causes one to be added to the binary number in ***AR***, so that the next word in sequence may be obtained from **ROM**. In APL the step might have been expressed as

$$\boldsymbol{AR} \leftarrow (10)\top((\perp \boldsymbol{AR}) + 1)$$

This form uses a disallowed primitive operator and gives no hint of the form of the combinational logic required to implement the operation. It *will not be allowed* in AHPL. The notation INC (***AR***) appears equally meaningless at this point, but it has the advantage of standard subroutine form. It represents a combinational logic network which causes ***AR*** to be incremented in one clock period. In effect, it represents the logic required to turn ***AR*** into a counter. In Chapter 7 we shall see how to express this network in subroutine form.

Step 6 causes a branch to step 8 if the reading of a 256-word sequence has just been completed. This requires a rather simple logical expression, since the last 8 bits of the first address of each sequence are all 0's. Steps 8, 9, and 10 reset ***ss*** to 0, place 0's in ***PC***, and return control to step 1 to await a request for another output sequence.

Step 7 is included to provide termination of an output sequence in the event that the operator causes ***ss*** to be reset to 0. This is accomplished by a branch to step 9. Otherwise, control returns to step 4 to read the next word of the sequence from **ROM**. ▮

Hopefully, the above example has answered some questions, but it has likely raised several others. Many of these questions will be answered in the next two chapters. In Chapter 6 we shall treat another control sequence design example, SIC, in a more leisurely manner. In Chapter 7 we shall present the control unit hardware required to implement control sequences.

PROBLEMS

In Problems 5.1–5.9 the result of carrying out the specified operations is to be determined. The following values for the operands are to be used:

$$w = 2 \quad u = 1 \quad x = 5 \quad y = -2$$

$$U = (1,0,0,1) \qquad V = (1,0,1,1)$$
$$W = (1,3,7,8) \qquad X = (0,1,-1,3)$$
$$Y = (2,4,8,16)$$

$$\mathbf{N} = \begin{vmatrix} 0 & 1 & 3 \\ 2 & -1 & 0 \\ 4 & 3 & 2 \\ 1 & -3 & 4 \end{vmatrix}$$

5.1 a) $z \leftarrow -y$ b) $z \leftarrow \times / W$
c) $z \leftarrow |y$ d) $Z \leftarrow u \vee U$

5.2 a) $Z \leftarrow x + X$ b) $Z \leftarrow u \wedge U$
c) $Z \leftarrow U/V$ d) $Z \leftarrow x \ulcorner Y$

5.3 a) $Z \leftarrow \overline{U}$ b) $Z \leftarrow U \wedge V$
c) $Z \leftarrow U \vee V$ d) $Z \leftarrow u \vee V$

5.4 a) $\mathbf{A} \leftarrow -\mathbf{N}$ b) $\mathbf{A} \leftarrow w \times \mathbf{N}$
c) $\mathbf{A} \leftarrow |\mathbf{N}$ d) $\mathbf{A} \leftarrow w \ulcorner \mathbf{N}$

5.5 a) $Z \leftarrow + / \mathbf{N}$ b) $Z \leftarrow \times // \mathbf{N}$
c) $z \leftarrow \wedge / U$ d) $Z \leftarrow + // |\mathbf{N}$

5.6 a) $Z \leftarrow U/Y$ b) $Z \leftarrow V/X$
c) $\mathbf{A} \leftarrow U//\mathbf{N}$ d) $\mathbf{A} \leftarrow (V/U)/\mathbf{N}$

5.7 a) $z \leftarrow +/(X > 0)$ b) $x \leftarrow \perp V$
c) $Z \leftarrow 5\perp//\mathbf{N}$ d) $Z \leftarrow V/((W + Y) = 7)$

5.8 a) $Z \leftarrow \alpha^3/W$ b) $Z \leftarrow \omega^2/Y$
c) $Z \leftarrow (\alpha^3 \wedge \omega^3)/W$ d) $\mathbf{A} \leftarrow \omega^2//\mathbf{N}$

5.9 a) $Z \leftarrow \top\perp U + 1$ b) $z \leftarrow 1 + \perp U$
c) $Z \leftarrow \top(\perp U + 1)$ d) $Z \leftarrow \top(1 + \perp U)$

5.10 Given two lists of numbers, X and Y. Write a concise program in APL to obtain those elements of Y having the same position numbers as those elements of X whose value is greater than 12.

5.11 It is desired to obtain that element of a matrix **A**, which is the minimum of the row-by-row maxima of the elements. Write a concise expression in APL for this element.

5.12 The number of combinations of n items taken k at a time may be computed from

$$C(n, k) = C(n - 1, k) + C(n - 1, k - 1)$$

where $C(n, 0) = C(n, n) = 1$.
a) Prove this assertion.
b) Write in APL a program which will compute $C(n, k)$ for all pairs n, k such that $k \leq n$.

5.13 A matrix, **M**, has 20 rows and 6 columns. Write in APL a program which will determine a scalar value, x, which is the number of a row in **M** such that the sum of the elements in that row is greater than or equal to the sum of the elements of every other row.

5.14 Design the AHPL control sequence for a system which will perform the reverse function of the system B in Section 4.8. It must assemble sequences of four 8-bit bytes as supplied by system C into 32-bit words to transmit to system A. Add any control flip-flops which may be required. Allow one dummy clock period in which system B does not change the contents of $\boldsymbol{LR}$ while system A reads this data.

5.15 Consider a matrix of 32 eighteen-bit words stored in individually accessible electronic registers. Write a valid AHPL transfer statement, which rotates the rows of the matrix, that is, row 0 → row 32 → row 31, etc. Recall that a single transfer may involve a matrix.

5.16 A digital communications buffer contains 32 eighteen-bit words. The buffer has its own control unit. Part of the function of the buffer is to check for longitudinal parity (that is, parity over the 32 bits in each bit position of the 32 words). If a parity error in one of the 18-bit positions is found, a flip-flop $\boldsymbol{pf}$ is to be set to 1. Write a partial control sequence which accomplishes this parity check in an economical sequential manner (see Problem 5.15). Add registers and flip-flops as needed.

5.17 Write a control sequence which will accomplish the operation discussed in example 5.2 sequentially. Use a 16-bit register, ***MA***, to store the address of a word to be obtained from memory. Assume that the AHPL statement $\boldsymbol{MD} \leftarrow \mathbf{M}^{\perp \boldsymbol{MA}}$ will cause the word addressed by ***MA*** to be placed in the memory data register ***MD***. Also assume that the contents of ***MA*** may be incremented, directly, using the combinational logic subroutine INC(***MA***).

REFERENCES

1. Iverson, K. E., *A Programming Language*, Wiley, New York, 1962.
2. Hellerman, Herbert, *Digital System Principles*, McGraw-Hill, New York, 1967.
3. Friedman, T. D., and Yang, S. C., "Methods Used in Automatic Logic Design Generator (ALERT)," *IEEE Trans. Computers*, Sept. 1969, p. 593.
4. Schorr, H., "Computer Aided Digital System Design and Analysis Using a Register Transfer Language," *IEEE Trans. Electronic Computers*, Dec. 1964, pp. 730–737.
5. Gentry, M., "A Compiler for AHPL Control Sequences," Ph.D. dissertation, University of Arizona, June 1971.

6

Machine Organization and Hardware Programs

6.1. INTRODUCTION

In Chapter 5 we introduced a new language, AHPL, with the justification that computer hardware could be described in terms of this language. Previously in Chapter 2 we discussed in detail a small digital computer, SIC. In this chapter we propose to design a computer which will function in the manner attributed to SIC in Chapter 2. The design will be expressed as a program in AHPL. Translation of this program into a hardware description or a logic block diagram must wait until Chapter 7.

We shall continue to use SIC as the vehicle to illustrate what is actually a completely general procedure. SIC is sufficiently simple that a reasonably complete design can be presented without burdening the reader with detail. There are, however, many important features of large scale computers which are not found in SIC. AHPL routines describing many of these features will be presented in later chapters. Having seen the details of a complete computer tied together in Chapters 6 and 7, the reader should be able to visualize the incorporation of these individual features into the overall design of a larger scale computer.

It is our conviction that AHPL is an excellent vehicle for teaching computer organization but is also a practical design language. A program has been developed to compile AHPL programs, i.e., to translate them into a logic block diagram form. In Chapter 7, however, our point of view will be to indicate the various correspondences between AHPL notation and computer hardware. Our goal will be to provide the reader with the tools required to carry out the translation process himself. Once he has progressed to this point the reader will have a basic understanding of computer organization.

6.2. REGISTER ORGANIZATION

The memory registers of SIC are shown in Fig. 6.1. The five registers discussed in Chapter 2 are included. The program counter is labeled ***PC***, the accumulator is labeled ***AC***, the instruction register is labeled ***IR***, and the index registers are labeled ***IA*** and ***IB***, respectively. In Chapter 4 we observed that two additional registers are required for the proper functioning of the random access memory. These are the memory address register ***MA*** and the memory data register ***MD***. ***AC***, ***IR***, and ***MD*** are 18-bit vectors while the remaining four registers contain 13 bits.

The memory will be designated by **M**, consisting for purposes of this discussion of 2^{13} row vectors of 18 bits each. Thus $\mathbf{M}^i$ will refer to row i as the ith numbered word in memory. The link, ℓ, will remain as a 1-bit register.

The execution of an instruction by the computer depicted in Fig. 6.1

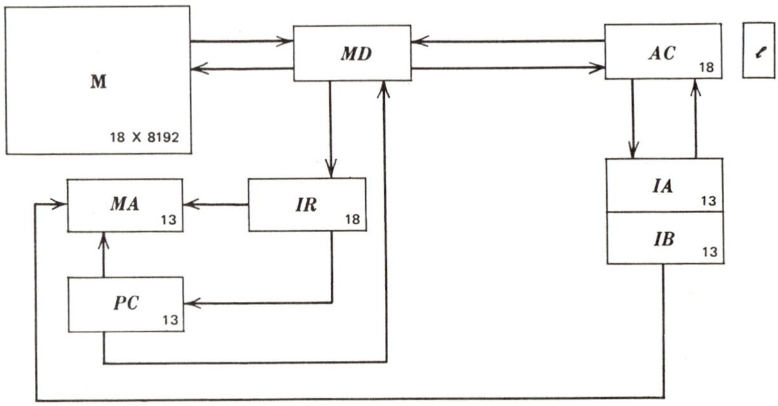

FIGURE 6.1. Register organization.

consists of a series of transfers of data from register to register. Several such register transfers will be required to accomplish a single machine language instruction such as LAC.

The registers in Fig. 6.1 are interconnected by arrows which indicate allowed data paths. Not shown are configurations of combinational logic which we shall label logic units. An adder is an example of a logic unit. The amount of hardware in a logic unit will often be comparable to that of a register. In general the logic units may be thought of as lying along the illustrated data paths. The contents of one or more registers may be routed through a logic unit and then into a receiving register. The receiving register may in some cases be one of the sending registers.

The AHPL program may be thought of as a control program. As we shall see in Chapter 7 this program represents a one-to-one correspondence to control unit hardware. In effect each assignment statement of the AHPL program will represent control of the transfer of information from one register to another.

In FORTRAN the only limitation on assignment statements is that a floating-point quantity may only replace a floating-point variable, and so on. By specifying data paths we place much tighter constraints on the allowable register transfers in an AHPL routine. Specification of data paths in advance is not a requirement of AHPL. Formally the designer need only list the registers in advance. He may specify transfers at will as he writes each AHPL routine. He need only ascertain that the same number of bits should appear in the vector on each side of a transfer statement. As we shall see, it is not even necessary to list the logic units in advance. These may be defined as individual statements of the hardware program written.

6.3. DATA PATHS

In practice the designer will often work out an overall hardware layout including registers, the principal logic units, and the allowed data paths prior to writing the control program. Three separate reasons may be cited for this practice. First, it provides the earliest possible estimate of overall hardware requirements and tends to minimize these requirements by encouraging the multiple use of the same data paths. Each potential data path avoided represents a saving of switching devices.

Second, certain relatively expensive logic units are often used with more than one set of arguments rather than using duplicate units. Provision must be made for switching these arguments at the input to the logic unit. This is usually accomplished by routing arguments through data buses. The connections to and from the bus must be specified prior to writing a control sequence. If we assume a pulse-oriented control unit, as we will throughout the book, a set of bus control flip-flops and decoding networks must be established using knowledge of the number of register connected to each bus. We shall disregard the possibility of busing in our introductory discussion of SIC, but shall consider it again later in the chapter.

A third reason for constraining data paths in advance is related to the translation of the control unit to hardware. More than one approach to hardware implementation of a control unit is possible. The first or *hard-wired* approach, which we shall discuss, does not necessarily constrain data paths. Another important approach may be termed *microprogramming*. Theoretically at least, the control unit of a microprogrammable computer may be altered after manufacture. Thus one machine could be adapted to a variety of special purpose applications or to emulate at the hardware level some other machine. Every microprogramming scheme limits the number of parameters available to a user in reconfiguring his machine. This always falls short of the arbitrary addition of data paths which would require a rewiring of the machine. Microprogramming will be the topic of Chapter 8.

The data paths in Fig. 6.1 are essentially those which will be utilized throughout the next several sections. As our purpose here is pedagogical we shall take no notice of these paths at this point. We shall proceed as if free to add register transfers at will.

We remind ourselves that each transfer step in the control sequence corresponds to a pulse from the control unit, which causes a register transfer. The hardware required to shift data from ***MD*** to ***AC*** is shown in simplified form in Fig. 6.2. This particular register transfer is a critical part of the instruction LAC. The OR gates provided at the input to the memory elements allow information to be transferred into the accumulator from various sources.

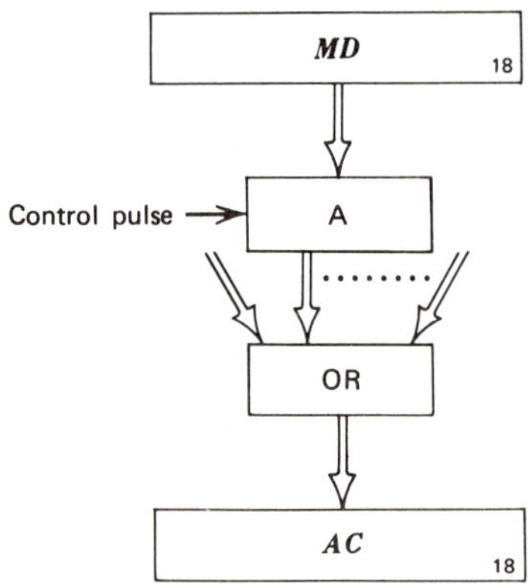

FIGURE 6.2. Register transfer.

Data lines from another register and a different control pulse could be routed to AND gates similar to those depicted at the output of ***MD***. The outputs of these gates would be connected to the same OR gates shown. As many configurations of this type may be attached to the OR gates as there are distinct data paths to ***AC*** specified by the control program.* Notice that Fig. 6.2 allows the propagation of pulses through the data network. This dictates the use of unclocked master-slave memory elements. We shall find it convenient throughout the book to assume all control signals to have the form of pulses. Thus with the exception of a short discussion in Section 7.10, all memory elements will be unclocked.

Gating the outputs of a logic unit into a register presents no further complications. As an illustration, the data path for the TAD instruction is shown in Fig. 6.3. Also included is the data path of Fig. 6.2. Note that the two control pulses shown in Fig. 6.3 arise in different parts of the control unit and will never both be 1 simultaneously. In fact the pulse lines are both 0 most of the time. The output of the adder, for example, is continuously available at the input to AND gate array A2. This adder output is of no interest at times other than short periods around the TAD pulse.

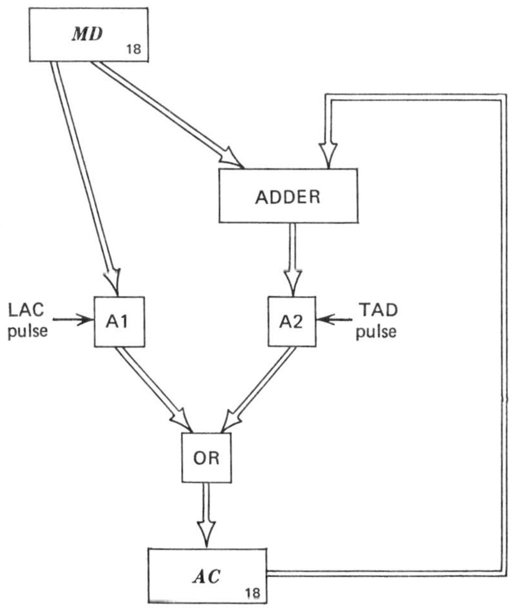

FIGURE 6.3. LAC and TAD register transfers.

* Electrically of course the number of inputs to an OR gate is limited. This limit is called *fan-in*.

Just before the advent of this pulse a valid sum of the numbers in ***MD*** and *AC* will appear at the adder output. This 18-bit sum will be gated into *AC* by the TAD pulse. As *AC* is assumed to be composed of master-slave flip-flops, the arguments at the input of the adder will remain undisturbed until after the TAD pulse has returned to zero.

Although indexing and busing have been omitted from the above discussion, at least one remark is in order. Suppose the adder is used in more than one operation. In this case the same output lines from this device will be connected to the input gating configuration of more than one register. As mentioned above, however, the registers will be unaffected except at the time of a control pulse intended to gate information into that register. No additional switching is required at the output of the adder. It is only necessary to provide switching buses at the input to assure that the proper arguments are supplied to this logic unit prior to the occurrence of a control pulse.

6.4. CLASSIFYING INSTRUCTIONS

We are now ready to proceed with the design of a control unit to generate control pulses of the form assumed in the previous section. Our approach will be to write an AHPL program containing a routine for the execution of each SIC instruction.

The instructions of any single-address machine can be divided into the following five categories:

1. Input/output
2. Operate
3. Read operand
4. Store
5. Branch without read

Instruction groups 3 and 4 are called *memory reference* instructions. Two references to the random access memory are required to accomplish these instructions. First the instruction must be read from memory, and then during the execution of the instruction a data word must be retrieved from or deposited in memory.

For the first, second, and fifth type of instruction a second memory cycle is not required. Various *input/output* instructions transfer data between the accumulator and peripheral equipment. This will require buffer registers and unique timing sequences. An I/O (Input/Output) cycle will usually require more time than an additional memory cycle. We shall defer a more detailed treatment of this problem until Chapter 10.

As defined in Chapter 2, *operate* instructions act on the contents of one of the electronic registers or execute a skip operation depending on the contents of one of these registers. Thus no operand is required from memory. Group 5 *branch* instructions require only that the address portion of the ***IR*** register be shifted to ***PC***. Thus a second memory reference is not required. These branch instructions may be unconditional or depend on the contents of certain registers (in the case of SIC only *AC* and ℓ). All instructions of this type fall into group 5.

Other branch (skip) instructions may depend on the contents of an addressed memory register. These instructions will be classed with the Read Operand instructions for purposes of this discussion. All instructions which require reading an operand from memory before commencing a logical operation are assumed to fall into group 3.

Instructions which call for storing the contents of some register or some fixed number in memory fall into group 4. In multiregister machines such as floating-point units, the contents of registers other than the accumulator may be transferred to memory.

The first memory reference is called the *fetch cycle*. This cycle, with the exception of indexing and indirect addressing, is common to all five groups of instructions. The fetch cycle is presented in detail in Fig. 6.4. The instructions are executed during what is termed, not surprisingly, *the execute cycle*. With the exception of JMP, execution is not detailed in Fig. 6.4. Once again the execute cycle involves a memory reference only for group 3 and 4 instructions. Details of the execute cycle for all but input/output (IOT) instructions will be presented in the next several sections.

During the fetch cycle the contents of the program counter, ***PC***, are first shifted to the memory address register, ***MA***. The memory responds with a read-write cycle as described in Chapter 4, leaving the addressed word in the memory data register, ***MD***. The contents of ***MD*** are subsequently transferred to ***IR***. If the instruction calls for indirect addressing, another memory reference is required as part of the *fetch* phase. The address portion of the contents of ***MD*** are thus shifted to ***MA***, and the new addressed data word is delivered to ***MD***.

As indirect addressing is not applicable to operate and IOT instructions, the control sequence for these instructions separates immediately following block 1 in Fig. 6.4. For indirect addressing, the last 13 bits of ***IR*** are placed in ***MA***, a memory cycle is executed, and the last 13 bits of ***MD*** replace the corresponding bits of ***IR***. Following the possible indirect addressing cycle, control diverges for the JMP instruction. As JMP is accomplished in only one register transfer, this transfer is detailed in block 27 of Fig. 6.4.

Notice that following the execution of instructions other than branch, control converges to cause the contents of the program counter to be increased by one. Next control returns to block 1 to begin the fetch cycle for

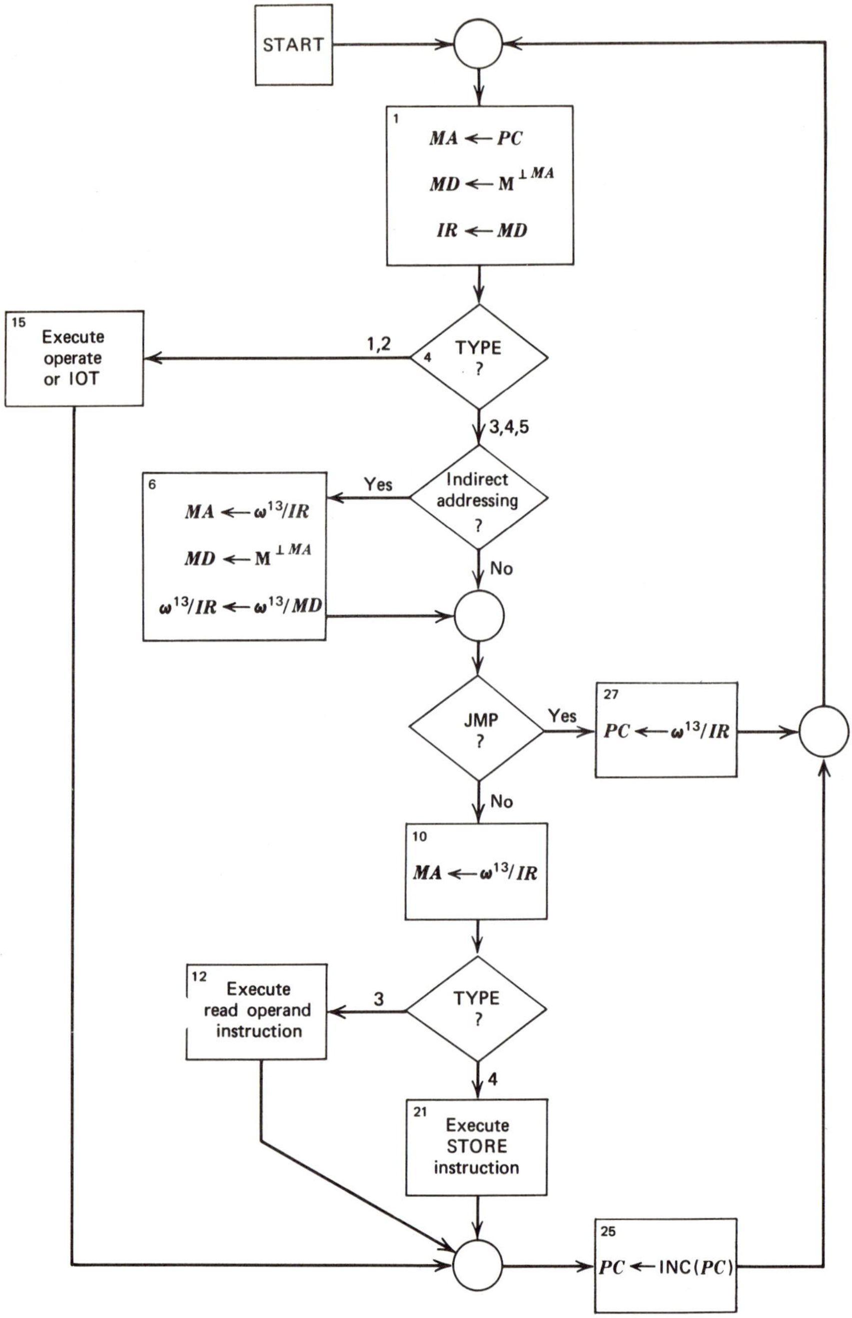

FIGURE 6.4. Overall control flow chart.

the next instruction. Once started this process continues indefinitely. The discussion of Fig. 6.4 will be continued in the next section after a necessary review of the bit codes of each instruction. We have now laid the necessary background for an instructive example.

Example 6.1

Design an indirect addressing cycle which will require one less register transfer (therefore requiring less time to accomplish) then the cycle illustrated in Fig. 6.4.

Solution. A solution is depicted in Fig. 6.5. The saving is achieved by eliminating block 10 of Fig.6.4. Rather than transferring $\boldsymbol{\omega}^{13}/\boldsymbol{MD}$ first to ***IR*** and then to MA, it is transferred directly to MA. This saving is not achieved without penalty. The reader will notice that two new data paths, one from ***MD*** to MA and the other from ***MD*** to ***PC***, are introduced in Fig. 6.5. The latter is made necessary by the

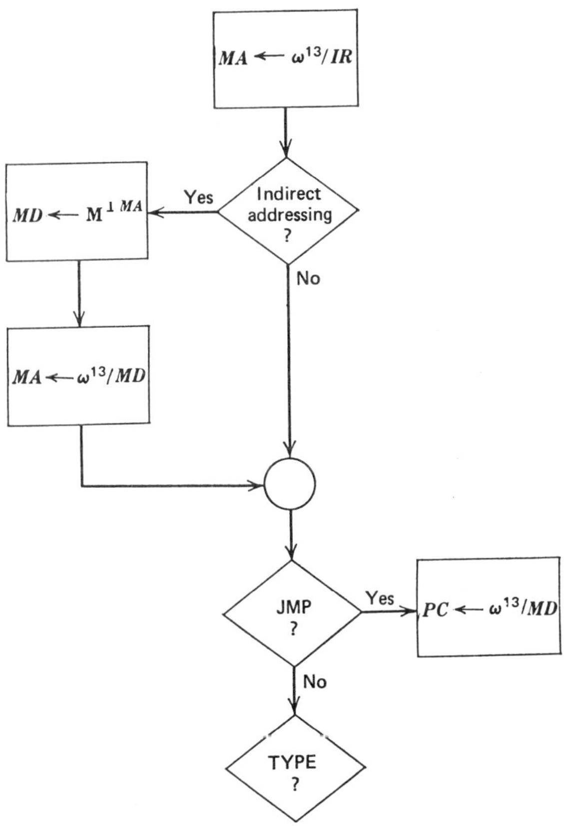

FIGURE 6.5. Alternate approach to indirect addressing.

JMP instruction since the new address has not been placed in the instruction register. Neither of these data paths is included in Fig. 6.1, and neither would otherwise be necessary in the design of SIC. Thus an additional array of AND gates would be required at the input of ***MA*** and another at the input of ***PC***. It may be that the frequency of use of indirect addressing and the relatively small time saving would not justify this additional hardware. ▮

6.5. AHPL CONTROL PROGRAMS

The reader probably cannot yet visualize the flow chart of Fig. 6.4 as a computer control unit. The complete picture must wait until the one-to-one correspondence between AHPL programs and control unit hardware is presented in Chapter 7. First we must interpret the branch symbols of Fig. 6.4 as AHPL statements and list program steps for the execute phase of the instructions. While branch statements require further explanation, the register transfers can be lifted directly from the flow chart and entered in a program listing.

The reader will recall from Chapter 2 that the bits of a SIC instruction word are grouped as follows. Bits 0–2 specify the operation code while bits

0–2	3	4	5–17
OP CODE			ADDRESS

5–17 specify the address for memory reference instructions. Bits 3 and 4 are used to specify indexing and indirect addressing. Bit combination 01 specifies indirect addressing, while 10 and 11 specify indexing, and 00 calls for neither indexing nor indirect addressing.

The instruction list is repeated in Fig. 6.6. The function of the first seven

Bits 0 1 2	Octal	Mnemonic	Group
0 0 0	0	ISZ	3
0 0 1	1	LAC	3
0 1 0	2	AND	3
0 1 1	3	TAD	3
1 0 0	4	JMS	4
1 0 1	5	DAC	4
1 1 0	6	JMP	5
1 1 1	7	Operate or I/O	1, 2

FIGURE 6.6. Instruction set.

instructions is as discussed in Chapter 2. If the OP code is 111, then bits 5–17 no longer refer to an address but may be used to specify particular input/output or operate instructions. The reader will note that the bit codings were carefully assigned to group the instructions. Notice that bit zero is 0 for all group 3 instructions. Bit zero is 1 and bit one is 0 for group 4 instructions. As will become apparent soon, these instruction bits control many of the branch operations in the AHPL program. The convenient bit assignments of Fig. 6.6 will simplify these operations.

As with any language, AHPL control programs need not necessarily be presented in flow chart form. The usual list of instructions in sequence will be more convenient. The first three register transfers of Fig. 6.4 and the branch corresponding to chart symbol 4 are listed as follows:

1. $\boldsymbol{MA} \leftarrow \boldsymbol{PC}$
2. $\boldsymbol{MD} \leftarrow \mathrm{M}^{\perp \boldsymbol{MA}}$
3. $\boldsymbol{IR} \leftarrow \boldsymbol{MD}$
4. $\perp(\alpha^3/\boldsymbol{IR}):7, (=,\neq) \rightarrow (29,5)$

Step 4 must accomplish a branch to a later point in the program for the case of operate and IOT instructions. If all three bits of the op code are ones, then $\perp(\alpha^3/\boldsymbol{IR}) = 7$ and control branches to step 29. Otherwise line 5 is the next program step.

Line 5 is another branch, this time to allow for indirect addressing. Indirect addressing is called for if $\boldsymbol{IR}_4$ is 1 (indexing will not be included at this point so bit 3 is assumed to be 0). For $\boldsymbol{IR}_4 = 1$, control continues to step 6. Otherwise it branches to step 9.

5. $\boldsymbol{IR}_4:1, (=,\neq) \rightarrow (6,9)$
6. $\boldsymbol{MA} \leftarrow \omega^{13}/\boldsymbol{IR}$
7. $\boldsymbol{MD} \leftarrow \mathrm{M}^{\perp \boldsymbol{MA}}$
8. $\omega^{13}/\boldsymbol{IR} \leftarrow \omega^{13}/\boldsymbol{MD}$

The three register transfers required for indirect addressing are as given in Fig. 6.4. It is intended that each register transfer in Iverson notation will correspond to a single hardware register transfer. That this is the case with steps 1 and 3 is evident. For step 6, for example, the control unit pulses only the last 13 bits of ***IR*** into ***MA***. In this case the first five bits would not be connected. No data register flip-flop will change state more than once during step 2. As we shall see in Chapter 7, this does not imply that the step will involve no sequential operations within the random access memory unit during its execution. For purposes of the control unit, the memory read cycle will be regarded as a single discrete operation. As this operation will require more real time than flip-flop register transfers, some approach to synchronization other than the basic clock will be required in the control unit. This will become clear in Chapter 7. Transfers between high speed electronic registers will be allowed only one clock interval.

The branch instructions will be accomplished through combinational logic gating within the control unit. Step 9, which represents a branch to separate group 3 and 4 instructions from group 5 instructions, may be written as follows:

$$9. \quad \rightarrow (((\overline{\boldsymbol{IR}}_0 \vee \overline{\boldsymbol{IR}}_1) \times 10) + ((\boldsymbol{IR}_0 \wedge \boldsymbol{IR}_1) \times 27))$$

If either of bits $\boldsymbol{IR}_0$ or $\boldsymbol{IR}_1$ is 0, then control branches to 10 for a group 3 or 4 instruction. If both bits are 1, then control branches to step 27 for the instruction JMP (control has already separated for IOT and Operate instructions). Since AHPL specifies the result of all Boolean operations as 1 or 0, we use + and × to generate a multivalued Boolean expression with 10 and 27 as logical constants. Alternatively one could have written

$$\rightarrow (10,27)_{\boldsymbol{IR}_0 \wedge \boldsymbol{IR}_1}$$

which would give the same results as 9. We shall see in Chapter 7 that expressions of the form of line 9 bear a closer correspondence to hardware. We shall see the form of line 9 in all but a few instances where other forms are used for brevity.

Program steps 10 and 11 place the address in $\boldsymbol{MA}$ and execute a branch to separate group 3 instructions from group 4:

$$10. \quad \boldsymbol{MA} \leftarrow \omega^{13}/\boldsymbol{IR}$$

$$11. \quad \rightarrow ((\overline{\boldsymbol{IR}}_0 \times 12) + (\boldsymbol{IR}_0 \times 21))$$

We are now ready to consider the execution phase of these instructions. For group 3 instructions, step 12 retrieves the data word from memory while step 13 separates control for the ISZ instruction from that for the other three instructions:

$$12. \quad \boldsymbol{MD} \leftarrow \mathrm{M}^{\perp \boldsymbol{MA}}$$

$$13. \quad \rightarrow (((\boldsymbol{IR}_1 \vee \boldsymbol{IR}_2) \times 14) + ((\overline{\boldsymbol{IR}_1 \vee \boldsymbol{IR}_2}) \times 16))$$

$$14. \quad \ell,\boldsymbol{AC} \leftarrow ((\overline{\boldsymbol{IR}}_1 \wedge (\ell,\boldsymbol{MD})) \vee (\overline{\boldsymbol{IR}}_2 \wedge (\ell,(\boldsymbol{MD} \wedge \boldsymbol{AC}))) \vee ((\boldsymbol{IR}_1 \wedge \boldsymbol{IR}_2) \wedge \mathrm{ADD}(\boldsymbol{MD},\boldsymbol{AC})))$$

$$15. \quad \rightarrow (25)$$

For the AND, TAD, and LAC instructions, some function of $\boldsymbol{AC}$ and $\boldsymbol{MD}$ must be gated into $\boldsymbol{AC}$. For ISZ a longer sequence will be required. If we choose to allow the function to be selected by a gating function of op code bit levels at the input of the $\boldsymbol{AC}$, then no distinction need be made between TAD, AND, and LAC by branches within the control unit. Line 14 implements the TAD, AND, and LAC operations. This is our first encounter with a *don't-care* condition. That is, step 13 only allows a branch to step 14 if one

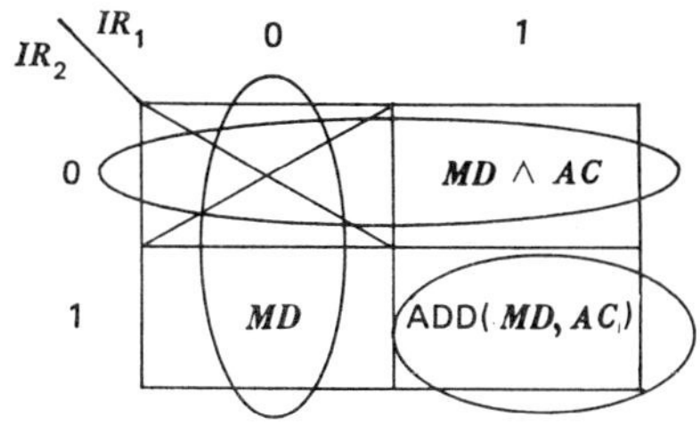

FIGURE 6.7. Karnaugh map for step 14.

of the bits IR_1 or IR_2 is 1. Thus at step 14, the case where $IR_1 = IR_2 = 0$ becomes a don't-care condition. The vector to be placed in ℓ,AC for various combinations of values of IR_1 and IR_2 is given in the vector Karnaugh map of Fig. 6.7. Two of the vector functional values take advantage of the don't-care condition, hence line 14. We notice the term ADD(MD,AC) appearing in the expression. This represents a combinational logic subroutine which generates the 19-bit arithmetic sum of MD and AC. In order that the syntax of line 14 be consistent we must specify the result of the ADD subroutine as a vector one bit longer than the length of AC.

The TAD instruction will usually require more than one clock time for execution. Since AND and LAC can be accomplished in one clock interval, one could choose to separately control all four read operand instructions. The following would be an alternative AHPL sequence:

13. $\rightarrow (20, 14, 16, 18)_{\perp \alpha^3 / IR}$
14. $AC \leftarrow MD$
15. $\rightarrow$ (convergence point)
16. $AC \leftarrow MD \wedge AC$
17. $\rightarrow$ (convergence point)
18. $\ell,AC \leftarrow$ ADD(AC,MD)
19. $\rightarrow$ (convergence point)

Either of these approaches is valid; and as we shall see in Chapter 7, the hardware difference is small.

Continuing with the former version, we may implement the ISZ instruction by the following sequence:

16. $MD \leftarrow$ INC(MD)
17. $M^{\perp MA} \leftarrow MD$
18. $(\vee / MD):0, (=, \neq) \rightarrow (19, 25)$
19. $PC \leftarrow$ INC(PC)
20. $\rightarrow (25)$

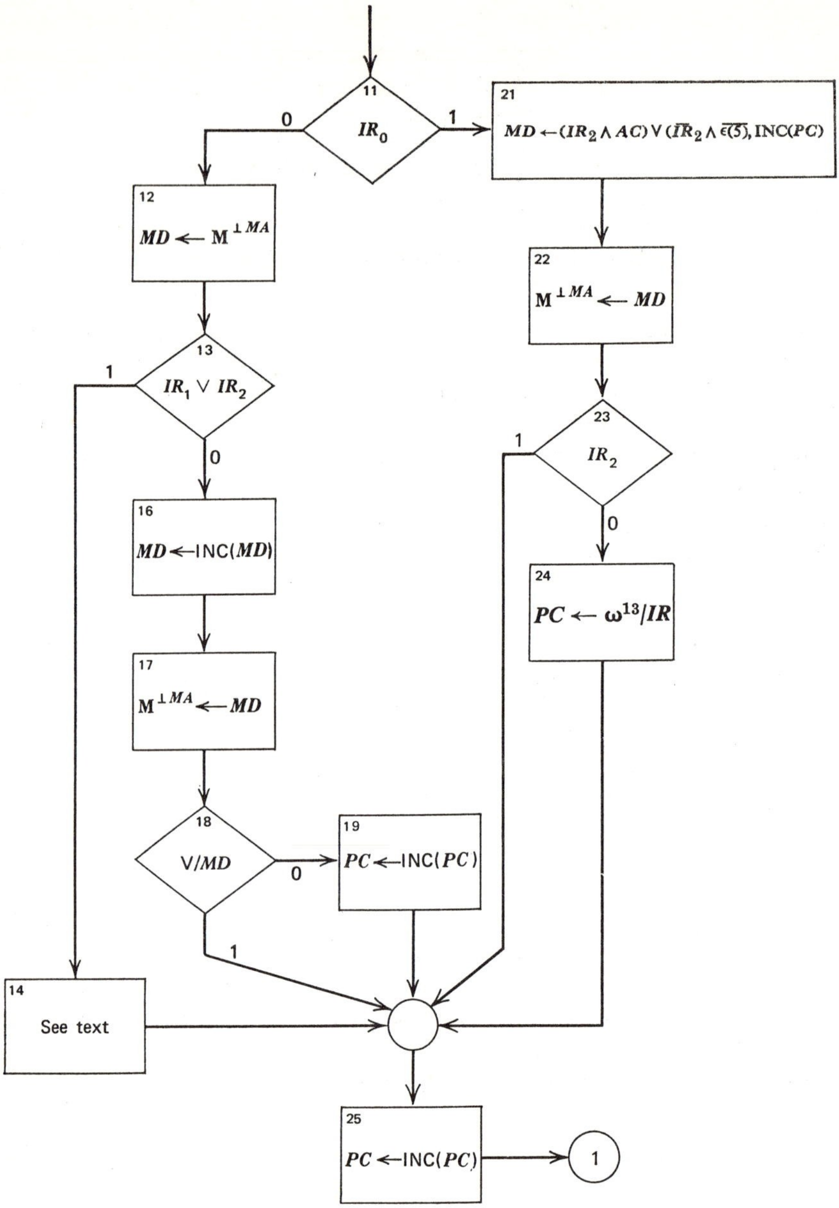

FIGURE 6.8. Execution of group 3 and 4 instructions.

The expression INC(MD) is another example of a combinational logic subroutine. Step 18 is the first instance where control branches as a function of a data word rather than an instruction. This will present no particular difficulty with respect to hardware implementation as we shall see in Chapter 7.

The instructions DAC and JMS have a common memory write cycle, so let us continue them as a single control sequence. Step 21 loads the memory data register with AC in the case of DAC and the contents of the program

21. $MD \leftarrow (IR_2 \wedge AC) \vee (\overline{IR}_2 \wedge (00000, \text{INC}(PC)))$
22. $\text{M}^{\perp MA} \leftarrow MD$
23. $\rightarrow ((IR_2 \times 25) + (\overline{IR}_2 \times 24))$
24. $PC \leftarrow \omega^{13}/IR$

counter in the case of JMS. The reader will recall that the contents of PC must be stored in memory by JMS so that the computer can return to the proper point in the program following the completion of the subroutine.

DAC is completed after the memory write cycle of step 22; and control branches to line 25, the point of convergence for instructions other than JMP. Step 24 concludes JMS by transferring the 13 address bits from IR to the program counter. The program counter will be incremented at step 25, and the next instruction will be taken from the memory location immediately following the one addressed by JMS.

25. $PC \leftarrow \text{INC}(PC)$
26. $\rightarrow (1)$
27. $PC \leftarrow \omega^{13}/IR$
28. $\rightarrow (1)$

The reader will recall that control converges at step 25 after the execution of any instruction but JMP. For these other instructions, $\perp PC$ is increased by one; and control returns to step one to begin another instruction. In the case of JMP, the last thirteen bits of IR are placed in PC at step 27; and control returns to step 1. As an aid to the reader, the execution cycles for group 3 and 4 instructions are depicted in flow chart form in Fig. 6.8.

6.6. GATING

As a further example of the gating associated with a register transfer we shall detail the switching associated with step 21 of the previous section. This step is repeated as follows:

$$MD \leftarrow (IR_2 \wedge AC) \vee (\overline{IR}_2 \wedge (00000, \text{INC}(PC)))$$

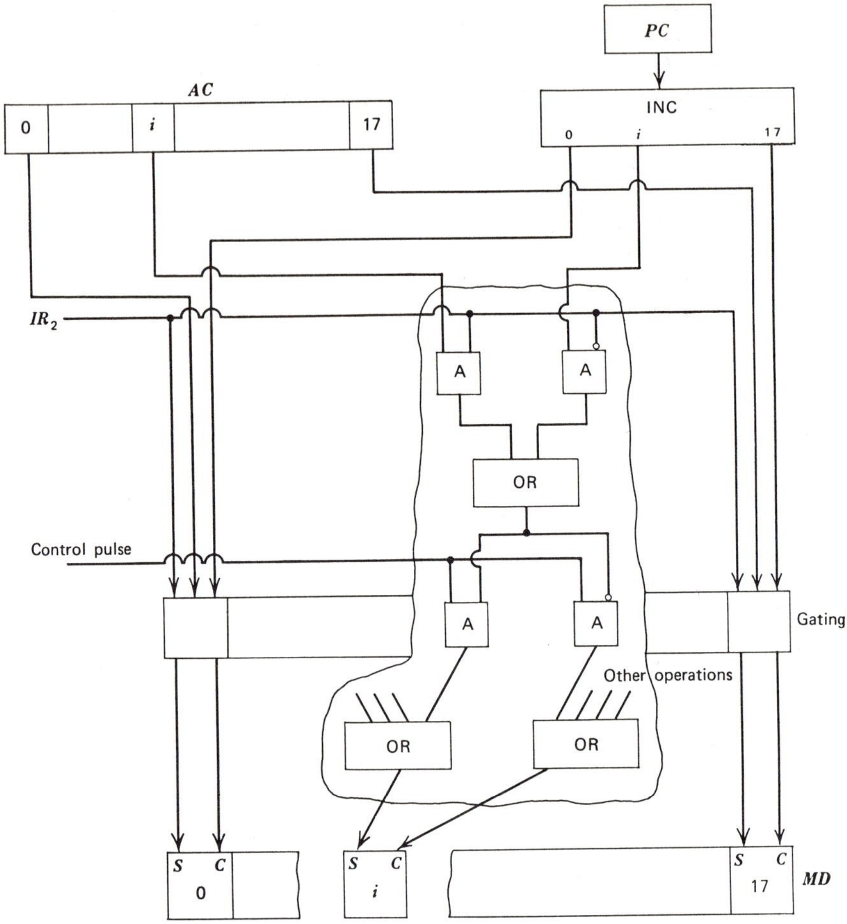

FIGURE 6.9. Gating into *MD* for store instructions.

The physical implementation of this register transfer is depicted in Fig. 6.9. The gating is shown in detail for only one flip-flop. The structure is similar for the remaining 17 flip-flops. Once again the OR gates at the input to the flip-flop will accommodate inputs corresponding to other transfers into ***MD***. Other possible control sequences for JMS and DAC can result in different switching configurations. This will be illustrated in the following example.

Example 6.2

Suppose that a computer with an instruction code similar to the one discussed above is to be designed so that the instructions JMS and DAC have separate control sequences. Express the control sequences for these instructions in AHPL. Since separate pulses will be available to trigger the input of ***MD*** for this instruction, redesign the input circuitry to a single flip-flop of Fig. 6.9.

Solution.

21. $IR_2 : 0\ (=, >) \rightarrow (22, 26)$
22. $MD \leftarrow 00000$, INC(PC)
23. $\mathbf{M}^{\perp MA} \leftarrow MD$
24. $PC \leftarrow \omega^{13}(IR)$
25. $\rightarrow (28)$
26. $MD \leftarrow AC$
27. $\mathbf{M}^{\perp MA} \leftarrow MD$
28. continue

Since separate triggering pulses are available, the first two levels of input logic are eliminated. The resulting configuration is illustrated in Fig. 6.10. As we shall see in Chapter 7, this alternative design will call for an increase in the number of components in the control unit. Since separate Set and Clear logic must be included (a pulse cannot be inverted), the saving in input logic is only one gate per flip-flop.

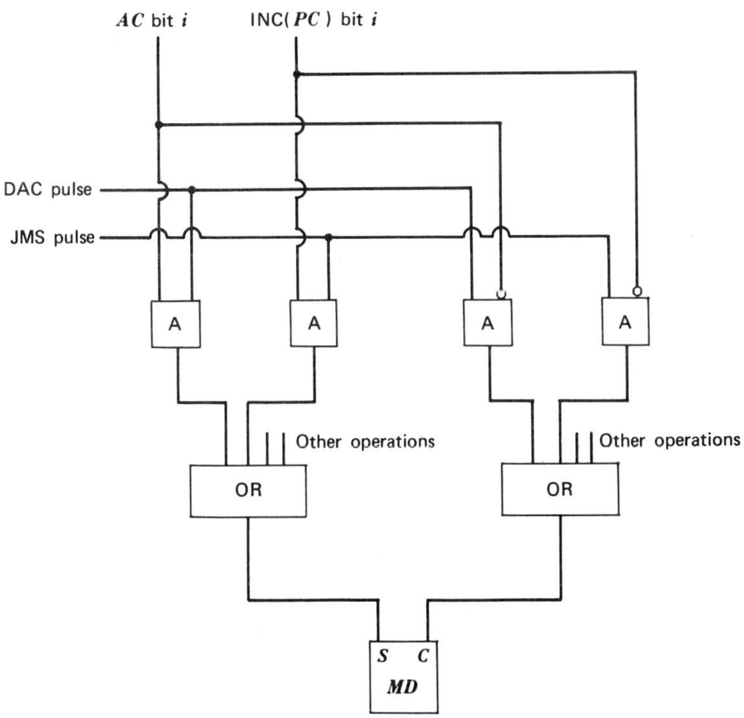

FIGURE 6.10. Alternate gating for store instructions.

Thus unless the improvement in speed facilitated by eliminating two levels of logic is critical, there is not a clear cut preference for either of the two possible designs. For three or more registers appearing in a single step, a design of the form of Fig. 6.9 will actually be the more economical. ▮

6.7. OPERATE INSTRUCTIONS

If bits 0, 1, and 2 of the op code are all 1's then another bit must be consulted to distinguish between I/O and operate instructions. Let us assume that bit 3 will be 1 for I/O instructions and 0 for operate instructions. Then the fourteen bits 4 through 17 may be used to specify the specific instruction. In this section only operate instructions will be considered.

The value of the operate instructions should be clear. By using the instruction bits normally set aside for addressing, we can specify a very large number of operations on the data registers of the machine. (In this case AC and ℓ.) In fact, using 14 bits we may specify 2^{14} or over 16,000 instructions. If we were to assign these instructions arbitrarily in a list of 16,000, it would be necessary for the programmer to refer to a dictionary in writing each instruction. Instead let us visualize each possible operate instruction as a sequence of lesser *microcoded* instructions.

Operate instructions do not require a time-consuming separate memory reference during execution. Similarly, individual microcoded segments can be accomplished in a single clock interval. Therefore they can reasonably be handled in sequential fashion. For SIC, each operate instruction will consist of three register transfers or branch operations executed in sequence. The execution cycle will still require less time than the fetch cycle.

Of the 14 available bits, one is applicable to all three *event times*. Five bits describe the first event time, and four bits describe each of the last two event times. The coding is tabulated in Table 6.1. The reader will quickly conclude that not all of the information available in 14 binary bits is utilized. Considerably fewer than 16,000 meaningful instructions can be assembled from Table 6.1. However, the coding scheme use is convenient both from the user's and from the designer's point of view; and a large number of instructions are possible.

Considerably more instructions are possible than the 18 listed in Fig. 2.4. Various schemes can be used for incorporating more of them into the assembly language. We shall not discuss that topic here. Any assembler will allow the programmer to specify an instruction in octal machine code as a last resort.

A general statement would be that any combination of bits which do not result in a logical conflict may be specified for the three event times. The valid combinations will become apparent as the design of the control sequences for operate instructions is worked out.

TABLE 6.1 Coding of Operate Instructions

Bit(s)		
4	0	If rotate is specified, the rotate is left
	1	Rotate right
	First Event Time	
5	0	No Rotate
	1	Rotate *AC*
6,7	00	NO OP
	01	Set Link
	10	Clear Link
	11	Halt
8,9	00	NO OP
	01	Set *AC*
	10	Clear *AC*
	11	Complement *AC*
	Second Event Time	
10	0	NO Rotate
	1	Rotate *AC*
11,12,13	000	NO OP
	001	SZL (also skips Third Event Time)
	010	DFA
	011	DFB
	100	DTA
	101	INA
	110	DTB
	111	INB
	Third Event Time	
14	0	NO Rotate
	1	Rotate *AC*
15	0	NO OP
	1	Skip if $\perp AC < 0$
16	0	NO OP
	1	Skip if $\perp AC = 0$
17	0	NO OP
	1	Skip if $\perp AC > 0$

Before we proceed to an example instruction, a few general comments regarding Table 6.1 are in order. Note that a rotation of three bits in either direction is possible if rotate is specified each event time. Bit 4 is applicable only if rotation is specified in one of the three event times. In that case it gives the direction of rotation. More than one operation can be accomplished in a single event time. For example, the link and accumulator could be cleared simultaneously during the first event time. Similarly, various combinations of SKIP instructions can be worked out using bits 15, 16, and 17. If bits 5–17 are all zero, then no operation will be performed. The option may be useful to a programmer in sequences designed to test for completion of asynchronous IOT Operations.

As an example, the instruction

$$7\ 0\ 5\ 6\ 0\ 6$$

would cause the link to be cleared and $\boldsymbol{AC}$ complemented followed by a rotation of $\boldsymbol{AC}$ left. If the resulting $\boldsymbol{AC}$ was less than or equal to zero, the next instruction would be skipped.

As we proceed with the development of the control sequencer, we shall tend to disallow bit combinations which would require more than one register transfer in sequence per event time. Our primary reason will be to avoid obscuring our discussion with detail. This might well be the approach in practice, as the problem of explaining the various sequences of operations to the user could easily outstrip the worth of the added versatility. A designer would be free, however, to allow considerably more complicated sequences of microcodes.

In Section 6.5 we saw that control branched to point 29 in the case of an operate or IOT instruction. At that point it is necessary to establish whether the instruction is operate or IOT. The operate sequence begins at step 30.

29. $\rightarrow ((\overline{\boldsymbol{IR}}_3 \times 30) + (\boldsymbol{IR}_3 \times ?))$

In accordance with the above paragraph, control is restricted to one of the 30 possible paths between point A and point D in Fig. 6.11. Branching to select a path between points A and B must begin at step 30. The rotate instruction is conveniently separated first. Step 31 separates the HALT instruction which is executed at step 32. The physical implementation of

30. $\rightarrow ((\overline{\boldsymbol{IR}}_5 \times 31) + (\boldsymbol{IR}_5 \times 35))$
31. $\rightarrow [((\overline{\boldsymbol{IR}_6 \wedge \boldsymbol{IR}_7}) \times 33) + ((\boldsymbol{IR}_6 \wedge \boldsymbol{IR}_7) \times 32)]$
32. HALT
33. $\boldsymbol{AC} \leftarrow (\overline{\boldsymbol{IR}}_8 \wedge \boldsymbol{AC}) \vee (\boldsymbol{IR}_9 \wedge \overline{\boldsymbol{AC}})$
    $\ell \leftarrow \boldsymbol{IR}_7 \vee (\boldsymbol{IR}_6 \wedge \ell)$

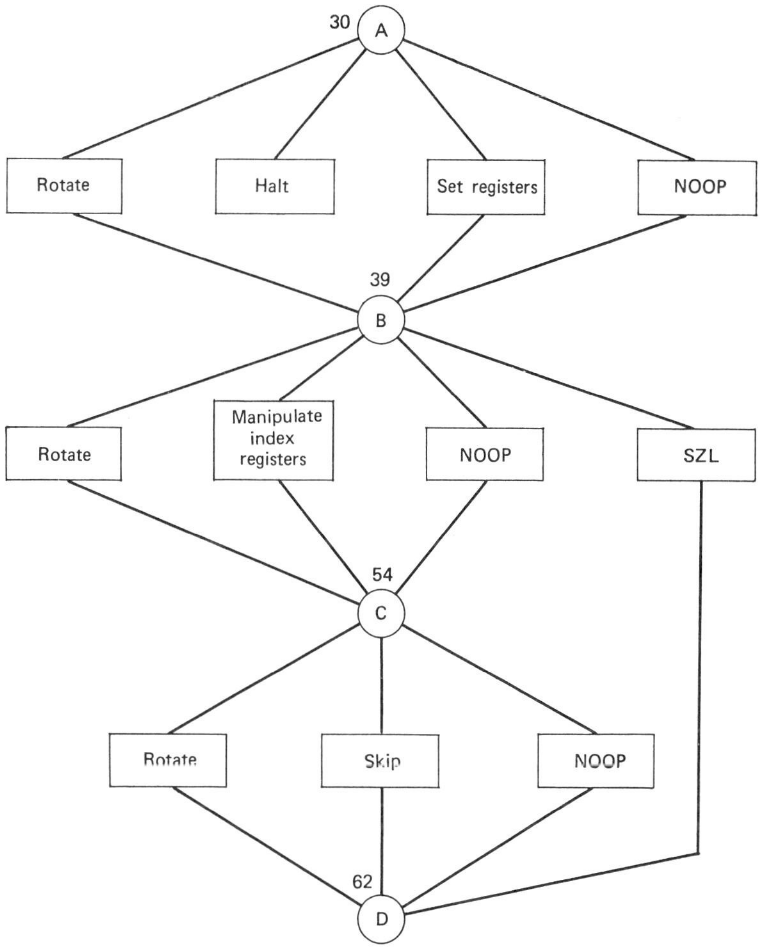

FIGURE 6.11. Flow chart for operate instructions.

HALT requires only that the control pulse be propagated no further in the control unit. The five possible operations on the link and ***AC*** are all expressed on the right at step 33. If nothing is changed in either ℓ or ***AC***, the operation is effectively NO OP.

The AHPL expressions in step 33 are determined by a modified Karnaugh map interpretation as given in Fig. 6.12. Notice the three separate terms specifying transfers into ***AC*** in step 33. Each corresponds to a particular set of values for $\boldsymbol{IR}_8$ and $\boldsymbol{IR}_9$. The right side of this transfer statement is not strictly a Boolean expression for the next value of ***AC***. No term is included, for example, corresponding to the left-most square of Fig. 6.12a which

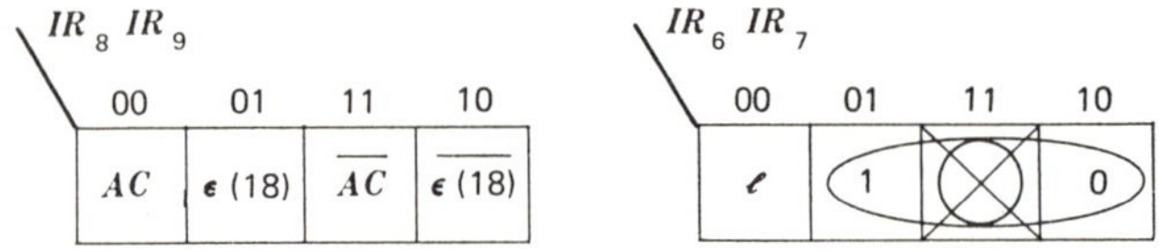

(a) Next values of AC (b) Next value of link

FIGURE 6.12. Next value maps.

specifies leaving the previous value of AC in AC. As we shall see in Chapter 7, the reason for ignoring this square of the Karnaugh map in step 33 is that no action, and therefore no control signal, is required. Similarly, a term corresponding to placing 0's in AC is included even though it could be eliminated by simple Boolean manipulation. The transfer expression for the link as derived from Fig. 6.12b may be even more discomforting to the switching theory purist. Again the left-most square of Fig. 6.12b, which specifies the link as unchanged, does not affect the transfer expression, while an obviously zero term is included. A "don't care" condition appears in Fig. 6.12b since a branch to the halt operation has already been included at step 31. The designation of the halt condition as $\boldsymbol{IR}_6 = \boldsymbol{IR}_7 = 1$ was deliberate so that minimal logic will be required to generate control signals for the link.

The generation of control signals corresponding to expressions like step 33 will be treated in Section 7.7. In that section the conditions in which AHPL transfer statements will depart from next-value Boolean expressions will be carefully defined.

For the rotate instruction it is necessary to inspect bit $\boldsymbol{IR}_4$ to determine the direction of rotation. The left or right rotations are accomplished at steps 36 and 38, respectively; and control converges at step 39. This corresponds

34. $\rightarrow (39)$
35. $\rightarrow ((\overline{\boldsymbol{IR}}_4 \times 36) + (\boldsymbol{IR}_4 \times 38))$
36. $\ell, AC \leftarrow 1 \uparrow (\ell, AC)$
37. $\rightarrow (39)$
38. $\ell, AC \leftarrow 1 \downarrow (\ell, AC)$

to point B of Fig. 6.11. In event time two, control is first separated for rotate, as before. The 8 instructions specified by $\boldsymbol{IR}_{11}$, $\boldsymbol{IR}_{12}$, and $\boldsymbol{IR}_{13}$ may be separated into four pairs. Notice that the destination register of DFA and DFB is AC, while the destination register of DTA and INA is IA, and the destination register of DTB and INB is IB. Thus each of these pairs may be executed as a single program step. Branching to the four steps is accomplished by step 40.

39. $\rightarrow((\overline{IR}_{10} \times 40) + (IR_{10} \times 50))$

40. $\rightarrow((\overline{IR}_{11} \wedge \overline{IR}_{12} \times 41) + (\overline{IR}_{11} \wedge IR_{12} \times 44)$
$\quad + (IR_{11} \wedge \overline{IR}_{12} \times 46) + (IR_{11} \wedge IR_{12} \times 48))$

41. $\rightarrow((\overline{(IR_{13} \wedge \bar{\ell})} \times 54) + ((IR_{13} \wedge \bar{\ell}) \times 42))$

42. $PC \leftarrow \mathrm{INC}(PC)$

43. $\rightarrow(25)$

If $IR_{13} = 1$ indicating SZL and $\ell = 0$, then the program counter is incremented causing the next instruction to be skipped. If the skip is successful, the third event time is skipped also to eliminate the possibility of skipping two instructions. Otherwise control proceeds directly from step 41 to event time 3. Execution of instructions DFA and DFB is accomplished at step 44. Similarly, DTA and INA are handled at step 46, and DTB and INB are

44. $\omega^{13}/AC \leftarrow (\overline{IR}_{13} \wedge IA) \vee (IR_{13} \wedge IB)$

45. $\rightarrow(54)$

46. $IA \leftarrow (\overline{IR}_{13} \wedge \omega^{13}/AC) \vee (IR_{13} \wedge \mathrm{INC}(IA))$

47. $\rightarrow(54)$

48. $IB \leftarrow (\overline{IR}_{13} \wedge \omega^{13}/AC) \vee (IR_{13} \wedge \mathrm{INC}(IB))$

49. $\rightarrow(54)$

handled at step 48. The 4-step rotate instruction will be identical to steps 35 to 38 as detailed for event time one. These steps would merely be repeated on lines 50 to 53.

50.
·
· Rotate
·

54. $\rightarrow((\overline{IR}_{14} \times 55) + (IR_{14} \times 58))$

Control is separated at step 54 for a third possible rotation. At step 55 the contents of the AC are examined to determine if a skip should be executed.

55. $\rightarrow((f \times 56) + (\bar{f} \times 25))$

Equation 6.1 is the logical expression generated in step 55. It is presented separately to avoid writing it twice. If the inequality specified in Table 6.1 is satisfied for one of bits IR_{15}, IR_{16}, and IR_{17}, which is specified as 1, then

$$f = ((AC_0 \wedge IR_{15}) \vee (\overline{\vee/AC} \wedge IR_{16}) \vee (\overline{AC}_0 \wedge (\vee/AC) \wedge IR_{17})) \qquad (6.1)$$

PC is incremented at step 56. Otherwise control passes to step 25, the point of convergence for all (except JMP) instructions.

56. ***PC*** ← INC(***PC***)
57. → (25)

Once again the rotate execution is the same as in event time one. Steps 58 to 61 are allowed for this operation. This completes the AHPL listing for the operate instructions.

58.
·
· Rotate
·
62. → (25)

The reader may wonder why the instructions for manipulating the index registers have been designed into the control unit while indexing itself has been omitted. The answer is merely convenience. It was desirable to present a complete picture of the implementation of the operate instructions. Only a few steps were required for index register manipulation. The design of SIC as presented so far is not entirely accurate. Indexing is part of the machine. We shall consider this subject in Section 6.9. Our goal will be to make it as easy as possible for the reader to fit the indexing sequences into the AHPL listing already presented.

6.8. BUSING OF ARGUMENTS

In Section 4.4 we presented only one reason, an economic one, for the use of busing, which is that busing permits the sharing of input switching logic between several destination registers. This switching logic then becomes the bus.

An additional reason for the use of busing emerges when the destination of the register selected by the bus is a combinational logic network such as an adder. Arguments for a combinational logic network must be selected by a level. Thus the switching network satisfies the description given for a bus in Section 4.4. For our pulse-oriented control unit, control levels must be obtained by setting bus control flip-flops. In this section we shall denote the placing of information on the buses by the setting or clearing of these bus control flip-flops.

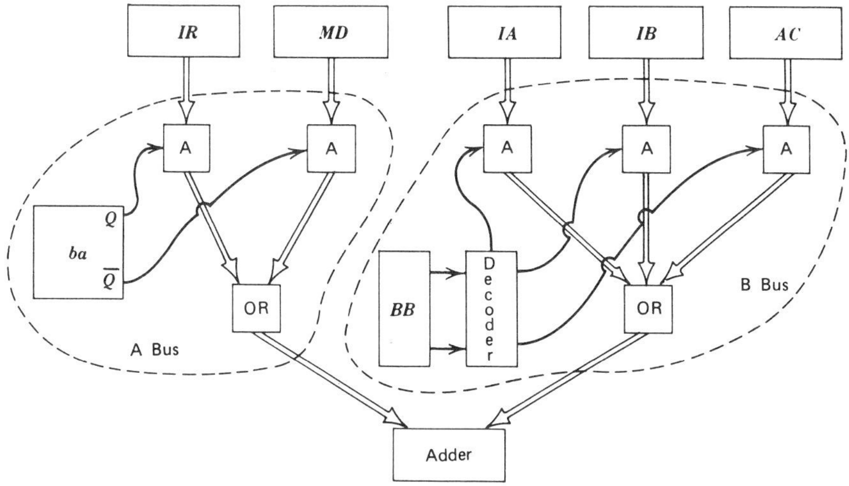

FIGURE 6.13. Input buses for SIC.

Because adders and other logic units may be expensive, it is generally desirable to provide for their use with various input and destination registers. A typical arrangement uses two input buses to provide switching of operands from various registers to various logic units. Such an arrangement for SIC is shown in Fig. 6.13. Later we shall allow other logic networks to share these same buses, but for now we shall concentrate our attention on the connections to the adder.

For SIC there are two input vectors, ***IR*** and ***MD***, to ***ABUS***; and three input vectors, ***IA***, ***IB***, and ***AC***, to ***BBUS***. The single flip-flop ***ba*** will serve to identify the desired input to ***ABUS***. If ***ba*** = 0, the input vector will be ***MD***. If ***ba*** = 1, the input vector will be ***IR***. The two-bit vector ***BB*** will be used to store the gating specification for ***BBUS***. Let ***BB*** = 00 specify input register ***IA***,* and let ***BB*** = 01 specify ***IB***,* and let ***BB*** = 11 specify ***AC***. ***BB*** = 10 will cause a vector of 0's to appear at the adder input. The ***BBUS*** configuration will differ from the ***ABUS*** only in that one additional input register must be accommodated and a decoder must be provided at the output of ***BB*** to generate three signals. Only the signal corresponding to the specified input register will be 1. A symbolic version of both ***ABUS*** and ***BBUS*** connected to the adder is given in Fig. 6.14.

The incorporation of ***ABUS*** and ***BBUS*** will require certain changes in the instruction TAD. It is now convenient to separate control for the AND and

* Actually 0,0,0,0,0, ***IA*** or 0,0,0,0,0, ***IB*** will be placed on the bus.

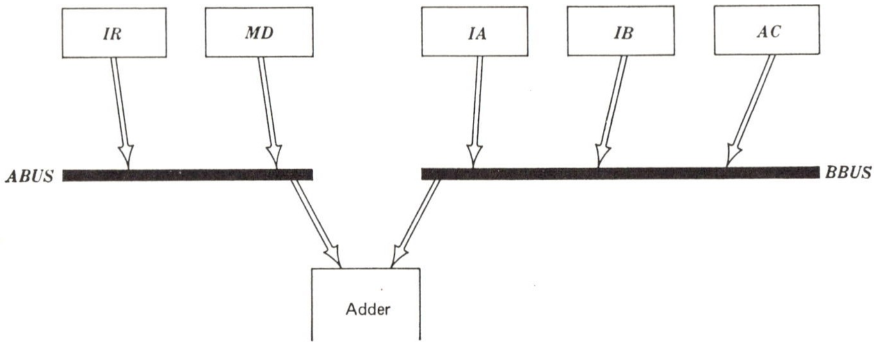

FIGURE 6.14. ***A* and *B* buses to adder.**

TAD instructions. At the penalty of increased execution time, LAC can be accomplished through the adder, thus eliminating the LAC switching circuitry from the input of *AC*. This is possible since ***BB*** = 10 will gate a vector of 0's through ***BBUS***.

We shall merely write a new AHPL routine to replace instructions 12–15 of Section 6.5, which execute the read operand commands. Instruction 13

12. $\boldsymbol{MD} \leftarrow \mathbf{M}^{\perp MA}$
13. $\rightarrow ((\boldsymbol{IR}_2 \times 14) + (\overline{\boldsymbol{IR}}_1 \wedge \overline{\boldsymbol{IR}}_2 \times 16) + (\boldsymbol{IR}_1 \wedge \overline{\boldsymbol{IR}}_2 \times 15))$
14. $\boldsymbol{ba}, \boldsymbol{BB} \leftarrow 0, 1, \boldsymbol{IR}_1$

groups TAD and LAC and separates AND and ISZ. Execution of ISZ remains as given in Section 6.5. Step 14 enters a 0 in ***ba*** to cause the contents of ***MD*** to be gated through ***ABUS***, and enters 10 or 11 in ***BB*** depending on whether the instruction is LAC or TAD. These instructions are then executed at step 14a.

14a. $\ell, \boldsymbol{AC} \leftarrow \text{ADD}(\boldsymbol{ABUS}, \boldsymbol{BBUS})$
14b. $\rightarrow (25)$

The arguments of the ADD subroutine are now specified as the outputs of ***ABUS*** and ***BBUS*** rather than as registers. The instruction AND is carried out separately at step 15.

15. $\boldsymbol{AC} \leftarrow \boldsymbol{MD} \wedge \boldsymbol{AC}$
15a. $\rightarrow (25)$

The bus configurations and instruction sequences presented above are accurate for SIC as presented in Chapter 2. The reader should notice that like combinational logic subroutines, the bus logic does not appear in the

AHPL description of the control unit. Strictly speaking it is necessary to define the buses and bus switching as separate subroutines.

It is sometimes desirable to include a multiplication instruction in machines comparable in size to SIC. As multiplication makes use of the adder, additional input registers to ***ABUS*** and ***BBUS*** will be required. We will discuss multiplication in Section 6.10 but will not fit this instruction into the framework of SIC. In the next section we shall make use of the busing configuration already developed to add the indexing capability to SIC.

6.9. INDEXING

Indexing takes place at the beginning of the initial fetch cycle. Indexing and indirect addressing cannot be specified simultaneously in SIC. Where more than 18 instruction bits are available this combination would probably be included. Indexing will affect the instruction JMP as well as the read operand instructions. It is possible to accomplish indexing in conjunction with steps 10 and 12 of Fig. 6.4. This would require switching the output of the adder into ***PC*** as well as ***MA***. Alternatively, the result of indexing could be gated back into ***IR*** prior to the branch at step 9. Although it is more time-consuming, we shall use the latter approach.

We need only allow for a three-way branch at step 5 and replace step 9 by a sequence of instructions. Step 5 becomes

5. $\rightarrow ((\boldsymbol{IR}_3 \times 9) + (\overline{\boldsymbol{IR}}_3 \wedge \boldsymbol{IR}_4 \times 6) + (\overline{\boldsymbol{IR}}_3 \wedge \overline{\boldsymbol{IR}}_4 \times 9\text{b}))$

The indexing routine begins at step 9. Step 9b is the point for branching to JMP following the indexing sequence. Following completion of indirect addressing at step 8 the next step must cause a jump to step 9b to avoid the indexing sequence. Like addition, the first step of indexing is to load ***ba*** and ***BB***. Indexing is accomplished by step 9a, and the branching between JMP

8a. $\rightarrow (9b)$
9. $\boldsymbol{ba}, \boldsymbol{BB} \leftarrow 1, 0, \boldsymbol{IR}_4$
9a. $\omega^{13}/\boldsymbol{IR} \leftarrow \omega^{13}/\text{ADD}(\boldsymbol{ABUS}, \boldsymbol{BBUS})$

and the memory reference instructions is accomplished by step 9b. In step 9, ***ba*** = 1 connects ***IR*** through ***ABUS***. If $\boldsymbol{IR}_4 = 0$, then ***BB*** = 00 gating ***IA***

9b. $\rightarrow ((\overline{\boldsymbol{IR}}_0 \vee \overline{\boldsymbol{IR}}_1 \times 10) + (\boldsymbol{IR}_0 \wedge \boldsymbol{IR}_1 \times 27))$

through ***BBUS***. If $\boldsymbol{IR}_4 = 1$, then ***IB*** is gated through ***BBUS***.

6.10. ADDRESSING SCHEMES

There are reasons why a memory addressing scheme may be made still more sophisticated than necessitated by the mere inclusion of indirect addressing. Multioperand instructions, as discussed in Chapter 1, are one possibility. Often it is desirable to add the contents of some register in addition to the index register to the address specified in an instruction. Sometimes this is made necessary by the lack of sufficient address bits in an instruction to address all of the available random access memory.

Suppose, for example, that only 10 address bits are provided but that 16 k words of memory are available. In order to form a 14-bit address it is necessary to add the contents of a special address register to the 10 address bits obtained from an instruction. Ordinarily it will not be necessary to change the contents of the special address register often, as execution can be confined to a 1k section of memory for many instructions in succession.

In some machines which have insufficient address bits, indirect addressing is relied on to permit accessing data or branching outside of small areas of memory. The term *page* has been used in some instances to refer to a small section of memory. Consider, as an example, a machine* with 4k twelve-bit words of memory. Only eight of the twelve bits are available for use as an address. Thus the memory must be divided into sixteen 256-word pages. The memory address register and program counter are designed to accommodate a complete 12-bit address. The most significant four bits of both registers remain unchanged as instructions are executed within a page. When an operation ventures out of a particular page via indirect addressing, a new 12-bit address is placed in ***MA***, or in the case of a branch, in both ***MA*** and ***PC***.

A special address register to add to every instruction address is useful in larger scale computers. It permits the *relocatability* of compiled programs within memory with a minimum of change. That is, a program may be compiled without foreknowledge of where it will be placed in memory. When loaded, the operating system need add only one instruction, which will cause the appropriate starting address to the placed in the special address register. A discussion of relocatability in Systems 360 and 370 may be found in Flores [1]. The following example illustrates an approach to the hardware handling of address formation.

Example 6.3

A control sequence is to be written for address formation in a machine which features indexing, indirect addressing, and relocatability. The total random access

* This configuration is a simplified version of the PDP-8. The PDP-8 includes one special page, which may be addressed directly from any other page.

IR_7	Indicates indirect addressing
IR_8	Indicates indexing
IR_9, IR_{10}, IR_{11}	Specifies number of index register
ω^{12}/IR	Instruction address
IM	$\rho_2(\mathrm{IM}) = 8$; each row is an 18-bit index register
REL	Relocation register—18 bits
MA	Memory address register—18 bits

FIGURE 6.15. Registers used in address formation.

memory contains 256k 24-bit words. Only the last 12 bits of an instruction may be used for addressing.

Solution. The registers pertinent to address formation together with their purposes and descriptions may be found in Fig. 6.15. Ignoring all but memory reference instructions, the following control sequence begins immediately after an instruction has been fetched and placed in IR.

1. $MA \leftarrow \mathrm{ADD}\ ((\overline{\epsilon(6)}, \omega^{12}/IR), REL)$
2. $\rightarrow ((IR_7 \times 3) + (\overline{IR}_7 \times 6))$
3. $MD \leftarrow \mathrm{M}^{\perp MA}$
4. $\omega^{12}/IR \leftarrow \omega^{12}/MD$
5. $MA \leftarrow \mathrm{ADD}\ ((\overline{\epsilon(6)}, \omega^{12}/IR), REL)$
6. $\rightarrow ((IR_8 \times 7) + (\overline{IR}_8 \times 8))$
7. $MA \leftarrow \mathrm{ADD}\ (\mathrm{IM}^{\perp(IR_9, IR_{10}, IR_{11})}, MA)$

The relocation register is added to the instruction address in step 1 and placed in MA. If neither indirect addressing nor indexing is called for, this is the final address of the operand. Steps 2–5 provide for the possibility of indirect addressing. Step 7 provides for the addition of the specified index register to the address, if indexing is called for. Busing, which was omitted for brevity, would certainly be used in practice. The resulting routine would be somewhat more complicated. We leave this as a problem for the reader.

The prospect of two successive additions (steps 5 and 7) to form the address in the event of indexing is not particularly inviting. The alternatives are a much more costly 3-argument adder or less flexibility in program relocation. To examine the second possibility let us suppose that memory is divided into 64 4k sections. Relocation will be limited to adding $a \times 2^{12}$ to each address, where a is an integer between 0 and 63 stored in 6-bit REL. Thus programs can be located at the beginning of each 4k section. Steps 5, 6, and 7 may then be combined to form

5. $MA \leftarrow \mathrm{ADD}\ ((REL, \omega^{12}/IR), IR_8 \wedge \mathrm{IM}^{\perp(IR_9, IR_{10}, IR_{11})})$

Step 1 would be modified also. ▮

6.11. MULTIPLE-CYCLE INSTRUCTIONS

The memory reference instructions considered so far were executed by a single transfer of information from one register to another register. The operate instructions required no more than three consecutive changes of state in a register. In later chapters, as we consider instructions useful in computers with particular problem distributions, we shall find that some instructions require many consecutive register transfers.

In general, the approach to designing the control sequencing hardware will be the same regardless of instruction complexity. Let us illustrate, using fixed-point multiplication as an example. There are various possible approaches to the multiplication of numbers which may be negative. Since storage may be in the form of one's-complements, two's-complements, or sign and magnitude, various schemes are used to effect multiplication in all of these formats. To preserve continuity let us defer a discussion of the various alternatives until Chapter 12.

The simplest, although not necessarily the fastest or least expensive, approach to multiplication is keeping track of signs and multiplying the magnitudes. Here let us assume that numbers are stored in two's-complement notation. Thus, prior to multiplication, the sign of the product will be determined; and all two's-complement negative numbers will be replaced by magnitudes.

Since the fixed-point multiplication of two 18-bit numbers may result in a 36-bit product, another register, the ***MQ*** register, must be added to store the 18 least-significant bits of the product. It will be necessary to count the number of bits of the multiplier which have been treated at any given stage in the process; so a 5-bit counter, designated ***MC***, will be added. The link will be used for storage of the sign. The described hardware configuration may be found in Fig. 6.16.

Only the basic data paths involved in multiplication are shown in Fig. 6.16. In practice, busing would very likely be used. However, to make the multiplication routine as clear as possible, it is desirable to omit program steps which load controlling registers for the various buses. We leave the rewriting of the routine to utilize busing of the arguments as a homework problem.

The multiplication instruction is not included in SIC. Similarly, several of the registers in Fig. 6.16 are not available in SIC. Therefore, let us visualize multiplication as part of another computer, encompassing all of the features of SIC but with an extended arithmetic capability, including multiplication.

Let us pick up the operation at a point in the control sequence following the fetch cycle and the identification of the instruction. The multiplier is in the

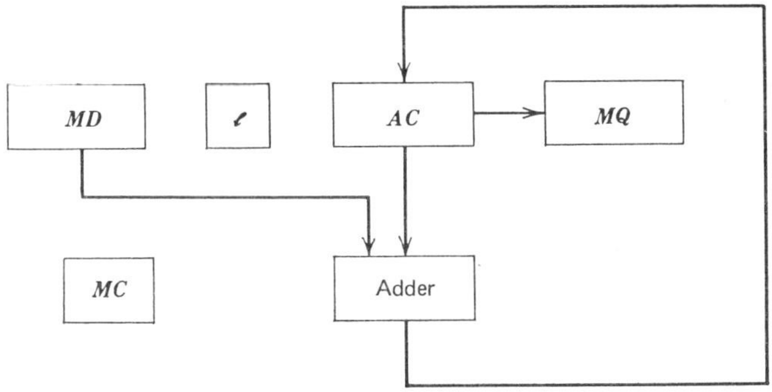

FIGURE 6.16. Multiplication hardware.

AC from the previous instruction. The multiplicand has just been read from storage and placed in ***MD***. Control has diverged to the point of the actual beginning of the instruction. The operation begins with the clearing of the link to prepare for sign determination. The first five steps convert the

1. $\ell \leftarrow 0$
2. $\rightarrow ((\overline{AC}_0 \times 5) + (AC_0 \times 3))$
3. $\ell, AC \leftarrow \overline{\ell}, \overline{AC}$
4. $\ell, AC \leftarrow \text{ADD}(AC, \epsilon^{17}(18))$
5. $MQ \leftarrow AC$
6. $AC \leftarrow MD$
7. $\rightarrow ((\overline{AC}_0 \times 10) + (AC_0 \times 8))$
8. $\ell, AC \leftarrow \overline{\ell}, \overline{AC}$
9. $\ell, AC \leftarrow \text{ADD}(AC, \epsilon^{17}(18))$
10. $MD \leftarrow AC$

multiplier to sign and magnitude form, leaving the magnitude in ***MQ*** and the sign in the link. The last five steps place the magnitude of the multiplicand in ***MD*** and leave the sign of the final product in the link. Two's-complements, where necessary, are obtained by complementing individual bits and adding one to the least significant bit. Notice that the link, which was initially reset to 0, is complemented once if the multiplier is negative and once if the multiplicand is negative. Thus, it ends up 0 if and only if the signs are the same.

Before proceeding, let us consider the basic multiplication process in some detail. Since the basic arithmetic process of a computer is addition, multiplication is generally carried out by successive addition. In this technique, the decimal multiplication of 203 × 576 would be carried out as shown in Fig. 6.17a. For the binary case, the process is even simpler since the only multiplier bits are zero or one. Thus, for each multiplier bit, the multiplicand

```
        576
      × 203
      -----
        576                 0110
        576                 0101
        576                 ----
       000                  0110
      576                  0000
      576                 0110
    -------               0000
(a) 116,828           (b) -------
                          0011110
```

FIGURE 6.17. Multiplication by successive addition.

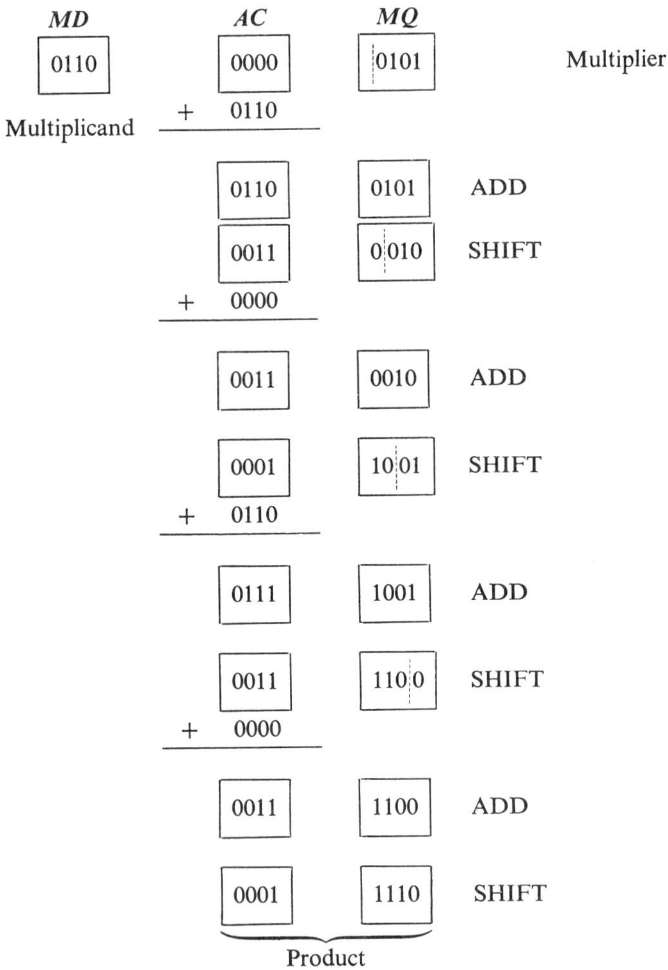

FIGURE 6.18. Computer mechanization of multiplication.

is either added once or not added at all. A typical binary multiplication is shown in Fig. 6.17b.

From this, it is seen that the basic binary multiplicative process involves inspecting each multiplier bit in turn, adding and shifting for a 1, and shifting without adding for a 0. As shown in Fig. 6.17, the partial products are successively shifted *left* before addition, finally resulting in a product having twice as many bits as the initial operands. This process would be impractical in a computer since it would require a double-length adder, e.g., a 36-bit adder for a machine with 18-bit operands.

To avoid this difficulty, addition, if required, is performed as each bit of the multiplier is inspected; and the resultant sum is then shifted *right*, providing a relative *left* shift of the next partial product. To provide for the double-length product, the ***AC*** and ***MQ*** registers are catenated for right shifting. The multiplier is initially loaded into ***MQ***, the multiplicand into ***MD***, with ***AC*** initially cleared. As the product is shifted into ***MQ***, the multiplier is shifted out, so that the multiplier bit to be inspected is always in the low-order position of ***MQ***. This process of multiplication is illustrated in Fig. 6.18, for the same multiplications as Fig. 6.17b. The dotted line in ***MQ*** indicates the boundary between the developing partial product and the remainder of the multiplier.

The first step in the implementation of this process stores a string of zeros, $\overline{\boldsymbol{\epsilon}(18)}$, in ***AC*** and sets the multiplication counter, ***MC***, to zero. This is followed by a loop which adds a product vector to ***AC*** and shifts the result right. This loop will be executed 18 times. When $\perp(\boldsymbol{MC}) = 18$, the process will terminate. Thus, at the conclusion of 18 cycles, the product will be found with the least significant bits in ***MQ*** and the remaining bits in ***AC***. The ***AC*** will not overflow at any step since the magnitude of the multiplicand is less than or equal to $2^{17} - 1$.

11. $\boldsymbol{MC}, \boldsymbol{AC} \leftarrow \overline{\boldsymbol{\epsilon}(5)}, \overline{\boldsymbol{\epsilon}(18)}$
12. $\perp \boldsymbol{MC}{:}18, (<, =) \rightarrow (13, 19)$
13. $\rightarrow ((\overline{\boldsymbol{MQ}_{17}} \times 14) + (\boldsymbol{MQ}_{17} \times 16))$
14. $\boldsymbol{AC}, \boldsymbol{MQ} \leftarrow 1 \overset{\circ}{\downarrow} (\boldsymbol{AC}, \boldsymbol{MQ})$
15. $\rightarrow (17)$
16. $\boldsymbol{AC}, \boldsymbol{MQ} \leftarrow 1 \overset{\circ}{\downarrow} ((\boldsymbol{\omega}^{18}/\mathrm{ADD}(\boldsymbol{AC}, \boldsymbol{MD})), \boldsymbol{MQ})$
17. $\boldsymbol{MC} \leftarrow \boldsymbol{INC}(\boldsymbol{MC})$
18. $\rightarrow (12)$

Notice that a separation of control is specified, depending on whether a given bit of the multiplier is 1 or 0. The reason for this is a physical one: the shift operation will require less time than the add followed by a shift (perhaps 5:1). Thus, if half the multiplier bits are zero, this approach will reduce the overall multiplication time by a factor of almost 2. Lines 14 and 16 could have been combined in the above sequence.

After consideration of all 18 multiplier bits, the contents of both $\boldsymbol{MQ}$ and $\boldsymbol{AC}$ are complemented if the link is 1. The process of adding one to complete the two's-complement is a somewhat cumbersome process. This alone might suggest looking for another approach to multiplication. For completeness, the following sequence, although awkward, does complete the process.

19. $\ell : 0\ (=,>) \rightarrow (26, 20)$
20. $\boldsymbol{MD} \leftarrow \overline{\boldsymbol{AC}}$
21. $\ell,\boldsymbol{AC} \leftarrow 0,\overline{\boldsymbol{MQ}}$
22. $\ell,\boldsymbol{AC} \leftarrow \mathrm{ADD}(\boldsymbol{AC},\boldsymbol{\epsilon}^{17}(18))$
23. $\boldsymbol{MQ} \leftarrow \boldsymbol{AC}$
24. $\boldsymbol{AC} \leftarrow \boldsymbol{MD}$
25. $\ell,\boldsymbol{AC} \leftarrow \mathrm{ADD}((\overline{\boldsymbol{\epsilon}(17)},\ell),\boldsymbol{AC})$
26. Exit to Next Instruction

6.12. SUMMARY

In this chapter we have presented a language in which the engineer can approach the design of a computer or a computer subsystem. It is not an algorithmic design procedure. The designer is not relieved of the responsibility of optimizing his AHPL description of the control unit for his application.

It is hoped, however, that this chapter and Chapter 7 will provide him with a place to start. So far, we have examined only those features of a computer which may be incorporated in a small machine, such as SIC. The number of additional features which might be added to a computer to improve its performance is far too great to allow them to be treated in a single textbook. We shall examine a few of them in the chapters which follow. We shall approach them through their control, using an AHPL sequence.

PROBLEMS

6.1 Select a familiar small scale computer and separate its instruction set into the five categories given in Section 6.4.

6.2 Multiple indirect addressing is possible. Such a scheme would allow an address obtained by indirect addressing to be the address of another address, which might be the data address or the address of another address, etc. SIC can easily be modified to allow this option by replacing $\boldsymbol{IR}_4$ as well as the address portion of $\boldsymbol{IR}$. Write an AHPL routine which will allow multiple indirect addressing, to replace steps 4–8 of Section 6.5.

6.3 Suppose a computer with a register configuration similar to that shown in Fig. 6.1 has an instruction JMP A if $AC \geq 0$, where A is the address portion of the instruction. Write in AHPL the control sequence of this instruction beginning at a point after control has diverged to separate this instruction from all other instructions.

6.4 Repeat Problem 6.3 for the instruction XOR, which means $AC \leftarrow AC \oplus MD$.

6.5 Many computers, particularly those which use one of the first two types of control approaches discussed in Chapter 4, branch at one point to form a separate control sequence for each individual memory reference instruction. Rewrite the portion of the SIC control sequence given in Section 6.5 so that the sequence for memory reference instructions are all separated at step 11. Compare the numbers of AHPL steps required by the two approaches.

6.6 Write an AHPL description of a machine similar to SIC, but with the instruction set given below. Consider all instructions except IOT and OPR. Assume the same instruction format as for SIC, including indirect addressing.

Op Code	Mnemonic	Meaning
000	OR	$AC \leftarrow MD \vee AC$
001	TAD	
010	JPA	Jump to Y if $\perp AC \geq 0$
011	JMP	
100	JMS	
101	DCA	Deposit and clear AC
110	IOT	
111	OPR	

6.7 A certain computer has only 8-bit instruction and data words. If bits 0, 1, and 2 of an instruction are all 1's, the instruction is an operate type instruction to be executed in two event times. Bits 3, 4, and 5 describe the first even time and bits 6 and 7 the second. If bits 3 is 1, then bits 4 and 5 prescribe rotate and shift (enter a 0 in evacuated bit position) operations as follows:

Bit 4	5		
0	0	Rotate AC	left
0	1	Rotate AC	right
1	0	Shift AC	left
1	1	Shift AC	right

The action of the second event time is specified by

Bit 6	7	
0	0	No operation
0	1	Set *AC*
1	0	Clear *AC*
1	1	Complement *AC*

Write an AHPL program specifying the control sequence for this operate instruction.

6.8 A certain computer has a memory, **M**, and the registers, ***MA***, ***MD***, ***PC***, ***AC***, and ***IR*** Bits 0, 1, 2, and 3 of an instruction specify the op code and bits 4 and 5 the level of indirect addressing (0, 1, 2, or 3). That is, if bits 4 and 5 are 10, the instruction

0000	10	*A*

means, for example, "*ADD the contents of the contents of the contents of A to the accumulator.*" The only four instructions which utilize indirect addressing are

Instruction bit	0	1	2	3	
	0	0	0	0	ADD
	0	0	0	1	Deposit *AC* in memory
	0	0	1	0	AND
	0	0	1	1	JMP unconditionally

Write an AHPL program specifying execution of an instruction in this machine. Begin your program with the preparation for the fetch cycle. Assume that the control sequence for the above four instructions will be separated from that of other instructions prior to indirect addressing. Continue your program from that branch point only for these four instructions. The steps accomplishing the indirect addressing should be included. The last step which need be shown is the step where control begins to diverge to separate the above instructions.

6.9 Recode the operate instruction word of SIC so as to allow up to six rotations per event time. Write an AHPL routine for this rotation operation which could be used in any of the three event times.

6.10 A certain computer makes no distinction between operate and memory reference instructions. All but the IOT instruction are accomplished through a form of microcoding on the basic op code. The first 7 bits are set up to specify the flow chart of the instruction cycle, as shown in Fig. P6.10. If $\boldsymbol{IR}_i$ controls a branch operation, the question is answered

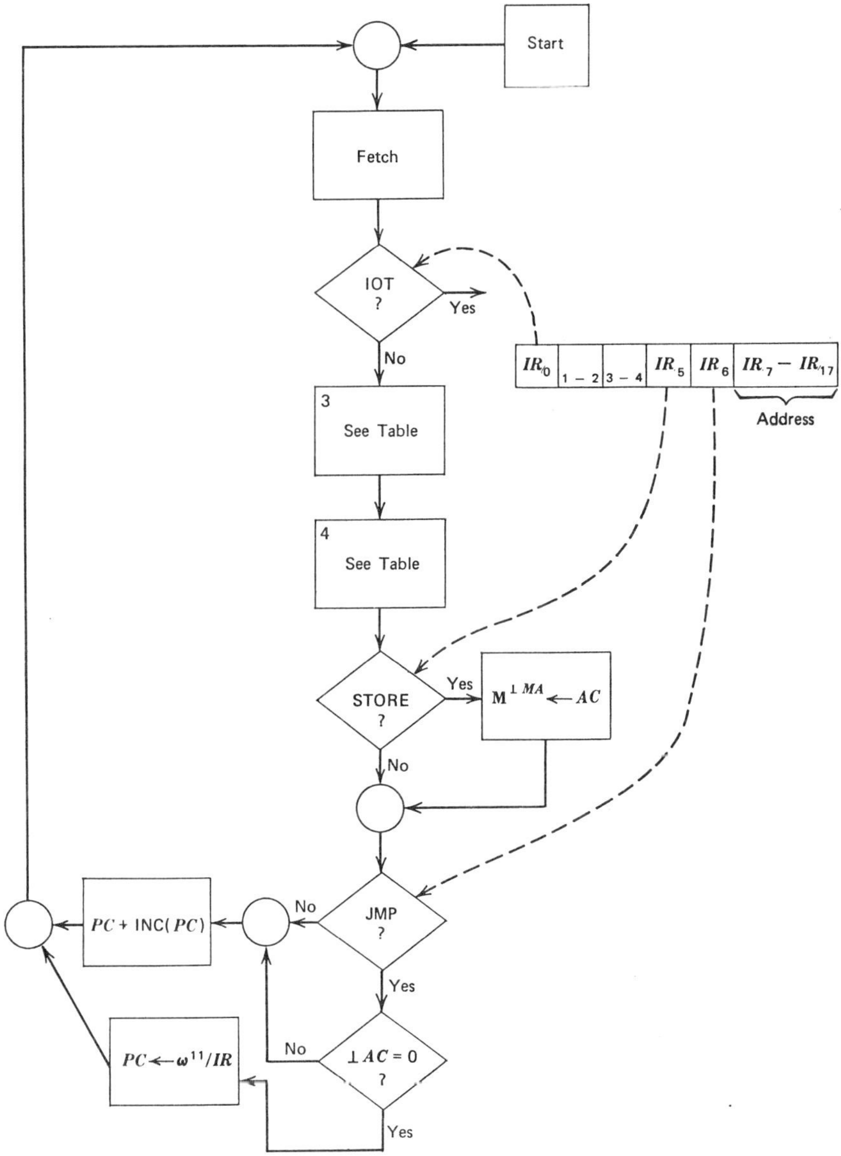

Start
Fetch
IOT
?
Yes
No
IR0
1 – 2
3 – 4
IR5
IR6
IR7 – IR17
Address
3
See Table
4
See Table
STORE
?
Yes
M⊥MA ← AC
No
JMP
?
No
PC + INC(PC)
Yes
No
⊥AC = 0
?
Yes
PC ← ω11/IR

FIGURE P6.10

yes if and only if $IR_i = 1$. Bits IR_1 and IR_2 specify the computation in block 3 as follows. Similarly, bits IR_3 and IR_4 specify the operations on AC in block 4. Although not necessarily a useful machine, this

IR_1	IR_2		IR_3	IR_4	
0	0	AND	0	0	$AC \leftarrow AC$
0	1	TAD	0	1	$AC \leftarrow \uparrow AC$
1	0	LAC	1	0	$AC \leftarrow \downarrow AC$
1	1	$AC \leftarrow AC$	1	1	$AC \leftarrow \overline{AC}$

computer illustrates that various combinations of instructions may be microcoded as a single memory reference instruction. Write an AHPL control sequence for all but the IOT instructions of this machine.

6.11 Draw a logic block diagram of the decoder which connects ***BB*** to ***BBUS*** described in Section 6.8.

6.12 Assume that the multiplication instruction in a computer must share the adder with the addition instructions and with indexing. Draw a symbolic diagram of ***ABUS*** and ***BBUS*** connected to the adder. Specify the number of bits and their coding in the controlling registers for each bus. Rewrite the multiplication instruction of Section 6.11 to accommodate busing.

6.13 Rewrite the control sequence of Example 6.2 to utilize busing.

6.14 In some computers the index registers are automatically incremented each time they are referenced; as a result, instructions like INA and INB are not required. This procedure may be called *autoindexing*.
   a) What are the advantages and disadvantages of this approach?
   b) How might one set up the instruction set so as to enjoy the advantages without the disadvantages?
   c) Rewrite the portion of the modified SIC control sequence given in Section 6.9 to provide for autoindexing.

6.15 Write the portion of the control sequence which forms the operand address for the 4k, 12-bit machine of Section 6.10. Include the handling of references and branches outside of the current page. Assume that indirect addressing is specified by $IR_3 = 1$.

6.16 Suppose the machine discussed in Problem 6.15 is modified so that only 7 bits are available to specify an operand address. Thus, there must now be 32 pages of 128 words each. The instruction bit IR_4 is now used as follows. If $IR_4 = 0$, the 7-bit address refers to the current page. If $IR_4 = 1$, the instruction refers to an address in the page with absolute addresses between 0 and 127. Important constants may thus be obtained from the first page at any time without indirect addressing. Rework Problem 6.15 with this modification.

6.17 The machine discussed in Problem 6.16 may be assumed to have the instructions and corresponding op codes tabulated in Fig. P6.17.

ISZ	000
AND	001
TAD	010
JMS	011
JMP	100
DAC	101
IO	110
Operate	111

FIGURE P6.17

Complete the design of the control sequence for this machine with the exception of input-output and operate instructions.

6.18 A computer is to be designed in which the basic word length is 8 bits. With this limitation it is impossible to fit both an op code and an address into a single word. Therefore, an instruction may consist of either one or two words. If it is an instruction which does not require an address, then the instruction will consist only of an op code, contained in one word. If it is an instruction requiring an address, the instruction will be contained in two words, the op code in the first word, the address, *Y*, in the next sequential location in memory. The significance of the first two bits of the op code, b_0 and b_1, will be as follows:

0 0	Operate instruction, no address required
0 1	IOT instruction, no address required
1 0	Memory reference instruction, direct addressing
1 1	Memory reference instruction, indirect addressing

For operate instructions, the remaining 6 bits are microcoded: bits 2,3,4 controlling event time 1, and bits 5,6,7 controlling event time 2, as follows:

Bits 2	3	4		
0	0	0	No op	NOP
0	0	1	Clear link	CLL
0	1	0	Set link	STL
0	1	1	Complement link	CML
1	0	0	Increment *AC*	INA
1	0	1	Clear *AC*	CLA
1	1	0	Set *AC*	STA
1	1	1	Complement *AC*	CMA

Bits 5	6	7		
0	0	0	No op	NOP
0	0	1	Skip if $AC \geq 0$	SPA
0	1	0	Skip if $AC < 0$	SMA
0	1	1	Skip	SKP
1	0	0	Rotate AC left	RAL
1	0	1	Rotate AC right	RAR
1	1	0	Not used	
1	1	1	Not used	

The memory reference instructions are also microcoded, but the number of event times depends on the code. If bit 2 is 0, the operation is a jump; if bit 2 is 1, the instruction calls for a register operation. The codes are given below.

MRI Codes

Bit	Value	Jumps (Bit-2=0)		AC Ops (Bit-2=1)	
3	0	No op		Load $\boldsymbol{MD}$	LMD
	1	Jump if AC=0	JZA	Store AC	DAC
4	0	No op		No op	
	1	Jump if AC>0	JPA	Clear AC	CLA
5	0	No op		No op	
	1	Jump if AC<0	JMA	$\boldsymbol{MD} \wedge \boldsymbol{AC}$	AND
6	0	No op		No op	
	1	Return jump, store contents of $\boldsymbol{PC}$ at $Y, Y+1$, take next instruction from $Y+2$	RJP	Two's-complement Add (ADD($\boldsymbol{MD}$, $\boldsymbol{AC}$))	TAD

Bit 7 is not assigned and is available for expanding the op codes. Part of the design task is to specify what should happen, in what order, if the programmer specifies two or more register operations in a single instruction. The memory size is 8k words. Means must be provided through indirect addressing to reference any word in memory. Assume the register configuration of Fig. 6.1, except for size and omitting the index registers; but you may add or delete registers or data paths as you wish, provided only that you be able to justify any changes.

a) Draw a hardware flow chart for the machine.

b) Write a detailed AHPL routine for the control sequences. Let IOT branch to an unspecified sequence.

6.19 This problem is concerned with writing the AHPL description of a two-address machine. That is, two arguments may be obtained from the random access memory or one argument can be read from memory and a result deposited in memory by one instruction. For simplicity, we assume that the random access memory contains only 2^{10} 24-bit words. Unless bits $\boldsymbol{IR}_0 = \boldsymbol{IR}_1 = \boldsymbol{IR}_2 = 1$, the instruction word will take the following form. It will be observed that indirect addressing is

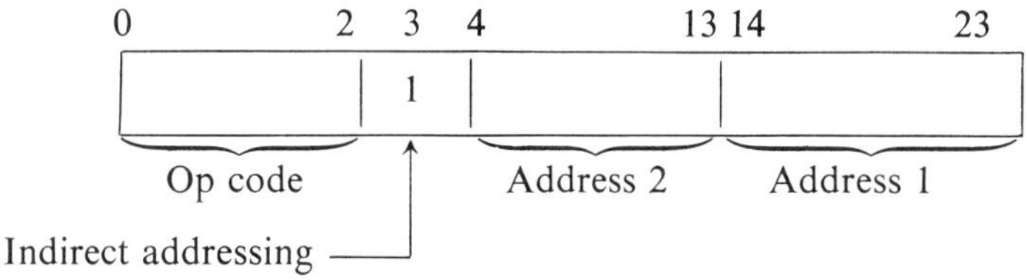

allowed while indexing is omitted for convenience. Arbitrarily we assume that when indirect addressing is specified that it refers to ADDRESS 1 only.

Of the seven possible memory reference instructions, two are of particular interest. These are

010	AND	AND the contents of the memory location specified by ADDRESS 1 with ***AC*** and deposit the result at the location specified by ADDRESS 2. ***AC*** is left unchanged.
011	JMP	JMP to ADDRESS 2 if and only if the contents of the location specified by ADDRESS 1 are ≥ 0.

The machine has a 24-bit instruction register, ***IR***, a single 10-bit memory address register, ***MA*** (only one memory access can be performed at a time), a 24-bit memory data register, ***MD***, a 24-bit accumulator, ***AC***, an extra 24-bit working register, ***WK***, and a 10-bit program counter, ***PC***. Write an AHPL sequence representing a hardwired control unit for the above machine. Include the fetch cycle and allow for indirect addressing. Carry through the execute cycle for only the two instructions AND and JMP listed above. Indicate the point where control diverges for the operate and I/O instructions represented by op code 111, and indicate the point where control for the instructions AND and JMP diverges from that of the other memory reference instructions.

REFERENCES

1. Flores, I., *Computer Organization*, Prentice-Hall, Englewood Cliffs, N.J., 1969.
2. Ware, W. H., *Digital Computer Technology and Design*, Wiley, New York, 1963.
3. Chu, Y. D., *Digital Computer Design Fundamentals*, McGraw-Hill, New York, 1962.
4. Flores, I., *Computer Logic*, Prentice-Hall, Englewood Cliffs, N.J., 1961.
5. Hellerman, Herbert, *Digital Computer System Principles*, McGraw-Hill, New York, 1967.
6. Gschwind, H. W., *Design of Digital Computers*, Springer-Verlag, New York, 1967.
7. Dietmeyer, D. L., *Logical Design of Digital Systems*, Allyn and Bacon, Inc., Boston, 1971.
8. Hill, F. J., and Peterson, G. R., *Introduction to Switching Theory and Logical Design*, Wiley, New York, 1968.

7

The Control Unit

7.1. INTRODUCTION

The basic function of the control unit is to furnish, at the proper times, the control pulses required to accomplish the register transfers described in Chapter 6. These pulses must appear on a multitude of separate lines destined to points within the arithmetic unit and elsewhere in the computer. The demands placed upon the control unit are illustrated by the pictorial diagram of Fig. 7.1. As shown, the primary input to the control unit is the master clock of the computer. The clock frequency may typically range between 1 and 100 MHz. Slower clock rates may be used in smaller special purpose machines where maximum computation speed is not a dominant design objective. Certain logic circuit technologies, such as MOS, may require slower clock rates.

At the upper end of the range of clock frequencies cited above, transmission line delay begins to become a limiting factor. Noting that the velocity of propagation of a pulse on a transmission line is approximately 3×10^8 m/sec, we conclude that a pulse is delayed 1 nsec by each foot of transmission line over which it passes between control unit and destination. At 100 MHz, clock pulses are separated by slightly less than 10 nsec. At this frequency, a difference of 2 or 3 ft in distances between the control unit and operand registers involved in consecutive data transfers would have a significant effect on the timing of these transfers. The use of integrated circuits reduces the size of the central processor, and therefore the distances between registers. Various

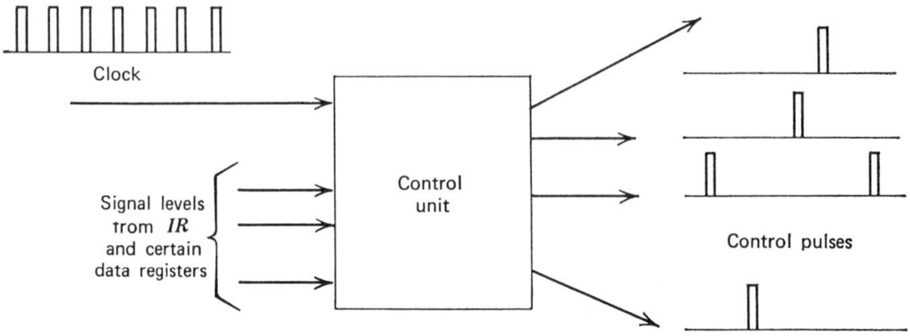

FIGURE 7.1. Control unit.

considerations, including the necessity of communications with physically large peripheral equipments, limit the advantage which can be realized from reducing machine dimensions. As logic circuits are available with delays less than 1 nsec, designers continue to look for further increase in clock frequencies. For clock frequencies above 100 MHz, special measures must be adopted to assure proper synchronization. This problem would take us too far afield for the present chapter.

The control pulses shown at the output of the control unit in Fig. 7.1 are all synchronized with input clock pulses. In effect, the control unit must select clock pulses occurring at particular time instants and gate them onto lines triggering register transfers scheduled to occur at those time instants. Our technique in this chapter will be one of physically implementing the flow chart of the AHPL description of the machine. The result will be a permanent hard-wired control unit.

A hard-wired control unit is not used in all computers. It is used in certain fast, large-scale machines. Smaller machines more often utilize a read-only memory as a control unit, a technique which may allow the modification of the control sequence through microprogramming. This approach will be the topic of Chapter 8.

As mentioned in Chapter 4, there are many approaches to the design of a hard-wired control unit. Some may use a multi-phase clock. Others will distribute control signals in the form of levels rather than pulses, as shown in Fig. 7.1. The reasons for choosing a particular approach are usually electronic circuit considerations and, therefore, outside of the scope of this book.

The implementation of the control unit used throughout the book will employ pulse delay elements to separate consecutive pulses by one clock period in time. An instruction sequence will be initiated by a single pulse which will then propagate through the control unit to cause the step-by-step execution of the control sequence. Following this pulse through a hardware block diagram of the control unit is much the same as tracing the AHPL sequence of a flow chart. The primary reason for choosing this form of control hardware is to provide the most graphic correspondence between the AHPL sequence and the control unit.

We shall denote the hardware translation of an AHPL sequence as a *control sequencer*. Sufficient detail is presented to permit the reader with some background in switching circuits to actually construct a control sequencer. An additional advantage of this type of control sequencer might be the simplification of maintenance procedures. Thus, even for short sequences, it may be chosen in preference to some other control unit with lower circuit cost.

7.2. THE CONTROL DELAY

Only two basic statement types, branches and register transfers, occur within AHPL programs. Specific circuit elements will represent these statement types in the control unit. A period of time must be allowed for the accomplishment of any register transfers. Direct transfers can be accomplished in one period of the master clock. Times for these operations are allotted by a very simple control unit element, which we shall call a *control delay*. There are two possible approaches to providing timing for AHPL statements which require longer than one clock period for execution. In one case control is synchronous, and for the other it is asynchronous.

We shall first describe the device which will provide a delay of one clock period. As mentioned, a single pulse distinct from the clock is propagated through the control network to generate each transfer pulse and to indicate the current point of activity. Thus a single control delay must have the input and output lines depicted as in Fig. 7.2a. The function of the circuit is described in the timing diagram of Fig. 7.2b. From time to time a control pulse from the control delay corresponding to a previous AHPL step will appear on the line labeled Pulse In. Due to propagation delay between control delays, the input pulse will be slightly delayed relative to a clock pulse.

The input pulse is routed immediately to cause the register transfer for AHPL step *m*. A subsequent transfer cannot occur until the control pulse has emerged on the line labeled Pulse out. Thus, step *m* will be allowed one clock period before its results can be required by another transfer.

The circuit implementation of the control delay must sense the overlapping clock and input pulses and generate an output pulse synchronized with the next clock pulse. The fundamental mode circuit shown in Fig. 7.3 will accomplish this function.

The design of this circuit, using traditional fundamental mode techniques, may be found in Reference [1]. Here we merely explain the functioning of the

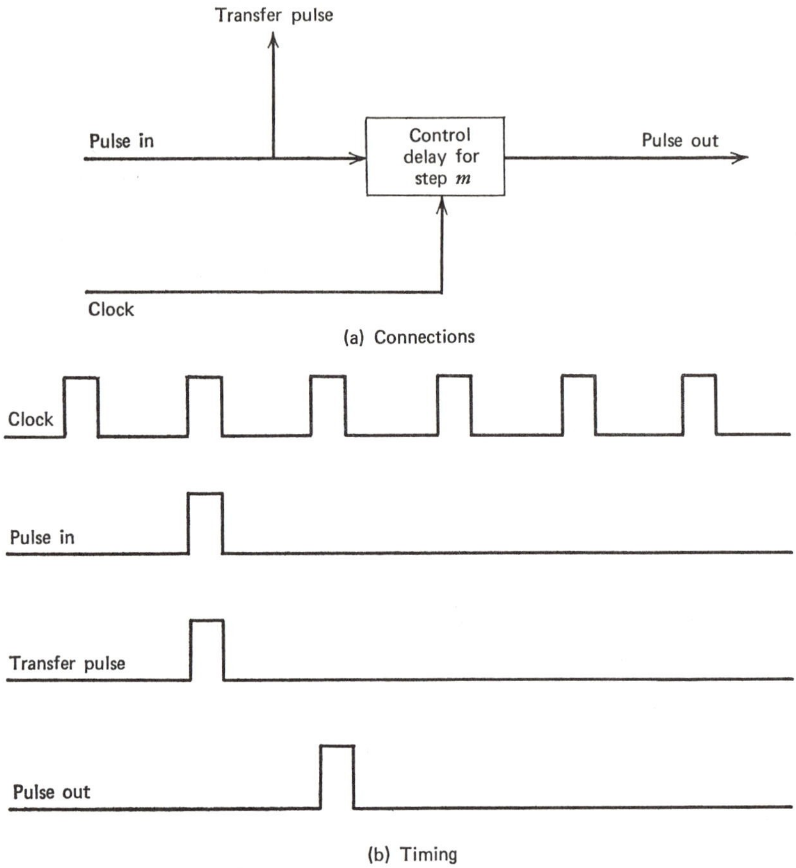

FIGURE 7.2. Control delay.

circuit as follows. The circuit has 3 inputs, the clock input labeled C, the control pulse input labeled x, and a master clear input. The pulse output is labeled z, and two points of particular interest within the circuit are labeled y and w. The function of the master clear is to assure that both y and z are 0 in all control delays prior to setting the computer in operation. Every control delay will remain in this state until excited by a control pulse on its input line, x. A single control pulse is initially entered somewhere in the control by depressing the START button. The circuit of Fig. 7.3 is a *sequential circuit*, as is usually the case where there is feedback. The output, z and the value, y, which are fed back to the circuit input, may be called *state variables*.

The logical output of each gate in the circuit prior to the appearance of a control pulse is shown in Fig. 7.3. The reader should verify these values. As

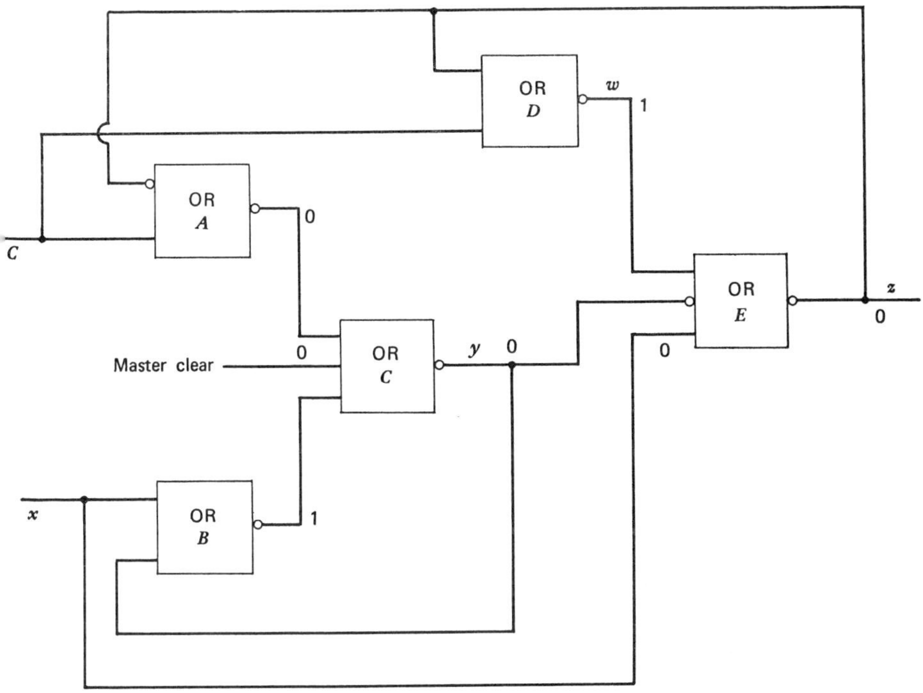

FIGURE 7.3. Control delay circuit.

mentioned previously, each x pulse will be slightly delayed relative to the clock pulse; but they will overlap. When a clock pulse occurs in the absence of a control pulse, the output, w, of gate D will go to 0; but the circuit output, z, and the other state variable, y, will not change. This is illustrated by the left-most clock pulse in the refined timing diagram of Fig. 7.4.

A control pulse arrives in conjunction with the third clock pulse. When this occurs, the state variable, y, will assume the value 1 but z will remain 0. The clock input will drive w to 0 also. Most important, when x and C return to 0, y will remain 1. Notice that C must return to 0 and w to 1 before x goes to 0, to prevent the occurrence of a stray output pulse. We have assumed this to be the case. A foolproof circuit, which would require only that x and C pulses overlap without regard to which occurs first, would require several additional gates.

With the occurrence of the fourth clock pulse, w will go to 0, this time causing z to go to 1. When C returns to 0, y will return to 0 first, and then z. The relative timing is carefully illustrated in Fig. 7.4. The reader will note that the circuit performs as desired. The output control pulse follows an input pulse with a delay of one clock period. Notice also that the output pulse goes to 0 significantly later than the corresponding clock pulse. Thus the assumed

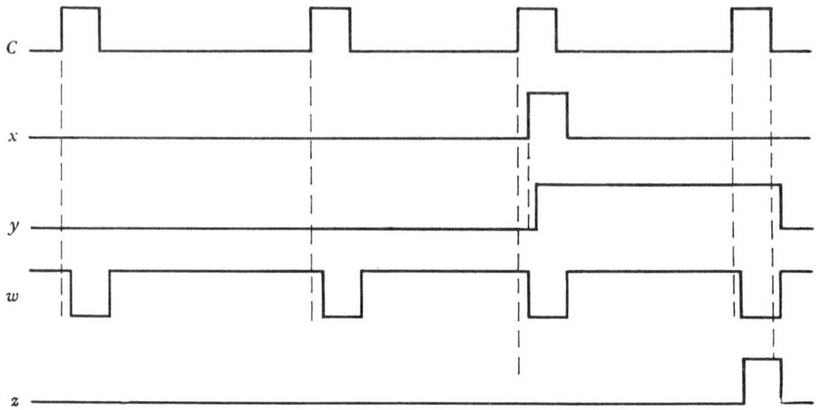

FIGURE 7.4. Timing within a control delay.

relation between clock pulse and input pulse will be satisfied for all control delays fed by this unit.

The reader who happens to have had a previous course in sequential circuits should have easily followed the above discussion. The less experienced reader can verify Fig. 7.4 by carefully calculating new outputs for each gate following each change of value anywhere within the network. Once the network is stabilized, he can move on to the next input change. He need only remember that an input change directly connected to a gate will take effect before a result of that input change which must propagate to the same gate through several prior levels of gating. Although a detailed analysis of Fig. 7.3 is not critical to subsequent sections, the reader will find the time devoted to such an analysis to be well spent.

As we construct control unit hardware it will not be necessary to show circuit details of the control delay. Similarly, it will not be necessary to show the clock input, as every control delay will be connected to the same clock source. In the remainder of the book we shall use the special symbol given in Fig. 7.5 to represent control delays.

7.3. ASYNCHRONOUS OPERATIONS

At this stage it will be illustrative to make a first attempt at translating an AHPL control sequence into a hardware control unit. We are at least able to handle synchronous register transfers.

The first four lines of the control sequence for SIC, as developed in Chapter 6, are reproduced in flow chart form as Fig. 7.6a. In Fig. 7.6b, we present as

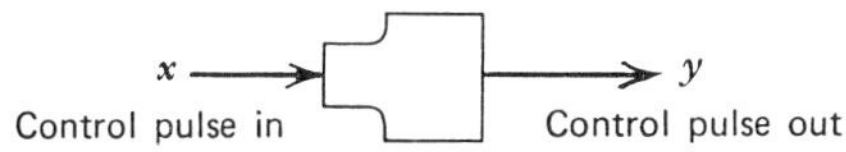

FIGURE 7.5. Symbol for a control delay.

much of the corresponding hardware as is provided for by the timing techniques developed so far. Beginning at the left, the starting mechanism is realized in the form of a single pulse generator. This device will produce a single control pulse synchronized with a clock pulse each time the start button is depressed. The pulse generator is a special case of a pulse synchronizing circuit to be presented later.

Next, we have a point of convergence of control. This merely requires the inclusion of an OR gate, so that a pulse arriving on either line will be transmitted to control delay number 1. Physically, an amplifying NOR gate would probably be employed to prevent voltage level deterioration. In order to avoid confusion, we neglect such physical considerations and use the simplest logic elements, usually AND, OR and NOT gates, throughout.

A control pulse which passes through the OR gate will be transmitted to the registers to trigger the transfer of the contents of ***PC*** to ***MA***. In addition, it will cause a control pulse to emerge at the output of the corresponding control delay one clock period later, allowing time for completion of the

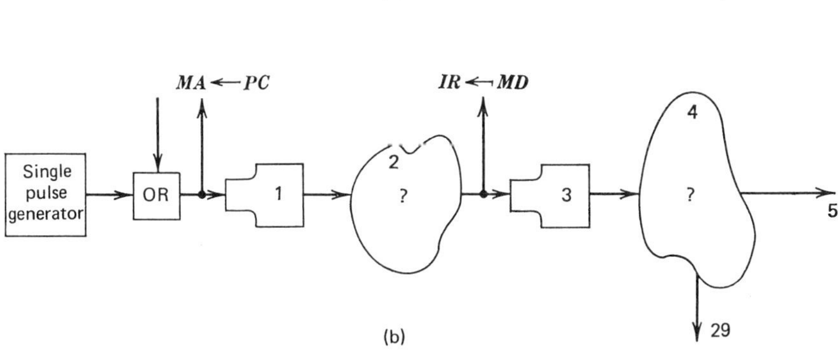

FIGURE 7.6. A first attempt at control hardware.

register transfer. This control pulse must now in some way cause the execution of AHPL step 2.

Step 2 calls for reading a word from the random access memory into the memory data register, ***MD***. If, as is commonly the case, the RAM is slower than the electronic registers, step 2 will require longer than one clock period to accomplish. Thus, some new timing technique must be introduced. After the completion of step 2, a control pulse must be supplied to trigger the transfer ***IR*** ← ***MD*** and simultaneously enter control delay 3. This latter transfer requires only one clock period, so its implementation calls only for control delay 3.

Following step 3, a branch instruction is encountered. Once again some new technique is required. The branch instruction will be the subject of the next section. Let us first consider the problem of timing for transfers which require several clock periods for execution.

Three forms of notation for synchronous transfers are given in Fig. 7.7, along with the corresponding control unit realization of each. Fig. 7.7a

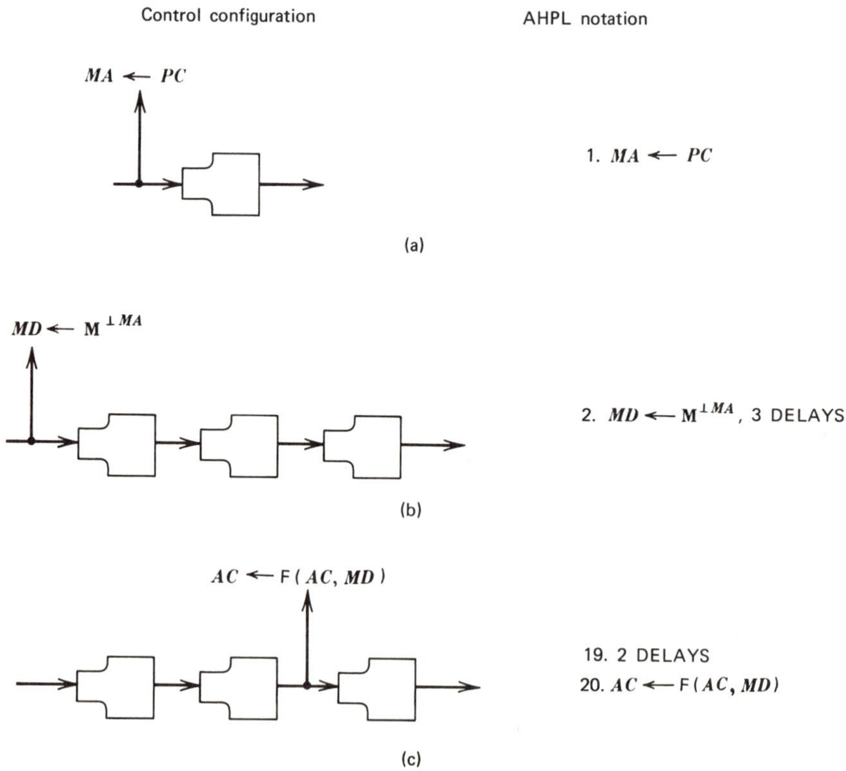

FIGURE 7.7. Synchronous timing notation.

illustrates the one-clock-period transfer already discussed. Situations such as step 2 in Fig. 7.6 may be handled as shown in Fig. 7.7b. Here it is assumed that three clock periods are required to place a vector from the RAM in ***MD***. Thus, after this transfer is initiated, the control pulse is required to pass through three control delays before another transfer pulse may be issued by the control unit. In the remainder of the book, the number of DELAYS (if other than one) required to accomplish a synchronous transfer will be part of the AHPL notation for that transfer. This is an example of the *comment* referred to in Chapter 5. On occasion, it will be desirable to specify a transfer step without delaying the rest of the control sequence one clock period while this transfer takes place. The following version of the notation in Fig. 7.7b will be used in such cases. Examples of the use of this notation will appear later.

$$\boldsymbol{A} \leftarrow \boldsymbol{B}, \quad \text{NO DELAY}$$

We shall see that some logic units will require data to propagate through many levels of combinational logic. Therefore, more than one clock period must be allowed. Once data has been placed in the proper argument registers and buses have been set where used, propagation through the logic unit may begin without further impetus from the control unit. Once the proper result has appeared at the output of the logic unit, it may be pulsed into the destination register in one clock period. An example is given in Fig. 7.7c, where two extra delays are required for formation of the vector function F. These two delays may be denoted in AHPL in a separate step immediately preceding the transfer step. This would have been the proper notation for step 14 of Section 6.5.

For steps which require many clock periods, or for which the execution time varies widely, some other technique is necessary. The method which we shall employ is shown in Fig. 7.8. An incoming pulse will cause the execution of whatever operation is specified by the AHPL step to begin. It will also set the output of a *SC* flip-flop to 1. In this state, the timing device is waiting for a return pulse signifying completion of the operation. The use of a flip-flop is only necessary to pin-point the place in the control unit where the completion pulse is to be received, or if a control level as well as an initiation pulse is required by the asynchronous operation. Typically the completion pulse will be returned to several control points which might have initiated the operation. The control flip-flop will allow the pulse to enter the control unit only at the proper point.

Consider the case of the core memory read operation as an example. The reader will recall from Chapter 3 that core memories are considerably slower than electronic logic, and their timing is generally completely independent of the master clock. Therefore, when a requested data word has been loaded into

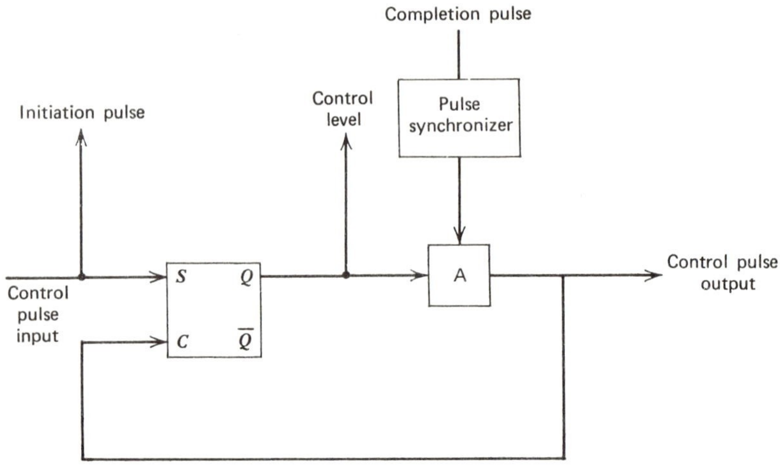

FIGURE 7.8. Asynchronous timing device.

the ***MD*** register, a completion pulse is issued by the core memory. Memory references may be requested at other steps in the control sequence. Each reference will cause a completion pulse to be sent to every possible request point in the control unit. The pulse will pass through the AND gate and enter the control unit only at the point where the WAIT flip-flop has been set to 1.

In the case of a core memory reference, a register transfer has been executed when a completion pulse is returned to the control unit. The corresponding AHPL step must denote the particular transfer, and that the transfer is asynchronous. This will be done as shown in expression 7.1:

$$2.\ \boldsymbol{MD} \leftarrow \boldsymbol{M}^{\perp \boldsymbol{MA}},\quad \text{WAIT} \tag{7.1}$$

In some cases a completion pulse will indicate only that a result vector is available at the output of a bus or a logic unit. This result must be transferred into a destination register as a separate step. This situation is represented by two AHPL steps as given by expression 7.2:

$$\begin{aligned} &19.\ \text{F}(\boldsymbol{MD}, \boldsymbol{AC}),\quad \text{WAIT} \\ &20.\ \boldsymbol{AC} \leftarrow \text{F}(\boldsymbol{MD}, \boldsymbol{AC}) \end{aligned} \tag{7.2}$$

The completion pulse arrives as part of the first of the two steps. The apparently redundant notation in this step is included to indicate that the completion pulse must be supplied by the logic unit which generates F. Either the initiation pulse or the control level shown in Fig. 7.8 may be used to enable the logic unit. We shall defer an illustration of an asynchronous logic unit until Chapter 11.

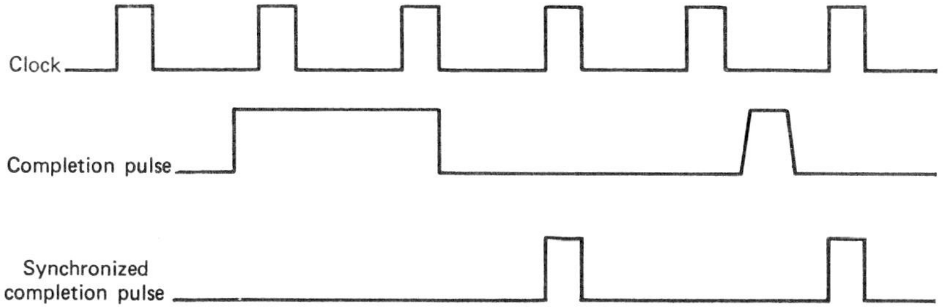

FIGURE 7.9. Pulse synchronization.

A pulse which is generated upon completion of an asynchronous operation may occur at any random point in the clock period. The result of allowing such a pulse to enter the control unit would be unpredictable. All pulses in the control unit must be approximately synchronized with the clock. The function of the pulse synchronizer in Fig. 7.8 is to generate an output pulse synchronized with the next clock pulse following the random input pulse. This is illustrated in the timing diagram of Fig. 7.9. The fundamental mode pulse synchronizer circuit will be presented in Chapter 9, where synchronization will be treated in detail. In effect, asynchronous control is a special case of communication between control units, the topic of Chapter 9.

Since there is no assumed phase relationship between the two input pulses, the pulse synchronizer circuit is more complicated than the control delay of Fig. 7.3. The fundamental mode design of the pulse synchronizer is also given in Reference [1].

In general, the use of the initiation pulse and the method of generation of the completion pulse will vary with the operation involved. The line marked *control level* (Fig. 7.8), which carries the state of the synchronous timing device, is sometimes utilized outside of the control unit. For clarity we repeat the illustration of Fig. 7.6b as Fig. 7.10, with an asynchronous timing device included to implement step-2 of the AHPL program.

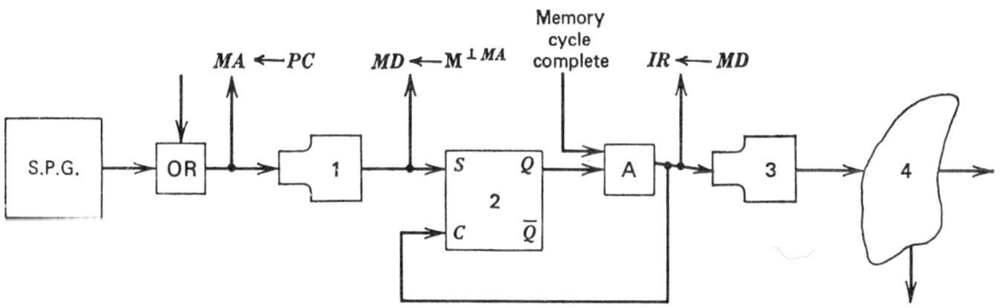

FIGURE 7.10. Read control.

7.4. TRANSLATING BRANCHING INSTRUCTIONS

With the exception of branch instructions, we have established a one-to-one correspondence between lines of AHPL and configurations of logic elements, memory elements, and control delays in the control sequencer. No time delay is required for a branch operation. The branch operation is merely a multiple-output combinational logic function of the pulse input, the instruction decoder, and various bits, or functions of bits, from the data registers. Let P be the pulse input and $X_1, X_2 \cdots X_k$ the level inputs. If there are m possible points to which control might branch, the functions must take the form $P \wedge f_1(X_1 \cdots X_k), P \wedge f_2(X_1 \cdots X_k), \cdots P \wedge f_m(X_1 \cdots X_k)$.

Except in the case of parallel processing, control cannot be transferred to two points simultaneously. We shall exclude parallel processing from our present discussion (see Chapter 9). Under this assumption, Eq. 7.3 must be satisfied for all i and j at every branch point, for every assignment of values to the variables $X_1, X_2, \ldots X_k$ which is not a "don't-care" condition:

$$f_i(X_1 \cdots X_k) \wedge f_j(X_1 \cdots X_k) = 0 \tag{7.3}$$

Since control must be routed somewhere, we have Eq. 7.4, which also need not be satisfied for any "don't-care" conditions:

$$\vee/[f_1(X_1 \cdots X_k), f_2(X_1 \cdots X_k). \ldots f_m(X_1, \ldots X_k)] = 1 \tag{7.4}$$

Now consider the generalized form of a branch statement, as shown in Eq. 7.5. The numbers $D_1, D_2, \ldots D_m$ are the destination line numbers of the branch. Equations 7.3 and 7.4 guarantee that Eq. 7.5 will always reduce

$$\rightarrow (D_1 \times f_1(X_1 \cdots K_k)) + (D_2 \times f_2(X_1 \cdots X_k)) \cdots + (D_m \times f_m(X_1 \cdots X_k)) \tag{7.5}$$

to the form of Eq. 7.6, where D_i is one of the destination line numbers.

$$\rightarrow(D_i) \tag{7.6}$$

As an example let us consider the equivalent of AHPL step 4 from Section 6.5. We have changed the form to conform to the general format of Eq. 7.5. Note the satisfaction of Eq. 7.3 and 7.4. The proposed hardware translation

$$4. \rightarrow (29 \times (\boldsymbol{IR}_0 \wedge \boldsymbol{IR}_1 \wedge \boldsymbol{IR}_2)) + (5 \times (\overline{\boldsymbol{IR}_0 \wedge \boldsymbol{IR}_1 \wedge \boldsymbol{IR}_2}))$$

of step 4 is given in Fig. 7.11b. The reader should be able to visualize the generalization of this configuration to handle any branch instruction of the form of Eq. 7.5. The flow chart branch symbol is given in Fig. 7.11a to assist the reader in visualizing the one-to-one correspondence between the flow chart and the control unit. The output line labeled 29 will be connected to the

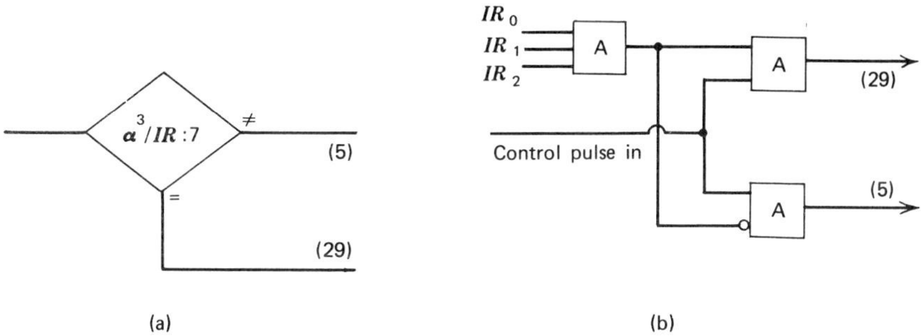

FIGURE 7.11. Branch logic.

input of the control delay representing step 29. Should a branch to step 29 occur somewhere else within the AHPL program, the lines would be routed through an OR gate, which would in turn be connected to the input of the appropriate control delay.

The hardware *control sequencer* for the first ten AHPL steps in the SIC control program is given in Fig. 7.12. This takes our discussion up to the execution phase in the control program. Notice the two OR gates in Fig. 7.12, one at the input to step 1 of the sequencer and the other prior to step 9. These are not specifically denoted in the AHPL sequence. Wherever control branches from more than one point in the sequence converge to the same step, an OR gate must automatically be included. Signal lines from steps 5 and 8 converge at step 9. One of the inputs to the OR gate at step 1 is the output of control delay 27, which allows a clock period for execution of the instruction JMP. Also connected to this OR gate are the start pulse and a line from the completion point of the other instructions. Note also in Fig. 7.12 that the Read Completion Pulse line is connected to two points in the sequencer.

One possible source of difficulty becomes apparent in Fig. 7.12. Notice that a path through strictly combinational logic exists from the output of control delay 3 to the input of control delay 10. A pulse propagating the length this path must pass through four gates, or four levels of logic. The effect of the corresponding delay merits some consideration. A pulse P_1 appearing at the output of delay 3 and the pulse P_2 arriving at the input of delay 10 are shown in Fig. 7.13. Clearly the significance of this delay will depend on the delay of individual gates and the clock frequency selected for the computer. The phase relationship of Fig. 7.13 reflects a relatively short clock period with respect to gate delay. This is characteristic of cases in which the clock is set at a maximum rate to maximize computation speed.

Notice that the pulse P_2 barely overlaps the clock pulse with which it is nominally synchronized. If there were more branch statements between

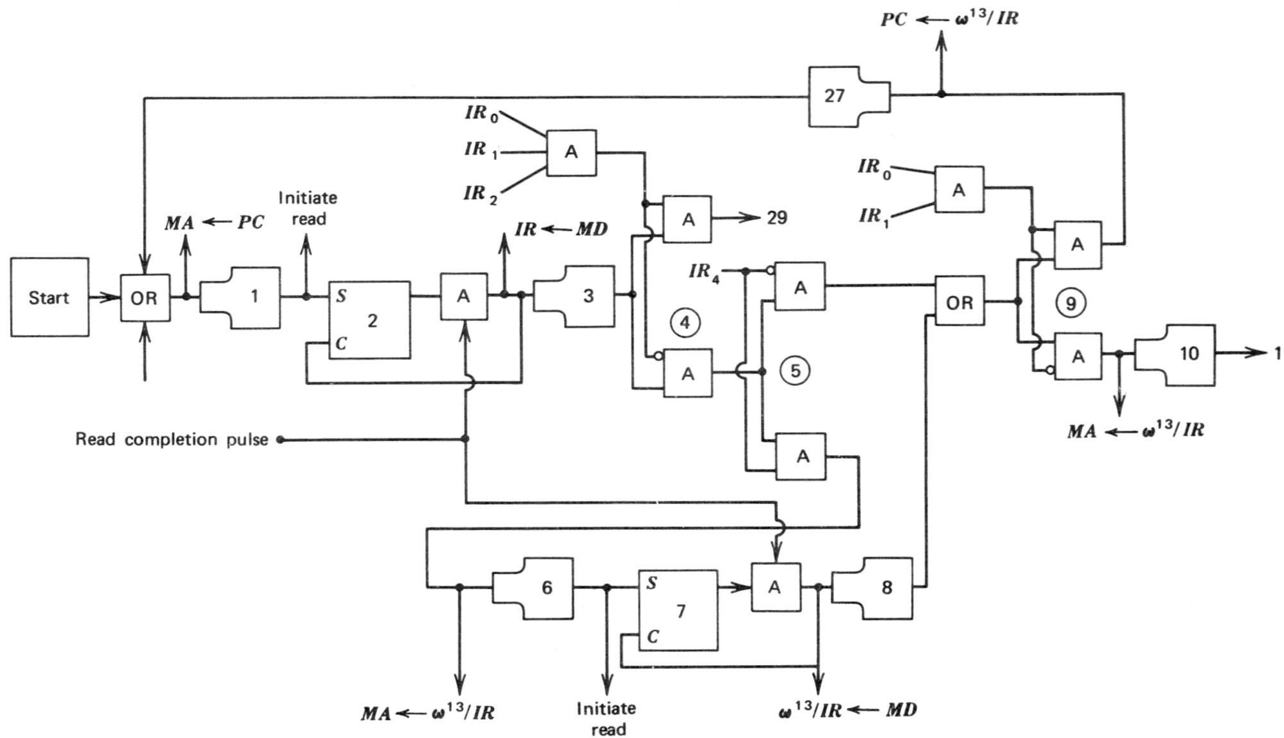

FIGURE 7.12. Partial control unit.

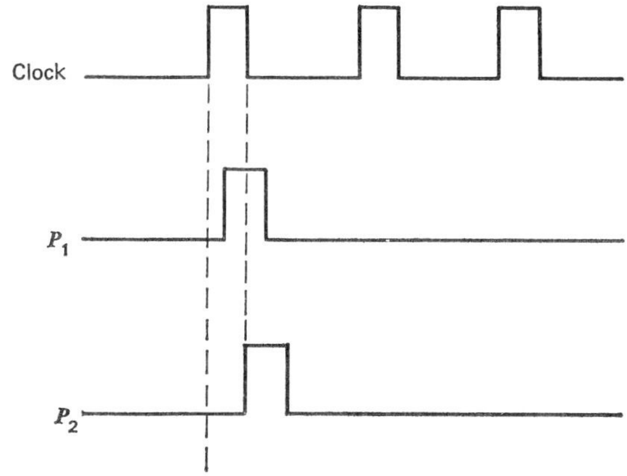

FIGURE 7.13. Delay of control pulses.

steps 3 and 10, the pulse P_2 might not overlap the corresponding clock pulse at all. This would, of course, violate the assumption made in designing the control delay and would lead to unpredictable performance. Widening the clock pulse can help in some cases; but for any clock frequency or pulse width, there is always a maximum tolerable pulse delay. A circuit with a longer delay in any pulse path will not work. A more complicated control delay than the one in Fig. 7.3 may be designed, so that control pulses need not overlap clock pulses. As is illustrated in example 7.1, there is still a maximum tolerable pulse delay.

Like other circuit problems the one discussed above is very much dependent on the particular technology in which the computer is constructed. In any real situation a constraint reflecting the maximum number of levels of control will be imposed. The reader may notice many configurations throughout the book where timing problems are a possibility. We shall not add confusion to our discussion by pointing out each instance. We leave it to the reader to analyze these situations in light of the discussion presented here.

Example 7.1

Illustrate the effect of delay in the worst case delay path of Fig. 7.12. Assume a clock frequency just above the allowable limit, given this worst path and a particular choice of circuit technology. Assume the use of control delays which do not require that their input pulses overlap a clock pulse. Any pulse which appears at the input of a control delay prior to the occurrence of a clock pulse will cause an output pulse to be generated synchronized with that clock pulse.

Solution. Let us use the block diagram notation introduced in Fig. 6.3 to display the connections at steps 27 and 1 to the inputs of *PC* and *MA*. To this configuration, as shown in Fig. 7.14, we have added an OR gate in the line connecting each

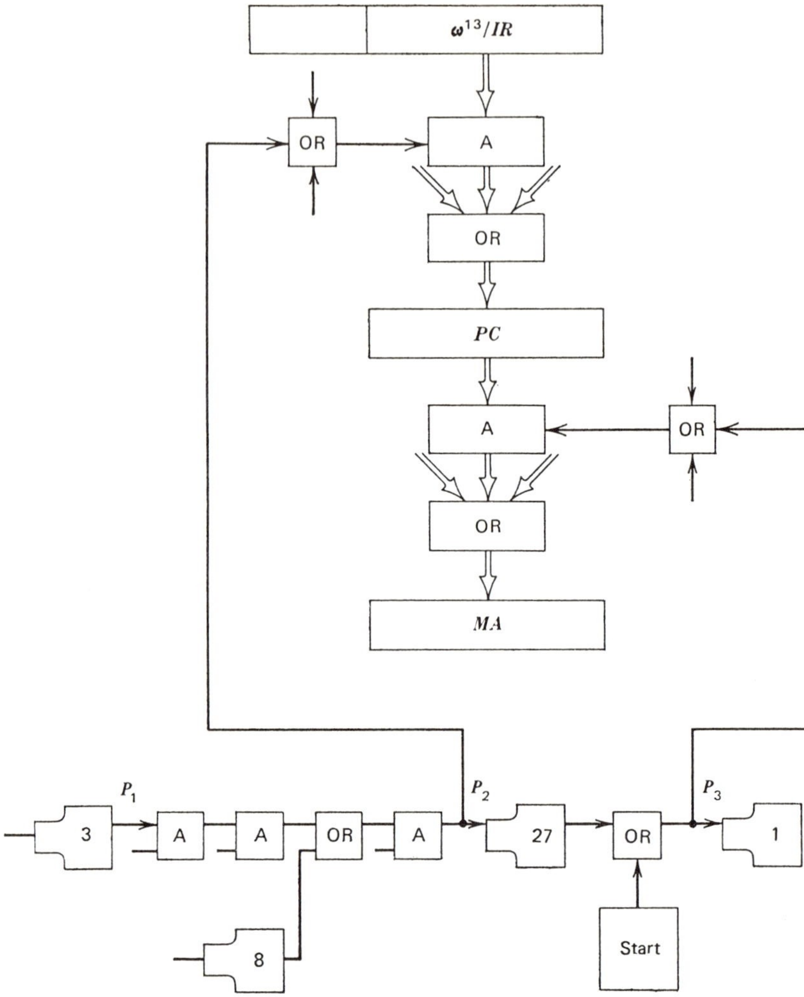

FIGURE 7.14. Transfer pulse connections.

transfer pulse to the register gating. In practice this OR gate will only appear if the exact same register transfer is called for from two points in the control unit. Although Fig. 7.12 does not indicate any further occurrences of the two register transfers depicted in Fig. 7.14, this is not the complete control unit; and these two transfers could be repeated elsewhere.

A timing diagram of the transfer from ***IR*** to ***PC*** is given in Fig. 7.15. Pulse P_1 represents the output of control delay 3 in Fig. 7.14, and pulse P_2 represents the input to control delay 27. Given the improved control delay discussed above, the phase relationship of P_2 itself is not the limiting factor. The possible problem is

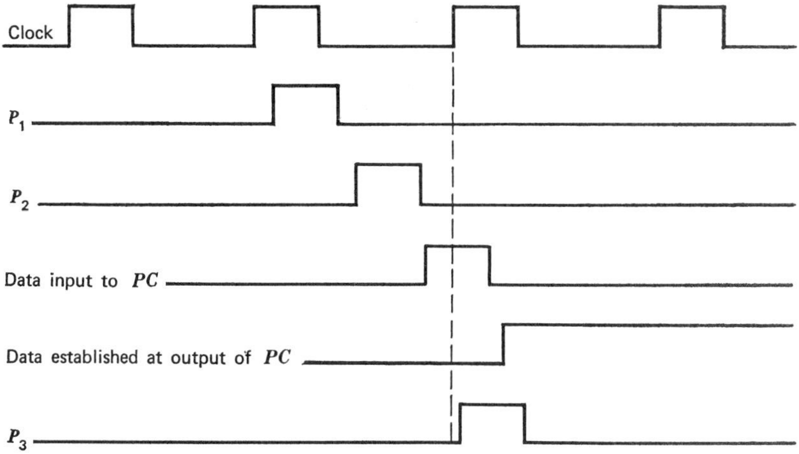

FIGURE 7.15. Register transfer timing for excessive clock frequency.

the time required for the propagation of a pulse through the path from the output of control delay 3 to the input of ***PC***. The pulse P_2 must pass through three additional levels of gating before reaching the inputs of the memory elements in ***PC***. In the process, the pulse is ANDed with the 13 data lines from ***IR***. The outputs of the master-slave memory elements in ***PC*** will not settle at their final values until after the input pulses return to 0. The time at which reliable data becomes available at the output of ***PC*** is illustrated by a level transition in Fig. 7.15.

A pulse synchronized with the third clock pulse of Fig. 7.15 will appear at the output of control delay 27. Following a delay through only one OR gate, this becomes the pulse P_3 shown on the last line of Fig. 7.15. Notice that P_3 triggers the new contents of ***PC*** into ***MA***. As shown in Fig. 7.15, at least the leading edge of P_3 occurs prior to the time the new data has settled at the output of ***PC***. This second data transfer *may* work anyway. The pulse P_3 may be delayed slightly through the illustrated OR gate before converging with the data from ***PC***. Although the data originally ANDed with the pulse is inaccurate, this situation will be corrected soon after the leading edge of P_3 and before the trailing edge. Possibly then, the correct data would wind up in ***MA*** anyway. This would depend on the actual gate delays and the type of memory elements used.

The situation would be worsened if some combinatorial logic function were to be executed on the data either prior to or following ***PC***. In practice, gate delays will not be identical. Particularly within LSI configuration a significant statistical variation is to be expected. A worst case combination of delays could considerably aggravate the problem depicted in the timing diagram of Fig. 7.15. Similarly, other situations will arise in which a single register will be involved in two consecutive data transfers. While the circuitry for one such transfer may be tuned to accommodate a maximum clock rate, it is not practical to attempt to manipulate circuit parameters at a large number of points within a computer.

In general we conclude that the clock rate assumed in Fig. 7.15 is not sufficiently "*conservative*." The establishment of a nominal clock rate is an important design decision in any computer project. Typically the designer will survey the control sequence (and combinational logic subroutines) so as to establish a clock rate which for the particular circuit technology to be employed will, in the worst case, avoid the difficulties discussed above. If one or two areas within the control sequence appear to be particularly troublesome, the system designer may be asked to modify those portions of his design. In actual practice more than one iteration may be required in this process. ▮

So far we have presented only a partial block diagram of the control unit for SIC. In the next several sections we shall consider some special problems involved in the process of translation to a control unit. Once this is done, the reader should be able to construct the complete control unit without difficulty.

7.5. COMBINATIONAL LOGIC SUBROUTINES

At several points in Chapter 6, combinational logic subroutines were defined but not explained further. We shall see that these subroutines may be realized in terms of combinational logic. In general, those steps which were detailed in Chapter 6 involved only register transfers or the transfer of very simple functions of two registers into a third register. As in the case of

$$AC \leftarrow AC \wedge MD$$

these simple functional transfers can be written on one line in AHPL.

Theoretically, any logical computation with the result transferred into a register can be written on a single line. For many functions, in particular the logical representation of arithmetic operations, sheer bulk makes this approach impractical. Some notation must be provided to permit the use of a sequence of AHPL steps to represent combinational logic. The system we propose for this purpose is that of a *combinational logic subroutine*.

We have mentioned that the process of translating an AHPL routine to a hardware control unit, with connections to previously declared registers, is very similar to the process of compilation of a program written in a high-level language. A program to automatically translate single line transfers and branch statements to hardware in the manner discussed in the previous sections of this chapter may be called a *hardware compiler*. The extension of this program to handle combinational logic subroutines will require it to function somewhat differently than an ordinary compiler. If loops are included in the combinational logic subroutine, the resultant compilation will appear in many ways like execution. We shall say that *the hardware compiler* realizes *a combinational logic subroutine*. The result of this execution is a hard-wired combinational logic network. Transfer statements in the control sequence will cause the compiler to connect the outputs of this network to data paths in the digital system. Branch statements may also cause such a network to be connected into the control sequencer.

Our initial illustration of a combinational logic subroutine will be a straight-line program. We shall add loops later to shorten the routines. Example 7.2 will illustrate the process of constructing a combinational logic network from a sequence of AHPL steps. This process may be carried out automatically. It is only necessary to somehow inform the hardware compiler when it encounters a combinational logic subroutine.

Example 7.2

The term *full adder* is used to refer to a circuit which accomplishes the addition of two corresponding binary bits, one from each argument vector connected to the input of the complete adder. This process entails accepting a carry bit from the full adder which adds the bits just lower in significance, and generating a carry to be used by the next most significant full adder. The ith components of the argument vectors may be labeled X_i and Y_i, while the carry from the previous position is C_{i+1}. The bit of the sum S_i corresponding to X_i and Y_i will be 1 if one or three of the bits X_i, Y_i and C_{i+1} are 1. The carry to the next full adder, C_i, will be 1 whenever two or more of the bits X_i, Y_i, and C_{i+1} are 1. Thus the Boolean expressions which describe the full adder are

$$C_i = (X_i \wedge Y_i) \vee (X_i \wedge C_{i+1}) \vee (Y_i \wedge C_{i+1})$$

$$S_i = [(X_i \vee Y_i \vee C_{i+1}) \wedge \overline{C_i}] \vee (X_i \wedge Y_i \wedge C_{i+1})$$

Devise a combinational logic subroutine describing the combinational logic of a full adder.

Solution. The input bits to a full adder will be labeled x and y, with the carry from the previous stage labeled cp. The output bits will be the sum bit, s, and the carry to the next stage, cn. As in most languages, the subroutine is prefaced by its name and a list of arguments. The notation in this example is informal, so the arguments and outputs are listed as simply as possible in the first line of the routine. Once the notation is formalized, the first line of the combinational logic subroutine will serve to alert the hardware compiler to the fact that arrows do not represent register

ARGUMENTS (x,y,cp) OUTPUTS (s,cn)

$sx \leftarrow x \wedge y$

$sy \leftarrow x \wedge cp$

$sz \leftarrow y \wedge cp$

$cn \leftarrow sx \vee sy \vee sz$

$cx \leftarrow x \wedge y \wedge cp$

$z \leftarrow x \vee y \vee cp$

$s \leftarrow (z \wedge \overline{cn}) \vee cx$

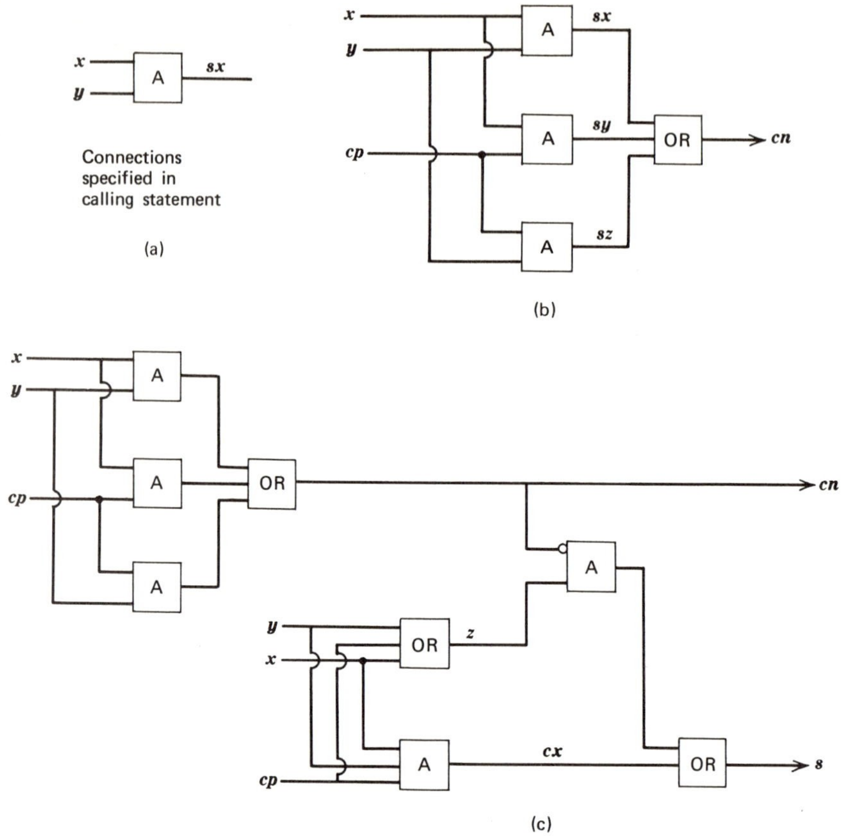

FIGURE 7.16. Full adder.

transfers but rather the input connection to a gate or an array of gates. This is the principal distinguishing feature of a combinational logic subroutine and is worth emphasizing. *In a combinational logic subroutine an arrow represents a wired connection, not a register transfer.*

The reader will notice that each step in the subroutine, with the exception of the last, represents a single gate. The process of translating the routine to hardware will consist of generating the individual gates in turn and connecting the inputs to already available signal points. The first few steps will usually call for connecting the logic function inputs to registers or other points within the existing hardware. These are specified as the calling point of the subroutine.

Fig. 7.16a shows the circuit after compilation of the first step of the subroutine. Fig. 7.16b shows the circuit after the first four steps, and Fig. 7.16c after the last step. The handling of the last step where three gates are specified in a single step presents no special problems. The order of gate generation is carefully set forth by the use of parentheses. Where convenient, the normal precedence of the AND operation will be observed. ▮

Three types of statements are used in combinational logic subroutines. The first, or identifying, statement and the RETURN statement at the end are included to set apart each routine in a list of such routines. The other seven statements in Example 7.2 are *wiring statements*. Much of the power of the combinational logic subroutine is derived from looping in the realization of the subroutine. To facilitate looping, a third type of statement, the *bookkeeping statement*, is allowed. Bookkeeping statements include APL branch statements and APL computations on subscripts. These are included only to specify the order of realization of wiring statements. The combinational logic network grows only with the realization of a wiring statement. A wiring statement must satisfy the following rules.

Rules for formulation of a wiring statement

1. The left and right sides of a wiring statement are connected by a left-pointing arrow.
2. The left side of a wiring statement is a vector (or scalar) representing the outputs (output) of a subnetwork formed by executing the statement.
3. The right side of a wiring statement is a vector Boolean function of its arguments which is directly realizable as logic subnetwork. That is, the only allowed primitive operators are $\wedge$, $\vee$, and NOT. Symmetric functions (which include exclusive OR) will be allowed (and used occasionally) as abbreviations of expressions involving only these operators.
4. Arguments may be constants (vectors of 0's and 1's), flip-flop or register outputs, variables specified by the left side of other wiring statements, or the outputs of other combinational logic subroutines. Variables may have subscripts, which are specified by bookkeeping statements.
5. Any subscripts of output or argument variables in a wiring statement about to be realized must have been fixed by already executed bookkeeping statements. All arguments of such statements must represent externally available logic lines or the outputs of subnetworks generated by previously-realized wiring statements.

For convenience we shall distinguish between subroutines and function subroutines in the call statements. We shall allow *any* subroutine to appear within a transfer statement as is the usual practice for function subroutines. The vector to be returned will be represented by the subroutine name in the calling statement.

We will retain the function subroutines as subroutines returning only one functional value. These will be indicated by strings ending in F. The function computed will share this subroutine name. It will be convenient to allow a hardware compiler to store an often-used function subroutine in circuit form. This would be particularly useful in the context of computer-aided design of large-scale integrated circuits. On occasion this feature may provide a helpful shortcut in our discussions.

The subroutine of Example 7.2 may be conveniently written as a pair of function subroutines as follows. One distinct feature of combinational logic subroutines is illustrated by this example. Notice that the subroutine SUMF calls the routine CARRYF. This amounts to connecting to the output of an existing network. A particular logic function of a fixed set of variables need be realized only once. If CARRYF is used later with different arguments, a

```
        FUNCTION CARRYF (x, y, cp)
        sx ← x ∧ y
        sy ← x ∧ cp
        sz ← y ∧ cp
    CARRYF ← sx ∨ sy ∨ sz
        RETURN
        FUNCTION SUMF (x, y, cp, CARRYF (x, y, cp))
        cx ← x ∧ y ∧ cp
         z ← x ∨ y ∨ cp
    SUMF ← (z ∧ CARRYF (x, y, cp)) ∨ cx
        RETURN
```

separate network must be realized. Once again we observe that realization of a combinational logic subroutine is not quite analogous to the compilation of an ordinary subroutine.

In a descriptive treatment such as this book, it is necessary to document the realization of a particular subroutine only once with one set of arguments. We can then use the subroutine at will with any argument. The reader should have no difficulty visualizing the realization of the required network. The reader will find that a few very important combinational logic subroutines will appear over and over again. In some cases changing the number of arguments will cause no significant changes in the form of a combinational logic network. The adder in Example 7.3 is an example of a subroutine which may be used for various numbers of arguments without re-examining the realization.

So far the only combinational logic subroutines considered have been straight-line programs. As will be shown in Example 7.3 and several additional examples in this chapter and Chapters 11, 12, and 13, the real power of the subroutine notation lies in the inclusion of loops.*

The combinational logic subroutine may seem a maze of details at this point. The reader should remind himself that he will not be required to deal with a compiler program which thrives on these details. The reader is the compiler for purposes of this discussion, and he may master these details at his own pace. Most of his questions will answer themselves as he considers the examples in this chapter.

Example 7.3

Write an AHPL listing of the combinational logic subroutine ADD(MD, AC).

Solution. A satisfactory routine may be listed as follows.

    1. CL SUBROUTINE ADD(MD, AC)
B 2. $C, S \leftarrow 19\rho 0,\ 18\rho 0$
    3. $C_{18} \leftarrow 0$
B 4. $i \leftarrow 17$
    5. $C_i \leftarrow \text{CARRYF}\,(AC_i, MD_i, C_{i+1})$
    6. $S_i \leftarrow \text{SUMF}\,(AC_i, MD_i, C_{i+1}, \text{CARRYF})$
B 7. $i \leftarrow i - 1$
B 8. $i{:}0\,(\geq, <) \rightarrow (5, 9)$
    9. $b \leftarrow (C_0 \oplus \ell)$
  10. ADD $\leftarrow b, S$
  11. RETURN

A glance at the above routine reveals several types of statements which have not been seen previously. In step 2 we use the RESHAPE operator to define the 19-bit carry vector, C, and the 18-bit sum vector, S. This statement will not declare a hardware register but will merely alert the hardware compiler to the dimensions of S and C (note B at the left). From the carry vector, only the most significant bit, C_0, will be connected outside of the adder. This is the bit which will be exclusive-OR'ed with the link. The 18-bit sum which a control pulse will cause to be gated into AC is represented by S. Recall that ADD(MD, AC) represented the 19-bit vector b, S in the control sequence of Chapter 6. This identification is made at step 10 so that the outputs of the adder may be connected to the appropriate AND-gate array.

Steps 2, 4, 7, and 8 are bookkeeping statements. A hardware compiler program would identify these statements by the B which must be placed at the left of the bookkeeping statement numbers.

Step 3 causes the input carry bit, C, to be connected to ground. This is shown in Fig. 7.17a. The second step, a bookkeeping instruction, merely establishes the

* Some readers may notice a similarity between combinational logic subroutines involving loops and iterative logic networks. See Section 16.4 of Reference [1].

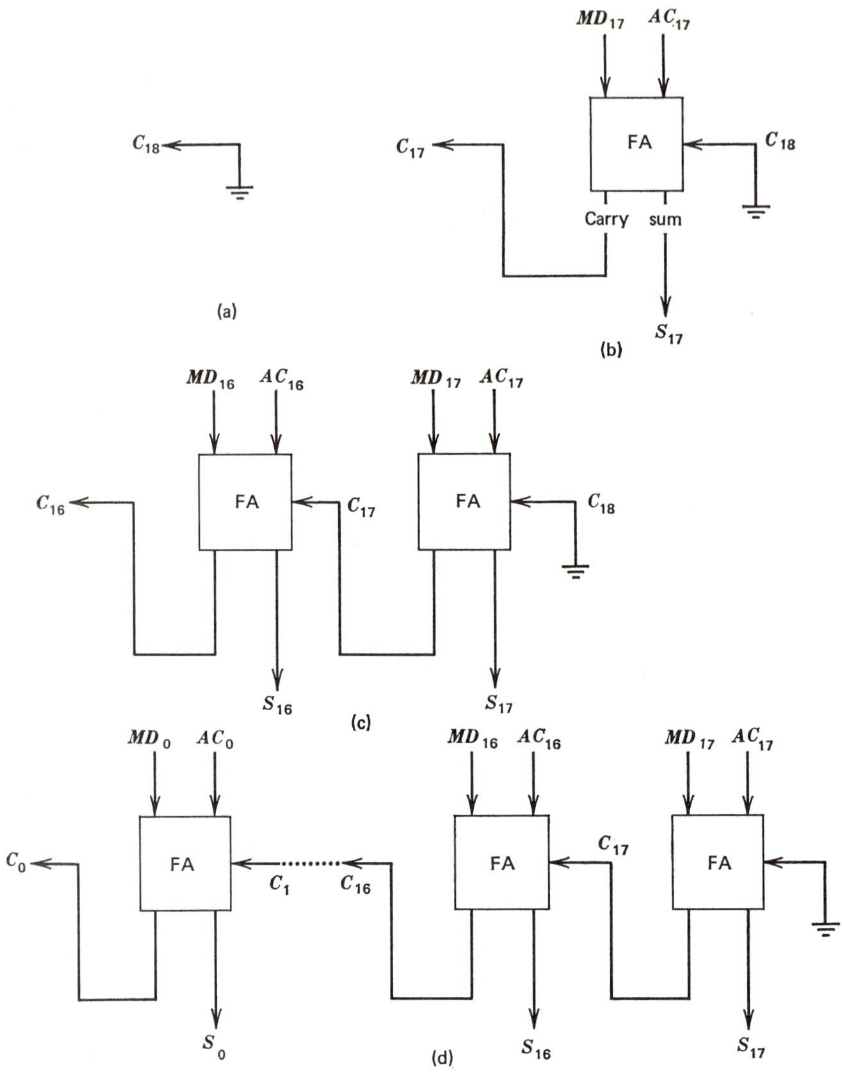

FIGURE 7.17. Generation of an 18-bit adder.

fact that the loop will be traversed 18 times. For $i = 17$, steps 5 and 6 cause the full-adder circuitry of Fig. 7.16b to be generated, with inputs AC_{17}, MD_{17}, and C_{18}, a sum output, S_{17}, and a carry output, C_{17}. This is symbolized by the block F. A. in Fig. 7.17b. The bookkeeping statements, 7 and 8, decrement i and return the compiler to step 5.

A second pass through steps 5 and 6 with $i = 16$ leaves the circuit as shown in Fig. 7.17c. Notice that the carry from the first full adder serves as an input to the second block. This process continues for 16 more passes through steps 5 and 6, finally yielding Fig. 7.17d. ▮

7.6. RETURN TO SIC CONTROL UNIT

In Section 7.4 a realization of the SIC control sequence was developed through step 10. Steps 11–15 are repeated as follows:

11. $\rightarrow((\overline{IR_0} \times 12) + (IR_0 \times 21))$
12. $MD \leftarrow M^{\perp MA}$
13. $\rightarrow((IR_1 \vee IR_2) \times 14) + ((\overline{IR_1 \vee IR_2}) \times 16)$
14. $\ell, AC \leftarrow ((\overline{IR_1} \wedge (\ell, MD)) \vee (\overline{IR_2} \wedge (\ell, (MD \wedge AC)))$
    $\vee ((IR_1 \wedge IR_2) \wedge \text{ADD}(MD, AC)))$, 5 DELAYS
15. $\rightarrow(25)$

Of most interest now is the use of the combinational logic subroutine ADD(*MD*, *AC*) in step 14. When this step is encountered by the hardware compiler, the adder network of Fig. 7.17 is generated from the subroutine, if not already available. Part of the compilation of step 14 consists of connecting the adder to the input switching to *AC*, as shown in Fig. 7.18. As the adder is synchronous, timing is provided by five control delays. The length of time required for a carry to propagate through the 18 full adders will be a function of the circuits employed. We assume that the designer has determined it to be the equivalent of five clock periods in this case.

Step 14 is the first instance of the general technique of using instruction bits (or data bits) within a transfer step to select the vector to be transferred.

The handling of the three operations AND, TAD, and LAC in a single statement necessitates the switching array labeled *SW* in Fig. 7.18. The switching for a single bit from this array is shown in Fig. 7.19a. The configurations of Figs. 7.18 and 7.19a presume that the control pulse must be ANDed with the vector, represented by the right side of step 14, as last step. This need not be the case. The control pulse is not specifically denoted in an AHPL expression. The control pulse could equally well be ANDed with the control bits, IR_1, and IR_2, first. The results branches the pulse to one of three separate lines as shown in Fig. 7.19b. In this way *SW* could be eliminated from Fig. 7.18 and replaced by two arrays of AND gates for each control pulse. In general, the configuration suggested by Fig. 7.19b would require slightly more gates but fewer total gate inputs. Integrated circuit technology will usually dictate the use of the form given in Fig. 7.19b where the choice is between a small number of arguments.

The network of Fig. 7.19b is similar to the network which would result if

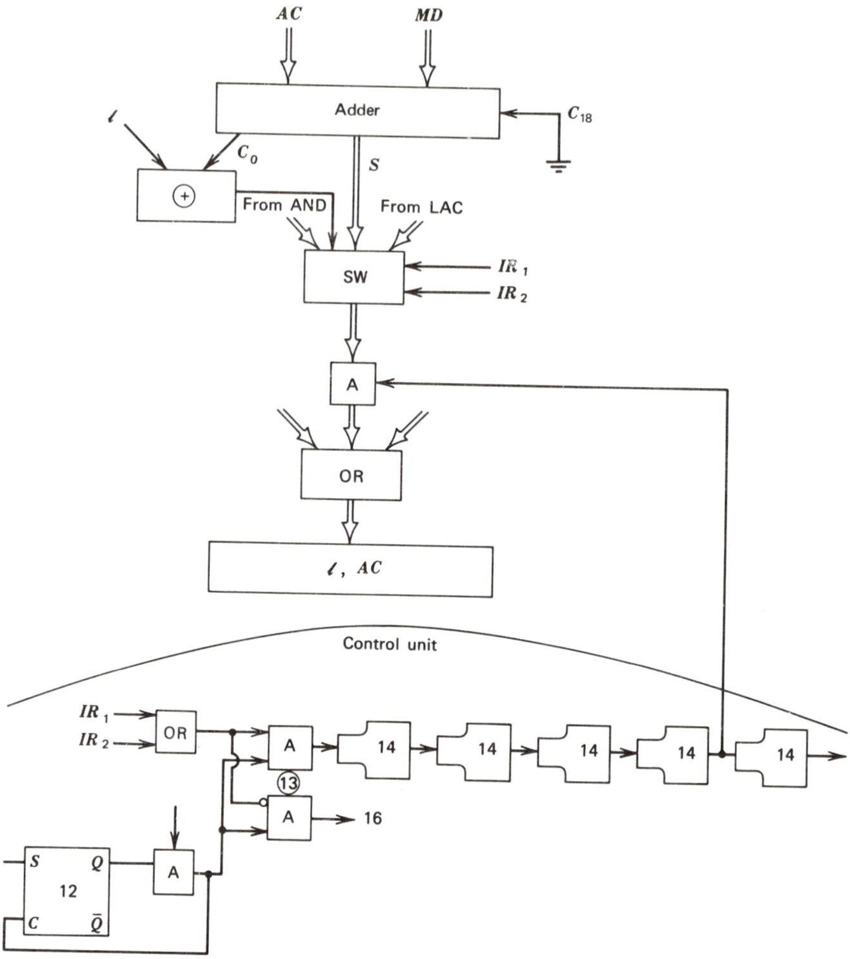

FIGURE 7.18. Control of the ADD operation.

the sequence branched to separate control for AND, TAD, and LAC as considered in Section 6.5. In both forms in Fig. 7.18, however, AND and LAC are slowed down to coincide with TAD.

7.7. A REFINEMENT

From here on, unless otherwise noted, where the vector to be transferred is specified by the values of one or more control levels, we shall assume the use of a network of the form given in Fig. 7.19b to generate the proper transfer pulse. To explore the implications of this choice, let us consider the various

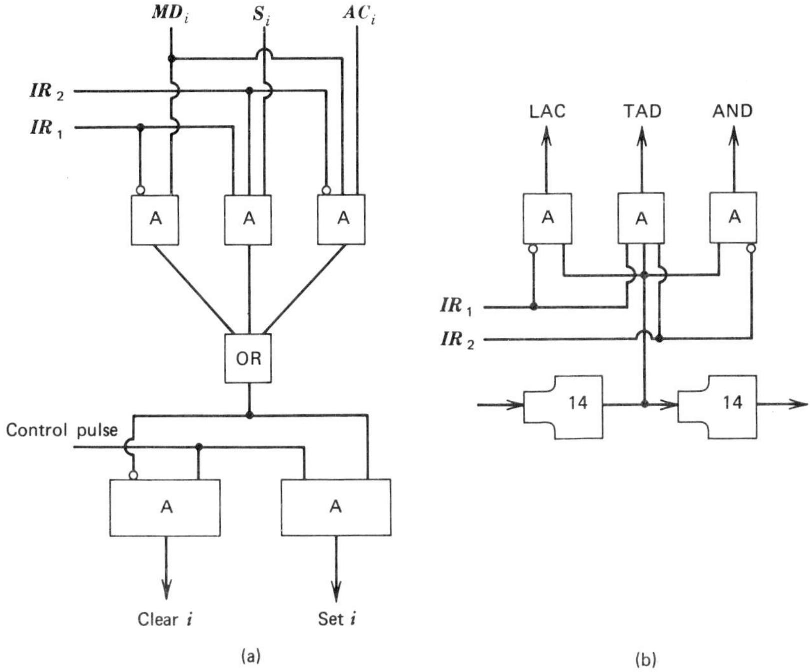

FIGURE 7.19. Alternates methods of using the control pulse.

types of vectors which might be transferred into an arbitrary register, A. Examples of all vector types which might affect the control hardware are given in the next-value Karnaugh map of Fig. 7.20. For simplicity the control variables are $\boldsymbol{a}$, $\boldsymbol{b}$, and $\boldsymbol{c}$. An AHPL transfer statement for this map is given as expression 7.7. Much as was done for step 33 in Section 6.7, terms are included only when the value of A is to be changed. As depicted, two of the

DATA COMPLEMENT

$$A \leftarrow ((\overline{\boldsymbol{b}} \wedge \boldsymbol{c}) \wedge \boldsymbol{B}) \vee ((\overline{\boldsymbol{a}} \wedge \boldsymbol{b} \wedge \boldsymbol{c}) \wedge (A \wedge \boldsymbol{B})) \vee ((\boldsymbol{a} \vee \boldsymbol{b} \vee \overline{\boldsymbol{c}}) \wedge \overline{A})) \quad (7.7)$$
$$\vee ((\overline{\boldsymbol{a}} \wedge \overline{\boldsymbol{c}}) \wedge \boldsymbol{\epsilon}(n)) \vee ((\boldsymbol{a} \wedge \boldsymbol{b} \wedge \boldsymbol{c}) \wedge \overline{\boldsymbol{\epsilon}(n)})$$

SET CLEAR

a \ bc	00	01	11	10
0	$\epsilon(n)$	B	$A \wedge B$	$\epsilon(n)$
1	A	B	$\overline{\epsilon(n)}$	$\overline{A}$

FIGURE 7.20. Next-values of A.

terms specify the transfer of data into A, one specifies the complementing of all flip-flops in A, one specifies setting all the flip-flops in A, and one specifies clearing these flip-flops.

The switching networks in Chapter 4 assumed that input vectors were always non-constant data vectors. The network may be simplified somewhat when the information to be placed in A is a constant or is $\overline{A}$ or A itself. As already mentioned, no control pulse at all is required in the latter case. If SC flip-flops are used, $\overline{A}$ must also be treated as data. In example 7.4 we shall see that the use of JK flip-flops greatly simplifies the handling of $\overline{A}$. When $\epsilon(n)$ is to be placed in A, it is not actually necessary to AND the control pulse with a vector of 1's. Instead, we merely route the control pulse directly to the set input of each flip-flop in A. Placing $\overline{\epsilon(n)}$ in A is similarly accomplished by routing the control pulse directly to the clear input of every flip-flop. A transfer of any other constant $\boldsymbol{K}$ into A can be handled by connecting the control pulse line to the set input of A_i if $\boldsymbol{K}_i = 1$, and to the clear input of A_i if $\boldsymbol{K}_i = 0$.

A section of a control unit for executing the transfer specified by expression 7.7 is given in Fig. 7.21. The control lines for accomplishing $A \leftarrow \epsilon(n)$ and $A \leftarrow \overline{\epsilon(n)}$ are shown connected to a typical flip-flop in A. These lines are identically connected to all other flip-flops in A. The more complicated data transfer connections follow the format given in Chapter 4.

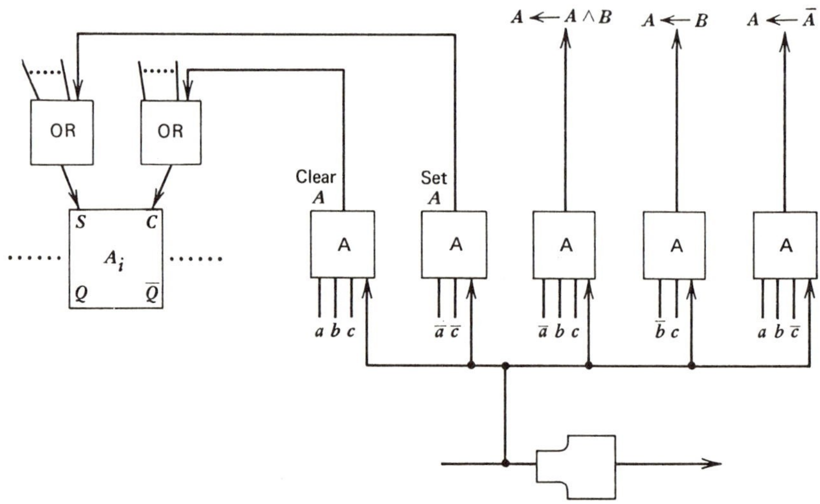

FIGURE 7.21. Control realization for expression 7.7.

Example 7.4

The portion of step 33 of Section 6.7 which involves operations on AC is repeated as expression 7.8. Construct a section of a control unit which will realize this expression. Assume that the accumulator

$$AC \leftarrow (\epsilon(18) \wedge (\overline{IR}_8 \wedge IR_9)) \vee ((IR_8 \wedge \overline{IR}_9) \wedge \overline{\epsilon(18)}) \vee ((IR_8 \wedge IR_9) \wedge \overline{AC}) \quad (7.8)$$

is an array of eighteen JK flip-flops.

Solution. JK flip-flops are distinguished from SC flip-flops by the fact that a simultaneous signal on both the J and K inputs will reverse the state. The Karnaugh map from which expression 7.8 was obtained is repeated as Fig. 7.22a. From this map the J and K signals are easily derived, as shown in Fig. 7.22b and c. Thus, $J = 1$ whenever AC is set to 1 or complemented, and $K = 1$ whenever AC is complemented or cleared. The very simple control circuit realization of Fig. 7.22d follows immediately from the J and K maps. ▮

A practical problem stands in the way of the use of JK flip-flops as called for in the above example. It is possible to design unclocked JK flip-flops by requiring that supposedly simultaneous J and K pulses at least overlap. However, only clocked devices requiring level J and K inputs are commonly available as integrated circuits. Most likely one would only take advantage of the flexibility of JK flip-flops by resorting to a level-oriented control unit of the form to be described in Section 7.10 and the Appendix.

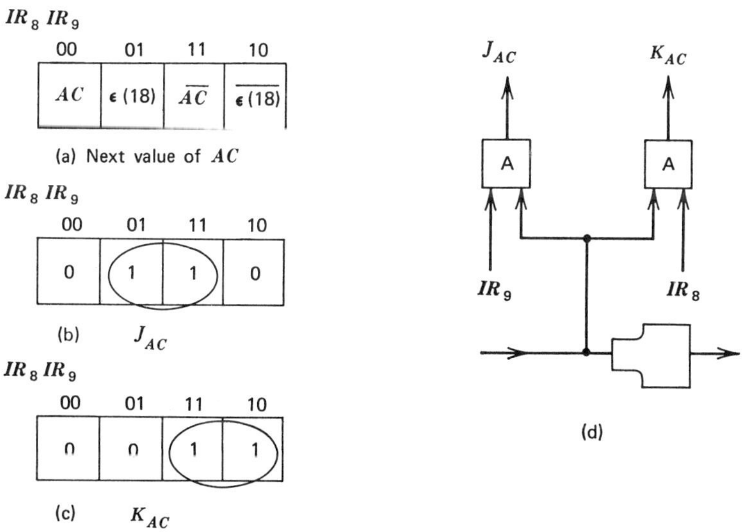

FIGURE 7.22. Operations on AC.

7.8. THE INCREMENT SUBROUTINE

To maintain perspective, we show the portion of the control unit specified by lines 10–16 of Chapter 6 in Fig. 7.23. If $IR_0 = 0$, an operand is read from memory. If $IR_1 = IR_2 = 0$, the ISZ command is implemented at step 16.

The realization of steps 16–20 calls for another combinational logic routine, INC. Step 16 calls for incrementing the ***MD*** register, and step 19 specifies incrementing ***PC***.

The program counter can be expected to be just that, a counter, with additional circuitry to permit inserting new locations for the JMP and JMS instructions. Normally, the memory data register will not be provided with a counting capability. The computer SIC has only two data registers, ***MD*** and ***AC***. Since the instruction ISZ requires that the operand be incremented while the contents of ***AC*** are left undisturbed, the operand must be updated in the ***MD*** register.

The increment subroutine in the notation of the ***MD*** register follows:

1. CL SUBROUTINE INC(***MD***)

B 2. $MDNEW \leftarrow 18\rho 0$

B 3. $i \leftarrow 17$

4. $MDNEW_i \leftarrow MD_i \oplus (\wedge/(\omega^{17-i}(18)/MD))$

B 5. $i \leftarrow i - 1$

B 6. $i:0\ (\geq, <) \rightarrow (4, 7)$

7. INC $\leftarrow MDNEW$

8. RETURN

Notice that the INC subroutine, as contrasted with the subroutine ADD, requires the outputs of no other functions as arguments. In fact, the only

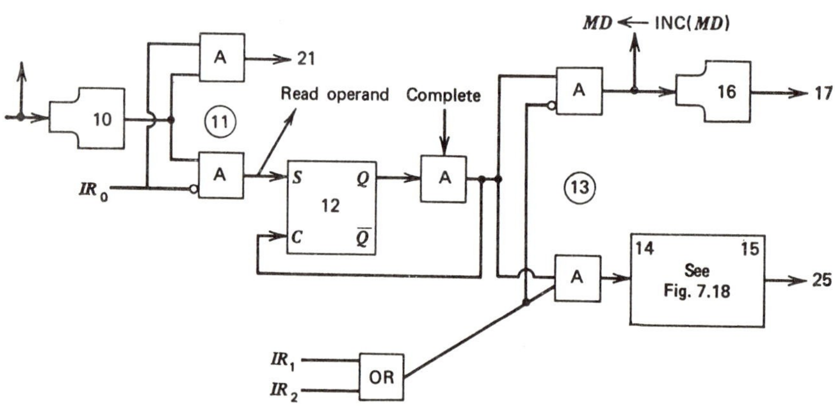

FIGURE 7.23. Control unit continued.

arguments are the bits in ***MD*** which will be changed by the subroutine. These new values of ***MD*** are represented temporarily in the form of ***MDNEW***, which is dimensioned in step 2. The reader will observe that a bit in a counter will change if all bits to the right of that bit are 1. Thus, step 4 generates a network expressing the next state of each bit $\boldsymbol{MD}_i$ in terms of this bit and all bits to the right. By traversing this step 18 times, the next-state networks for all 18 bits are generated. The overall effect of the subroutine on a bit $\boldsymbol{MD}_i$ is given by Eq. 7.9. From this equation, we see that $\boldsymbol{MD}_i$ will be complemented if Eq. 7.10 is satisfied and will remain unchanged otherwise.

$$\boldsymbol{MD}_i \leftarrow \boldsymbol{MD}_i \oplus (\wedge/(\boldsymbol{\omega}^{17-i}(18)/\boldsymbol{MD})) \tag{7.9}$$

$$\wedge/(\boldsymbol{\omega}^{17-i}(18)/\boldsymbol{MD}) = 1 \tag{7.10}$$

In step 19 we see INC(***PC***). The subroutine for incrementing the program counter is similar to INC (***MD***) except that step 3 is replaced by $i \leftarrow 12$ since the program counter has only 13 bits, all of which are involved in the count. The construction of a control unit block diagram for AHPL steps 16–20 will be left to the student.

In step 21, INC(***PC***) is routed directly to ***MD***. For this operation the same network which is generated for $\boldsymbol{PC} \leftarrow INC(\boldsymbol{PC})$ may be used. It is only necessary to connect the outputs of this network through an array of AND gates to the inputs of ***MD***. As usual, the other input to the AND gates is the step 21 transfer pulse from the control unit. For compactness we omit this step from Fig. 7.24 which shows the reconvergence of control from the three

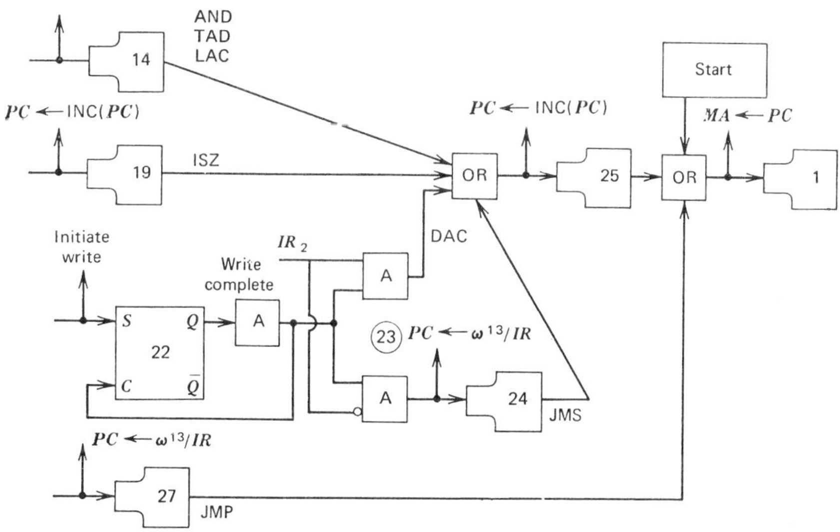

FIGURE 7.24. Convergence of control.

separate paths for the types 3, 4, and 5 instructions. The upper two paths, from delays 14 and 19, represent the group 3 sequences, while the paths through timing devices 22 and 27 represent groups 4 and 5, respectively. Group 3 and 4 sequences converge at delay 25 to cause the program counter to be incremented. As illustrated, control converges for all instructions at the input of control delay 1 to begin the fetch cycle of the next instruction.

Example 7.5

Use a version of the combinational logic subroutine presented in this section to generate the logic block diagram of a 4-bit counter.

Solution. The essential AHPL steps modified for 4-bit vectors, $\boldsymbol{CT}$, are given as follows:

B 1. $i \leftarrow 3$
   2. $\boldsymbol{CTNEW}_i \leftarrow \boldsymbol{CT}_i \oplus (\wedge/(\omega^{3-i}(4)/\boldsymbol{CT}))$
B 3. $i \leftarrow i - 1$
B 4. $i{:}0\,(\geq, <) \rightarrow (2, 5)$

As usual, a transfer pulse is required to gate the logical values $\boldsymbol{CTNEW}$ into the counter register $\boldsymbol{CT}$. In effect, the counter will count these transfer pulses modulo 16.

The first pass through the above routine generates $\boldsymbol{CT}_1$. For $i = 3$ and $3 - i = 0$, we have Eq. 7.11 from the definition of the AND reduction operator. Thus

$$\wedge/(\omega^0(4)/\boldsymbol{CT}) = 1 \tag{7.11}$$

$\boldsymbol{CTNEW}_3 = \boldsymbol{CT}_3 \oplus 1$, as shown in Fig. 7.25a. It should be clear that for this special case the exclusive-OR gate could be replaced by an inverter. The exclusive-OR block normally represents a configuration of three NAND gates and an inverter. A second pass through the routine generates the bit $\boldsymbol{CTNEW}_2$, leaving the circuit as shown in Fig. 7.25b. For $i = 2$, step 2 reduces to Eq. 7.12. AND gates are actually

$$\boldsymbol{CT}_2 \oplus (\wedge/(\omega^1(4)/\boldsymbol{CT})) = \boldsymbol{CT}_2 \oplus \boldsymbol{CT}_3 \tag{7.12}$$

required at the input to the exclusive-OR gates for bits $\boldsymbol{CTNEW}_0$ and $\boldsymbol{CTNEW}_1$. This is illustrated in Fig. 7.25c. The circuit in this figure is the result of two more passes through the above routine and adding the circuitry required to allow the transfer pulse to trigger $\boldsymbol{CTNEW}$ into the register $\boldsymbol{CT}$. ∎

7.9. THE SHIFT REGISTER

In order to allow for implementation of the rotate instructions, the $\boldsymbol{AC}$ must be provided with the capability of shifting in both directions. The gating necessary to permit shifting in either direction is illustrated in Fig. 7.26. The

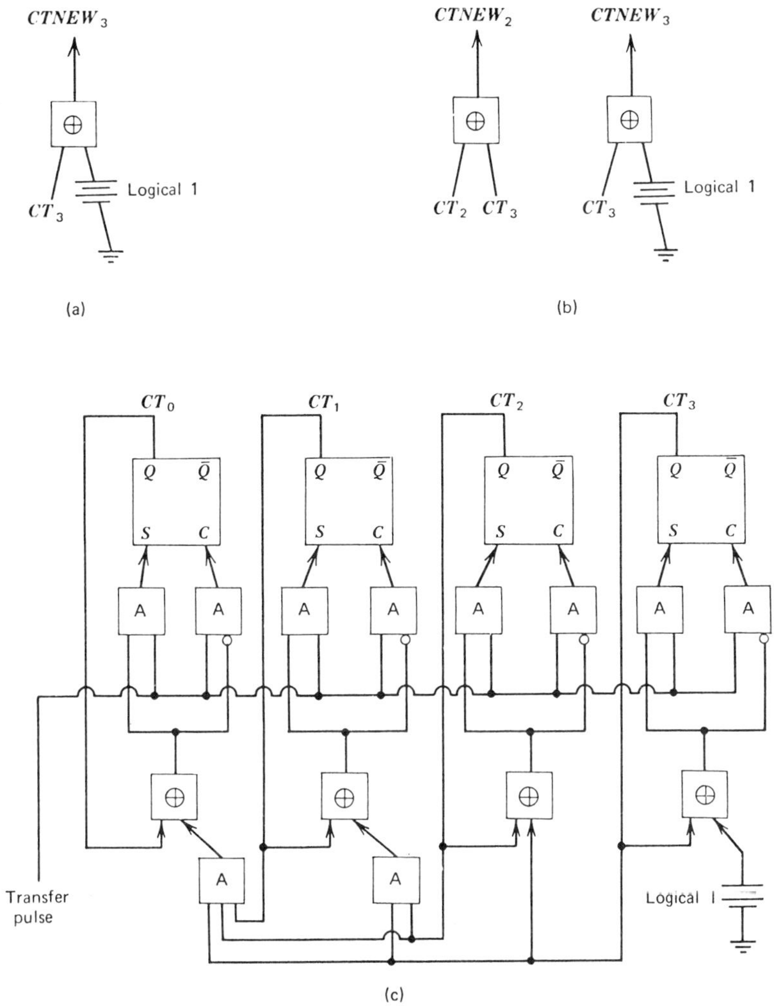

FIGURE 7.25. Four-bit counter. (The reader may notice that the exclusive-OR units can be eliminated by using T flip-flops or JK flip-flops.)

input gating is shown only for a single flip-flop from *AC*. This gating must, of course, be duplicated for each flip-flop in *AC* and the link, with inputs taken from the flip-flops immediately on the left and right. The link is connected to AC_0 and AC_{17}. Thus *AC* becomes a left-right shift register. The rotate right and rotate left pulses, each one of which drives all 19 flip-flops, are generated by the section of the sequencer corresponding to the operate sequence of Section 6.7.

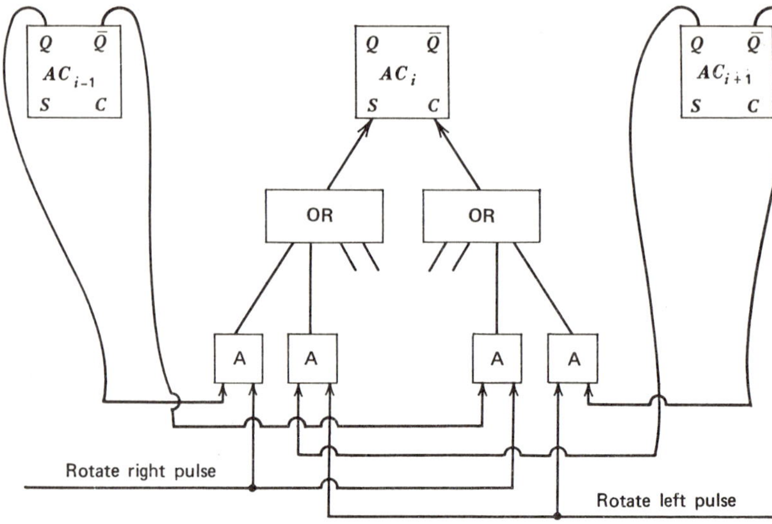

FIGURE 7.26. Left and right shift capability.

The control sequencer for rotation in the first event time is detailed in Fig. 7.27. The other event times are represented as single blocks in the figure. The reader will recall that step 30 is the first step in the operate sequence following the separation of control for input/output instructions. Notice that rotate left and rotate right lines may be generated in the sequencer for each event time. These are connected to OR gates, the outputs of which provide the rotate pulse lines shown in Fig. 7.26.

Example 7.6

Notice that bit $\boldsymbol{IR}_4$ is used in all three event times to separate the rotate right and rotate left control pulses, and that separate control delays are required for shifts in the two directions. Make use of this observation to design an AHPL sequence for rotate which will simplify Fig. 7.27.

Solution. Let us generate a rotate pulse in each event time and use bit IR_4 to distinguish between right and left rotation after the rotate pulse lines from the three event times have converged. For event time 1 we merely replace steps 35–38 by a single step. This process may be repeated in the other two event times. As a pulse leaving the control unit is not assigned an identity as a variable, our simple

30. $\rightarrow ((\overline{\boldsymbol{IR}}_5 \times 31) + (\boldsymbol{IR}_5 \times 35))$

.

.

.

35. $\ell, AC \leftarrow (\overline{\boldsymbol{IR}}_4 \wedge \uparrow(\ell, AC)) \vee (\boldsymbol{IR}_4 \wedge \downarrow(\ell, AC))$

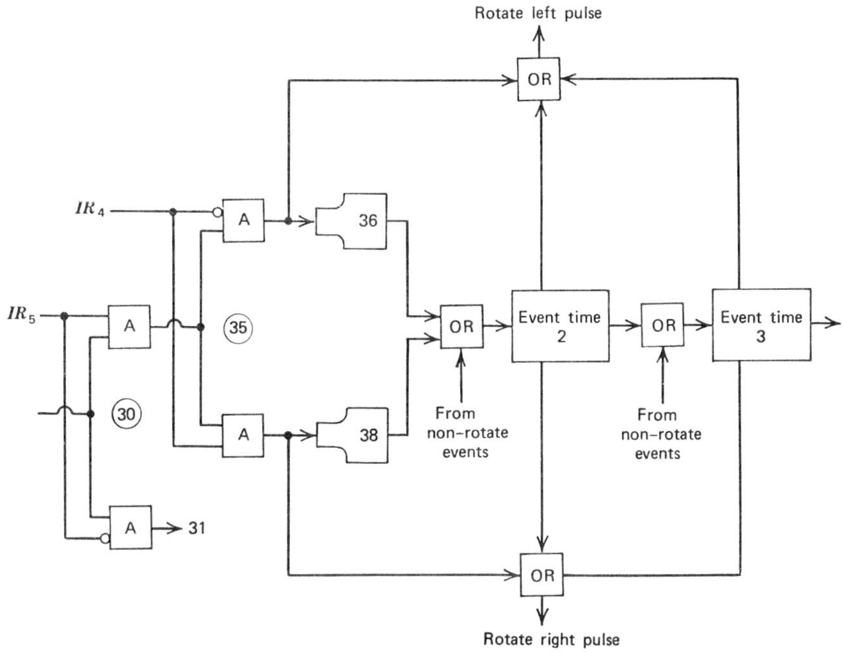

FIGURE 7.27. Rotate control.

system of notation breaks down. Rather than define a translation process, we shall merely present the hardware configuration and suggest it to the reader as a useful technique for certain situations.

The single rotate pulses which emerge at step 35 in event time, and at similar points in the other two event times, converge at an OR gate prior to being separated into left and right rotate pulses by IR_4. This is illustrated in Fig. 7.28. The reader will note that this configuration results in a saving of three control delays, two branching networks, and an OR gate over the network in Fig. 7.27. ∎

Most of the control networks required by operate instructions are similar to those already considered for memory reference instructions. We shall leave further translation of the operate control sequence to the reader.

7.10. ANOTHER FORM OF CONTROL HARDWARE*

The purpose of this section is to explore the possibility of designing a control unit which will issue control levels rather than pulses. The reader will recall from Section 4.9 that there are advantages to using flip-flops featuring a third

* This section is not necessary for continuity. Readers without prior background in clock mode sequential circuits may have some difficulty with the level output control unit.

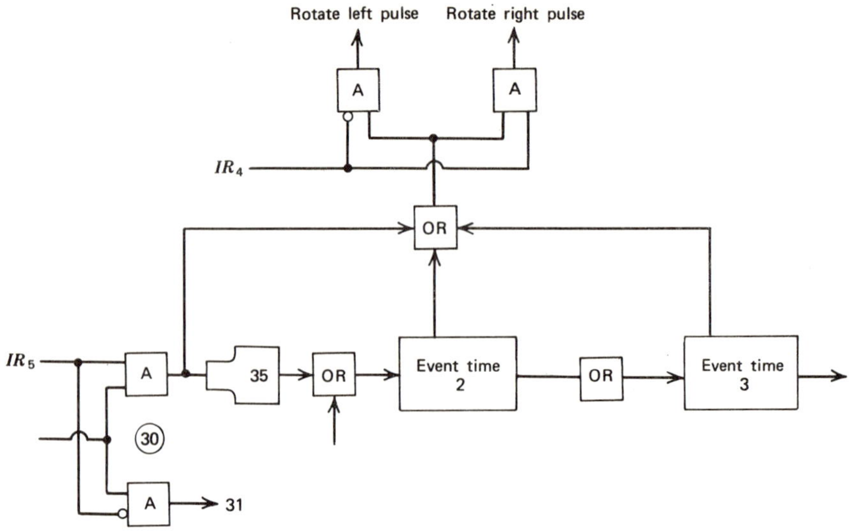

FIGURE 7.28. Alternate rotate control.

input directly connected to a low-impedance clock line. The function of the clock is to trigger into the flip-flops that information which is routed to its inputs by control levels. The very simple control sequence of Section 4.8 will serve as an example for comparing the two forms of control unit.

The sequence of Section 4.8, with two changes, is repeated as follows. Notice that branch statements are now expressed in AHPL rather than FORTRAN.

1. $\rightarrow((\boldsymbol{ready} \times 3) + (\overline{\boldsymbol{ready}} \times 2))$
2. 2 DELAYS, $\rightarrow(1)$

Also, two control delays are inserted in the waiting loop at step 2. A pulse circulating in a loop consisting only of branch instructions is an electronically unstable situation. One delay of the type given in Fig. 7.3 will not suffice,

3. $\boldsymbol{SR} \leftarrow \alpha^8/\boldsymbol{LR}$
4. $\boldsymbol{full} \leftarrow 1$
5. $\boldsymbol{SR} \leftarrow \omega^8/(\alpha^{16}/\boldsymbol{LR})$
6. $\boldsymbol{full} \leftarrow 1$
7. $\boldsymbol{SR} \leftarrow \omega^8/\alpha^{24}/\boldsymbol{LR})$
8. $\boldsymbol{full} \leftarrow 1$
9. $\boldsymbol{SR} \leftarrow \omega^8/\boldsymbol{LR}$
10. $\boldsymbol{full} \leftarrow 1$
11. $\boldsymbol{ready} \leftarrow 0$
12. $\rightarrow(1)$

since the design assumption for that circuit ruled out input pulses in two consecutive clock periods. Clearly, a more complicated control delay, not subject to this assumption, could be designed.

The above control sequence may be translated directly to the control sequencer of Fig. 7.29. The reader will recall that a memory element, ***ready***, was used to allow system *A* to indicate that a word had been placed in ***LR***. A second memory element, ***full***, was provided to signal system *C* that a byte should be taken from ***SR***. Since ***ready*** is sampled by and can be cleared by the control unit, this memory element is shown with the control unit in Fig. 7.29. The data registers, ***SR*** and ***LR***, and the ***full*** indicator are not shown. Intuitively, the string of eight delays for steps 3–10 seems inefficient. Alternatively, a 2-bit counter might have been used to count through the sequence of four transfers from ***LR*** to ***SR***, much the same as was done in multiplication. The design of this version, which will require four less control delays than Fig. 7.29, will be left as a problem for the reader.

Now let us assume that levels, rather than pulses, are required as outputs from the control sequencer. This can be accomplished by replacing the control delays of Fig. 7.29 with master-slave *S-C* memory elements. Figure 7.30 compares the function of these two devices in a control sequencer. Notice that a pulse coinciding with clock pulse 2 appears at the input to the control delay, while a level input overlapping clock pulse 2 appears at the input to the *S-C* memory element. As discussed previously, a pulse appears at the output, Z_1, of the control delay coinciding with clock pulse 3. The situation is similar for the master-slave flip-flop. Since the set input is 1 when clock pulse 2 arrives, this pulse sets the output, Z_2, to 1. Thus the level propagates through the memory element much the same as the pulse propagated through the control delay. The pulse on Z_1 can be used to cause a register transfer. Similarly, the level on Z_2 can be used to route data to the input of a register. These data will then be triggered into the register by clock pulse 3. Since Z_1 coincides with clock pulse 3, the two register transfers would occur at approximately the same time. Notice that the control levels remain 1 for only one clock period. When a control level returns to 0, it causes the control level of the succeeding memory element to be cleared to 0 by the next clock pulse.

Relying on this one-to-one correspondence, we replace the control delays of Fig. 7.29 with master-slave flip-flops to obtain Fig. 7.31. The latter control unit will cause a digital system using clocked flip-flops to function in the same manner as the original system controlled by Fig. 7.29. For clarity, the six memory elements of steps 5–10 have been replaced by a single block, representing six flip-flops, in Fig. 7.31. Also, with the use of master-slave flip-flops, only one such element is required in the waiting loop of steps 1 and 2. The heavy lines in the figure represent connections to the clock.

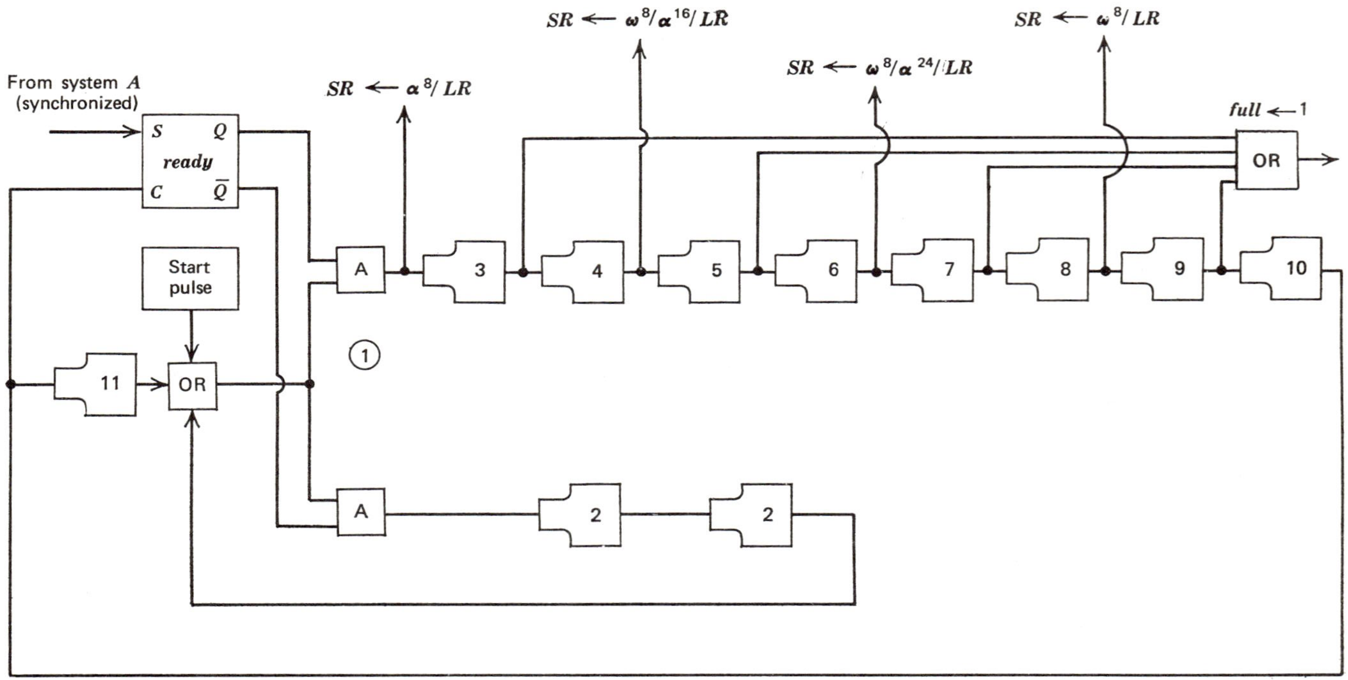

FIGURE 7.29. Control sequencer for word disassembler.

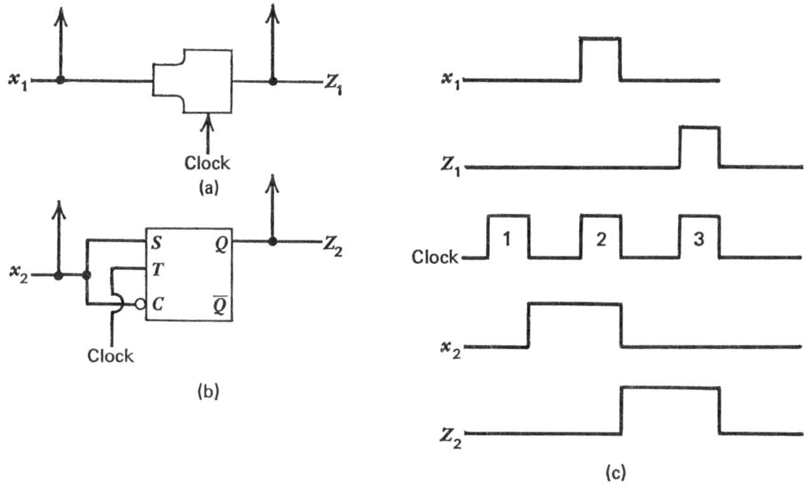

FIGURE 7.30. Replacing control delay with master-slave flip-flop.

The control unit of Fig. 7.31 is a clock-mode sequential circuit. In this form, minimization procedures can formally show the equivalence of sequencers that accomplish the same function. For example, one might reduce the configuration of Fig. 7.31 to coincide with the form mentioned earlier that uses a 2-bit counter.

A minimal-state control unit may be described by reasoning as follows. Of the ten (not counting *ready*) memory elements in Fig. 7.31, one and only one of them will have a 1-output at any given time. Thus the control sequential circuit can reach only ten of the 2^{10} possible states. Therefore, a 10-state (four flip-flops) equivalent control unit is possible. This 10-state control unit is *not necessarily better*, however. While using only four flip-flops this version would contain vastly more combinational logic. At the same time, the one-to-one correspondence between AHPL steps and blocks in the control unit, which can be most helpful in testing and maintenance, is lost. The trade-off between memory elements and combinational logic is ever-present in control unit design. The ultimate in a combinational logic approach is microprogramming, to be discussed in the next chapter.

This section has been included only to emphasize the variety of possible approaches to control unit construction. Many factors, including electronic circuit considerations, will influence a designer's choice of control hardware. From here on, our purpose will be to investigate a variety of digital system organizations. In doing this we shall continue to visualize a pulse-oriented control unit. To avoid going too far afield in this chapter we have included an Appendix as a discussion of the details of implementation of a digital system

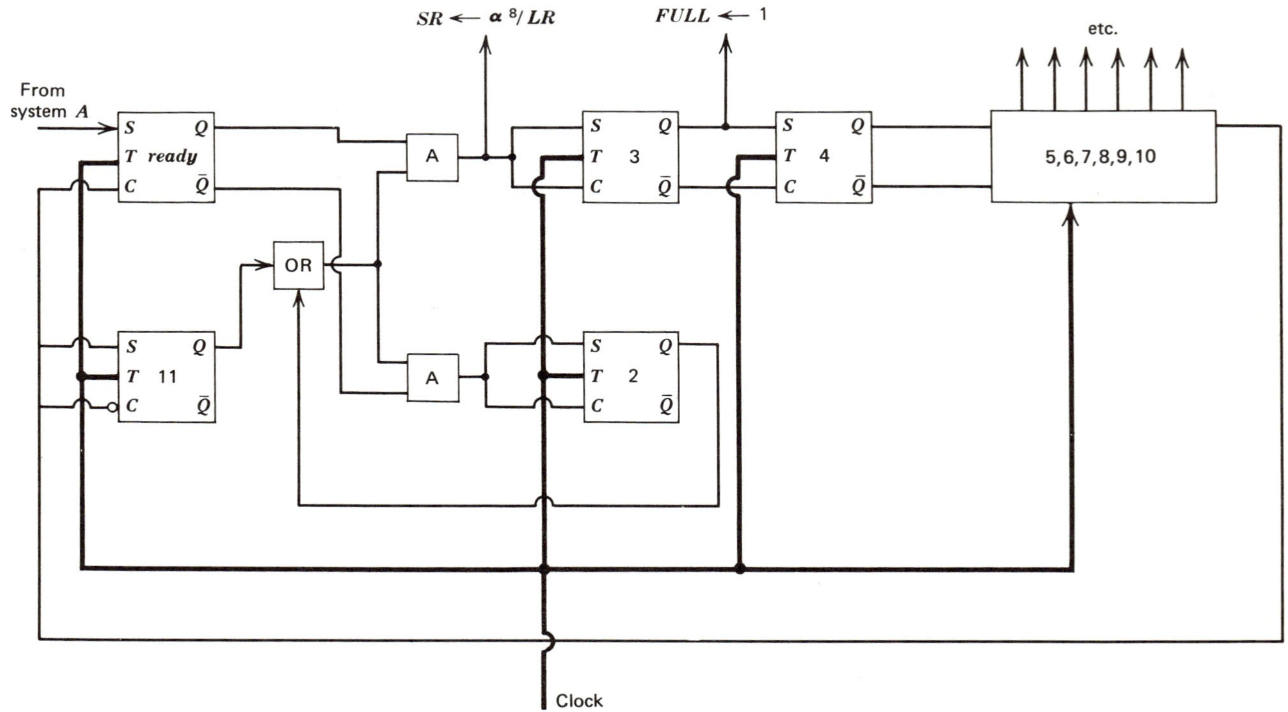

FIGURE 7.31. Level-oriented control unit.

with a level-oriented control unit. The electrical engineer facing an immediate design problem may wish to consider the Appendix at this point.

7.11. SEQUENCES INVOLVING LOOPS

This section will consider a multiplication control sequencer. The detail of the first 10 control instructions will not be shown. The reader should be able to supply this with little difficulty. The situation is the same for steps 19–28, which establish the sign of the result.

Like the instruction list, the control sequencer for accomplishing the actual multiplication is surprisingly simple. The sequencer for steps 11–18 is detailed in Fig. 7.32. The multiplication counter, ***MC***, may be set to zero with a clear pulse on each flip-flop. If counts greater than 18 are considered as don't-cares, a Karnaugh map analysis will show that a count of 18 may be expressed as a function of only two bits, $MC_0 \wedge MC_3$. Four of the five addition delays are not shown in detail. The control pulse will circulate in the feedback loop until all 18 multiplier bits have been considered. Note that a control delay is saved by allowing convergence of control prior to the final control delay of the ADD sequence.

An alternative arrangement in which the result of the addition is placed in the ***AC*** with one transfer pulse, and rotated with a second pulse, would permit

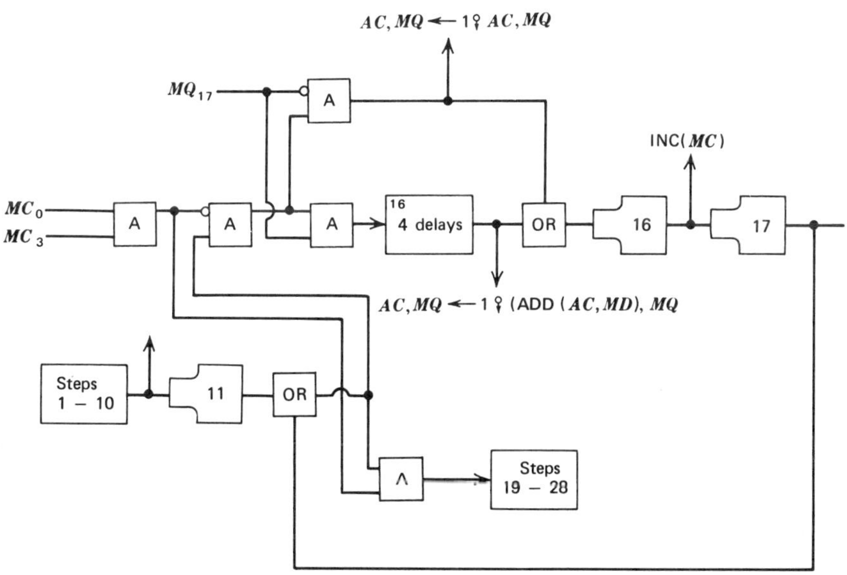

FIGURE 7.32. Multiplication.

control to converge for the rotation operation. This approach is specified by the following instruction sequence.

13. $\leftarrow (\boldsymbol{MQ}_{17} \times 14 + \overline{\boldsymbol{MQ}_{17}} \times 15)$
14. $AC \leftarrow \text{ADD}(AC, MD)$
15. $AC, MQ \leftarrow 1 \updownarrow (AC, MQ)$
16. $MC \leftarrow \text{INC}(MC)$

Example 7.7

Where economy is of first importance, it is possible to accomplish addition serially using only a single full adder. The hardware configuration for this process is shown in Fig. 7.33.

In addition to the full adder, a carry flip-flop to store the carry between the addition of successive pairs of bits, and a 5-bit counter ***ADC*** to keep track of the number of shifts, must be included. The addition is accomplished by adding the least significant bits of ***MD*** and ***AC***, storing the sum in ℓ, the carry in the ***c*** flip-flop and then shifting right. After 18 such shifts the sum will appear in the ***AC***, and any overflow will be stored in ***c***. The following is the control sequence for serial addition

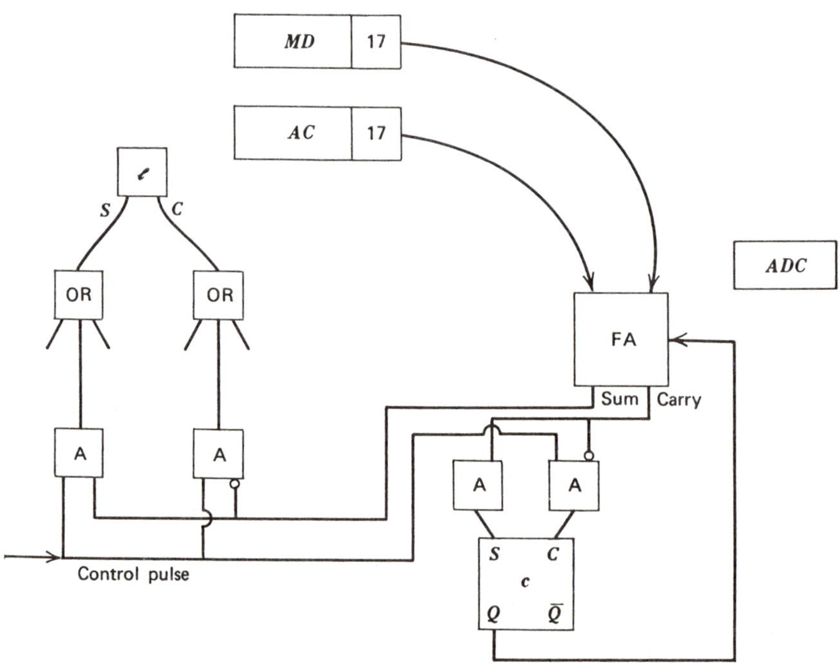

FIGURE 7.33. Serial addition.

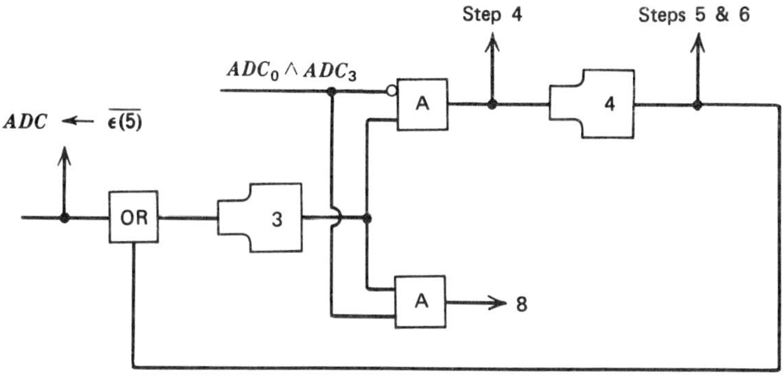

FIGURE 7.34. Serial addition control.

in AHPL. We begin after the operand has been read into the ***MD*** register and control has branched to the first step of the ADD sequence.

1. $c \leftarrow 0; \ell \leftarrow 0$
2. $ADC \leftarrow \overline{\epsilon(5)}$
3. $\perp ADC{:}18, (\geq, <) \rightarrow (8, 4)$
4. $\ell, c \leftarrow \text{SUMF}(AC_{17}, MD_{17}, c), \text{CARRYF}(AC_{17}, MD_{17}, c)$
5. $\ell, AC, MD \leftarrow \updownarrow(\ell, AC), \updownarrow MD$
6. $ADC \leftarrow \text{INC}(ADC)$
7. $\rightarrow (3)$

The control sequencer for serial addition is given in Fig. 7.34. Once again, steps 5 and 6 could have been written on the same line.

The timing system which we have used thus far requires a minimum of two control delays in a closed feedback loop. If master-slave flip-flops are used in all registers, it may be possible to execute the Shift, ADD, and Increment Add Counter all at the same time. The master-slave arrangement assures that the *i*th bits still appear at the outputs of AC_{17} and MD_{17}, to permit reliable completion of the *i*th addition while the next bits are being shifted into these two flip-flops. ∎

For purposes of comparison, we shall assume one clock period per bit of serial addition. We shall let the time delay of a single gate be t_d seconds. Typically a pulse of length $2t_d$ would be required to set a flip-flop. In addition, time must be allowed for propagation through 3 or 4 levels of gating while the clock pulse is 0. Thus a single clock interval would be αt_d sec, where α is about 5 or 6 or more in conservative systems.

For synchronous addition, sufficient time must be allowed for propagation through two levels of gating per bit and one additional clock cycle for updating the accumulator. Thus for an *n*-bit word length, the required delay time for synchronous addition is given by Eq. 7.13.

$$T_{syn} = 2nt_d + \alpha t_d = (2n + \alpha)t_d \tag{7.13}$$

For serial addition, n clock times are required; and the total elapsed time is given by Eq. 7.14. If

$$T_{ser} = n\alpha t_d \tag{7.14}$$

$\alpha = 6$ and $n = 32$, for example, one has

$$T_{syn}(6, 32) = 70t_d \tag{7.15}$$

and

$$T_{ser}(6, 32) = 192t_d$$

For large n we have

$$\lim_{n\to\infty} \frac{T_{syn}}{T_{ser}} = \frac{2}{\alpha} \tag{7.16}$$

In Chapter 11 we shall consider some approaches to increasing the speed of addition. As we shall see, the adder speed is critical since addition is the core of all arithmetic operations. Serial adders have been used in a few minicomputers. They are very common in desk calculators where speed is not critical and where information is stored in serial form, in shift registers or delay lines.

7.12. DECODING NETWORKS

So far we have not discussed a network realization of the frequently-used expression

$$\mathbf{M}^{\perp MA}$$

This expression has appeared on both the left and right side of AHPL statements. We shall see that this expression appearing on the right may be directly replaced by a pair of combinational logic subroutines. No special complications are encountered. The use of $\mathbf{M}^{\perp MA}$ on the left of AHPL statements has provided the only example of variable control of the destination of a register transfer. Some notational problems will appear as we attempt to analyze this situation in more detail.

Proceeding with the simplest case first, we recall from the descriptive treatment of Chapter 3 that a decoding network is a critical part of any memory addressing scheme. A decoding network with n inputs has 2^n outputs. For every combination of values of the n inputs there will be a corresponding output line which will take on the value 1. All other lines will have the value 0. A distinct line will correspond to each combination of values. Two decoding networks are shown in Fig. 7.35.

A simple network of the form of Fig. 7.35a will accomplish the decoding function for a small number of variables. Typically only one inverter will be used for each variable. Separate inverters are shown at the inputs of individual AND gates in Fig. 7.35a to simplify the drawing. A direct extention

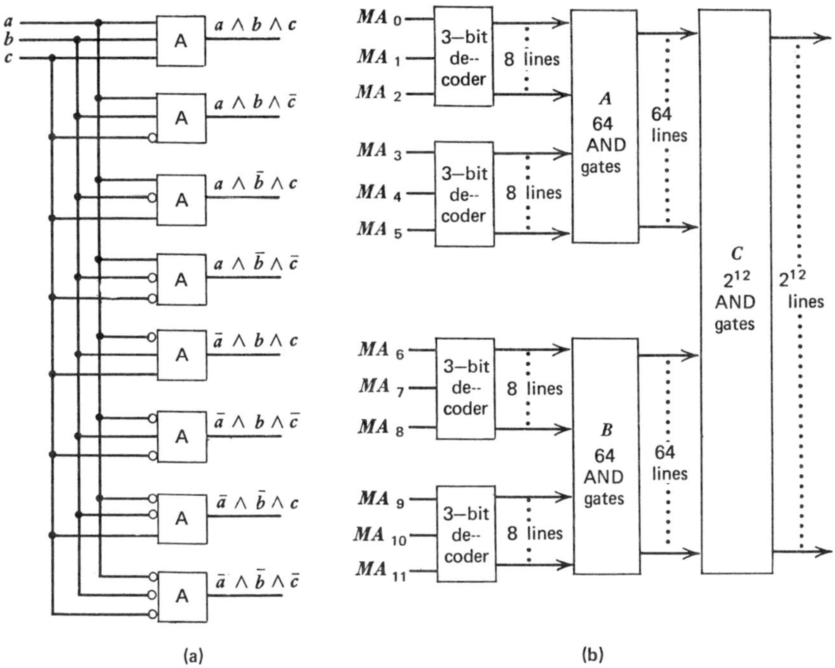

FIGURE 7.35. Decoding networks.

of this type of network for the case of a large number of input lines would be inefficient. The cost of a gate in an LSI network increases almost proportionally to the number of inputs.

Typically, a large decoder will be constructed as shown in Fig. 7.35b. In this particular case a 12-bit memory address register is decoded. The first level of decoding consists of four of the 3-bit decoders shown in Fig. 7.35b. The next level is made up of 2-input AND gates. Each of the 64 output lines of network *A*, for example, comes from an AND gate with a unique pair of input lines, one from the upper 3-bit decoder and one from the lower 3-bit decoder. The situation is similar for networks *B* and *C*. It should be clear that the cost of the first two levels of the decoder is small compared to the cost of the 2^{12} 2-input AND gates in network *C*. In Chapter 8 of Reference [1], it is demonstrated that this is the most economical approach to large decoding networks.

Throughout the book, we shall denote decoding networks by the combinational logic subroutine DECODE. We shall use the same notation for any number of input lines. Separate networks are, of course, required for each distinct set of arguments. A simple version of DECODE, which will realize a network of the form of Fig. 7.35a, is given below. The first line of DECODE specifies the input vector A. The second line recognizes that $2 * \rho A$ (exponentiation) outputs are required.

1. CL SUBROUTINE DECODE (A)
B 2. $\boldsymbol{B} \leftarrow (2 * \rho A)\rho 0$
B 3. $i \leftarrow 0$
4. $\boldsymbol{B}_i \leftarrow \wedge/[(\top i)/\boldsymbol{A}, (\overline{\top i})/\overline{\boldsymbol{A}}]$
B 5. $i \leftarrow i + 1$
B 6. $i:(2 * \rho A), (\geq, <) \rightarrow (7, 4)$
7. $\boldsymbol{DECODE} \leftarrow \boldsymbol{B}$
8. RETURN

Step 4, which generates each of the 2^n outputs individually, is the critical step. At first glance, $(\top i)$ and $(\overline{\top i})$ may seem to be invalid operations in combinational logic subroutines. Note, however, that i is not an argument but a bookkeeping variable. Thus, $(\top i)$ and $(\overline{\top i})$ are merely bookkeeping vectors, which select complemented and uncomplemented literals. We leave it to the reader to trace through the routine for $\rho A = 3$. The result should be a network of the form given in Fig. 7.35a.

There is one further step involved in reading a vector from a memory matrix. The 2^n outputs of the decoding network must be ANDed with each of the 2^n memory vectors. The resulting 2^n vectors are then OR'ed, resulting in the desired word appearing at the input of a memory data register. A tiny portion of the selection network for a semiconductor memory is shown in Fig. 7.36. The first three bits of only two words are shown. The OR gates will actually have 2^n inputs (n is the number of bits in the address register), and would almost certainly be a wired OR gate, as illustrated in Chapter 4.

If we allow $\boldsymbol{Y}$ to be the output vector from a decoder, the following combinational logic subroutine will generate a selection network for the semiconductor memory $\mathbf{M}$. Analysis of this subroutine will be left to the reader.

1. CL SUBROUTINE SELECT ($\mathbf{M}$, $\boldsymbol{Y}$)
B 2. $i \leftarrow 0$
3. $\boldsymbol{Z}^i \leftarrow \boldsymbol{Y}_i \wedge \mathbf{M}^i$
B 4. $i \leftarrow i + 1$
B 5. $i:\rho_2\mathbf{M}, (<, \geq) \rightarrow (3, 6)$
6. $\boldsymbol{SELECT} \leftarrow \vee//\boldsymbol{Z}$
7. RETURN

We now observe, for example, that

$$MD \leftarrow \mathbf{M}^{\perp MA} \tag{7.17}$$

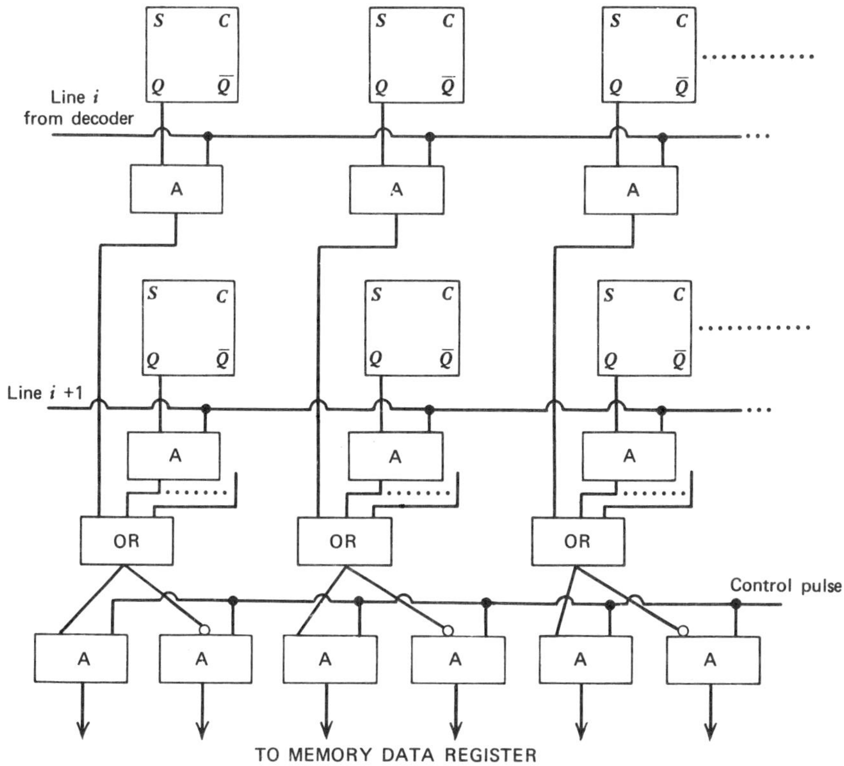

FIGURE 7.36. Memory select.

may be replaced by

$$MD \leftarrow \text{SELECT}\ (\mathbf{M},\ DECODE(MA)) \tag{7.18}$$

The subroutines have been included primarily for completeness. We shall continue to use the abbreviated notation. Subroutines are not particularly suitable for describing large random access memories. The semiconductor memory, as treated in Chapter 4, used the same wires to handle the input and output. Core memories do not use gates in the selection process. Many other electronic economies have been used for which an attempt at subroutine description would be futile. The function of any of these memories may be hidden behind the notation of expression 7.17. As only a few RAM's are included within any system, they may conveniently be treated as special cases.

In later chapters we shall refer to several small but high-speed electronic memory matrices. For such cases expression 7.17 may be correctly interpreted as an abbreviation of expression 7.18.

We now turn our attention to the problem of writing in memory. The same decoding network is almost always used in both the read and write operation. The complication lies with the select process, which must route control pulses in the case of the write operation. Up to this point all transfer statements except $\mathbf{M}^{\perp \boldsymbol{MA}} \leftarrow \boldsymbol{MD}$ have been into a fixed destination register. Which register would receive the data has never been a function of other information in the digital system. Clearly the variable destination statement $\mathbf{M}^{\perp \boldsymbol{MA}} \leftarrow \boldsymbol{MD}$ must be detailed in terms of elementary statements with a similar capability.

Consider the network depicted in Fig. 7.37. It should be evident that this circuit will transfer the contents of register $\boldsymbol{A}$ to either register $\boldsymbol{B}$ or to register C, depending on the value of the function f. If $f = 0$, the destination will be $\boldsymbol{B}$. If $f = 1$, the destination will be $\boldsymbol{C}$. f is the output of some combinational logic network and may be a function of any number of variables.

We introduce the form given in expression 7.19 as the AHPL representation of Fig. 7.37.

$$(\bar{f} * \boldsymbol{B}) \vee (f * \boldsymbol{C}) \leftarrow \boldsymbol{A} \tag{7.19}$$

The notation may be extended to more than one functional value as given by expression 7.20. To hold the proliferation of notational problems in check we require that no more than one of the F_i be 1.

$$(F_1 * \boldsymbol{B}) \vee (F_2 * \boldsymbol{C}) \vee (F_3 * \boldsymbol{D}) \vee (F_4 * \boldsymbol{G}) \leftarrow \boldsymbol{A} \tag{7.20}$$

For single element registers, the notation of expressions 7.19 and 7.20 would be ambiguous. A hardware compiler would require information to

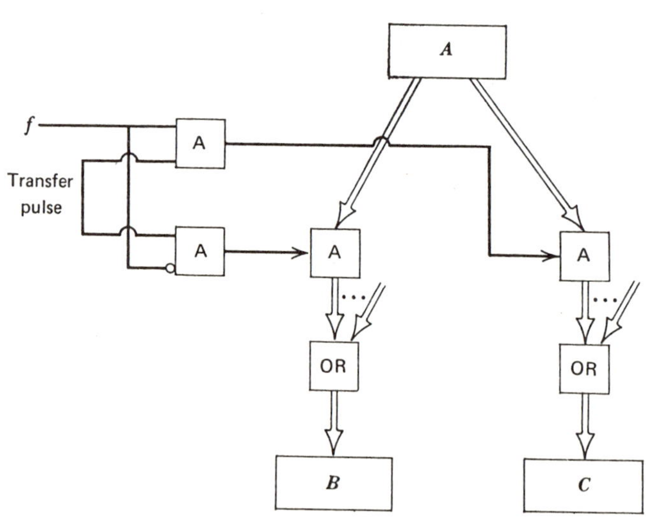

FIGURE 7.37. Variable destination transfer.

distinguish destination memory elements from the controlling functions. As we shall make infrequent use of the notation, we sidestep the problem.

Quite arbitrarily, we extend the notation of expression 7.20 to handle a large number of destination registers by letting

$$\text{DEST } (F, \mathbf{M}) \leftarrow$$

mean

$$(F_0 * \mathbf{M}^0) \vee (F_1 * \mathbf{M}^1) \vee \cdots \vee (F_n * \mathbf{M}^n) \leftarrow$$

Therefore, $\mathbf{M}^{\perp \boldsymbol{MA}} \leftarrow \boldsymbol{MD}$ may be expressed as

$$\text{DEST } (\text{DECODE}(\boldsymbol{MA}), \mathbf{M}) \leftarrow \boldsymbol{MD}$$

It is hoped that the above development has helped the reader to visualize the circuit interpretation of $\mathbf{M}^{\perp \boldsymbol{MA}} \leftarrow \boldsymbol{MD}$. We shall continue to use this abbreviated notation.

The subroutine DECODE which was developed in this section will appear frequently in succeeding chapters.

7.13. A COMPLETE DESIGN EXAMPLE*

So far in Chapters 6 and 7, we have been concerned exclusively with the computer SIC. Because of the scope of this system, it may not have seemed like a single design problem to the reader. The discussion of SIC should, however, have equipped the reader with the tools required to make the design decisions in less complicated systems.

It remains to illustrate how these tools can be applied step-by-step to arrive at the design of a complete digital system. We shall do this in terms of a small priority storage unit which might be used to store a queue of instructions awaiting execution in a large overall system.

Although this priority store would form a part of some larger system, we will design it as a complete self-contained system. We assume that the clocks of this unit may be synchronized with the main system clock, so transfers to and from the priority store are synchronized with internal transfers.

The reader with a special interest in special-purpose systems may wish to consider some of the topics in Chapter 15 after reading the following example.

Example 7.8

A control sequence is designed for a priority store. This system is to provide temporary storage for 32 18-bit words on a priority basis. The left-most 3 bits of

* This section may be omitted without loss of continuity

each word indicate the priority of that word, priority 7 being highest. An input/output data register ***DR*** which can be loaded internally and externally must be provided. Two control flip-flops, ***a*** and ***b***, must also be included. The following status conditions are indicated by the corresponding values of ***a*** and ***b***.

a	***b***	
0	0	idle, waiting for external request
0	1	input data present in ***DR***
1	0	output data desired
1	1	output data available in ***DR***

A memory space becomes available when the word it contains is placed in ***DR***. Words below this space in memory must then he shifted up to fill the space. In this way new words are always entered at the bottom of the stack. When a request is made for data output, the highest priority word available is to be placed in ***DR***. If more than one word of this priority is present, the one nearest the top of the stack is selected.

Two additional control flip-flops are required. If all 32 words in the store are full, a third flip-flop, ***full***, will be set to 1 to discourage requests to input data to the store. If there are no data words in the store, a flip-flop ***empty*** is set to 1 to prevent read requests. We assume that these flip-flops are examined by the external system before a read or write request is made.

Design this system assuming that a relatively slow system response time is tolerable. Add registers and flip-flops as required.

Solution. As usual the first step is to determine a list of all storage devices which will be required in the design. Next we should list the important combinational logic subroutines required. Once these steps have been accomplished, we can proceed to write the control sequence.

For this example most of the rest of the hardware will depend on the approach chosen for the implementation of the 32 word × 18-bit store itself. The number of words in the store (32) falls in the gray area where RAM and register memory overlap, so that a variety of possible approaches might be considered.

First we assume that only a single copy of our system is to be produced so that it would not be economical to design a special LSI (large scale integrated circuit) unit. Of the various approaches using "off the shelf" parts which might be considered, we shall mention only three. The approach which would offer greatest flexibility would use 32 × 18 individual IC flip-flops (2–4 per package). In this way we could connect to the inputs and outputs of individual registers at will. A second approach would be to use a standard small RAM which might be available in the form of two or three IC's on a printed circuit card. A third approach might involve a bank of eighteen 32-bit integrated circuit shift registers. If standard parts are available, either of the latter two approaches will be more economical than the individual flip-flop approach.

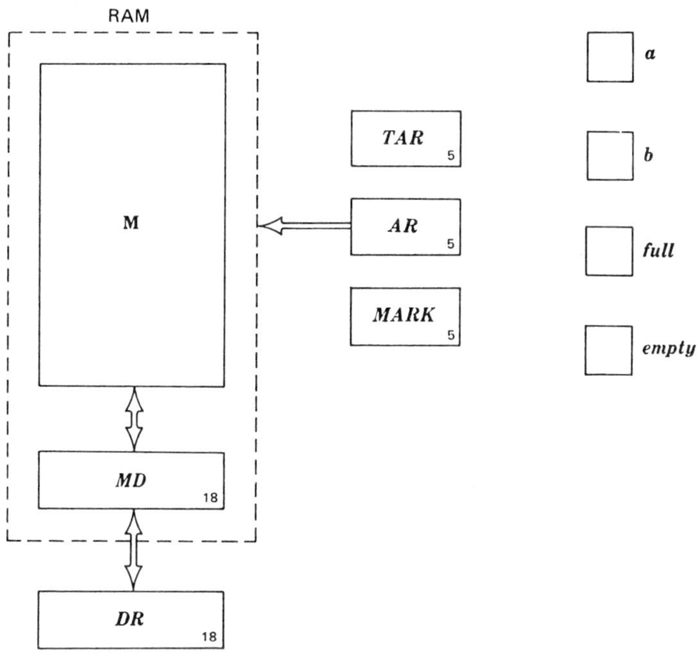

FIGURE 7.38. Storage hardware for priority store.

We now assume that discussions with vendors have led us to select a 32-word RAM as the primary component of our system. With this choice we must accept the usual constraints imposed by a RAM, that data may be entered and received only through the memory data register ***MD***. As shown in Fig. 7.38, ***MD*** is part of the RAM. Addresses must reach the RAM on five level lines as shown. Therefore, an external 5-bit address register, ***AR***, must be provided.

Two additional 5-bit registers are required. The register ***MARK*** contains the address of the first available space at the bottom of the data list. The basic strategy in servicing a READ request will be to store the highest priority word found so far in ***DR***. As the memory is searched from address 0 to $\perp$ ***MARK***, ***DR*** will be updated as higher priority words are found. The 5-bit trial address register ***TAR*** must contain the address of the word in ***DR*** at the end of the search. Data words below this address must be shifted up to fill this space.

For comparing the priority of words in the store we use the combinational logic subroutine LARGER ($\alpha^3/\boldsymbol{MD}$, $\alpha^3/\boldsymbol{DR}$). LARGER = 1 if and only if $\perp\alpha^3/\boldsymbol{MD} > \perp\alpha^3/\boldsymbol{DR}$.

The first three steps in the control sequence implement a one-period loop waiting for a READ or WRITE request. If ***b*** is set to 1 from outside the system, control branches to step 4 to enter the word in ***DR*** at the bottom of the stack. This is accomplished by using the contents of ***MARK*** as the address of the write operation, after which ***MARK*** is incremented.

1. $\rightarrow ((\bar{b} \times 2) + (b \times 4))$
2. $\rightarrow ((\bar{a} \times 3) + (a \times 11))$
3. 1 DELAY $\rightarrow (1)$
4. $MD \leftarrow DR$; $empty \leftarrow 0$
5. $AR \leftarrow MARK$
6. $\mathrm{M}^{\perp AR} \leftarrow MD$
7. $MARK \leftarrow \mathrm{INC}(MARK)$
8. $\rightarrow ((\vee/MARK \times 10) + (\overline{\vee/MARK} \times 9))$
9. $full \leftarrow 1$
10. $b \leftarrow 0, \rightarrow (1)$

Following a WRITE operation it is possible that the stack may contain 32 entries. If so, $MARK = \overline{\epsilon(5)}$. A check is made for this possibility at step 8, and if the stack is indeed full, the flop-flop ***full*** is set to 1 at step 9.

If ***a*** is found to be 1 at step 2, control branches to step 11 to begin service of a READ request. Steps 11–18 accomplish the search for the maximum priority word nearest the top of the stack. This sequence begins with 0's in both ***TAR*** and ***AR*** so that they both point at the first word in memory, as depicted in Fig. 7.39a. Following step 18, the desired word is in ***DR*** and the address of this word is stored in ***TAR***, as depicted in Fig. 7.39b. ***AR*** contains the same address as ***MARK***.

11. $AR \leftarrow \overline{\epsilon(5)}$; $full \leftarrow 0$; $TAR \leftarrow \overline{\epsilon(5)}$
12. $MD \leftarrow \mathrm{M}^{\perp AR}$
13. $DR \leftarrow MD$
14. $AR \leftarrow \mathrm{INC}(AR)$
15. $\rightarrow ((\vee/AR \oplus MARK) \times 16) + (\overline{\vee/AR \oplus MARK} \times 19)$
16. $MD \leftarrow \mathrm{M}^{\perp AR}$
17. $\rightarrow (\mathrm{LARGER}\,(\alpha^3/MD, \alpha^3/DR) \times 18) + (\overline{\mathrm{LARGER}\,(\alpha^3/\mathrm{MD}, \alpha^3/\mathrm{DR})} \times 14)$
18. $DR \leftarrow MD$, $TAR \leftarrow AR$, $\rightarrow (14)$

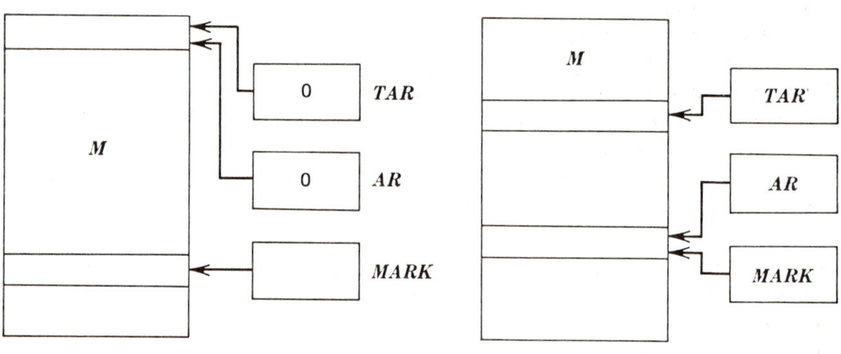

(a) (b)

FIGURE 7.39. Search of stack.

Steps 19–29 shift each word in the stack below the space marked ***TAR*** in Fig. 7.39b up one space. It is possible that the read operation has emptied the stack. If so, ***empty*** is set to 1 at step 29.

19. $AR \leftarrow TAR$
20. $AR \leftarrow \mathrm{INC}(AR)$
21. $\rightarrow ((\vee/AR \oplus MARK) \times 22) + (\overline{\vee/AR \oplus MARK} \times 26)$
22. $MD \leftarrow \mathrm{M}^{\perp AR}$
23. $AR \leftarrow \mathrm{DEC}(AR)$
24. $\mathrm{M}^{\perp AR} \leftarrow MD$
25. $AR \leftarrow \mathrm{INC}(AR); \rightarrow (20)$
26. $AR \leftarrow \mathrm{DEC}(AR)$
27. $MARK \leftarrow AR$
28. $\rightarrow (\vee/MARK \times 30) + (\overline{\vee/MARK} \times 29)$
29. $empty \leftarrow 1$

At step 30 ***b*** is set to one to signal that the requested data word is waiting in ***DR***. Steps 31 and 32 cause control to wait in a loop until the word is removed from ***DR*** and ***a*** and ***b*** reset to 0.

30. $b \leftarrow 1$
31. $\rightarrow ((\overline{a \vee b}) \times 1) + ((a \vee b) \times 32)$
32. 1 DELAY $\rightarrow (31)$ ∎

7.14. SUMMARY

In this chapter we have provided one means by which an AHPL sequence can be interpreted as a computer control unit. In the process we have treated many of the problems which arise in any approach to control unit design. In particular we have considered the details of timing very carefully. Our approach allows us to consider the timing problem only once, rather than coming back to it repeatedly in various situations.

In attempting to adhere to a single standard procedure, we have undoubtedly overlooked many possible circuit economies. Often, possible savings will be a function of the particular technology involved. We take it for granted that a designer would use our approach only to provide a beginning. He would then go on to make changes to achieve the most economical control unit and arithmetic unit consistent with performance specifications.

The order of presentation was chosen for pedagogical reasons. There is nothing sacred about specifying registers, writing the AHPL sequence, and translating to form the control unit, in that order. In practice, several iterations back and forth through these activities may be required before a design is complete.

In the next chapter we shall consider another approach to implementation of a control unit called *microprogramming*. Efficient production methods make microprogramming using read-only memories an attractive approach to economical control unit design. Microprogramming has become almost the standard practice. Hard-wired delay elements, as discussed in this chapter, will continue to be required to control subsequences where many consecutive high-speed register transfers are specified.

PROBLEMS

7.1 A pulse synchronizer circuit is given in Fig. P7.1. Construct a timing diagram for the circuit showing the clock input, the sense pulse, y_3, y_2, y_1, and the output, Z. Verify that the circuit will generate a pulse synchronized with the clock corresponding to each input pulse longer than a clock period.

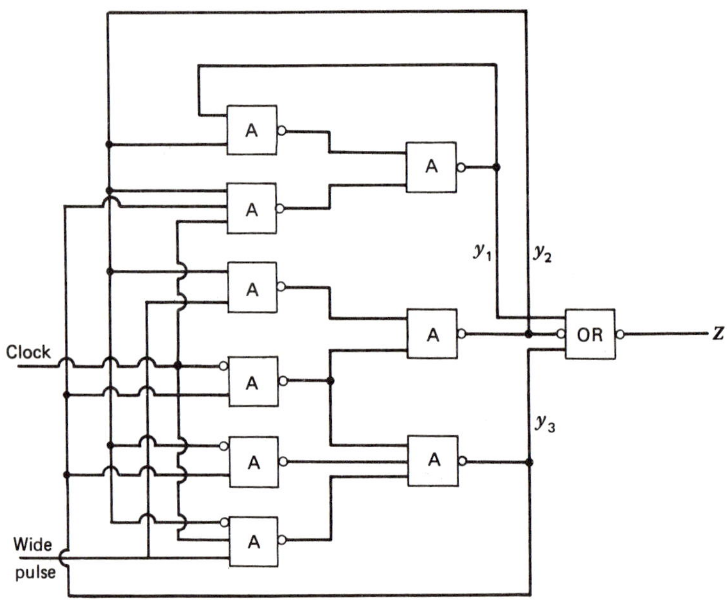

FIGURE P7.1

7.2 What are the implications of using NOR gates to provide for convergence of control rather than OR gates? Redesign the control delay of Fig. 7.3 to accommodate inverted input pulses without increasing the total number of gates.

7.3 Translate the control sequence for the machine tool controller of Example 5.3 into a hardware control sequencer.

7.4 Construct a block diagram of the control sequencer corresponding to the partial control sequence of Example 6.1.

7.5 Construct a block diagram of the control sequencer, for the machine of Problem 6.6, for memory reference instructions.

7.6 Construct a block diagram of the control sequencer for the machine of Problem 6.7.

7.7 Translate the following partial control sequence into a hardware control sequencer.

1. $\boldsymbol{B} \leftarrow \boldsymbol{A}$
2. $\rightarrow ((\boldsymbol{B}_0 \times 3) + (\overline{\boldsymbol{B}}_0 \times 6))$
3. $\boldsymbol{B} \leftarrow$ FUNCTION $(\boldsymbol{B}, \boldsymbol{C})$, WAIT
4. $\rightarrow ((\text{TEST}\ (\boldsymbol{B}) \times 1) + (\overline{\text{TEST}\ (\boldsymbol{B})} \times 6))$
5. $\boldsymbol{C} \leftarrow \mathbf{M}^{\perp \boldsymbol{B}}$, WAIT
6. $\boldsymbol{A} \leftarrow \downarrow \boldsymbol{C}$
7. $\rightarrow (1)$

7.8 Write the combinational logic subroutine for a full adder which uses only two levels of combinational logic in the generation of the sum bit. Construct a logic block diagram.

7.9 A step, $\ell \leftarrow EVEN\ (\boldsymbol{AC})$, in the main AHPL control sequence uses the combinational logic subroutine EVEN. This subroutine generates one bit, which is a 0 if there are an odd number of 1's in the 18 bits in the accumulator. This bit is to be 1 if there are an even number of 1's in $\boldsymbol{AC}$. Write the combinational logic subroutine EVEN. (Hint: Although this is not necessarily the most economical approach, use the following recursive relation: $\boldsymbol{EV}_i$ is 1 if and only if there are an even number of 1's in the vector $\omega^{18-i}/\boldsymbol{AC}$. Then

$$\boldsymbol{EV}_i = \boldsymbol{AC}_i \oplus \boldsymbol{EV}_{i+1}$$

and

$$\boldsymbol{EV}_{17} = \overline{\boldsymbol{AC}_{17}}$$

Indicate bookkeeping steps in the usual manner.

7.10 It is possible to write a combinational logic subroutine to accomplish sign and magnitude multiplication? The results, but not necessarily the method, should be the same as given in Section 6.11. If possible, suggest an approach (write out some sample logical expressions). Is your approach practical?

7.11 The execution of AND and LAC instructions will be more efficient if the control for these instructions is separated from the TAD instruction. Construct the block diagram of the control sequencer associated with these three instructions as three separate branches. Begin your sequencer at a point just prior to the branch into the three mentioned instruction sequences.

7.12 Translate the AHPL sequence of Example 6.3 into a hardware control sequencer.

7.13 Suppose the addition of two 18-bit numbers is to be broken into nine additions of two bits from each number. Thus, the inputs to a double full adder may be considered to be X_n, Y_n, X_{n-1}, Y_{n-1}, and C_{n+1}. Determine, using Karnaugh maps, Boolean expressions for the three outputs of the adder S_n, S_{n-1}, and C_{n-1}. Compare the speed of an arrangement of nine of these units as a synchronous adder with the usual 18-bit synchronous adder. Construct the block diagram of the control sequencer for addition consisting of nine serial operations of one double full adder.

7.14 Construct the block diagram implementing AHPL steps 12–15 of Section 6.8, in which busing is employed.

7.15 Rewrite the control sequence of Example 7.8 substituting a 3 bit register, to store a priority value only, in place of ***DR***. Let ***MD*** be connected to the I/O lines in place of ***DR***.

7.16 (For the student with background in sequential circuits.) Construct a minimal-state equivalent of the level-oriented control sequencer of Fig. 7.31.

7.17 Construct a level-oriented version of the control unit developed in Problem 7.7.

7.18 Write, in AHPL, the control sequence for multiplication in a machine possessing only a serial adder and the necessary registers. Construct a block diagram of the corresponding control sequencer.

7.19 A random sequence generator is driven by an external clock source. The nature of the random generator is unknown except that its only output, z, may change levels only when triggered by an external clock pulse. A pulse will not necessarily cause a level change, however. A special purpose computer is to be designed employing a 1 MHz clock. This computer is to provide an output clock to drive the random process at a frequency of 1 kHz. The computer must also compute the number of level changes in the random process each second. The computer must also compute and display the average number of level changes per second over the first 2^8 seconds following the depression of its start button. Specify the necessary hardware and construct a block diagram of the control sequencer for this special-purpose computer. Accomplish division by shifting.

7.20 What will happen in SIC if the START button is depressed a second time while the computer is in operation? Suggest a remedy for this problem. Sketch the section of interest in the revised control unit.

7.21 Write a combinational logic subroutine which will generate a decoding network similar to the one given in Fig. 7.35a but using only one inverter per literal.

7.22 Write a combinational logic subroutine which will generate the decoding network of Fig. 7.35b.

7.23 Redesign the control sequence which led to Fig. 7.29. Provide a 2-bit counter which will count through the sequence of four byte transfers. At least four control delays should be saved.

REFERENCES

1. Hill, F. J., and Peterson, G. R., *Introduction to Switching Theory and Logical Design*, Wiley, New York, 1968.

2. Goddard, J., "Compiling Combinational Logic Subroutines," M.S. Thesis, University of Arizona, 1971.

3. Gschwind, H. W., *Design of Digital Computers*, Springer-Verlag, New York, 1967.

4. Dietmeyer, D. L., *Logical Design of Digital Systems*, Allyn and Bacon, Boston, 1971.

5. Breuer, M. A., "General Survey of Design Automation of Digital Computers," *Proc. IEEE*, Vol. 54, Dec. 1966, pp. 1708–1721.

6. Gerace, G. B., "Digital System Design Automation—A Method of Designing a Digital System as a Sequential Network System, *IEEE Trans. Computers*, Vol. C-17, Nov. 1968, pp. 1044–1061.

8

Microprogramming

8.1. INTRODUCTION

The concept of a microprogram was first presented by M. V. Wilkes of Cambridge University Mathematical Laboratory in 1951 [1, 2, 3, 4]. This may seem particularly remarkable if one recalls that the vacuum tube and the relay were the only switching devices available at that time. This was only eight years after the introduction of the first electrical computing machine, which incidently utilized the relay as the principal component. The concept was utilized infrequently until the introduction of the IBM System 360 in 1964. All but the fastest and most sophisticated model in the 360 series relied on microprogramming in the control unit design. A primary reason for this approach was to permit reasonably efficient emulation of earlier IBM computers on the System 360. The assurance that existing customer programs could be used directly on the new computer was no doubt a valuable marketing technique for IBM.

In Chapter 6 we learned to express the control function for a digital system as a sequence of AHPL steps very much like a program. Why not store this program in some type of memory and read the AHPL steps out in program sequence? Each time such an AHPL step is read it could cause a branch (within the AHPL program) or a register transfer within the computer. This is microprogramming. In effect the control unit of a microprogrammable computer consists principally of a memory rather than a large network of control delays. Most often this memory will be a read-only memory (ROM).

The instructions stored in the ROM are called *microinstructions*. Each microinstruction corresponds to an AHPL step. Usually a ROM will be cheaper than a read-write memory with the same access time.

In addition to possible economy, other advantages of a microprogram include the possibility of modifying the instruction code and the apparent architecture of the machine. Also, a ROM may make possible cheaper storage and faster execution of frequently used subroutines such as multiplication, division, and, in the case of scientific applications, trigonometric functions. In the early stages of the design process the designer must carefully weigh the above factors against certain drawbacks, to be pointed out in succeeding sections, in the context of the intended application for his proposed computer. He will then decide to what extent, if any, he will utilize microprogramming in the design of the control unit.

8.2. CONTROLLING THE MICROPROGRAM

It is easy to say "store the AHPL program in read-only memory," but how is this done? There are two basic problems we must consider. First, some correspondence must be established between the vectors of 1's and 0's which can be stored in memory and the AHPL program steps. Second, we must control the reading of program steps from memory and their execution. Clearly it is impossible to avoid including a certain amount of hard-wired control circuitry.

In Fig. 8.1a we see a simplified diagram of the essential items of SIC hardware. The items of hardware which would be found in a microprogrammable version of SIC are shown in Fig. 8.1b. The most important observation to make from Fig. 8.1 is that the two versions of SIC are identical except for the control units. Even the terminal characteristics of the control unit are the same. That is, precisely the same sequence of transfer pulses appear on the same control lines in both versions. Only the means by which these control signals are generated is different.

The performance similarity of microprogrammed machines and non-microprogrammed machines should not be pushed too far. The control sequences for the two machines of Fig. 8.1 must necessarily be identical as both machines were defined to be SIC. This is not to say that the type of control unit, microprogrammed or hard-wired, will not influence the layout of the other parts of a digital system. As we shall see in subsequent sections, the choice of a microprogrammable control unit of realistic cost will impose certain constraints on the form of a control sequence which can be implemented. These constraints are not imposed by a hard-wired control sequencer.

The control sequencer of Fig. 8.1a is replaced by a ROM, two registers

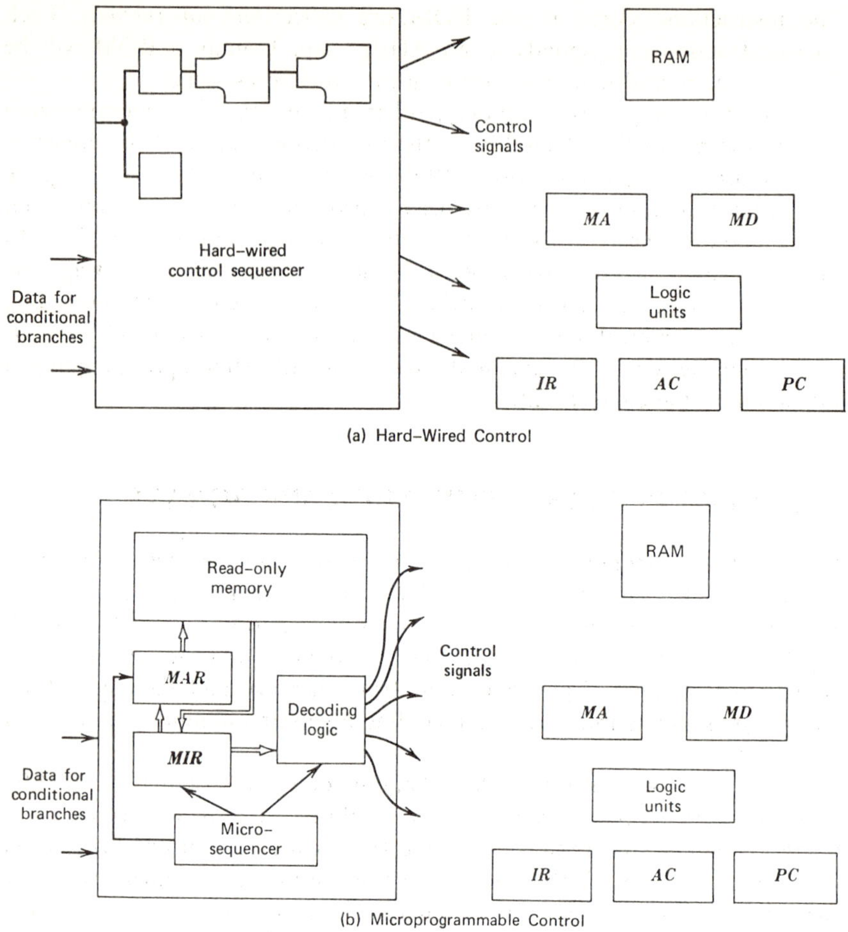

FIGURE 8.1. Two types of control unit.

MAR and ***MIR***, a *micro sequencer*, and a network of decoding logic. Much of this chapter is devoted to demonstrating how these components might function as a control unit. The microsequencer is a small hard-wired control sequencer. This is necessary to facilitate the transfer of vectors between the ROM, ***MIR***, and ***MAR*** within the control unit. Only instructions are stored in the read-only memory.* Therefore, a word may be read from the ROM directly into the

* For some machines this constraint is modified to permit the reading of constants from the ROM.

microinstruction register, ***MIR***. No special memory data register for the read-only memory is required. ***MIR*** stores the microinstruction currently being executed. This microinstruction will either cause a transfer pulse to be issued from the control unit or will cause a branch within the control sequence. The *microaddress register*, ***MAR***, functions as both a program counter and an address register for the read-only memory. Again this is possible because every address is the address of an instruction. The reader may observe that a microprogrammable control unit is almost a computer within a computer.

There are inputs to the control unit, which serve to control conditional branches within the *microprogram*. Very often these lines, which are shown in Fig. 8.1b, come from the instruction register, ***IR***.

It is the decoding logic of Fig. 8.1b, in conjunction with the microsequencer, which makes it possible to interpret the vector in ***MIR*** as an AHPL step. Our approach here will be to gradually uncover the structure of these units and the reasons why they are so structured. We will not start by showing all the details of the coding of a microinstruction, but rather will specify these details only as they arise naturally in the discussion.

In general, the execution of a microinstruction is a two-step process:

1. Place a word from the ROM in ***MIR***.
2. Issue a control pulse and/or update ***MAR***.

If no asynchronous transfers are specified, two clock periods are required per microinstruction. By contrast, in a machine with a hard-wired control sequencer, synchronous transfers require only one clock period; and branches within the control sequence require no clock periods. Various sophistications can be added to lessen the time penalty inherent in microprogramming. We shall see in Section 8.4 that the penalty is less severe in bus oriented machines. It is safe to say that a machine with a hard-wired sequencer can always be made to operate faster than an apparently identical machine which employs microprogramming.

There are three basic types of microinstructions which must be separated by the microsequencer. These are branch operations, synchronous transfers, and asynchronous transfers. We assume that if $\boldsymbol{MIR}_0 = 1$, the microinstruction is a branch. If $\boldsymbol{MIR}_0 = 0$, the microinstruction calls for a register transfer. For transfer microinstructions $\boldsymbol{MIR}_1 = 0$ indicates synchronous transfers, and $\boldsymbol{MIR}_1 = 1$ indicates asynchronous transfers.

Because of the above alternatives, the *microcontrol sequence*, i.e., the sequence which is executed by the microsequencer to control the execution of a microinstruction, will require more than two steps. The basic form of the microsequence is listed below. The corresponding microsequencer is illustrated in Fig. 8.2. It controls the functioning of the control unit.

1. $MIR \leftarrow \mathbf{ROM}^{\perp MAR}$

2. $\rightarrow (MIR_0 \times 3 + \overline{MIR}_0 \times 5)$

Branch 3. $MAR \leftarrow$ WHAT(MIR, data outside control unit)

4. $\rightarrow (1)$

5. $\rightarrow (MIR_1 \times 6 + \overline{MIR}_1 \times 8)$

Asynchronous Transfer 6. $MAR \leftarrow$ INC(MAR);
DEST (MIR) $\leftarrow$ ORIG(MIR), WAIT

7. $\rightarrow (1)$

Synchronous Transfer 8. $MAR \leftarrow$ INC(MAR);
DEST(MIR) $\leftarrow$ ORIG(MIR)

9. $\rightarrow (1)$

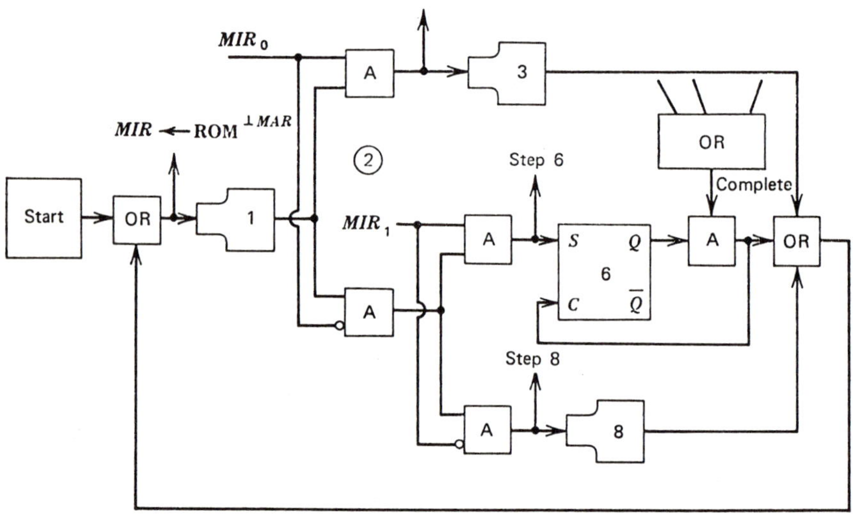

FIGURE 8.2. Minimal microsequencer.

In the above microsequence WHAT, DEST, and ORIG figuratively represent combinational logic subroutines which decode the bits in ***MIR***. Step 1 causes the microinstruction stored at the address specified by ***MAR*** to be read from the read-only memory matrix, **ROM**. Step 2 causes a branch in the microsequence to separate branch- and transfer-type microinstructions. Step 5 is a branch which separates synchronous and asynchronous transfers.

Step 3 executes a branch-type microinstruction by placing a new address in ***MAR***. Note that a branch in the control sequence (but not the microsequence) now consumes a finite number of clock periods (2), much the same as an assembly language branch. The subroutine representation WHAT merely indicates the formation of an address vector as a function of bits in ***MIR*** and information stored in registers outside of the control unit. If the branch is unconditional, a subset of the bits in ***MIR*** would most likely be transferred directly to ***MAR***. The unconditional branch is illustrated in Example 8.1. Further treatment of the more complicated conditional branches will wait until the next section.

Example 8.1

Suppose that the addresses at which microinstructions are stored in the **ROM** are the binary equivalents of the numbers of the corresponding AHPL steps. Thus the AHPL step

$$\rightarrow (67)$$

might be represented by the microinstruction

1XXXXX000001000011

The five bits represented by X will be specified so as to indicate that the branch was unconditional. When the above vector is read into ***MIR***, the decoding network will sense from these five bits that the branch was unconditional and cause the rightmost 12 bits to be placed in ***MAR***. The 12 bits are the binary equivalent of 67. The next microinstruction to be read from the ROM will come from location 67. ∎

Notice that steps 6 and 8 of the microsequence are identical except that "WAIT" is appended to step 6. The significance of this difference is apparent in Fig. 8.2. Each time an asynchronous transfer is initiated, memory element 6 is set to 1. All completion pulses from asynchronous operations are routed to the single OR gate labeled "COMPLETE" in the figure. By contrast, control delay 8 allows one clock period for every synchronous transfer.

The functions of pulses which leave the microsequencer at points 6 and 8 are not yet clear. From the listed microsequence we see that one function of these pulses is to increment ***MAR*** to the address of the next instruction in sequence. In addition they pass through the microinstruction decoding network, emerging on one of the control lines leaving the control unit. The bits of the microinstruction in ***MIR*** must in some way specify which transfer is to be executed. This transfer is symbolized by expression 8.1. Somehow the bits in ***MIR*** must be used to select the register (or bus or logic unit) which will

$$\text{DEST}(\boldsymbol{MIR}) \leftarrow \text{ORIG}(\boldsymbol{MIR}) \tag{8.1}$$

serve as the origin of the vector to be transferred. This selection is symbolized by ORIG(***MIR***). Similarly the register to receive the vector must be specified by bits in ***MIR*** as expressed by DEST(***MIR***). In effect both choices are made as the decoding network for ***MIR*** causes the transfer pulse to leave the control unit on the correct one of the large number of possible control lines.

Example 8.2

In small microprogrammable machines the number of transfers which can take place at any point in the control sequence may be fewer than the number of bits in ***MIR***. In this case, each bit of ***MIR*** can correspond to a distinct transfer. Then the portion of the decoding network which routes transfer pulses becomes trivial. Suppose that the last few bits of ***MIR*** specify transfers as given in Fig. 8.3a. The

$$\begin{array}{ll} \text{If } MIR_{17} = 1 & A \leftarrow B \\ \text{If } MIR_{16} = 1 & A \leftarrow C \\ \text{If } MIR_{15} = 1 & D \leftarrow E \end{array}$$

(a)

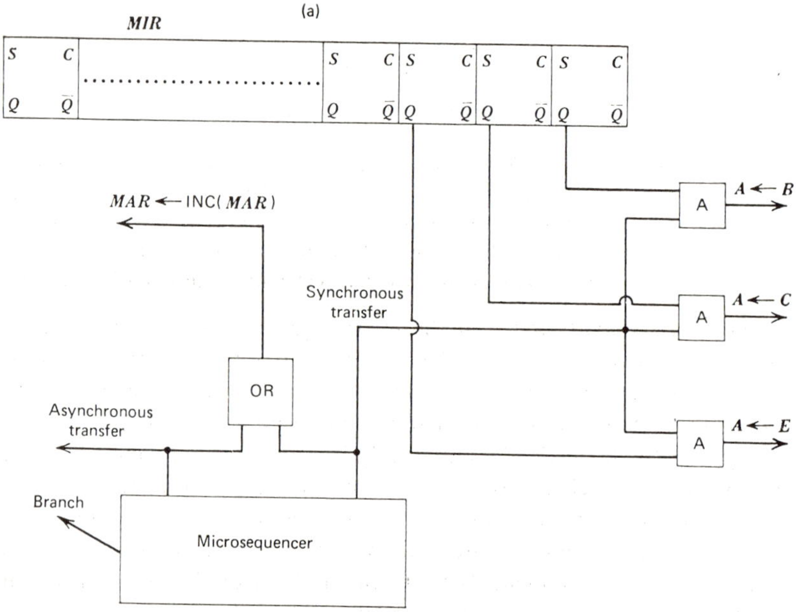

(b)

FIGURE 8.3. Typical synchronous transfers.

portion of the microprogrammable control unit which effects these three particular transfers is depicted in Fig. 8.3b. The microsequencer of Fig. 8.2 is represented by a single block in Fig. 8.3b. ▮

Let us visualize once again the control unit as a sequential circuit. In a microprogrammable control unit the number of states is fixed as the product of the number of states of ***MIR***, the number of states of ***MAR***, and the four states of the microsequencer. Since the contents of the ROM are not altered in the course of the execution of a microprogram, the ROM has only one fixed state. The ROM really represents an array of combinational logic which, in conjunction with the decoding network, specifies the output and next state of the control unit as a function of the present state.

A microprogrammable control unit is a close approximation of a minimal-state control unit. Correspondingly, the amount of combinational logic required is very large. Combinational logic is least expensive when in the form of a read-only memory. The uniformity of the ROM makes possible many efficiencies in the manufacturing process. Consequently the principal advantage of a microprogrammable control unit is economy. Another possible advantage of microprogramming is that the control sequence can be altered by substituting sections of the read-only memory.* It is likely, however, that this option is discussed in the literature far more than it is exercised in practice.

8.3. A MICROPROGRAMMED SIC

We have laid the basis for the discussion of a fairly sophisticated microprogrammable control unit as might be used in a System 360 or 370. As we shall see, economics dictates a stripped down version for a machine as small as SIC. There are no conceptual problems associated with using the control unit of Fig. 8.1b in any machine. It is instructive to investigate the microprogramming of a complete machine. We therefore use SIC, which we already have well in mind.

For the present, busing and indexing will be disregarded. The ROM word length will be the same as for main memory, 18 bits. There is no necessity for the two memories to have the same word length since they are completely independent, but 18 bits turns out to be adequate for this simple machine. We will assume that the access time of the ROM is approximately as long as a single clock period. The clock frequency has been chosen so that a single register transfer can conveniently be accomplished in a single clock period. The validity of our assumption will depend on the particular technologies chosen for the ROM and the high-speed registers. One would expect this situation to characterize certain cases where a very large cheap ROM is employed.

Under the assumed timing constraints, we conclude that the steps making up the individual event times for the operate instructions should not be stored

* The control memory is not always a read-only memory. If a read-write memory is used, the control sequence can be very easily modified. In this case these modifications are much more likely to be made. For example, a special control sequence could be placed in the control memory for purposes of diagnostic testing of the system.

in the ROM. Since only one register transfer is executed during each event time, we conclude that an entire operate instruction can be executed in less time than one access to the ROM. Thus we shall include a hard-wired control sequence to execute the operate instructions.

We shall depart from the principal control sequence as described in Figs. 6.5 and 6.7 only to the extent that control will branch to accomplish the LAC, AND, and TAD operations of step 14 in separate steps and the JMS and DAC operations of step 21 in separate steps. At the end of our discussion we shall find reasons to criticize the approach used here. In Section 8.4 we shall move on to consider an approach more typical of actual practice.

Let us consider first the branch operations within the control sequence. Each such branch is either unconditional or is determined by some Boolean

MIR_1	MIR_2	MIR_3	MIR_4	Branch Function, f
0	0	0	0	UNCONDITIONAL
0	0	0	1	IR_1
0	0	1	0	IR_2
0	0	1	1	IR_3
0	1	0	0	IR_4
0	1	0	1	IR_0
0	1	1	0	$IR_0 \wedge IR_1$
0	1	1	1	$IR_1 \wedge IR_2$
1	0	0	0	$IR_0 \wedge IR_1 \wedge IR_2$
1	0	0	1	$IR_1 \vee IR_2$
1	0	1	0	$\vee/MD$
1	0	1	1	
1	1	0	0	
1	1	0	1	
1	1	1	0	
1	1	1	1	

(a)

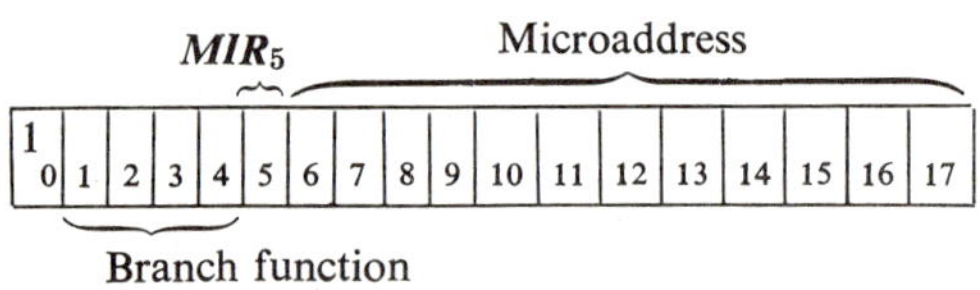

Branch to microaddress if and only if

$$f \oplus MIR_5 = \bar{f} \wedge MIR_5 \vee f \wedge \overline{MIR_5} = 1$$

(b)

FIGURE 8.4. Branch operations.

function of the instruction bits or, in one case, a function of the bits in ***MD***. The reader can satisfy himself that all branch operations in the control sequence of Section 6.5 are specified by one of the Boolean functions listed in the right-most column of Fig. 8.4a. Counting the unconditional branch, there are eleven branch functions in all. Thus these functions can be identified by four information bits. These bits can be inserted in the microinstructions stored in the ROM. They are decoded as bits $\boldsymbol{MIR}_1$, $\boldsymbol{MIR}_2$, $\boldsymbol{MIR}_3$, and $\boldsymbol{MIR}_4$ in the microinstruction register. Bit $\boldsymbol{MIR}_0$ is used to distinguish between branch and transfer microinstructions. If $\boldsymbol{MIR}_0 = 0$, it is a transfer; and if $\boldsymbol{MIR}_0 = 1$, it will be a branch. We are separating branch and transfer instructions in this example primarily for convenience of explanation.

Every branch in the main SIC control sequence of Section 6.5 is bidirectional, with one of the two possible next steps following immediately after the branch instruction in sequence. Thus we need only specify the branch function, f, the location of the alternate next step which does not follow in sequence, and a bit to assign functional values (1 or 0) to the two alternatives. If and only if the function, f, and the bit $\boldsymbol{MIR}_5$ have opposite values, control branches to the address specified. That is, $\boldsymbol{MIR}_5 = 0$ indicates that a jump will take place if the branch function is satisfied. $\boldsymbol{MIR}_5 = 1$ indicates a jump when the branch function is not satisfied. If $f = \boldsymbol{MIR}_5$, control passes to the next microinstruction in sequence. In effect we can use each function listed in Fig. 8.4 or its complement to specify a branch. As only eleven branch functions are found in an elementary SIC, five branch codes are unused in Fig. 8.4a. The complete branch instruction word is given in Fig. 8.4b. Since 12 bits are allowed to specify the microaddress, as many as 2^{12} instructions in the ROM can be reached by a branch.

The 14 transfer operations which occur within the sequence of Section 6.5 are tabulated in Fig. 8.5. The order of listing of these transfers is arbitrary. Since the number of transfers is fairly small, we assign a bit of the microinstruction to specify each transfer. This technique is often used in small machines employing a transformer ROM, so as to simplify the decoding of the microinstruction.

In addition to the transfer bits, the left-most three bits of ***MIR*** have a special function. $\boldsymbol{MIR}_0$ must be 0 to indicate a transfer microinstruction. If bit $\boldsymbol{MIR}_1 = 1$, the transfer is asynchronous. If bit $\boldsymbol{MIR}_1$ is 0 and $\boldsymbol{MIR}_2$ is 1, an operate instruction is to be executed. The microsequencer must wait while the operate instruction is accomplished by a hard-wired sequencer. If $\boldsymbol{MIR}_2 = 0$, the remaining bits in the table will cause the corresponding transfers to be accomplished. One bit in the 18-bit ROM word is left unused.

Using the tables of Figs. 8.4 and 8.5, we can translate the AHPL instructions of Section 6.5 into microcode form for storage in read-only memory. A program to accomplish this task would be somewhat less complicated than the

Transfer Operation	Specifying Bit in *MIR*
$MA \leftarrow PC$	3
$MD \leftarrow \mathrm{M}^{\perp MA}$	4
$IR \leftarrow MD$	5
$MA \leftarrow \omega^{13}/IR$	6
$\omega^{13}/IR \leftarrow \omega^{13}/MD$	7
$AC \leftarrow MD$	8
$AC \leftarrow MD \wedge AC$	9
$l,AC \leftarrow \mathrm{ADD}(MD,AC)$	10
$MD \leftarrow \mathrm{INC}(MD)$	11
$\mathrm{M}^{\perp MA} \leftarrow MD$	12
$PC \leftarrow \mathrm{INC}(PC)$	13
$MD \leftarrow AC$	14
$MD \leftarrow 00000, \mathrm{INC}(PC)$	15
$PC \leftarrow \omega^{13}/IR$	16
UNUSED	17

(a)

MIR_0	MIR_1	MIR_2	Type of Transfer
0	0	0	Synchronous transfer
0	0	1	Wired operate instruction execution
0	1	0	Asynchronous transfer
0	1	1	IOT TRANSFER (IGNORED)

(b)

FIGURE 8.5. Transfer microinstructions.

hardware compiler proposed in Chapter 7. It would merely be required to generate a coded version of each AHPL instruction. Since address assignment would not be required, this program would, in that respect, be simpler than an assembler. An example of the assembly of a short sequence is given in Fig. 8.6. The vertical lines separate the six branch description bits from the 12 address bits in the case of branch microinstructions. The three bits which describe the type of transfer are similarly separated from the 15 bits which specify individual transfers.

Line 19, for example, is a synchronous transfer, so bits MIR_0, MIR_1, and MIR_2 are all zero. The particular transfer is specified by $MIR_{13} = 1$, in agreement with Fig. 8.5a. Line 20 is an unconditional branch, so the left-most five bits of the microinstruction are 10000. The address is 25, as we assume

AHPL Instruction	Microcode
16. $MD \leftarrow \mathrm{INC}(MD)$	000 | 000 000 001 000 000
17. $\mathrm{M}^{\perp MA} \leftarrow MD$	010 | 000 000 000 100 000
18. $\rightarrow (\overline{\vee/MD} \times 19 + (\vee/MD) \times 25)$	110 100 | 000 000 011 001
19. $PC \leftarrow \mathrm{INC}(PC)$	000 | 000 000 000 010 000
20. $\rightarrow (25)$	100 000 | 000 000 011 001

FIGURE 8.6. Example of microcode assembly.

that the microinstructions are stored in the ROM locations corresponding to the step numbers.

The microcontrol sequencer required to execute the microinstructions of Figs. 8.4 and 8.5 will be a somewhat modified version of Fig. 8.2. The microcontrol sequence follows. We leave it for the reader to translate this sequence to hardware. A particular modification of Fig. 8.2 is that the ROM read operation given in step 1 must be controlled asynchronously. The reader will recall that for this example a less expensive but slower ROM was assumed which required five clock periods for a read operation.

Step 2 separates control for branch and transfer operations. The branching sequence begins at step 2. Whether a branch is actually executed depends on a Boolean function, g, which is easily understood although it contains a large number of terms. The four bits MIR_1, MIR_2, MIR_3, and MIR_4, which identify the branch condition functions, must be decoded to form all 16 minterms (only 11 are used). Each conjunction of one of these minterms with the

1. $MIR \leftarrow \mathrm{ROM}^{\perp MAR}$
2. $\rightarrow (MIR_0 \times 3 + \overline{MIR_0} \times 5)$
3. $MAR \leftarrow (\bar{g} \wedge \mathrm{INC}(MAR)) \vee (g \wedge \omega^{12}/MIR)$
4. $\rightarrow (1)$
5. $\rightarrow (((\overline{MIR_1} \wedge \overline{MIR_2}) \times 9) + (MIR_1 \times 11) + (MIR_2 \times 6))$
6. $\rightarrow$ (OPERATE SEQUENCE), WAIT
7. $MAR \leftarrow \mathrm{INC}(MAR)$
8. $\rightarrow (1)$
9. $MAR \leftarrow \mathrm{INC}(MAR)$; $\mathrm{DEST}(MIR) \leftarrow \mathrm{ORIG}(MIR)$
10. $\rightarrow (1)$
11. $MAR \leftarrow \mathrm{INC}(MAR)$; $\mathrm{DEST}(MIR) \leftarrow \mathrm{ORIG}(MIR)$, WAIT
12. $\rightarrow (1)$

corresponding condition function (exclusive-OR'ed with MIR_5) calls for a branch when equal to 1. We thus write g as given by Eq. 8.2. The first term of g represents the unconditional branch, so only the MIR bits appear. The second term expresses the branch which depends on IR_1 as given by line 2 of Fig. 8.4a.

$$\begin{aligned} g = {} & (\overline{MIR}_1 \wedge \overline{MIR}_2 \wedge \overline{MIR}_3 \wedge \overline{MIR}_4) \\ & \vee (\overline{MIR}_1 \wedge \overline{MIR}_2 \wedge \overline{MIR}_3 \wedge MIR_4 \wedge (IR_1 \oplus MIR_5)) \\ & \quad \vdots \\ & \vee MIR_1 \wedge \overline{MIR}_2 \wedge MIR_3 \wedge \overline{MIR}_4 \wedge ((\vee/MD) \oplus MIR_5) \end{aligned} \tag{8.2}$$

Notice that MIR_5 specifies whether the branch will occur if IR_1 is 1 or whether it will occur when IR_1 is 0. Also shown is the term corresponding to the last jump condition listed in Fig. 8.4a. The reader is left to use this table to supply the remaining terms.

The first of the three types of transfer operations is listed at step 6. This step represents the complete hardware sequencer for the execution of an operate instruction. Following this sequence, control branches to step 7 to increment ***MAR***. It is still not convenient to detail the complete logic for the transfer instructions in the control sequence. In effect, the ORIG subroutine represents a complex branching network to route pulses to appropriate points to accomplish the various register transfers.

Only three of the transfers listed in Fig. 8.5a are asynchronous. We shall therefore illustrate a portion of the selection network for this case in Fig. 8.7. The synchronous case is left to the reader. Bits 4, 10, and 12 route the initiate pulse to cause the READ, ADD, and WRITE operations, respectively, to

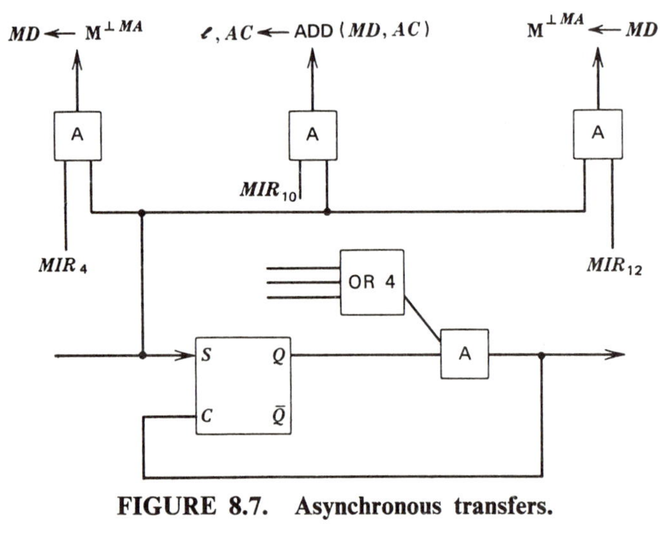

FIGURE 8.7. Asynchronous transfers.

begin. The completion pulse from whichever of the transfers is executed passes through OR-gate 4 to re-enter the control unit.

8.4. MICROPROGRAMMING A BUS-ORIENTED MACHINE

The advantages of microprogramming may not seem apparent to the reader from the example of the previous section. There we added a massive ROM to replace most of a fairly simple hard-wired control unit. In the process we have increased the execution time for each instruction considerably.

The discussion of the previous section was intended primarily as an introduction to some of the problems of controlling microprograms. The control unit discussed did not take advantage of the large ROM available. Once the hard-wired portion of the microprogram control unit has been included, it need not be increased, regardless of the number of microinstructions stored in the read-only memory. It would seem, then, that the efficient use of microprogramming would imply sequences of microinstructions to execute complex operations such as multiplication, division, or other arithmetic or logical operations. The only exception to this observation might be in certain small machines, where small transformer ROM's with limited branching capability have been used to reduce the cost of the control units. Various specialized circuit techniques, which will not be discussed here, were used in these cases to effect economies.

Although the op code could be changed, it would probably be difficult to devise microinstructions for the machine of Section 8.3 to substantially expand its performance beyond that of SIC. Only one branch condition which was a function of data registers was included, and only those register transfers specifically used in SIC were allowed. In order to permit a larger class of possible register transfers, data busing is almost universally used within machines employing microprogramming.

In this section we shall include the index registers ***IA*** and ***IB***, busing, and certain additional branch conditions in a more general microprogrammable machine which could include SIC as well as a much broader capability. Similarly, operate instructions could be microprogrammed. We will still assume a 3-bit op code, which could be, but would not necessarily be, the SIC op code, depending on the microprogram. In this way we can use the eleven familiar branch conditions of Fig. 8.4a, adding five additional conditions based on data registers. The augmented list of branch conditions is given in Fig. 8.8. The interpretation of microinstruction bits remains as given in Fig. 8.4b.

It is assumed here that unused bit combinations in operate instructions will

MIR_1	MIR_2	MIR_3	MIR_4	Branch Function f
0	0	0	0	UNCONDITIONAL
0	0	0	1	IR_1
0	0	1	0	IR_2
0	0	1	1	IR_3
0	1	0	0	IR_4
0	1	0	1	IR_0
0	1	1	0	$IR_0 \wedge IR_1$
0	1	1	1	$IR_1 \wedge IR_2$
1	0	0	0	$IR_0 \wedge IR_1 \wedge IR_2$
1	0	0	1	$IR_1 \vee IR_2$
1	0	1	0	$\vee/MD$
1	0	1	1	$\vee/AC$
1	1	0	0	AC_0
1	1	0	1	MQ_{17}
1	1	1	0	I
1	1	1	1	$\vee/(MC \oplus MAX)$

FIGURE 8.8. Augmented branch conditions.

be used to specify complex operations such as multiplication. These operations cannot involve memory references, but must merely manipulate the contents of the high-speed registers. There is much to be said, of course, for a longer word length, which would allow four or more bits to specify the op code.

The reader may observe that still more branch functions will be required if operate instructions are to be identified and accomplished using microprogramming. Thus, more than four bits in ***MIR*** would be needed to code these branches. The difficulty of providing sufficient branching capability is a basic limitation of microprogramming. We shall consider this problem further in subsequent sections. For now we sidestep the problem. Examples and homework related to this section will usually call for writing microprograms for individual assembly language instructions, beginning at a point after the sequences have been separated for individual instructions.

The register configurations and bus connections for the expanded SIC are given in Fig. 8.9. The index registers are now 18 bits, so they can be used for temporary storage as well as indexing. Three buses are used. The 18-bit A and B buses serve as argument buses. The 19-bit O bus, or output bus, also serves as the path for all direct transfers between registers. An *exclusive-OR* logic unit, designated XOR, has been provided. Most machines include this bit-by-bit operation. We shall find it convenient in various problems and examples. INC is included twice so that every argument which can be connected to either

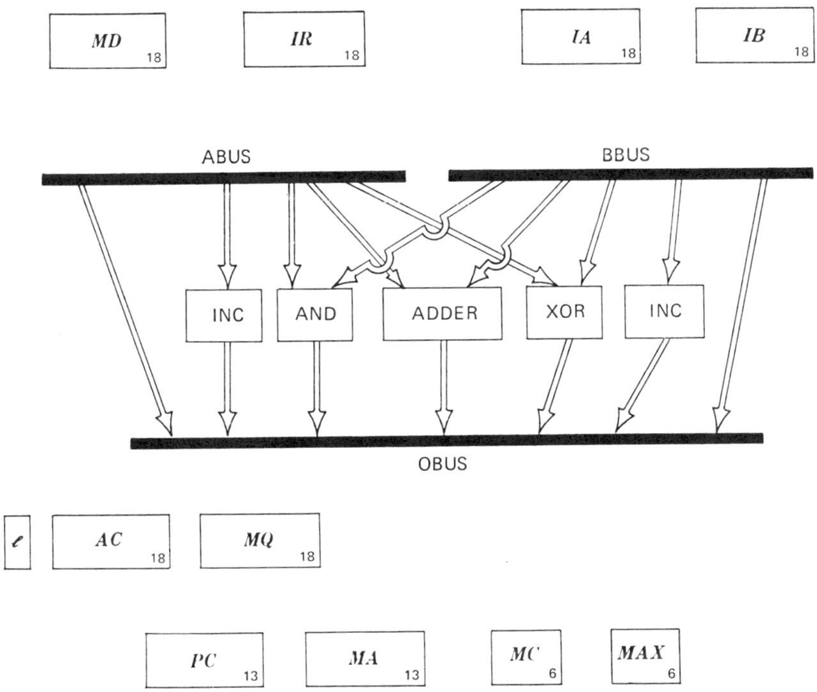

FIGURE 8.9. Register and bus configuration.

bus can be incremented. Only the interconnections between buses and logic units are shown in Fig. 8.9. Not shown are the register connections into the *A*, *B*, and *O* buses and the output connections from the ***OBUS***. The connections between registers and buses will be specified in several tables to follow. The very large number of such connections would so clutter the diagram of Fig. 8.9 as to make it useless.

In some cases, registers connected to the inputs and outputs of buses contain fewer bits than specified for the buses themselves. All such cases will be assumed to satisfy the following conventions. If a register with fewer bits than a bus is connected to a bus, the register is aligned at the right of the bus and the left-most bus bits are connected to zeros. For example, connecting ***PC*** to the ***OBUS*** accomplishes the operation given by Eq. 8.3. Note that the ***OBUS*** is a 19-bit bus.

$$\boldsymbol{OBUS} \leftarrow 000000, \boldsymbol{PC} \tag{8.3}$$

If the output of a bus is pulsed into a register with fewer bits, once again the bus and register are aligned on the right. The left-most bus bits are merely connected to nothing. Thus a microinstruction which specifies a transfer from the ***OBUS*** to ***MC*** causes the action given in Eq. 8.4. Notice that we

$$MC \leftarrow \omega^6(19)/OBUS \qquad (8.4)$$

have found it useful to specify ***MC*** as a 6-bit register. This register may be used to provide a count of the number of steps completed in a variety of operations.

The left-most three bits of ***MIR*** are used to identify types of transfers, as shown in Fig. 8.5. MIR_3 is unused. The next 3 bits of ***MIR*** (4–6) will be used to specify the input connections to the ***ABUS***. Bits MIR_7 and MIR_8 specify the input connections to the ***BBUS***. The outputs of the ***ABUS*** and ***BBUS*** are connected to the four logic units as shown in Fig. 8.9. The bit combinations corresponding to particular connections to the ***ABUS*** and ***BBUS*** are given in Fig. 8.10.

The ***OBUS*** is intended to supply a path for all register transfers. Therefore, one would expect a very large number of possible input and output connections to this bus. Five bits of ***MIR*** (9–13) are used to identify the input to the ***OBUS***. The last 4 bits of ***MIR*** (14–17) specify the output connections from the ***OBUS***. The bit combinations corresponding to particular connections to the ***OBUS*** are given in Fig. 8.11.

The layout of Fig. 8.11 provides a clue to our overall point of view. Notice that the output connections for the ***OBUS*** are listed in the form of register transfers. In fact, these are the only actual register transfers which can take place in the execution of a microinstruction. The execution of each microinstruction is accomplished in two steps. The first step utilizes bits 4 to 13 of ***MIR*** to gate a data vector to the output of the ***OBUS***. This vector may be either a register or the combinational logic function of two registers, depending on the particular bits in ***MIR***.

This flow of data through the buses is determined by output lines from

ABUS inputs				BBUS inputs		
MIR_4	MIR_5	MIR_6		MIR_7	MIR_8	
0	0	0	***MD***	0	0	***IA***
0	0	1	$\epsilon^{17}(18)$	0	1	***IB***
0	1	0	***MC***	1	0	***AC***
0	1	1	***PC***	1	1	$\overline{\epsilon(18)}$
1	0	0	***IR***			
1	0	1	$\epsilon^{14,16}(18)$			
1	1	0	$\epsilon^{11,12,15}(18)$			
1	1	1	$\epsilon^{8,9,10,11,12,14}(18)$			

FIGURE 8.10. Connections to *ABUS* and *BBUS*.

MIR_9	MIR_{10}	MIR_{11}	MIR_{12}	MIR_{13}	Input Connection
0	0	0	0	0	$ABUS$
0	0	0	0	1	$\ell,\overline{AC}$
0	0	0	1	0	$\overline{\ell},AC$
0	0	0	1	1	$\overline{\ell},\overline{AC}$
0	0	1	0	0	ℓ,AC
0	0	1	0	1	$\overline{MQ}$
0	0	1	1	0	MQ
0	0	1	1	1	$BBUS$
0	1	0	0	0	$\overline{ABUS}$
0	1	0	0	1	INC($ABUS$)
0	1	0	1	0	INC($BBUS$)
0	1	0	1	1	AND($ABUS,BBUS$)
0	1	1	0	0	ADD($ABUS,BBUS$)
0	1	1	0	1	XOR($ABUS,BBUS$)
0	1	1	1	0	$\epsilon(19)$
0	1	1	1	1	$\overline{BBUS}$
1	0	0	0	0	$MD \leftarrow \mathrm{M}^{\perp MA}$
1	0	0	0	1	$\epsilon^{3,4,5,6,7,8}(18)/MIR$
1	0	0	1	0	$\mathrm{M}^{\perp MA} \leftarrow MD$

(a)

MIR_{14}	MIR_{15}	MIR_{16}	MIR_{17}	Output Connection
0	0	0	0	$MD \leftarrow \omega^{18}/OBUS$
0	0	0	1	$IR \leftarrow \omega^{18}/OBUS$
0	0	1	0	$IA \leftarrow \omega^{18}/OBUS$
0	0	1	1	$IB \leftarrow \omega^{18}/OBUS$
0	1	0	0	$PC \leftarrow \omega^{13}/OBUS$
0	1	0	1	$MQ \leftarrow \omega^{18}/OBUS$
0	1	1	0	$MC \leftarrow \omega^{6}/OBUS$
0	1	1	1	$MA \leftarrow \omega^{13}/OBUS$
1	0	0	0	$\ell,AC \leftarrow OBUS$
1	0	0	1	$\ell,AC \leftarrow \downarrow(OBUS)$
1	0	1	0	$\ell,AC \leftarrow \uparrow(OBUS)$
1	0	1	1	$AC,MQ \leftarrow \overset{\circ}{\downarrow}(\omega^{18}/OBUS,MQ)$
1	1	0	0	$AC \leftarrow \omega^{18}/OBUS$
1	1	0	1	$\ell \leftarrow \omega^{1}/OBUS$
1	1	1	0	$AC \leftarrow \omega^{\perp MAX}/OBUS$
1	1	1	1	$MAX \leftarrow \omega^{6}/OBUS$

(b)

FIGURE 8.11. Connections to *OBUS*.

three decoders whose inputs are ***MIR*** (4–6), ***MIR*** (7–8), and ***MIR*** (10–13), respectively. For example, a data word will be gated onto the ***ABUS*** by the one line from the 8-output decoder (inputs ***MIR*** (4–6)) whose logical value is 1. The second step transfers bits from the ***OBUS*** into one of the registers, as listed in Fig. 8.11b. The first step takes place when a transfer micro-instruction is read from the **ROM** into ***MIR***. Thus, as in the previous two sections, only two clock periods are required to execute a microinstruction. The clock period required to set connections to the buses is the same clock period in which a microinstruction is read from the **ROM**. Since the use of busing slows the machine with hard-wired control, the time penalty attributable to microprogramming, as compared to hard-wired control, is less for a bus-oriented machine.

The only exception to the two-step sequence are the read and write in memory operations. Busing is not involved in these operations. Quite arbitrarily, two of the bit combinations in Fig. 8.11a are used to specify read and write. When these bit combinations are decoded, no information is pulsed from the ***OBUS***; and bus inputs are immaterial.

A survey of Figs. 8.10 and 8.11 will indicate that any register transfer which was employed in any SIC memory reference or operate instruction has been provided for. A very large number of other transfers are also possible. In particular, bit combination 10001 causes $\epsilon^{3,4,5,6,7,8}(18)/$***MIR*** to be connected to the input of the ***OBUS***. Thus, 6-bit constants for counting and indexing may be entered into the various registers from the **ROM**. The branch functions listed in Fig. 8.8 have been selected so that the multiplication operation can be accomplished by microprogramming. These additional tests of the data registers should be sufficient to permit most other operations of interest compatible with the SIC register configuration. The faster **ROM**, together with the bus oriented approach, will necessitate some changes in the micro-control sequencer of Section 8.3. These changes will be left as a problem for the reader.

From Fig. 8.11b, it will be noted that there is a considerable amount of signal processing done between the ***OBUS*** and *AC*. In particular, *AC* may receive data from the ***OBUS*** over three different paths, i.e., direct, rotated right, and rotated left. This will require 3-input OR gates at the inputs to *AC*. In a sense, this duplicates the function of the ***OBUS***, which is to collect data from a variety of sources for distribution to registers.

In other circumstances, economy and convenience might dictate doing all processing between the ***ABUS*** or ***BBUS*** and the ***OBUS***; so the ***OBUS*** may be connected directly to the destination registers without intermediate gating. This would particularly be true where the ***OBUS*** drives many registers, e.g., a bank of general-purpose registers. Otherwise, the OR-gating at the multiple registers would essentially comprise another complete bus.

With the machinery thus set up, consideration of examples of microprograms which can be accomplished by the expanded SIC would seem to be the next order of business. Clearly, however, we do not want to examine strings of 1's and 0's as we discuss these microprograms. In the next section we shall consider a version of APL as a possible assembly language for microprogramming. We shall not find it difficult to translate these AHPL programs to microcode where necessary. In instances where a large variety of microprograms are to be written for a machine in production, the authors strongly recommend the use of a microassembler program. Such a program will be dependent on the machine to be microprogrammed but will not be difficult to write. As only line-by-line translation is required, many of the usual difficulties in writing an assembler are avoided. Certainly such a program will be much less complicated than the hardware compiler mentioned previously.

8.5. AN ASSEMBLY LANGUAGE FOR MICROPROGRAMS

Each transfer microinstruction accomplishes two distinct operations. The first is the establishing of the input data vector on the ***OBUS***. Except for the case of addition, this first step is accomplished at the time the microinstruction is read into ***MIR*** from the **ROM**. An additional period of time must be allowed for the propagation delay through the adder. Once the vector on the ***OBUS*** is established, the second step transfers this vector into a register. It is therefore convenient to let each coded transfer microinstruction be represented by two AHPL steps, the first to establish the vector on the ***OBUS***, the second to transfer this vector to a register. Both of these operations must be consistent with Figs. 8.10 and 8.11. The branch microinstructions, which may specify only those branch conditions listed in Fig. 8.8, will be represented by only one AHPL step. For easy reference we name the resulting language MICRAL, microassembly language.

As a first example let us express the multiplication sequence of Section 6.11 in MICRAL. Only the first step of each transfer microinstruction is numbered. We begin with the sign determination routine. The reader should refer to the routine of Section 6.11 and notice that it is being reconstructed in a nearly step-by-step fashion.

1. $\boldsymbol{OBUS} \leftarrow \overline{\epsilon(19)}$
   $\ell \leftarrow \omega^1/\boldsymbol{OBUS}$
2. $\boldsymbol{AC}_0{:}0,\ (=) \rightarrow (5)$
3. $\boldsymbol{OBUS} \leftarrow \bar{\ell}, \overline{\boldsymbol{AC}}$
   $\ell, \boldsymbol{AC} \leftarrow \boldsymbol{OBUS}$

A problem would seem to arise in the first microinstruction. The reader will notice that no provision is made for a direct connection of $\overline{\epsilon(19)}$ to the ***OBUS***. However, by connecting the ***OBUS*** to the output of the ***BBUS*** and routing $\overline{\epsilon(18)}$ to the ***BBUS***, this result is accomplished indirectly. (When a data vector is routed to $\omega^{18}/\boldsymbol{OBUS}$ only, a zero automatically appears on the $\boldsymbol{OBUS}_0$ output.) This will be a much-used technique, as none of the arguments connected to the ***ABUS*** and ***BBUS*** are directly connected to the ***OBUS***. The ***ABUS*** and ***BBUS*** connections are not explicitly expressed in MICRAL. In general, the necessary ***ABUS*** and ***BBUS*** connections are fixed when the input to the ***OBUS*** is specified. These connections are automatically provided by the microassembler. The microprogrammer need only check the tables to verify that the desired connections are possible. In some cases, for the sake of economy, it is necessary to route a single argument through the ***ABUS*** or ***BBUS*** directly to the ***OBUS***.

We modify the branch in step 2 to reflect the fact that, if the branch condition is not satisfied, control always proceeds to the next step in sequence. The complement of the bit immediately to the right of the colon can be entered directly as bit 5 of the microinstruction by the assembler.

4. $\boldsymbol{OBUS} \leftarrow \text{ADD}(\epsilon^{17}(18), AC)$
   $\ell, \boldsymbol{AC} \leftarrow \boldsymbol{OBUS}$

5. $\boldsymbol{OBUS} \leftarrow \boldsymbol{AC}$
   $\boldsymbol{MQ} \leftarrow \omega^{18}/\boldsymbol{OBUS}$

6. $\boldsymbol{OBUS} \leftarrow \boldsymbol{MD}$
   $\boldsymbol{AC} \leftarrow \omega^{18}/\boldsymbol{OBUS}$

7. $AC_0{:}0, (=) \rightarrow (10)$
8. $\boldsymbol{OBUS} \leftarrow \overline{\ell}, \overline{\boldsymbol{AC}}$
   $\ell, \boldsymbol{AC} \leftarrow \boldsymbol{OBUS}$

9. $\boldsymbol{OBUS} \leftarrow \text{ADD}(\epsilon^{17}(18), AC)$
   $\ell, \boldsymbol{AC} \leftarrow \boldsymbol{OBUS}$

10. $\boldsymbol{OBUS} \leftarrow \boldsymbol{AC}$
    $\boldsymbol{MD} \leftarrow \omega^{18}/\boldsymbol{OBUS}$

Step 11 of Section 6.11 must be replaced by two separate two-step microinstructions. As we see, the ***OBUS*** approach virtually excludes parallel operations. In general, we shall find that microprograms will include more steps and require more time for execution than hard-wired sequences. Microprograms, however, will require significantly less time than purely software approaches to the same operation.

11. $\boldsymbol{OBUS} \leftarrow \overline{\epsilon(19)}$
    $\boldsymbol{AC} \leftarrow \omega^{18}/\boldsymbol{OBUS}$
12. $\boldsymbol{OBUS} \leftarrow \overline{\epsilon(19)}$
    $\boldsymbol{MC} \leftarrow \omega^{6}/\boldsymbol{OBUS}$

We have provided a single branch condition which compares $\perp \boldsymbol{MC}$ with $\perp \boldsymbol{MAX}$. The vector ***MAX*** may be set to any value from 0 to 63 in advance. This is accomplished in step 13 by placing bits 3–8 of ***MIR*** on the ***OBUS*** as provided by line 18 of Fig. 8.11a. The corresponding AHPL step should be easily recognizable by an assembler.

13. $\boldsymbol{OBUS} \leftarrow \top(18)$
    $\boldsymbol{MAX} \leftarrow \omega^{6}/\boldsymbol{OBUS}$
14. $\vee/(\boldsymbol{MC} \oplus \boldsymbol{MAX}):0, (=) \rightarrow (21)$
15. $\boldsymbol{MQ}_{17}:1, (=) \rightarrow (18)$
16. $\boldsymbol{OBUS} \leftarrow \boldsymbol{AC}$
    $\boldsymbol{AC}, \boldsymbol{MQ} \leftarrow \downarrow((\omega^{18}/\boldsymbol{OBUS}), \boldsymbol{MQ})$

Step 16 takes advantage of a transfer operation set up especially for the multiplication instruction. The output of the ***OBUS*** and the contents of ***MQ*** are rotated right together. The ***MQ*** register is not connected to a bus.

17. $\rightarrow (19)$
18. $\boldsymbol{OBUS} \leftarrow \mathrm{ADD}(\boldsymbol{MD}, \boldsymbol{AC})$
    $\boldsymbol{AC}, \boldsymbol{MQ} \leftarrow \downarrow((\omega^{18}/\boldsymbol{OBUS}), \boldsymbol{MQ})$
19. $\boldsymbol{OBUS} \leftarrow \mathrm{INC}(\boldsymbol{MC})$
    $\boldsymbol{MC} \leftarrow \omega^{6}/\boldsymbol{OBUS}$
20. $\rightarrow (14)$

The reader will recall that step 20 concludes the multiplication of the absolute values of the arguments. The following sequence takes the two's-complement of ***AC***, ***MQ*** if the sign of the product is to be negative.

21. $\ell:0, (=) \rightarrow (30)$
22. $\boldsymbol{OBUS} \leftarrow \overline{\boldsymbol{AC}}$
    $\boldsymbol{MD} \leftarrow \omega^{18}/\boldsymbol{OBUS}$
23. $\boldsymbol{OBUS} \leftarrow \overline{\boldsymbol{MQ}}$
    $\boldsymbol{AC} \leftarrow \boldsymbol{OBUS}$
24. $\boldsymbol{OBUS} \leftarrow \overline{\epsilon(19)}$
    $\ell \leftarrow \omega^{1}/\boldsymbol{OBUS}$
25. $\boldsymbol{OBUS} \leftarrow \mathrm{ADD}(\epsilon^{17}(18), \boldsymbol{AC})$
    $\ell, \boldsymbol{AC} \leftarrow \boldsymbol{OBUS}$

26. ***OBUS*** ← ***AC***
    MQ ← ω^{18}/***OBUS***
27. ***OBUS*** ← ***MD***
    AC ← ω^{18}/***OBUS***

Step 25 of the original sequence uses the link as part of one of the arguments of addition. The tables of Fig. 8.10 do not provide for this situation, so this instruction must be replaced by a branch and the addition of a fixed argument to *AC*.

28. ℓ:0 (=) → (30)
29. ***OBUS*** ← ADD($\epsilon^{17}(18)$, *AC*)
    ℓ, ***AC*** ← ***OBUS***
30. End of Sequence.

Example 8.3

Like SIC, most modern computers store data and perform arithmetic operations in straight binary form. Always present, then, is the problem of converting to and from binary-coded-decimal notation for communication with the outside world. It is often necessary to recognize 6- to 8-bit alphanumeric characters as decimal digits and to convert strings of such digits to binary form. For purposes of illustration we shall simplify the problem as follows. Assume that the right-most 16 bits of ***MQ*** represent four binary-coded-decimal digits. Write a sequence of microinstructions which will convert this four-digit number to binary form.

Solution. Our approach to the problem is suggested by the last three ***ABUS*** arguments listed in Fig. 8.10. We note that

$$\perp \epsilon^{14,16}(18) = \perp(1, 0, 1, 0) = 10_{\text{base ten}}$$
$$\perp \epsilon^{11,12,15}(18) = 100_{\text{base ten}}$$

and

$$\perp \epsilon^{8,9,10,11,12,14}(18) = 1000_{\text{base ten}} \tag{8.5}$$

The four-digit number $D_3D_2D_1D_0$ which must be converted to binary may be represented as

$$D_3 \times 1000_{\text{base ten}} + D_2 \times 100_{\text{base ten}} + D_1 \times 10_{\text{base ten}} \times D_0 \tag{8.6}$$

If each of the D_i and the powers of ten are replaced by their binary equivalents and the above computation performed, the result will be the binary equivalent of $D_3D_2D_1D_0$. Suppose for example that $D_1 = 9$. In this case the binary equivalent of $D_1 \times 10$ is given by Eq. 8.7.

$$\begin{aligned} \top(D_1 \times 10_{\text{base ten}}) &= 1001 \times (1010) \\ &= 1010000 \times 1 + 101000 \times 0 + 10100 \times 0 + 1010 \times 1 \\ &= 1010000 + 1010 = 1011010 \end{aligned} \tag{8.7}$$

Thus the conversion process is very similar to multiplication. Each bit of the BCD digit multiples the power of ten expressed in binary. This process is carried out for all four digits with the results added together. As in multiplication, we consider each bit of $\boldsymbol{MQ}$ beginning at the right. The vector $\boldsymbol{AC}$, $\boldsymbol{MQ}$ is rotated right each step. The following sequence handles the right-most eight bits, or two decimal digits. The reader is left to complete the microprogram for the remaining eight bits. Step 9, which realigns the partial sum after the first digit multiplication, requires that a new input connection to the $\boldsymbol{OBUS}$ be added to the list in Fig. 8.11a.

1. $\boldsymbol{OBUS} \leftarrow \overline{\epsilon(19)}$
   $\boldsymbol{AC} \leftarrow \omega^{18}/\boldsymbol{OBUS}$
2. $\boldsymbol{OBUS} \leftarrow \top(4)$
   $\boldsymbol{MAX} \leftarrow \omega^{6}/\boldsymbol{OBUS}$
3. $\boldsymbol{OBUS} \leftarrow \overline{\epsilon(19)}$
   $\boldsymbol{MC} \leftarrow \omega^{6}/\boldsymbol{OBUS}$
4. $\boldsymbol{MQ}_{17}:0,\ (=) \rightarrow (6)$
5. $\boldsymbol{OBUS} \leftarrow \mathrm{ADD}(\epsilon^{17}(18), \boldsymbol{AC})$
   $\boldsymbol{AC} \leftarrow \omega^{18}/\boldsymbol{OBUS}$
6. $\boldsymbol{OBUS} \leftarrow \boldsymbol{AC}$
   $\boldsymbol{AC}, \boldsymbol{MQ} \leftarrow \overset{\circ}{\downarrow}(\omega^{18}/\boldsymbol{OBUS}), \boldsymbol{MQ})$
7. $\boldsymbol{OBUS} \leftarrow \mathrm{INC}(\boldsymbol{MC})$
   $\boldsymbol{MC} \leftarrow \omega^{6}/\boldsymbol{OBUS}$
8. $\bot \boldsymbol{MC} : \bot \boldsymbol{MAX}\ (\neq) \rightarrow (4)$
9. $\boldsymbol{OBUS} \leftarrow \omega^{15}/\boldsymbol{AC}, \alpha^{4}/\boldsymbol{MQ}$
   $\ell, \boldsymbol{AC} \leftarrow \boldsymbol{OBUS}$
10. $\boldsymbol{OBUS} \leftarrow \overline{\epsilon(19)}$
    $\boldsymbol{MC} \leftarrow \omega^{6}/\boldsymbol{OBUS}$
11. $\boldsymbol{MQ}_{17}:0,\ (=) \rightarrow (13)$
12. $\boldsymbol{OBUS} \leftarrow \mathrm{ADD}(\epsilon^{14,16}(18), \boldsymbol{AC})$
    $\boldsymbol{AC} \leftarrow \omega^{18}/\boldsymbol{OBUS}$
13. $\boldsymbol{OBUS} \leftarrow \boldsymbol{AC}$
    $\boldsymbol{AC}, \boldsymbol{MQ} \leftarrow \overset{\circ}{\downarrow}((\omega^{18}/\boldsymbol{OBUS}, \boldsymbol{MQ})$
14. $\boldsymbol{OBUS} \leftarrow \mathrm{INC}(\boldsymbol{MC})$
    $\boldsymbol{MC} \leftarrow \omega^{6}/\boldsymbol{OBUS}$
15. $\bot \boldsymbol{MC} : \bot \boldsymbol{MAX}\ (\neq) \rightarrow (11)$
16. etc. ▮

The reader may feel that the design of the machine described in the previous section has been tuned to the two examples which we have examined so far. To a certain extent he is correct in this assertion, although sufficient options are available to permit the writing of a large array of useful microprograms. Certainly the last three arguments listed as available to the $\boldsymbol{ABUS}$ have limited utility. Other microprograms may require other constant vectors. A desirable modification of our machine would be a special transfer instruction which could read 18-bit constants from the ROM into high-speed registers. This would imply the addition of registers which could store these constants temporarily as well as adding to the overall capability of the machine. Another improvement would be the provision for more flexibility in branch microinstructions. These are the topics of the next sections.

8.6. FURTHER FLEXIBILITY

The reader will recall that bit $\boldsymbol{MIR_3}$ was unused in the transfer microinstructions of Section 8.4. Let us use this bit, together with $\boldsymbol{MIR_1}$ and $\boldsymbol{MIR_2}$, to broaden the scope of transfer instructions. We shall merely redefine the significance of these three bits. No attempt will be made at redefining the connections listed in Figs. 8.10 and 8.11 to take advantage of these changes.

Consider the bit assignments as listed in Fig. 8.12. The first row of Fig. 8.12 specifies the new operation. If bit $\boldsymbol{MIR_1} = 0$, the 12 bits $\boldsymbol{MIR_2}$ to $\boldsymbol{MIR_{13}}$ specify a complete 12-bit **ROM** address. The 18-bit constant vector specified by this address is read into a special data register, ***SDR***, the output of which is connected to the ***OBUS***. Bits $\boldsymbol{MIR_{14}}$ to $\boldsymbol{MIR_{17}}$ cause this constant vector to be pulsed from the ***OBUS*** to a register according to Fig. 8.11b. Thus a very large number of constants may be stored in the **ROM**. These constants can be used for masking or in arithmetic operations.

The reader will recall that ***MAR*** serves as the microprogram counter as well as the microaddress register. Thus bits 2–13 of ***MIR*** are not placed in ***MAR***. For simplicity we shall merely assume the input to the address decoder can be switched by combinational logic to bits 2–13 of ***MIR***. An extra clock period is allowed for this operation in Fig. 8.13. We shall use $\boldsymbol{OBUS} \leftarrow \mathbf{ROM}^{\perp K}$ in MICRAL to refer to obtaining a constant from location $\perp K$ of the **ROM**.

As will be illustrated in Problem 8.11, it is often desirable to compare a data word with a list of constants stored in the **ROM**. This function can be greatly facilitated by adding an indexing capability for addresses in the **ROM**. To do

MIR_0	MIR_1	MIR_2, MIR_3, MIR_4 to MIR_{13}		MIR_{14} to MIR_{17}
0	0	Bits 2–13 specify a location in the **ROM**		***OBUS*** output
0	1	0	0	Synchronous transfer
0	1	0	1	Asynchronous transfer
0	1	1	0	Wired control
0	1	1	1	Bits 4–17 specify IOT transfer

FIGURE 8.12. Types of transfers.

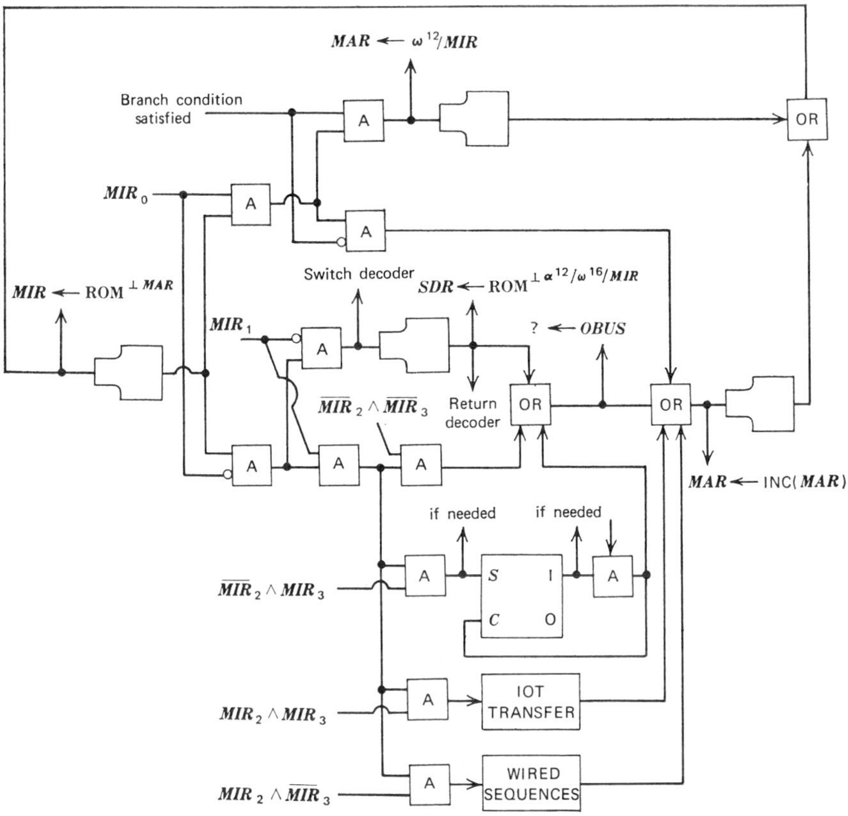

FIGURE 8.13. Modified microsequencer.

this would require inclusion of an address register for the **ROM** separate from the program counting ***MAR***. One approach would be to separate the **ROM** into a microprogram section and a separate section for storage of constants. The two sections would have completely separate address registers and decoders. We leave the reader to follow up these observations and restrict our further discussion to the simpler configuration described by Figs. 8.12 and 8.13.

The next second and third rows of Fig. 8.12 specify synchronous and asynchronous register transfers which are controlled as discussed in Section 8.4. Particular short sequences of operations often arise in large machines for which microprogram control is awkward and excessively time-consuming. A microinstruction whose left-most four bits are 0110 will cause control to pass to a short hard-wired sequencer. Bits 4 to 17 may be used to distinguish between such sequences and to determine branching within the sequences.

Control converges at the end of all such sequences to cause ***MAR*** to be incremented and a new microinstruction to be read from **ROM**.

Additional registers and buses may be required for IOT instructions. If the left-most four bits of ***MIR*** are 0111, then bits 4–17 may be used to specify a completely different set of transfers, which may be part of input/output instructions. In some machines, busing and execution will not be separated for IOT operations. We have chosen to do so in the case of the expanded SIC, in order to provide for the inclusion of input/output without treating the subject in detail at this point.

We have added so many options that a fairly elaborate hard-wired micro-program controller is necessary. Such a control unit is depicted in Fig. 8.13.

8.7. BRANCHING IMPROVEMENTS

In the previous section we had no difficulty in providing for the coding of any register transfers which appeared at all useful. At the same time it was remarked that the branching code was insufficient to handle the decoding of operate instructions. In general it is the conditional AHPL branch operation which is most severely constrained by a microprogramming approach. The SIC control sequence of Chapter 6 liberally used instruction bits and data bits to branch at various points within the sequence. The wired approach makes it possible to connect directly to any bit or combination of bits of any registers in the machine to control a branch operation. For large machines with several high-speed data registers, the amount of information embodied in a particular branch condition is overwhelming. Consider, for example, a machine with 16 registers of 32 bits each. Let f_i be the Boolean function which gates a pulse through a particular path of a particular branch operation. The number of possible ways to specify this function is given in Eq. 8.8.

$$N(f_i) = 2^{2^{16(32)}} = 2^{2^{512}} \tag{8.8}$$

Thus, in the most general case, 2^{512} bits would be required to specify the function. Another $\rho(\boldsymbol{MAR})$ bits would be required to provide the address of the next microinstruction in the event the branch condition is satisfied. Compared to assembly language, a much larger number of branch functions are required in microprogramming.

In a microprogramming approach, the branch function and the branch address must be specified by the bits in ***MIR***.* Clearly not all of the functions

* This can be avoided as was done in the original Wilkes model by simply not placing branch microinstructions in ***MIR***. Instead, a new address is pulsed directly into ***MAR*** each time a transfer is executed. Each word line from the decoder contains the same spatial information as found in the hard-wired control unit. If switching is allowed on these word lines, then the designer has complete freedom in assigning branch conditions. An example of this form of microprogrammable control unit will be provided in Section 8.8.

enumerated in Eq. 8.8 would be of interest. However if the designer of a large machine enjoyed the freedom of the hard-wired control approach, he would likely specify more branches than could be coded in a microinstruction if a large block of bits were set aside for the branch address.

We have not even discussed multiple branches as yet. Often it is desirable to provide a conditional branch to more than two points in the microprogram. When one considers the possibility of providing bits to specify more than one address in a microinstruction, the need for some other approach becomes obvious. There are many ways to add to the flexibility of branch commands. Two such schemes will be presented in this section. Both achieve this greater branching capability at the price of one or more of the following: more complexity in the microsequencer, more time required to execute the desired branch, and wasted space within the **ROM**.

Scheme I. Branch microinstructions in a particular system, employing an 18-bit, 2^{15}-word **ROM**, may take one of four forms depending on $\boldsymbol{MIR_1}$ and $\boldsymbol{MIR_2}$. These formats are illustrated in Fig. 8.14.

The first format specifies an unconditional branch to any address in the **ROM**. The second format is a two-option branch, with one option being the next instruction in sequence. Eight bits are provided to specify a branch function from a fairly long list of 2^8 such functions. If the branch condition

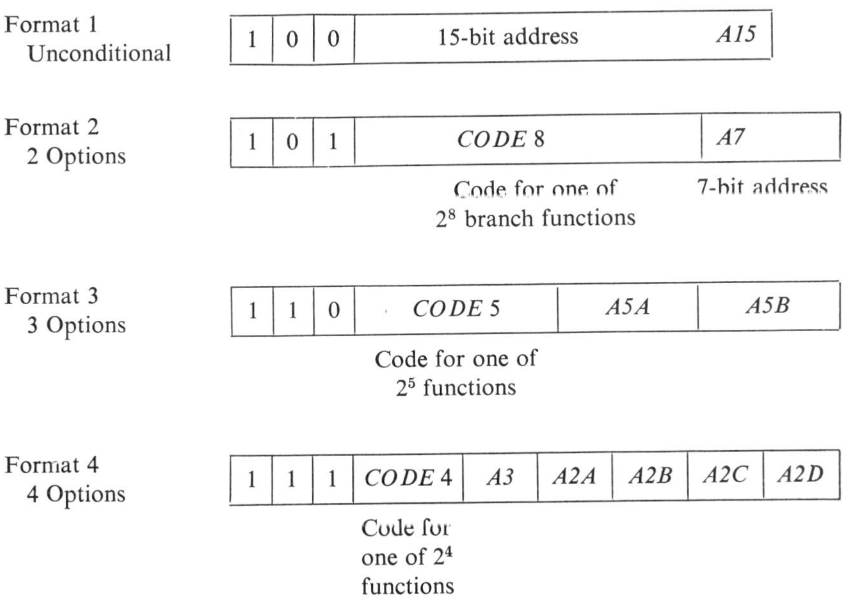

FIGURE 8.14. Branch instruction formats.

is satisfied, the new 15-bit address is formed as given by expression 8.9.

$$MAR \leftarrow (\alpha^8/MAR), A7 \tag{8.9}$$

Notice that the most significant eight bits of ***MAR*** are not changed. The first two formats together provide an improvement over the approach of the previous sections. The longer list of branch functions is achieved at the price of only an occasional extra microinstruction.

Example 8.4

Suppose that the current address of a microprogram employing the branching scheme of this section is 32575 octal. From here it is desired to branch to 40000 if a branch condition, $f = 1$, is satisfied, and to continue in sequence otherwise. The two step operation may be expressed in MICRAL as follows:

Octal address	
32575	f:1, ($\neq$) → 32577
32576	→ (40000) ▮

The format-3 branch instruction provides for 32 possible three-way branches. Depending on functional values, the next microinstruction is taken from the next address in sequence or from an address formed from *A5A* or *A5B*. Either of these 5-bit vectors can be used as the least significant five bits of an address as was done for format 2.

Format 4 provides for a four-way branch, as specified by one of 16 branch functions. The most significant three bits of the new address will always be *A3*, the next two bits will be *A2A* or *A2B* or *A2C* or *A2D*, and the last 10 bits will always be zeros.

Most any 3- or 4-way branch can be accomplished using a format-3 or -4 branch microinstruction together with one or more unconditional branches. The principal disadvantage of the scheme discussed above is the long lists of branch functions. These lists would be difficult to remember. In addition, the associated decoding logic would be very costly.

Scheme II. The limitations mentioned above can be overcome by not storing the complete address of either alternative next instruction as bits of the branch microinstruction in the **ROM**. Instead, this address can be assembled from bits in various registers. Thus the branch is a function of these data bits, and multiple branches are possible.

We shall describe one possible approach to assembling a branch address. With this introduction the reader should be able to develop any number of similar schemes. Our approach is not optimized for any particular computer or for any prospective set of microprograms. In fact, it may not be particularly

BLOC1	MIR_4, MIR_5, MIR_6, MIR_7
BLOC2	Assembled from zeros and the value of one of eight functions of various data bits
BLOC3	A special 4-bit register
BLOC4	0 or 1 $\ell, \bar{\ell}$, 0, or 1 $MQ_{17}, \overline{MQ}_{17}$, 0, or 1 $AC_0, \overline{AC}_0$, 0, or 1
BLOC5	IR_0, IR_1, IR_2 IR_3

FIGURE 8.15. Available blocks of microaddress bits.

good in any application. It is convenient to explain, however, and it illustrates most types of options available to the designer.

As before, a **ROM** address will consist of twelve bits. We shall assemble this address by selecting three 4-bit blocks from a set of five such blocks and ordering them in a manner prescribed by the bits of the microinstruction. These blocks of 4 bits are taken from a variety of sources. The five available blocks of bits are listed in Fig. 8.15.

The 18-bit branch microinstruction is used to specify and assemble these blocks into a 12-bit address. The bits of MIR are utilized as shown in Fig. 8.16.

There are three bits which specify the assembly of blocks into an address. One bit combination specifies an unconditional transfer, so only seven permutations of three of the five blocks are allowed. These are given in Fig. 8.17 along with the bit combination which specifies each. For example, if bits MIR_1, MIR_2, and MIR_3 are all zero, then the address of the next microinstruction becomes

BLOC3(4 Bits), MIR_4, MIR_5, MIR_6, MIR_7, BLOC4(4 Bits)

Depending on how the bits of block 4 are assigned, this instruction would cause a branch to one of 16 adjacent addresses. If MIR_1, MIR_2, and MIR_3 are all 1, ω^{12}/MIR is taken as the address of an unconditional transfer.

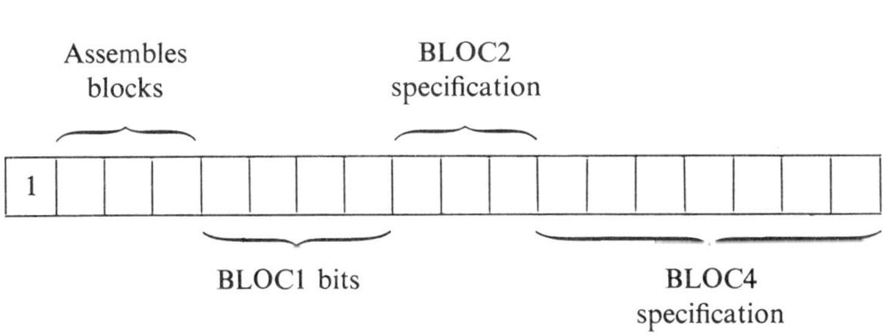

FIGURE 8.16. Branch microinstruction.

MIR_1	MIR_2	MIR_3	First 4 Address Bits	2nd 4 Bits	3rd 4 Bits
0	0	0	Block 3,	Block 1,	Block 4
0	0	1	3,	1,	2
0	1	0	1,	3,	2
0	1	1	3,	4,	1
1	0	0	3,	4,	5
1	0	1	1,	5,	4
1	1	0	1,	3,	4
1	1	1	Unconditional Transfer		

FIGURE 8.17. Assembly of a microaddress.

The last seven bits of ***MIR*** are used in a way which permits a great deal of flexibility in the composition of BLOC4. The bits of BLOC4 are assigned as shown in Fig. 8.18. Only three bits are available to control the composition of BLOC2. We, therefore, use the bits to choose one of eight functions of the data vectors. These functional values are inserted in BLOC2 as shown in Fig. 8.19. A particular f_i might be any useful function of the bits in the data register. For example, $\vee/\boldsymbol{AC}$ would very likely be included.

The reader will immediately see ways to improve the scheme described herein. Our purpose has been to suggest a general approach and certain specific techniques which a designer may find useful in a particular design situation. One possibility, which we have not considered, would be the inclusion of blocks of bits from the present contents of ***MAR*** in an extended version of Fig. 8.17. No doubt the final choice of a branching scheme for a proposed computer would be the result of interaction between individuals or groups working on different aspects of the system design. One would expect modifications as the overall design of the computer progressed.

MIR_{11}	0	1		
$BLOC4_0$	0	1		
MIR_{12}, MIR_{13}	00	01	10	11
$BLOC4_1$	0	1	ℓ	$\bar{\ell}$
MIR_{14}, MIR_{15}	00	01	10	11
$BLOC4_2$	0	1	MQ_{17}	$\overline{MQ}_{17}$
MIR_{16}, MIR_{17}	00	01	10	11
$BLOC4_3$	0	1	AC_0	$\overline{AC}_0$

FIGURE 8.18. Assignment of bits in BLOC4.

MIR_8,	MIR_9,	MIR_{10}	$BLOC2_0$,	$BLOC2_1$,	$BLOC2_2$,	$BLOC2_3$
0	0	0	0	0	0	f_1
0	0	1	0	0	0	f_2
0	1	0	0	0	0	f_3
0	1	1	0	0	0	f_4
1	0	0	0	0	f_5	0
1	0	1	0	0	f_6	0
1	1	0	0	0	f_7	0
1	1	1	0	0	f_8	0

FIGURE 8.19. Composition of BLOC2.

Consider, as an example, the branch microinstruction of Fig. 8.20a. Bits 1, 2, and 3 are 101; so the next address is given by blocks 1,5, and 4. BLOC1 is specified by the branch microinstruction as 1001. Since the last seven bits of ***MIR*** are 0, BLOC4 is composed of all 0's. The four bits forming the center of the next address are taken as the first four bits of the instruction register, ***IR***. Presumably these bits are the op code of the instruction under execution. Thus, the 16-way branch provides a method of simultaneously separating control into separate sequences for 16 instruction types. The addresses of the next microinstructions are the first words of 16 consecutive 16-bit blocks. The addresses of the first words in each block range from 4400 to 4760 octal.

It is assumed that the 16 separate instruction sequences will require no more than 16 operations before reconvergence or further branching. Certain of the alternate instructions sequences will likely require fewer than 16 operations. Thus, unused **ROM** locations may remain in the various blocks. One of the unpleasant implications of any branch scheme of the type discussed in this section is that the use of these randomly distributed **ROM** locations elsewhere in the microprogram is very awkward.

Consider as a second example the microinstruction stored at 7430 in the

Assembles blocks   BLOC2 Specification

1 1 0 1 1 0 0 1 0 0 0 0 0 0 0 0 0 0

BLOC1   BLOC4

(a)

1, 0, 0, 1, IR_0, IR_1, IR_2, IR_3, 0, 0, 0, 0

(b)

FIGURE 8.20. Sixteen-way branch.

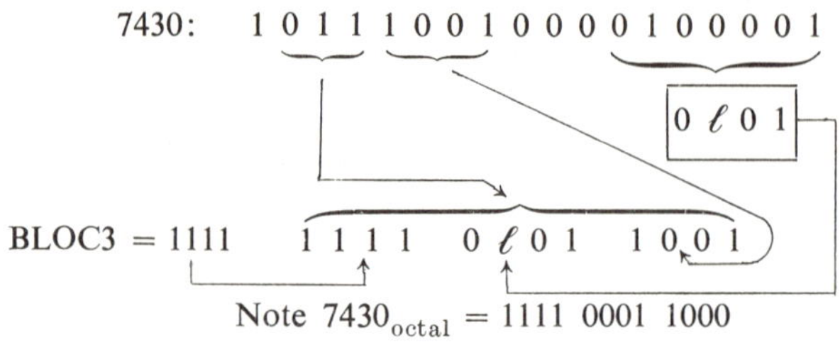

FIGURE 8.21. Single condition branch.

ROM, as shown in Fig. 8.21. Bits 1, 2, and 3 of ***MIR*** are 011, so the address of the next microinstruction is composed of blocks 3, 4, and 1, respectively. The BLOC3 register contains 1111 as shown in the figure. Similarly the block 1 bits from ***MIR*** are placed in ***MAR*** as shown. The last seven bits of ***MIR*** specify block 4 as 0ℓ01, as indicated in the box in Fig. 8.21. These bits are also placed in ***MAR*** as indicated. Notice that if the link is zero, the 12 bits inserted in ***MAR*** differ from the original bits only in bit MAR_{11}. Thus if $\ell = 0$, the next instruction in sequence is executed. If $\ell = 1$, control branches to location 7531 of the **ROM**.

Thus, it is possible to accomplish the simple single condition branch used exclusively in previous sections. Clearly such branches cannot be specified with complete flexibility. The reader will agree that the expression of the branch microinstructions for this approach in MICRAL, or any other assembly language, will be awkward; and the writing of the necessary assembler much more difficult.

8.8. AN ECONOMICAL MICROPROGRAMMABLE CONTROL UNIT

In the last three sections we have discussed a fairly sophisticated form of microprogramming. We have assumed that the advantage of microprogramming lay in the use of fairly complex microprograms for functions which would otherwise be accomplished by software. Certainly the case of a large number of microinstructions would be required to justify the complex microsequencer and decoder implied by the development in these three sections.

Not all microprogrammable machines are described by the above paragraph. In certain small machines microprogramming is used for reasons of economy only. The read-only memory in such machines contains enough microinstructions to provide the control sequences for the basic assembly language operations only. In this section we shall make a sequence of design decisions which will lead to what may be the most economical small microprogrammable control unit. We assume that the basic clock rate of the machine is slow enough that any **ROM** technology is acceptable.

In Chapter 7 we indicated that a minimal-state control unit would have no more states than steps in the control sequence. If the **ROM** is completely utilized, there is a one-to-one correspondence between steps in the control sequence and states in ***MAR***. Thus let us re-examine the function of ***MIR***. Perhaps it is redundant. Can a vector in **ROM** as selected by ***MAR*** serve to control a transfer or a branch without ever being placed in another register? The answer is technology-dependent. In all but certain semiconductor **ROM**'s, data will appear on the output lines in the form of pulses. Although a semiconductor **ROM** is fairly expensive, one might delete ***MIR*** from the configuration of Section 8.3, and with a few other modifications wind up with a reasonably inexpensive control unit. This will be left as a problem for the reader.

If the output of a **ROM** is pulses, can these pulses be used directly to effect register transfers and branches in the control unit? Only in the case of a transformer-coupled **ROM** are these pulses of sufficient magnitude to be used in the computer without benefit of an array of amplifiers or a data register like ***MIR***. A transformer **ROM** requires only a number of cores equal to the number of bits in a single microinstruction. Given the modest speed requirement, we chose the transformer-coupled **ROM** as the overall most economical alternative.

Pulses cannot be decoded. That is, pulses are not allowed to simultaneously appear on more than one input of a gate. Therefore, we must have a bit in the ROM word for each possible transfer. Similarly, an encoded list of branch functions cannot be used. The bits used in the previous section to specify the type of microinstruction will not be required since separate cores are provided for all branches and transfers. Busing can be used in conjunction with this type of control unit only if separate microsteps are provided for the setting of bus control flip-flops prior to each transfer.

A control unit of this type is illustrated in Fig. 8.22. A core is provided for each possible transfer, and a set of cores equal to the number of bits in ***MAR*** is provided to permit branching. Every microinstruction will accomplish a branch as well as a transfer. Often the branch will be merely an unconditional branch to the next microinstruction in sequence. Conditional branches must not depend on registers which are affected by a simultaneous transfer operation.

Typical microinstructions are represented by lines from the decoder labeled "Word *a*" and "Word *b*" in Fig. 8.22. A pulse on line *a* will induce a pulse on the sense winding shown for the second core from the left. The sense line will route the pulse out of the control unit to cause the transfer $\boldsymbol{B} \leftarrow \boldsymbol{A}$.

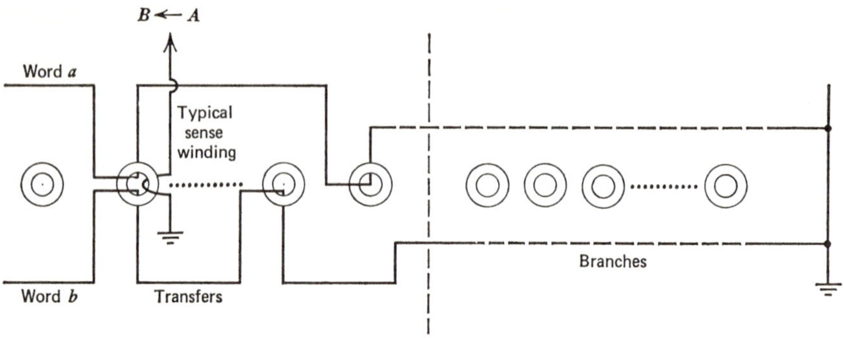

FIGURE 8.22. Implementation of two microinstructions.

Although not shown, a sense line is provided in each of the other cores. Each of the sense windings in the section of the **ROM** labeled "Transfers" is used to control a separate register transfer. Notice that line *a* also passes through various cores in the branching section. A detailed illustration of the branching function will be given in Fig. 8.23. Line *b* passes through two transfer cores as well as through the branch section. That two parallel register transfers are accomplished simultaneously should cause no problem.

Two cores are included in the branch section of the **ROM** corresponding to each flip-flop in ***MAR***. Since every microinstruction will include a branch, each line from the decoder will pass through either the core corresponding to the SET or the core corresponding to the CLEAR input of each of these flip-flops. The simplest case of an unconditional branch is illustrated in Fig. 8.23a. A conditional branch is illustrated in Fig. 8.23b. In this case the address of the next microinstruction depends on the value of ∨/***MD***. Branches with any number of alternative destinations may be handled similarly. Notice that the pulse of the word line passes directly through the branching network. When word lines are handled in this manner, there is a one-to-one correspondence between word lines and control delay outputs in a hard-wired control unit. Thus there is no sacrifice in branching flexibility in this type of microprogram control unit. When a **ROM** word is pulsed into a ***MIR***, this one-to-one correspondence is lost. Thus when a branch is decided on the basis of the contents of ***MIR*** alone, significant information is being ignored.

The microsequencer becomes trivial for control units which do not use ***MIR*** and in which branch and transfer operations are combined. Each microinstruction requires only one clock period, and the microsequencer need not distinguish between types of microinstructions. Therefore, a microsequencer is not needed at all. The clock itself may be substituted for the output of the microsequencer and used to drive the **ROM**.

Variations of the control unit just described have been used frequently in

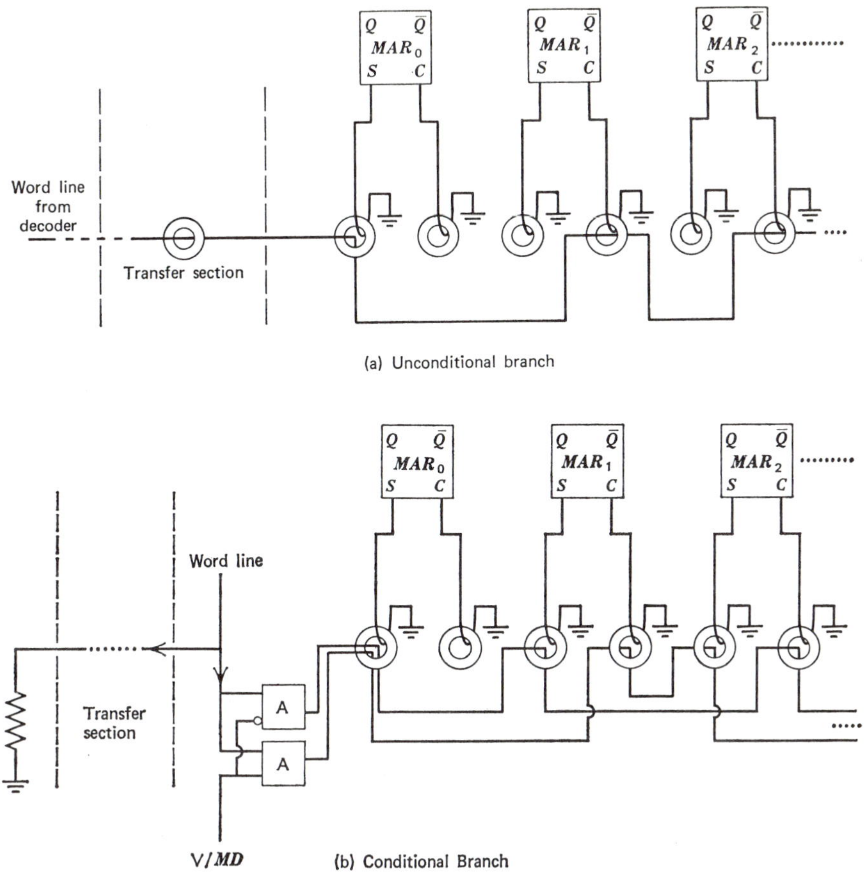

FIGURE 8.23. Branching in a transformer-coupled ROM.

minicomputers. Their simplicity and economy is inviting for machines requiring relatively short control sequences.

For machines utilizing long complex control sequences, with many branches using the same branch function, a **ROM** data register like ***MIR*** is in order. Otherwise the length of **ROM** words will grow to the point of making the **ROM** uneconomical. Where busing is used extensively, there is little time or hardware penalty associated with the use of ***MIR***. Most of the flip-flops, along with the extra clock period to set them, are required anyway to route information through the buses. Economics usually dictates that more sophisticated machines operate at higher clock frequencies. This requirement will usually eliminate transformers, which cannot be operated at clock rates much above 1 MHz.

8.9. OBSERVATIONS

Microprogramming is a widely-used method of controlling the execution of machine language instructions. It can be applied at a variety of levels with hard-wired control sequencers of greater or lesser complexity for controlling microprogram execution. The simplest application of microprogramming would limit the use of branching within the microprogram to separating all instructions at the beginning of the execution sequences. Assembly language branches could be accomplished by merely making a transfer to the program counter, ***PC***, dependent on a data bit. We saw in Section 8.4 that a more elaborate microprogramming approach could be justified only by storing routines, which would otherwise be part of system software, in a large **ROM**.

Where a **ROM** is used in the control unit, the overall machine speed is limited by the access time of the **ROM**. Thus, wherever the cost per computation is a governing factor, the access time of the **ROM** must be of the same order of magnitude as the time required for a data transfer between high-speed registers. The clock rate would probably be specified according to this access time of the **ROM**. If the resulting clock period is significantly longer than the delay of the register transfers, the system will not be operating at maximum efficiency.

The cost-speed trade-off of the read-only memory is critical. While the speed of the **ROM** must be consistent with the speed of the other electronics, it must be sufficiently cheap to justify its use in place of a completely hard-wired control unit.

In order to improve machine speed it is often found desirable to fetch a succeeding microinstruction from the **ROM** while one microinstruction is being executed. This overlap is similar to the more general notion of instruction lookahead, which will be discussed in Chapter 14. As is the case for lookahead, a branch microinstruction may cause a succeeding microinstruction already read from the **ROM** to go unused.

Microprograms will usually include a large number of branch operations. This can be verified by noticing the frequency of branches on the AHPL sequence of Chapter 6. In the hard-wired control unit, a branch instruction does not require a clock period. If every other operation were a branch, a 50% saving in execution time could be achieved if special references to the **ROM** memory for branch operations could be eliminated from the microprogramming approach. Thus branch and transfer operations are often combined in a single microinstruction, as in Section 8.8, even though a register performing the function of ***MIR*** is included. The original Wilkes model followed this approach.

Whether or not branch and transfer operations should be combined depends on the frequency of branch operations and the cost of lengthening the **ROM** word to accommodate both operations. In the case of a transformer **ROM** with no ***MIR***, this cost is negligible. The same number of transformers must be provided whether the two types of operations are done together or separately. A way to express the cost added to the **ROM** might be in the cost of storing 0's. A combined transfer and increment ***MAR*** microinstruction will contain mostly 0's in the branch section (in fact, mostly zeros altogether). It costs nothing but wire to store a 0 in a transformer **ROM**. The situation is quite different in a semiconductor **ROM** where an active device must be provided for each bit. This device is open-circuited in the last stage of the manufacturing process if the bit is 0.

Microprogramming has been used in the design of multifunction desk calculators. In some cases the microprogram is stored in a read-write memory. In some such machines additional memory locations are provided for short programs written by the user. This practice provides the user with a rather difficult assembly language, namely microcode. Clearly the microprogramming options must be severely limited in this case to make the language at least tractable for the casual programmer.

PROBLEMS

8.1 It has been deemed desirable to change the instruction list of the microprogrammed SIC of Section 8.3 to agree with the list given for Problem 6.6. Write a control sequence for the execute phase of the memory reference instructions listed in Problem 6.6, which can be assembled in a one-to-one fashion into the microcode of Section 8.3. Use AHPL. Assemble the microcode of the short sequence of steps necessary to implement the OR instruction. Let the unused bit 17 of ***MIR*** (see Fig. 8.5) specify the transfer $AC \leftarrow \overline{AC}$. Let 1011 specify a branch with branch function, AC_0. (Hint: It may be necessary to generate two simultaneous control pulses which will interchange ***MD*** and *AC*.)

8.2 Translate the 12-step microprogram control sequence of Section 8.3 to a hard-wired control sequencer.

8.3 Supply the third, fourth, and fifth terms of the sum-of-products expression given by Eq. 8.2.

8.4 Discuss why a microprogrammable control unit cannot by itself be called a computer.

8.5 In terms of the machine described in Section 8.3, write a more detailed transfer statement using realizable combinational logic subroutines which can take the place of the figurative

$$\text{DEST}(MAR) \leftarrow \text{ORIG}(MIR)$$

(Hint: It may be necessary to list all registers in a matrix and use SELECT and DECODE.) Sketch the logic block diagram of the hardware described by your subroutine.

8.6 The microprogrammable bus-oriented machine described by Figs. 8.8, 8.10, and 8.11 is to be microprogrammed to form a special purpose computer for information retrieval applications. One special instruction is to be included which will search a list of words in the random access memory, beginning with the address specified by register ***IA***. If one of these words is the same as the contents of index register ***IB***, the in-instruction will terminate by leaving the corresponding address in ***IA***. If no matching word is found, the instruction will leave $\overline{\epsilon(18)}$ in ***IA***. The number of words in the list is assumed to have been previously deposited in the register ***MAX***.

Write a microprogram for the execution of the single instruction discussed above (since no address is required it is coded like an Operate instruction) in MICRAL. It may be necessary to use at least one branch function not listed in Fig. 8.8. Do not worry about the ***MIR*** code specifying this function.

8.7 Refer to the microprogrammable bus-oriented machine of Section 8.4 of the textbook. Write in MICRAL a control microprogram which will divide (discarding the remainder) a 17-bit positive integer in ***AC*** by $2^{\perp MAX}$. A number between 0 and 15 has been placed in ***MAX*** by a previous sequence. The answer will be left in ***AC***. Microcode two instructions only: the first transfer microinstruction appearing in your sequence and the first branch microinstruction appearing in your sequence. Add branch functions to Fig. 8.8 if necessary.

8.8 A proposed computer is to have 2^{13} 16-bit words of random access memory. Certain memory reference instructions are to be two address instructions. For example, an instruction might call for adding the contents of two locations in the random access memory and leaving the result in a high-speed register. The machine will have eight high-speed registers, one of which must serve as a program counter and two of which must serve as an instruction register. The remaining five may serve as data registers (the output of the random access memory could be connected to a bus), accumulators, index registers, or whatever. A link is associated with only one register. The last 26 bits of the instruction registers contain the 13-bit addresses of the two arguments. The left-most 6 bits may be used to specify the op code, indexing, and indirect addressing. The 26 address bits of the instruction register double as the memory address registers. Thus a fetch cycle would call for placing the contents of ***PC*** in the first 13 address bits and $\top(\perp PC + 1)$ in the other 13-bit address register.

Set up a system of buses to handle data in the machine under microprogram control. Devise a system of microprogram control branches and transfer operations to allow as much flexibility as possible. Use a 24-bit **ROM**. Make your specifications sufficiently complete to allow unambiguous coding of microinstructions.

8.9 Devise a suitable instruction list for the machine discussed in Problem 8.8. Include an instruction which will add two arguments from the random access memory and place the result in a high-speed register. Also include an instruction which will take the two's-complement of a 16-bit word from a random access memory location and place the result in another location of the random access memory. Write microprograms for these instructions in an appropriate APL-like microassembly language.

8.10 Write in MICRAL the microprogram for the instruction fetch operation in the microprogrammed bus-oriented SIC. Provide for both indexing and indirect addressing.

8.11 Consider the microprogrammable machine of Section 8.4 modified only to the extent that transfers are controlled as shown in Figs. 8.12 and 8.13. Suppose the right-most eight bits of the ***AC*** is a coded character which is the same as one of 20 eight-bit characters stored at consecutive locations in the **ROM**. Write in MICRAL a sequence of microinstructions which will compare ***AC*** with the list of characters until the identical character is found. A number between 1 and 20, which identifies this character, is to be left in ***IA***. Note that no indexing capability is available for addresses in the **ROM**. If necessary, branch functions may be added to the list of Fig. 8.8.

8.12 Assume the same hardware configuration described in Problem 8.11. Write in MICRAL a sequence of microinstructions which will accomplish the conversion of a 13-bit binary number stored initially in ω^{13}/AC into four binary-coded-decimal digits.

8.13 Design the hard-wired control sequencer for the microprogrammable configuration described in Section 8.4. Do not include modifications added in later sections.

8.14 Complete the last half of the microprogram for converting four BCD digits to a binary number as given in Section 8.5.

8.15 Suggest improvements to the branching scheme of Section 8.6. Design an alternate scheme that will take advantage of all 18 bits of the branch microinstruction for each possible assembly of a 12-bit **ROM** address.

8.16 Rewrite the microcontrol sequence of Section 8.3 for use with a semiconductor **ROM** which does not require ***MIR***. Assume that the output $\mathbf{ROM}^{\perp MAR}$ is in the form of properly synchronized levels rather than pulses.

8.17 Write the control sequences for the SIC operate instructions in MICRAL. Expand the list of branch operations as needed.

8.18 Are transformers for conditional branches as discussed in Section 8.8 actually required? Suggest an alternate hardware configuration.

8.19 Assume that a control unit is to be constructed using an **ROM** which will cost 1¢ per bit regardless of the length of a word. Suppose 1 step in the control sequence out of four is a branch. Twenty bits will be required to microcode a transfer operation, and 20 bits will be required to microcode a branch. Compute the costs of the **ROM** for separate branch and transfer operations, and for branches and transfers combined in the same microinstruction. Assume a total of 4000 branch and transfer steps in the control sequence. Assume that the cost of storing 0's is also 1¢ per bit. Neglect the decoder. What will be the percentage decrease execution time achieved by combining branches and transfers. If the cost of the **ROM** is 10% of the cost of the overall machine, compare the cost performance ratios for the two approaches.

8.20 Redesign the microcontrol sequencer of Fig. 8.13 to provide a separate address register ***CAR*** for constants stored in the **ROM**. Assume that this register can be reset, indexed, and loaded from the ***OBUS*** by hard-wired control ($\alpha^4/\boldsymbol{MIR} = 0110$). Rework Problem 8.11 assuming this capability.

REFERENCES

1. Husson, S. S., *Microprogramming Principles and Practice*, Prentice-Hall, Englewood Cliffs, N.J., 1970.

2. Wilkes, M. V., "The Best Way to Design an Automatic Calculating Machine" Report of Manchester University Computer Inaugural Conference, July, 1951, pp. 16–18.

3. Wilkes, M. V., and Stringer, J. B., "Microprogramming and the Design of the Control Circuits in Electronic Digital Computers," *Proc. Comb. Phil. Soc.*, Vol. 49, Part 2, 1953, pp. 230–238.

4. Wilkes, M. V., Renwick, W., and Wheeler, D., "The Design of a Control Unit of an Electronic Digital Computer," *Proc. IEE*, Vol. 105, Pt. B, 1958, p.121.

5. Gerace, G. B., "Microprogram Control for Computing Systems," *IRE Trans. Elec. Computer*, Vol. EC-12, 1963.

6. Tucker, S. G., "Emulation of Large Systems," *Commun. ACM*, Vol. 8, No. 12, Dec. 1965.
7. Foglia, H. R., McDermid, W. L., and Peterson, H. E., "Card Capacitor—A Semi Permanent Read Only Memory," *IBM J. Res. Development*, Vol. 5, No. 1, 1961.
8. Bush, G. H., "Microprogramming," IBM Technical Report, No. 00-158L, SDD Division, Poughkeepsie, New York, March 7, 1967.
9. *A Guide to the IBM System 370, Model 165*, GC20-1730-0, June, 1970.

9

Intersystem Communications

9.1. INTRODUCTION

All large data processing facilities constitute a network of interacting vector-handling digital systems. Each of these systems includes at least an elementary control unit. These systems with their control units might be regarded as a set of separate intelligences organized to cooperate in accomplishing a computational task. One might observe a tenuous analogy with an industrial organization or committee of people, united to work on a particular problem.

Fortunately the coordination of digital systems is less difficult, and their individual capacities are used more efficiently than is the case with most committees of people. The intelligence of certain digital systems (such as tape transports) is so rudimentary that they can function only in close communication with another system. In a computation facility there is nearly always a very strong committee chairman, usually but not always the central processor, which closely coordinates the activity of the individual digital systems.

Prior to our first major encounter with system interaction in the discussion of input/output in Chapter 10, it will be desirable to develop a means of describing intersystem communications. The problem of interconnecting two systems and providing for their communication is called *interfacing*. Problems arise in interfacing at the circuit design level, the sequential circuits level, and at the systems level. Although very real to the person who must design an interface, circuit problems, such as level conversion and impedance matching, can be conveniently divorced from a systems treatment. The sequential circuit problem involved in interfacing is *synchronization.* The discussion of this problem in Section 9.4 will be applicable throughout the book.

The remainder of the chapter will be devoted to an analysis of communications at the systems level. Some representation of the communications activity must be integrated into AHPL. As will be apparent, we shall be still less concerned with automatic hardware generations at the multi-system level. Data lines and control lines which interconnect systems, will be defined in the *metalanguage* (English) rather than in AHPL. This is, of course, consistent with the usual practice of constructing digital systems separately and connecting them as a final step.* The timing of communications between systems is part of the control function. We must, therefore, provide notation for sending and receiving signals in AHPL.

Closely related to multiple control is the notation of parallel processing. Parallel operations can be specified at several levels. The simplest of parallel operations can be handled with the notation already available. In its most sophisticated form, parallel processing clearly involves multiple control. It is an intermediate form, *parallel sequences* of operations, which shall be considered in the next section. As parallel sequences become longer and more complex, the distinction between this format and multiple control becomes less clear.

9.2. PARALLEL OPERATIONS

No one can avoid the observation that performing a set of computing operations simultaneously or in parallel will require a shorter time than performing the same operations in sequence. In every context the degree of parallelism is limited by operations whose arguments are dependent on the results of other operations. In some cases this dependence is unavoidable. In others it is a function of a particular analysis or approach to a problem. It is often difficult to ascertain which is the case.

There are many ways in which parallelism can be built into a computer. The simplest, perhaps, is the processing of bits of data words simultaneously in arithmetic or logical operations, rather than serially. This form of parallelism is almost universal. Only in special-purpose computers, which are locked into situations where continuous availability is required but computation

* Individually controlled systems are not always mounted in physically separate units. Certain system pairs must be mounted in very close (inches) proximity to maximize communications speed.

speed is unimportant, can the small savings in cost permitted by serial-by-bit operation be justified.

Other commonly employed parallelisms include simultaneous I/O and execution of different programs in a batch processing environment. Occasionally more than one complete central processor share the same peripherals and memory, and operate in parallel. Where look-ahead is employed, it is possible to have more than one assembly language instruction in various stages of execution at one time. The overall time saving achieved by this technique is heavily dependent on having an object program with a minimum of interdependence between consecutive operations. Another technique, which is even more problem dependent, involves the use of a single control unit to control the functioning of an array of processors which perform almost identical computations. The last two approaches will be discussed in Chapters 14 and 15.

The benefit to be derived by executing assembly language instructions in parallel is contingent on factors beyond the control of the logical designer. Such, however, is not the case for the sequence of register transfers making up the execution of an individual instruction. In the latter case, parallelism of register transfers should be maximized. This observation is underscored where high-speed solid state main memories or scratch-pad memories are employed. One cannot, then, point to slow memory cycles as determining execution times, making sequential register transfer times relatively unimportant.

In earlier chapters clarity was emphasized. Transfers were specified as parallel only where this did not interrupt the discussion. As a general rule the designer should arrange the AHPL sequence so as to minimize the number of control delays and asynchronous WAIT's in each path through the control sequencer.

The notation which has been introduced thus far provides for simultaneous individual transfers but not simultaneous sequences. The most complicated case which can as yet be handled is illustrated by the following sequence. The corresponding hardware is shown in Fig. 9.1. In effect, two synchronous and an asynchronous operation are initiated simultaneously. The OR gate is included so that control can branch from other points to step 2. As many simultaneous

1. $\boldsymbol{A} \leftarrow \text{INC}(\boldsymbol{A})$; $\boldsymbol{B} \leftarrow \uparrow \boldsymbol{C}$, NO DELAY
2. $\boldsymbol{MD} \leftarrow \boldsymbol{M}^{\perp \boldsymbol{MA}}$, WAIT

synchronous transfers as desired may be included in parallel with one asynchronous operation. The situation is not basically different for a set of individual transfers in parallel with a sequence.

Now suppose it is desired to allow two sequences of transfers to be carried out in parallel. We need no new notation or hardware unless at least one of

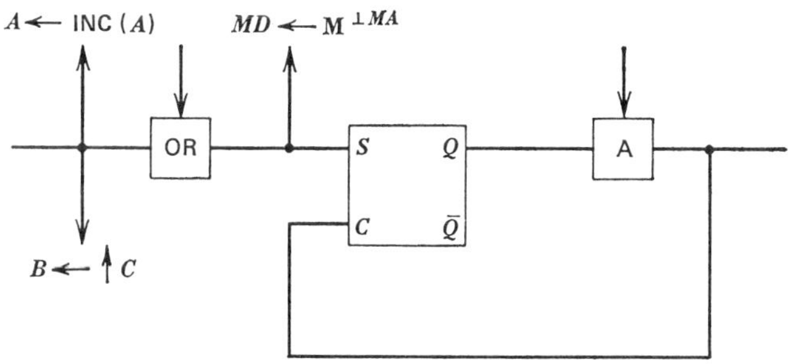

FIGURE 9.1. Simple parallel transfers.

the sequences involves an asynchronous transfer. Suppose, for example, that it is desired that the following two sequences be carried out in parallel:

1. $\boldsymbol{A} \leftarrow \mathrm{INC}(\boldsymbol{A})$	1. $\boldsymbol{D} \leftarrow \downarrow\boldsymbol{A}$
2. $\boldsymbol{B} \leftarrow \uparrow\boldsymbol{A}$	2. $\boldsymbol{E} \leftarrow \mathrm{INC}(\boldsymbol{D})$
3. $\boldsymbol{C} \leftarrow \boldsymbol{\omega}^5/\boldsymbol{B}$	

These sequences may be merged in the established notation as follows:

1. $\boldsymbol{A} \leftarrow \mathrm{INC}(\boldsymbol{A})$; $\boldsymbol{D} \leftarrow \downarrow\boldsymbol{A}$
2. $\boldsymbol{B} \leftarrow \uparrow\boldsymbol{A}$; $\boldsymbol{E} \leftarrow \mathrm{INC}(\boldsymbol{D})$
3. $\boldsymbol{C} \leftarrow \boldsymbol{\omega}^5/\boldsymbol{B}$

This tactic cannot be applied where asynchronous transfers are involved since the timing synchronism of the individual steps is destroyed. In this case it is necessary to permit more than one control pulse to propagate simultaneously through parallel paths in the control unit. Suppose we have the following situation where the contents of an index register are added asynchronously to $\boldsymbol{AC}$, while a reference to memory is being executed. The separate sequences each include a synchronous transfer as well.

To handle this situation while still writing all AHPL steps in a single list we introduce some new notations:

1. $\boldsymbol{PC} \leftarrow \boldsymbol{\omega}^{13}/\boldsymbol{AC}$, DIVERGE (A2, B2)
A2. $\boldsymbol{MA} \leftarrow \boldsymbol{PC}$
A3. $\boldsymbol{MD} \leftarrow \mathbf{M}^{\perp \boldsymbol{MA}}$, WAIT
A4. $\rightarrow (5)$
B2. $\boldsymbol{AC} \leftarrow \mathrm{ADD}(\boldsymbol{AC}, \boldsymbol{IA})$, WAIT
B3. $\boldsymbol{AC} \leftarrow \downarrow\boldsymbol{AC}$
5. CONVERGE (A4, B3)
6.

A hardware mechanism must be provided for a single control sequence which continues following the execution of the parallel sequences. Often it is known

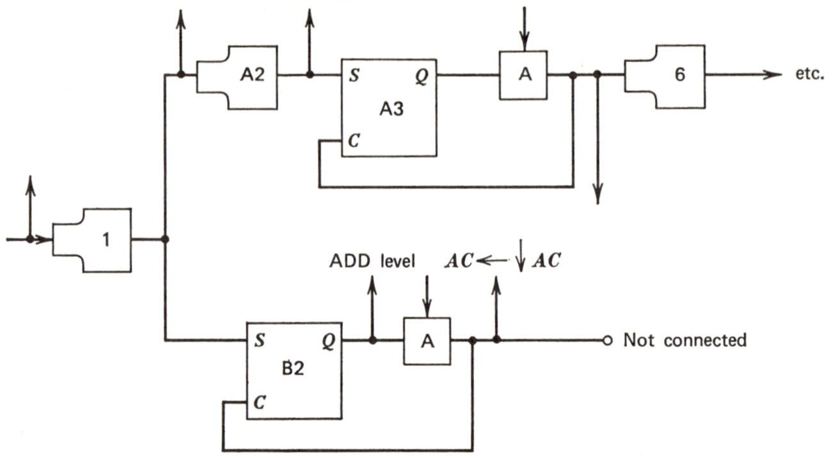

FIGURE 9.2. Convergence with known timing relation.

that one or the other of the sequences will always be completed first. Then convergence may be handled by terminating the faster path at a dead end. In Fig. 9.2 it is assumed that sequence B will always be completed first. In this case there is no actual hardware element corresponding to the convergence step (step 5).

In many cases the relative completion times of two or more parallel sequences may be unknown. In this case a special fundamental mode designed convergence circuit must be provided. The symbol and application of such a circuit are illustrated very simply in Fig. 9.3.

The output of the convergence circuit shown in Fig. 9.3 will be a pulse, synchronized with the second of two input pulses to arrive. Depending on gate

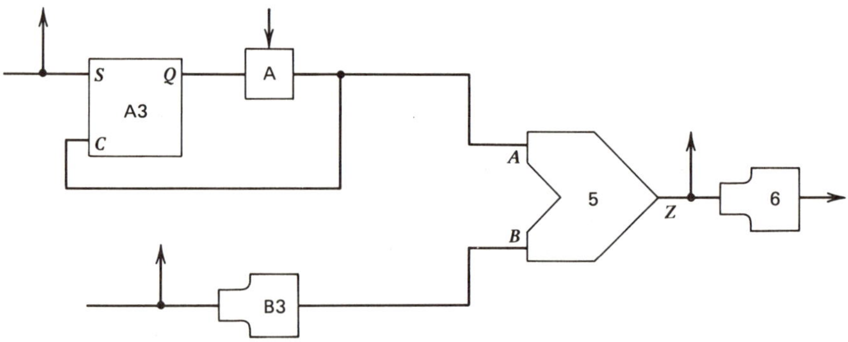

FIGURE 9.3. Convergence of arbitrary sequences.

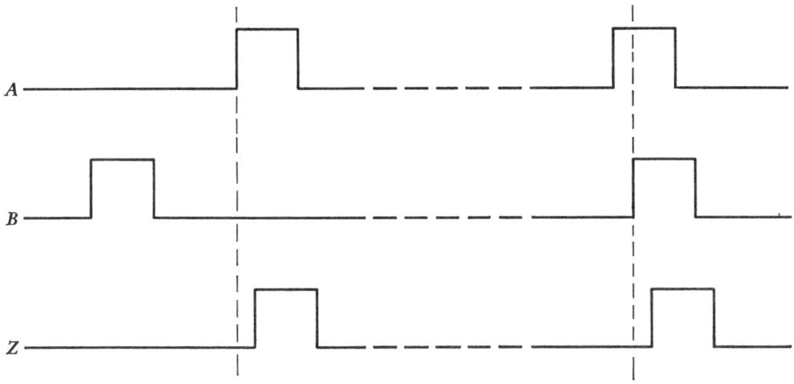

FIGURE 9.4. Timing diagram for convergence circuit.

delays and the clock frequency, it might be necessary to delay the output pulse one clock period. A typical timing diagram under the assumption of no one clock period delay is presented in Fig. 9.4. We will not be concerned here with the detailed design of the circuit. We leave it as a homework problem for those students with previous background in sequential circuit design.

We shall utilize the notation for divergence and convergence of control, as introduced above, as part of AHPL in the succeeding sections of this chapter. We will not give further attention to the particular hardware approach to convergence. In a design context it may be desirable to further refine the AHPL notation to identify the type of convergence circuit. Our attention throughout the remainder of the book will be restricted to developing control sequences. It will be convenient to not be concerned with the relative time required by parallel paths. Thus we use the same notation for all cases and leave the decision as to whether a hardware convergence circuit is needed to the "translation to hardware" step.

Example 9.1

A digital process controller is to be designed. The principal difference between this controller and the machine tool controller of example 5.2 is that this controller must operate at the maximum possible data transfer rate. The register configuration for the controller is shown in Fig. 9.5. While the flip-flop ***run*** is 1, words are read continuously and in sequence from **M**. Each word is to be added to a constant which is stored in register ***KK***, and then placed in register ***CR***. The vectors are read from ***CR*** asynchronously by the external system at varying data rates up to the maximal possible. The data transfers from ***CR*** are controlled by means of pulse communications. The digital controller supplies a ***ready*** pulse when a vector is placed in ***CR***. The external system responds with a completion pulse as it reads this data.

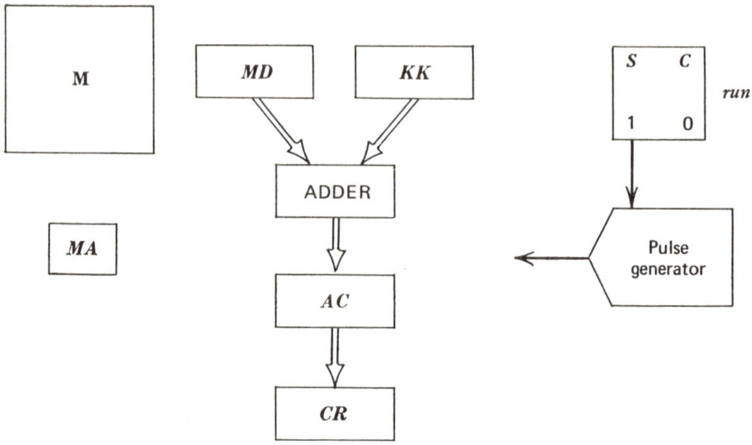

FIGURE 9.5. Registers for process controller.

The registers ***MA***, ***KK***, and the flip-flop *run* are all connected to panel switches. The initial address and the constant to be added can be inserted manually. When the flip-flop *run* is cleared, the digital system should stop. When ***run*** goes from 0 to 1, a control pulse is supplied to the control unit by a pulse generator as shown.

Solution. We shall examine two possible designs for the control unit of the process controller. The control sequences are given in Fig. 9.6. The sequence of Fig. 9.6a is straight forward. First a word is read from memory, then it is added to the constant in ***KK***, and then it is placed in the register ***CR***. The notation of step 6 indicates that a ***ready*** pulse is supplied to the external system and control waits at step 6 for a completion pulse in response. If ***run*** = 1, control returns to step 2 to read the next word from memory.

The disadvantage of the sequence of Fig. 9.6a is that three time-consuming operations read from memory, addition, and the asynchronous transfer are done

1. START
2. $\boldsymbol{MD} \leftarrow \mathrm{M}^{\perp \boldsymbol{MA}}$, WAIT
3. $\boldsymbol{MA} \leftarrow \mathrm{INC}(\boldsymbol{MA})$
4. $\boldsymbol{AC} \leftarrow \mathrm{ADD}(\boldsymbol{MD}, \boldsymbol{KK})$
   6 DELAYS
5. $\boldsymbol{CR} \leftarrow \boldsymbol{AC}$
6. line ***ready*** ← PULSE, WAIT
7. $\rightarrow (\boldsymbol{run} \times 2 + \overline{\boldsymbol{run}} \times 8)$
8. HALT

(a)

2. DIVERGE (A3, B3, C3)

A3. $\boldsymbol{MD} \leftarrow \mathrm{M}^{\perp \boldsymbol{MA}}$, WAIT
A4. $\rightarrow (5)$
B3. $\boldsymbol{AC} \leftarrow \mathrm{ADD}(\boldsymbol{ARG}, \boldsymbol{KK})$ 6 DELAYS
B4. $\rightarrow (5)$
C3. line ***ready*** ← PULSE, WAIT

5. CONVERGE (A4, B4, C3)
6. $\boldsymbol{MA} \leftarrow \mathrm{INC}(\boldsymbol{MA})$; $\boldsymbol{ARG} \leftarrow \boldsymbol{MD}$; $\boldsymbol{CR} \leftarrow \boldsymbol{AC}$
7. $\rightarrow (\boldsymbol{run} \times 2 + \overline{\boldsymbol{run}} \times 8)$
8. HALT

(b)

FIGURE 9.6. Control sequences for process controller.

sequentially. In the sequence of Fig. 9.6b, these three operations are done in parallel for three different data words. One additional register, ***ARG***, has been added to store one argument of the adder. In this way no register is involved in more than one of the three primary time-consuming operations. Each word from memory must pass through each of the three steps sequentially. However, while one data word is being read from ***CR***, a second word is being readied for output through the addition of ***KK***, and a third data word is being read from memory. With each pass through the control sequence, each of three words advance one step in the process. After convergence, step 5 moves the data ahead and increments ***MA***.

ARG would be unnecessary if all three of the principal operations discussed above were synchronous, requiring only one clock period. In this case, expression 9.1 would be a legitimate step. Since at least one of these operations is asynchronous,

$$\boldsymbol{MD} \leftarrow \mathrm{M}^{\perp \boldsymbol{MA}};\ \boldsymbol{AC} \leftarrow \mathrm{ADD}(\boldsymbol{MD}, \boldsymbol{KK}) \tag{9.1}$$

expression 9.1 might result in a change in ***MD*** while addition is in progress. A similar observation could be made to justify the need for separate registers ***CR*** and ***AC***. ∎

9.3. WHERE IS CONTROL?

As the user looks from the outside of a large digital system, he sees many input and output ports which seem to be simultaneously absorbing and disgorging information. From the users' manuals he learns of many internal activities which are said to take place simultaneously. What is controlling all of these activities? How is it that these activities seem to cooperate rather than compete? Are these parallel operations controlled by a single intelligence or several?

That parallel control sequences and separate control might not be totally different can be argued in terms of the figurative model shown in Fig. 9.7. A portion of a control sequencer featuring three parallel sequences is represented by Fig. 9.7a. Only the paths of propagation of the control pulse within the control unit are depicted. The transfers which take place are left to the imagination of the reader.

Figure 9.7b differs from Fig. 9.7a only in that the individual parallel branches have become more complicated. A control pulse can circulate in a path containing a loop for long periods of time. Where such is the case for two or more loops, one might argue that the pulse convergence circuit serves to provide occasional communications between the separate control sequences embodied in these loops.

In Fig. 9.7c the individual control loops have been formally separated to form distinct control units. Two-way communications between these separate

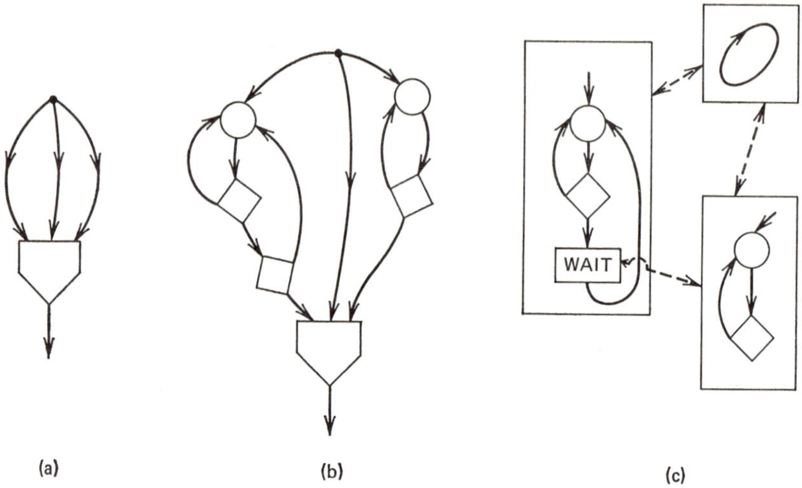

FIGURE 9.7. Parallel sequences and multiple control.

control units is indicated by the dashed arrows. Presumably this communications capability is more flexible than could be provided by depending on the pulse convergence circuit. To go further in comparing the details of interloop communications between Figs. 9.7a and 9.7b would be esoteric at best. The primary purpose of the rest of this chapter will be to develop the model suggested by Fig. 9.7c.

Recall once more that the three parallel paths, in the parallel control sequence of Example 9.1, worked with three disjoint sets of registers. Only in step 6 of Fig. 9.6b, after the three paths have converged, does a transfer involve registers from more than one of these sets. This is a method, not necessarily the only method, of insuring the satisfaction of what we shall label Rule 9.1.

Rule 9.1 A single register can be the destination of no more than one transfer in the same clock period.

As pointed out in Chapter 4, the result of trying to transfer two vectors into a register simultaneously is unpredictable and cannot be tolerated. Rule 9.2 applies to registers which may be the destination of an asynchronous transfer. Recall that precautions were taken to assure satisfaction of this rule in Example 9.1.

Rule 9.2 The contents of a register must not be read at a time when they might be in the process of change due to an asynchronous transfer.

When control is separated into two or more distinct control units as in Fig. 9.7c, the register arrays are usually separated and associated with the

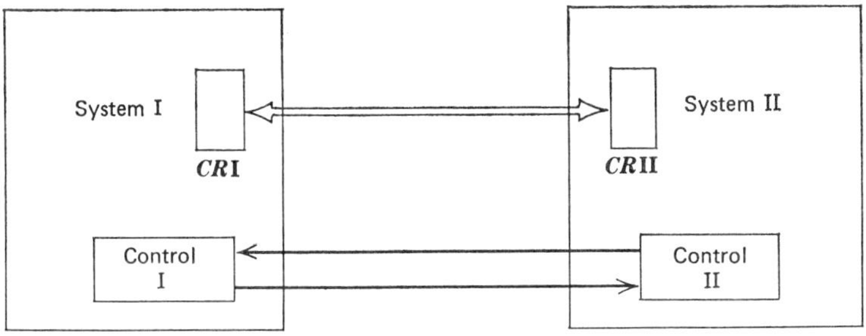

FIGURE 9.8. System interaction.

individual control units. The result is two separate subsystems. In order that there be interaction between the systems, certain registers must be provided which can be accessed by both systems. As suggested by the communications registers, ***CR I*** and ***CR II*** in the model of Fig. 9.8, such a register remains part of one of the systems.

In order to assure that Rules 9.1 and 9.2 are satisfied and to assure that data transfers between the two systems via ***CR I*** and ***CR II*** are meaningful, some means must be provided so that each of the control units can *know* what the other is doing to ***CR***. We shall find it convenient to use the term *know* in reference to control units from time to time in our discussion.

Defn. 9.1 A control unit may be said to *know* a piece of information related to its function if this information is properly coded and stored so that it may be used to influence branch operations within this control unit.

Knowledge fitting into this category can be interchanged in vector form through the ***CR***'s. As we shall see in Section 9.5, some information must be transmitted in the form of control pulses in order to coordinate the vector transfers between systems. These control lines are indicated by single lines in Fig. 9.8. Reference to pulse communications has been made in several of the examples already considered.

9.4. SYNCHRONIZATION

Until now it has been assumed that all systems considered were timed by the same clock and that the physical distance between the subsystems was small. If either of these assertions is *not* true, a new set of problems arises. Suppose a pulse from a separately clocked control unit II in Fig. 9.8 arrives at control unit I to indicate that a vector has just been placed in ***CR I***. This pulse may clear a WAIT flip-flop and introduce an unsynchronized control pulse into control unit I. Depending on the design of the control

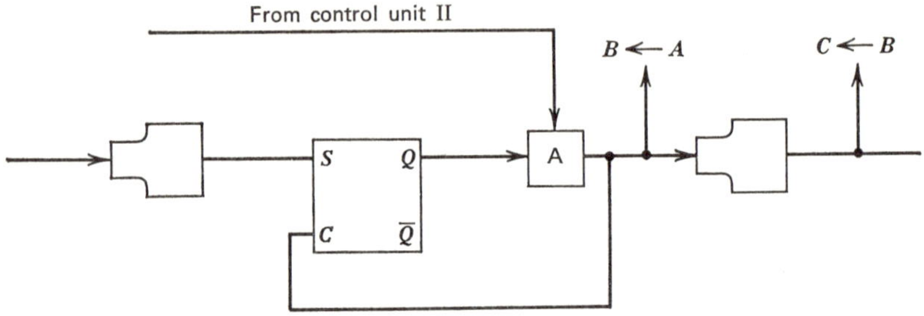

FIGURE 9.9. Unsynchronized pulse in control unit I.

delay, the effect could be an indeterminate output from the control delay reached by this pulse. The pulse could also initiate a transfer which might not be completed before the results were required by a succeeding transfer, as suggested in Fig. 9.9.

Unsynchronized data levels in the communications registers can sometimes cause problems also. Certain applications call for periodically checking a communications register without being instructed to do so by a pulse communication. An example is the interrupt register to be discussed in Chapter 10. The transfer of data into a communications register which can be so freely sampled must be carefully synchronized with a clock pulse.

The synchronization of levels is easily accomplished as shown in Fig. 9.10a. A vector of data lines from a register or bus from another system is shown at the input of a subsystem. The synchronization mechanism is shown for only one line. Synchronization is accomplished by merely clocking the signal levels into an input register, using the internal clock of the receiving system. The logic level on the input lines may change at any time, even during a clock pulse. This pulse may or may not succeed in triggering the level changes into the register. If not, the change in register output is delayed one clock period. Typically the level on an input line will remain unchanged for several clock periods. In any case, whatever the register output, it will always be synchronized with the clock and internal control signals.

The system of Fig. 9.10a would be most commonly used where the individual lines in the vector are independent. Difficulty can arise if a vector representing a binary number, for example, is transferred in this way. The level changes may not appear at the subsystem boundary at precisely the same point in time. If the appearance of a binary vector approximately coincides with a clock pulse, some of the level changes may be clocked into the register while others may wait for the next clock pulse. If the register is sampled in the interim an error may result.

Consider the machine tool controller of Chapter 5. The normal sequence of numbers transmitted to the controller might vary only slowly in magnitude. It

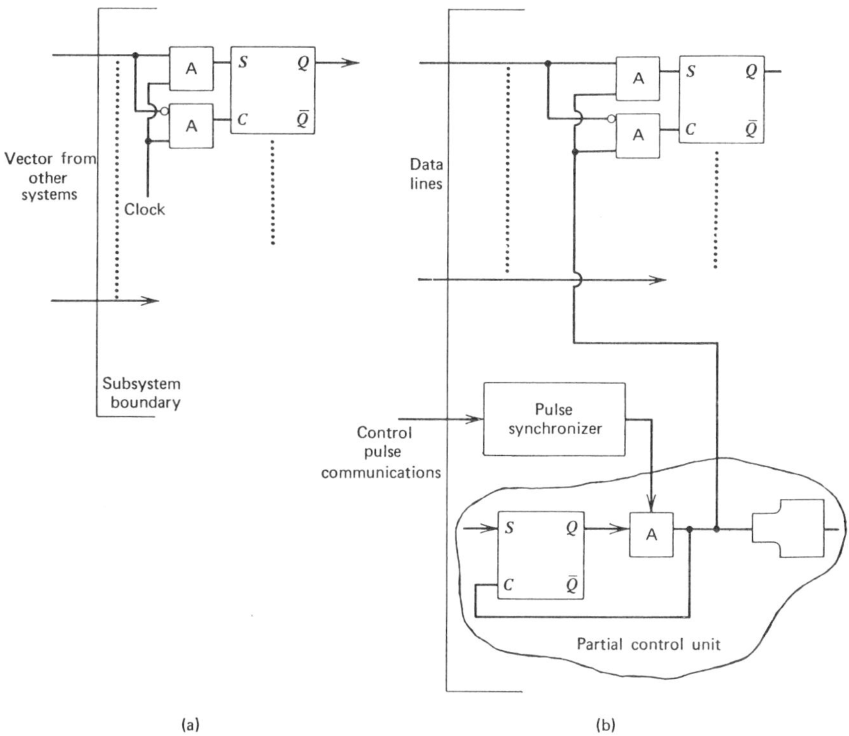

FIGURE 9.10. Synchronizing data transfers.

might be tempting to supply the numbers to the tool in sequence to be synchronized as shown in Fig. 9.10a. In this way no control communications would be required. Suppose two consecutive data numbers expressed in octal are 007765 followed by 010043. If the second number were only partially clocked into the tool register, some such number as 017767 might reside there for one clock period. This number is appreciably greater than the two correct numbers, which are close together in magnitude. An undesired transient in the movement of the controller might be the result. This problem could be most easily avoided by letting a control pulse from the controller place data in the tool register. Thus, only one control unit would be involved; and no synchronization would be required.

If two systems are physically close and timed by a single clock, it is common for the control unit of the sending system to pulse information into registers in the receiving system. Where the systems are physically remote or timed by separate clocks, so that synchronization is required, this approach is rarely used. Most commonly, a communications pulse is provided to the control unit of the receiving system to indicate when new information has arrived on the data lines. When such a pulse is received, the control unit may treat the data lines as if they were a bus within the receiving system. The vector on the data lines may be pulsed by the control unit into any register.

As illustrated, figuratively, in Fig. 9.10b, the synchronization problem is transferred to the pulse line. As discussed at the beginning of the section, an unsynchronized pulse cannot be allowed to enter a control unit. The circuit required to synchronize a control pulse is somewhat more complicated than the single flip-flop required to synchronize a logic level. An approach to pulse synchronization is most easily discussed in terms of the circuit of Fig. 9.11a which utilizes two *S-C* flip-flops. The input pulse is used to set the first flip-flop (output y_1) to 1. The level y_1 cannot be gated with a clock pulse to generate a synchronized pulse, as it too is unsynchronized. A partial pulse could result. The level y_1 is very much analogous to the input level in the level synchronizer

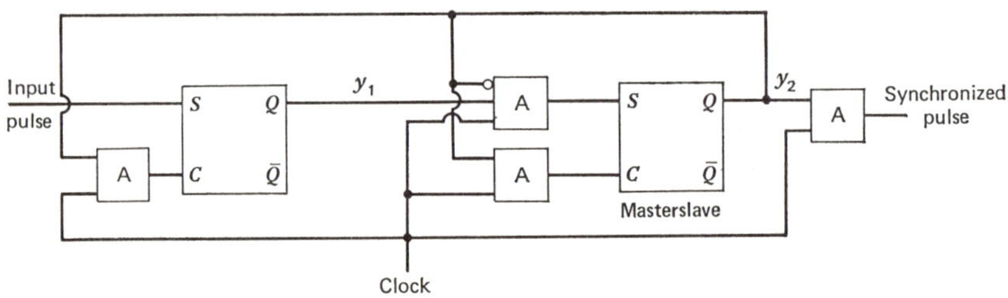

(a)

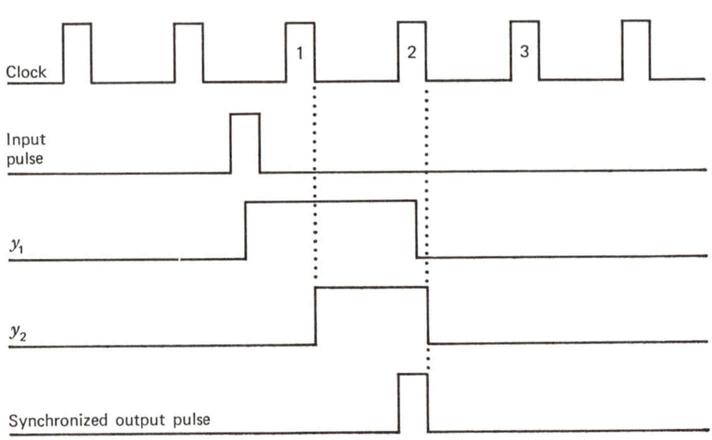

(b)

FIGURE 9.11. Pulse synchronization.

of Fig. 9.11a. This level is used to set a second *S-C* flip-flop at the time of the next clock pulse, labeled 1 in Fig. 9.11b. The synchronized level, y_2, can then be used to gate a synchronized pulse as illustrated.

Note that the clock pulse labeled 2, which generates the synchronized pulse, also clears both flip-flops, y_1 and y_2 to 0. This readies the circuit to accept another input pulse. Although the input pulse need not be as narrow as shown, it must have returned to 0 before clock pulse 3 arrives. As a general observation, some control communications must always be in the form of pulses, so as to discretely separate each data vector in sequence. Each pulse will cause a separate action by the control unit. Depending on the form of the synchronizing circuit, these pulses could be several clock periods wide; but in some sense they must be pulses.

The right-most flip-flop of Fig. 9.11a must be a master-slave flip-flop, since its inputs are a direct function of its outputs. The left-most flip-flop could be merely two cross-coupled NOR gates. Thus the total number of gates used in Fig. 9.11a, including those used to implement the flip-flops, is 12. There are three state variables or feedback loops in the circuit: y_1, y_2, and the internal loop of the master-slave flip-flop.

The level mode designed pulse synchronizer of Fig. 9.12 is slightly more economical in that it utilizes only 10 gates. More important, it will generate a synchronized output pulse one clock period sooner, in most cases. The output from this circuit will be a pulse, synchronized with the first clock pulse following, but not overlapping, each input pulse. Where rapid response

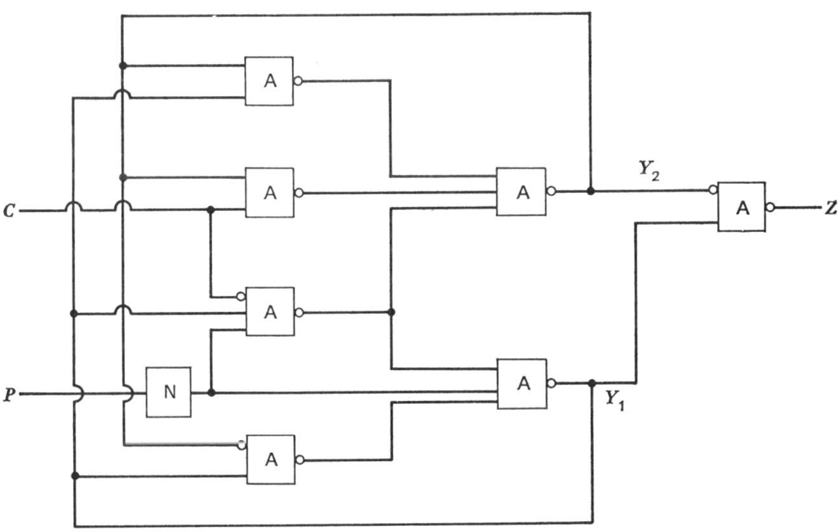

FIGURE 9.12. Faster responding pulse synchronizer.

is important, the circuit of Fig. 9.12 would clearly be preferable. In other applications where the extra clock period is not critical, the easily constructed circuit of Fig. 9.11 could be used with perhaps extra confidence. In some cases the extra clock period may be desirable to allow sufficient time for the data to arrive.

9.5. CONVENTIONS

Control pulses will be transmitted between systems as parts of two types of activity. In one case the pulse will enter the control unit at a WAIT point in the second system. In the second case the pulse will be used to set (or clear) any flip-flop (or place data in a register) of the receiving system. A flip-flop which is set in this way can be referred to by the control unit of the receiving system at will. This same flip-flop may also be set or cleared by the receiving system itself.

For both of these cases, a pulse synchronizer as shown in either Fig. 9.11 or Fig. 9.12 will be included where required by separate clocks or physical distances. No reference to the synchronizer will be made in the control sequence of either system.

The notation in the control sequence of a unit which sends a pulse to a WAIT point in another system will be that given in Fig. 9.13a. It is assumed that the line y will be identified in the discussion as a line which connects the two control units. Various types of notation will be allowed for keeping track of communications lines. Special statements would be required to identify these lines in an AHPL program intended for automatic translation to hardware. We shall not include such statements in our discussion. Our point of

line $y \leftarrow$ PULSE

(a) Sending pulse from control unit

$A \leftarrow B$, WAIT for y PULSE

(b) Receiving pulse in control unit

(In central processor)	$z \leftarrow 1$
(In unit one)	$B \leftarrow A$

(c) Transmitting data in pulse form

$MD \leftarrow IOBUS$
$MD \leftarrow A$ (From unit one)

(d) Receiving data levels

FIGURE 9.13. Notation for intersystem communication.

view will be to keep the number of communications lines referred to in a given section to a minimum, so they can be conveniently identified in the discussion.

A typical sequence associated with the receiving of a communications pulse by a control unit is shown in Fig. 9.13b. This resembles the notation previously used to indicate a WAIT for an asynchronous transfer, except that the line on which the return pulse is to be expected is indicated specifically. Once again it is implicit that line y passes through a pulse synchronizer if required, prior to connection to the control unit. The notation of Fig. 9.13b is easily extended to permit waiting for a pulse on either one of two lines. (See Problem 9.7.)

The pulsing of data into a flip-flop or register in another system may be denoted as shown in Fig. 9.13c. Whenever a transfer to an external system is specified, the receiving system is denoted in parenthesis on the left side of the transfer statement. This liberal use of English text in AHPL would make the writing of a hardware compiler very difficult. Once again our purpose here is to make the meaning of notation as self-evident as possible. The allowed comments would be much more limited in a version of AHPL actually destined for automatic translation to hardware.

The notation of Fig. 9.13c will be used rarely to specify the transfer of data vectors between unsynchronized systems. An expensive pulse synchronizer on every set or clear line is implied. The notation will prove quite convenient, however, to specify setting or clearing individual flip-flops. In this case only one pulse synchronizer is implicit in the notation.

As discussed in the previous section, most data transfers will be controlled as shown in Fig. 9.10b. The receiving control unit will pulse the data from a set of lines which carry the data vectors in the form of levels. These levels may come directly from the sending system or from a bus interconnecting several systems. Two forms of notation specifying the use of these levels are shown in Fig. 9.13d. The text in parenthesis on the right side of the lower transfer statement indicates that the data vector is taken from a set of lines connected to the output of register A in unit 1.

9.6. DATA TRANSFER RATES

If two systems are synchronized, data can be transmitted for finite periods of time at the rate of one data vector per clock pulse.* This requires that the

* In very fast systems, a new timing problem can arise when an attempt is made to synchronously read data from and pulse data into a register in the same clock period. Control pulses from different control units may not be precisely synchronized. To eliminate the possibility of trouble requires the use of still more complicated memory elements, edge-sensing master-slave flip-flops.

receiving system interrogate a flip-flop or register, in a branch operation, in the same clock period that the transfer takes place. The flip-flop or register would indicate whether or not a new data vector had been placed in the communications register. The branch might compare a counter with the number of vectors to be transferred. This number could have been stored in advance. Alternatively, the branch might depend on a single flip-flop which is set (or cleared) by the sending system as a vector is placed (or not placed) in ***CR*** each clock period.

Suppose that two systems are driven by the same clock but that there is a transmission delay of somewhat less than a clock period between the two systems. Two such systems must be called unsynchronized. Data transfers can still take place at the rate of one vector per clock period, if the transmission delay on the data lines is as great as that on the pulse line. In fact, the transmission delay may act as a stabilizing factor with respect to the problem cited by the most recent footnote.

It is possible to consider long transmission lines as storage media on which sequences of data vectors can propagate simultaneously. When used in this mode, the transmission line must be treated as a separate system with an elaborate interface at each end. As noise becomes a problem, an error checking capability is usually part of this interface.

Transmission lines between subsystems in close physical proximity are not usually considered as storage media. In this case, a data vector must be removed from the line before another vector can be placed on the line. Thus, if r is the number of clock periods delay in transmission, the maximum data transfer rate is $1/r$ vectors per clock period.

All data transmissions discussed so far may be called *non-responsive*. That is, a response was not required from the receiving system corresponding to each data vector transmitted. Non-responsive transmission requires that the receiving system be able to handle data as rapidly as it can be provided by the sending system. Usually the length of the sequence of vectors which can be received without response is limited. Typically, knowledge of the number of vectors (within the allowable limit) to be transmitted in a block is communicated between the control units prior to transmission of the data.

A *responsive* data transmission will be defined as satisfying the following sequence of events. A set of data levels together with a control pulse are transmitted by the sending system. The control pulse enables the receiving system to pulse the data vector into its communications register ***CR***. After the data has been removed from ***CR***, or used in some way by the receiving system, a pulse is returned to the sending system to indicate this fact. Only after receipt of this pulse, can another data vector be placed on the transmission line. One clock period or several may be required to free the communications register in the receiving system. The process may be asynchronous.

Clearly the data transfer rate will always be slower where responsive transmission is used. There is no choice, however, if a long or indeterminate period of time is required to free the receiving communications register.

Example 9.2

Write the control sequences required to transmit a series of vectors from a semiconductor memory, **SM**, in one system, to a slower core memory, **CM**, in another system. Assume that a vector can be read from **SM** in one clock period.

Solution. The outputs of ***MD***, which serves as the memory data register of the sending system, are routed to the register, ***CR***, in the receiving system. The memory address registers for the core memory and semiconductor memory are ***CMA*** and ***SMA*** respectively. A pulse on line ***ready*** tells the receiving system that a vector is available in *MD*. A pulse on line ***empty*** tells the sending system that ***CR*** is free.

The control sequences for the actual data transfers are given in Fig. 9.14. No sequence for setting initial addresses or counting transfers is shown. It is interesting to determine the time required to transmit each data vector. Let us begin with the reading of a word from **SM** in a single clock period, T_c. Next we allow time for synchronizing the ***ready*** pulse in the receiving unit. At best this requires a clock period, T_c. A third clock period is required to place the data vector in ***CR***. We let αT_c represent the time required for the asynchronous write in core memory operation. Before a second word can be read from **SM**, one more clock period is required for synchronizing the response pulse on line ***empty***. The total time required for transferring one vector is given by Eq. 9.2. If the data could be removed from ***CR***

$$\text{Responsive transfer time} = (4 + \alpha)T_c \tag{9.2}$$

in one clock period the transfer time would reduce to $5T_c$. This is the minimum time required for the responsive transmission of a vector between two unsynchronized systems.

Notice that the memory address registers were incremented in parallel with the transfer operations. The same would be the case for any bookkeeping operations required to count the number of transfers.

For completeness, the hardware block diagram implied by the above sequences is given in Fig. 9.15. ∎

(a) Sending

1. $MD \leftarrow \text{SM}^{\perp SMA}$
2. line ***ready*** ← PULSE
3. *SMA* ← INC(*SMA*)
4. WAIT FOR ***empty*** PULSE
5. → 1

(b) Receiving

1. WAIT FOR ***ready*** PULSE
2. ***CR*** ← ***MD*** (From Unit 1)
3. $\text{CM}^{\perp CMA}$ ← ***CR***, WAIT
4. line ***empty*** ← PULSE
5. ***CMA*** ← INC(***CMA***); → 1

FIGURE 9.14. Memory-to-memory transfer sequences.

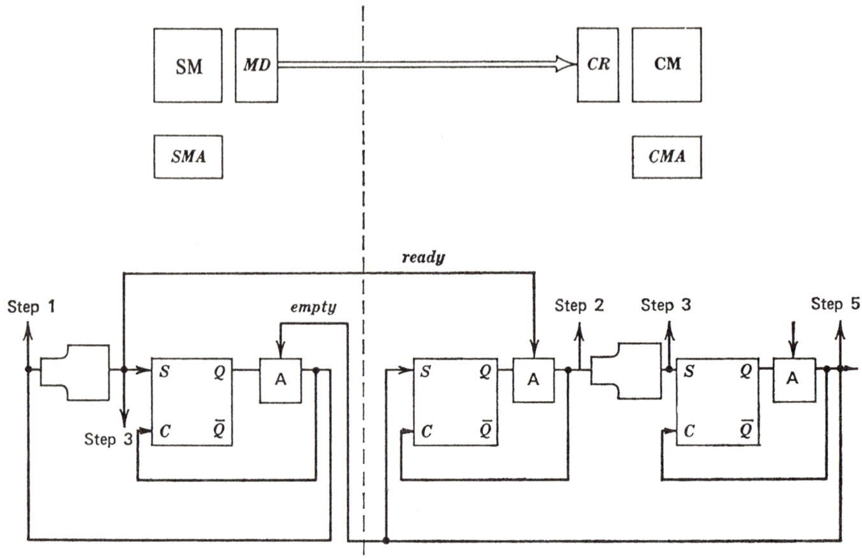

FIGURE 9.15. Memory-to-memory transfer hardware.

9.7. A TAPE TRANSPORT CONTROLLER

In Chapter 10 we shall consider the interconnection of a medium-scale digital computer and its associated peripheral equipments. The viewpoint will be one of looking out from the central processor. The peripheral equipments themselves will not be considered in detail. The example in this section illustrates how the control unit design for a typical peripheral equipment might be approached. In addition, it serves to illustrate the use of conventions defined earlier in this chapter.

One of the special characteristics of I/O devices is that the data format is generally different from that used in the central processor or main memory. On magnetic tape, information is arranged in characters of six to twelve bits (see Fig. 3.26); and the same sort of arrangement is used on paper tape. Punched cards generally consist of 80 columns of 12 positions each, normally read one column at a time. For teletypewriters, information arrives one character at a time. High-speed printers may require that all the characters for one line (100 to 150 characters) be supplied at one time, or they may accept data one character at a time.

The word length of main memory, i.e., the number of bits accessed in a single read-write cycle generally matches none of these I/O data formats. It is therefore necessary to provide means of assembling smaller data groups into larger, and disassembling larger data groups into smaller, as data flows between memory and the I/O devices. This assembly and disassembly may be done by the central processor; but it is more common to provide separate assembly and disassembly logic within the individual I/O devices, for two reasons. First, a single computer may have to communicate with many different types of I/O devices, each with its own special requirements, so that supplying sufficient flexibility in a single CPU would be difficult. Second, providing all these data conversion services would leave the CPU with little time to do anything else. Although a small computer like SIC might use the CPU for these activities, for reasons of economy, we will assume that the central processor accepts and supplies data only in the word length of main memory, and that all assembly, disassembly, and data conversion operations are performed by the I/O devices themselves.

The assembly of data in a tape transport is part of the READ operation. We shall consider the design of the read control sequence in detail. We leave it to the reader to fill in the details for control sequences for other commands. A tape transport is a very complicated device. Only those hardware items which directly influence our discussion will be introduced. For details the reader is referred to Reference [1].

We assume a tape transport with independent control. It is connected to the central processor via a 36-bit ***IOBUS*** on which data words can pass in both directions and a 12-bit command status bus, ***CSBUS***. The tape transport will receive commands from the central processor and transmit a status vector on ***CSBUS***. As indicated in Fig. 9.16, the contents of the tape data register, ***TDR***, are gated onto the ***IOBUS*** when ***tdriobus*** = 1. The tape transport is also connected to the central processor by an interrupt pulse line and some other

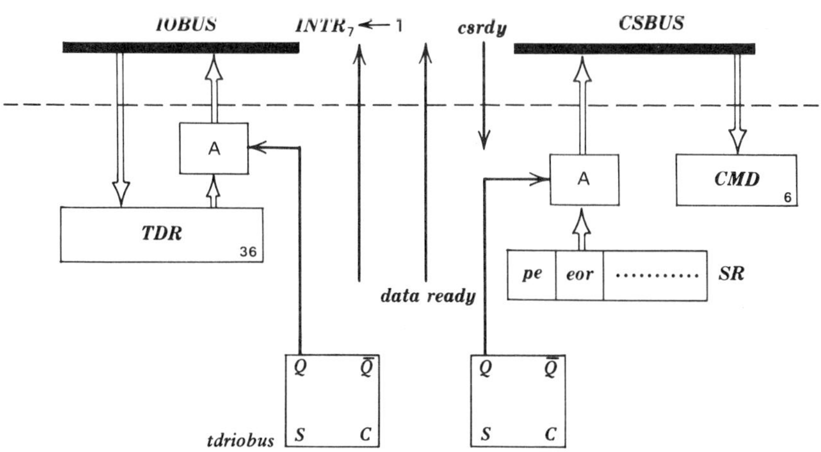

FIGURE 9.16. Connections to tape transport.

pulse lines, including a ***data ready*** line. The 12-bit status register, ***SR***, is actually a configuration of individual flip-flops, a parity error flip-flop, ***pe***, an end of record flip-flop, ***eor***, etc.

The one input pulse line of interest is ***csrdy***. A pulse on this line indicates that a command is waiting on ***CSBUS***. As indicated in the following control sequence, the tape transport stands idle until a pulse appears on this line. When a pulse appears, every peripheral device examines bits 3–5 (arbitrarily we assume that only eight devices are connected) of the ***CSBUS*** to see if the command is intended for that device. This is accomplished by step 2 of the control sequence for the tape transport. For convenience the tape transport has been assigned device number 7.

1. WAIT for ***csrdy*** PULSE
2. $\rightarrow[(\wedge/\omega^3/\alpha^6/\boldsymbol{CSBUS}) \times 4 + \overline{(\wedge/\omega^3/\alpha^6/\boldsymbol{CSBUS})} \times 3]$
3. ONE DELAY,$\rightarrow$(1)
4. $\boldsymbol{CMD} \leftarrow \omega^6/\boldsymbol{CSBUS}$
5. $\rightarrow[(\text{DECODE}_0(\boldsymbol{CMD}) \times 6) + (\text{DECODE}_1(\boldsymbol{CMD}) \times 19) + \cdots]$

If the command is not for device 7, the WAIT for ***csrdy*** flip-flop is set again following step 3 (a simpler control unit would result if the pulse were kept out of the control unit unless bits 3–5 were all ones). If the command is for the tape transport, the last 6 bits of ***CSBUS*** are placed in ***CMD*** by step 4. This register is decoded to determine the specific instruction for the tape transport. We assume that the command is READ if all 6 bits are zero. In this case, control branches to step 6 where the READ control sequence is presented in detail. The sequences for other commands, such as WRITE, BACKSPACE, REWIND, or PROVIDE STATUS, are not continued.

Figure 9.17 shows the simplified read circuits for a magnetic tape unit in which data is recorded in 6-bit units and the computer word length is 36 bits. Although there are six information bits in each character, there are seven bits actually recorded on tape, the seventh bit providing odd parity over the character. The seven bits of each character are entered into the *tape read register*, ***TRR***, and are also OR'ed to form the *sprocket signal*,* which provides timing control for the *read control logic*. Since parity is odd, there is always at least one 1 in each character, so the sprocket signal will be 1 whenever a character is being loaded into ***TRR***. All seven bits go to the parity check logic, which provides a 1-output if the parity is not odd.

The sprocket signal is not necessarily synchronized with the tape transport

* The term *sprocket signal* is apparently derived from the sprocket holes in paper tape, which actually control the mechanical movement of the tape; it has become fairly standard in referring to magnetic tape. The sprocket signals serve the same function as the signals derived from the timing track of a disc, that of marking the position of each character.

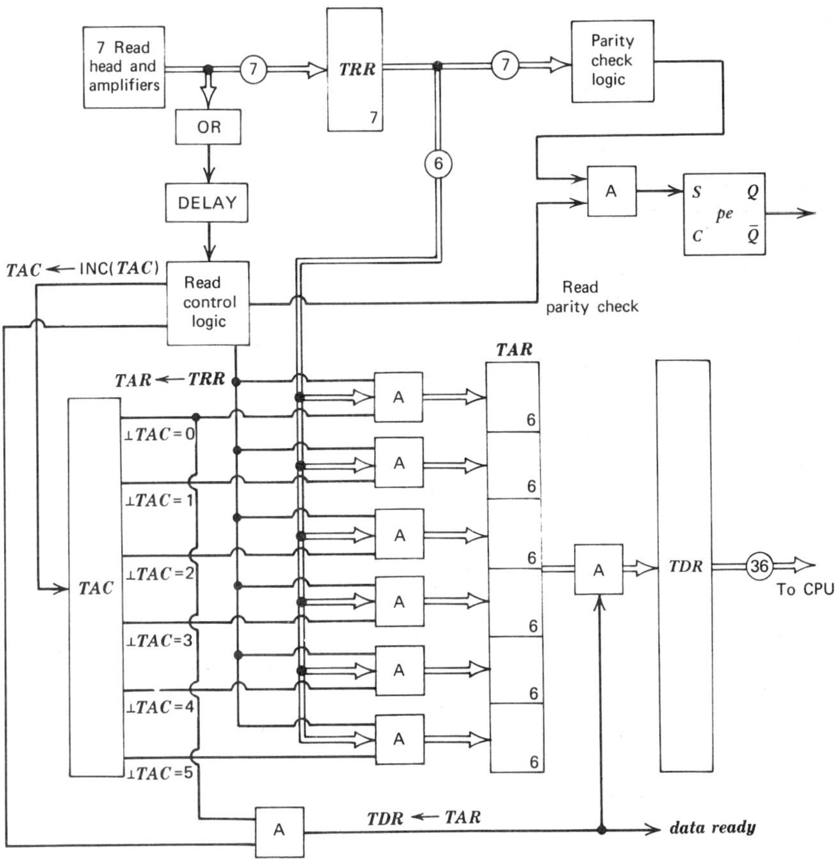

FIGURE 9.17. Magnetic tape read logic.

clock. Therefore, execution of the READ sequence will not be synchronized with the clock. This is not the case for other commands. The WRITE command uses the clock to generate the current used in writing bits on the tape.

Step 6 causes the tape drive to start moving by setting the drive control flip-flop, ***forward***, to 1. Step 7 clears the status register, creates a path from ***TDR*** to the ***IOBUS***, and clears the tape assembly counter, ***TAC***. The assembly of characters into a word is controlled by ***TAC***. The control unit waits at step 8

6. ***forward*** ← 1; ***begin*** ← 1
7. ***tdriobus*** ← 1; ***SR*** ← $\overline{\epsilon(12)}$; ***TAC*** ← 0, 0, 0
8. WAIT FOR SPROCKET PULSE DON'T CLEAR

until the first sprocket pulse appears. The comment DON'T CLEAR indicates that the WAIT flip-flop is left in the 1 state so that subsequent sprocket pulses will enter at this point until the READ operation has been completed. Each sprocket pulse will propagate through the control network disappearing following steps 15 or 16.

The record gap allows the tape to come up to speed before the first sprocket pulse enters the READ control unit. Actually each sprocket pulse is delayed so that it can be used to control the character which has just been entered in the tape read register, ***TRR***. Each pulse propagates clear through the control unit so no control delays are necessary. With each sprocket pulse, the READ control issues a signal, $\boldsymbol{TAR} \leftarrow \boldsymbol{TRR}$, to transfer the character into the *tape assembly register*, ***TAR***. This signal, together with the $\perp \boldsymbol{TAC} = 0$ signal, gates the six data bits from ***TRR*** into the first six bits of ***TAR***. The READ control then increments ***TAC*** to 1, so that the next character is loaded into the second six bits of ***TAR***. This process continues until all six characters have been assembled into a 36-bit word. If $\boldsymbol{TAC} = 0$, the contents of ***TAR*** are transferred into ***TDR*** just before new data is entered in ***TAR*** (except for first pulse when $\boldsymbol{begin} = 1$). Simultaneously a ***data ready*** signal is supplied to the CPU,

9. $\rightarrow[((\wedge/\overline{\boldsymbol{TAC}}) \wedge \overline{\boldsymbol{begin}} \times 10) + (\overline{(\wedge/\overline{\boldsymbol{TAC}}) \wedge \boldsymbol{begin}} \times 11)]$
10. $\boldsymbol{TDR} \leftarrow \boldsymbol{TAR}$; line $\boldsymbol{dataready} \leftarrow$ PULSE, NO DELAY
11. $\rightarrow[(\text{EVEN}(\boldsymbol{TRR}) \times 12) + (\text{ENDREC}(\boldsymbol{TRR}) \times 17) + (\overline{\text{EVEN}}(\boldsymbol{TRR}) \wedge \overline{\text{ENDREC}}(\boldsymbol{TRR}) \times 13)]$
12. $\boldsymbol{pe} \leftarrow 1$, NO DELAY
13. $\text{DEST}(\boldsymbol{TAC}, \boldsymbol{TAR}) \leftarrow \omega^6/\boldsymbol{TRR}$, NO DELAY
14. $\perp \boldsymbol{TAC}{:}5, (=, \neq) \rightarrow (16, 15)$
15. $\boldsymbol{TAC} \leftarrow \text{INC}(\boldsymbol{TAC})$; $\boldsymbol{begin} \leftarrow 0$; DEAD END
16. $\boldsymbol{TAC} \leftarrow 0, 0, 0$; DEAD END
17. $\boldsymbol{eor} \leftarrow 1$; $\boldsymbol{control\ 8} \leftarrow 0$; $\boldsymbol{forward} \leftarrow 0$
18. (In Central Processor) $\boldsymbol{INTR}_7 \leftarrow 1, \rightarrow (1)$

The combinational logic subroutine EVEN checks for even parity. ENDREC checks for the special end of record character, and DEST selects the proper block in ***TAR*** to receive the 6-bit character. Only a lateral parity check is performed for simplicity. Once an end-of-record character is encountered, control jumps to step 17 to terminate the READ operation. The transfer, $\boldsymbol{control\ 8} \leftarrow 0$, resets the wait flip-flop corresponding to step 8, so that no extraneous sprocket pulses can pass through this section of the control sequence.

Following completion of the READ operation, the interrupt flip-flop corresponding to the tape transport in the central processor is set. Eventually the central processor will respond to the interrupt by requesting a status vector to determine whether the READ was terminated by a parity error or end-of-record mark. Control returns to step 1 to await a request for status or

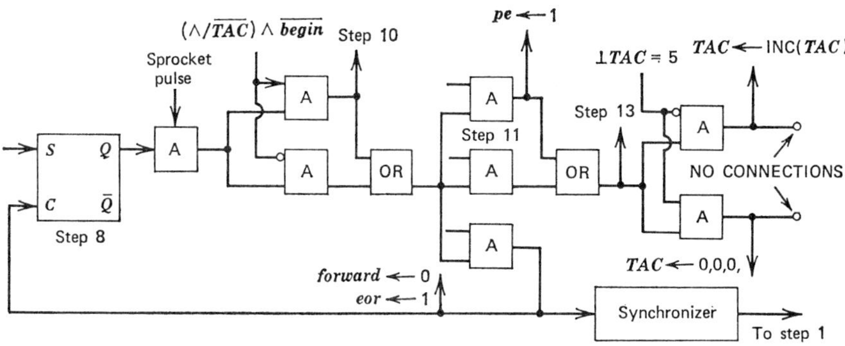

FIGURE 9.18. Control sequencer for READ.

some other command. What takes place when a parity error is detected is a function of the software operating system. The simplest procedure would be to simply call for a rereading of the record. In some cases redundant characters may be written into records to provide for actual location and correction of errors by software. See Chapter 8 of Reference [2], as well as Reference [3].

Since the hardware implementation of the control sequence just described is somewhat unusual, it is included as Fig. 9.18. It might seem that timing problems could arise due to the numerous branching networks through which each sprocket pulse must propagate. The network should work, since the clock period is long and a pulse to read from a register will never be a delayed version of a pulse intended to write in the same register.

The ***TDR*** is not absolutely necessary, as information could be transferred directly from ***TAR*** to the CPU. However, the use of the extra register gives the computer more time to respond. In a typical tape reader, characters might be read at a rate of one every 30 μsec. Thus, within 30 μsec after the sixth character of one word has been loaded, ***TAR*** must be cleared to receive the first character of the next word. Loading the word into ***TDR*** gives the CPU six character times (180 μsec) to pick up the word. This procedure of using extra, or *buffer*, registers to increase the time available to the computer to respond to a data request is very common. In some cases a small *buffer memory* may be provided in which a number of words can be collected for group transfer to main memory.

The logic for a write operation would be basically similar. A *tape disassembly counter*, ***TDC***, would gate successive 6-bit groups from a *tape disassembly register*, ***TDA***, into a 7-bit *tape write register*, ***TWR***. These six bits would also go to the *parity generate* logic, which generates the parity bit and loads it into the seventh bit position of ***TWR***. On most tape units, separate read and write heads are provided, the read heads coming after the write heads. To provide a check against error, the word is read into ***TRR*** immediately after it has been written and compared with the contents of ***TWR***. A ***write error*** signal will be issued if the contents of the two registers do not agree.

In addition to being assembled and disassembled, data are sometimes converted from one form to another by the I/O devices. A common example occurs in card readers and punches. Data are recorded on cards in two common forms, binary, and Hollerith. In the binary form, each position of each column corresponds to a single bit: 0 if it is not punched, 1 if it is. Thus, a single 80-column card can contain up to 960 bits of information.

However, the most common arrangement of data on cards is one character per column, in the Hollerith code. Since there are twelve positions in a column, the Hollerith code is a 12-bit-per-character code, which has certain advantages in mechanical card-handling equipment, such as sorters. Within computers, 6- or 8-bit codes are more efficient for alphanumeric characters. The code conversion could be done in the CPU; but it is generally more efficient to do it in the card reader or punch as a part of the assembly or disassembly operation.

The card is read, one column at a time, as the card passes continuously under the read station. In the Hollerith mode, as each character (column) is read, the 12-bit Hollerith code is fed into a coding circuit which puts out the corresponding computer code for that character. The re-coded characters are then assembled into registers having the same word length as the main memory. The assembled words may be transmitted to the CPU one at a time, as in the tape unit discussed above, or all 80 characters may be assembled into a group of registers, or buffer memory, before transmission to the CPU. For example, if the computer used a 6-bit internal code and 36-bit words, the contents of the entire 80 columns, sometimes referred to as the *card image*, could be assembled into 14 words, with only two characters in the last word.

PROBLEMS

9.1 All of the registers appearing in the following hypothetical AHPL sequence have the same number of bits. Rewrite the sequence so that as many as possible of the operations can take place in parallel. Utilize the notation of Section 9.2. If the average time required

1. $\boldsymbol{A} \leftarrow \boldsymbol{B}$
2. $\boldsymbol{C} \leftarrow \text{FCT}(\boldsymbol{A})$, 3 DELAYS
3. $\boldsymbol{D} \leftarrow \boldsymbol{M}^{\perp \boldsymbol{B}}$, WAIT
4. $\boldsymbol{F} \leftarrow \text{ADD}(\boldsymbol{B}, \boldsymbol{D})$, 4 DELAYS
5. $\boldsymbol{LR} \leftarrow \text{ADD}(\boldsymbol{G}, \boldsymbol{H})$, 4 DELAYS
6. $\boldsymbol{B} \leftarrow \boldsymbol{F} \wedge \boldsymbol{C}$, $\rightarrow (1)$

by the asynchronous memory reference is six clock periods, compare the time required for one pass through the above serial sequence and through the equivalent parallel sequence.

9.2 A certain special purpose computer has only single address memory reference instructions. Even the IOT operations are memory reference. As in SIC, the left-most three bits specify the op code, and bits 3 and 4 specify indexing or indirect addressing. The only jump instruction is JPA, which causes a jump to the addressed instruction if and only if $\perp AC \leq 0$. In the programs used by this special-purpose computer, it has been shown that one in every ten instructions is JPA. Write in AHPL a control sequence for the *fetch* cycle and preparation for and termination of the *execute* cycle in this machine. The fetch of the next instruction should be accomplished in parallel with execution of the current instruction. Provide for holding up the fetch cycle while a JPA is executed. Make sure that the fetch will not interfere with use of the memory in the execution of any instruction. Assume a semiconductor memory with an access time of two clock periods. Do not include an indexing capability.

9.3 Discuss the possibility of parallel control sequences in a microprogrammed machine. Can parallel sequences exist within the microprogrammed control unit? How? Can parallel sequences be used outside the microprogrammed control unit? Can separate control units be employed in a microprogrammed machine? How?

9.4 (For students with background in sequential circuit design.) Use fundamental mode techniques to design the pulse convergence circuit shown in Fig. 9.3.

9.5 Suggest a modified AHPL notation for parallel sequences which will clearly indicate when a convergence circuit is needed. Make the notation as straightforward and self-explanatory as possible.

9.6 Construct a complete timing diagram for the pulse synchronizer shown in Fig. 9.12.

9.7 A data communications (long distance) terminal includes its own control unit. The portion of the control unit which will cause received data to be stored in the memory of a minicomputer is to be designed. Data will pass in only one direction. Receiving data is a high-priority operation for the minicomputer. When a full buffer of data is available, the computer suspends all other activity while storing this data in memory. Connections between the terminal and the computer are shown in Fig. P9.7. The semiconductor buffer in the terminal contains (when full) 32 8-bit characters. Pairs of consecutive characters are combined to be stored as 16-bit words in the minicomputer memory. These words

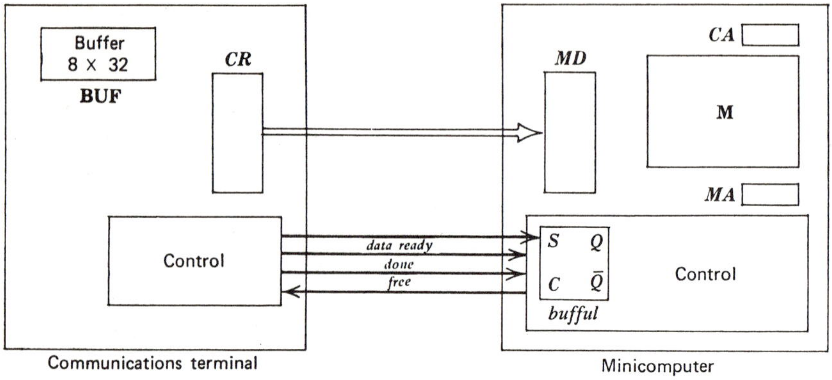

FIGURE P9.7

can be transferred directly from ***CR*** in the terminal to ***MD*** in the minicomputer. The first portion of the terminal control sequence is concerned with communications on a telephone line so that the 32 8-bit characters are properly placed in the buffer. After the buffer has been filled, a pulse from the terminal will cause a flip-flop, ***bufful***, in the computer to be set to 1.

a) Write the last portion of the control sequence for the terminal beginning with the step which generates the set ***bufful*** pulse. This sequence will interact with the computer to cause the 32 characters to be stored in memory. After a word has been placed in ***CR***, a ***data ready*** pulse is sent to the computer. The computer responds with a pulse on line ***free*** after it places the word in ***MD***. After the buffer has been emptied, a pulse on line ***done*** is sent to the computer.

b) At step 1 in the control sequence, prior to the fetch operation, the computer pauses to examine the contents of ***bufful***. If ***bufful*** = 0, the instruction fetch is carried out. If ***bufful*** = 1, control branches to step 100 to provide communications with the terminal. Write step 1. Write the sequence, beginning at step 100, which writes the data in memory. The next address at which data are to be stored in memory is available in ***CA***. This address is kept current by software, when a transfer sequence is not in progress.

c) Construct a hardware block diagram of the interacting control units, similar to Fig. 9.15. (Hint: A variation of the notation in Fig. 9.13 so that control can wait for a pulse on either one of two lines might be helpful.)

9.8 Write in AHPL the WRITE control sequence for the tape transport of Section 9.7. Postulate any additional hardware which may be required.

Note that the tape transport clock is used to generate current pulses for writing on tape, so no separate WRITE control unit is required. Why then aren't the pulses synchronized with the clock when read back?

9.9 Write in AHPL the control sequence for the BACK SPACE (One Record) command for the tape transport of Section 9.7. Postulate any additional hardware required.

9.10 Write in AHPL the REWIND control sequence for the tape transport of Section 9.7.

9.11 Translate the READ control sequence of Fig. 9.18 to a hard-wired control sequencer. Show the connection to the sprocket pulse. Notice that no control delays are required. Cite any instances (if there are any) where an improper phase relationship between control pulses might cause the unit to malfunction.

REFERENCES

1. Bycer, B. B., *Digital Magnetic Tape Recording: Principles and Computer Applications*, Hayden Book Company, New York, 1965.
2. Hill, F. J., and Peterson, G. R., *Introduction to Switching Theory and Logical Design*, Wiley, New York, 1968.
3. Wallner, Arthur, "Error Detection for Peripheral Storage Devices," *Computer Design*, Jan. 1972, p. 57.

10

Interrupt and Input/Output

10.1. INTRODUCTION

In this chapter we are concerned basically with the problem of communicating with the computer. Input/output (I/O) devices are those devices by means of which the computer communicates with the "outside world." Interrupt is a part of the communication problem because we must get the computer's "attention" before we can communicate with it. Interrupt procedures enable us to notify the computer during normal processing operations that special conditions exist which require the computer to put aside its current program as quickly as possible and institute special steps to deal with the special conditions. Input/output operations are not the only reasons for interrupt, but they are probably the most common. Also, the special machine instructions dealing with interrupt are usually grouped with I/O instructions, so it seems logical to consider interrupt and I/O together.

Among the more common I/O devices are card readers and punches, printers, teletypewriters, and paper tape punches and readers. These are all electromechanical devices of great complexity, but details of how they are constructed will not be considered here. We are concerned only with how the computer communicates with these devices. With regard to communications with the computer, all these devices have three special characteristics which account for the special nature of the I/O problem. First, their operation is completely asynchronous with respect to the central processor. Second, their speed of operation is many orders of magnitude slower than that of the central processor. For example, the data rate of a typical card reader would be 300 words per second, compared with a typical CPU rate of a million operations per second. Third, their data format is usually quite different from that of the central processor.

From the standpoint of communication with the CPU, magnetic tape, disk, and drum are generally considered to be I/O devices because they share these same three special characteristics. We have previously considered these three types of devices as memory, but this is simply a matter of point of view. These devices are memory in the sense that the CPU can store information in them and later retrieve it without human intervention; but they are I/O in the sense of requiring special techniques to deal with their characteristics of slow, asynchronous operation and special data formats.

There is probably more variation from computer to computer in the areas of interrupt and I/O design than in any other area of computer design. This being the case, we cannot hope to cover all possible techniques. In line with our belief that learning best proceeds from the specific to the general, we shall develop specific "typical" interrupt and I/O systems, and then comment on the variations and options open to the designer.

10.2. INTERRUPT SYSTEM FOR SIC

There are many possible situations which can require interruption of the main computer program. *Internal* interrupts usually are caused by various types of error conditions, such as arithmetic overflow, or invalid memory address. *External* interrupts arise because of requests from I/O devices for attention. The occurrence of these conditions may generate only transient signals, so we need a means of storing the fact that the condition has occurred. For this purpose we shall provide an *interrupt* register, ***INTR***, with one position set aside for each interrupt condition specified by the designer. Thus, one position might indicate arithmetic overflow, another a memory fault, etc. In addition we shall occasionally need *status indicators*, which are simply individual flip-flops which are set to indicate that some special condition exists. These indicators shall be denoted by names ending in ***f***, such as ***intf***, ***einf***, etc.

The designer's decision as to what conditions shall be provided for in the ***INTR*** register determines what conditions might possibly cause interrupts. It is also desirable that the programmer should be able to exercise control over which conditions will actually be allowed to cause an interrupt under various conditions. In particular, the programmer may wish to establish priority among various I/O devices. For example, it may be desired to ignore a request from a slow device, such as a card reader, if a faster device, such as a disk, is already being processed.

To provide this programmer control over interrupts we establish a *mask* register, ***MR***, having the same number of positions as ***INTR***. By means of a special command, to be discussed later, the programmer can set or clear any position of the mask register as desired. If a position of ***MR*** is set to 1, the corresponding position of ***INTR*** is *enabled*, i.e., when it is set by an interrupt request, it may in turn set the interrupt indicator, ***intf***. If a position of ***MR*** is 0, the corresponding position of ***INTR*** is *disabled*, so that its setting has no effect on ***intf***. The logic by which this is accomplished is shown in Fig. 10.1.

When a condition demanding interrupt occurs, the CPU should respond as quickly as possible. In most computers, the interrupt will occur as soon as the instruction currently being executed has been completed, before fetching a new instruction. Thus, before entering a new fetch cycle, the control unit should check to see if an interrupt has been requested. Referring back to Fig. 6.4, we see that a new fetch is initiated in SIC when the control unit returns to step 1 after incrementing ***PC*** (step 25) or loading a jump address into ***PC*** (step 27). Once during each instruction cycle, control must interrogate the masked interrupt signals (***MIS***) and set the interrupt indicator, ***intf***,

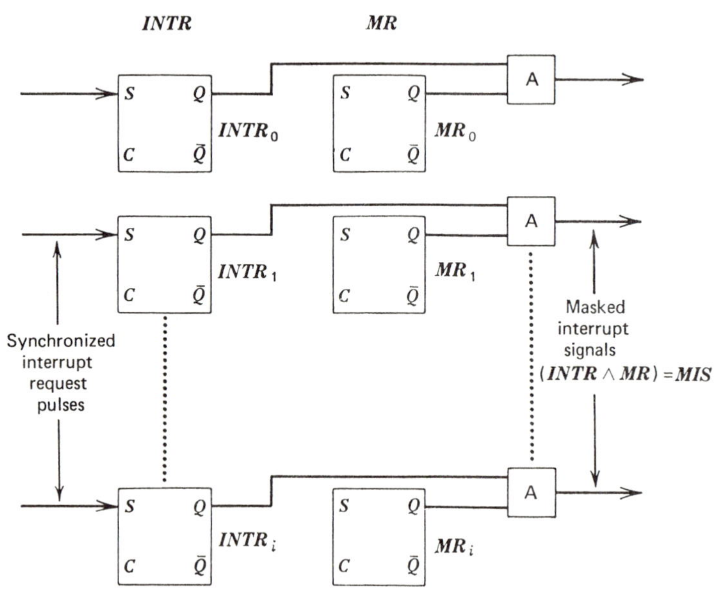

FIGURE 10.1. Masking of interrupt requests.

if any are present. We then insert a new step 1, to cause a branch into an interrupt sequence if ***intf*** is set. The interrogation of the ***MIS*** should come at the latest point common to all instructions, immediately before the branch at step 4. The modified control sequence will then be as shown below. Step 63 is the start of the interrupt sequence; ***enif*** is the *enable interrupt* indicator,

START

1.	$\rightarrow((\overline{intf} \times 1a) + (intf \times 63))$		$\leftarrow$ (new)
1a.	$MA \leftarrow PC$	no change	
2.	$MD \leftarrow M^{\perp MA}$	no change	
3.	$IR \leftarrow MD$	no change	
3a.	$intf \leftarrow ((\vee/(INTR \wedge MR)) \wedge enif)$		$\leftarrow$ (new)
4.	as before		

which provides a "master control" of the interrupt system. Its use will be more fully explained later. The modifications to the hardware flow chart and the control unit logic are shown in Fig. 10.2.

The first step in the interrupt sequence is to clear ***enif*** and ***intf*** to prevent any more interrupts until the machine is in a position to deal with them. The interrupt request must be processed by a software subroutine. The hardware must place the address of the proper subroutine in the program counter so that this routine can take over. To do this the hardware must first determine which interrupt source requires attention. The programmer has determined, by setting ***MR***, which interrupt sources are to be enabled; but it is possible that more than one enabled interrupt can occur at the same time. For example, suppose that when ***INTR*** is interrogated (step 3a), there are enabled signals present for both an overflow and an I/O request. This will result in ***intf*** being set, and the control unit will branch to the interrupt sequence when it returns to step 1; but which request should be dealt with first?

We shall establish priority by means of a logic circuit such that the interrupt source connected to $INTR_0$ will have highest priority, the source at $INTR_1$, next highest priority, etc. The priority circuit is described by the combinational logic subroutine PRI(A), where A is the vector of masked interrupt signals; and the output is an ρA-element vector, only one bit of which can take on the value 1 at any time. The combinational logic subroutine is given in Fig. 10.3a. The resultant circuit for a 4-bit interrupt system is shown in Fig. 10.3b. Note that an enabled interrupt signal at any bit position is complemented and applied to AND gates at all lower-priority positions, thus blocking any lower-priority interrupts. This system establishes a fixed priority with regard to ***MR*** and ***INTR***; but the user can usually exercise some control over which interrupt sources are connected to which position in the ***INTR*** register. In particular, some of the ***INTR*** positions will correspond to various I/O channels, and the user will usually have considerable freedom in assigning various I/O devices to various channels.

Before turning control over to a software subroutine for dealing with the interrupt request, the current contents of ***PC*** must be stored to provide for returning to the interrupted program. We will permanently reserve two positions in memory for each interrupt line, one for storing the contents of ***PC***, the other for a jump command. For SIC, let us assume nine bits in the ***INTR*** register and assign locations 00010 and 00011 to $\boldsymbol{INTR}_0$, 00012 and 00013 to $\boldsymbol{INTR}_1$, 0014 and 00015 to $\boldsymbol{INTR}_2$, etc.

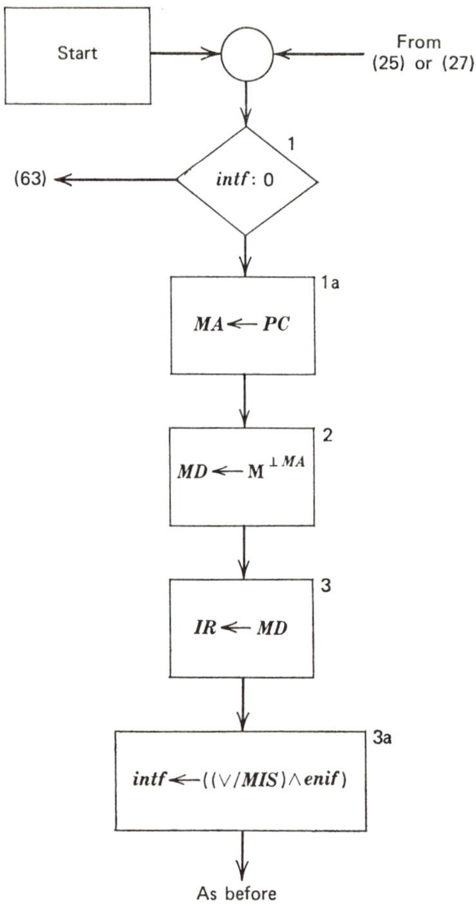

(a) Modified flow chart

FIGURE 10.2. Modifications for interrupt detection.

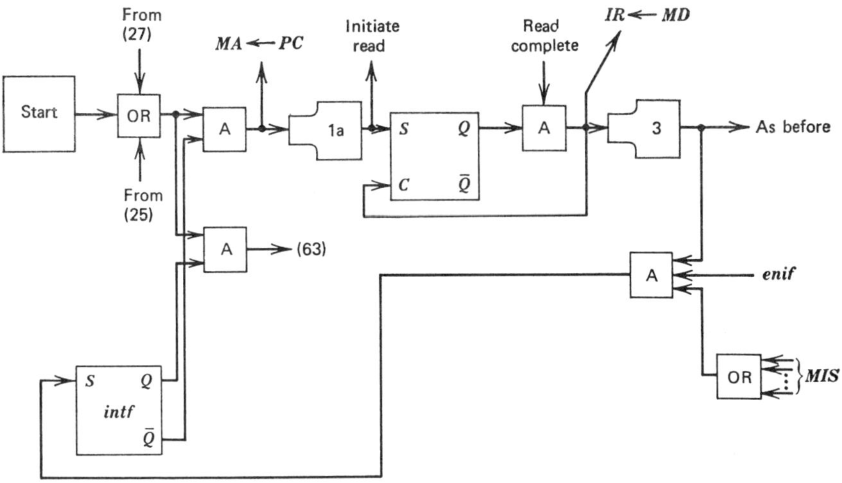

(b) Modified control logic

FIGURE 10.2 ***Continued***

CL SUBROUTINE PRI(A)

	1.	$\boldsymbol{B}_0 \leftarrow A_0$
B	2.	$k \leftarrow 1$
	3.	$\boldsymbol{B}_k \leftarrow A_k \wedge (\wedge/(\boldsymbol{\alpha}^k/\bar{A}))$
B	4.	$k \leftarrow k+1$
B	5.	$k : \rho A, (<, \geq) \rightarrow (3,6)$
	6.	PRI $\leftarrow \boldsymbol{B}$

(a) Combinational logic subroutine

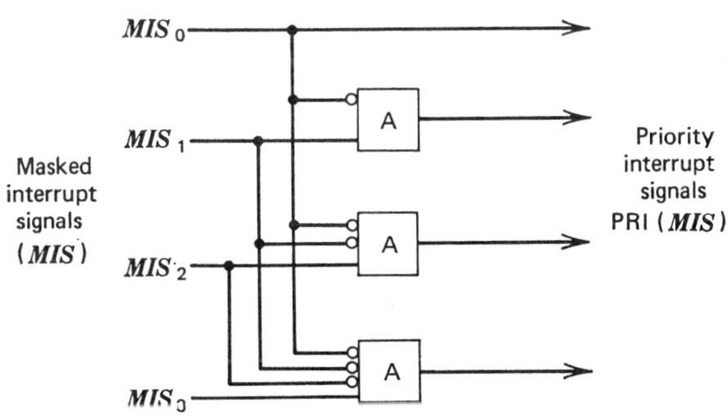

(b) Four-bit network

FIGURE 10.3. Interrupt priority circuit.

Since only one of the outputs of PRI can take on a 1 value at any one time, this output identifies the source making the interrupt request. The signal PRI($\boldsymbol{INTR} \wedge \boldsymbol{MR}$) will be fed to another logic circuit, the address coding circuit, ADDR(A), which will produce the address of the first memory location set aside for the interrupt source originating the request. For example, if the interrupt request had come from the source assigned to $\boldsymbol{INTR}_0$, ADDR = 00010. This address will be loaded into $\boldsymbol{MA}$ and $\boldsymbol{IR}$, and the current contents of $\boldsymbol{PC}$ will be stored at the addressed location. The address will then be transferred from $\boldsymbol{IR}$ to $\boldsymbol{PC}$ and incremented; and a normal fetch cycle will then be entered. This fetch will then take the jump instruction from the second assigned location, e.g., 00011 if ADDR(PRI($\boldsymbol{INTR} \wedge \boldsymbol{MR}$)) = 00010. The programmer will have previously entered a jump instruction at this location, to jump to an appropriate subroutine for dealing with interrupts from the source initiating the request. This sequence, starting at step 63, is shown below.

63. $\boldsymbol{intf}, \boldsymbol{enif} \leftarrow 0, 0$
64. $\omega^{13}/\boldsymbol{IR} \leftarrow \text{ADDR}(\text{PRI}(\boldsymbol{INTR} \wedge \boldsymbol{MR}))$
65. $\boldsymbol{MA} \leftarrow \omega^{13}/\boldsymbol{IR};\ \boldsymbol{MD} \leftarrow \boldsymbol{PC}$
66. $\text{M}^{\perp \boldsymbol{MA}} \leftarrow \boldsymbol{MD}$
67. $\boldsymbol{PC} \leftarrow \omega^{13}/\boldsymbol{IR}, \rightarrow (25)$

The reader may note that the above sequence is similar in some respects to the JMS (jump to subroutine) sequence, and it is possible that some economy might result from sharing hardware between these two sequences. However, we are here concerned with the basic processes involved, rather than minor simplifications in circuitry.

The first step in the above sequence, the clearing of ***intf*** and ***enif***, is necessary to prevent the control unit from re-entering the interrupt sequence instead of fetching the next (jump) instruction, and to inhibit any further setting of ***intf*** until the programmer indicates that further interrupts are to be allowed. This is essential as the programmer must have complete control over what, if anything, is to be allowed to interrupt the interrupt program.

The reader should note carefully that the hardware sequence discussed above does not really do anything "about" the interrupt. It establishes priority among interrupts, identifies the source, and initiates a jump to a program for dealing with the interrupt. From this point on, what happens is entirely at the discretion of the programmer, and is thus largely beyond the scope of this book. However, for purposes of a fuller understanding of the interrupt process, it may be useful to discuss briefly the steps that might be involved in a typical interrupt program.

The first portion of the interrupt program may involve inquiries to find out more about the nature of the interrupt condition. For example, an I/O unit may interrupt for several reasons such as parity error, end-of-file, etc. However, each channel will probably be allocated only one position in ***INTR***; so it cannot directly indicate the nature of the interrupt condition. For this purpose, the programmer will use STATUS INPUT commands (to be discussed later) to interrogate the interrupting channel as to the exact reason for the interrupt.

Having determined the exact reason for the interrupt, the interrupt program will then take the appropriate action to deal with the interrupt condition, as specified by the programmer. If this action will require the use of the arithmetic registers, then their contents will have to be stored in order to preserve the status of the interrupted program.

One of the most difficult aspects of interrupt programming is the handling of interrupts which come in during an interrupt program. If there are no interrupt sources of such urgency that they cannot wait until the current interrupt has been processed, the program will simply leave the interrupt system disabled. Note that interrupt requests arriving while the interrupt system is disabled are not lost. They will still set the appropriate positions of ***INTR***, and may be responded to whenever the interrupt is enabled.

In some situations, such as real-time process control, there may be interrupt requests of such urgency that response cannot be delayed until the current interrupt program is completed. In this case the program will re-enable the interrupt system, changing ***MR*** as required to reflect the priorities of the interrupt program. Also, the procedure for dealing with an interrupt of an interrupt may be different from that for dealing with an interrupt request from the same source but coming during the main program. The programmer may alter the interrupt program, or change the jump address associated with the interrupt source, to cause a jump to a different program.

When the appropriate action has been completed, the interrupt system will be disabled and the restoration of the main program started. It is important that the interrupt be disabled during the beginning and ending of the interrupt routine. If the computer is interrupted while in the midst of switching programs, it will be virtually impossible to keep track of the program status. The next-to-last step in the interrupt routine will reset ***MR*** for the main program, and set ***enif*** to enable the interrupt system. The final command will be an indirect jump to the location where the ***PC*** contents were stored, to return control to the main program. For example, if the interrupt originated through $INTR_0$, the final command of the interrupt program will be

JMP I 00010

which causes a jump to the address stored in 00010, i.e., the contents of ***PC*** at the time the interrupt was initiated.

Note carefully that additional interrupts cannot occur until after the jump command has been executed. Prior to the next-to-last command, the interrupt has been disabled, i.e., both ***enif*** and ***intf*** have been cleared. This prevents ***intf*** from being set during the execution of the next-to-last command, ensuring that the jump command will be executed. The setting of ***enif*** will make possible the setting of ***intf*** during the execution of the jump command, if an interrupt signal is present; but this will not cause an interrupt until the next fetch, after completion of the jump command. This two-step enabling procedure, effectively delaying the enable for a full instruction cycle, is absolutely essential.

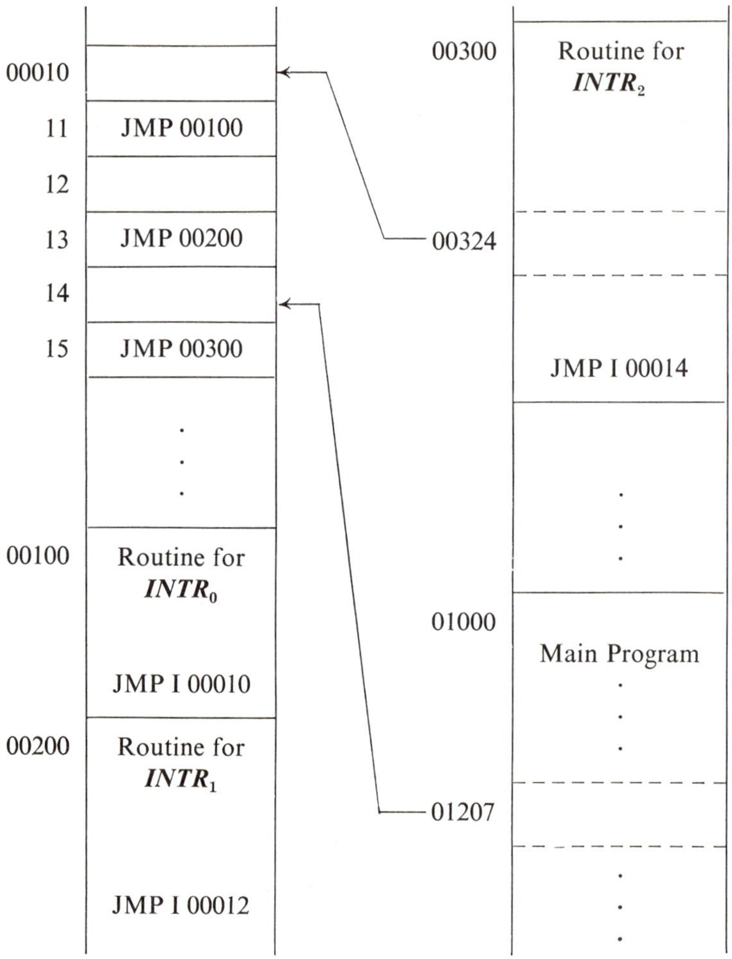

(a)

FIGURE 10.4. Typical interrupt routines.

Address	Contents
00300	$MR \leftarrow 10000000$
	$INTR_2 \leftarrow 0$, $enif \leftarrow 1$
	⋮
00375	$intf \leftarrow 0$, $enif \leftarrow 0$
00376	$MR \leftarrow 11100000$, $enif \leftarrow 1$
00377	JMP I 00014

(b)

FIGURE 10.4 ***Continued***

In order to clarify the above, let us consider a specific interrupt situation. In the execution of a certain program, assume that only the first three interrupt sources, $INTR_0$, $INTR_1$, and $INTR_2$ are enabled. The routines for dealing with these interrupts start at locations 00100, 00200, and 00300, respectively, and the main program starts at 01000, as shown in Fig. 10.4a. Accordingly, locations 00011, 00013, and 00015 contain jumps to 00100, 00200, and 00300, while the last steps in the corresponding interrupt routines are indirect jumps through 00010, 00012, and 00014.

Assume that during the execution of instruction 01205 of the main program, $INTR_2$ is set by an interrupt request. At step 3a of the next fetch cycle, $INTR$ is checked and $intf$ is set as a result of $INTR_2$ having been set. The instruction at 01206 will then be executed. At the start of the next fetch cycle (for instruction 01207), $intf$ will cause a branch to step 63, the start of the interrupt sequence. Steps 64 and 65 will load 00014, corresponding to $INTR_2$, into MA, and step 66 will load the address of the next instruction in the main program, 01207, into location 00014. Step 67 will load address 00014 into PC and this will be incremented at step 25, causing the next instruction to be fetched from 00015. This instruction, JMP 00300, causes a jump to the routine for dealing with $INTR_2$.

Fig. 10.4b shows some of the specific instructions in the routine for dealing with $INTR_2$. Since we have not yet defined a format for the interrupt instructions, we indicate in this figure what is to be done without regard to SIC assembly format. Let us assume that only $INTR_0$ is to be allowed to interrupt the interrupt in this case. So the first step in the interrupt routine is to reset the mask register accordingly. The next instruction clears $INTR_2$, since the request is now being responded to, and sets ***enif***, to re-enable the interrupt sequence. Succeeding steps, which will deal with the interrupt request, will depend on the nature of the interrupt.

Next assume that $INTR_0$ is set during the execution of instruction 00322 of the interrupt routine. Thus during the fetch of 00323 ***intf*** will be set. This will in turn cause address 00324 to be stored at 00010, followed by a jump at 00011 to 00100, to deal with $INTR_0$. On completion of the routine for $INTR_0$, the execution of JMP I 00010 will return control to 00324, to continue with the routine for $INTR_2$.

On completion of whatever steps are required to deal with $INTR_2$, ***intf*** and ***enif*** are cleared at 00375, disabling the interrupt system in preparation for return to the main program. At 00376, ***MR*** is reset as appropriate for the main program and ***enif*** is set. Finally, 00377 makes the indirect jump through 00014 to 01207, returning to the main program. Even though a position of ***INTR*** might be set during the execution of 00375 or 00376, ***intf*** could not be set until step 3a of the fetch of 00377, preventing a branch to the interrupt sequence until step 1 of the fetch following completion of the jump back to the main program.

To conclude this section we must consider the commands necessary for controlling the interrupt system. Rather than specify many different commands we shall specify just one, *interrupt control*, INT, and use the same microcoding technique used for the operate instructions, in which specific bits control specific operations. In this manner the programmer is given the maximum flexibility in constructing his own interrupt instructions. INT will be one of the I/O class of instructions for which bits 0–3 are all 1's. For INT,

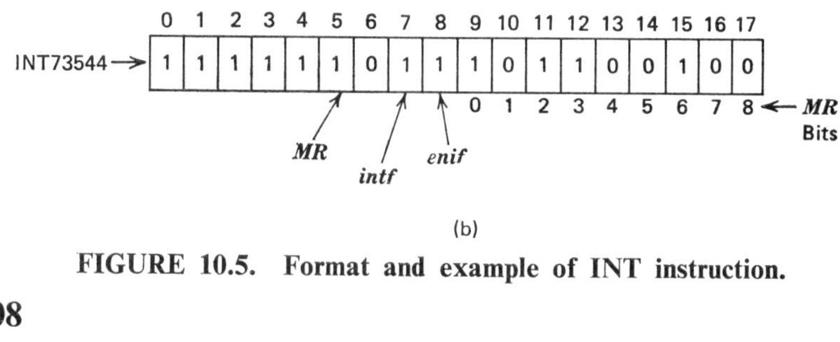

FIGURE 10.5. Format and example of INT instruction.

bit-4 will also be 1, the remaining bits having the significance shown in Fig. 10.5a.

Operations on ***MR*** or ***INTR*** are indicated by 1's in bits 5 or 6. If bit 7 is 1, ***intf*** is cleared; if bit 7 is 0, ***intf*** is left alone. Bit 8 indicates the desired setting for ***enif***. Bits 9–17 correspond to bits 0–8 of ***MR*** or ***INTR***. If bit 5 is 1, bits 9–17 indicate the desired setting of ***MR***. If bit 6 is 1, 1's in bits 9–17 indicate the positions of ***INTR*** which are to be cleared. Any combination of 1's and 0's in bits 5–15 is permitted. For example, the instruction shown in Fig. 10.5 would clear ***intf***, set ***enif***, and enable bits 0, 2, 3, and 6 of ***MR***. Consideration of the hardware and control logic necessary for implementing this instruction will be deferred to a later section, in which we consider the entire I/O sequence.

10.3. BASIC DATA TRANSFER OPERATIONS

Any data transfer operation will involve some or all of the following steps:

1. Check to see if device is available.
2. When device becomes available, activate.
3. Transfer data.
4. Deactivate.

The first step is to check to see if the desired I/O device is available. It might seem at first consideration that the CPU should "know" if it is using the device, but this is not always the case. Because I/O is slow and inefficient, software operating systems try to group I/O activities and fit them in at convenient times; as a result there may well be conflicting requests for the same device from different parts of a single program or even from different programs. It is thus desirable to have the CPU issue an inquiry as to the status of the device. This inquiry can be made in two ways: by status report or by interrupt.

In the first method, the CPU requests a status report from the I/O device and tests this report to see if the device is available, i.e., not busy with some other I/O activity. If it is busy, it executes the next command, which is a jump back to the status request, causing the CPU to remain in a loop, checking the status of the device, until it becomes available. When the status report indicates that the device is available, the jump instruction is skipped, fetching a new instruction to initiate data transfer.

The above method is undesirable unless the I/O device is certain to be immediately available, since it puts the CPU into a holding loop pending availability of the device. This can be avoided by using an interrupt inquiry. In this method, a special I/O control instruction requests the I/O device to enter an interrupt request when it becomes available. Various I/O devices may be allotted positions in the ***INTR*** register, which may be enabled by a suitable INT command. However, there are a number of reasons why an I/O device might issue an interrupt request, such as parity error, end-of-file, device available, etc. A special control instruction is therefore required to instruct the I/O device as to the conditions for which it should issue an interrupt request. After the above instruction has been issued, the program may go on to other tasks, until it is interrupted as a result of the device becoming available.

The exact nature of the second step, activating the device, will depend on the device, and in some cases may be skipped altogether. For example, console typewriters and CRT displays are in standby, "ready to go" anytime they are available, and no activation step is necessary. On the other hand, in devices like tape units and card readers, the mechanical motion must be started, the type of code (binary, Hollerith, etc.) indicated, error indicators that are to generate interrupts enabled, etc. Similar comments apply to the deactivate step. Devices such as console typewriters and CRT displays automatically go back to standby when the transfer is complete. In a tape unit, however, the end-of-file mark must be inserted, tape motion stopped, interrupt indicators cleared, etc.

The third step, the actual transfer of the data, may be carried out by three distinct methods which we shall designate as *programmed*, *buffered*, and *direct memory access* or *DMA*. In the programmed mode of transfer, the execution of one or more instructions, fetched from memory, is required for the transfer of each word. For devices requiring no activation step, the instruction to which the program skips as a result of the device becoming available will be a READ or WRITE command to the device.

Devices requiring activation, such as tape units, generally transmit data in blocks of words, with words being transferred at a rate which is asynchronous and slow with respect to the CPU operations. In such cases the last step in the activate sequence will be to issue an instruction to interrupt when ready to transfer a word. When the interrupt signal is received, the CPU goes into an interrupt procedure as described in previous sections, storing the interrupted program, fetching instructions to transfer a word, and restoring the interrupted program. This procedure continues, with the main program being interrupted for each word transfer, until the desired number of words has been transferred, at which time the device will be deactivated.

The programmed data transfer procedure is very inefficient since it requires a full interrupt procedure, including storage and restoration of the interrupted program, for every word transferred. For a buffered (hardware-controlled) transfer, we add sufficient control logic to eliminate the need for fetching special instructions when a word is to be transferred, plus enough additional data paths so that the main program need not be disturbed. When a word is to be transferred, execution of the main program will be suspended until the transfer is complete; but no special steps need be taken to preserve the main program. In essence, a buffered transfer is a special interrupt procedure which requires no instructions to be fetched.

Buffered transfer is used only when a number of words are to be transferred to or from a specific area in memory, usually referred to as the *buffer area.* In some computers a certain special area of memory is permanently reserved for buffer operations, but this technique is inconvenient from a programming point of view. Usually the programmer may specify the size and location of the buffer area. For each device to be buffered, two locations in memory are permanently reserved for storing the addresses of the buffer area. Prior to activating the buffer, the programmer will store in these locations either the first or last address of the buffer area and the number of words in the buffer area.

When the buffer is in operation, a special signal will be issued by the I/O device whenever it is ready to transfer a word. This signal will function as a special interrupt signal, transferring control to a special buffer sequence when the execution of the current instruction is complete. The buffer sequence will read the address and word count from memory, determine from them the current buffer address, transfer the word in or out of memory, update the word count and check to see if the buffer is complete (no more words to be transferred), and then return control to the main program. All of this is done by hard-wired or microprogrammed control, i.e., no instructions are fetched and sufficient extra hardware is provided so that the main program will not be affected in any way.

While buffer transfer is certainly faster than programmed transfer, we must keep in mind that the relative speeds of the CPU and the I/O devices set an upper limit on how many devices can be serviced simultaneously. When a device makes a buffer request, it must wait for the current instruction to be executed; and in the worst case, it may have to wait for the instruction with the longest execution time. For example, suppose the longest execution time in SIC were 5 μsec and the execution time of the buffer sequence were 2 μsec. Then the fastest rate at which we could guarantee to service buffer channels would be once every 7 μsec. If there were eight buffer channels active, of equal priority and being serviced in a fixed sequence, the fastest data rate we could guarantee to handle from any single device would be one word every 56 μsec. This might not be fast enough for some devices. In that case it would be necessary to reduce the number of active buffer channels.

Even with a limited number of buffers, the buffered transfer may not be fast enough for such devices as drums or fast parallel discs. We see that there are two main factors limiting the speed of the buffer operation. First, some

CPU hardware, such as the adder and ***MD***, is shared with the main program, forcing us to wait until the execution of an instruction is completed. Second, one or more memory accesses are required to determine the buffer address. With direct memory access (DMA), we can eliminate these delays by providing separate registers for the buffer addresses and sufficient extra logic and data paths to allow all aspects of the actual data transfer to take place completely independently of the CPU. Then, whenever the CPU is not actually accessing memory, the I/O channel can "steal a memory cycle" from the CPU.*

Each DMA channel must be provided with two address registers, one for the last-word address and one for current-word address. There must be sufficient arithmetic logic for processing and updating the addresses. This logic will generally be shared by several channels. Although it is not essential, there will usually be a second *port*, or *entrance*, to the memory, consisting of separate data and address registers. Sometimes ***MA*** and ***MD*** are shared by the CPU and the DMA channels, but this slows the operation and complicates the problem of deciding when the channel may have access to memory. We will consider it "true" DMA only if a second memory port is provided. Finally, there must be certain amount of priority logic to control the access of the CPU and channels to the memory. In the simplest case this will be a MEMORY BUSY signal to prevent a new access until the current access is complete, access otherwise being on a "first-come, first-served" basis.

Whenever the I/O device is ready to transfer a word, the current-word address will be loaded into the I/O memory address register; and if it is an input, the word will be transferred from the I/O device to the I/O memory data register. A request for a memory read or write will then be made. As soon as memory is free, the addressed location will be accessed. If the operation is output, the word will be transferred from the I/O memory data register to the I/O device. The current-word address will then be updated and compared to the last-word address to determine if the desired number of words has been transferred. If not, the operation continues; if so, the CPU will be interrupted to initiate the deactivate sequence. Since the CPU and the channel are sharing the memory on an equal basis, the worst case access time will simply be twice the memory cycle time.

10.4. INPUT/OUTPUT INTERCONNECTIONS

There are two classes of information that must be transferred between the CPU and the I/O devices, data, and control or status information. The most

* Another popular name for DMA is "*cycle stealing*" access.

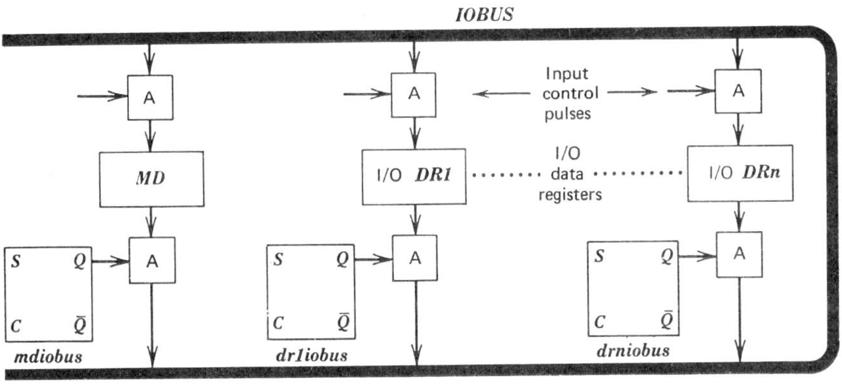

FIGURE 10.6. I/O bus interconnections.

common arrangement for data transmission is the *I/O bus*, which from a logical point of view simply consists of a set of n lines providing bidirectional transfer of n-bit words between ***MD*** in the CPU and the data registers of the I/O devices, as shown in Fig. 10.6. If there are no direct transfers between I/O devices, the principal saving achieved by the use of an I/O bus is in cabling. As shown in Fig. 10.6, the bus is routed serially from device to device, rather than routing two cables between each device and the central processor. In addition, the switching located at the input to the central processor is simpler (although the switching at each I/O device is more complicated).

Since the registers connected to the bus are located in separate devices, a single bus control register and decoder cannot be used. As shown in Fig. 10.6, a separate flip-flop controls the path between each device data register and ***IOBUS***. These flip-flops are set and cleared locally by the device control units. Clearly a procedure must be provided by which one device, usually the central processor, issues bus control commands, so that no more than one register is connected to the bus at a given time. The names assigned to bus control flip-flops are intended to suggest their function (e.g., ***mdiobus*** in the central processor).

For clarity of discussion we shall use two separate notations in AHPL for connecting the output of a register to a bus. For example,

$$\textbf{\textit{mdiobus}} \leftarrow 1$$

and

$$\textbf{\textit{IOBUS}} \leftarrow \textbf{\textit{MD}}$$

shall both mean connect the output of ***MD*** to ***IOBUS***. The latter form will often be used for emphasis. These notations will be used whenever convenient throughout the book.

For output, ***mdiobus*** = 1 gates the contents of ***MD*** onto ***IOBUS***. A pulse generated by the addressed I/O device then gates the bus contents into its data register. For input, the bus control flip-flop in the appropriate I/O device is set to 1 to place the contents of its data register onto ***IOBUS***. The CPU then issues a pulse to transfer the bus contents into ***MD***. From an electronic point of view, the I/O bus may be quite complex, including amplifiers, level-shifters, etc.; but the net logical results are as described above.

In addition to the I/O bus, there must be paths provided for transmission of control information between the CPU and the I/O devices, which we shall refer to as the *control/status* lines. There are two distinct modes of interconnection possible. First, there may be a separate set of control/status lines to each I/O device, as shown in Fig. 10.7a. In this case the CPU addresses a specific I/O device by placing signals on the appropriate set of lines, and determines which I/O device is signaling by noting which lines are active.

Second, there may be a single set of control/status lines connecting to all I/O devices, as shown in Fig. 10.7b. With this arrangement, the control/status lines must include a set of address lines, with each device assigned an

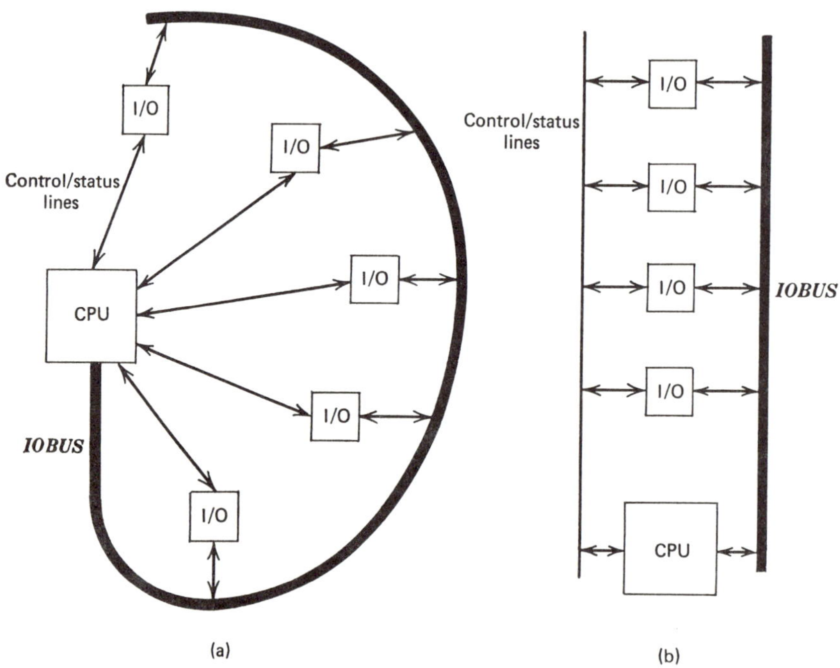

FIGURE 10.7. Basic types of control/status connections.

address, or *selector code*. To address a device, the CPU places its selector code on the address lines. Each device is equipped with a decoding circuit, by means of which it recognizes its own code and upon receipt of which it will gate in information from the other control/status lines. When a device signals the CPU, it must transmit its own code as a means of identification. Logically there is little real difference between the two methods; and often a combination is used, some control/status lines being common to all I/O devices, others running to single devices.

The choice between common or individual control/status lines depends largely on the degree to which various I/O devices may interfere with each other on common lines. For programmed transfer, common lines are most frequently used because all transfers take place under the complete control of the CPU, which can therefore control access to the lines so as to prevent interference. In buffered transfer, however, transfer takes place at the request of the I/O devices; and separate buffered devices may make requests for service at the same time. It is usual practice to provide separate control/status lines for each buffered device, with sequencing of their requests handled by the CPU.

If enough separate control/status lines and logic are provided for buffering of four devices at a time, for example, we will say that four *buffer channels* are provided. This nomenclature is perhaps unfortunate since the word "channel" suggests a completely separate set of lines, data and control/status, for each device. Sometimes, especially in earlier machines, this has been the case, which probably accounts for the use of the name "channel." However, even though buffer requests may occur simultaneously, only one word at a time can be transferred in or out of memory, so only one set of data lines, the I/O bus, is needed. Thus the arrangement shown in Fig. 10.7a is the most common for buffer channels. By contrast, the DMA channel, which is completely self-controlled, is a completely distinct channel, even to a separate memory port, as discussed in the previous section.

10.5. I/O SYSTEM FOR SIC

To provide a specific example of the I/O concepts discussed in previous sections, we shall now develop an I/O system for SIC to provide programmed and buffered transfer. The basic block diagram of SIC, with the I/O system added, is shown in Fig. 10.8. We assume up to eight I/O devices, all connected for programmed transfer through the I/O bus and control/status lines. Additional buffer control lines are provided for four buffer channels. The purpose of the various additional registers will be explained as we develop the various control sequences.

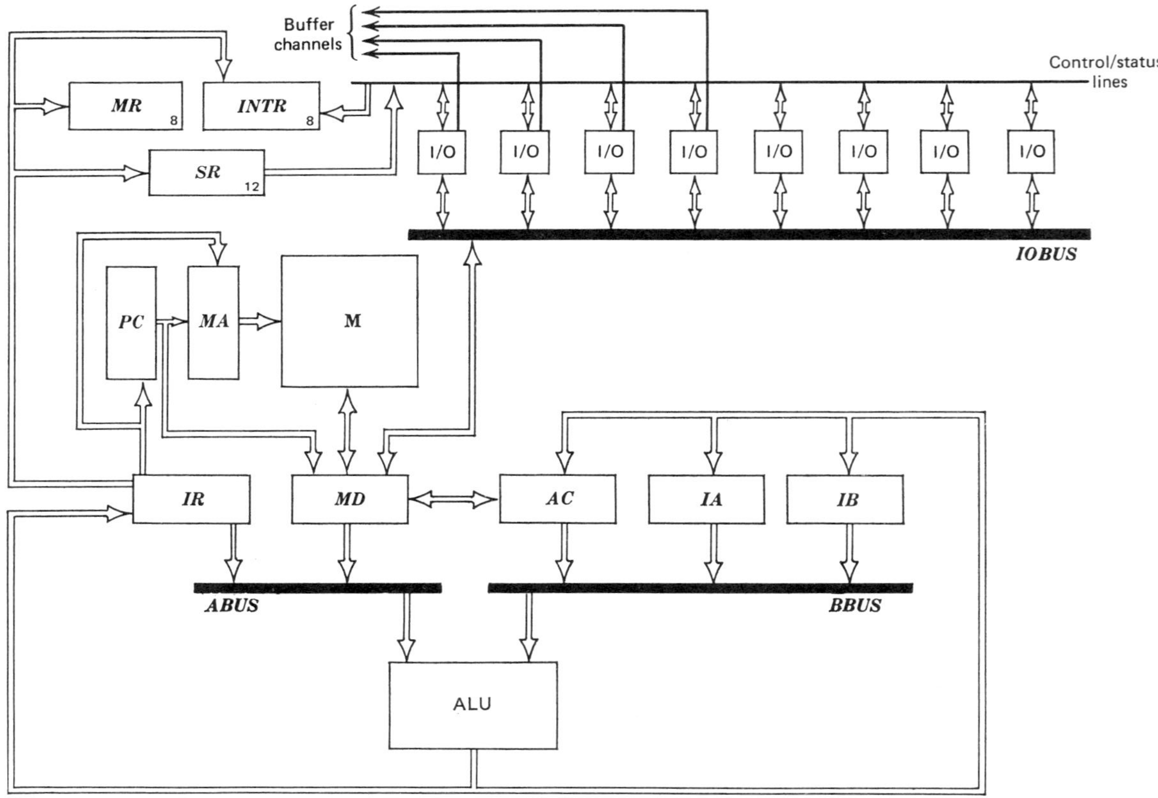

FIGURE 10.8. Basic block diagram of SIC with I/O circuits added.

There will be seven instructions included in the I/O group, i.e., instructions for which the first four bits are all 1. One of these, INT, used for controlling the interrupt system, has already been explained. The other instructions will be TSR (Test Status Register), ABn (Activate buffer on device *n*), and four IOT (Input/Output Transfer). All of these instructions are listed in Fig. 10.9.

The control/status lines consists of the *control/status bus*, ***CSBUS***, the *interrupt lines*, and several special signaling lines. The 12-bit ***CSBUS*** provides bidirectional transfers of control/status information between the I/O devices

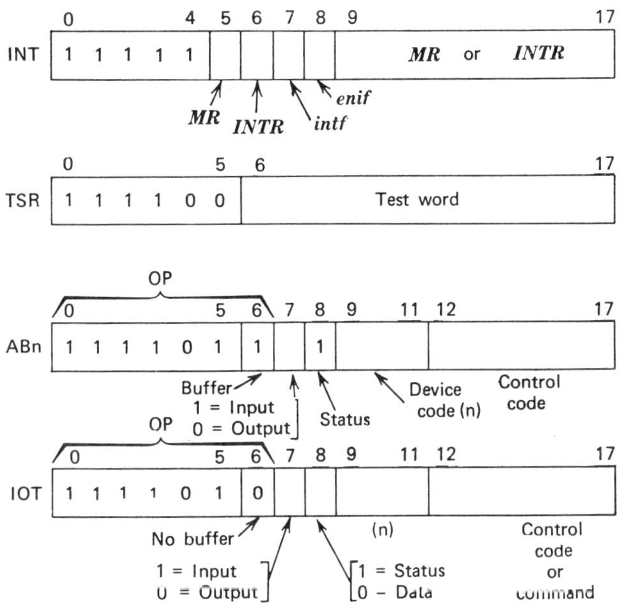

(a) Instruction formats

Mnemonic	Octal Code	Meaning
INT	76	Set interrupt system
TSR	74	Test status register
ABn	755*n*	Activate buffer for device *n*
ODn	750*n*	Output data to device *n*
OCn	751*n*	Output command to device *n*
IDn	752*n*	Input data from device *n*
ISn	753*n*	Input status from device *n*

(b) Mnemonics, codes, and interpretation

FIGURE 10.9. I/O class instructions.

and the 12-bit *status register*, ***SR***. Eight interrupt pulse lines provide for interrupt signaling from the I/O devices to the corresponding assigned positions of ***INTR***. The special signaling lines are ***cprdy*** and ***csrdy***, which provide for pulse signaling from the central processor, and ***iordy*** pulse lines from the I/O devices, which indicate response to a command from the central processor. The 18-bit *input/output bus*, ***IOBUS***, provides bidirectional data transfer between the I/O devices and ***MD***. The buffer channels will be discussed later.

The INT command has already been discussed, and the setting up of a control sequence to implement this command will be left as an exercise for the reader (see Problem 10.1). The TSR command is a skip instruction which will provide the means of branching on the basis of status information received from an I/O device. Bits 6–17 of the instruction correspond to bits 0–11 of the status register. Wherever these bits are 1, the corresponding bits of the status register will be tested. If any of the tested bits are 1, the next instruction will be skipped; if not, the next instruction will be executed. The implementation of this command will also be left to the reader (Problem 10.2).

For the ABn and IOT commands, bits 6–17 of the instruction are first sent to the status register, ***SR***, and thence to the addressed device. What happens then depends on the instruction. The sequence for the ABn command will be discussed later. There are four IOT commands, OUTPUT COMMAND, INPUT STATUS, OUTPUT DATA, and INPUT DATA.

The status and command instructions are used in the activate and deactivate steps of the I/O process. For OUTPUT COMMAND, no further action is necessary by the CPU. The addressed I/O device treats the control code, bits 12–17, as an instruction, specifying what action is to be taken. For INPUT STATUS, the addressed I/O device will transmit status information to the status register, to be tested by means of the TSR command. The data commands are used for programmed data transfer. For OUTPUT DATA, a word is sent from ***AC*** to ***MD*** and thence, via ***IOBUS***, to the addressed device. For INPUT DATA, the addressed device transmits a word via ***IOBUS*** to ***MD*** and then to ***AC***. Since ***MD*** must be used for buffered transfers, the ***IOBUS*** is connected to this register rather than directly to ***AC***.

A partial flow chart of the I/O sequence, dealing primarily with the IOT commands, is shown in Fig. 10.10. The branches at steps 4 and 29, part of earlier sequences, are shown simply to relate the I/O sequence to those already developed. The I/O sequence starts at step 68 with branches to the INT and TSR sequences.

68. $\rightarrow ((\overline{IR}_4 \times 69) + (IR_4 \times \text{INT Seq}))$
69. $\rightarrow ((IR_5 \times 70) + (\overline{IR}_5 \times \text{TSR Seq}))$

At step 70, bits 6–17 of the instruction are sent to ***SR*** and then gated onto

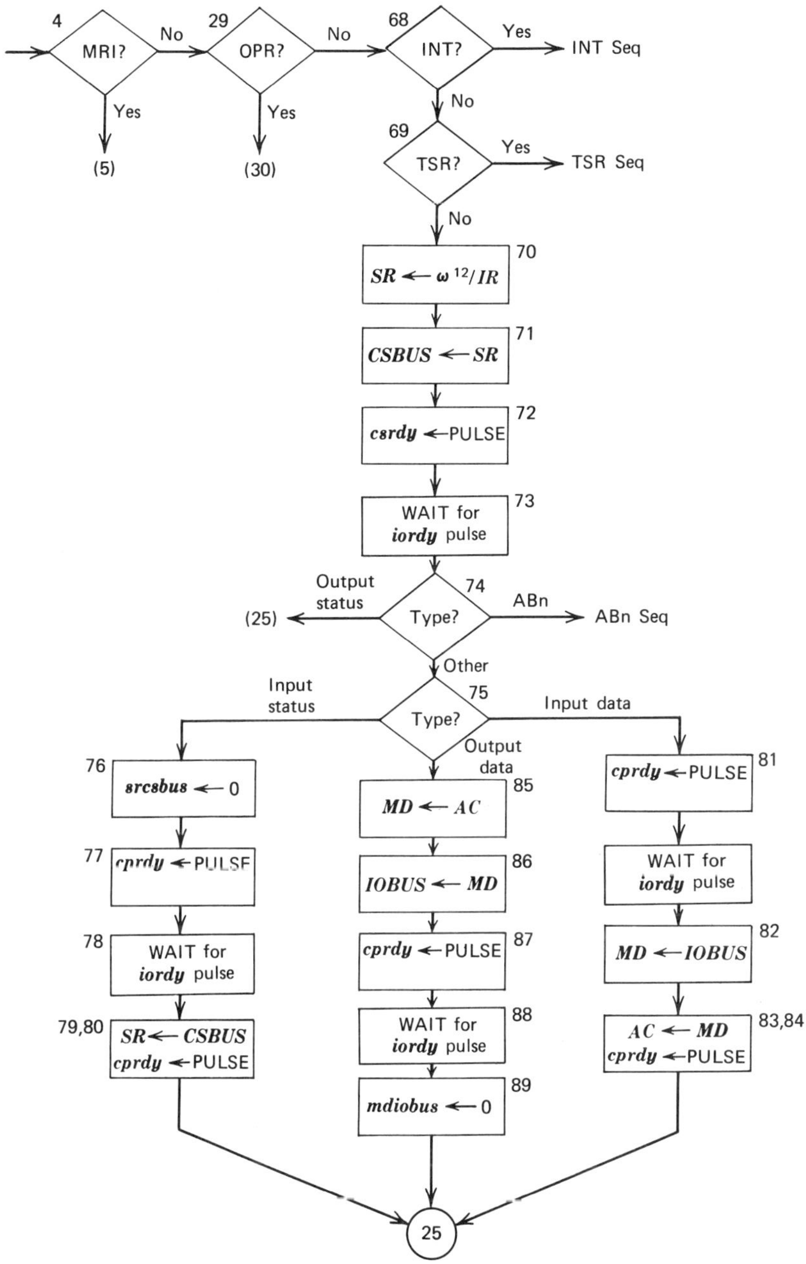

FIGURE 10.10. Partial flow chart of I/O sequence.

the ***CSBUS*** (step 71). The command-status ready line, ***csrdy***, is then pulsed in step 72.

70. $\boldsymbol{SR} \leftarrow \omega^{12}/\boldsymbol{IR}$
71. $\boldsymbol{CSBUS} \leftarrow \boldsymbol{SR}$
72. line ***csrdy*** ← PULSE

The line ***csrdy*** is constantly monitored by all I/O devices. When a pulse appears on this line, all devices check the device code (on bits 3–5 of ***CSBUS***) to see which device has been addressed. The addressed device will then check the other bits of ***CSBUS*** to see what action is required. When the appropriate action has been initiated, it acknowledges receipt of the instruction by returning a pulse on the *I/O ready* line, ***iordy***, to permit the program to continue beyond step 73.

73. WAIT for ***iordy*** PULSE

Steps 74 and 75 branch on the basis of the type of command. For ABn, the branch is to a special sequence for that command, to be discussed later. For OUTPUT COMMAND, the execution is complete; so the branch is to step 25, to increment ***PC*** and proceed to the next instruction. The other three types of IOT instruction each require a separate sequence.

74. $\rightarrow(((\overline{\boldsymbol{IR}}_6 \wedge \overline{\boldsymbol{IR}}_7 \wedge \boldsymbol{IR}_8) \times 25) + (((\boldsymbol{IR}_7 \vee \overline{\boldsymbol{IR}}_8) \wedge \overline{\boldsymbol{IR}}_6) \times 75) +$
    $(\boldsymbol{IR}_6 \times \text{ABn Seq}))$
75. $\rightarrow(((\boldsymbol{IR}_7 \wedge \boldsymbol{IR}_8) \times 76) + ((\boldsymbol{IR}_7 \wedge \overline{\boldsymbol{IR}}_8) \times 81) + ((\overline{\boldsymbol{IR}}_7 \wedge \overline{\boldsymbol{IR}}_8) \times 85))$

The sequence for INPUT STATUS starts at step 76 with the clearing of the ***CSBUS***. This is accomplished by clearing the flip-flop, ***srcsbus***, which controls the path between ***SR*** and the ***CSBUS***. The CPU then issues a pulse on the *cpu ready* line, ***cprdy***. Note the purposes of the three signaling lines.

76. ***srcsbus*** ← 0
77. line ***cprdy*** ← PULSE
78. WAIT for ***iordy*** PULSE

The *command-status ready* line, ***csrdy***, is used to initiate a command, and causes all I/O devices to check the device code being transmitted. The *CPU ready* line, ***cprdy***, is used to signal an already-selected unit that it should proceed with the next step in the sequence for the instruction being executed. The *I/O ready* line, ***iordy***, is used for acknowledgment signals from the selected I/O device to the CPU indicating that the desired action has been completed. Whenever the CPU sends out a signal which requires an acknowledgment, it will wait for a return pulse on ***iordy***.

When the selected I/O device receives the ***cprdy*** signal, it will gate the requested status information onto ***CSBUS***, and return a pulse on ***iordy***. Control then proceeds to step 79, which gates the contents of ***CSBUS*** into ***SR***, moves on to step 80, which signals the I/O device to clear ***CSBUS***, and exits to step 25 to prepare for the next instruction. Note that responsive signaling, i.e., waiting for a return signal on ***iordy***, is used not to insure

79. ***SR*** ← ***CSBUS***
80. line ***cprdy*** ← PULSE, → (25)

that the signal has been received, but to insure that the device has had sufficient time to perform the desired steps. At step 80, the control unit is exiting to the fetch of another instruction, so there is no question that the device will have time to clear the bus, hence no need to wait for a reply.

The sequence for INPUT DATA starts at step 81 with the issue of a pulse to the I/O device indicating that it should place a data word on ***IOBUS***. When the device indicates by a return pulse that this has been done, the word is gated into ***MD*** and then to ***AC***, followed by issue of a pulse to cause the device to clear the ***IOBUS***.

81. line ***cprdy*** ← PULSE, WAIT for ***iordy*** PULSE
82. ***MD*** ← ***IOBUS***
83. ***AC*** ← ***MD***
84. line ***cprdy*** ← PULSE, → (25)

The sequence for OUTPUT DATA starts at step 85 by transferring a data word from ***AC*** to ***MD*** and onto ***IOBUS***. A pulse is issued to notify the I/O device that the word is ready. When the I/O device acknowledges receipt of the word, the CPU clears the ***IOBUS*** and exits.

85. ***MD*** ← ***AC***
86. ***IOBUS*** ← ***MD***
87. line ***cprdy*** ← PULSE
88. WAIT for ***iordy*** PULSE
89. ***mdiobus*** ← 0, → (25)

10.6. BUFFER CHANNELS FOR SIC

A partial block diagram of SIC, including only those portion used in buffer operations, is shown in Fig. 10.11. The reader will recall that buffer operations take place between instructions, and must be performed in such a manner that the main program is not affected. Therefore, all registers whose status must be preserved from one instruction to the next have been deleted from Fig. 10.11 to emphasize that they are not available for buffer operations.

Since only three of the regular registers, ***MD***, ***MA***, and ***IR*** are available,

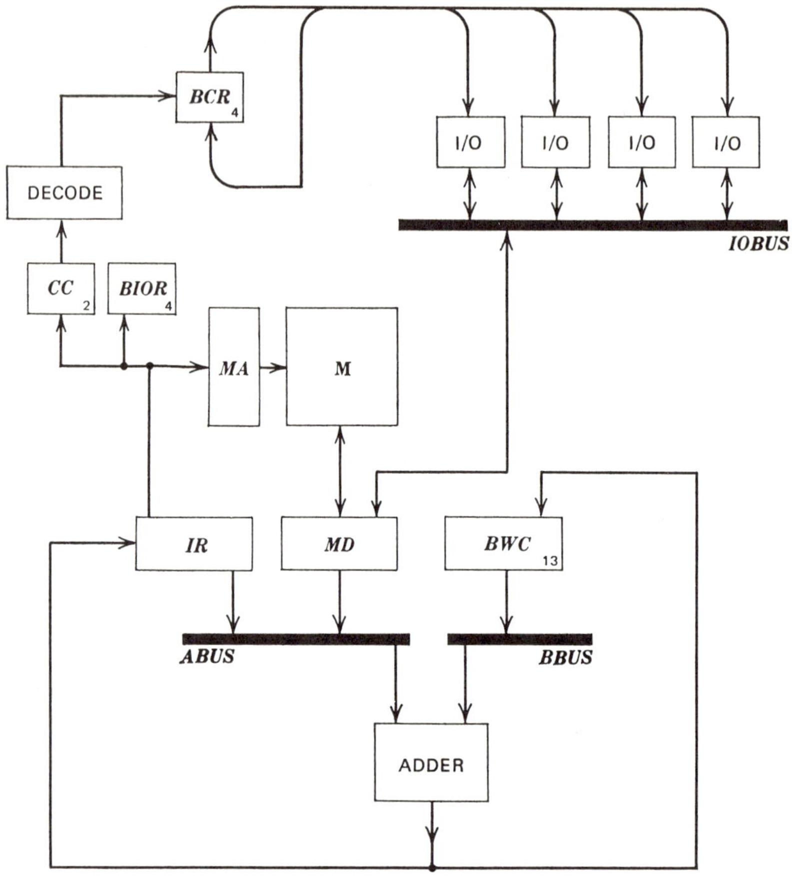

FIGURE 10.11. Block diagram, buffer section of SIC.

certain special registers have to be added for buffer processing. The *buffer word counter*, ***BWC***, is a 13-bit register used in processing the buffer addresses. There are two 4-bit registers, each having one bit for each of the four buffer channels. The positions of the *buffer I/O* register, ***BIOR***, will indicate if the corresponding channel is engaged on input or output, using 1 for input, 0 for output. The positions of the *buffer channel ready* register, ***BCR***, will be set by signals from the corresponding channel, requesting the attention of the central processor. The *channel counter*, ***CC***, is a 2-bit counting register which will contain the number of the buffer channel currently being processed.

The buffer channel lines consist of three groups of four lines each, one line in each group for each channel. Note that the buffer channels do not share common signaling lines, as in the case of the control/status lines. Since the buffered devices are completely independent of one another, there would be no way of preventing them from interfering with one another if they shared common signaling lines. On the other hand, even for buffered transfer the actual data transfer takes place under CPU control, so ***IOBUS*** may be used. A set of *buffer channel ready* lines transmits pulses from the buffered devices to the SET inputs of the corresponding positions of the buffer channel ready register, ***BCR***.

When the activate buffer command, ABn, is executed, the lower 12 bits of the instructions are sent to ***SR*** and thence to the addressed device by steps 70–72 of the I/O sequence. The 1 in position $\boldsymbol{IR_6}$ will inform the device that a buffer is to be activated; it will then take the appropriate steps. In addition, the CPU must take certain steps in activating the buffer. The ABn sequence starts at step 90 by transferring the number of the buffer channel to be activated to the channel counter, ***CC***. The device code is contained in bits 9–11 of the instruction. We will assume that only the devices assigned codes 0,1,2, or 3 may be buffered, so bits 10–11 suffice to identify the buffer channel. To simplify notation in the programs, we shall denote the number of the channel being processed as n, noting that

$$n = \perp \boldsymbol{CC}$$

The ABn sequence ends with the setting of $\boldsymbol{BIOR}_n$ to indicate whether an input or output buffer has been activated.

90. $\boldsymbol{CC} \leftarrow \boldsymbol{IR}_{10},\boldsymbol{IR}_{11}$
91. $\boldsymbol{BIOR}_n \leftarrow \boldsymbol{IR}_7;$ $\quad\quad \rightarrow (25)$

Whenever an active channel is ready to transfer a word, it transmits a pulse to set $\boldsymbol{BCR}_n$ to 1. Whenever the control program returns to step 1 to start the fetch of a new instruction, it first checks ***BCR*** to see if any buffer requests have been made. For this purpose we insert a new step 1 to branch to the buffer sequence if any positions of ***BCR*** have been set.

1. $\rightarrow(((\vee/\boldsymbol{BCR})\times 92)+(\overline{(\vee/\boldsymbol{BCR})}\times 1a))$ $\quad\quad \leftarrow$ (new)

1a. $\rightarrow((\overline{\boldsymbol{intf}}\times 1b)+(\boldsymbol{intf}\times 63))$

1b. $\boldsymbol{MA} \leftarrow \boldsymbol{PC}$ $\quad\quad$ no change

2. as before

.

.

A flow chart of the buffer sequence is shown in Fig. 10.12. The first requirement is to determine which channel (or channels) made the buffer

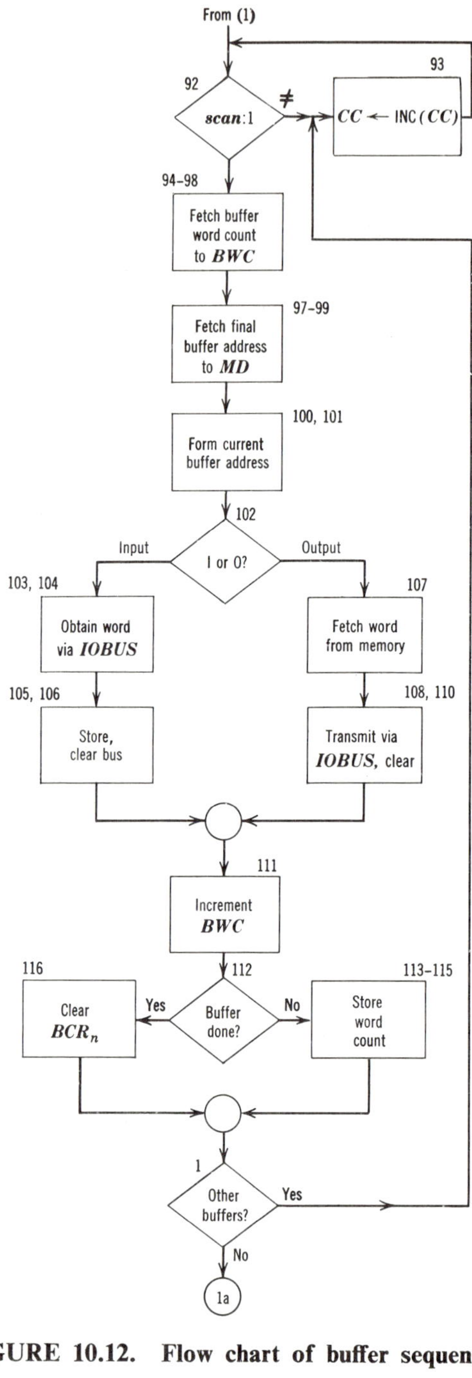

FIGURE 10.12. Flow chart of buffer sequence.

request. The ABn sequence sets ***CC*** to the number of the channel being activated; but if more than one channel is activated, there is no assurance that the contents of ***CC*** correspond to the channel making the buffer request. For this purpose we use a scanner circuit, as shown in Fig. 10.13. The output of ***CC*** is applied to a decoder circuit, which produces a signal on one of four lines that corresponds to the binary value of the contents of ***CC***. The outputs of the decoder are ANDed with the output of ***BCR***, and the outputs of the AND gates are OR'ed. Thus, only if the position of ***BCR*** corresponding to the contents of ***CC*** is set will there be a 1-output from the circuit. If there is not, ***CC*** is incremented, "scanning" ***BCR*** until a set position is found. This stops the scan; so ***CC*** now contains the number of the set position of ***BCR***. It is possible that more than one position of ***BCR*** may be set, in which case the scanner circuit will stop at the first one encountered.

Step 92 checks to see if the scanner output is 1; if it is not, we increment ***CC*** (step 93). A scanner output of 1, indicating that ***CC*** contains the number of a channel making a buffer request, causes a branch to step 94. For each buffer channel the programmer must have previously stored two items of in-

92. $\rightarrow((\textit{\textbf{scan}} \times 94) + (\overline{\textit{\textbf{scan}}} \times 93))$
93. $CC \leftarrow \mathrm{INC}(CC), \rightarrow (92)$

formation, the final address of the buffer area and minus the number of words in the buffer area. For this purpose we permanently reserve two locations in

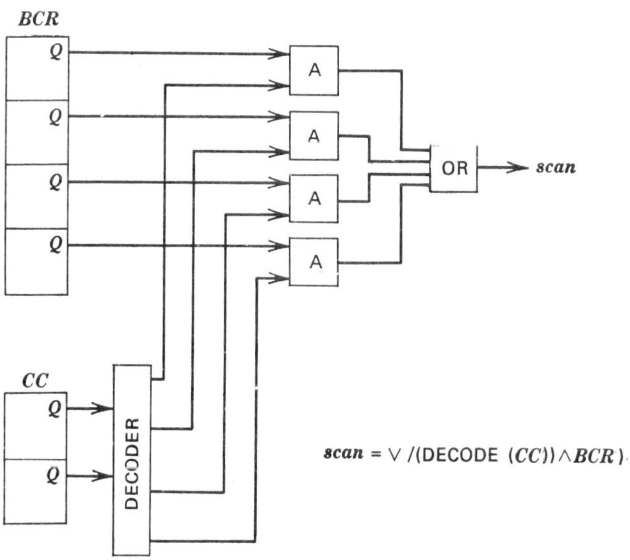

FIGURE 10.13. BCR scanner.

memory for each channel: locations 00040 and 00041 for Channel 0, locations 00042 and 00043 for Channel 1, etc. The first location of each pair will hold the negative word count, the second the final address.

To generate these addresses we use a coding circuit, BADDR, of the same type used for the interrupt circuits. The input to BADDR is ***CC***, which contains the number of the channel being processed. This address is sent via ***IR*** to ***MA***, and the negative word count is fetched (steps 94–96). The address is then incremented (step 97) and sent to ***MA***, and the word count is sent to ***BWC*** (step 98). The final address is then fetched into ***MD*** (step 99).

94. $\omega^{13}/\boldsymbol{IR} \leftarrow \mathrm{BADDR}(\boldsymbol{CC})$
95. $\boldsymbol{MA} \leftarrow \omega^{13}/\boldsymbol{IR}$
96. $\boldsymbol{MD} \leftarrow \mathrm{M}^{\perp \boldsymbol{MA}}$; WAIT
97. $\omega^{13}/\boldsymbol{IR} \leftarrow \mathrm{INC}(\omega^{13}/\boldsymbol{IR})$
98. $\boldsymbol{MA} \leftarrow \omega^{13}/\boldsymbol{IR}$; $\boldsymbol{BWC} \leftarrow \boldsymbol{MD}$
99. $\boldsymbol{MD} \leftarrow \mathrm{M}^{\perp \boldsymbol{MA}}$; WAIT

Adding the negative word count to the final address gives the current buffer address, which is sent to ***MA*** in preparation for fetch or storage of the buffer data word (steps 100–101).

100. $\omega^{13}/\boldsymbol{IR} \leftarrow \mathrm{ADD}(\boldsymbol{MD},\boldsymbol{BWC})$
101. $\boldsymbol{MA} \leftarrow \omega^{13}/\boldsymbol{IR}$

Next $\boldsymbol{BIOR}_n$ is checked to see if the operation is input or output (step 102). If input, a pulse is sent out on line $\boldsymbol{BFRDY}_n$. ***BFRDY*** is a set of four lines, one to each buffered device, by means of which the CPU notifies the I/O device when it should take the next step in the buffering sequence. The control sequence of the I/O must keep track of what the next step is at each point in the sequence. When the I/O device has taken the appropriate action, it returns a pulse on the ***resume*** line to notify the CPU. In this case the I/O device will gate the word to be transferred onto the ***IOBUS***, and return a ***resume*** pulse, enabling the program to continue (step 104). At step 105, the word is transferred to ***MD*** and another pulse sent out on $\boldsymbol{BFRDY}_n$, notifying the I/O device that the word has been accepted and the ***IOBUS*** should be cleared. The word is then stored (step 106).

102. $\rightarrow((\boldsymbol{BIOR}_n \times 103)+(\overline{\boldsymbol{BIOR}}_n \times 107))$
103. line $\boldsymbol{BFRDY}_n \leftarrow$ PULSE
104. WAIT for ***resume*** PULSE
105. $\boldsymbol{MD} \leftarrow \boldsymbol{IOBUS}$; line $\boldsymbol{BFRDY}_n \leftarrow$ PULSE
106. $\mathrm{M}^{\perp \boldsymbol{MA}} \leftarrow \boldsymbol{MD}$; WAIT, $\rightarrow (111)$

For output, the data word is obtained from memory (step 107). At step 108 it is gated onto the ***IOBUS***, and a pulse is sent out on $\boldsymbol{BFRDY}_n$ to notify the

I/O device that it is ready. When the I/O device acknowledges receipt of the word with a pulse on ***resume***, the program proceeds to step 110 to clear ***IOBUS*** and again pulse $\boldsymbol{BFRDY}_n$, this time as an indication that the transfer has been completed.

107. $\boldsymbol{MD} \leftarrow \mathrm{M}^{\perp \boldsymbol{MA}}$; WAIT
108. $\boldsymbol{IOBUS} \leftarrow \boldsymbol{MD}$; line $\boldsymbol{BFRDY}_n \leftarrow$ PULSE
109. WAIT for ***resume*** PULSE
110. $\boldsymbol{mdiobus} \leftarrow 0$; line $\boldsymbol{BFRDY}_n \leftarrow$ PULSE

At step 111, having completed the input or output transfer, the negative word count is incremented, thus decreasing its absolute value. This count is checked at step 112 to see if it has reached 0, which would indicate that the desired number of words has been transferred. If not, the updated word count is stored (steps 113–115). If so, then $\boldsymbol{BCR}_n$ is cleared to prevent further servicing of the buffer at step 1; and a pulse is emitted on line $\boldsymbol{BFEND}_n$ notifying the I/O device that the buffer is complete and it should take appropriate steps to deactivate (step 116).

111. $\boldsymbol{BWC} \leftarrow \mathrm{INC}(\boldsymbol{BWC})$
112. $\perp \boldsymbol{BWC}$:0, $(=, \neq) \rightarrow (116, 113)$
113. $\omega^{13}/\boldsymbol{IR} \leftarrow \mathrm{BADDR}(\boldsymbol{CC})$; $\boldsymbol{BCR}_n \leftarrow 0$
114. $\boldsymbol{MA} \leftarrow \omega^{13}/\boldsymbol{IR}$; $\boldsymbol{MD} \leftarrow \boldsymbol{BWC}$
115. $\mathrm{M}^{\perp \boldsymbol{MA}} \leftarrow \boldsymbol{MD}$; WAIT, $\rightarrow (1)$
116. $\boldsymbol{BCR}_n \leftarrow 0$; line $\boldsymbol{BFEND}_n \leftarrow$ PULSE; $\rightarrow (1)$

When the system returns to the main sequence, step 1 checks to see if any more buffer requests are waiting to be serviced. Recall that buffer requests are completely asynchronous with respect to one another, so that more than one request could have been present when this buffer cycle was started, or more could have come in during this buffer cycle. Note that $\boldsymbol{BCR}_n$ was cleared in the above sequence; so another request is indicated by any other positions being set, i.e., by $\vee/\boldsymbol{BCR} = 1$. In this event, control returns to step 92 to resume the scan of ***BCR***. Only when all buffer requests have been serviced will the program continue to step 1a.

Note that step 1 gives buffer requests priority over other interrupts or the fetching of new instructions. If buffer requests arrive fast enough, step 1 could result in the CPU being completely monopolized by buffer operations. This assignment of top priority to buffer operations is the general practice. Buffered devices are generally fast, and failure to service them before another word is available or required will result in the loss of data.

Finally, the reader should note that we have not attempted to optimize the I/O or buffer sequences with regard to speed, in the interest of maintaining the maximum possible clarity of exposition. There are many places where operations could be overlapped, particularly with memory cycles, to speed up the sequences.

10.7. THEME AND VARIATIONS

As noted in the introduction to this chapter, there are probably as many different types of interrupt and I/O systems as there are different models of computers. So far we have discussed only the essential features of the most commonly-used types of systems. If we compare the three basic types of I/O systems, we may note a theme here, that the speed of the I/O system is proportional to the amount of extra hardware provided for I/O. Conversely, we may state that the speed of I/O transfer is inversely proportional to the degree that CPU hardware is shared by I/O and non-I/O operations.

There is an essentially continuous spectrum of designs, ranging from a completely shared CPU to completely independent I/O channels, and any division into categories is to some degree arbitrary. Nevertheless, the classification we have made is based on fairly clear-cut distinctions. In the programmed transfer, each transfer of a word requires a formal interrupt of the main program and fetching of special instructions. In the buffered transfer, the main program is not interrupted and no instructions are fetched; but some hardware is shared, so transfers may occur only between execution of main program instructions. In the DMA transfer, the only hardware shared is the memory itself; and the main program will be "unaware" of the I/O activities except to the degree that it may occasionally have to wait longer for memory than would otherwise be the case.

Even though these distinctions are fairly sharp, there are obviously many possible variations. At one extreme, programmed transfer may involve even less separate hardware than we proposed for SIC. We may eliminate the status register and the control/status lines and route all information, data or control/status, via the I/O bus and the accumulator or some other arithmetic register. Possibly the ultimate example of this approach is the "unibus" concept, in which all registers, both CPU arithmetic and control registers and I/O data registers, communicate through a single common bus. Thus, a transfer in or out of an I/O register is no different than a transfer in or out of any other register. This scheme has a certain straightforward simplicity, but the total lack of special hardware for handling I/O would increase the chance of the machine being monopolized by I/O operations.

Intermediate between the programmed and buffered approaches would be one in which instructions would have to be fetched for each transfer, but enough extra registers and logic would be provided so that the main program would not have to be disturbed. Similarly, we can achieve a compromise between buffered and DMA operation. Note that three memory references were required to process the address in the buffer sequence developed for SIC. By providing a separate register for each channel, to hold the word count, we could reduce this to one reference per transfer. By providing two registers per channel, we can eliminate all memory references for address processing.

The DMA approach can be extended by providing separate control logic to handle all phases of I/O—inquiry, activation, and deactivation, as well as the actual transfer. When this is done, the resultant collection of hardware is often referred to as the *channel controller*; and it is essentially a special-purpose computer, sharing memory with the CPU. When an I/O operation is desired, the CPU transfers one instruction to the channel controller, simply indicating which I/O device is to be used and the size and location of the buffer area, and then leaves all the details to the controller.

Channel controllers vary enormously in capacity and complexity. In systems that are primarily I/O oriented, such as interactive time-sharing systems, the controllers may actually be more complex than the CPU, and may even be in control, telling the CPU what to do, rather than the other way round. In some cases, the CPU and channel controller may be different model computers, one selected for its I/O capabilities, one for its processing capabilities. These machines communicate through access to a common memory. An interesting example of this approach is found in the CDC 6000 and 7000 series machines, which consist of one central processor and ten peripheral processors. The peripheral processors, which handle all I/O activities, are small, completely independent computers, each with its own small memory but also sharing access to the main memory with the CPU. Features of these machines will be discussed in more detail in Chapter 14.

An interesting and important variation on the interrupt procedure is the use of the *program status word*, PSW. When an interrupt takes place, the status of the interrupted program must be preserved by storing appropriate information, such as the contents of the ***PC*** register. When the program is restored, the ***MR*** register must be restored to the appropriate condition, which implies that the desired mask register setting is stored in an instruction in the interrupt program. Further, setting up the interrupt requires putting a new address into ***PC*** and a new setting of the ***MR***.

From the above, we see that replacing a main program with an interrupt program, or, for that matter, replacing any program with any other program, requires the exchange of certain information. To make this exchange as systematic as possible, we specify a *program status register*, ***PSR***, which will at all times contain the information which must be preserved in order to preserve the status of any type of program. The ***PSR*** will basically consist of the catenation of the ***PC*** register, the ***MR***, and various indicators, the exact nature of which will depend on the computer. The contents of this register are referred to as the program status word, PSW.

Associated with interrupt source will be a reserved location in memory, in which the programmer will store the PSW for the interrupt program associated with that source. The PSW will contain the starting address of the interrupt program, the desired mask register setting, and such indicator settings as may be required. When an interrupt occurs, the CPU simply exchanges PSW's, storing the current PSW of the interrupted program in the second reserved location and loading the PSW of the interrupt program into ***PSR***. The reader should note that there is nothing basically new here. This same information must be exchanged in any interrupt procedure; the PSW concept makes this exchange somewhat more systematic than it might otherwise be. This approach is very important as it is used in IBM Systems 360 and 370 and all the many imitators of those systems.

PROBLEMS

10.1 Devise a control sequence to implement the INT command in SIC, assuming hard-wired control.

10.2 Repeat 10.1, for the TSR command.

10.3 The interrupt system discussed in Section 10.2 utilizes fixed priority from the point of view of the programmer. Devise a system whereby the priority assigned to various positions of ***INTR*** can be controlled by the programmer. Consider both the hardware requirements and any additional instructions that might be required. Having specified the hardware and the instructions required, write the control sequence to implement the instructions.

10.4 The programmed data transfer sequence for SIC discussed in Section 10.5 moves data through ***AC***, thus creating problems with regard to the preservation of the interrupted program. Devise a system whereby programmed data transfer will not involve any general-purpose register except ***MD***. Note that this may require modifications to the MRI instruction set. If so, determine the nature of any such modifications.

10.5 Assume the speed of the buffer sequence for SIC is to be increased by providing word-count registers, ***BWC1*** to ***BWC4***, for each channel. This will eliminate two memory references per buffer cycle. Revise the ABn and buffer sequences as required to accommodate this change.

10.6 Continue Problem 10.5, assuming that the buffer speed is to be further improved by providing last word address registers, ***LWA1*** to ***LWA4***, for each channel.

10.7 Design a buffer control for an I/O device to be used with the SIC buffers described in Section 10.6. To generalize the problem, assume a data register, ***DR***, connected to the ***IOBUS***. The buffer control should be considered separate from the I/O device "proper." The I/O device will assemble and disassemble words in a separate register, ***AR***. The buffer will initiate or acknowledge transfers between ***DR*** and ***AR***. Specify clearly the connection of all indicators and registers in the buffer control to the lines to the CPU and write the control sequence for the buffer control.

10.8 Repeat Problem 10.7, except now assume the I/O device is the tape transport for which the READ sequence was given in Section 9.7 and the WRITE sequence was developed in Problem 9.8. Write a complete control sequence, including the READ, WRITE, and buffer sequences.

10.9 Write a control sequence for a card reader. Assume that the card is stepped from one column position to the next by control pulses at a rate determined by the controller. As each column is read, the Hollerith code is converted into a 6-bit character code. The full card image is stored in 27 18-bit words, with one character position left unused in the last word. When a full card image has been assembled, it is to be transmitted to the CPU under buffer control. Once the buffer has been initiated, it proceeds fast enough that reading the next card may be commenced without waiting for completion of the full 27-word transfer.

10.10 Ten MOS shift registers containing 2^{16} bits each are arranged to provide a bulk storage peripheral device for SIC. All that the reader need understand about an MOS shift register is that each time a control pulse is applied, the 2^{16} bits are rotated one position. At all times, only one bit is observable and only this bit can be altered externally. As a unit the shift registers form a 2^{16} character by 10-bit memory designated **SRM**. Only the character currently in $\mathbf{SRM}^0$ can be read out or modified. A 16-bit register ***SRC*** contains the number of the character currently in $\boldsymbol{SRM}^0$. A character numbering system of ***SRC*** is required so that SIC can request information by providing a starting address. The only two AHPL steps which will be interpreted as affecting **SRM** and ***SRC*** are

$$\mathbf{SRM} \leftarrow \Uparrow \mathbf{SRM};\ \boldsymbol{SRC} \leftarrow \mathrm{INC}\ (\boldsymbol{SRC})$$

and

$$\mathbf{SRM}^0 \leftarrow \text{ANY TEN BITS}$$

These transfers may be repeated as many times as required in a control sequence. The outputs of ***SRC*** and $\mathbf{SRM}^0$ may be connected to branch and transfer circuitry as required.

The first 9 bits of each of two consecutive characters correspond to an 18-bit SIC word. The tenth bit is used to form even parity over the character. A control sequence for the bulk storage peripheral is to be designed which provides for the transfer of blocks of information in either direction between SIC and the **SRM** by program-controlled transfer only. The number of the first character in a block transfer will be provided to the peripheral as the last 16 bits of the ***IOBUS*** in an ODn (assume n = 0) instruction just prior to the transfer.

There are just four CPU commands to which the bulk storage controller (device 0) must respond. The command appearing on the control status bus and the subsequent I/O operation for each are described below. Following the execution of each operation, the controller must be ready to respond to any one of the four commands. Typically a control code 00 operation will be followed by a sequence of either data input or data output steps. The only status information required by IS_0 is the contents of a parity error flip-flop which is set any time a parity error in an output character from the peripheral is detected. The 00 command causes the parity error flip-flop to be cleared.

OD_0	Control Code: 00 (octal) = First Character Command $\omega^{16}/$***IOBUS*** = Number of First Character of a Block
OD_0	Control Code: 01 (octal) = Output Command Data on ***IOBUS***
ID_0	Control Code: 02 (octal) = Input Command ***IOBUS*** ← DATA
IS_0	Control Code: 03 (octal) = Input Status Command ***CSBUS*** ← STATUS

Design the bulk storage peripheral (only) so that it will interface with the SIC IOT configuration as described in this chapter. Use the buses and control pulse lines provided in the description of SIC.

11

High-Speed Addition

11.1. INTRODUCTION

One of the main concerns of the computer designer is obtaining the highest possible operating speed, subject to various technical and economic constraints. As we have seen, the adder plays a central role in the operation of the computer, and is thus a major factor in determining the overall speed of most machines. As a result, the design of high-speed adders has been the subject of exhaustive study from the very beginning of the computer era.

Over the years a number of fast-adders have been developed, but today the majority of fast-adder designs utilize some version of the *carry look-ahead* principle. The carry look-ahead adder was first described by Weinberger and Smith [1] in 1956. The design was further refined in the design of the *Stretch* computer; this version was described by MacSorley [2] in a 1961 article which is the basic reference on the subject. Flores (1963) [3] presented the first description in a textbook, and his description is probably the most complete to date.

A particular problem of notation arises in describing adders. It is standard practice in articles on adders to number the bit positions starting with the least-significant-digit (l.s.d) position as bit 0, the next most significant as bit 1, etc. However, as we have seen, the practice in numbering registers is exactly the opposite, the most-significant-digit (m.s.d.) position being bit 0. The former convention is convenient from a point of keeping the equations simple since we start writing equations with the l.s.d. position. If we adopt the latter convention, in a ρ-bit adder the l.s.d. is bit (ρ-1), the next digit is bit (ρ-2), etc., which makes for very cumbersome notation. To keep things as simple as possible while remaining consistent with the register notation, throughout this chapter we shall discuss a fixed-length adder of 64 bits, from bit 0 (m.s.d.) to bit 63 (l.s.d.). The reader should have no trouble adapting the equations to adders of any other length, and we feel that the slight loss of generality will be more than compensated for by the advantages of a consistent system of notation.

11.2. RIPPLE-CARRY ADDER

The simplest form of parallel adder is the ripple-carry adder, which consists of full-adders connected as shown in Fig. 11.1. The combinational logic subroutine generating this adder was presented in Section 7.5, but we wish to analyze it in detail at this time to set the stage for the discussion to follow. The adder combines an addend and an augend, $\boldsymbol{A}$ and $\boldsymbol{B}$, to develop a sum, $\boldsymbol{S}$. A given full adder, in the jth bit position, receives the jth bits of the addend and augend, $\boldsymbol{A}_j$ and $\boldsymbol{B}_j$, together with a carry-in from the next-least-significant digit, $\boldsymbol{C}_{j+1}$, and produces the sum bit, $\boldsymbol{S}_j$, and the carry-out, $\boldsymbol{C}_j$. The truth table for a full adder is shown in Fig. 11.2, and the equations for the sum and carry bits are given in Eqs. 11.1 and 11.2.

$$\boldsymbol{S}_j = (\boldsymbol{A}_j\wedge\bar{\boldsymbol{B}}_j\wedge\bar{\boldsymbol{C}}_{j+1})\vee(\bar{\boldsymbol{A}}_j\wedge\bar{\boldsymbol{B}}_j\wedge\boldsymbol{C}_{j+1})\vee(\bar{\boldsymbol{A}}_j\wedge\boldsymbol{B}_j\wedge\bar{\boldsymbol{C}}_{j+1})\vee(\boldsymbol{A}_j\wedge\boldsymbol{B}_j\wedge\boldsymbol{C}_{j+1}) \quad (11.1)$$

$$\boldsymbol{C}_j = (\boldsymbol{A}_j\wedge\boldsymbol{B}_j)\vee(\boldsymbol{A}_j\wedge\boldsymbol{C}_{j+1})\vee(\boldsymbol{B}_j\wedge\boldsymbol{C}_{j+1}) \quad (11.2)$$

Note that these equations are written in the second-order sum-of-products form; so there are two levels of gating (AND-OR) between input and output. If we let the delay through a single level of gating be Δt, then the delay in a single stage is $2\Delta t$, which is the minimum possible. We assume that all bits

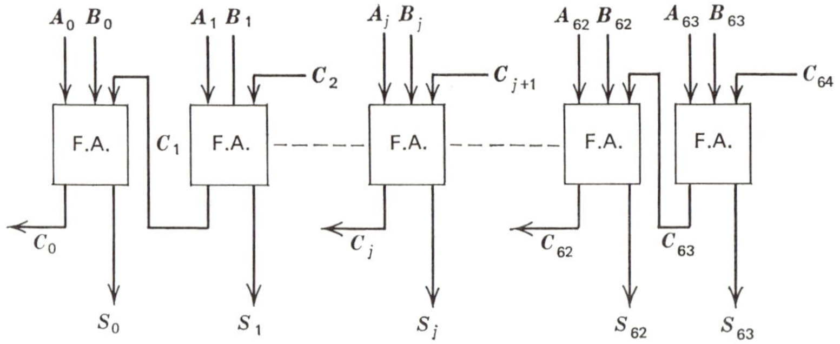

FIGURE 11.1. Basic ripple-carry adder.

A_j	B_j	C_{j+1}	S_j	C_j
0	0	0	0	0
0	0	1	1	0
0	1	0	1	0
0	1	1	0	1
1	0	0	1	0
1	0	1	0	1
1	1	0	0	1
1	1	1	1	1

FIGURE 11.2. Truth table for full adder.

of the addend and augend arrive at the same time, but each individual adder cannot develop its sum until $2\Delta t$ after it receives the carry from the previous stage. Further, if the addend bit is 1 and the augend bit 0 (or vice versa) the carry-out will not be developed until $2\Delta t$ after the arrival of the carry-in. In the worst possible case the carry may have to propagate ("ripple-through") the adder from one end to the other, with a delay of $2\Delta t$ in each stage and a total delay of $\rho 2\Delta t$ for the whole adder. The worst case will rarely occur; if the addend and augend bits are both 0 or both 1, then the output carry is independent of the input carry. But we must allow for the worst case. Thus, for a 64-bit adder, we must allow $128\Delta t$ for addition; and even with very fast electronics, this can be an intolerable delay. As a result, the ripple-carry adder will generally be found only in small, inexpensive computers.

11.3. THE MINIMUM-DELAY ADDER

A basic theorem of Boolean algebra states that any Boolean function, no matter how complex, can be realized in a second-order (sum-of-products or product-of-sums) form. All the bits of the addend and augend are assumed to be available simultaneously, so there would seem to be no theoretical reason why we can't develop a second-order equation for each sum bit and eliminate the delays of carry propagation. Let us investigate this possibility for the 64-bit adder.

For the l.s.d. position we have

$$S_{63} = (A_{63} \wedge \bar{B}_{63} \wedge \bar{C}_{64}) \vee (\bar{A}_{63} \wedge B_{63} \wedge \bar{C}_{64}) \vee (\bar{A}_{63} \wedge \bar{B}_{63} \wedge C_{64}) \vee (A_{63} \wedge B_{63} \wedge C_{64}) \quad (11.3)$$

and

$$C_{63} = (A_{63} \wedge B_{63}) \vee (A_{63} \wedge C_{64}) \vee (B_{63} \wedge C_{64}) \quad (11.4)$$

For the next stage we have

$$S_{62} = (A_{62}\wedge\bar{B}_{62}\wedge\bar{C}_{63})\vee(\bar{A}_{62}\wedge B_{62}\wedge\bar{C}_{63})\vee(\bar{A}_{62}\wedge\bar{B}_{62}\wedge C_{63})\vee(A_{62}\wedge B_{62}\wedge C_{63}) \tag{11.5}$$

Substituting Eq. 11.4 into Eq. 11.5 to eliminate the propagated carry* we have

$$\begin{aligned} S_{62} = {} & (A_{62}\wedge B_{62}\wedge A_{63}\wedge B_{63})\vee(A_{62}\wedge B_{62}\wedge A_{63}\wedge C_{64})\vee(A_{62}\wedge B_{62}\wedge B_{63}\wedge C_{64}) \\ & \vee(A_{62}\wedge\bar{B}_{62}\wedge\bar{A}_{63}\wedge\bar{B}_{63})\vee(A_{62}\wedge\bar{B}_{62}\wedge\bar{A}_{63}\wedge\bar{C}_{64})\vee(A_{62}\wedge\bar{B}_{62}\wedge\bar{B}_{63}\wedge\bar{C}_{64}) \\ & \vee(\bar{A}_{62}\wedge B_{62}\wedge\bar{A}_{63}\wedge\bar{B}_{63})\vee(\bar{A}_{62}\wedge B_{62}\wedge\bar{A}_{63}\wedge\bar{C}_{64})\vee(\bar{A}_{62}\wedge B_{62}\wedge\bar{B}_{63}\wedge\bar{C}_{64}) \\ & \vee(\bar{A}_{62}\wedge\bar{B}_{62}\wedge A_{63}\wedge B_{63})\vee(\bar{A}_{62}\wedge\bar{B}_{62}\wedge A_{63}\wedge C_{64})\vee(\bar{A}_{62}\wedge\bar{B}_{62}\wedge B_{63}\wedge C_{64}) \end{aligned} \tag{11.6}$$

Here we have a second-order equation exclusively in terms of the original inputs to the adder; so S_{62} will be developed with the same delay as S_{63}. However, Eq. 11.3 requires only four 3-input AND gates while Eq. 11.6 requires twelve 4-input AND gates. If we carry the same process on further, we find that S_{61} requires four 4-input and twenty-four 5-input gates, and S_{60} requires four 4-input, eight 5-input, and forty-eight 6-input AND gates. It is obvious that the number and size of gates very rapidly becomes totally impractical. S_0 would require approximately 10^{20} gates!

11.4. THE CARRY LOOK-AHEAD PRINCIPLE

We have seen that the ripple-carry adder is too slow and the minimum-delay adder impractical, so we look for something in between. In one sense, we need to find a way to factor the equations of the minimum-delay adder into groupings of practical size. There are an infinite number of ways of factoring the equations, and many have been tried; but the most successful designs all utilize the *carry look-ahead* principle.

We begin by taking a slightly different approach to the implementation of the individual full adder. Notice from Fig. 11.2 that if $A_j = B_j = 0$, then $C_j = 0$ regardless of the value of C_{j+1}. Similarly, if $A_j = B_j = 1$, then $C_j = 1$ regardless of C_{j+1}. If $A_j \neq B_j$, then the carry-out C_j is the same as the carry-in C_{j+1}. In the latter case we say that the carry propagates through stage j. Where the carry-out of stage j is a 1 regardless of the carry-in, we say that stage j is a *generate* stage. This interpretation of an adder stage is given in Fig. 11.3.

* The input carry to the first stage, C_{64}, is used in complement arithmetic, and is assumed to be available at the same time as the addend and augend.

A_j	B_j	C_j	
0	0	0	
0	1	C_{j+1}	Propagate stage
1	0	C_{j+1}	Propagate stage
1	1	1	Generate stage

FIGURE 11.3. Carry propagation.

Stage j is a generate stage if and only if G_j as defined by Eq. 11.7 is 1:

$$G_j = A_j \wedge B_j \tag{11.7}$$

Stage j is a propagate stage if and only if P_j as defined by Eq. 11.8 is 1:

$$P_j = A_j \oplus B_j = (A_j \wedge \bar{B}_j) \vee (\bar{A}_j \wedge B_j) \tag{11.8}$$

From Fig. 11.3 we observe that we have a carry out of stage whenever $G_j = 1$ or when $P_j = 1$ and there is a carry into stage j. This yields Eq. 11.10 as an expression for C_j.

$$C_j = (A_j \wedge B_j) \vee (((A_j \wedge \bar{B}_j) \vee (\bar{A}_j \wedge B_j)) \wedge C_{j+1}) \tag{11.9}$$

$$C_j = G_j \vee (P_j \wedge C_{j+1}) \tag{11.10}$$

It is also possible to express the sum S_j as a function of G_j, P_j, and C_{j+1}. This is most easily accomplished by algebraic manipulation of the basic expression for S_j.

$$S_j =$$

$$(A_j \wedge \bar{B}_j \wedge \bar{C}_{j+1}) \vee (\bar{A}_j \wedge B_j \wedge \bar{C}_{j+1}) \vee (\bar{A}_j \wedge \bar{B}_j \wedge C_{j+1}) \vee (A_j \wedge B_j \wedge C_{j+1}) \tag{11.11}$$

$$= (((A_j \wedge B_j) \vee (\bar{A}_j \wedge \bar{B}_j)) \wedge C_{j+1}) \vee (((A_j \wedge \bar{B}_j) \vee (\bar{A}_j \wedge B_j)) \wedge \bar{C}_{j+1})$$

$$S_j = (\bar{P}_j \wedge C_{j+1}) \vee (P_j \wedge \bar{C}_{j+1}) \tag{11.12}$$

Equations 11.12 and 11.10 are certainly simpler in form than the original sum and carry equations, but it is not yet evident what effect they will have on the speed or complexity of the circuit. For this purpose let us now apply these equations to the design of the 64-bit adder, starting as usual with the l.s.d. position:

$$\begin{aligned} S_{63} &= (\bar{P}_{63} \wedge C_{64}) \vee (P_{63} \wedge \bar{C}_{64}) \\ S_{62} &= (\bar{P}_{62} \wedge C_{63}) \vee (P_{62} \wedge \bar{C}_{63}) \\ S_{61} &= (\bar{P}_{61} \wedge C_{62}) \vee (P_{61} \wedge \bar{C}_{62}) \\ S_{60} &= (\bar{P}_{60} \wedge C_{61}) \vee (P_{60} \wedge \bar{C}_{61}) \end{aligned} \tag{11.13}$$

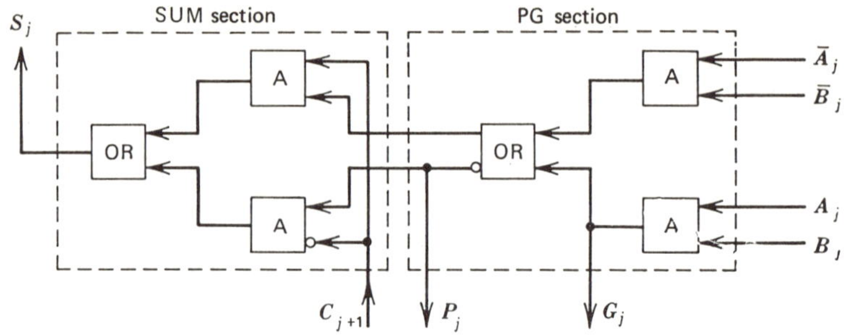

FIGURE 11.4. Full-adder circuit.

The sum equations obviously all have the same form so we shall implement them with a special form of full-adder circuit, as shown in Fig. 11.4. For later convenience, we shall divide this circuit into two sections, the *PG section* and the *SUM section*, as shown.

The carry-in terms to the sum circuits will be developed as shown in the following equations:

$$C_{63} = G_{63} \vee (P_{63} \wedge C_{64}) \tag{11.14}$$

$$\begin{aligned} C_{62} &= G_{62} \vee (P_{62} \wedge C_{63}) \\ &= G_{62} \vee (P_{62} \wedge G_{63}) \vee (P_{62} \wedge P_{63} \wedge C_{64}) \end{aligned} \tag{11.15}$$

$$\begin{aligned} C_{61} &= G_{61} \vee (P_{61} \wedge C_{62}) \\ &= G_{61} \vee (P_{61} \wedge G_{62}) \vee (P_{61} \wedge P_{62} \wedge G_{63}) \vee (P_{61} \wedge P_{62} \wedge P_{63} \wedge C_{64}) \end{aligned} \tag{11.16}$$

These three equations are implemented in the carry look-ahead (CLA) unit, shown in Fig. 11.5. (This unit also implements some additional equations, which will be discussed shortly.) Since the CLA unit may be used with any set of four bit-positions, we have used generalized subscripts in Fig. 11.5. For implementation of the above equations, $j = 63$.

The interconnection of the CLA unit with the adder units for bits 60–63 is shown in Fig. 11.6. Noting that each unit (SUM, PG, CLA) is a second-order circuit, we can analyze the propagation delays. Let us consider the worst case, a carry generated in bit 63 and propagated through to bit 60. The carry is generated in PG_{63} with a delay of $2\Delta t$, propagated through the CLA to C_{61} in $2\Delta t$, and propagated through SUM_{60} to develop S_{60} in $2\Delta t$, for a total delay of $6\Delta t$. This compares with a delay of $8\Delta t$ for ripple-carry through four bits. This is only a minor improvement; but this is just the beginning of the design, as we shall see.

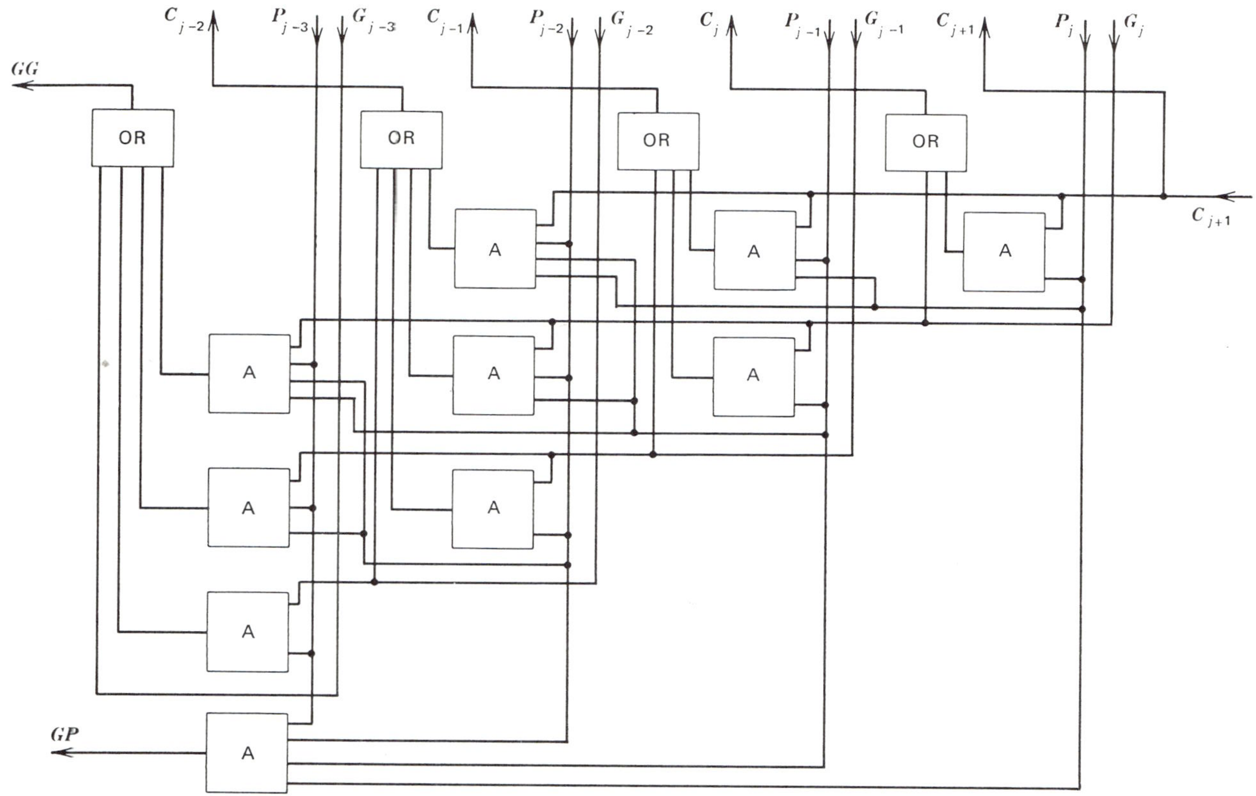

FIGURE 11.5. Carry look-ahead unit.

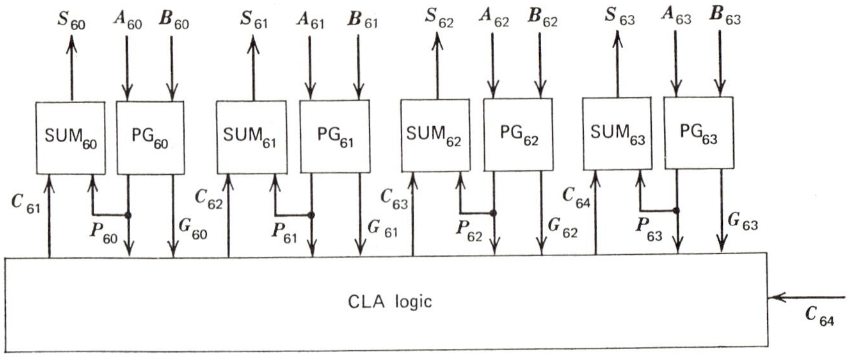

FIGURE 11.6. Complete adder for bits 60–63.

If we examine Eqs. 11.14, 11.15, 11.16, we see that they are iterative in form; and there is no reason why we could not continue the same process to write equations for C_{60}, C_{59}, etc. These equations would also be second-order, so the CLA unit could be extended to cover more bits, with no increase in delay. However, as we increase the number of bits, the size and number of gates also increases. C_{61} requires 4-input gates, C_{60} would require 5-input gates, C_{59} would require 6-input gates, etc. So the number of bits the CLA unit can cover is limited by the fan-in capability of our gates. Circuit technology makes it generally impractical to go beyond about eight bits in the basic CLA unit.

11.5. GROUP CARRY LOOK-AHEAD

As the next step in our design, we shall divide the 64-bit adder into 4-bit groups, bits 0–3 comprising group 0, bits 4–7, group 1, etc. We then define *group generate*, GG, and group propagate, GP, terms, as shown below for group 15 (bits 60–63). The group generate term corresponds to the situation

$$GG_{15} = G_{60} \vee (P_{60} \wedge G_{61}) \vee (P_{60} \wedge P_{61} \wedge G_{62}) \vee (P_{60} \wedge P_{61} \wedge P_{62} \wedge G_{63}) \quad (11.17)$$

$$GP_{15} = P_{60} \wedge P_{61} \wedge P_{62} \wedge P_{63} \quad (11.18)$$

where a carry has been generated somewhere in the group and all more-significant positions are in the propagate condition, so that the carry propagates on out of the group. The group propagate corresponds to the condition where all bits in the group are in the propagate condition, so that a carry into the group should pass right through the group. Note that these terms are implemented by the left-most five gates in the CLA unit (Fig. 11.5).

Next, we note that there is a carry out of the group if a carry is generated in the group and propagated out or if there is a carry into the group which is propagated through the group. Thus we can define the *group carry*, GC_{15}, which is equal to C_{60}, by the following equation:

$$C_{60} = GC_{15} = GG_{15} \vee (GP_{15} \wedge GC_{16}) \tag{11.19}$$

where $GC_{16} = C_{64}$, the carry into the group. In a similar fashion we can develop equations for the group carries from succeeding 4-bit groups.

$$\begin{aligned} C_{56} = GC_{14} &= GG_{14} \vee (GP_{14} \wedge GC_{15}) \\ &= GG_{14} \vee (GP_{14} \wedge GC_{15}) \vee (GP_{14} \wedge GP_{15} \wedge GC_{16}) \end{aligned} \tag{11.20}$$

$$\begin{aligned} C_{52} = GC_{13} &= GG_{13} \vee (GP_{13} \wedge GC_{14}) \\ &= GG_{13} \vee (GP_{13} \wedge GC_{14}) \vee (GP_{13} \wedge GP_{14} \wedge GC_{14}) \\ &\quad \vee (GP_{13} \wedge GP_{14} \wedge GP_{15} \wedge GC_{16}) \end{aligned} \tag{11.21}$$

Except for the names of the variables, Eqs. 11.19, 11.20, and 11.21 are seen to be identical to Eqs. 11.14, 11.15, and 11.16. Thus the group carry terms can be developed by the same type of CLA circuit as used for the ordinary carries (Fig. 11.5). The interconnection of adders and CLA units for bits 48–63 is shown in Fig. 11.7. (The group carry unit is labeled GCLA for purposes of identification, but is the same circuit as the CLA units.)

Now let us consider the delay for these 16 bits, again considering the worst case. The carry is generated in PG_{63} in $2\Delta t$, propagates through CLA_{15} to develop GG_{15} in $2\Delta t$, through $GCLA_3$ to develop GC_{13} in $2\Delta t$ and through CLA_{12} to develop C_{48} in $2\Delta t$. Thus the carry propagation delay in Fig. 11.7 is $8\Delta t$ compared to $32\Delta t$ for 16 bits of a ripple-carry adder. We are now beginning to see some significant improvements in delay times, but we are not done yet.

11.6. SECTION CARRY LOOK-AHEAD

We now divide the 64-bit adder into four 16-bit sections and define *section generate*, SG, and *section propagate*, SP, terms, in a manner exactly analogous to the group terms. These equations will be seen to have the same form as

$$SG_3 = GG_{12} \vee (GP_{12} \wedge GG_{13}) \vee (GP_{12} \wedge GP_{13} \wedge GG_{14}) \vee (GP_{12} \wedge GP_{13} \wedge GP_{14} \wedge GG_{15}) \tag{11.22}$$

$$SP_3 = GP_{12} \wedge GP_{13} \wedge GP_{14} \wedge GP_{15} \tag{11.23}$$

Eqs. 11.17 and 11.18 for the group generate and propagate terms. Thus the

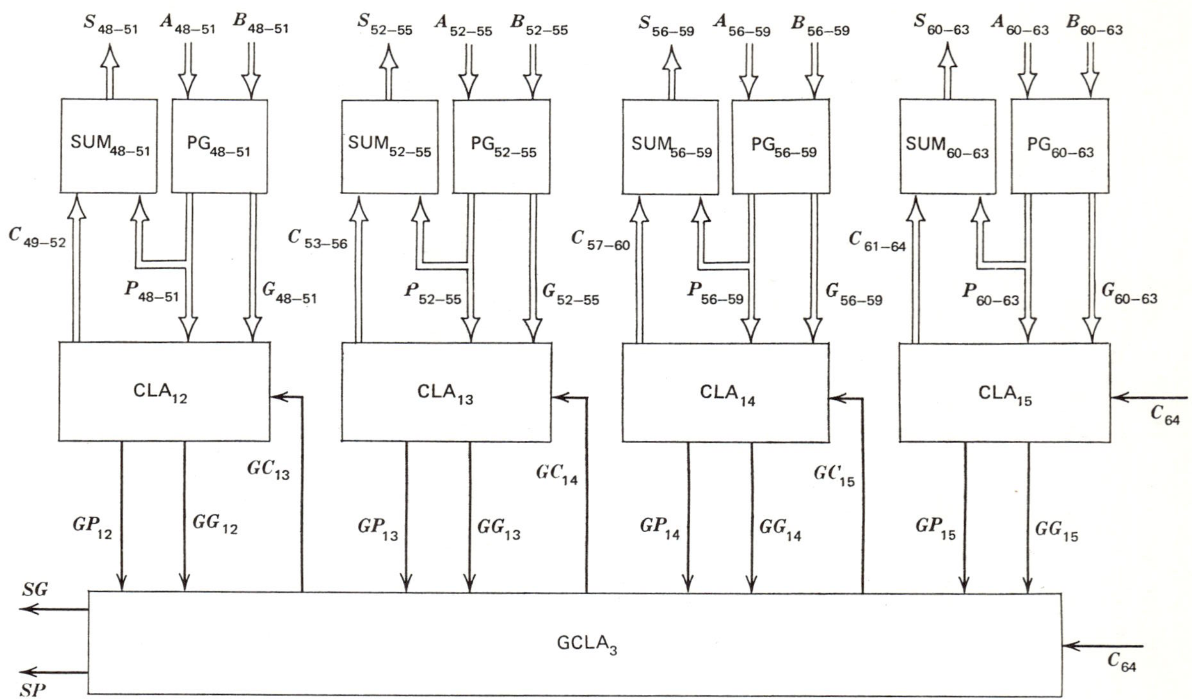

FIGURE 11.7. 16-Bit adder with group carry look-ahead.

five left-most gates of Fig. 11.5 will form SG and SP terms when the inputs are GG and GP terms. The SG and SP outputs from GCLA are shown in Fig. 11.7.

We now develop equations for *section carry-out* in the same manner as for the group carry-outs. These equations are seen to have the same form as

$$C_{48} = GC_{12} = SC_3 = SG_3 \vee (SP_3 \wedge SC_4) \tag{11.24}$$

$$\begin{aligned} C_{32} &= GC_8 = SC_2 = SG_2 \vee (SP_2 \wedge SC_3) \\ &= SG_2 \vee (SP_2 \wedge SG_3) \vee SP_2 \wedge SP_3 \wedge SC_4) \end{aligned} \tag{11.25}$$

$$\begin{aligned} C_{16} &= GC_4 = SC_1 = SG_1 \vee (SP_1 \wedge SC_2) \\ &= SG_1 \vee (SP_1 \wedge SG_2) \vee (SP_1 \wedge SP_2 \wedge SG_3) \\ &\quad \vee (SP_1 \wedge SP_2 \wedge SP_3 \wedge SC_4) \end{aligned} \tag{11.26}$$

those for the original CLA unit, so the same form of circuit can be used again, with one small change. Since there will be no further levels of look-ahead, the final output carry, C_0, must be developed. To develop this term,

$$\begin{aligned} C_0 = SG_0 &\vee (SP_0 \wedge SG_1) \vee (SP_0 \wedge SP_1 \wedge SG_2) \vee (SP_0 \wedge SP_1 \\ &\wedge SP_2 \wedge SG_3) \vee (SP_0 \wedge SP_1 \wedge SP_2 \wedge SP_3 \wedge SC_4) \end{aligned} \tag{11.27}$$

connect a SC_4 input to the gate on Fig. 11.5 which develops GP, and connect the output of this gate to the OR gate which develops GG on Fig. 11.5; this gate will now develop C_0. The complete block diagram of the 64-bit adder with three levels of carry look-ahead is shown in Fig. 11.8.

Applying the same sort of analysis as before, the reader should be able to convince himself that the worst case delay through this adder would be $14\Delta t$, compared to $128\Delta t$ for the 64-bit ripple-carry adder. Thus we have achieved about a nine-to-one improvement in speed, certainly a worthwhile accomplishment. However, we must also consider the cost of this speed improvement. An exact cost analysis would depend on the hardware chosen, but a good measure of the cost of a logic circuit is the total number of gate terminals (inputs and outputs) since this number will generally be proportional to the total number of active devices.

The full-adder of Fig. 11.4 has 22 terminals, giving a total of 1408 for 64-bits. The CLA unit of Fig. 11.5 has 56 terminals; and there are 21 CLA units in the complete adder of Fig. 11.8. Including the two extra inputs in the SCLA required for C_0, this gives a grand total of 2586 terminals for the complete adder. The cost of a ripple-carry adder will depend on the full adder configuration chosen. The simplest circuit known to the authors [4] has 27 terminals, giving a total of 1728 terminals for 64 bits. Thus, for less than a 50% increase in cost, we have achieved about a nine-to-one increase in speed, a remarkable speed/cost trade-off.

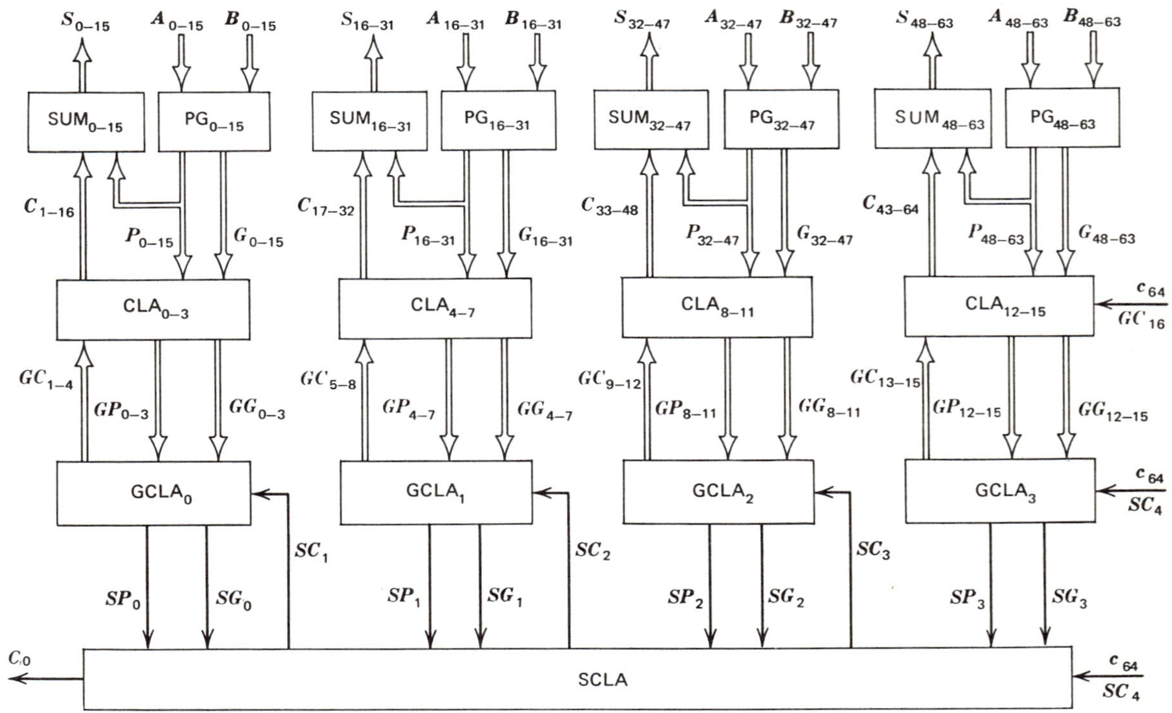

FIGURE 11.8. 64-Bit adder with three levels of carry look-ahead.

11.7. GENERATION OF ADDER LOGIC BY COMBINATIONAL LOGIC SUBROUTINE

We have now completed our discussion of the principles of the carry look-ahead adder, but we have actually generated only a sample of the equations describing it. The structure of the adder is highly repetitive in form, with the same form of equations occurring many times; so it is ideally suited to description by a combinational logic subroutine. The adder is made up of two basic types of units, the full-adders and the CLA units. The full-adders are quite simple and need only be duplicated 64 times. If we consider the equations for the CLA units, Eqs. 11.14, 11.15, and 11.16, for example, we see that they are iterative in form. If we let $\boldsymbol{C}_{64} = \boldsymbol{G}_{64}$, then each equation consists of a $\boldsymbol{G}$ term and one or more products of $\boldsymbol{G}$ and $\boldsymbol{P}$ terms. Since this same form of carry equation occurs in all the CLA units, at all levels, it is convenient to develop a subroutine to generate the carry terms. This is shown in Fig. 11.9.

The inputs to the subroutine are $\boldsymbol{P}$ and $\boldsymbol{G}$, the vectors of the carry and propagate terms developed by the full-adders; *cin*, the carry-in to the group, e.g., $\boldsymbol{C}_{64}$ for CLA_{15}; i, the index of the carry bit being developed; and j, the index of the carry-in to the group. A trace of this program for $\boldsymbol{C}_{62}$ is shown in Fig. 11.10. In this program, h is the counter on the index of the $\boldsymbol{G}$ term in each product, and m is the counter on terms in each product.

The inputs to the ADD($\boldsymbol{A}$, $\boldsymbol{B}$, $\boldsymbol{c}$) subroutine are the addend and augend, $\boldsymbol{A}$ and $\boldsymbol{B}$, and the carry-in, $\boldsymbol{c}$. The outputs are the sum, $\boldsymbol{S}$, and the output

CL SUBROUTINE CARRY ($\boldsymbol{P}$, $\boldsymbol{G}$, *cin*, i, j)

	0. $\boldsymbol{G}_j \leftarrow \boldsymbol{cin}$
	1. $\boldsymbol{sum} \leftarrow 0$
B	2. $h \leftarrow j$
	3. $\boldsymbol{prod} \leftarrow \boldsymbol{G}_h$
B	4. $m \leftarrow h$
B	5. $m \leftarrow m - 1$
B	6. $m : i, (<) \rightarrow (8)$
	7. $\boldsymbol{prod} \leftarrow \boldsymbol{prod} \wedge \boldsymbol{P}_m, \rightarrow (5)$
	8. $\boldsymbol{sum} \leftarrow \boldsymbol{sum} \vee \boldsymbol{prod}$
B	9. $h \leftarrow h - 1$
D	10. $h : i, (\geq) \rightarrow (3)$
	11. CARRY $\leftarrow \boldsymbol{sum}$
	12. RETURN

FIGURE 11.9. Combinational logic subroutine for CARRY.

i	j	h	m	G_{64}	prod	sum
62	64	64	64	C_{64}	C_{64}	0
			63		$P_{63}\wedge C_{64}$	
			62		$P_{62}\wedge P_{63}\wedge C_{64}$	
			61			$P_{62}\wedge P_{63}\wedge C_{64}$
		63	63		G_{63}	
			62		$P_{62}\wedge G_{63}$	
			61			$(P_{62}\wedge G_{63})\vee(P_{62}\wedge F_{63}\wedge C_{64})$
		62	62		G_{62}	
			61			$G_{62}\vee(P_{62}\wedge G_{63})\vee(P_{62}\wedge P_{63}\wedge C_{64})$
		61				CARRY $\leftarrow$ sum

FIGURE 11.10. Trace of CARRY(P, G, C_{64}, 62, 64).

carry, C_0. The reader will recall from the discussion of complement arithmetic that the operands may be the true or complemented form of the numbers in the input registers, the carry-in may be 0 or 1, and overflow may be signaled by the presence or absence of a carry-out, all depending on the signs of the operands and whether the operation is addition or subtraction. We will assume that all decisions with regard to these matters are made by external logic. Thus, the adder could be used with any type of number representation, signed-magnitude, two's-complement, or one's-complement, with all decisions with regard to the nature of the inputs and the interpretation of the outputs left to external logic.

The complete ADD subroutine is shown in Fig. 11.11. The first two statements specify the number of bits in the adder and the number of bits per CLA group. Thus the program can be used for different size adders just by changing these two statements. Statements 2 and 3 give the number of groups and the number of sections. Statements 4–8 define the dimensions for the various vector variables. Step 9 establishes the input carry as the carry-in to the SCLA unit. Steps 10–12 initialize the counters on sections, groups, and bits, respectively. In each case, i signifies the number of the unit being processed and j the number of the input to that group or section. Steps 13 and 15 set up the linkage between the section, group, and bit carry numbers, e.g., $C_{16} = GC_4 = SC_1$, etc. Steps 14, 16, and 17 decrement the section, group, and bit counters.

The loop from step 17 to step 22 develops the G, P, S, and C terms. The decision at step 21 breaks out of the loop when a group of k bits has been completed. Steps 23 and 24 develop the group generate and propagate terms. Step 25 sets j equal to i since the carry now being generated is the

SUBROUTINE ADD(A, B, c)

B 0. $n \leftarrow 64$
B 1. $k \leftarrow 4$
B 2. $ng \leftarrow n \div k$
B 3. $ns \leftarrow ng \div k$
4. $\boldsymbol{G} \leftarrow \boldsymbol{P} \leftarrow \boldsymbol{S} \leftarrow n_\rho 0$
5. $\boldsymbol{C} \leftarrow (n+1)_\rho 0$
6. $\boldsymbol{GG} \leftarrow \boldsymbol{GP} \leftarrow \boldsymbol{GC} \leftarrow (ng)_\rho 0$
7. $\boldsymbol{SG} \leftarrow \boldsymbol{SP} \leftarrow (ns)_\rho 0$
8. $\boldsymbol{SC} \leftarrow (ns+1)_\rho 0$
9. $\boldsymbol{SC}_n \leftarrow c$
B 10. $is \leftarrow js \leftarrow ns$
B 11. $ig \leftarrow jg \leftarrow ng$
B 12. $i \leftarrow j \leftarrow n$
13. $\boldsymbol{GC}_{jg} \leftarrow \boldsymbol{SC}_{is}$
B 14. $is \leftarrow is-1$
15. $\boldsymbol{C}_j \leftarrow \boldsymbol{GC}_{ig}$
B 16. $ig \leftarrow ig-1$
B 17. $i \leftarrow i-1$
18. $\boldsymbol{G}_i \leftarrow \boldsymbol{A}_i \wedge \boldsymbol{B}_i$
19. $\boldsymbol{P}_i \leftarrow \overline{\boldsymbol{G}_i \vee (\bar{\boldsymbol{A}}_i \wedge \bar{\boldsymbol{B}}_i)}$
20. $\boldsymbol{S}_i \leftarrow (\boldsymbol{P}_i \wedge \bar{\boldsymbol{C}}_{i+1}) \vee (\bar{\boldsymbol{P}}_i \wedge \boldsymbol{C}_{i+1})$
B 21. $i:(j-k), (=) \rightarrow (23)$
22. $\boldsymbol{C}_i \leftarrow$ CARRY($\boldsymbol{P},\boldsymbol{G},\boldsymbol{C}_j,i,j$), $\rightarrow (17)$
23. $\boldsymbol{GG}_{ig} \leftarrow$ CARRY($\boldsymbol{P},\boldsymbol{G},\boldsymbol{G}_{j-1},i,j-1$)
24. $\boldsymbol{GP}_{ig} \leftarrow \wedge/(\alpha^{j-1} \wedge \omega^{n-1})/\boldsymbol{P}$
B 25. $j \leftarrow i$
B 26. $ig:(jg-k), (=) \rightarrow (28)$
27. $\boldsymbol{GC}_{ig} \leftarrow$ CARRY($\boldsymbol{GP},\boldsymbol{GG},\boldsymbol{GC}_{jg},ig,jg$), $\rightarrow (15)$
28. $\boldsymbol{SG}_{is} \leftarrow$ CARRY($\boldsymbol{GP},\boldsymbol{GG},\boldsymbol{GG}_{jg-1},ig,jg-1$)
29. $\boldsymbol{SP}_{is} \leftarrow \wedge/(\alpha^{jg-1} \wedge \omega^{ng-ig})/\boldsymbol{GP}$
B 30. $jg \leftarrow ig$
31. $\boldsymbol{SC}_{is} \leftarrow$ CARRY($\boldsymbol{SP},\boldsymbol{SG},\boldsymbol{SG}_{js},is,js$)
B 32. $is:0, (>) \rightarrow (13)$
33. ADD $\leftarrow \boldsymbol{SC}_0,\boldsymbol{S}$
34. HALT

FIGURE 11.11. Subroutine ADD.

carry-in to the next group. Step 26 checks to see if the section is complete. If not, step 27 develops the group carry, and the program returns to step 15 to process the next group. When a section is complete, the branch at step 26 leads to steps 28–31 which develop the section terms. Step 32 checks to see if the adder is complete; if not, the program returns to step 13 to process the next section.

11.8. THE CARRY-COMPLETION ADDER

There is another type of adder which applies a completely different approach, and therefore deserves some comment. We have noted that the worst case, the carry propagating from one end of the adder to the other, will occur only with certain combinations of operands. In most cases there will be stages in either the *generate* or *no propagate* condition every few bits, so that any given carry is likely to propagate through only a few stages. It has been shown [5] that the average maximum carry length for a 64-bit adder is about seven bits. Thus, the *average* time for addition in a ripple-carry adder would be about $14\Delta t$, the same as for the full CLA adder designed in previous sections.

In the carry-completion adder, circuitry is added to detect when all carries have fully propagated and issue a completion signal. Upon receipt of the completion signal, the computer can then go on to the next step, without waiting to allow time for the rare worst case. A carry-completion adder of typical design [3] has a cost about half-way between that of the ripple-carry and the CLA adders. This type of adder has been used in a few machines, but has not met with much acceptance. The main problem is that it is difficult to make effective use of the time "saved" by the carry-completion adder. If the add time is fixed, we can schedule other things to be going on at the same time. But if the add times may vary over a range of 64-to-1, it becomes very difficult to synchronize other operations with the adder.

11.9. SUMMARY

The carry look-ahead adder has been considered in detail for two reasons: first, it is probably the most popular form of fast adder; second, it is a classic example of the ingenious application of logic design to the problem of obtaining increased speed at minimum cost.

The validity of the first reason may change with time due to developments in device technology. However, it is interesting to note that the carry look-ahead principle, which was first applied to vacuum-tube circuits, has also been applied to integrated circuits, resulting in CLA adders nearly a thousand times faster than the original vacuum-tube versions. A design principle which has remained viable while component speeds have increased by several orders of magnitude has certainly demonstrated some intrinsic validity.

On the other hand, as basic logic speeds continue to increase, the ordinary ripple-carry adder may become so fast compared to other system components, such as memory, that the CLA adder will be less attractive economically. But whatever the future may bring for the CLA adder, the logic design principles it illustrates will remain important. The careful analysis of the arithmetic process and the resultant factoring of the equations into iterative forms are basic ideas which will remain applicable to any technology.

REFERENCES

1. Weinberger, A., and Smith, J. L., "The Logical Design of a One-Microsecond Adder Using One-Megacycle Circuitry," *IRE Trans. Elec. Computers*, Vol. EC-5, No. 2 (June 1956), pp. 65–73.
2. MacSorley, O. L., "High-Speed Arithmetic in Binary Computers," *Proc. IRE*, Vol. 49, No. 1 (Jan. 1961), pp. 67–91.
3. Flores, I., *The Logic of Computer Arithmetic*, Prentice-Hall, Englewood Cliffs, N.J., 1963, Chaps. 4, 5, 6.
4. Maley, G. A., and Earle, J., *The Logic Design of Transistor Digital Computers*, Prentice-Hall, Englewood Cliffs, N.J., 1963, p. 163.
5. Hendrickson, H. C., "Fast High-Accuracy Binary Parallel Addition," *IRE Trans. Elec. Computers*, Vol. EC-9, No. 4 (Dec. 1960), pp. 469–79.

12

Multiplication and Division

12.1. SIGNED MULTIPLICATION

In Chapter 6 the multiplication of negative numbers in complement form was accomplished by first determining the sign of the product, converting the operands to magnitude form, and then carrying out the multiplication. For numbers stored in one's-complement form, this conversion can be accomplished by merely reading the operand bits from the complement side of each flip-flop in the respective register. Thus, for one's-complement machines, sign and magnitude provides a satisfactory approach to multiplication.

In the two's-complement system, the process of complementing requires extra addition cycles, which may be considered to consume time unnecessarily. Recall that in Chapter 6 multiplication was initiated with the multiplicand in the ***MD*** register and the multiplier in the ***AC*** register. As the multiplication progressed, the multiplier was first transferred to ***MQ*** and the product was gradually formed in ***AC*** and shifted, least-significant bit first, into the ***MQ*** register. At the conclusion of this operation, the product is found spanning ***AC*** and ***MQ***.

We now propose to carry out multiplication in the same manner without first converting the operands to magnitude form. Thus ***MD*** and ***MQ*** may contain two's-complement numbers. As we shall see, it will be necessary to

a	b	$\perp MQ$	$\perp MD$	Desired Result $\perp(AC, MQ)$
+	+	a	b	ab
+	−	a	$2^n - \|b\|$	$2^{2n} - a \cdot \|b\|$
−	+	$2^n - \|a\|$	b	$2^{2n} - \|a\| \cdot b$
−	−	$2^n - \|a\|$	$2^n - \|b\|$	$\|a\| \cdot \|b\|$

FIGURE 12.1

modify the hardware program slightly. Our goal in doing so will be to accomplish any corrections in the same time intervals as the basic shift and add operations.

We see in Fig. 12.1 a tabulation of the possible contents of ***MD*** and ***MQ***. We let a and b represent the respective numerical values, which may be either positive or negative. If both a and b are positive, then two's-complement and signed-magnitude multiplication are identical. As we shall see, the program to be specified for two's-complement multiplication will reduce to the program of Chapter 6 for this case.

Now consider the second case; the multiplier is still positive but the multiplicand is negative, so the product should be negative. Recall that the basic multiplication process consists of repeated cycles of adding the multiplicand to partial products in AC, followed by right shifts of the new partial product. If we add a negative multiplicand in the proper complement form to negative partial products in the proper complement form, the result will be a negative product in the proper complement form.

We already know that complement addition works, so the only special precaution we must observe is to see that the shifting process produces a proper complement. Assume that the number y is loaded into an n-bit ***AC*** register, i.e.,

$$\perp AC = y$$

If we shift this number one place right, the effect is to reduce the value by 2^{-1}, i.e.,

$$\perp (\updownarrow AC) = 2^{-1} \times y$$

The correct complement form for the negative value of the shifted quantity would be a binary vector such that

$$\perp AC = 2^n - 2^{-1}y$$

Now suppose that the complement of y, $2^n - y$, has been stored in AC and is shifted one place right. The result is

$$\perp (\updownarrow AC) = 2^{-1}(2^n - y) = 2^{n-1} - 2^{-1}y$$

which is not the correct complement of the shifted number. To correct it we must add 2^{n-1}, which gives

$$2^{n-1} - 2^{-1}y + 2^{n-1} = 2^n - 2^{-1}y$$

that is, a 1 is inserted in the vacated most-significant-digit position.

In summary, for both cases where the multiplier is positive, we add the multiplicand and shift, the only difference being that a 0 is inserted in the vacated position for positive multiplicand and a 1 for negative multiplicand. This is equivalent to saying that the inserted bit is equal to the multiplicand sign; so the desired shifting can be accomplished by the statement

$$\boldsymbol{AC,MQ} \leftarrow \boldsymbol{MD}_0,(\boldsymbol{\omega}^{2n-1}/\overset{\circ}{\downarrow}(\boldsymbol{AC,MQ}))$$

Next we consider the situation where the multiplier is negative. When this occurs, both the multiplier and multiplicand are complemented, thus giving the proper sign for the product. The complementation can be accomplished without lengthening the multiplication process. Recall that in the routine of Chapter 6 the multiplier is inspected one bit at a time to determine whether the multiplicand is to be added to the current partial product. We also recall that a bit-by-bit algorithm for taking the two's-complement of a number was discussed in Chapter 2. The bits of the number are examined and corrected sequentially from right to left. Until a 1 is encountered, 0's are left unchanged. The first 1 from the right is also left unchanged, but all remaining bits are complemented. We will use this complementing process for each bit of the multiplier as that bit is used to control addition of the multiplicand to the partial product.

With a negative multiplier, the sign of the product will be the opposite of the sign of the multiplicand. Thus, if the multiplicand is positive, it must be complemented to the negative form before adding in order to produce a negative product, and vice-versa for a negative multiplicand. Noting that an alternate procedure for taking the two's-complement is to take the logical complement (one's-complement) and add 1 in the least-significant-digit position, we see that the multiplicand can be complemented as it is added to the partial product. We need only gate the complement of ***MD*** to the adder and insert a 1 on the input-carry line. Finally, the proper shifting algorithm must be followed, inserting 0 when a positive product is to be developed and 1 when the product is to be negative.

On the basis of the above discussion, we can now set up a flow chart for the complete signed-multiplication procedure, as shown in Fig. 12.2. As in Chapter 6, we will assume 18-bit registers and will assume that we start with the multiplier in ***AC*** and the multiplicand in ***MD***.

Steps 1 and 2 check for zero operands, in which case steps 18 and 19 set

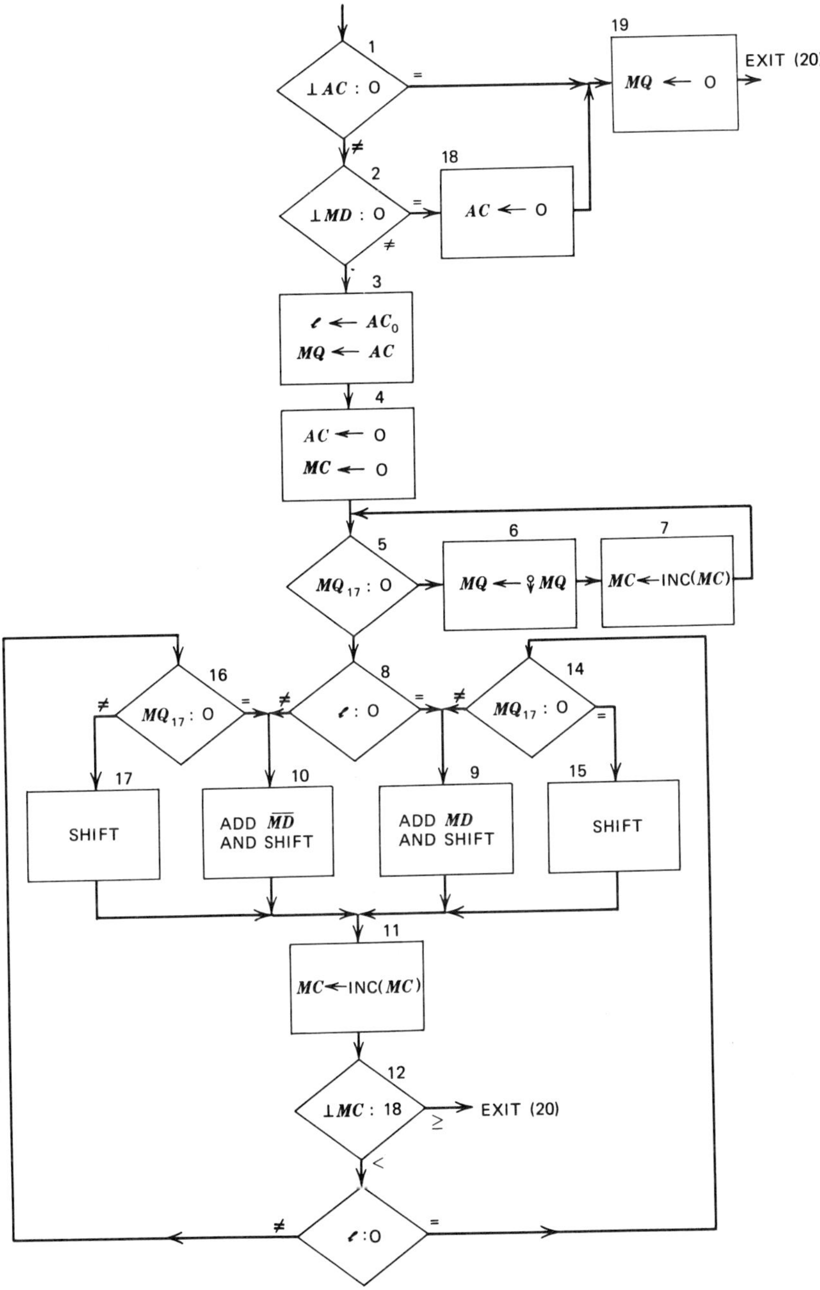

FIGURE 12.2. Flow chart of signed multiplication.

the product to zero and exit:

1. $\perp AC$:0, $(=,\neq) \rightarrow (19,2)$
2. $\perp MD$:0, $(=,\neq) \rightarrow (18,3)$

Step 3 stores the multiplier sign in the link and transfers the multiplier to ***MQ***. The storage of the multiplier sign is required because the shifting will move the sign into a different position of ***MQ*** after every cycle. Step 4 clears ***AC*** and the multiplication counter, ***MC***:

3. $\ell \leftarrow AC_0$; $MQ \leftarrow AC$
4. $AC \leftarrow \overline{\epsilon(18)}$; $MC \leftarrow \overline{\epsilon(5)}$

Step 5 commences the actual multiplication by checking the least-significant digit of the multiplier. As long as the multiplier bits remain zero, the product is to remain zero, regardless of the ultimate sign of the product. Thus we remain in the steps 5, 6, 7 loop, shifting only the multiplier, until the first 1 of the multiplier is encountered:

5. MQ_{17}:0, $(=,\neq) \rightarrow (6,8)$
6. $MQ \leftarrow \overset{\circ}{\downarrow} MQ$
7. $MC \leftarrow \mathrm{INC}(MC), \rightarrow (5)$

Step 8 checks the sign of the multiplier to determine whether the true or complemented contents of ***MD*** should be added. For a positive multiplier, step 9 adds the true contents of ***MD*** to ***AC*** and shifts right, inserting MD_0 in the vacated position. For a negative multiplier, step 10 adds the complement of the contents of ***MD*** and shifts right, inserting $\overline{MD}_0$ in the vacated position:

8. ℓ:0, $(=,\neq) \rightarrow (9,10)$
9. $AC,MQ \leftarrow MD_0, (\omega^{35}/\overset{\circ}{\downarrow}(\mathrm{ADD}(AC,MD,0),MQ)), \rightarrow (11)$
10. $AC,MQ \leftarrow \overline{MD}_0,(\omega^{35}/\overset{\circ}{\downarrow}(\mathrm{ADD}(AC,\overline{MD},1),MQ))$

Whichever addition was made, step 11 increments the multiplication counter and step 12 checks to see if the multiplication is complete. If not, step 13 checks the multiplier sign, branching to step 14 for positive multiplier, to step 16 for negative multiplier. Step 8, which also checks the multiplier sign, is encountered only on the first 1 in the multiplier, which must be treated differently from succeeding 1's for negative multipliers.

11. $MC \leftarrow \mathrm{INC}(MC)$
12. $\perp MC$:18, $(<,\geq) \rightarrow (13,20)$
13. ℓ:0, $(=,\neq) \rightarrow (14,16)$

For positive multipliers, step 14 checks the current least-significant bit of the multiplier, branching to step 15 for a shift if it is 0 and to step 9 for add-and-shift if it is 1. Step 16 makes a similar check for negative multipliers, branching to step 17 for a shift for a 1-bit or to step 10 for add-and-shift for a 0-bit.

14. MQ_{17}:0, $(=,\neq) \rightarrow (15,9)$
15. $AC,MQ \leftarrow MD_0$, $(\omega^{35}/\updownarrow(AC,MQ))$, $\rightarrow (11)$
16. MQ_{17}:0, $(=,\neq) \rightarrow (10,17)$
17. $AC,MQ \leftarrow MD_0$, $(\omega^{35}/\updownarrow(AC,MQ))$, $\rightarrow (11)$
18. $AC \leftarrow \overline{\epsilon(18)}$
19. $MQ \leftarrow \overline{\epsilon(18)}$
20. EXIT

After each shift or add-and-shift, control returns to step 11 to increment *MC* and check for completion. Steps 18 and 19 set the product to zero for zero operands as determined in steps 1 and 2.

12.2. MULTIPLICATION SPEED-UP—CARRY-SAVE

The time-saving offered by the technique discussed in the last section is relatively small. At best, it eliminates two additions required for complementing; and since there may be n additions required for an n-bit multiplier, this is a minor saving. It is often included since it requires little extra hardware. In order to make any significant reductions in multiplication time, we must reduce either the number of additions or the addition time. If multiplication is to be provided, we will almost certainly use a fast adder, such as the CLA adder discussed in the last chapter; but the necessity for n complete additions will still make multiplication relatively slow. Many techniques for multiplication speed-up have been proposed, most of which are discussed in Flores [1]. We shall consider only a few of the more significant and representative techniques.

Certainly the best method of speed-up, in terms of cost/performance ratio, is the *carry-save* technique. This technique provides very significant increases in speed with relatively little extra hardware, and there are few multipliers of any size which do not include this feature in some form. The basic notion of carry-save is simple. The addition process may be visualized as developing a set of sum and carry bits, shifting of the carry bits right, and updating the sum and carry bits. The process continues until the carry has been formed and shifted $n - 1$ times. This is actually a synchronous interpretation of the usual carry propagation process. Now suppose a series of numbers is to be added together, one at a time. Since addition is associative, the process is not changed if the next argument is added at the same time as the shifted carry. The process continues, with a new carry word formed and

	0000 1011	*AC, MQ*	
	0000	*CS*	
	1111	*MD* · 1	Step 1
1st Partial sum	1111 1011	*AC, MQ*	
	0000	*CS*	
Shift	01111 101	*AC, MQ*	
	1111	*MD* · 1	Step 2
2nd Partial sum	10001 101	*AC, MQ*	
	0111	*CS*	
Shift	010001 10	*AC, MQ*	
	0000	*MD* · 0	Step 3
3rd Partial sum	001101 10	*AC, MQ*	
	0100	*CS*	
Shift	0001101 1	*AC, MQ*	
	1111	*MD* · 1	Step 4
4th Partial shift	1010101 1	*AC, MQ*	
	0101	*CS*	
Shift	01010101	*AC, MQ*	Step 5
Propagate add	10100101	*AC, MQ*	

$1011 \times 1111 = 10100101$

FIGURE 12.3. Example of carry-save multiplication.

shifted with each addition, until the list of numbers to be added is exhausted. From that point the carry is allowed to propagate normally through $n - 1$ stages to complete the arithmetic.

Multiplication is an example of the process described above with the ith argument consisting of the multiplicand shifted $i - 1$ bits to the left if the ith bit of the multiplier is 1. Otherwise the ith entry is zero. The process is illustrated for a simple example in Fig. 12.3. The process consists of four steps of additions to the partial product, followed by a fifth step, representing completion of the carry propagation. In this figure we have shown the computer form of the process, with the relative left shift of the carry-save word, ***CS***, and the multiplicand actually provided by a right shift of the partial product. The ***CS*** word is shown boxed for emphasis, and the space in the ***AC,MQ*** word indicates the boundary between partial product and the shifted remainder of the multiplier.

In analyzing the example, note that the contents of the ***AC,MQ*** registers, in each step prior to the last, do not represent the binary sum of the three inputs, but rather represent the bit-by-bit exclusive-OR'ing of the three input vectors. For example, at step 2,

$$(1,0,0,0,1) = (1,1,1,1,0) \oplus (0,0,0,0,0) \oplus (0,1,1,1,1)$$

and the carry bits, 0111, are shifted and added in step 3. The reader should follow the process step-by-step; and if necessary, check by carrying out the multiplication in the usual manner.

In most computers the same adder is used for multiplication as for all other operations involving addition, so provision must be made to modify this adder when carry-save is to be implemented. If we assume an 18-bit ripple-carry adder, the configuration for carry-save would be as shown in Fig. 12.4. The output-carry from each stage, instead of going directly to the input-carry line of the next stage, is stored in a position of the ***CS*** register. On the next cycle, this stored carry will become the input-carry to the same stage. It might seem that each stage of the ***CS*** register should provide the input-carry to the next stage to the left, until we recall that the partial sum is shifted to the right before the next cycle, providing the logical equivalent of a left shift of the carries. A two-level switching network on each carry-input can be added so that the same adder can function as given in Fig. 11.1 or Fig. 12.4, depending on the value of a single control signal.

The basic control program for carry-save multiplication can now be written. Note that steps 2 and 3, representing formation of the carries and partial sums, occur simultaneously and are written on separate lines solely

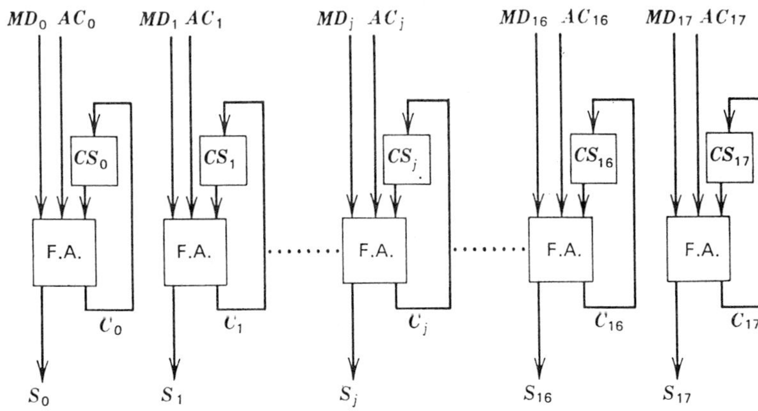

FIGURE 12.4. Ripple-carry adder converted to carry-save adder.

for clarity. Also note that circuitry of the adder would require gating to

1. $MC \leftarrow \overline{\epsilon(5)}$; $CS \leftarrow \overline{\epsilon(18)}$
2. $AC \leftarrow AC \oplus CS \oplus (MD \wedge MQ_{17})$,   NO DELAY
3. $CS \leftarrow (CS \wedge AC) \vee (CS \wedge (MD \wedge MQ_{17})) \vee (AC \wedge (MD \wedge MQ_{17}))$
4. $AC,MQ \leftarrow \overset{\circ}{\downarrow}(AC,MQ)$
5. $MC \leftarrow \mathrm{INC}(MC)$
6. $\perp MC$:18, $(<,\geq) \rightarrow (2,7)$
7. $AC \leftarrow \mathrm{ADD}(AC,CS)$

convert from a conventional adder to a carry-save adder, and the complete program would probably include the setting and clearing of some sort of indicator to control this gating.

The above program considers the multiplication of magnitudes only. We leave it as an exercise for the reader to modify the signed-multiplication routine to incorporate carry-save. Carry-save can be used with virtually any type of adder or other type of speed-up method.

12.3. MULTIPLE-BIT SPEED-UP TECHNIQUES

So far we have assumed that only one multiplier bit is to be handled each cycle. By carrying out multiplication for several bits at a time, the number of cycles can be reduced. This will reduce the overall multiply time if extra hardware is provided to process multiple bits in the same time as single bits. First, we must provide for multiple shifts in the same time as single shifts; and second, we must provide means of adding multiples of the multiplicand in a single addition cycle.

The simplest multiple-bit technique is *shifting over zeros*. We inspect two or more of the multiplier bits. If they are all zero, we make a multiple shift over the corresponding number of bits. The speed advantage of this technique depends on the statistical likelihood that strings of zeros of various lengths may occur. The technique is fairly simple and frequently used.

A closely-related technique is *shifting over ones*. Assume we have three ones in a row in the multiplier. Essentially, this requires adding seven times the multiplicand, which can be accomplished by *subtracting* the multiplicand, shifting three places—which multiplies by eight—and then adding the multiplicand. Since this method requires two addition cycles, there must be at least three consecutive ones before it is worth doing; it is therefore less popular than shifting over zeros.

Next let us consider the handling of arbitrary pairs of multiplier bits. If at a given step the least-significant-multiplier bits are 00, a 2-bit shift is carried out. If the bits are 01, the multiplicand is added and then a 2-bit shift is made. If the bits are 10, there are two possible techniques. The first is to revert to the single-bit method, i.e., make a single shift to take care of the 0 and then pair the 1 with the next bit in the multiplier for the next cycle. Alternatively, we can shift the multiplicand one position to the left as it enters the adder—thus multiplying it by two—and then make a 2-bit shift of the sum. If the bits are 11, there are also two possibilities. We can add, shift once, and pair the second 1 with the next multiplier bit. Or we can provide a special register, ***TR***, in which we store three times the multiplicand at the start of the multiplication cycle. Then when 11 occurs, we add ***TR*** to the partial product and shift twice. Note that the use of ***TR*** and the use of multiplicand shifting will require the addition of an extra bit-position to ***AC*** and the adder.

A control sequence for bit-pair multiplication, using ***TR*** and multiplicand shifting, is shown below. Note in step 4 that the shift of the multiplicand is

1. $\boldsymbol{AC} \leftarrow \boldsymbol{MD}, 0$
2. $\boldsymbol{TR} \leftarrow \mathrm{ADD}(\boldsymbol{AC},(\mathbf{0},\boldsymbol{MD}))$
3. $\boldsymbol{MC} \leftarrow \overline{\epsilon(5)};\ \ell,\boldsymbol{AC} \leftarrow \overline{\epsilon(20)}$
4. $\ell,\boldsymbol{AC},\boldsymbol{MQ} \leftarrow ((\overline{\boldsymbol{MQ}_{16}} \wedge \overline{\boldsymbol{MQ}_{17}}) \wedge (2 \overset{\circ}{\downarrow} (\ell,\boldsymbol{AC},\boldsymbol{MQ})))$
   $\vee((\overline{\boldsymbol{MQ}_{16}} \wedge \boldsymbol{MQ}_{17}) \wedge (2 \overset{\circ}{\downarrow} (\mathrm{ADD}(\boldsymbol{AC},(\mathbf{0},\boldsymbol{MD})))))$
   $\vee((\boldsymbol{MQ}_{16} \wedge \overline{\boldsymbol{MQ}_{17}}) \wedge (2 \overset{\circ}{\downarrow} (\mathrm{ADD}(\boldsymbol{AC},(\boldsymbol{MD},\mathbf{0})))))$
   $\vee((\boldsymbol{MQ}_{16} \wedge \boldsymbol{MQ}_{17}) \wedge (2 \overset{\circ}{\downarrow} (\mathrm{ADD}(\boldsymbol{AC},\boldsymbol{TR}))))$
5. $\boldsymbol{MC} \leftarrow \mathrm{INC}(\boldsymbol{MC})$
6. $\perp \boldsymbol{MC}: 19,\ (<,\geq) \rightarrow (4,7)$
7. $\ell,\boldsymbol{AC},\boldsymbol{MQ} \leftarrow 2 \overset{\circ}{\downarrow} (\ell,\boldsymbol{AC},\boldsymbol{MQ})$

not a register shift (indicated by $\overset{\circ}{\downarrow}$ or $\underset{\circ}{\uparrow}$), but is a "shift during transfer," provided by appropriate gating in the transfer path from ***MD*** to the adder. It is indicated by the use of the catenated vector, (**0**,***MD***) or (***MD***,**0**), as arguments for the ADD function.

An alternate scheme for handling bit-pairs, known as *ternary* multiplication, is discussed by Flores [1].

Groups of three multiplier bits can be handled by techniques quite similar to those discussed above. In the table of Fig. 12.5 are listed the actions taken for various bit combinations. We see that this method requires the capability for both single and double shifts of ***MD***, and single shifts of ***TR***. For bit-triplets 101 and 111, we revert to bit-pair methods, letting the third bit form part of the next triplet. Alternatively, we could provide special registers for storing $5 \times (\perp \boldsymbol{MD})$ and $7 \times (\perp \boldsymbol{MD})$.

One might expect to achieve further improvement by handling more than three bits at a time. However, extending the above approach directly would imply the use of a large number of registers to store the products of the

Multiplier Bits	Action
0 0 0	Triple shift
0 0 1	Add ***MD***, triple shift
0 1 0	Add 2 × ***MD***, triple shift
0 1 1	Add ***TR***, triple shift
1 0 0	Add 4 × ***MD***, triple shift
1 0 1	Add ***MD***, double shift
1 1 0	Add 2 × ***TR***, triple shift
1 1 1	Add ***TR***, double shift

FIGURE 12.5. Bit-triplet multiplication.

multiplicand and various prime numbers. To compute the contents of these registers serially prior to the multiplication would tend to negate any speed advantage which might be obtained. At some point one would expect a decrease in speed with the consideration of additional bits.

Alternatively, the multibit partial products could be expressed as a combinational logic subroutine. These products could then be added to the contents of ***AC,MQ***, employing carry-save. Each addition of an r-bit partial product would be followed by a shift of r-bits. This approach will be considered in Section 12.5. Until recently, such lavish use of combinational logic would have been prohibitively expensive. With the continuing decrease in cost of large-scale integrated circuits, such approaches are becoming practical. The limiting case is a completely combinational-logic multiplier.

12.4. SPEED ANALYSIS

Before proceeding further it will be instructive to derive some expressions which will allow us to compare the speed of various multiplier configurations. In order to carry out this analysis, it is necessary to make some assumptions regarding the speed of various operations relative to the basic clock rate of the computer. Let σ represent the propagation delay through two levels of logic. The time required to change the contents of a register will then be on the order to 2σ to 4σ, depending on the logic family used. To allow time for logical operations during transfer and some tolerance for stray delays, the clock period might typically be set to $\tau_c = 8\sigma$. As we saw in the last chapter, the carry propagation time for a very fast adder might be $\tau_p = 7\sigma$. On this basis we will assume that a shift operation requires one clock period, an add-and-shift operation, two clock periods.

First let us consider bit-by-bit multiplication without carry-save. If the multiplier bit is 0, we shift in one clock period; if it is 1, we add and shift in two clock periods. The probabilities of a multiplier bit being 1 or 0 are both 0.5. Therefore the average time for accomplishing multiplication is given by Eq. 12.1:

$$T_1 = 0.5N\tau_c + 0.5N(2\tau_c) = 1.5N\tau_c = 12N\sigma \tag{12.1}$$

where N is the word length. Becoming slightly more general, suppose a slower adder were employed, requiring k clock periods to complete an addition. In this case, Eq. 12.1 takes the form of Eq. 12.2:

$$T_1 = 0.5N\tau_c + 0.5N(k\tau_c) = \frac{N\tau_c}{2} \times (1 + k) \tag{12.2}$$

If carry-save is employed, the partial-add requires a delay of only σ; so each cycle except the last requires only one clock period for a partial-add and shift. Thus the time for an N-bit multiplication is given by Eq. 12.3:

$$T_2 = (N - 1)\tau_c + k\tau_c = (N - 1 + k)\tau_c \tag{12.3}$$

For $k = 2$, we have $T_2 = (N + 1)\tau_c$, which approaches $\frac{2}{3}T_1$ for large N. For a slower adder ($k > 2$), the improvement achieved by carry-save is more noticeable.

Consider next the bit-pair process described in the previous section. Let us assume $k = 2$ and that carry-save is not employed. Thus $N/2$ cycles will be required. Since an addition is required in all but the case where both multiplier bits are zero, three-quarters of the cycles will require two clock periods while one-quarter will require one period. Therefore the average bit-pair multiplication time is given by Eq. 12.4. The $2\tau_c$ on the right accounts for the

$$T_3 = \frac{N}{2}[0.75(2\tau_c) + 0.25\tau_c] + 2\tau_c = (0.875N + 2)\tau_c \tag{12.4}$$

addition time necessary to compute the contents of the ***TR*** register. If bit-pairs and carry-save are used, only one clock period is required for all but the last of the $N/2$ shift cycles. For this case we express the multiplication time in Eq. 12.5.

$$\begin{aligned} T_4 &= \left(\frac{N}{2} - 1\right)\tau_c + 2\tau_c + 2\tau_c \\ &= \left(\frac{N}{2} + 3\right)\tau_c \end{aligned} \tag{12.5}$$

For bit-triplets with carry-save, the average multiplication time is given by Eq. 12.6,

$$T_5 = \left(\frac{N}{2.75} + 3\right)\tau_c \tag{12.6}$$

Multiplication Scheme	Multiplication Time	Time for $N = 64$
Bit-by-bit	$1.5N\tau_c$	$96\tau_c$
Bit-by-bit with carry-save	$(N + 1)\tau_c$	$65\tau_c$
Bit-pairs	$(0.875N \times 2)\tau_c$	$58\tau_c$
Bit-pairs with carry-save	$\left(\frac{N}{2} + 3\right)\tau_c$	$35\tau_c$
Bit-triplets with carry-save	$\left(\frac{N}{2.75} + 3\right)\tau_c$	$26\tau_c$

FIGURE 12.6. Multiplication times for 2 clock periods per addition ($2\tau_c$).

The derivation of this expression will be left as an exercise. The various expressions for multiplication times are summarized in the table in Fig. 12.6.

12.5. LARGE, FAST PARALLEL MULTIPLIERS

For a large, fast machine with a heavy investment in memory and peripheral equipment, an additional investment in logic circuitry to speed up arithmetic and increase the machine's throughput is usually considered money well spent. The time for multiplication can be decreased from the level discussed in the previous sections by decreasing the number of intermediate storage times required. This must be accomplished while holding the propagation time preceding each storage time to a minimum.

Consider the "paper-and-pencil" multiplication of two 4-bit binary numbers, shown below as a specific example and in general terms. The P terms represent the bit-by-bit partial products, i.e., $P_{33} = X_3 \wedge Y_3$, $P_{23} = X_2 \wedge Y_3$, $P_{32} = X_3 \wedge Y_2$, etc. The multiplication process can be divided into two parts, the development of the array of partial products and the summation of these partial products.

```
       1011                         X0  X1  X2  X3
       1101                         Y0  Y1  Y2  Y3
       ----                        ----------------
       1011                        P03 P13 P23 P33
      0000                     P02 P12 P22 P32
     1011                  P01 P11 P21 P31
    1011               P00 P10 P20 P30
   --------           ---------------------------------
   10001111           Z0  Z1  Z2  Z3  Z4  Z5  Z6  Z7
```

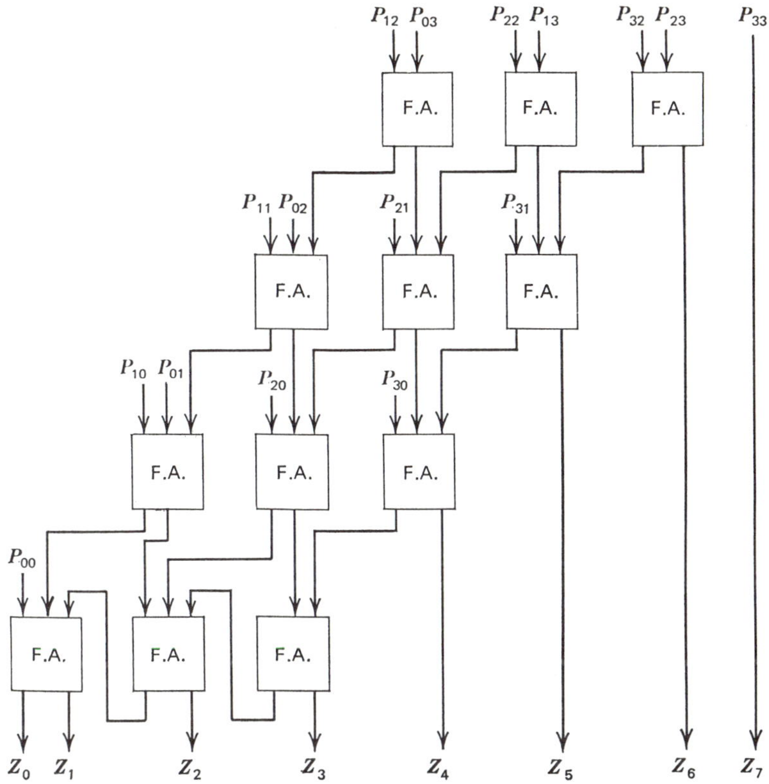

FIGURE 12.7. Four-bit, four-operand combinational carry-save adder.

The array of partial products can be developed in the time of a single gate delay, $\sigma/2$, by an array of N^2 AND gates for the multiplication of two N-bit numbers. With all N^2 partial product terms available simultaneously, the addition of these terms can then be carried out in a single combinational logic adder, with no intermediate storage. The speed of the addition is limited primarily by adder complexity considered to be economically feasible.

The most straightforward multiple-operand adder is the combinational carry-save adder, shown in Fig. 12.7. This circuit consists of an array of full-adders. In the top row of adders, the first two rows of partial products are partially added. The sums and carries from this addition are combined with the third row of partial products in the second row of adders. These sums and carries are in turn combined with the last row of partial products in the third row of adders. The last row of adders ripple the carries through to complete the addition. Note that the worst case for carry propagation would be through a path of six adders, for a delay of 6σ. The complete multiplication, including formation of the partial product in an array of 16 AND gates, summation of the partial products, and shifting or storage of the product, can thus be completed in $2\tau_c$. This compares with a time of $5\tau_c$ for the sequential carry-save multiplier, for four bits.

This basic technique can be extended to any number of bits, with an additional delay of 2σ for each additional bit. The general relationship is

$$\tau_p = 2(N - 1)\sigma$$

Thus, assuming $\tau_c = 8\sigma$, as before, the time for a 64-bit multiplication would be $16\tau_c$, compared with a low of $26\tau_c$ for the methods previously discussed. Also note that this assumes ripple-carry for completion of the addition. The use of carry look-ahead in the last stage would reduce the time to $9\tau_c$.

While this approach can theoretically be extended to any number of bits, the cost may become prohibitive for large numbers of bits, even with large-scale integrated circuits. For 64-bits, this technique requires an array of 4096 AND gates and an array of 4032 full-adders for the ripple-carry version. As an alternative, we could use a combination of combinational and sequential techniques. In one large machine, using 48-bit words, the multiplier is divided in half. The multiplicand is first multiplied by the lower half of the multiplier, using a 24 × 48 array of AND gates to form the partial products and an array of adders to form 72-bit partial-sum and partial-carry terms, which are saved in registers. The same arrays are then used to multiply the multiplicand by the upper half of the multiplier, forming two more 72-bit partial-sum and partial-carry terms. The four partial terms are then added in a 4 × 96 carry-save adder to form two 96-bit partial-sum and partial-carry terms, which are then added in a 96-bit carry look-ahead adder to form the complete product. Depending on the exact form of the adder arrays, the time for this technique would be about $12\tau_c$.

There are many other possible ways of reducing multiplication time. Considering the complexity of the operation, it is hardly surprising that a tremendous variety of techniques have been used; and many more will doubtless be developed in the future. We have tried here to indicate the basic ideas behind some of the more popular techniques, not to provide an exhaustive survey. Further, no general evaluation of the various techniques is practical, since so much depends on the characteristics of the system in which the multiplier is being used.

12.6. DIVISION

In most computers, division is a considerably slower operation than multiplication. Its logical nature is such that it does not lend itself to speed-up as well as multiplication; and it occurs less frequently than multiplication in the general mix of problems, so that slow speed can be better tolerated. In the machine using the complex 48-bit multiplication scheme described earlier, division takes four times as long as multiplication.

The basic technique of division is the comparison, or trial-and-error, method. In decimal division, we compare the divisor to the dividend or current partial remainder, estimate how many times it "fits," and then check the estimate by multiplying the divisor by the quotient digit and subtracting the resultant product from the partial remainder. If it doesn't "fit," we make a new estimate, hence the name "trial-and-error."

Binary division is considerably simpler since the quotient bit is either 0 or 1. If the divisor is smaller than the partial remainder, the quotient bit is 1 and we subtract; if it is larger, the quotient bit is 0 and we do not subtract. An example of "paper-and-pencil" binary division of two 7-bit (including sign) numbers is shown in Fig. 12.8.

Consideration of this example indicates several special problems of division. First, placement of the binary point in the quotient requires not only knowledge of the position of the binary point in the divisor and dividend, but also some information as to the relative magnitudes of the two operands. For example, both divisor and dividend can be fractional (binary point to the left, as in Fig. 12.8); but if the divisor is smaller than the dividend, the quotient will not be fractional. It is usual to assume both operands fractional, and to require that the divisor be larger than the dividend, thus ensuring a fractional quotient. Provisions to ensure this condition may be included in either the hardware or software of the machine. We will assume that this condition is met in the remainder of this chapter.

In the manual technique, we determine whether or not to subtract by a

```
                0.101110
        0.011010)0.010011
                 -011010      Divisor larger than dividend, shift
                 -------
                  001100      Subtract, enter 1
                   011010     Shift divisor, enter 0
                  -011010     Shift divisor
                  -------
                    010110    Subtract, enter 1
                   -011010    Shift divisor
                   -------
                     010010   Subtract, enter 1
                    -011010   Shift divisor
                    -------
                      001010  Subtract, enter 1
                       011010 Shift divisor, enter 0
```

FIGURE 12.8. Binary division, trial-and-error method.

visual comparison of the shifted divisor and partial remainder. Unfortunately, the usual method of comparing the magnitudes of two numbers in a computer is to subtract one from the other and note the sign of the result. Thus, we must subtract on every cycle. Further, since a negative difference will be indicated by a carry-out of the most-significant digit position, we must allow time for the carry to propagate all the way through; so carry-save is ruled out.

In the manual technique, we shift the divisor right to make it smaller than the partial remainder. In a computer, since the adder is fixed in position relative to the registers, we accomplish the same result by shifting the partial remainder left. As we do so, we shift the quotient into the ***MQ*** register.

MD	0011010		Initial contents of registers
AC, ***MQ***	0010011	0000000	
	0100110	0000000	Shift *AC*, ***MQ***, enter sign at MQ_6
	0001100	0000000	Subtract *AC* − ***MD***
	0011000	0000001	Shift, enter 1 at MQ_6
	0110000	0000010	Shift, enter 0 at MQ_6
	0010110	0000010	Subtract *AC* − ***MD***
	0101100	0000101	Shift, enter 1
	0010010	0000101	Subtract *AC* − ***MD***
	0100100	0001011	Shift, enter 1
	0001010	0001011	Subtract *AC* − ***MD***
	0010100	0010111	Shift, enter 1
	0101000	0101110	Shift, enter 0

FIGURE 12.9. **Computer division by trial-and-error method.**

Figure 12.9 illustrates the computer implementation of division for the same example as Fig. 12.8.

The process starts with the divisor in ***MD***, the dividend in *AC*, and the ***MQ*** register cleared. In the following we will assume positive operands, and will write the AHPL statements for 18-bit division as we describe the process. Since the divisor is known to be larger than the dividend, step 1 shifts *AC*,***MQ*** and enters the sign-bit of the quotient (0 for this example) in the vacated position.

1. $AC,MQ \leftarrow \underset{0}{\uparrow} AC,MQ;\ MC \leftarrow 0$

Step 2 examines the result of a trial subtraction. Note that we have to make a subtraction in any case; but the subtraction is "completed," in the sense of entering the result into *AC*, only if the difference is positive, i.e., the divisor "fits" into the partial remainder. Note that the subtraction is accomplished by using the logical (one's) complement of ***MD*** and injecting a 1 on the input-carry line.

2. $\alpha^1/(\mathrm{ADD}(AC,\overline{MD},1)):0,\ (=,\neq) \rightarrow (3,5)$

Step 3 enters the difference into *AC*, and step 4 shifts *AC*,***MQ***, entering a 1 into ***MQ***. These two steps can be combined, but we have shown them separate for clarity. At step 5, if the subtraction did not work, *AC*,***MQ*** is shifted, with a 0 entered in ***MQ***.

3. $AC \leftarrow \mathrm{ADD}(AC,\overline{MD},1)$
4. $AC,MQ \leftarrow (\alpha^{35}/(\underset{0}{\uparrow} AC,MQ)),1, \rightarrow (6)$
5. $AC,MQ \leftarrow \underset{0}{\uparrow} AC,MQ$

Step 6 increments the multiplication counter, ***MC***, which we assume was set to zero at the start; and step 7 checks to see if the division is complete. At the finish, the quotient is in ***MQ*** and the remainder in *AC*. The designer may add a step to switch their positions if it is desired that all arithmetic operations terminate with the answer in *AC*. In this discussion we have considered only positive operands. We will leave it as an exercise for the

6. $MC \leftarrow \mathrm{INC}(MC)$
7. $(\perp(MC)):18,\ (<,=) \rightarrow (2,8)$
8. EXIT

reader to devise procedures for handling negative operands.

As we mentioned earlier, it is relatively difficult to increase the speed of division significantly; but we might indicate the general nature of a few techniques that have been used. One technique is known as *non-performing* division. The basic idea is to find some faster method of comparing the magnitudes of two numbers than subtracting them. One possibility is to use some type of carry-completion adder, in which a change in the sign of the difference can be detected in less time than it takes to complete the subtraction. Or one might provide a combinational circuit for comparing the magnitudes of two numbers. With the increasing availability of large-scale integrated circuits this last approach may be the most attractive.

The concept of shifting over 0's can be applied to division, but practical application requires that the divisor be normalized. For example, if the divisor is 0.1xxxxxxxxx and the dividend is 0.00001xxx, we can see that four shifts will be required before a subtraction can possibly be successful. Thus we can shift four places and enter four 0's in the quotient before trying a subtraction. On the other hand, if there were leading 0's in the divisor, it would be more difficult to determine how many shifts should be made.

Shifting over 1's and other multi-bit techniques, analogous to those used in multiplication, are possible; but they are so complex that their practicality is questionable. The interested reader is referred to Flores [1] for a full discussion.

12.7. SUMMARY

Our goal in this chapter has been to suggest some of the problems and options available in the implementation of multiplication and division. We have not attempted to provide all of the information which may be required to make a design decision. The reader will, hopefully, have gained sufficient insight to consider in more detail the various aspects of multiplication and division as the need arises. As before, we have utilized AHPL as much as possible, so that the reader will retain the confidence that he can fill in the details of a hardware realization in a straightforward way.

We have restricted ourselves to fixed-point arithmetic. Floating point is the topic of the next chapter. As we shall see, however, most of the material of this chapter is applicable to floating point. It is only necessary to add a few registers for handling the exponents and some additional control logic.

PROBLEMS

12.1 Suppose a special purpose computer is to be designed which will be called upon frequently to compute x^3 in fixed point. The number x may be positive or two's-complement. Write an AHPL routine for accomplishing this operation. The sign should be developed directly as part of the multiplication operation, as discussed in Section 12.1. Assume an 18-bit word length.

12.2 Rewrite the carry-save routine of Section 12.2 to allow for two's-complement multipliers and multiplicands.

12.3 Improve the AHPL routine of Section 12.2 by adding a hardware capability to detect strings of 0's in the multiplier and providing for a multiple shift of that number of bits in *AC*.

12.4 Refer to the time for bit-by-bit multiplication with carry-save given in Fig. 12.6. Develop a similar expression valid where the capability for shifting over unlimited strings of 0's is provided. Assume only one clock period is required to shift over a string. Suppose that the hardware could not detect strings longer than five bits. How would this affect your expression?

12.5 Compile a table similar to Fig. 12.5 for bit-quadruplet multiplication. How many multiple multiplier registers would you recommend? What would be the average number of bits handled in a cycle by this scheme?

12.6 Develop an expression for the multiplication time of a multiplier using bit-triplets without carry-save.

12.7 Modify the AHPL routine for elementary division in Section 12.6 to allow for negative arguments.

12.8 Write an AHPL routine for division which allows for shifting over strings of 0's. Assume that both divisor and dividend are positive.

REFERENCES

1. Flores, Ivan, *The Logic of Computer Arithmetic*, Prentice-Hall, Englewood Cliffs, N.J., 1963.

2. Chu, Yaohan, *Digital Computer Design Fundamentals*, McGraw-Hill, New York, 1962.

3. Habibi, A., and Wintz, P. A., "Fast Multipliers," *IEEETEC*, Vol. C-19, Feb. 1970, pp. 153–157.

4. Pezaris, S. D., "A 40-ns 17-Bit by 17-Bit Array Multiplier," *IEEETEC*, Vol. C-20, April 1971, pp. 442–448.

5. Braun, E. L., *Digital Computer Design*, Academic Press, New York, 1963.

6. Ling, H., "High-Speed Computer Multiplication Using a Multiple-Bit Decoding Algorithm," *IEEETEC*, Vol. C-19, Aug. 1970, pp. 706–710.

13

Floating-Point Arithmetic

13.1. INTRODUCTION

Floating-point notation is the computer equivalent of the familiar scientific notation. For example, rather than writing the speed of light as

$$300{,}000{,}000 \text{ m/sec}$$

we generally write

$$3 \times 10^8 \text{ m/sec}$$

or the FORTRAN equivalent

3.0E08

Virtually all high-level programming languages provide for this type of notation, and provision for handling numbers in this form can be included either in the software (the compiler) or in the hardware. We are concerned in this chapter with the hardware procedures for handling numbers in this form.

All our discussions of computer arithmetic up to now have assumed *fixed-point* operation.* The radix (decimal or binary) point is not physically

* This should not be confused with the *fixed format* (F format) of FORTRAN, which concerns only the form of the numbers for input-output.

present in a computer register, but its assumed position clearly must be known. When we add two numbers together, such as

$$\begin{array}{r} 36.81 \\ +1.041 \\ \hline 37.851 \end{array}$$

the decimal points must be aligned, whatever the length of the numbers. When we add the contents of two registers, the corresponding bit-positions are combined; so we must assume the same position for the radix point in both registers for the results to have any meaning.

It is general practice in computers to assume the radix point immediately to the left of the most-significant-digit, as was done for the division process in Chapter 12. The chief reason for this practice is to preserve alignment of the radix point in multiplication and division. For example, consider multiplication in a computer with 3-digit decimal registers. Multiplication inherently produces a double-length product;

$$\begin{array}{r} 0.361 \\ \times 0.483 \\ \hline 0.174363 \end{array}$$

but our registers are only 3-digits, so we can retain only the three most-significant-digits. We note that the decimal point in the product is in the correct position, to the left of the m.s.d. With any other position of the decimal point in the multiplier and multiplicand, the decimal point of the product would be in the wrong position.

Not all numbers are fractions, so how can we use a fixed-point computer? The answer is that, at input, each number must have a scale factor assigned to it to convert it to a fraction. Thus 531 will have a scale factor of 1000 assigned, and will enter the machine as 0.531. This assignment is done by the loading program and must be done even for floating-point machines. The difference between fixed- and floating-point machines is in what is done with the scale factor after it is assigned. In a fixed-point machine, the programmer must keep track of the scale factor and take it properly into account in all operations. This can be done, but it is very complicated. When compilers are written for fixed-point machines, the scaling is provided in the compiler; so users of the machine writing in the high-level language are not aware of the problem.

While it is possible to handle scaling problems by programming, the resultant programs or compilers tend to be inefficient because of the many extra steps required to keep track of the scale factors. In floating-point machines we substitute hardware for software, or in some cases we microprogram the computer to handle the scale factors. The scale factors become part of the data words and are handled automatically by the hardware. The resultant hardware is relatively complex and obviously adds to the cost of the computer. However, the operation of the machine is so much more efficient that floating-point hardware is usually considered a good investment and is omitted only on small computers.

Another important reason for floating-point is the increased range of the computer. Consider a fixed-point computer with 48-bit word length. With one bit reserved for the sign, the range of numbers that can be represented is $\pm 2^{47}$, which is approximately $\pm 10^{14}$. Though this seems very large, there are many classes of problems for which it is inadequate. For example, in electronic circuit problems we frequently deal with resistance in megohms (10^6) and capacitance in picofarads (10^{-12}), a range of values of 10^{18}, too large for a 48-bit fixed-point machine.

In floating-point, each data word A is divided into two parts, the mantissa and the exponent. If A stores a positive floating-point variable a, then a is given by

$$a = \perp \mathbf{AM} \times 2^{\perp \mathbf{AE}}$$

where $\mathbf{AM}$ and $\mathbf{AE}$ are the mantissa and exponent, respectively. In a typical 48-bit machine, the mantissa might be 37 bits including sign, and the exponent 11 bits. Now the range of numbers that can be represented is

$$\pm 2^{36} \times \pm 2^{2^{11}} = \pm 2^{36} \times \pm 2^{2048} \approx \pm 10^{630}$$

The increase in range has a cost in accuracy, since we have lost 11 bits of precision, or about three decimal digits. However, 36 bits still provide about 10 decimal digits of accuracy, adequate for most problems. In addition, most machines with floating-point arithmetic also provide fixed-point arithmetic for greater accuracy, and may also provide double-precision arithmetic for even greater accuracy.

13.2. NOTATION AND FORMAT

The first decision we have to make in designing a floating-point system is the number of bits to be used in the exponent. This depends to an extent on the total word length, but is generally between seven and fourteen bits. The choice obviously involves a compromise between range and accuracy. For our examples in this chapter, we shall specify a 48-bit machine with 11-bit exponents.

The next question is the arrangement of the various parts of the data word. The most common arrangement places the sign of the mantissa in the bit-0 position, followed by the exponent and then the mantissa, as shown in Fig. 13.1. The separation of the mantissa and its sign may seem awkward, but this

Mantissa Sign	Exponent	Mantissa	Typical Order
as	*AE*	*AM*	
	1 11	12 47	Bit numbers for examples in this chapter

FIGURE 13.1. Floating-point data format.

arrangement offers some advantages. First, the bit-0 position will be the sign for fixed-point format; and this position may be specially set up for sign manipulation. Since the mantissa is handled as a fixed-point number, it seems reasonable to preserve its sign position. Similarly, the right-most bit position is set up for receiving the input carry required in certain complement arithmetic, so it is desirable to keep the l.s.d. of the mantissa in this position. Third, the exponent is more significant than the mantissa, so placing the exponent to the left of the mantissa means that relative magnitude comparisons can be made by the same algorithms as for fixed-point numbers. We will therefore adopt the format shown in Fig. 13.1. Notice in the figure that the sign of the mantissa (i.e., the sign of the floating-point number) is denoted separately as ***as***; ***as***,***AM*** will be considered to be in two's-complement form.

Next, consider the matter of exponent representation. Obviously we must provide for both positive and negative exponents. The most straightforward approach is to use the same representation used for the mantissa and fixed-point numbers, i.e., signed magnitude, two's-complement, or one's-complement, as the case may be, with the exponent sign in the m.s.d. position of the exponent section (bit 1 in the format of Fig. 13.1). This system has been used in many machines.

Another system of representation, known as *biased exponents*, adds a positive constant to each exponent as the floating-point number is formed, so that internally all exponents are positive. For example, with an 11-bit exponent section, 2^{10} is added to each exponent, so that (in octal notation) exponents range from 0000 to 3777 with 2000 corresponding to a true exponent value of zero. There are at least two major reasons for the use of biased exponents. One is that the absence of negative exponents may provide some simplification of the exponent arithmetic.

The second factor relates to the manner in which zero is represented in floating-point form. Formally, zero times anything is zero, so that the exponent associated with a zero mantissa is apparently arbitrary. In some machines, when a computation results in a zero mantissa, the exponent is left at whatever value it happens to have, resulting in a "dirty" zero. However, as we shall see later, dirty zeros may result in a loss of significance in some computations. As a result, most machines assign the smallest possible exponent to a zero mantissa, producing a "clean" zero. With unbiased exponents, the smallest possible exponent is the most negative possible exponent; but with biased exponents it is zero. The floating-point representation of zero is then the same as the fixed-point, i.e., all zeros. This means that the same circuitry and the same commands can be used to test for zero, regardless of the type of arithmetic. The biased exponents corresponding to various floating-point values are shown in Fig. 13.2. Note that -2^{10} and $2^{10} - 1$ are the smallest and largest possible exponents, respectively.

Finally, note that there is no particular problem converting to and from the biased form. Numbers have to be converted between decimal and floating-point binary on input and output in any case, and the biasing of the exponent does not make the conversion any more difficult.

Another question about representation arises from the fact that in floating-point notation there is no unique representation for a given number. For example, 0.5×10^2 and 0.05×10^3 represent the same number. Since the number of bits (or digits) in a register is fixed, we obviously reduce the number of possible significant digits if we carry along non-significant leading zeros. Therefore, it is standard practice on input of floating-point numbers to adjust the exponent so that the leading bit or digit of the mantissa is non-zero. Numbers in this form are said to be *normalized*.

Now consider the subtraction of one normalized number from another.

$$\begin{array}{r} 0.10011 \times 2^9 \\ -0.10010 \times 2^9 \\ \hline 0.00001 \times 2^9 \end{array}$$

The result is un-normalized. In most machines post-normalization is performed after every operation, to ensure that all operands are always in the normalized form. In the above example, the result would be normalized to 0.1×2^5. There are some who feel that post-normalization is undesirable

Floating-Point Number	***AE***	$\perp$***AE***
$\perp AM \cdot 2^{-2^{10}}$	0,0,0,0,0,0,0,0,0,0,0	0
$\perp AM \cdot 2^{0}$	1,0,0,0,0,0,0,0,0,0,0	2^{10}
$\perp AM \cdot 2^{2^{10}-1}$	1,1,1,1,1,1,1,1,1,1,1	$2^{11} - 1$
$\perp AM \cdot 2^{b}$	$1,(10)\top b$	$2^{10} + b$
$\perp AM = 0$	0,0,0,0,0,0,0,0,0,0,0	0

FIGURE 13.2. Biased exponent representation.

because it may hide a progressive loss of significance in a sequence of calculations. Most computers either use normalized arithmetic at all times or else offer the programmer the choice of using it or not. We shall use it in all our examples.

13.3. FLOATING-POINT ADDITION AND SUBTRACTION

In this section we shall develop an AHPL routine for handling floating-point addition and subtraction. The emphasis will be on presenting an understandable treatment of the arithmetic operations without worrying about details of the hardware configuration. The existence of necessary registers, data paths, and combinational logic circuits will be assumed. In the last section of the chapter a specific hardware configuration will be developed.

In these analyses, two input operands will be $\boldsymbol{A}$ and $\boldsymbol{B}$, the result will be $\boldsymbol{C}$, and the sign, exponent, and mantissa sections will be denoted by adding the letters $\boldsymbol{s}$, $\boldsymbol{E}$, or $\boldsymbol{M}$, respectively. Thus, the operand $\boldsymbol{A}$ is made up of the catenation of its three components.

$$\boldsymbol{A} \leftarrow \boldsymbol{as},\boldsymbol{AE},\boldsymbol{AM}$$

For addition and subtraction, the exponents must be equal before the mantissas can be added or subtracted. For example, if $\boldsymbol{A} = 0.111010 \times 2^7$ and $\boldsymbol{B} = 0.101010 \times 2^5$, then $\boldsymbol{B}$ must be converted to 0.001010×2^7 before the mantissas can be combined. Thus the first steps are to compare the exponents, subtract the smaller from the larger, and then shift the mantissa having the smaller exponent right a number of places equal to the difference between the exponents.

Note that significant digits will be lost from the number shifted; and if the difference between exponents is larger than the number of digits in the mantissa, the smaller number will be shifted right out. In the above example, if $\boldsymbol{B} = 0.101010 \times 2^1$, then after shifting to equalize exponents, $\boldsymbol{B} = 0.000000 \times 2^7$. Thus, if the difference between the exponents is larger than the number of digits in the mantissa, the answer is taken as equal to the larger operand.

This pre-shifting also accounts for the loss of significance with dirty zeros. Assume that one operand is a dirty zero with a large exponent and the other is a non-zero number with a small exponent. Then the non zero operand may be shifted right out, giving an incorrect zero answer.

After exponent equalization, the mantissas are added or subtracted in the usual fashion. If the result overflows, the mantissa is shifted one place right and the exponent increased by one. The control sequence then checks for *exponent overflow*. If the exponent of the inputs was the largest possible for the machine, then increasing it by one as a result of mantissa overflow will result in exponent overflow, indicating a result too large to be represented by the computer.

If there is no mantissa overflow, a check is made to see if the result is normalized. If not, the result is shifted left until a non-zero digit appears in the m.s.d. position, decreasing the result exponent by one for each shift. In the event of an all-zero result, the post-normalization step should be skipped. After normalization, a check for *exponent underflow* is required. If the input exponent was close to the most negative possible, decreasing it further for normalization may result in underflow, indicating that the result is too small to be represented by the computer.

The complete flow chart for this process is shown in Fig. 13.3. At step 1 the exponents are compared. For this purpose we assume the existence of three combinational logic functions indicating the relative magnitudes of the two exponents.* Alternatively, the comparison could be made by subtracting

$$\begin{aligned}\text{AEG} &\leftarrow ((\perp \boldsymbol{AE}) > (\perp \boldsymbol{BE}))\\ \text{AEB} &\leftarrow ((\perp \boldsymbol{AE}) = (\perp \boldsymbol{BE}))\\ \text{AEL} &\leftarrow ((\perp \boldsymbol{AE}) < (\perp \boldsymbol{BE}))\end{aligned}$$

one exponent from the other and checking the sign of the result; but we shall assume the faster combinational approach here (see Problem 13.1).

1. $\rightarrow ((2 \times \text{AEG}) + (6 \times \text{AEB}) + (7 \times \text{AEL}))$

Branching to step 2 if the $\boldsymbol{A}$ exponent is greater, $\boldsymbol{BE}$ is subtracted from $\boldsymbol{AE}$ and the result compared to the number of bits in the mantissas (step 3):

2. $\boldsymbol{CE} \leftarrow \text{ADD}(\boldsymbol{AE}, \overline{\boldsymbol{BE}}, 1)$
3. $(\perp \boldsymbol{CE}):36, (<, \geq) \rightarrow (5,4)$

Recall that subtraction is accomplished by adding the two's-complement of the subtrahend to the minuend, and that the two's-complement of a number is equal to the logical complement (one's-complement) plus 1 on the carry-in line. This requires no extra time as the 1 is added in as part of the regular add cycle. If the branch at step 3 determines the difference in exponents to exceed the number of mantissa bits, the larger argument is used as the result and the computation is complete (step 4). Otherwise, the mantissa corresponding to the smaller exponent is shifted right at step 5. This shift may be

* The above statements simply define the three functions in the simplest algebraic terms using relational operators. The design of the actual combinational logic subroutines required to implement them is left as an exercise (see Problem 13.3).

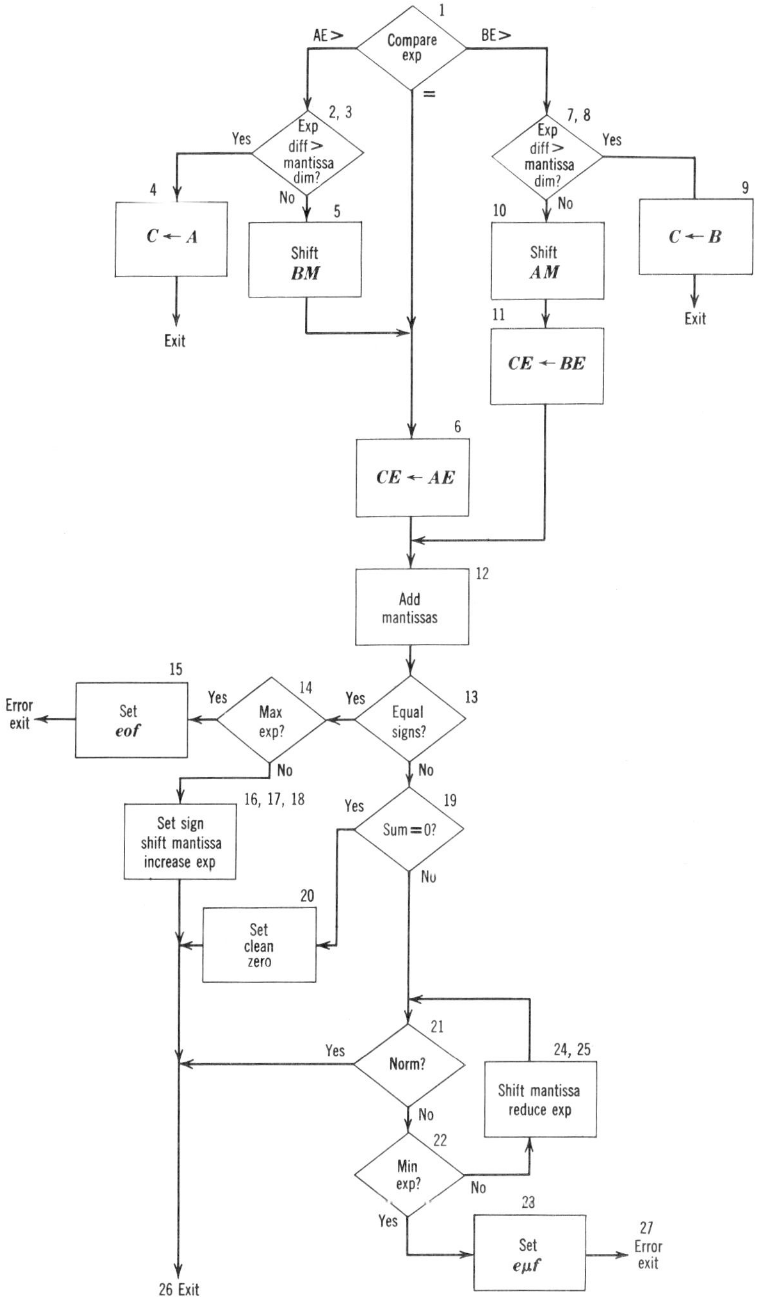

FIGURE 13.3. Flow chart of floating ADD.

carried out sequentially (one bit per clock pulse) or as a single variable length shift. The latter method is faster but more costly. At step 6, the result exponent is set equal to the larger exponent:

4. $\boldsymbol{C} \leftarrow \boldsymbol{A}, \rightarrow (26)$
5. $\boldsymbol{BM} \leftarrow (\bot\, \boldsymbol{CE})\, \overset{\circ}{\downarrow}\, \boldsymbol{BM}$
6. $\boldsymbol{CE} \leftarrow \boldsymbol{AE}, \rightarrow (12)$

Steps 7–11 accomplish the same functions for the case where ***BE*** is the larger exponent. When the exponents are equal, the sum exponent is equal to either operand exponent, hence the branch to step 6 for the case of equal exponents

7. $\boldsymbol{CE} \leftarrow \mathrm{ADD}(\overline{\boldsymbol{AE}}, \boldsymbol{BE}, 1)$
8. $(\bot\, \boldsymbol{CE}) : 36,\ (<, \geq) \rightarrow (10,9)$
9. $\boldsymbol{C} \leftarrow \boldsymbol{B}, \rightarrow (26)$
10. $\boldsymbol{AM} \leftarrow (\bot\, \boldsymbol{CE})\, \overset{\circ}{\downarrow}\, \boldsymbol{AM}$
11. $\boldsymbol{CE} \leftarrow \boldsymbol{BE}$

could equally well branch to step 11.

At step 12, the addition of the mantissas is carried out. At step 13, the signs of the operands are compared to determine what post-addition corrections may be required:

12. $\boldsymbol{cs}, \boldsymbol{CM} \leftarrow \mathrm{ADD}(\boldsymbol{as}, \boldsymbol{AM}; \boldsymbol{bs}, \boldsymbol{BM}; 0)$
13. $\boldsymbol{as} : \boldsymbol{bs},\ (=, \neq) \rightarrow (14,19)$

Since we are assuming normalized operands (magnitude ≥ 0.5), addition of operand of like sign will always produce overflow (magnitude ≥ 1.0), requiring a right shift of the mantissa and an incrementing of the exponent. Step 14 checks to see if the sum exponent already has the maximum value. If it does, incrementing it would produce exponent overflow; so the exponent overflow indicator, ***eof***, is set and control exits the routine (step 15).

14. $(\wedge / \boldsymbol{CE}) : 1,\ (=, \neq) \rightarrow (15,16)$
15. $\boldsymbol{eof} \leftarrow 1, \rightarrow (27)$

If there is no exponent overflow, steps 16, 17, and 18 shift the mantissa, set the sum sign, and increment the sum exponent. The setting of the sign is necessary because the additive overflow will prevent the adder from automatically producing the correct sign, as it would otherwise do.

16. $\boldsymbol{CM} \leftarrow \overset{\circ}{\downarrow}\, \boldsymbol{CM}$
17. $\boldsymbol{cs} \leftarrow \boldsymbol{as}$
18. $\boldsymbol{CE} \leftarrow \mathrm{INC}(\boldsymbol{CE}), \rightarrow (26)$

If the signs of the operands were not equal, a check is made at step 19 for a zero mantissa. If $\boldsymbol{CM} = 0$, ***CE*** is set to zero to provide a clean zero (step

20). Since there can be no overflow for addition of oppositely-signed numbers, the sign bit produced by the adder will be correct.

19. $(\vee/\boldsymbol{CM}):0, (=,\neq) \rightarrow (20,21)$
20. $\boldsymbol{CE} \leftarrow \overline{\epsilon(11)}, \rightarrow (26)$

Step 21 checks for an un-normalized result. For positive numbers, we wish to bring a 1 into the m.s.d. position; for negative numbers in complement form, it is just the opposite: a normalized number has a 0 in the m.s.d. position. Thus, in normalized numbers, the most significant bit and the sign bit will be opposite.

21. $\rightarrow (((\boldsymbol{CM}_0 \oplus \boldsymbol{cs}) \times 26) + (\overline{(\boldsymbol{CM}_0 \oplus \boldsymbol{cs})} \times 22))$

If the result is not normalized, a check is made to see if the exponent is already zero (step 22), in which case decrementing it would produce exponent underflow, indicated by setting the exponent underflow indicator, ***euf*** (step 23).

22. $\rightarrow (((\overline{\vee/\boldsymbol{CE}}) \times 23) + ((\vee/\boldsymbol{CE}) \times 24))$
23. $\boldsymbol{euf} \leftarrow 1, \rightarrow (27)$

If there is no underflow, the mantissa is shifted (step 24), the exponent is decremented (step 25), and control is returned to step 21 to see if the result is now normalized. The normalization process continues in this manner until the result is normalized.

24. $\boldsymbol{CM} \leftarrow \underset{0}{\uparrow}\boldsymbol{CM}$
25. $\boldsymbol{CE} \leftarrow \text{DEC}(\boldsymbol{CE}), \rightarrow (21)$
26. NORMAL EXIT
27. ERROR EXIT

Small computers such as SIC generally do not have a SUBTRACT instruction, and subtraction is accomplished by taking the complement of the subtrahend by program steps. If a computer is large enough to have a floating-point unit, however, it will certainly have a SUBTRACT instruction. Providing this feature requires sufficient extra hardware to take the two's-complement of subtrahend, which we will assume to be the ***B*** operand in terms of the previous discussion.

Recalling our previous discussion of subtraction by addition of the two's-complement of the subtrahend, we can change the floating-add routine to a subtract routine by changing just three steps. Step 9 is modified to generate the complement of ***BM*** as the mantissa of the result for the case where the ***B*** exponent is so much larger than the A exponent that the answer is simply $-\perp B$.

9. $C \leftarrow bs, BE, \text{ADD}(0, \overline{BM}, 1), \rightarrow (26)$

Step 12 is modified so that the adder will perform subtraction, as discussed

12. $cs, CM \leftarrow \text{ADD}(as, AM; bs, \overline{BM}; 1)$

above; and step 13 must be changed, since the addition of like-signed num-

13. $as : bs\ (=, \neq) \rightarrow (19, 14)$

bers is equivalent to the subtraction of oppositely-signed numbers, and vice versa. With these changes, the program will produce the difference, $\perp C = \perp A - \perp B$.

13.4. FLOATING-POINT MULTIPLICATION AND DIVISION

For floating-point multiplication we add the exponents and multiply the mantissas. The mantissa multiplication may be done by any of the various methods discussed in the previous chapter, and thus may be fairly simple or quite complex. In other respects floating multiplication is somewhat simpler than floating addition or subtraction, as there are fewer special conditions to worry about. There is no preshifting required and no possibility of mantissa overflow.

A flow chart for floating multiplication is shown in Fig. 13.4. Step 1 checks for either operand equal to zero, and sets the product to zero at step 2 if this condition occurs.

1. $\overline{(\vee / AM \vee \vee / BM)} : 1, (=, \neq) \rightarrow (2, 3)$
2. $C \leftarrow \overline{\epsilon(48)}, \rightarrow (21)$

Step 3 adds the exponents. Note that the link must be connected to receive any additive overflow. Since both exponents are biased by the addition of 2^{10}, the exponent sum will have to be corrected by subtracting 2^{10}. Before doing this, however, a check is made for exponent overflow and underflow. Overflow will occur if the exponent sum is larger than $2^{11} - 1 + 2^{10}$, so that the subtraction of 2^{10} will leave an exponent larger than the largest legal biased value, $2^{11} - 1$. We leave it to the reader to satisfy himself that this condition will be indicated by both the link and the most significant digit of

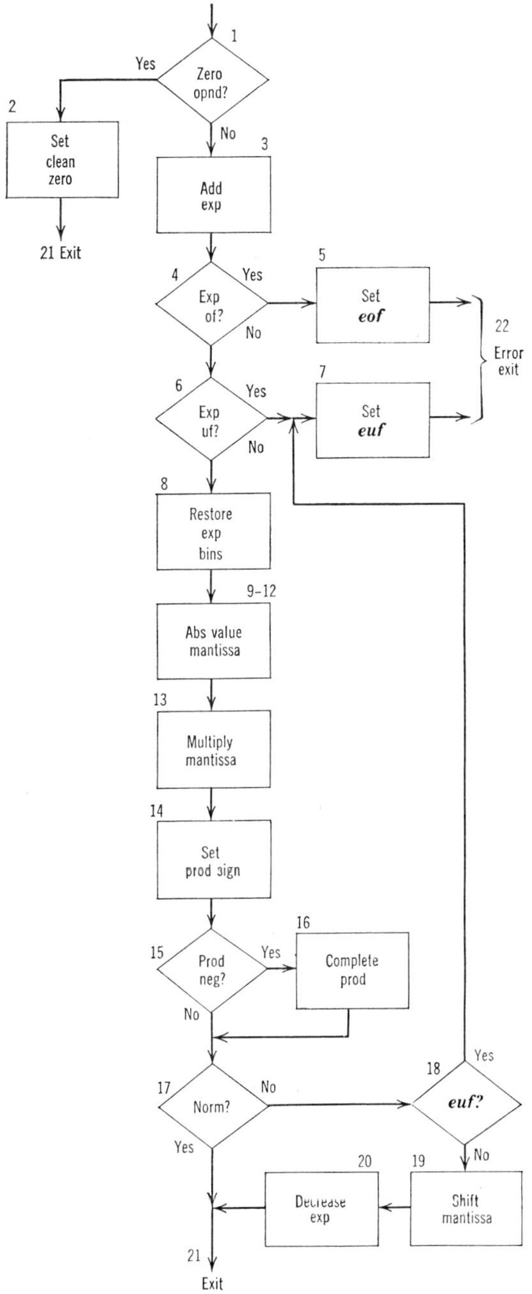

FIGURE 13.4. Flow chart of floating multiply.

CE being 1. Step 4 checks for this condition, and step 5 sets the ***eof*** indicator if the condition occurs.

3. $l,CE \leftarrow \mathrm{ADD}(AE,BE,0)$
4. $\rightarrow (((l \wedge CE) \times 5) + (\overline{(l \wedge CE)} \times 6))$
5. $eof \leftarrow 1, \rightarrow (22)$

If both of these bits are 0, the subtraction of 2^{10} will produce exponent underflow, i.e., a biased exponent less than zero. Step 6 checks for this condition, and step 7 sets the ***euf*** indicator, if appropriate.

6. $\rightarrow (((\overline{l \vee CE}) \times 7) + ((l \vee CE) \times 8))$
7. $euf \leftarrow 1, \rightarrow (22)$

If neither overflow nor underflow occurs, the exponent is corrected. Since the two's-complement (2^{11}'s complement) of 2^{10} is 2^{10}, this is accomplished at step 8 by adding 2^{10}, with the carry-out ignored.

8. $CE \leftarrow \mathrm{ADD}(1, \overline{\epsilon(10)}; CE; 0)$

As discussed in the last chapter, there are ways of handling complemented operands directly in multiplication; but we shall use the technique of recomplementing negative operands and multiplying magnitudes. Steps 9–12 complement negative operands.

9. $\rightarrow (as \times 10 + \overline{as} \times 11)$
10. $AM \leftarrow \mathrm{ADD}(\overline{AM}, \overline{\epsilon(36)},1)$
11. $\rightarrow (bs \times 12 + \overline{bs} \times 13)$
12. $BM \leftarrow \mathrm{ADD}(\overline{\epsilon(36)}, \overline{BM}, 1)$
13. $CM \leftarrow \mathrm{MULTIPLY}(AM, BM)$ Sequence

At step 13 we multiply the mantissa magnitudes by any one of the magnitude multiplication methods discussed in the previous chapters. Here existing notation is inadequate since a multiplication routine is a complete program, requiring a complete sequence of operations involving the arithmetic registers rather than a single logic circuit, as is the case with the combinational logic subroutines. Step 13 should be regarded simply as a convenient shorthand notation. In the complete AHPL program for a specific hardware configuration, the designer would insert here the complete sequence of steps required for multiplication.

Steps 14–16 set the sign of the product and complement the product mantissa if it is negative.

14. $cs \leftarrow as \oplus bs$
15. $\rightarrow ((cs \times 16) + (\overline{cs} \times 17))$
16. $CM \leftarrow \mathrm{ADD}(\overline{CM}, \overline{\epsilon(36)},1)$

Step 17 checks to see if the product mantissa is normalized. If not, step 18 checks for zero exponent, indicating exponent underflow. If there is no underflow, steps 19 and 20 shift the mantissa and reduce the exponent. Note that only one normalization shift is necessary; the smallest normalized operand is 0.1000 . . . . . , so the smallest possible product is 0.01000 . . . . . .

17. $(CM_0 \oplus cs)\!:\!1,\ (=,\neq) \rightarrow (21,18)$
18. $(\vee/CE)\!:\!1,\ (=,\neq) \rightarrow (19,7)$
19. $CM \leftarrow \underset{0}{\uparrow} CM$
20. $CE \leftarrow \mathrm{DEC}(CE)$
21. NORMAL EXIT
22. ERROR EXIT

Division is very similar. The exponents are subtracted and the mantissas divided. A zero divisor leads to an overflow, a zero dividend to a zero quotient. We shall leave the writing of a program for floating-point divide as an exercise for the reader.

13.5. HARDWARE ORGANIZATION FOR FLOATING-POINT ARITHMETIC

In the previous sections the exact hardware configurations were not specified. Separate registers were assumed for all operands and results, and no separate *MQ* register was specified for multiplication. In practice, the register layout for floating-point multiplication and division is quite similar to the layout for the corresponding fixed-point operations.

Considering the complexity of the floating-point processes, it is hardly surprising that there are many different hardware arrangements used for implementation. As a general rule, the same registers and adder used for fixed-point or integer arithmetic are used for processing the mantissas. The variety lies chiefly in the way the exponents are handled. One possibility is to "split" the registers electronically, so that the same registers are used for all parts of the floating-point data words. An alternate approach, which is probably more commonly used, is to *unpack* the exponents and place them in separate registers.

Even if separate mantissa and exponent registers are used, the arithmetic and logic circuits may be split, or shared by the mantissa and exponent registers. Alternately, completely separate arithmetic and logic facilities may be provided for the exponent processing. Just which approach is used may depend on the manner in which address modification, particularly indexing, is handled. If index addition is done in the main adder, then the main adder will probably also be used for both exponent and mantissa processing. If a

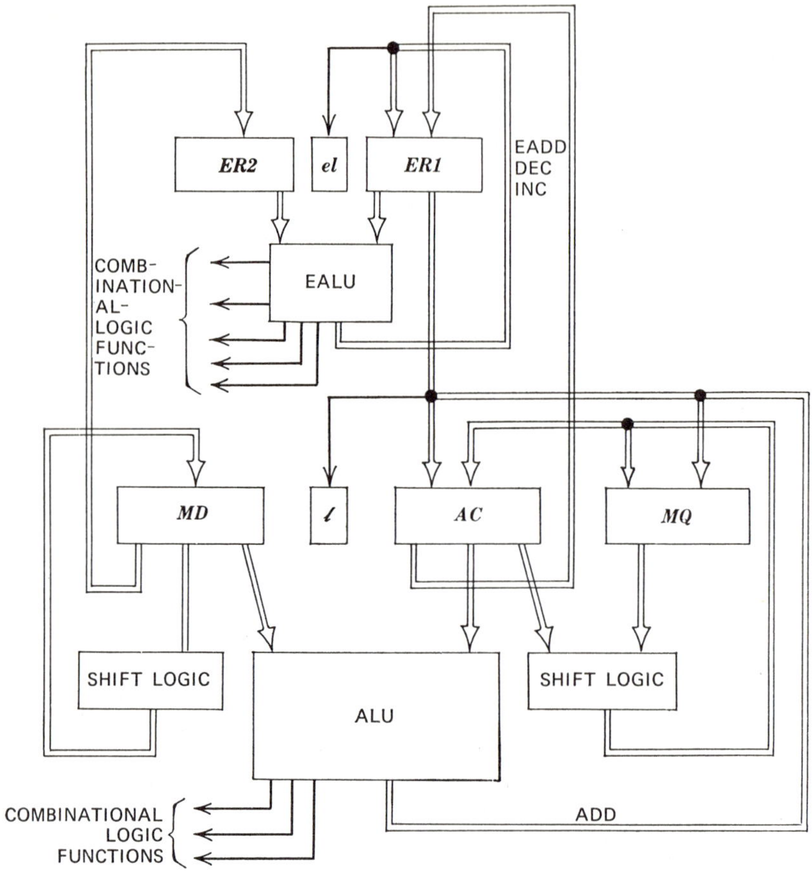

FIGURE 13.5. Basic block diagram, floating-point hardware.

separate adder is used for index addition, this adder will probably also be used for exponent processing. This latter alternative is particularly attractive if the exponents and the index quantities are comparable in size, which they often are.

One possible organization for floating-point operation is shown in Fig. 13.5. This arrangement provides much greater clarity in analyzing the various aspects of floating-point than does any shared-hardware approach. The mantissas will be handled in the same three 48-bit registers that would be used for fixed-point, or integer, arithmetic: ***MD***, the memory data register; ***AC***, the accumulator register; and ***MQ***, the multiplier-quotient register. All three registers will be provided with logic for 1-bit right or left shifts; and ***AC*** and ***MQ*** may be connected for shifting, if desired.

Rather than indicate just an adder, we indicate an arithmetic-logic unit, ALU. As we have seen in our analysis of the floating-point operations, it is necessary to be able to detect certain special conditions, such as a mantissa equal to zero. These conditions will be detected by combinational logic circuits with the appropriate register positions as inputs. Often these logic circuits may be wholly or partially realized by sharing the logic of the adder. For example, in a carry look-ahead adder, the condition of equal signs would be indicated by $\overline{P}_0=1$. For this reason we simply specify the ALU, a package of combinational logic to realize the desired functions.

ER1 and ***ER2*** are 11-bit exponent registers connected to bits 1–11 of the ***AC*** and ***MD*** registers. Exponent processing is handled by the exponent arithmetic-logic unit, EALU, which, in addition to exponent arithmetic, provides a variety of combinational logic functions such as the AEG, AEB, and AEL functions discussed earlier. INC and DEC provide for counting up and counting down in the ***ER1*** register. EADD is any conventional adder, with the output carry connected to a special link ***el***, for detection of exponent overflow or underflow, as discussed earlier.

We have shown in Fig. 13.5 only those registers and interconnections actually involved in the execution of the floating-point operations. As we have indicated, the exponent logic might well be used for index addition and other aspects of address processing; but we are not concerned with such matters here. We have also omitted any paths required for fetching the operands. A floating-point command normally includes the fetching of one operand from memory, with the other operand having been placed in the appropriate register by previous commands. For example, addition would start with one operand already in the ***AC*** register, with the other to be fetched from memory and loaded into the ***MD*** register as a part of the Floating-Add sequence. The first steps in execution would *unpack* the arguments in ***AC*** and ***MD***, placing the exponents in ***ER1*** and ***ER2***. The control sequence of Section 13.3 would then follow, modified as necessary to fit the specific hardware configuration (see Problem 13.4). The sequence would conclude by *packing* (assembling) the complete floating-point sum in ***AC***.

PROBLEMS

13.1 In Section 13.3, it was pointed out that the exponents could be compared by subtracting and checking the sign of the difference. Since alignment of unequal exponents requires subtraction of exponents to determine the number of shifts required, this seems like an attractive alternative. However, there will be some time penalty, for two reasons.

First, if the larger exponent is subtracted from the smaller, the difference will be the complement of the number of shifts required. Second, if the exponents are equal, no subtraction is required to determine the number of shifts.

a) Modify the control sequence for addition as required to compare exponent magnitudes by subtraction.

b) Investigate the time penalty involved in this method, as a function of the probability that the two exponents are equal. Assume that, when they are unequal, the probabilities are equal for one or the other being the larger.

Note that the answers to both parts may depend on the way the shifting is done, one bit at a time, or all at once.

13.2 Note that in considering the shifting of the mantissas after addition we have taken no account of the sign of the result. Is this correct? Should the same numbers be entered in the vacated positions for both true and complement forms? Indicate any special considerations in the control sequence or hardware layout that may be required to ensure proper shifting.

13.3 Write combinational logic subroutines to implement the functions AEG, AEB, and AEL discussed in Section 13.3.

13.4 Adapt the control sequence for Floating-Add to the hardware configuration of Fig. 13.5. Start with the operands in the ***AC*** and ***MD*** registers. Include steps to unpack the operands and pack the sum. Convert all operand designations to the appropriate register designations. Define any combinational logic functions required. Note that ***AC*** and ***MQ*** are equipped for shifting only one bit at a time.

13.5 Repeat Problem 13.4 for the Floating-Multiply sequence of Section 13.4. Start with the multiplier in ***AC*** and the multiplicand in ***MD***. Use the basic add-and-shift multiply routine described in Chapter 6 for the mantissa multiplication.

13.6 Write a control sequence for division, in the same general form as the multiplication sequence of Section 13.4, i.e., in terms of general operands rather than a specific hardware configuration.

13.7 Repeat Problem 13.5 for the Floating-Divide sequence developed in Problem 13.6. Start with the dividend in ***AC*** and the divisor in ***MD***. Use the basic division technique of Chapter 12 for division of the mantissa magnitudes.

14

Features of Large, Fast Machines

14.1. OVERVIEW

With the exception of the discussion of arithmetic in the last three chapters, we have restricted our treatment to elementary computers. In this chapter we turn our attention to large machines which are designed to accomplish many computations per unit time and as much computation as possible per unit cost.

Many large computer systems are operated in either the batch processing or the time-sharing mode. In both situations a queue of programs awaiting execution is always present at the input terminals to the system. Thus the computer system takes on many of the characteristics of a production process. The goal becomes to maximize the number of jobs (weighted of course by their complexity) which are inputed to the system and executed per unit of time. A measure of accomplishment of this goal is called the machine's *throughput*.

The raw material of the production process is programs rather than parts of an automobile to be assembled together. Programs as contrasted to sets of automobile parts are conceived and constructed independently by many different individuals, with little thought given to the convenience of the production process. Some of the largest installations can afford the luxury of assigning different types of jobs to different machines. Other batch-oriented installations attempt to improve throughput by spacing jobs in time, according to memory requirements or other apparent features which provide information as to job type. It is, of course, impossible to completely anticipate the requirements of a program until it is executed. In general, it is the same flexibility which makes the computer program so very useful that renders it so hard to treat as a production item. Perhaps more than any other one feature it is the conditional branch instruction which limits the applicability of mass production techniques on program execution.

There are two obvious approaches to improving a machine's throughput. The speed with which the central processor can perform arithmetic can be increased. It is also possible to increase the speed at which data can be moved about in the machine. This includes input/output rates, memory access times, etc. In general, an efficient machine represents a balance between the two capabilities. For example, it would be wasteful of computation capability to utilize an extremely fast central processor with a slow random access memory and a minimum input/output capability. When a central processor is forced to stand idle for significant periods of time because the system I/O is unable to deliver programs or carry off results fast enough, we say the system is *I/O bound.* Because batch processing facilities must handle many small programs and many I/O-oriented data processing assignments, such systems usually operate I/O bound.

The speed of all computer functions can be increased by increasing component speed. In Chapters 11, 12, and 13 we saw that the speed of arithmetic operations could be increased up to a point by using more complex logic. Component speeds are limited by the state of the art, and a point of diminishing returns is always reached in speeding up individual arithmetic operations. *In this chapter we will be concerned with further increasing computer throughput by organizational innovation.*

As pointed out, data movement is the more frequent limiting factor on throughput. Therefore, in the first part of the chapter we shall investigate organizational techniques for speeding data flow. Sections 14.2 through 14.6 deal with this topic. In Sections 14.7, 14.8, and 14.9 we shall investigate organizational innovations aimed at increasing the number of computations per unit time which can be performed by a central processor. In general, we shall try to organize machines so that more than one computation can be accomplished simultaneously or in parallel. We shall find that it is impossible to completely separate computation and data movement. Thus there will be considerable interrelation between the two sets of sections. The chapter concludes with a section devoted to byte-oriented machines. These machines are of interest because of their wide application to business data processing.

In Fig. 14.1 we see a block diagram of a computer system which will allow us to outline the data flow problem in more detail. Here we classify the major subunits of a computer system into three sections according to

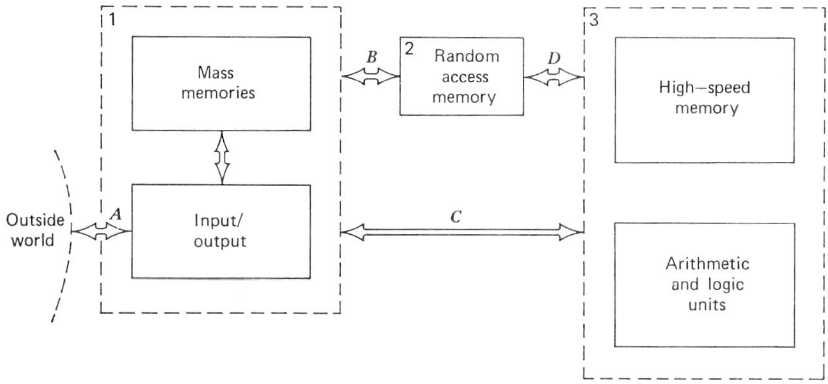

FIGURE 14.1. Data flow.

response time. A memory unit is included in each section. As mentioned in Chapter 3, the capacity and speeds of the three memory units vary inversely. The high-speed memory in block 3 has the smallest capacity while the mass memories of block 1 are slowest. The random access memory is intermediate in both categories. The set of memories of differing characteristics may be termed a *memory hierarchy*. In some systems it is possible to divide the hierarchy into more than three blocks. For example, the mass memory is assumed to include both magnetic disc and magnetic tape memories, which have different speeds and capacities. Three blocks are convenient for this discussion, however.

The high-speed memory may consist of a few data registers, as will be discussed in Section 14.2, or a larger number of registers capable of accommodating instructions or data, as discussed in Section 14.5. In the latter case it may take on many of the characteristics of the random access memory. Reading and writing in the memory in block 3 may be accomplished in a single clock period. It is likely that considerations such as LSI chip area and power requirements will always place a cost premium on the components of the high-speed memory. One would, therefore, expect to find in most systems a slower, cheaper, and larger capacity RAM, as shown in block 2, regardless of the organization of the high-speed memory.

Block 3 is organized so as to attempt both to minimize the cost per computation and to maximize the number of computations per unit time. Both of these parameters will be optimized for sequences of operations carried on entirely within block 3. Unfortunately, such utopian situations will be highly temporary in most real-world job environments. The overall system throughput must depend on the flow of information along paths *B*, *C*, and *D* in Fig. 14.1. Ideally, path *C* will be used only rarely, so as to avoid slowing block 3 to the data rates achievable by the devices in block 1. Thus data flow will normally be along the path *ABD* when the system is operating routinely in the batch mode.

Clearly data flow along path *A* will occur simultaneously with other system functions without interfering in any way. This is possible primarily because the system demands the right to accept programs from users and to furnish results at its own convenience. Many organizations have been devised which will relieve the central processor in block 3 of the responsibility of data flow on path *B*. One of these will be discussed in Section 14.9. Thus, jobs can be placed in a queue in the random access memory to be executed in order by the central processor, with the results independently removed after execution. This procedure is, of course, complicated by programs which demand large shares of the RAM or use auxiliary storage.

With independent control, data flow along path *B* will depend on the capacity of block 1 to provide data and the capacity of block 3 to execute programs. The cost per computation will be lowest when these capacities are matched. A quantitative model of this relation may be found in Hellerman [2]. The more common situation finds the capacity of block 1 to provide programs and data less than the capacity of block 3. We have already referred to this situation as I/O bound.

Path *D* is intimately involved in program execution. The high-speed memory of block 3 may contain both instructions and data; so short sequences may be executed entirely within block 3. When a branch to an instruction in the RAM of block 2 occurs, however, it often becomes necessary to replace a sequence of instructions in the high-speed memory in as little time as possible, without requiring block 3 to wait. Similarly, it may be possible to transfer arrays of data from the RAM to the high-speed memory at a data rate exceeding the maximum of the access rate for individual words in the RAM.

In Section 14.3 we shall consider a method of organizing the random access memory so that the reading and writing of individually addressed words may be overlapped. Not only will this increase effective data rate, but this same organization will permit communication with the memory by more than one processor. Like each of the topics of this chapter, the approach of Section 14.3 may be included in a system design at the option of the designer. The designer must decide whether the performance improvement to be expected from the inclusion of one of these features is sufficient to justify the cost.

14.2. REGISTER SYMMETRY AND MULTIADDRESS INSTRUCTIONS

Among the most time-consuming aspects of instruction execution are the continual references to the main random access memory for instructions and data. As solid-state random access memories become common, an improvement in access time will be inevitable. However, the speed-cost trade-off will remain. Economics will continue to force the use of slower, cheaper technologies for the main memory than are used for the high-speed registers within the central processor. In the next several sections we shall discuss a number of organization techniques intended to minimize the time consumed by accesses to the main memory.

One approach to reducing the number of memory references was incorporated into most third-generation machines. By adding a small number of registers to form a very small high-speed memory, it is possible to reduce both the number of instruction fetches and the number of data requests from the RAM. The number of instruction fetches is reduced through the use of multiaddress instructions. A single ADD instruction, for example, might cause an argument at address A to be added to an argument obtained from address B and the result placed in address C. Because all three of these addresses are part of one instruction word, two instruction fetches are avoided. Multiaddress instructions were mentioned earlier and were first considered in the early days of computing. Their efficient application, however, depends on the use of the small set of high-speed data registers. It will usually be impractical to employ instruction words long enough to specify three addresses in the RAM. The number, or address, of a high-speed register can be specified by just a few bits. Where data in the high-speed registers can be used repeatedly, the number of data requests to the RAM is also reduced. Clearly the relative improvement which may be achieved by this approach is program dependent.

The diagram in Fig. 14.2 is suggestive of a multiregister configuration for a large general-purpose computer. We have resorted to many notational simplifications in order to leave the diagram tractable. Single arrows are used to indicate vector data paths, and registers as well as logic units are grouped together in banks. An arrow from a register bank to a bus, for example, should be interpreted as representative of the network of connections of individual registers to the bus.

The configuration at the left handles logical and integer operations while that at the right handles the more complex arithmetic operations. Notice that the special registers ***IR***, ***MA***, and ***PC*** can serve as logic and integer arguments.

Two separate busing configurations are provided, one for simple fixed-point and logical operations and one for multiplication, division, and floating-point instructions. The general-purpose registers at the right, labeled ***LR1***, etc., would generally be longer than the ***SR*** registers, to accommodate the longer floating-point operands. Notice that the ***OBUS*** at the input to the long registers is split into two sections. This makes it possible to provide

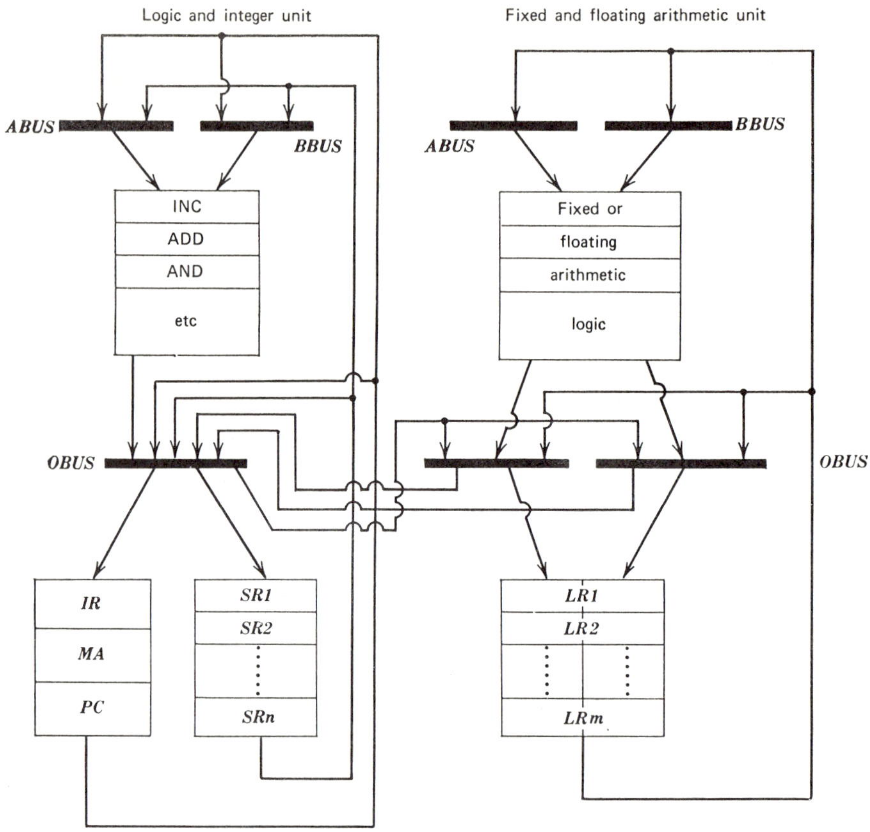

FIGURE 14.2. Multiregister configuration for large machine.

communication with the short register ***OBUS***. The number of ***LR*** and ***SR*** registers is variable. Under certain circumstances, the numbers ***n*** and ***m*** may be quite large.

Clearly, many of the complexities involved in the execution of instructions on the configuration of Fig. 14.2 remain unmentioned. No purpose would be served by attempting to treat such a mass of details here. We have presented this configuration first only because it is typical of what may be found in certain existing large-scale computers.

Let us remove completely the right-hand busing configuration from Fig. 14.2 and further specify 13 short registers, plus registers ***IR***, ***MA***, and ***PC*** as registers 13, 14, and 15, so that these registers may be addressed in the same manner as the ***SR*** registers. The modified configuration as depicted in Fig. 14.3 is something of a super-minicomputer which we can describe in

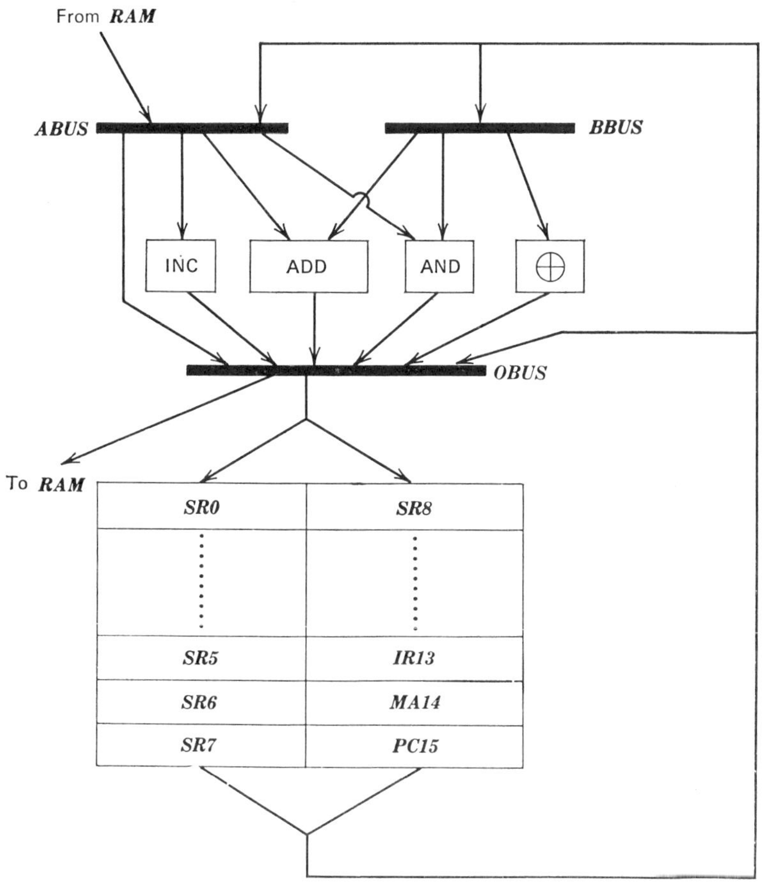

FIGURE 14.3. Simplified multiregister configuration.

more detail. Notice that the data lines from memory are connected to the ***ABUS*** with a direct connection between the ***ABUS*** and ***OBUS*** to provide for loading any of the 16 registers from memory.

For convenience we assume 24-bit words throughout. We shall allow two types of instruction words. The first type, shown in Fig. 14.4a, provides for obtaining an argument from or depositing a result in the random access memory. The second type of instruction, illustrated in Fig. 14.4b, calls for obtaining both arguments from the 16 data registers and placing the result in one of these registers.

Indexing, as indicated by bit 3, is possible where a reference to the random access memory is specified. If $\boldsymbol{IR}_3 = 0$, bits 4–7 may be used to specify some form of indirect addressing. Any of the 16 data registers may be used as an

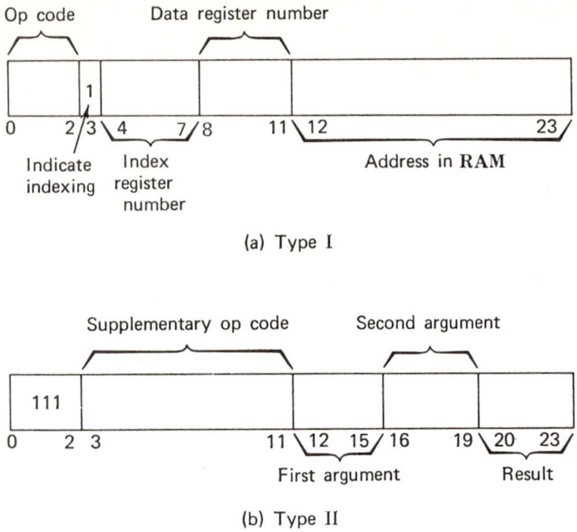

FIGURE 14.4. Instructions for configuration of Fig. 14.3.

index register, as specified by bits 4–7, if $IR_3 = 1$. Consider the instruction

$$2 \quad 4 \quad 4 \quad 3 \quad 0 \quad 0 \quad 4 \quad 0 \qquad \text{(octal)} \tag{14.1}$$

Using the SIC op code, we may interpret this instruction as calling for AND-ing the contents of the word in **RAM** with the contents of SR_3. The address of the word in **RAM** is given by 40 plus the contents of SR_2. The result must replace the argument in SR_3.

We can express the above sequence of transfers in AHPL if we represent the 16 data registers as the rows of a matrix **SR**. This implies, for example, that

$$\mathbf{SR}^3 = SR3$$

and

$$\mathbf{SR}^{15} = PC$$

The following sequence begins with the execution phase of the instruction given by expression 14.1. The execution sequences of other Type I instructions will be similar.

1. $ABUS, BBUS \leftarrow (\overline{\epsilon(12)}, \omega^{12}/IR, \overline{\epsilon(12)}, \omega^{12}/(\mathbf{SR}^{\perp \omega^4/\alpha^8/IR}))$
2. $MA \leftarrow \text{ADD}(ABUS, BBUS)$ 4 DELAYS
3. $ABUS \leftarrow \mathbf{M}^{\perp MA}$; $BBUS \leftarrow \mathbf{SR}^{\perp \alpha^4/\omega^{16}/IR}$ WAIT
4. $\mathbf{SR}^{\perp \alpha^4/\omega^{16}/IR} \leftarrow ABUS \wedge BBUS$

Type II instructions are indicated by an op code consisting of three 1's.

The particular type II instructions are specified by bits 3–11. A large number of type II instructions are possible, including most functions accomplished by SIC operate instructions. The three sets of four bits at the right of the type II instruction indicate the data registers containing the arguments of each operation, together with the register into which the result is to be deposited.

The following sequence accomplishes a Type II AND operation. It is quite similar to the Type I AND sequence presented above except that no memory reference is required and the result need not replace either argument. No indexing is carried out.

1. $\boldsymbol{ABUS} \leftarrow \mathrm{SR}^{\perp \alpha^4/\omega^{12}/\boldsymbol{IR}}$; $\boldsymbol{BBUS} \leftarrow \mathrm{SR}^{\perp \alpha^4/\omega^8/\boldsymbol{IR}}$
2. $\mathrm{SR}^{\perp \omega^4/\boldsymbol{IR}} \leftarrow \boldsymbol{ABUS} \wedge \boldsymbol{BBUS}$

A slight notational problem merits mention at this point. Notice that the ***OBUS*** is not mentioned in either of the above sequences. The output of the AND gate, for example, must be connected to the ***OBUS*** at the same time that the input arguments are connected to the ***ABUS*** and ***BBUS***. The operation is not specified as AND until step 2. Rather than complicate step 1 we assume that in the process of translating to hardware one can look ahead to step 2 for an indication of the ***OBUS*** connection. Note that this convention differs from that established for the microassembly in Chapter 8. This is tolerable in light of the differing functions of the hardware translation and microassembly.

The savings to be achieved by reducing the number of memory references required by execution cycles seems less significant when we remind ourselves that a memory reference is still required for fetching each instruction. One would clearly like to reduce the average fetch time also. This is a more difficult problem, which will be approached by techniques presented in some of the next few sections.

14.3. MULTIPLE MEMORY BANKS

The speed at which a magnetic core RAM may be operated is limited by physical considerations. The situation is only slightly more complex for a large semiconductor RAM. Once the cost per bit to be allowed for such a memory is fixed by design decision, the available technologies are constrained and a limit on the operating speed is the result.

There will always be applications of a random access memory in which its overall performance cannot be improved beyond a point dictated by the basic read and write times. There are circumstances, however, where the need for information from two consecutive memory locations becomes known at one time. It is possible to organize a slow random access memory so that

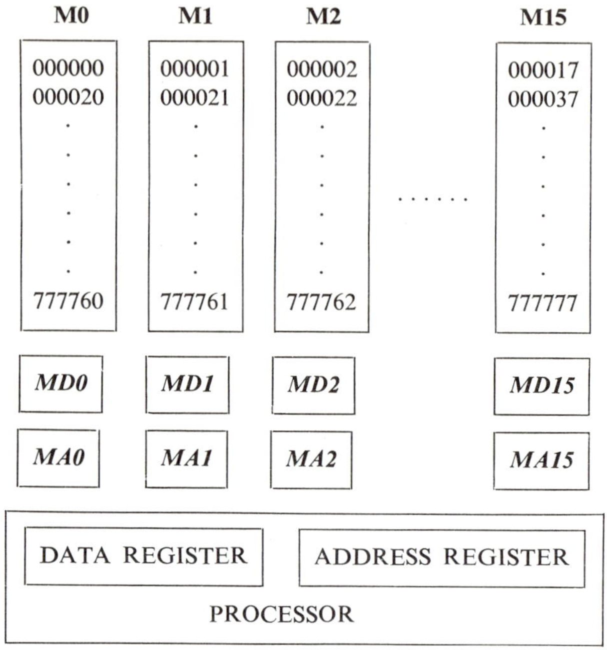

FIGURE 14.5. Interleaved memory banks.

several such memory references can be handled almost simultaneously. We shall first accomplish this by dividing the memory into several independent banks. The method of assigning addresses to these banks is called *interleaving*.

A memory consisting of 16 interleaved banks is partially depicted in Fig. 14.5. The complete memory contains 2^{18} words, 2^{14} in each bank. The assignment of memory addresses is shown in octal in the figure. Notice that the first overall address, 000000, is found in **M0**, while the next address, 000001, is found in **M1**, with 000002 in **M2**, etc. Thus the first 16 addresses are distributed over the 16 banks, the second 16 are similarly distributed, etc. This is interleaving.

A sophisticated central processor will often find it advantageous to obtain the contents of several consecutive addresses from memory simultaneously. Typically this information will be transferred to a scratch-pad memory. The reader will see more clearly how these blocks of data may be used in succeeding sections.

It should be apparent that the memory in Fig. 14.5 can be in the process of retrieving up to 16 consecutive data words simultaneously. The feasibility of this set up depends on a disparity between the access time of the individual memory banks and the basic clock period of the central processor. Suppose, for example, that core or MOS memories with access times of 500 nsec are used, while the clock period is 20 nsec. Thus, as many as 25 high-speed register transfers could be accomplished while a word was obtained from a memory bank.

Suppose the processor in Fig. 14.5 becomes aware of a need to read data from several consecutive memory addresses. It begins by placing the first address in the processor address register shown. It can place a second address in this register while the master memory controller routes the first address to the memory address register of the appropriate memory bank. This process can continue until an address in the processor address register is found to be located in a memory bank which is busy servicing a prior request. In the case of the transfer of a very long block of data, the memory controller will begin transferring data into the processor data register at the same time new addresses are routed to other memory banks.

The writing of the control sequence for the memory in Fig. 14.5 will be left as a problem for the reader. In the next section a control sequence will be written for a somewhat more complicated situation.

An alternate approach to 16 interleaved banks would be organizing the memory with words equal in length to 16 processor words. When a block of processor words are requested, a long word is read from memory and broken into segments as it is transferred to the processor. For several reasons (left to the insight of the reader) this approach is less flexible than interleaving.

14.4. INTERLEAVED BANKS WITH MULTIPLE ENTRY POINTS

Once the decision has been made to include multiple memory banks in a system, an additional advantage accrues: the memory can be accessed simultaneously from more than one entry point. These entry points may be connected to separate processors in a multiprocessing situation. Alternatively, they can be regarded as DMA points to speed up I/O operations and accomplish this in parallel with the execution of other programs. In this section we will construct a control sequence for a four-bank memory with four entry points. This sequence should serve to illustrate problems which will occur in other complex multipath data routing situations.

Our basic configuration will consist of four separate memory banks as illustrated in Fig. 14.6. Each bank has a separate memory data register and memory address register as shown. Any of the four memory banks may communicate with any of four entry points through the respective communications address register, *CA*, and communications data register, ***CD***. The

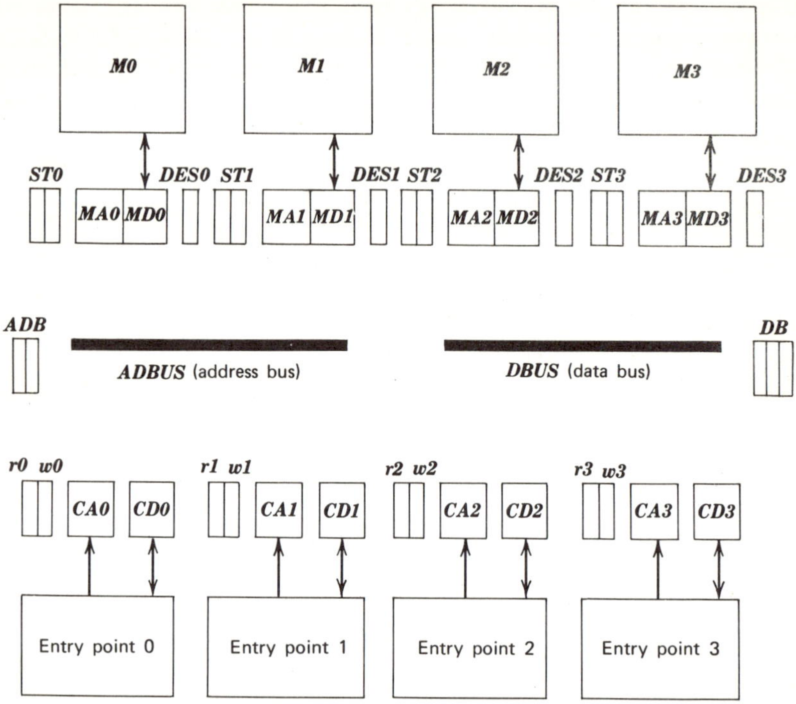

FIGURE 14.6. Memory layout.

memory unit and the processors are operated from the same clock source. Thus a processor can place a word in its ***CA*** register in one clock period, and this word may be taken from the register in the next clock period by memory control. The data communications process may take place in either direction through a ***CD*** register.

Two flip-flops, ***r*** (***r0*** to ***r3***) and ***w***, are associated with each ***CA*** register for control purposes. If the corresponding ***r*** flip-flop is set to 1, a read is being requested. If ***w*** = 1, a word to be written in memory is waiting in the communications data register with the address in the corresponding address register. If ***r*** = ***w*** = 0, the address and data communications registers are available to the entry point control unit. This indicates to the processor that it must take the next action.

The transfer of addresses between the ***CA*** and ***MA*** registers is accomplished by way of the bus, ***ADBUS***. The input to the ***ADBUS*** is controlled by the 2-bit register, ***ADB***. If ***ADB*** = 00, ***CA0*** is connected to the ***ADBUS***. If ***ADB*** = 01, ***CA1*** is connected, and so on. Data is routed between the memory data registers and the ***CD*** registers by way of the ***DBUS***. Because

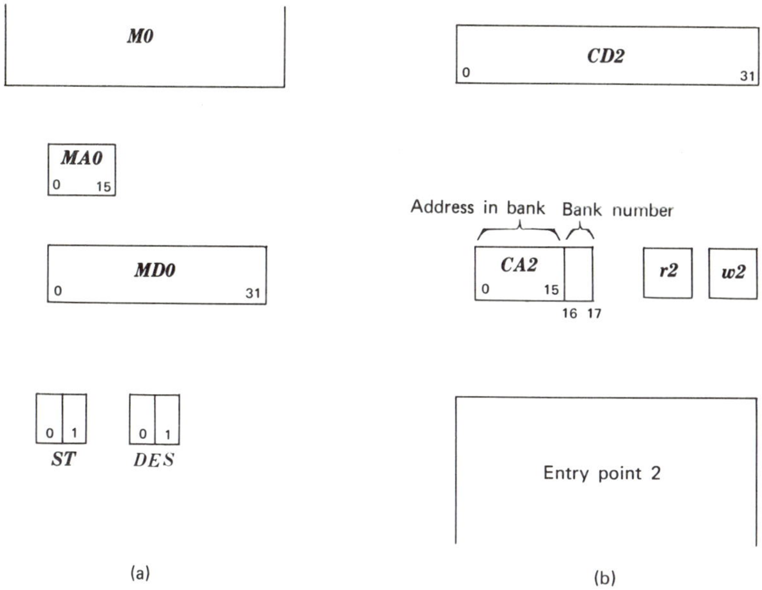

FIGURE 14.7. Typical memory bank and communications hardware.

data pass through the ***DBUS*** in both directions, a 3-bit register, ***DB***, is required to specify the eight possible input connections to this bus. Bit combinations 000 to 011 specify the ***DBUS*** inputs as ***MD0*** through ***MD3***, respectively. Bit combinations 100 to 111 indicate input connections from ***CD0*** through ***CD3***, respectively.

Some provision must be made for keeping track of which entry point is currently served by a given memory bank, so that a word read out can be routed to the proper ***CD*** register. As the time required to access memory or to write in memory is many clock periods, it is possible for all four memory banks to be simultaneously in the process of retrieving four separate data words for the same entry point. Therefore, we include a 2-bit register ***DES*** with each memory bank element to identify the entry point which will receive the word, if any, currently being read from the memory bank. Also associated with each bank is a 2-bit status register, ***ST***. If ***ST*** = 00, the bank is inactive. The status register will be 01 whenever a write or read operation is in progress. If ***ST*** = 10, the bank has just completed a read operation; and the data is waiting in the memory data register.

The hardware associated with a typical memory bank **M0** is detailed in Fig. 14.7a. The hardware associated with a typical entry point is given in Fig. 14.7b. Notice in particular that the communications address register, ***CA2***, contains 18 bits, while the memory address register has space for only 16 bits.

000000	000001	000002	000003
000004	000005	000006	000007
000010			
⋮	⋮	⋮	⋮
777774	777775	777776	777777
M0	**M1**	**M2**	**M3**

FIGURE 14.8. Address distribution.

The two least-significant-bits in ***CA2*** indicate the number of the bank containing the requested data, while the most-significant 16 bits specify the address within the bank. Thus each bank contains the data for every fourth address, as illustrated in Fig. 14.8, where the addresses are listed in octal.

If the other three entry points are not requesting data at a given time, one processor can supply four consecutive addresses to the four memory banks in only two clock periods per address. We make the assumption that if an entry point requests four words to be read from memory, this point will be ready to receive the words as they become available. Otherwise the data words may not be transferred to ***CD*** in the same order as requested. In general, the control sequencers must in some way keep track of the requests for data which they have made. In particular, a processor must not attempt to write in a bank if a read request is outstanding.

We are now ready to begin consideration of the control sequence for our multibank memory. Control of this unit may be thought of as managing traffic through the address and data buses. In order to avoid slowing the process unnecessarily we must permit simultaneous transfers on the two buses. As depicted in Fig. 14.9, the control sequence is divided into two sections. The first part of the sequence will accept a new READ request an simultaneously deliver the data from a completed READ. The upper left path in Fig. 14.9 specifies the interrogation of each entry point for a possible READ request. The first request encountered is set up by passing the address to the appropriate memory bank through the ***ADBUS***. At the same time, a word may be returned to an entry point through the ***DBUS***. Control for the latter activity is depicted in the upper right path of Fig. 14.9.

Following the processing of no more than one read request and one data return, control converges to permit a search for a possible WRITE request. We represent control convergence in the flow chart by the hardware symbol

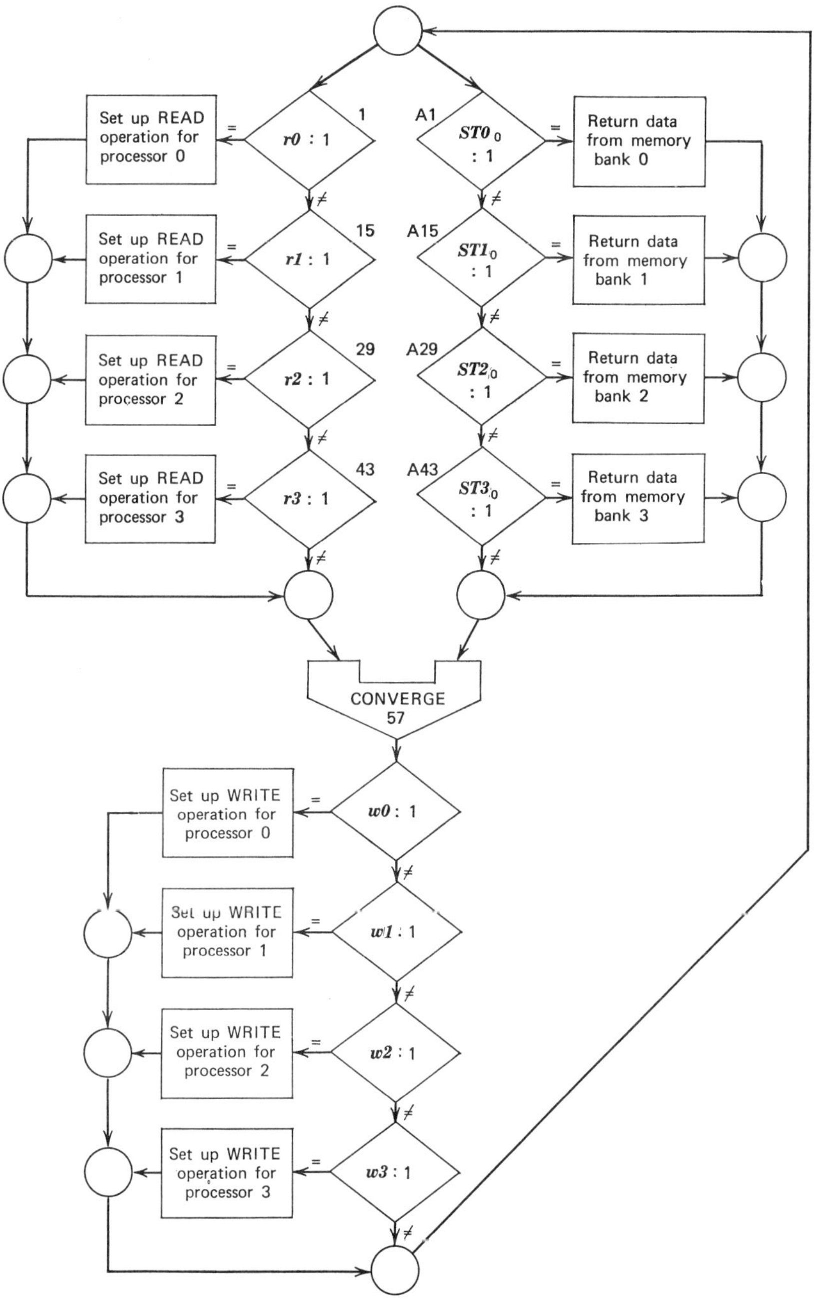

FIGURE 14.9. Bus control for interleaved memory.

for this operation. Only the first WRITE request encountered is set up by the lower sequence in Fig. 14.9. Write requests are considered separately since both data and an address must be passed to a memory bank. This ties up both buses, precluding any parallel transfer.

The reader may notice a priority system built into the flow chart in which the lower numbered entry points and memory banks enjoy highest priority. It may even appear that repeated requests from the high-priority units will be honored, effectively causing the low-priority units to be ignored. This will *not* be the case. The actual read and write times for the memory banks are much longer than the time required for several passes through the bus control sequence. Each transfer of address or data between processor and memory bank takes only one clock period.

The details of the control sequence implementing a typical READ request (entry point 0) are given below. Sequences for the other entry points are similar. If a read request by entry point 0 is encountered at step 1, then step

1. $\rightarrow (r0 \times 2) + (\overline{r0} \times 15)$
2. $\rightarrow (3, 6, 9, 12) \perp (CA0_{16}, CA0_{17})$
3. $\rightarrow ((\overline{STO_0} \wedge \overline{STO_1}) \times 4) + (\overline{(\overline{STO_0} \wedge \overline{STO_1})} \times 15)$
4. $ADB, DES0, ST0, r0 \leftarrow 0, 0, 0, 0, 0, 1, 0$
5. $MA0 \leftarrow ADBUS$; bank 0 ← READ PULSE, → (57)

2 causes a four-way branch, depending on the bank addressed by ***CA0***. If that bank is inactive, step 4 causes the appropriate status changes and connects the ***ADBUS*** for the transfer of the address from ***CA0*** to the proper memory address register (***MA0*** for the case shown). Step 5 carries out the address transfer and sends a read pulse to bank 0. Three separate 3-step sequences, 6–8, 9–11, and 12–14, are required to handle cases where banks 1, 2, and 3, respectively, are addressed. Steps 15–56 process requests made by the other three entry points.

The concurrent sequence for returning data is given by steps A1 to A14. Steps A1 to A5, as shown, handle returns from bank 0. Similar sequences in steps A15 to A56 will service the remaining three memory banks. Step A2 causes a branch, depending on the destination of the data as stored in

A1. $\rightarrow (STO_0 \times A2) + (\overline{STO_0} \times A15)$
A2. $\rightarrow (A3, A6, A9, A12) \perp DES0$
A3. $DB, ST0, \leftarrow 0,0,0,0,0$
A4. $CD0 \leftarrow DBUS$; *line* ***read complete*** ← PULSE
A5. $\rightarrow (57)$

DES0. Step A3 establishes bus connections and returns the status of the memory bank to idle. Step A4 transmits the desired data word to the communications register, ***CD0***, and announces this with a *read complete* pulse.

Control converges at step 57 to service a possible WRITE request by entry point 0:

57. Converge (56, A56)
58. $\rightarrow (59 \times wo) + (72 \times \overline{wo})$
59. $\rightarrow (60, 63, 66, 69)_{\perp(CA0_{16}, CA0_{17})}$
60. $\rightarrow ((\overline{ST0_0} \wedge \overline{ST0_1}) \times 61) + (\overline{(\overline{ST0_0} \wedge \overline{ST0_2})} \times 72)$
61. $DB, ADB, ST0, wo \leftarrow 1,0,0,0,0,1,0$
62. $MA0, MD0 \leftarrow ADBUS, DBUS$; *line* **write** (bank 0) $\leftarrow$ PULSE
63. DIVERGE (1,A1)

Steps 63–71 handle the cases where banks 1, 2, and 3 are addressed. Steps 72–113 handle WRITE requests made by entry points 1, 2, and 3. The above sequence is not necessarily the fastest or most efficient. A pass through the sequence will require at most four clock periods. If the memory read-write cycle is 50 to 100 times the clock period (a possibility), the four clock period service time is not significant. If the read-write cycle is 10 or fewer clock periods, this delay may become significant. Clearly a speed improvement could be realized by replacing the buses with direct transfers. Further improvement might be realized by eliminating the transfers altogether in favor of combinational logic routing of addresses. The result, of course, would be a formidable combinational logic network.

The hardware configuration discussed above was made as general as possible to illustrate the techniques involved. If certain of the entry points can be satisfied with lower grade service, various less costly approaches can be used. Where a larger number of memory banks are interleaved, a saving could be realized by advancing addresses from address register to address register in shift register fashion, until a match of bank identification bits is obtained. Data could be shifted out in the same fashion. The number of variations of such schemes is almost endless.

14.5. SCRATCH-PAD MEMORIES

We use the term *scratch pad* to refer to a high-speed memory which is not in itself of sufficient size to satisfy the RAM requirement for the system in which it is found. There are several ways in which a scratch pad, sometimes called a buffer memory, may be organized. Some of these approaches will be discussed in this section. The portion of Fig. 14.1, which depicts path *D* between the large RAM and the scratch pad is reproduced as Fig. 14.10. The simplest example of scratch-pad memory organization is the register array discussed in Section 14.2. The number of data registers which can be included in these arrays is limited. Three-argument instructions can only be used for

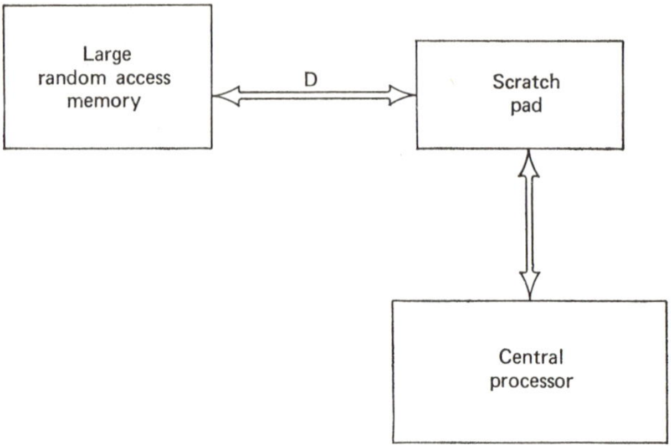

FIGURE 14.10. Scratch-pad memory.

small arrays. In addition, it is difficult for the programmer to use larger high-speed arrays efficiently. Thus we look for alternative organizations for high-speed scratch pads.

However the scratch pad is organized, the goal is to make the average access time for words requested by the central processor as near as possible to the access time of the scratch pad itself. This bound on the average access time can never be actually achieved, as the central processor will invariably request some items stored not in the scratch pad but in the large RAM. The slowing effect of references to the RAM may be lessened in the following three obvious ways. Point 3 was the topic of the previous section.

1. Keep the ratio of RAM references to scratch-pad references as small as possible.
2. Overlap references to RAM with other central processor activities. Anticipate requirements for items from RAM in advance.
3. Organize the RAM so that the average data transfer rate is greater than the reciprocal of the access time.

The three points are not independent. A certain anticipation of information requirements as well as multiple use of items placed in the scratch pad are implied if sequences of items are to be profitably obtained from the RAM at an increased transfer rate.

In this section we are primarily concerned with point 1. Clearly the number of references to the large RAM is reduced as the size of the scratch pad is increased. We may assume that the cost per bit of the scratch pad is considerably greater than that of the RAM. As the scratch pad is increased in size, the point of diminishing returns on the cost-performance curve is reached for a scratch pad with significantly less capacity than the RAM.

Critical to the organization of a small scratch pad is any advance knowledge which might exist as to the need for information from the RAM. In certain cases a program to be executed can be provided with this kind of information by the programmer. Instructions for block transfers along path D could be inserted in the program and performed in parallel with arithmetic and logical operations. For such cases a scratch pad organized merely as a fast random access memory would be satisfactory. However the burden of providing for these block transfers cannot be passed on to the higher language programmer. The result is an extremely difficult problem for the systems programmer.

If the possibility of providing such insight within the program is discounted, what information remains as to when and if a block transfer should be performed and on what data? There is some. For example, if one word is requested from the RAM, there is a significant probability that subsequent memory locations will be accessed in the immediate future. The instruction look-ahead feature, discussed in the next section, is based on this observation. Problems remain as to how many locations to transfer, where to put the information in the scratch pad, and how to inform the central processor of its new location.

All of the above problems are solved by organizing the scratch pad in a manner so that it is completely *transparent* to the programmer. That is, the programmer may assume that he is working with the large RAM only. To the programmer every memory reference will seem to be to the RAM. The only external indication of the scratch pad will be the shorter than predicted average execution time for programs. To make the scratch pad transparent we shall organize it as an *associative memory*. In an associative memory, a data word is not obtained by supplying an address which specifies the location of that data word in memory. Instead, an identifying descriptor is provided to memory. The memory is then searched until an exact match is found between the submitted descriptor and a descriptor associated with a data word. When a match is found, the corresponding data word becomes the desired memory output. A descriptor may be part of each data word, or the descriptors may be stored separately. The human mind is often thought of as an associative memory. As an individual dwells on a particular thought, related thoughts seem to flow from memory into his consciousness.

An associative memory might be organized so that many data words will be associated with one descriptor. Here each descriptor will be unique, so that only one output data word will be obtained at each memory reference. The memory search in an associative memory may be sequential, or the input descriptor may attempt to match all stored descriptors simultaneously.

A sequential search would be prohibitively slow in an associative memory intended for use in a high-speed processor. If the search is parallel, the large amount of combinational logic required will severely limit the size of an associative memory. Prior to 1970, logic costs made a combinational associative memory out of the question.

For convenience we shall detail the design of a relatively small, 256-word associative scratch-pad memory. This memory will be operated in conjunction with a 256k-word slow random access memory. The registers required for the implementation of this memory are shown in Fig. 14.11.

In addition to the matrix, **AM**, which constitutes the data storage, there are two additional 256-row matrices, **AA** and **UC**. Each word stored in **AM** is also stored in the RAM. The address of $\mathbf{AM}^i$ in the RAM is stored in $\mathbf{AA}^i$. Thus a word retrieved from RAM which is requested by the central processor is also stored in the associative memory. The probability that this word will be requested again in the immediate future by the processor is much higher than 2^{-18}, the average request probability of a word in RAM. When the same word is subsequently requested from the associative memory, it will be obtained in only two clock periods. Empirical studies on machines with associative memories have shown that up to 95% of the words requested by the processor have been found in the associative memory. Thus the associative memory can provide a considerable speed improvement.

The 256-word memory will fill up quickly, so it is necessary to provide a mechanism by which words which have not recently been accessed may be

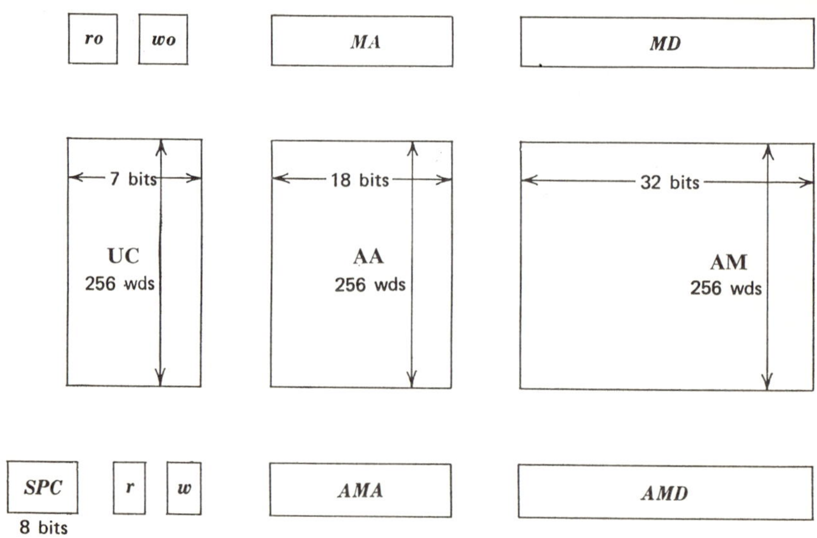

FIGURE 14.11. Associative memory.

replaced. Keeping track of the history of accesses is the function of counter matrix **UC**. Corresponding to each word in **AM**, there is a 7-bit counter in **UC**. Each time $\mathbf{AM}^i$ is accessed $\mathbf{UC}^i$ is set to $2^7 - 1$. With each access of **AM**, the counters corresponding to words not accessed are decremented by 1. When a counter reaches zero, it remains at that count unless set to $2^7 - 1$. Since there are 256 counters with a maximum count of 128, and only one counter is set each access, at least half of the counters will contain zero at any given time. A word will not be deleted from the associative memory unless the corresponding count is zero.

Of the remaining hardware in Fig. 14.11, ***AMA*** and ***AMD*** are the address register and data registers, respectively, for the associative memory. The registers ***MA*** and ***MD*** serve this function in the RAM. The control flip-flop, ***r***, will be set to 1 whenever the central processor determines that a word must be read from RAM. When the associative memory is ready to receive a word from RAM, then ***ro*** is set to 1. The flip-flops, ***w*** and ***wo***, serve similar functions with respect to writing in RAM. The remaining register in Fig. 14.11 is an 8-bit space counter, ***SPC***, which specifies the number of the word in **AM** which may next be deleted.

There are many possible approaches to designing control for the associative memory. Since only two clock periods are required to access the associative memory itself, we shall let this be accomplished by the central processor's control unit. If an access to RAM is required, control for this function is the responsibility of the *associative memory control unit*. As we shall see, part of this function will be carried out after the complete pulse has been returned to the central processor. The most convenient approach to the required simultaneous but totally independent operations would seem to be two separate control units.

First we consider the simpler memory reference routines in the control sequence. Where a read-from-memory is required, the address is placed in ***AMA*** and control branches to the read sequence, as given in expression 14.3.

$$\rightarrow (1) \qquad \text{WAIT} \tag{14.3}$$

For convenience we start the read sequence at step 1. This causes a branch to

1. $\rightarrow(\vee/(\text{ASSOC}(\mathbf{AA},\boldsymbol{AMA}) \times 2)) + (\overline{\vee/\text{ASSOC}(\mathbf{AA},\boldsymbol{AMA})} \times 5)$
2. $\boldsymbol{AMD} \leftarrow \text{ASSOC}(\mathbf{AA},\boldsymbol{AMA}) \,//\, \mathbf{AM};\ \mathbf{UC} \leftarrow \text{DECZ}(\mathbf{UC})$

step 2 if the word desired is in **AM**. The key operation is the combinational logic subroutine ASSOC(**AA**,***AMA***) which generates a 256-bit vector by comparing the rows of **AA** with ***AMA***. For example, if $\mathbf{AA}^i$ contains the same address as ***AMA***, the ith component of the vector ASSOC will be 1. No more than one component of the vector will ever be 1, as all the addresses in **AA** are different. If none of the rows of **AA** match ***AMA***, $\vee/(\text{ASSOC}(\mathbf{AA},\boldsymbol{AMA})$

will be 0, causing a branch to step 5. The details of the combinational logic subroutine, ASSOC, will be left as a problem for the reader.

At step 2 the vector ASSOC is used to select the row of **AM** which contains the desired information, and place it in the associative memory data register. Also at step 2, all 256 counters in **UC** (unless already zero) are decremented. The Z in DECZ symbolizes the fact that zero is the minimum count.

As the requested data word is now in ***AMD***, control is returned to the request points while the counter corresponding to the referenced word is set to $2^7 - 1$. For those cases where the desired word is not in **AM**, steps 5 and 6

3. ***return** lines* ← PULSE; ASSOC(**AA**,*AMA*) // **UC** ← $\epsilon(7)$
4. DEAD END
5. $r \leftarrow 1$
6. associative memory control ← PULSE; WAIT
7. → (3)

set r to 1 to indicate a desired read from RAM and transfer control to the associative memory control sequencer. When the read has been accomplished and the word from RAM placed in ***AMD***, control returns to the request point, just as before. As the above sequence is an interesting example of a subsequence within a subsequence, we depict the corresponding hardware in Fig. 14.12. The sequencer for writing in **AM** is very similar, except that the

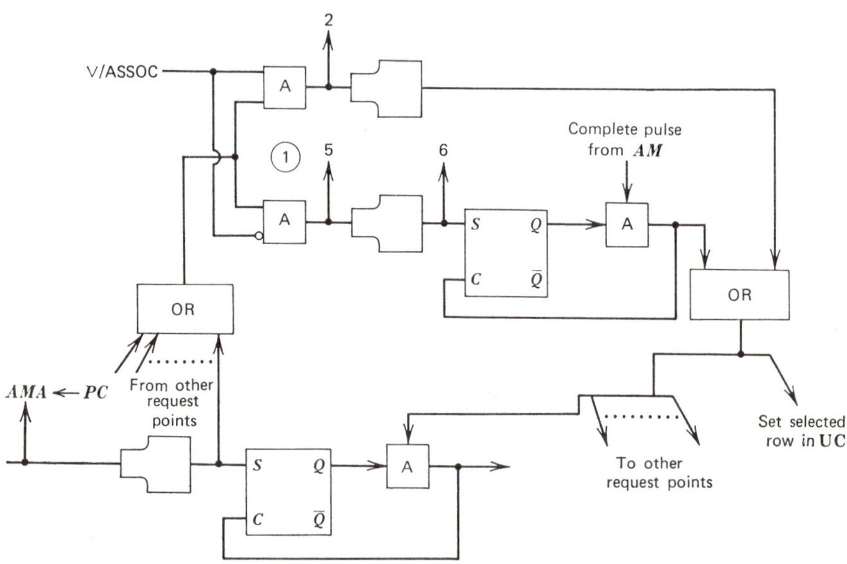

FIGURE 14.12. Control for READ from AM.

following is substituted for step 2.

2. ASSOC(**AA**,***AMA*** // **AM**) ← ***AMD***, **UC** ← DECZ(**UC**)

The associative memory control sequencer begins with a convergence step. The "mop-up" steps, following the last reference to RAM, may or may not have been completed prior to a subsequent request to RAM. These steps must be complete and a new request made before control passes beyond step 1. At step 2 control separates for the read and write in RAM operations. The

1. CONVERGE (PROCESSOR, 15)
2. $\to(r \times 3 + w \times 7)$
3. ***MA***,***ro*** ← ***AMA***, 1
4. ***MD*** ← $\mathbf{M}^{\perp \boldsymbol{MA}}$
5. ***AMD*** ← ***MD***
6. → (8)
7. ***MA*** ← ***AMA***; ***MD*** ← ***AMD***

read operation is accomplished asynchronously in steps 3–5, leaving the data in ***AMD***. No write in RAM is actually performed. Step 7 only prepares for writing in the RAM later at step 13.

Only one word is read at step 4. A better approach in the case of a READ would call for transferring a short block of information from the portion of RAM immediately following an addressed word into the associative memory. As the processor will often refer to successive memory words in sequence, this approach can save many separate references to RAM. (See Problem 14.11.)

Control may be returned to the central processor at this point, while the associative memory is simultaneously updated. As mentioned previously, the 8-bit counter ***SPC*** is used to indicate the word in **AM** which is slated for replacement. As the central processor may have used this word since the last reference to RAM, a check is made to see that the vector in **UC** identified by ***SPC*** is still zero. If not, ***SPC*** is incremented until a zero vector is encountered.

8. processor line ***complete***←PULSE; ***r***,***w*** ← 0,0
9. $\to(\vee/(\text{DECODE}(\boldsymbol{SPC})//\mathbf{UC}) \times 10) + (\overline{\vee/(\text{DECODE}(\boldsymbol{SPC})//\mathbf{UC}} \times 12)$
10. ***SPC*** ← INC(***SPC***)
11. → (9)
12. DECODE(***SPC***)//(**AA**,**AM**) ← ***MA***,***MD***;
    MA,***MD*** ← DECODE(***SPC***)//(**AA**,**AM**)
13. $\mathbf{M}^{\perp \boldsymbol{MA}}$ ← ***MD***   WAIT, → (1)

Once this is accomplished, the contents of ***MA*** and ***MD*** are interchanged with locations in **AA** and **AM** specified by SPC. At step 13 the word purged from **AM** is written back in the RAM. A control pulse must be returned to the convergence unit at step 1, before another request pulse from the processor can pass that point.

14.6. VIRTUAL MEMORY

Somewhat analogous to the associative scratch pad is *virtual memory*. While the scratch pad is included to shorten the effective access time of memory references, virtual memory is an organizational technique for increasing the apparent size of the random access memory. That is, the number of random access addresses available to the programmer is substantially greater than the number of locations in the physical RAM. These additional data are actually stored in a semi-random access memory (SRAM). The actual location of a particular data word is transparent to the programmer. Hence the term, *virtual memory*. To be of any value the virtual memory control must operate so as to make the probability large that a piece of data will be residing in RAM when it is requested.

A typical organization of a SRAM and a RAM to form a large virtual memory is given in Fig. 14.13. The SRAM is organized into 512 blocks of 2^{12} words each, for a total of 2^{21} addressable words. The RAM is organized into 32 banks, also of 2^{12} words each. At any point in time (unless in the process of a swap) each bank of RAM will contain an updated copy of one of the 16 blocks of SRAM shown in the column above it in Fig. 14.13. The first and last address of each block of SRAM is shown in octal in the figure.

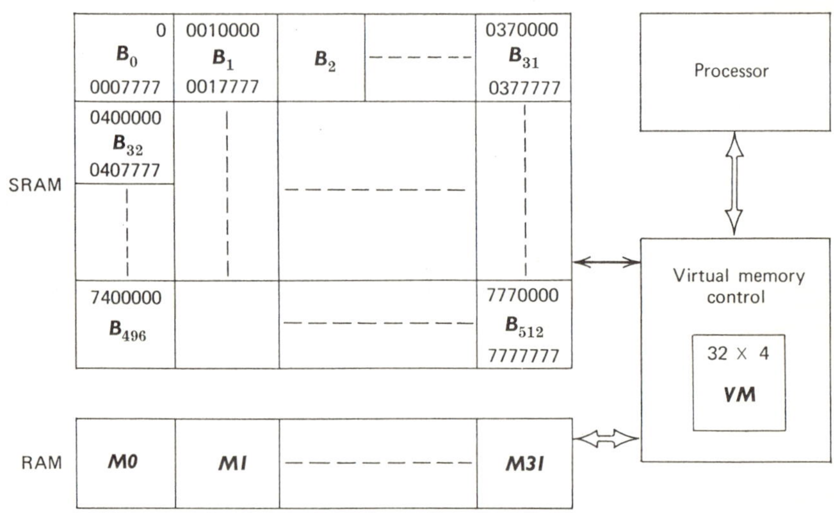

FIGURE 14.13. Typical virtual memory organization. (Block numbers are in decimal. Addresses are in octal.)

Notice that consecutive blocks in SRAM are listed horizontally. The result is a form of block interleaving. That is, it is possible to place 32 consecutive blocks, or 2^{17} consecutive memory locations, in RAM. In a batch processing environment this may include one or more complete programs.

The advantage of virtual memory is that any of the 2^{21} addresses in SRAM can be referenced by the programmer at anytime. Whenever a reference is made to a block not in RAM but in column *I* of SRAM, the virtual memory controller causes this block to be written in bank **MI** of RAM. The block already in RAM is first rewritten in the area of the SRAM from which it had been taken earlier. The matrix **VM** in the virtual memory controller is used to indicate the block stored in each bank of RAM. One row of **VM** corresponds to each bank of RAM. The four bits, $\mathbf{VM}^i$, constitute the *block address* of the block currently stored in **MI**. The block address consists of the four most-significant-bits common to all addresses in the block. The controller must search **VM** each time a memory request is made. This search must be accomplished using combinational logic only. If the addressed block is already in RAM, the reference is completed immediately. If not, a block swapping operation is initiated.

In the above discussion we have described most of the functions of the virtual memory controller. We leave the actual writing of the control sequence as a problem for the reader. We have described only a typical virtual memory organization. It is not necessarily optimal. In practice, one would expect to make a careful statistical study of average time consumed swapping blocks. One would then design the system using a block size which would minimize swap time in the anticipated application. As an alternative, one might choose not to identify the banks of the RAM with particular columns in SRAM. If blocks could be placed in the RAM bank with a record of least use, the RAM would become associative at the block level. In this case, the virtual memory controller would very much resemble the scratch-pad controller of the previous section.

14.7. INSTRUCTION LOOK-AHEAD

The savings achieved by minimizing the number of storage references during instruction execution can never seem quite satisfying as long as a reference to memory is required by the fetch phase of each instruction. If a scratch-pad memory is not used, one might attempt to reduce the number of fetch cycles which require reference to the main RAM by allowing short sequences of instructions to be stored in high-speed electronic registers, as were data in Section 14.2. If the number of *look-ahead* registers is sufficiently large, short loops in the program can be traversed entirely within the look-ahead unit. Where a buffer memory with an access time equivalent to the look-ahead registers is used, the same saving may be achieved by looping within the buffer memory. This assumes block transfers into the buffer, as discussed in Problem 14.12. As the buffer memory may in some cases be quite large, the likelihood of storing a complete loop within the buffer is great.

Thus, if a buffer is used, a very large number of registers within the look-ahead unit would be redundant. There is further advantage in a look-ahead unit with a few registers, however. The time consumed by the memory references may be approximately cut in half by overlapping the fetch and execution phases. That is, while one instruction is being executed, the next instruction can be fetched, placed in the instruction register, and readied for execution. This approach would be particularly advantageous where more than one word from memory are required to form an instruction. As other aspects of this machine are well understood, we can most simply illustrate the design of this simple form of look-ahead unit in terms of SIC. In practice, it is unlikely that this feature would be included in such an otherwise elementary computer.

Given the simple 8k memory originally provided for SIC, very little could be accomplished by adding a look-ahead unit. We must have the possibility of obtaining an instruction word and data word from memory simultaneously, or serially in a very short time period. This would imply an interleaved RAM, a buffer memory, or both. For purposes of illustration we replace the original SIC memory with a four-way interleaved memory of the form described in Section 14.3. The memory will be identical to the one in Section 14.4 except that the four banks will contain 2^{11} or approximately 2k 18-bit words each. The memory address registers will, therefore, be 13 bits. Only two of the entry points to the memory will be used in the discussion. The other two ports might be used for DMA input/output transfers, although the additions to SIC as found in the chapter on I/O will be disregarded here. A scratch-pad memory will not be included in the design.

Given the above configuration, the principal payoff of the look-ahead unit to be discussed will be simultaneous fetch and execution memory references approximately 75% of the time. On the average, 25% of the data addresses will be found in the same bank as the instruction addresses. The resulting design will be the most elementary form of a look-ahead unit, but it should serve as an introduction to some of the awkward problems which are created when look-ahead is included in a design.

Other than the memory, the only registers added to facilitate look-ahead are shown in Fig. 14.14. The instruction register ***IR1*** contains the instruction under execution, while ***IR2*** and ***IR3*** are provided for the next two instructions in sequence. If at the beginning of the control sequence the special flip-flop ***sh*** (short) contains a 0, the registers ***IR1*** and ***IR2*** contain the next two instructions in order. If ***sh*** = 1, only ***IR1*** contains the proper instructions.

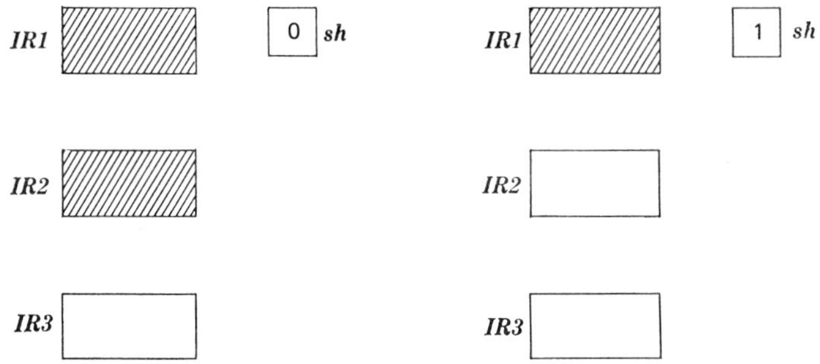

(a) (b)

FIGURE 14.14. Instruction look-ahead hardware.

These two situations are illustrated in Fig. 14.14a and b. We shall see that ***sh*** will be 1 following a jump or skip instruction.

The control sequence will cause the instruction in ***IR1*** to be executed while at the same time causing the next two instructions to be placed in ***IR2*** and ***IR3***. The program counter will contain the address of the next instruction to be obtained from memory, whether this instruction is to be placed in ***IR2*** or ***IR3***. The first step separates control for the JMP instruction. In effect, the execution of JMP and determination of the next instruction are the same operation.

1. $\rightarrow ((\boldsymbol{IR}1_0 \wedge \boldsymbol{IR}1_1 \wedge \overline{\boldsymbol{IR}1_2}) \times 21) + (\overline{(\boldsymbol{IR}1_0 \wedge \boldsymbol{IR}1_1 \wedge \overline{\boldsymbol{IR}1_2})} \times 2)$
2. DIVERGE (A3, 3)

A3.—AX Execution

AX + 1. $\rightarrow (13)$

Step 2 causes control to diverge to accomplish execution and fetch simultaneously. The A sequence executes all but the conditional skips at the end of the ISZ instruction and in the last event time of operate instructions. The execution sequence uses memory communications registers ***CA1*** and ***CD1***.

3. $\boldsymbol{CA0}, \boldsymbol{ro} \leftarrow \boldsymbol{PC}, 1$
4. $\rightarrow (\boldsymbol{sh} \times 5 + \overline{\boldsymbol{sh}} \times 11)$
5. $\boldsymbol{PC} \leftarrow \text{INC}(\boldsymbol{PC})$
6. 2 DELAYS
7. $\rightarrow (\boldsymbol{ro} \times 6 + \overline{\boldsymbol{ro}} \times 8)$
8. $\boldsymbol{CA0}, \boldsymbol{ro} \leftarrow \boldsymbol{PC}, 1$
9. WAIT FOR COMPLETE PULSE
10. $\boldsymbol{IR}2, \boldsymbol{wo} \leftarrow \boldsymbol{CD0}, 0$
11. WAIT FOR COMPLETE PULSE
12. $\boldsymbol{IR3} \leftarrow \boldsymbol{CD0}$
13. CONVERGE

Step 3 provides the memory communications register with the address of the next instruction. If ***sh*** = 0, control branches to step 11 to wait for the remaining instruction to be retrieved. This instruction is subsequently placed in ***IR3***. If ***sh*** = 1, the program counter is incremented and control circulates in a loop until ***CA0*** is free to accept another address. The second address is supplied at step 8. Control then waits for both instructions, placing the first in ***IR2*** and the second in ***IR3***. Notice that at step 10 only ***wo*** is reset to 0 since the processor does not know whether the second address has as yet been accepted by memory from ***CA0***. There is no danger of saddling memory with a dummy read operation, however, as only one memory bank is addressed.

Control converges at step 13 to permit completion of any possible skip operation. We leave the combinational logic determining the skip operation to the reader. We merely define the function, *f*, which is to be 1 if and only if any sort of skip instruction is called for *and* the skip condition is satisfied.

14. $\rightarrow (f \times 15 + \bar{f} \times 17)$
15. ***IR1***, ***IR2***, ***sh*** ← ***IR2***, ***IR3***, 1
16. → (18)
17. ***sh*** ← 0
18. ***IR1***, ***IR2*** ← ***IR2***, ***IR3***

If ***f*** = 1, the instructions are advanced in the look-ahead unit at step 15 and ***sh*** is set to 1. If ***f*** = 0, ***sh*** is cleared to 0. At step 18 the instructions are advanced for all cases. Thus the instructions were advanced twice in the case of a skip.

19. ***PC*** ← INC(***PC***)
20. → (1)

Prior to step 19 the ***PC*** is always set at the last instruction already entered in the look-ahead unit. After ***PC*** is incremented at step 19, it contains the address of the next instruction to be obtained from memory.

Control branched at step 1 to step 21 for separate execution of the JMP instruction. Indirect addressing is possible, and is provided for by steps 23, 24, and 25. Step 26 completes the jump operation by placing the new

21. ***CA0***, ***PC***, ***ro*** ← $\omega^{13}/\boldsymbol{IR}$, $\omega^{13}/\boldsymbol{IR}$, 0
22. WAIT FOR MEMORY COMPLETE PULSE
23. $\rightarrow (\boldsymbol{IR1}_3 \times 24 + \overline{\boldsymbol{IR1}_3} \times 26)$
24. ***CA0***, ***PC***, ***ro*** ← $\omega^{13}/\boldsymbol{CD0}$, $\omega^{13}/\boldsymbol{CD0}$, 1
25. WAIT
26. ***IR1***, ***sh*** ← ***CD0***, 1
27. → (19)

instruction in ***IR1*** and setting ***sh*** to 1. As the address of this instruction has already been inserted in ***PC***, the situation is the same as at step 18 following a skip instruction. This completes the discussion of the elementary look-ahead unit.

If a scratch-pad memory is included in a computer, the actual execution of certain longer instructions will be more time-consuming than the instruction fetch or the data fetch operation. In this case, further advantage would be realized by overlapping the execution phases of several instructions. This approach would considerably complicate the design of the look-ahead unit. Some instructions use as arguments the result computed by the immediately previous instructions. Other sequences of instructions are independent. It would be the responsibility of the look-ahead unit to distinguish these two situations and to allow the execution of instructions only after the required arguments become available. Further complication is introduced by conditional branch instructions. These will either terminate a sequence of overlapping instructions or possibly cause partially computed results to be discarded.

The above example should have made clear the fact that the design of a control sequence for even an elementary look-ahead unit is quite involved. The difficulties involved in handling jump and skip instructions were apparent. As we shall note in the next section, the handling of these instructions in a more sophisticated look-ahead unit requires a very powerful memory organization. We conclude this section with an example applying look-ahead in microprogramming.

Example 14.1

Design a microinstruction look-ahead unit which will make possible the execution of one microinstruction per clock pulse.

Solution. For purposes of this example, we ignore asynchronous transfers and use the earliest notation given for microsequences in Chapter 8. If we ignore the possibility of branch operations, the following single step forms a complete microsequence. This sequence is very similar to the three instruction register look-ahead

1. $\boldsymbol{MAR}$, $\boldsymbol{MIR}$, DEST($\boldsymbol{MIR}$) $\leftarrow$ INC($\boldsymbol{MAR}$), ROM$^{\perp \boldsymbol{MAR}}$, ORIG($\boldsymbol{MIR}$)
2. $\rightarrow$ (1)

unit discussed in this section. Consider the three typical microinstructions depicted in Fig. 14.15. Three instructions are involved in each step of the microsequencer. Microinstruction 1 is executed while microinstruction 2 is placed in ***MIR*** and the address of microinstruction 3 is placed in ***MAR***. During the next time step, microinstruction 2 is executed, and so on.

If microinstruction 1 is a branch, it cannot be handled by the sequence above. Regardless of the approach, it is impossible to place the next instruction, as

Microinstruction 1	Executed
Microinstruction 2	Placed in ***MIR***
Microinstruction 3	Address placed in ***MAR***

FIGURE 14.15. Sequence of three microinstructions.

specified by the branch, in ***MIR*** in one time step. The best possible timing will be achieved by the following sequence. (Note MIR_0 distinguishes between branch and

1. $\rightarrow (MIR_0 \times 4 + \overline{MIR_0} \times 2)$
2. $MAR, MIR,$ DEST(MIR) $\leftarrow$ INC(MAR), $\mathrm{ROM}^{\perp MAR}$, ORIG(MIR)
3. $\rightarrow (1)$
4. $MAR \leftarrow$ WHAT(MAR, data outside control unit)
5. $MAR, MIR \leftarrow$ INC(MAR), $\mathrm{ROM}^{\perp MAR}$
6. $\rightarrow (1)$

transfer microinstructions.) Two time steps are required to accomplish a jump instruction. ▮

14.8. EXECUTION OVERLAP

So far we have limited our discussion of throughput improvement to speeding up the movement of data. If many of these innovations are included in the design of a machine, the execution of instructions by the central processor can become the bottleneck. A preferable situation would have the data movement and computation capabilities approximately matched. In this section we begin our discussion of organizational techniques for speeding up instruction execution.

The notion of operating a computer like an assembly line with an unending series of instructions in various stages of completion has intrigued designers for many years. The instruction look-ahead problem, as discussed in the last section, and the hardware costs involved acted to keep the idea on the shelf during the early history of computing. With the advent of LSI this concept has been reexamined and in some cases put into practice. Our goal in this section will be to define the reservation control and routing system for a computer featuring simultaneous execution of instructions. Once again our system is only intended to suggest one possible approach. We begin by considering an example of overlap within a single *functional unit.*

Example 14.2

Design a multiplication unit capable of an average execution rate of one 18-bit multiplication per clock period and which will complete a given multiplication operation in three clock periods.

Solution. The reader will recall from Chapter 11 that many approaches to multiplication are possible, some requiring considerable combinational logic. We propose here a simple approach which satisfies the problem statement. No claim is made that this is a particularly efficient approach in terms of the cost of the combinational logic required. The method is illustrated in Fig. 14.16.

The multiplier is shown as composed of six strings of 3 bits each. The first step of the multiplication process computes, in parallel, six partial products by performing multiplication of each 3-bit segment times the multiplicand, ***MTND***. Each product consists of 36-bits with the significant bits of each partial product vector shifted left 3 bits (multiplied by 8) from those of the product immediately above. Those memory elements in the 36-bit products which always contain zeros would not be included in the actual physical implementation.

The second step of the operation will consist of adding ***P1***, ***P2***, and ***P3*** to form ***SUM1*** and adding ***P4***, ***P5***, and ***P6*** to form ***SUM2***. The last step consists of merely adding ***SUM1*** and ***SUM2***. Two very fast adders are assumed, which can perform the additions in a single clock period. Note that a complete carry propagation must be provided for each step. Once again we point out that quite likely breaking the process up in some other manner might permit a shorter carry propagation. The approach here was chosen for reasons of simplicity.

The registers required are illustrated in Fig. 14.17. The multiplier is stored in the register, ***MLTR***. Five control flip-flops, ***c1***, ***c2***, ***c3***, ***c4***, and ***c5***, are included to control the flow of information through the multiplier. The values of ***c1*** and ***c5*** are supplied externally, while ***c2***, ***c3***, and ***c4*** are under control of the multiplier control unit. ***c1*** = 1 indicates the presence of arguments in ***MTND*** and ***MLTR***, ***c2*** = 1 indicates that a set of six partial products are stored, ***c3*** = 1 indicates the existence of numbers in ***SUM1*** and ***SUM2***, and ***c4*** = 1 indicates the existence of a

MTND Multiplicand
A, B, C, D, E, F Multiplier in 3-bit segments

$P1 = (36)\top(\perp MTND \times \perp F)$
$P2 = (36)\top(\perp MTND \times 8 \times \perp E)$
$P3 = (36)\top(\perp MTND \times 64 \times \perp D)$ 36-bit partial products
P4 etc.
P5
P6

PROD

FIGURE 14.16. Multiplication in six segments.

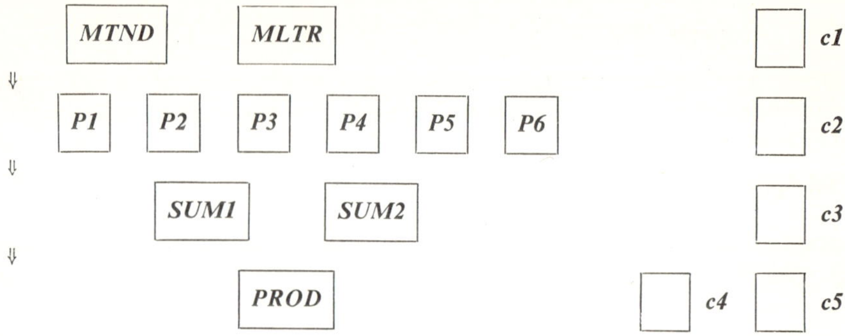

FIGURE 14.17. Registers for multiplication.

product in ***PROD***; ***c5*** = 1 indicates that the present stored product will remain in ***PROD*** after the next clock period.

1. $PROD \leftarrow \mathrm{ADD}(SUM1, SUM2) \wedge \overline{c4 \wedge c5};$
   $SUM1, SUM2 \leftarrow (\mathrm{ADD3}(P1,P2,P3), \mathrm{ADD3}(P4,P5,P6)) \wedge \overline{c3 \wedge c4 \wedge c5};$
   $P1,P2,P3,P4,P5,P6 \leftarrow \mathrm{TIMES}(MTND,MLTR) \wedge \overline{c2c3 \wedge c4 \wedge c5};$
   $c4,c3,c2 \leftarrow c3 \vee (c4 \wedge c5), c2 \vee (c3 \wedge c4 \wedge c5), c1 \vee (c2 \wedge c3 \wedge c4 \wedge c5)$
2. $\rightarrow (1)$

The multiplication control routine consists of a single step as shown. As discussed in Chapter 9, the control unit might consist of only combinational logic connected directly to the clock. At every clock period in which arguments are entered in ***MTND*** and ***MLTR***, a 1 is entered in ***c1***. With each clock pulse, the contents of the registers at each level in Fig. 14.14 are replaced by more nearly completed results in the next lower level of registers. An exception occurs if the external reservation control indicates, by inserting a 1 in ***c5***, that the result currently in ***PROD*** will not be removed during a given step. In this case, information will be advanced within the multiplication unit only insofar as empty registers exist within the unit. ▮

Execution overlap is facilitated by programming so that many consecutive instructions specify the same operation on different arguments. This is the assumption in the CDC STAR (see Section 15.9). Under these circumstances, execution overlap is referred to as *pipelining*. We shall find it convenient to refer to the array of registers containing arguments on which computation is in various stages of completion as *pipelines*.

Let us assume that a particular computer has only two arithmetic functional units, multiplication and division, which require more than one clock period for execution. Execution overlap for multiplication is as discussed in the above example. The division unit will accept arguments every four clock periods, while requiring twelve clock periods to complete a given computation.

Several additional logic units which require only one clock period for execution also exist within the machine.

Consider the look-ahead and reservation control unit required to manage this setup. Space will not permit complete development of this design, but we shall attempt to illustrate some of the complications involved. Let us assume that the machine under discussion has at least ten general-purpose data registers, along the lines discussed in Section 14.2. These are labeled *a* through *j*, as shown in Fig. 14.18a. In Fig. 14.18b we see ten arbitrary operations strung together to form an assembly language program. Although written in a distortion of APL, each step corresponds to a plausible assembly language operation. The lettered arguments refer to numerical values stored in the general-purpose data registers, while three arguments are identified by their location in RAM. These three arguments may or may not be in the associative memory.

We assume that following a branch operation, the ten instructions of Fig. 14.18 were placed in the look-ahead unit. From the point of view of the look-ahead unit, we have the unusual good fortune of only one branch instruction out of ten instructions. Let us proceed to identify the tasks which must be accomplished by the look-ahead unit during each time period. We assume that nothing has previously been done for any of these instructions. The pipelines are empty, etc.

During step 1, arguments *f* and *g* must be entered into the division pipeline. They must be somehow tagged so that the result will be recognized later. An identifier must in some way be associated with register ***e***, so that this register will not be used as an argument for the next 12 clock periods. Memory references must be initiated for the three arguments stored in RAM. The instructions must be shifted ahead in the look-ahead unit with a memory reference initiated to replace instruction 10. These last operations, which must be repeated each step, will not be mentioned again.

a	*f*
b	*g*
c	*h*
d	*i*
e	*j*

(a) Data Registers

1. $e \leftarrow f \div g$
2. $a \leftarrow g + b$
3. $a \leftarrow a + c$
4. $c \leftarrow a \times d$
5. $d \leftarrow b \times d$
6. $b \leftarrow a \times (\mathrm{RAM}^{353432})$
7. $g \leftarrow d \times a$
8. $c{:}(\mathrm{RAM}^{353433}), (\geq, <) \rightarrow (9, (\mathrm{RAM}^{357777}))$
9. $h \leftarrow e \times c$
10. $b \leftarrow g \div a$

(b)

FIGURE 14.18. APL-like assembly language program.

Instructions 2 and 3 are conveniently executed in one step each. At steps 4 and 5, two sets of arguments are entered into the multiplication pipeline. If the data word in memory location 353432 was in the associative memory, all but the register ***PROD*** of the multiplication pipeline would be filled at step 6.

At first glance it would appear that a multiplication pipeline will be completely filled at step 7. However, the look-ahead unit must observe that the argument, ***d***, is tagged and that the new value has not yet emerged from the multiplication pipeline. The control unit must wait two clock periods before instruction 7 can be initiated.

In the meantime, look-ahead control advances to step 8. Conveniently, the new value of ***c*** emerges from the multiplication pipeline at this step, so that it may be compared with the contents of memory location 353433 if available. If ***c*** is smaller, a new string of instructions must be placed in the look-ahead unit while the instructions prior to 8 are completed.

If ***c*** is larger, instruction 9 may be initiated. Depending on holdups in prior instructions, the new value of ***e*** may or may not have emerged from the division pipeline. Also at step 9, instruction 7 may be initiated as the argument, ***d***, is now available.

Clearly the design of a control unit able to keep track of all of the details discussed above would be a formidable task, and many of the details, particularly those involving new instructions being entered in the look-ahead unit, were not even mentioned.

The above discussion reflected an attempt to handle one instruction per time step. Considering all that must be done, it would be difficult indeed to realize this goal in the actual design of a look-ahead unit. Nonetheless it is necessary if one processor is to have any chance of keeping up with the multiplication pipeline. Given the achievement of the goal of one instruction per time step, it is doubtful that one processor could have more than one computation in the pipeline often enough to be worth the cost of the multiplication unit. Filling the pipelines would require an extremely cooperative programmer or compiler.

Given the possibility of multiprocessing, execution overlap may be viewed in a different light. This is the topic of the next section.

14.9. MULTIPROCESSING

In the previous section it was implied that in order to justify the cost of highly combinational arithmetic functional units, they must be kept reasonably busy. Whether this is so or not is an economic question. Factors, such as the cost of LSI, on which an answer to such a question might be based change continuously.

If the answer is "yes, they must be kept busy," then two approaches are possible. One approach is to use the computer system primarily in an environment of special problems in which the proportion of arithmetic operations to other instructions is greater than average. The highly parallel ILLIAC IV, which will be discussed in Chapter 15, is based on the premise that this is possible. Unfortunately there may be only a few such special problem environments which can afford a large-scale machine.

The other approach is to increase the rate of execution of instructions to a point at which the utilization of a particular functional unit is sufficient to justify its inclusion. In the case of the multiplication unit of the previous section, satisfactory utilization may mean only intermittent occurrences of more than one computation in the pipeline. The notion of continuously full pipelines within a general-purpose computing system may be wishful thinking.

The look-ahead unit, touched on in the previous section, represents an effort to increase the utilization rate of functional units. There it was assumed that only one program was in the process of execution at a given time. Relaxing this assumption leads to the concept of *multiprocessing*. That is, let us postulate a set of n separate control units, each executing a separate program in central memory. Such a system is illustrated in Fig. 14.19. The processors share the items requiring the heaviest investment: namely, the very large random access memory, peripheral equipments, and certain highly combinational functional units. The several processors should have less trouble keeping the pipelines filled than a single look-ahead unit.

The advantage of the system in Fig. 14.19 is efficiency. The obvious disadvantage is that it is so large, and therefore so expensive, as to be of interest to relatively few installations. Perhaps it could be sold in modular, or building block, fashion. Unfortunately, the purchaser of a single processor would find at least some hardware in his system, for which the only justification is that it will make an n processor system operate more efficiently.

With the intention of returning to the system of Fig. 14.19 later, let us consider multiprocessing as a general term. This term has been given different meanings in different contexts. For example, multiprocessing has been used in a purely software sense to refer to an operating system switching back and forth from the execution of one program to another. Some advantage may be derived from this technique if one program under execution arrives at a point where extensive I/O is required. Where DMA is employed, there can be simultaneous operations contributing to the execution of two programs. As no more than one instruction can be fetched and considered for execution at a given time, the above technique is properly referred to as *multiprogramming*. The term multiprocessing is reserved to refer to separate hardware control units executing separate programs simultaneously.

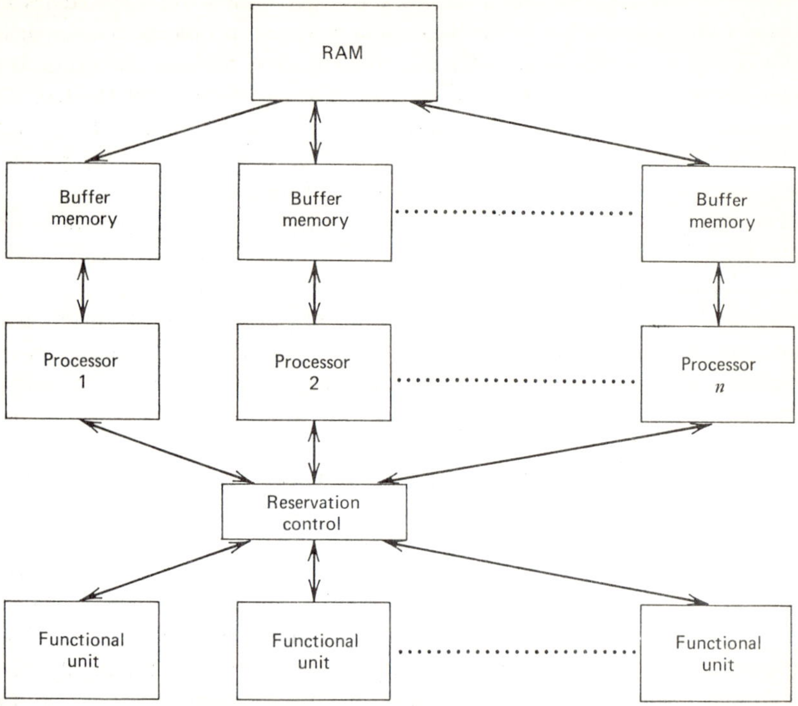

FIGURE 14.19. Multiprocessing.

Various forms of actual hardware multiprocessing may be found in existing machines. One of the earliest examples may be found in the CDC 6400 which is organized along the lines depicted in Fig. 14.20. Here the central processor executes programs simultaneously with ten *peripheral processors*. The peripheral processors handle the chores of managing input/output, preparing programs for execution, and loading the main memory. No functional units are shared by the central processor and the peripherals. The main random access memory is not shared, in the sense that only the central processor executes programs in this memory. The peripheral processors merely load and unload central memory. There is extensive hardware sharing among the peripheral processors. It might even be argued that the specialized design employed actually binds the ten peripheral processors together as one processor under a single control unit. For further details the reader is referred to the CDC reference manuals. In any case there are at least two independent control units in Fig. 14.20.

We now return to consider the configuration of Fig. 14.19 in more detail. The question might arise as to why the RAM is shared, rather than providing

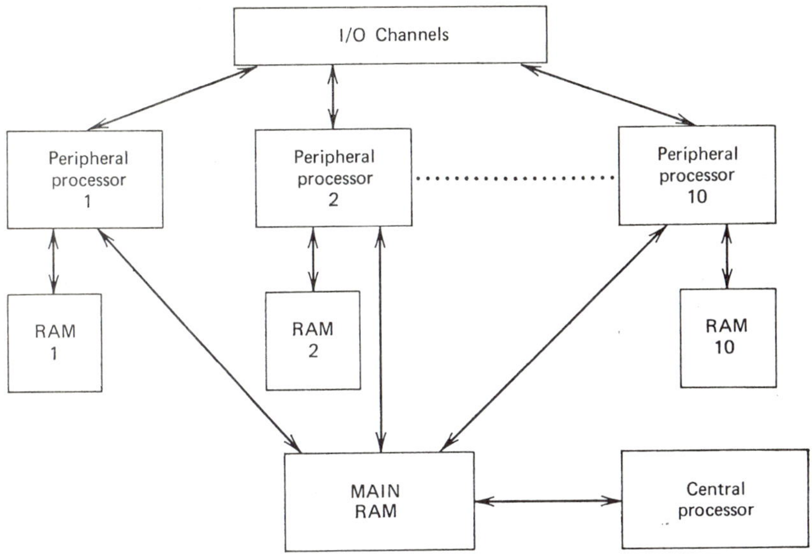

FIGURE 14.20. Input/output multiprocessing.

a separate smaller RAM for each processor. The reason is greater flexibility. If certain processors use less than their share of memory, this memory is available to a larger program which may be in the process of execution by another processor. Certain programs may even require the entire large memory. While this situation would idle all but one processor, it still might be more economical than a frequent shuffling of overlays in a smaller memory.

Dedicating the entire configuration of Fig. 14.19 to a single program raises the question "Why can't all of the processors work in parallel on the same program?" Clearly if a program is serial in nature, that is, if most program steps depend on results of immediately preceding steps, it is not possible for more than one processor to work on the problem at a given time. But perhaps many problems are not all that serial. Perhaps they just look that way after being reduced to program form. Which problems can be formulated for parallel processing given the latitude to change even the numerical techniques or models used? Which, if any, programs written in the usual manner in a high-level language could be compiled for parallel processing? How difficult would be the writing of such a compiler? These are questions which the authors cannot answer but which must be faced by a designer contemplating a system relying on parallel processing for efficiency. Some work in this direction has been accomplished in research in support of ILLIAC IV. A section of Chapter 15 will be devoted to ILLIAC IV.

One more feature of Fig. 14.19, the reservation control block, merits further consideration. The interaction of more than one separate control unit has been encountered in the text. In most cases this was a limited cooperative interaction between a processor and a supporting peripheral equipment. In Fig. 14.19 the processors are completely independent and competitive. That, at some point in time, two processors will attempt to supply arguments to one functional unit simultaneously, is unavoidable. At the minimum, some priority network must be included. More likely, the reservation control will be a separate control unit similar to the memory bank control of Section 14.4.

The reservation control cannot afford the luxury of sequential searching for requests, as was the case in the memory control. It must complete service of each request for a functional unit in only one or two clock periods. In the process it must determine the priority of conflicting requests, check availability of the functional unit, and tag arguments so that results may be returned to the correct processor. Simultaneous with servicing requests, it must return computed results. Again, no more than one or two clock periods can be allowed for this operation. Space limitations preclude presentation of the design of the reservation control. The design of a stripped-down version will be left as a problem for the reader.

14.10. VARIABLE WORD-LENGTH COMPUTERS

All of the machine organizations we have studied so far have assumed that all operations involve operands of a fixed length. No matter how complex the organization, we have assumed that each memory access involves one complete operand. The choice of the word length for such a machine necessarily involves a number of compromises. In Chapter 1 we discussed the compromises involved in choice of word length, memory size, and instruction complexity. With regard to operand size, the word length should be large enough to handle the largest operands anticipated but not so large as to waste excessive memory space on operands of average size.

For typical engineering and scientific computations, in which data are primarily numeric and the precision of data does not vary widely, reasonable compromises on a fixed word length are possible. However, in many business data processing applications, the size of basic data items varies over too wide a range to make any single word length satisfactory.

First, the size of numeric data items may vary widely. For example, an inventory program may involve thousands of individual item prices, requiring only a few digits each, and a small number of inventory totals, each requiring many digits. Even more of a problem is the fact that most data in business problems consist of alphanumeric characters. A single data item, such as a name or address, may require twenty or thirty characters; but such operations as sorting and editing require the ability to access and process individual characters.

Alphanumeric characters are coded in combinations of six to eight bits, the most common length being eight bits, with an 8-bit data unit generally referred to as a *byte*. We could, thus, provide for processing individual characters in a fixed word-length machine by making the basic word length equal to one byte, i.e., eight bits. However, this arrangement would require separate instructions for each byte processed, a requirement that would lead to intolerably long programs for even simple data processing problems. (Although the problems are not exactly the same, the reader who has tried to write character-handling programs in ordinary FORTRAN will have some conception of the difficulties involved.)

One answer to the problem of achieving efficient processing of character-oriented programs is provided by a *variable word-length* organization, in which single instructions may specify operands of any number of bytes to be processed one byte at a time. Thus the word length will always be some multiple of eight, and a word will be referenced by addressing the first byte in the word. Because machines with this organization are most useful for business data processing, they have been traditionally referred to as "business" computers, in contrast to "scientific," or fixed word-length, computers.

Since a complete operand may be very long, up to 256 bytes in typical variable word-length computers, it is not practical to provide an accumulator capable of storing a complete operand. Without an accumulator to serve as the implied source of one operand and implied destination of the results, the one-address instruction is impractical. For this reason, most variable word-length computers use two-address replacement instructions. For example, an ADD instruction would have the basic format

ADD	LOCA	LOCB

and the meaning, "Add the operand found in LOCA to the operand found in LOCB and store the sum in LOCA, replacing the first operand." The replacement aspect of this format causes difficulties when it is necessary to preserve both operands, so it might seem that the three-address format would be preferable. However, since variable word-length machines require addressing down to the byte level, they require such long addresses that three-address instructions would generally be impractically long.

Although addressing is at the byte level, this does not mean that the memory should be byte-oriented. If the basic memory word length is one byte, then n accesses will be required for an n-character operand; and since memory is relatively slow, this is very undesirable. Most variable word-length machines access several bytes at a time, with four bytes (32 bits) probably being the most common memory word length. This is the length we shall assume for the remainder of this chapter. It might seem that we are defeating our original objective of conserving memory space by using a 4-byte word, but operands of less than four characters will occur relatively infrequently. Our primary concern in the variable word-length organization is to provide for handling very long operands with reasonable efficiency.

Next let us consider the implications of our choice of memory word length on the addressing problems. First, we note that addressing to the byte level will require two more bits than addressing to the word level, with four bytes per word. For example, with a memory of 128k words, there will be 512k bytes, requiring 19-bit addresses. Two addresses will, therefore, require 38 bits; so an instruction cannot be fitted into a single memory word. We can make two accesses to memory for each instruction fetch, but we would like to avoid that if possible.

One way to reduce the number of address bits required in the instruction is *base-addressing*. We divide the 128k words of memory into 64 segments of 2k words each, and specify a 6-bit *base-address register*, into which we place the six most-significant-bits of the address of the first word in the 2k segment we wish to address. The address in the instruction then need specify only which byte out of 8k (2k words of four bytes each) is desired, which requires only 13 bits; so our two addresses will fit into a single memory word.

While this scheme saves address bits, it is inconvenient from the programmer's point of view. Anytime he wants an operand or instruction not in the current 2k segment, he must reset the base-address register. This problem may be alleviated by having several base-address registers, and adding bits to the instruction to indicate which one is to be used. For example, we could have four base-address registers and add two bits to the instruction to designate which one is to be used. An instruction could then access any of 8k words in memory, in any four 2k groups in memory.

With the two bits added for base-address designation, we need 28 bits for addressing, leaving four bits for the op code for memory reference instructions. This might be sufficient, but we have not yet indicated the length of the operands. The addresses will specify the first bytes in each operand, but the number of bytes must also be specified. There are two methods used to specify operand length. The most obvious is to add bits to the instruction, but this gets us right back into problems with the instruction length. A widely used alternative is to use a special symbol, the *word mark*, in the operand itself, to identify the last byte. There are a variety of ways of coding the word mark, but the simplest is to set aside one bit position in each byte, which will be 1 only for the last byte of an operand.

Let us now consider a partial organization and instruction sequence for a computer embodying the features discussed above. The memory word length will consist of 128k words of 32 bits (four bytes) each. The instruction format will be as shown below. *BA* is the number of the base-address register. The

OP	*BA*	ADDRESS *A*	ADDRESS *B*
0 3	4 5	6 18	19 31

two low-order bits of each address will be the byte number, i.e., 00 will signify the first byte in the word (bit 0 to bit 7), 01 will signify the second byte (bit 8 to bit 15), etc. The catenation of the upper eleven bits in the address the six bits of the specified base-address register will form the address of the word in memory. Operands will start with the byte addressed and will be processed from left to right in each word, through consecutive memory locations, until the word mark is encountered. The word mark will be a 1 in the high-order bit of a byte.

A partial block diagram of the computer is shown in Fig. 14.21. There are two 32-bit operand registers, ***MDA*** and ***MDB***, and two 1-byte operand registers, *A* and *B*, which provide the operands for the ALU. The ALU provides the logic to carry out various operations such as AND, OR, ADD, etc. The results go to a third 1-byte register, ***C***, from which they are returned to ***MDA***. The byte counters, ***BCA*** and ***BCB***, are 2-bit counters to keep track

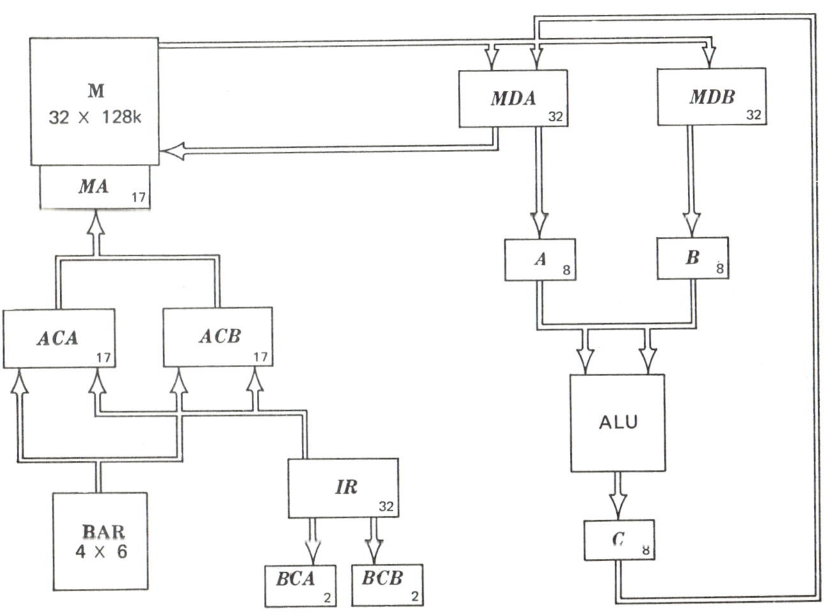

FIGURE 14.21. Partial block diagram of variable word-length computer.

of which bytes in ***MDA*** and ***MDB*** are currently being processed. The instruction register, ***IR***, holds the 32-bit instruction currently being executed. ***BAR*** is the matrix of four 6-bit base-address registers. The two 17-bit address counters, *ACA* and *ACB*, keep track of the addresses of the operand words.

Now let us consider the control sequence for the implementation of typical memory reference instruction. These instructions will obtain variable length arguments specified by addresses *A* and ***B***, perform a logical or arithmetic computation, and place the result in the memory space specified by address *A*. We will assume that the instruction has been fetched and loaded into ***IR*** and that the base-address registers have been loaded by previous instructions. The basic flow chart of the sequence is shown in Fig. 14.22.

We start with step 5, assuming that the first four steps fetched the instruction and branched to the appropriate sequence. Steps 5 and 6 form the initial word addresses from the upper eleven bits of the addresses in the instruction and the six bits of the selected base-address register. Step 7 loads the low-

5. $ACA \leftarrow \mathrm{BAR}^{\perp(IR_4,\, IR_5)},\ \alpha^{11}/\omega^{26}/IR$
6. $ACB \leftarrow \mathrm{BAR}^{\perp(IR_4,\, IR_5)},\ \alpha^{11}/\omega^{13}/IR$
7. $BCA \leftarrow \alpha^2/\omega^{15}/IR;\ BCB \leftarrow \omega^2/IR$
8. $MA \leftarrow ACA$
9. $MDA \leftarrow \mathrm{M}^{\perp MA}$
10. $MA \leftarrow ACB$
11. $MDB \leftarrow \mathrm{M}^{\perp MA}$

order two bits of each address into the byte counters. Steps 8 to 11 fetch the first words of the two operands from memory. Step 12 loads the appropriate

12. $A \leftarrow \mathrm{BYSEL}(BCA,MDA);\ B \leftarrow \mathrm{BYSEL}(BCB,MDB)$
13. $C \leftarrow \mathrm{ALOP}(A,B,\alpha^4/IR)$
14. $\mathrm{BYSEL}(BCA,MDA) \leftarrow C$

bytes into *A* and *B*. BYSEL is a combinational logic subroutine to select the desired byte from ***MDA*** or ***MDB*** as determined by the contents of the byte counters. At step 13, ALOP represents the appropriate operation by the ALU, as specified by the op code. We are assuming any "byte-by-byte" operation, i.e., one in which there is no carry over from one byte to the next. At step 14 the result from *C* is returned to the appropriate byte destination in *MDA*.

This completes the operations on one byte. The remainder of the sequence consists of "bookkeeping" operations to sequence through the remaining bytes of the operands. Step 15 checks to see if the end of the operand has been reached. For this example we assume that both operands are the same

15. $A_0:1,\ (=,\neq) \rightarrow (16,18)$
16. $MA \leftarrow ACA$
17. $\mathrm{M}^{\perp MA} \leftarrow MDA,\ \rightarrow$ (Fetch next instruction)

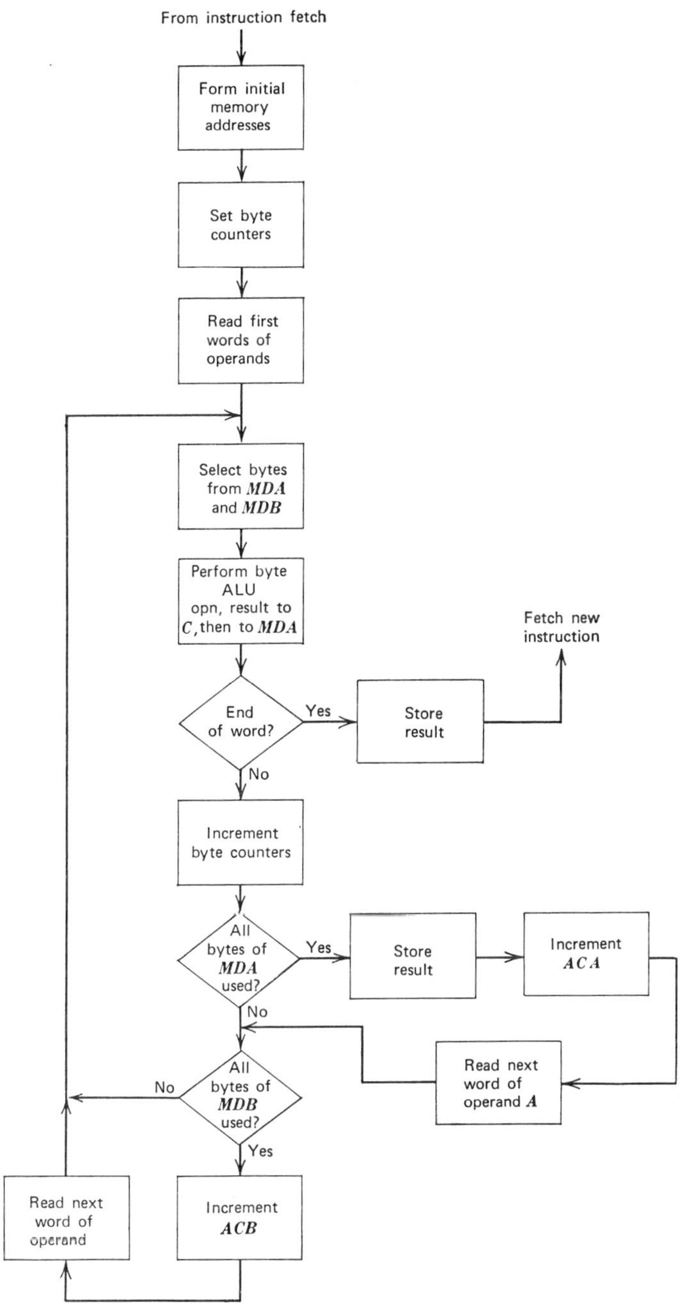

FIGURE 14.22. Flow chart of typical *MRI* sequence in variable word-length computer.

length, so the byte of operand *A* just processed is checked for an end-of-word mark. If an end-of-word mark is sensed, steps 16 and 17 store the result, and branch to fetch a new instruction. If the end of the operands has not been

18. $BCA \leftarrow \text{INC}(BCA);\ BCB \leftarrow \text{INC}(BCB)$
19. $(\bot BCA):0,\ (=,\neq) \rightarrow (20,25)$
20. $MA \leftarrow ACA$
21. $\mathrm{M}^{\bot MA} \leftarrow MDA$
22. $ACA \leftarrow \text{INC}(ACA)$
23. $MA \leftarrow ACA$
24. $MDA \leftarrow \mathrm{M}^{\bot MA}$
25. $(\bot BCB):0,\ (=,\neq) \rightarrow (26,12)$
26. $BCB \leftarrow \text{INC}(BCB)$
27. $MA \leftarrow BCB$
28. $MDB \leftarrow \mathrm{M}^{\bot MA},\ \rightarrow (12)$

reached, step 18 increments the byte counters and step 19 checks to see if all the bytes in ***MDA*** have been processed. The byte counters are modulo-2 counters, with the sequence 00, 01, 10, 11, then returning to 00. If the counter reads 00 after incrementing, all bytes in the word have been processed. In that event, the result in ***MDA*** is stored, ***ACA*** is incremented, and the next word of operand *A* read out. Steps 25–28 check to see if the operand in ***MDB*** has been fully processed and read out a new word if required. After any new word has been accessed, control returns to step 12 to continue the byte processing, Note that independent byte counters are provided, on the assumption that the two operands need not start in the same byte-position of a word.

Another distinct feature of the variable word-length computer is the manner of performing arithmetic. In the fixed word-length computer, numeric operators are fully converted from decimal to binary on input, e.g., 169 is converted to 10101001, so there is no correlation between any specific binary bits and any specific decimal digits. Performing this conversion to a variable word-length format is considerably more complicated. Therefore, numeric operators, like alphanumeric, are converted into binary code on a digit-by-digit basis. There are a variety of codes used, but the most common is the direct 4-bit binary equivalent, generally referred to as binary-coded-decimal, or BCD. Thus, the BCD equivalent for 169 would be 0001 0110 1001. (The spaces between digits are shown only for clarity, and would not be present in the computer.) Since a decimal digit requires only four bits for code, there is a question of how best to arrange them in 8-bit bytes. They may be stored one digit to a byte in the low-order four bits, with the upper four bits 0 except in the case of end-of-word mark, or they may be packed two digits to a byte.

The use of BCD representation obviously requires that arithmetic be done

Decimal	Binary	BCD
73	1001001	0111 0011
62	0111110	0110 0010
135	10000111	0001 0011 0101

FIGURE 14.23. Addition in decimal, binary, and BCD.

on a digit-by-digit basis. To illustrate the difference, the addition of two numbers is shown below in both binary and BCD. In the BCD mode, addition in each digit position forms a BCD sum digit, with a carry into the next digit if the sum exceeds nine. The addition of two BCD digits is generally done in two steps. First, the digits are added as conventional 4-bit binary numbers, producing a 4- or 5-bit binary sum. If the sum exceeds nine, a carry is stored for addition to the next digit position; and the sum digit is corrected to the correct BCD value. The correction is done by adding binary six to the sum. We will leave it to the reader to satisfy himself that adding binary six to a binary number between 10 and 18 will produce the correct BCD value of the lower-order digit in the four lower-order bits of the sum.

To further illustrate the process of addition, as well as some other features of variable word-length computers, let us consider the process of addition in a computer of the IBM System/360–370 family, as in Example 14.3. The various models of System/360–370, although "program-compatible," differ considerably in details of organization and functioning; thus the following should be considered as representative rather than exactly descriptive of any particular computer.

Example 14.3

System/360–370 computers can operate in either a fixed or variable word-length mode. For operations in the variable word-length mode, instructions are in the *SS* (Storage-to-Storage) format, and have the same replacement meaning as covered above. There are two important distinctions between the *SS* instructions and those discussed earlier. First, four bits are used to designate one of up to 16 possible base-address registers, and a separate base-address may be specified for each address. Second, the length of the operand, up to 256 bytes, is specified in the instruction, so that no word marks are needed.

The *SS* format is shown in Fig. 14.24. The total length of the instruction is six

OP	Length	BAA	Address A	BAB	Address B
←1→	←1→	$\frac{1}{2}$	←$1\frac{1}{2}$→	$\frac{1}{2}$	←$1\frac{1}{2}$→

FIGURE 14.24. *SS* instruction format.

bytes (48 bits) and the lengths of the various segments are shown in bytes in Fig. 14.24. The memory word length in various System/360–370 models may be 16, 32, or 64 bits; so the fetch of an *SS* instruction may require one, two, or three memory accesses. We shall again assume a 32-bit memory word length, requiring two accesses for an *SS* instruction, with the right half of the second word being discarded. BAA and BAB are the designators for the base-address registers. As before, the lower-order two bits in the addresses will designate the byte address, with the upper ten forming the lower-order portion of the word address. The base-address registers are 24 bits in length, and are *added* to the 10-bit addresses from the instruction, to generate 24-bit addresses.

The register configuration will be only slightly different from that shown in Fig. 14.21. The ***ACA***, ***ACB***, and ***MA*** registers will be 24 bits in length, and the dimensions of **BAR** will be 16 × 24. There will be one new register, ***LR***, an 8-bit counter used to keep track of the number of bytes processed; and the ***C*** register will be nine bits, to provide for storage of the carry. Also, we will assume a direct path from memory to ***IR*** for instruction fetches.

Since the fetch process is somewhat more complex, we shall include it in our program. The first two steps read the first word, containing the op code, length, and first address, into *IR*.

1. $MA \leftarrow PC$
2. $IR \leftarrow \mathbf{M}^{\perp MA}$
3. $\rightarrow ((IR_0 \wedge IR_1) \times 4) + (\overline{(IR_0 \wedge IR_1)} \times \text{Non-SS})$
4. $ACA \leftarrow (\mathbf{BAR}^{\perp(\alpha^4/\omega^{16}/IR)}, \alpha^{10}/\omega^{12}/IR)$
5. $BCA \leftarrow \omega^2/IR$

An *SS* instruction is indicated by the first two bits of the op code being 1. Step 3 checks for this condition, and branches to other sequences if the instruction is not of the *SS* type. Step 4 forms the word address of the first operand in ***ACA*** and step 5 loads the byte address into ***BCA***. Steps 6–10 fetch the second word of the instruction and load ***ACB*** and ***BCB***.

6. $PC \leftarrow \text{INC}(PC)$
7. $MA \leftarrow PC$
8. $\omega^{16}/IR \leftarrow \alpha^{16}/\mathbf{M}^{\perp MA}$
9. $ACB \leftarrow (\mathbf{BAR}^{\perp(\alpha^4/\omega^{16}/IR)}, \alpha^{10}/\omega^{12}/IR)$
10. $BCB \leftarrow \omega^2/IR$

Step 11 loads the operand length (in bytes) into ***LR***, and steps 12–15 load the first words of the operands into ***MDA*** and ***MDB***.

11. $LR \leftarrow \omega^8/\alpha^{16}/IR$
12. $MA \leftarrow ACA$
13. $MDA \leftarrow \mathbf{M}^{\perp MA}$
14. $MA \leftarrow ACB$
15. $MDB \leftarrow \mathbf{M}^{\perp MA}$

Step 16 checks the op code and branches accordingly. The remainder of our program will consider the sequence for ADD only. In System/360–370 computers, decimal digits may be stored one or two to a byte; but for arithmetic operations they are packed two to a byte, in standard BCD code. The decimal adder, which we shall call by the combinational logic subroutine DECADD, combines two digits of each operand and an input carry from the previous two digits, to form two digits of the sum and an output carry. To accommodate these, the $\boldsymbol{C}$ register is enlarged to nine bits, with the output carry going to $\boldsymbol{C}_0$.

17. $\boldsymbol{C}_0 \leftarrow 0$
18. $\boldsymbol{A} \leftarrow \text{BYSEL}(\boldsymbol{BCA}, \boldsymbol{MDA})$; $\boldsymbol{B} \leftarrow \text{BYSEL}(\boldsymbol{BCB}, \boldsymbol{MDB})$
19. $\boldsymbol{C} \leftarrow \text{DECADD}(\boldsymbol{A}, \boldsymbol{B}, \boldsymbol{C}_0)$
20. $\text{BYSEL}(\boldsymbol{BCA}, \boldsymbol{MDA}) \leftarrow \omega^8/\boldsymbol{C}$

Step 17 sets the input carry to zero, step 18 moves the proper bytes into $\boldsymbol{A}$ and $\boldsymbol{B}$, step 19 carries out the addition, and step 20 stores the two digits of sum, leaving the input carry for the next two digits in $\boldsymbol{C}_0$. This completes the addition of two digits, and the remainder of the program consists of the "bookkeeping" operations required to sequence the digits through the added in the proper sequence.

Step 21 decrements the byte count in $\boldsymbol{LR}$ by one, and step 22 checks to see if the end of the operands has been reached. If so, steps 23 and 24 store the final word of the result and exit to the next instruction fetch.

21. $\boldsymbol{LR} \leftarrow \text{DEC}(\boldsymbol{LR})$
22. $(\perp \boldsymbol{LR}):0, (=, \neq) \rightarrow (23, 25)$
23. $\boldsymbol{MA} \leftarrow \boldsymbol{ACA}$
24. $\mathbf{M}^{\perp \boldsymbol{MA}} \leftarrow \boldsymbol{MDA}, \rightarrow$ (Fetch Next Instruction)

The remaining steps in the program are the same as presented previously, except for the direction of sequencing through the successive bytes and words. When processing alphanumeric characters, it is convenient to proceed from left to right, as one does in reading or writing normal text. But arithmetic operation must proceed from right to left, starting with the least-significant-digit. When data are read in, they are normally read from left to right, as they would appear, for example, on punched cards; and they are stored in sequentially increasing locations in memory. One could store decimal numbers in the opposite order; but this would be very inconvenient as it would mean specifying in advance whether those data may be considered only as alphanumeric or decimal. It is more usual to specify that arithmetic operations will sequence through the operands in the opposite direction. To accomplish this, the byte counters and address counters are decremented instead of incremented. Except for this, steps 25–35 of this example correspond exactly to steps 18–28 of the previous presentation.

25. $\boldsymbol{BCA} \leftarrow \text{DEC}(\boldsymbol{BCA})$; $\boldsymbol{BCB} \leftarrow \text{DEC}(\boldsymbol{BCB})$
26. $(\perp \boldsymbol{BCA}):3, (=, \neq) \rightarrow (27, 32)$
27. $\boldsymbol{MA} \leftarrow \boldsymbol{ACA}$
28. $\mathbf{M}^{\perp \boldsymbol{MA}} \leftarrow \boldsymbol{MDA}$
29. $\boldsymbol{ACA} \leftarrow \text{DEC}(\boldsymbol{ACA})$

30. $MA \leftarrow ACA$
31. $MDA \leftarrow M^{\perp MA}$
32. $(\perp BCB)$:3, $(=, \neq) \rightarrow (33, 18)$
33. $ACB \leftarrow$ DEC(ACB)
34. $MA \leftarrow ACB$
35. $MDB \leftarrow M^{\perp MA}, \rightarrow (18)$ ∎

As the previous examples illustrate, the internal organization and functioning of the variable word-length computer will be considerably more complex than that of the fixed word-length machine. Nevertheless, the increased efficiency of these machines for business-oriented problems generally justifies the increased complexity. For example, decimal arithmetic is definitely slower than binary. However, business processing generally involves a great many I/O operations and character-oriented operations and relatively few arithmetic operations. Thus, the relative inefficiency of arithmetic operations is more than compensated for by the greater efficiency of I/O conversions using the BCD format.

One of the biggest problems in this type of computer is the time penalty involved in the multiple memory accesses, and a great variety of techniques have been applied to minimize this penalty. One common technique is the use of a split-cycle in memory, to take advantage of the fact that since the *A* operand is to be replaced, there is no reason to rewrite it after reading. Rewriting typically requires about 60% of the time of a full memory cycle in a core memory, and a split-cycle allows one the option of reading without rewriting. Thus, the *A* operand is read first in a read-only operation, leaving the location cleared. The *B* operand is then read, and the rewrite takes place while processing continues. When ready, the result is stored in the already-cleared location with a write-only operation. The net result is a saving of one memory cycle out of three. The reader can probably identify other points in the program where memory accesses can overlap processing steps.

Interrupts also present a special problem in this type of computer. We have seen that certain interrupts must be serviced in a relatively short time. With the variable word-length organization, the duration of any given operation is unpredictable; so it may be necessary to interrupt in the middle of the execution of an instruction. Preserving the status of an incompletely-executed instruction will obviously be more difficult than for one that has been completed.

The relative merits of the two types of organizations, fixed and variable word-length, is still a subject of considerable debate. IBM has, in a sense, avoided the debate by providing both types of operations in the System/360–370 machines. Naturally, providing both types of operations requires even more complex organization than providing either separately. However, as advances in integrated circuits make ever-more-complex functions available at ever-decreasing cost, it is quite possible that the general trend in computer design will be toward more-and-more complex machines.

14.11. SUMMARY

In this chapter, as has been the case throughout most of the book, the emphasis has been on how to design rather than on what to design. Various factors which influence design decisions in large machines have been pointed out, but no systematic procedure for evaluating these factors has been presented. The reader can no doubt see the advantage of an analytical model which will indicate whether such features as associative memories, look-ahead, pipelining, or multiprocessing should be employed in a given design. Models of this type have in fact been developed, but have generally been very complex and applicable only to specific situations.

Rather than attempting to present a representative sampling of decision models, we merely call the reader's attention to their general use. As the costs implied by a design decision in the computer area are often very great, the designer must endeavor to take advantage of any analytical aids available.

PROBLEMS

14.1 Write in AHPL the control sequences for Type I and Type II increment instructions in terms of the hardware configuration of Fig. 14.3.

14.2 Write in AHPL the control sequence for the complete fetch cycle of the machine in Fig. 14.3. Continue the sequence for Type I and Type II instructions to the point where control must separate for the execution of individual instructions.

14.3 Consider a machine whose slow, large-capacity RAM is arranged in blocks of 16 words. Each time a request is made for one of the words in a block, the entire block is read into a memory data register in one operation. Suppose a single central processor will request words from this memory at a rate exceeding the reciprocal of the read time of this memory. Often the requests will be for data from consecutive memory locations and can be serviced at an increased rate. Write a control sequence for this memory so that it will satisfy as nearly as possible the needs of the mentioned central processor. Define control and data registers as needed.

14.4 Compare the efficiencies of the memory of Problem 14.3 with the multiple-bank arrangement of Fig. 14.5. Form a conjecture as to their respective abilities to satisfy the requests of a processor which may request data at a rate four times the reciprocal of the memory cycle time. How might hard data be obtained to substantiate this conjecture? Supply some details.

14.5 Write the combinational logic subroutine ASSOC. This routine was used in Section 14.5.

14.6 Write a control sequence which will handle all memory references in the 16-bank configuration of Fig. 14.5.

14.7 Define the control lines between the Main Control Sequencer memory routine and the associative memory controller in Section 14.5. Modify step 6 of the memory routine and step 8 of the associative memory controller to provide for pulses on these specific lines.

14.8 Combine the control sequences of Section 14.5 so that all memory references are handled by a Memory Control Sequencer. All memory references in the main control sequence will require a transfer of control to this unit. Write this sequence in AHPL. Discuss the advantages and disadvantages of this approach.

14.9 Step 14 of Section 14.7 uses a Boolean function, f, to control whether or not a skip is to be executed. Write a Boolean algebraic expression for f.

14.10 Write in AHPL a control sequence for the virtual memory controller shown in Fig. 14.13. Define additional address and data registers as needed.

14.11 The associative memory controller of Section 14.5 requests only one word at a time from the RAM. Modify the control sequence so that each request for a word in RAM will cause the three succeeding words to be placed in the associative memory as well. Assume that the associative memory is dealing with an interleaved multibank RAM, so that these transfers can take place approximately in parallel.

14.12 Consider a look-ahead unit similar to the unit discussed in Section 14.7, but containing a block of 16 instruction registers, so that small loops can be contained within the unit. Assume the instructions are replaced as a block after the last one is executed, or upon a jump out of the block. Write an AHPL control sequence for this look-ahead unit. Assume a 16-bank RAM but no scratch pad. Execution of the first instruction in a new block should begin as soon as it is received from memory.

14.13 Design the control sequence to a single computer which will appear as eight separate copies of SIC. Consider memory reference instructions only. The machine will have a 64k core memory. Devise an economic technique for achieving an access time for each processor equal to the overall access time of the machine. (Hint: Consider CDC 6400 peripheral processors.)

14.14 Write the control sequence for the reservation control in Fig. 14.19. Assume that each request for a functional unit must be accomplished in no more than two clock periods.

14.15 For a shift command in a variable word-length computer, only one address is needed. System/360 computers use several formats for shift instructions; one is the same as the *SS* format (Fig. 14.24) except that the *B* address is omitted. For such a command, the shift is one digit left or right, the direction of shift being indicated by the last bit of the op code: 0 indicating right and 1, left. Write a control sequence for shifting in a machine having the configuration described in Example 14.3.

14.16 Multiplication in a variable word-length computer may be done as follows: the first digit of the multiplicand is multiplied by the first digit of the multiplier; the low-order digit of the resultant product is stored in the low-order position of the product location; the second digit being saved for the next cycle; the second digit of the multiplicand is then multiplied by the first multiplier digit; the low-order digit of this product is added to the carry from the first multiplication, the sum being stored in the second digit position of the product location. This procedure is repeated until the multiplicand is completely multiplied by the first multiplier digit. The same process is then carried out for the second multiplier digit, with the resultant partial product, shifted one place left, being added to the first partial product. This is repeated for each multiplier digit in turn until the multiplication is completed. Assume a machine having the configuration of Example 14.3 and the SS instruction format of Fig. 14.24. Since both the multiplier and multiplicand must be preserved for the entire sequence, the product cannot replace either operand. Assume that operand *A* is the multiplier, operand *B* is the multiplicand, and the product is to be stored in the appropriate number of sequential locations immediately following the multiplicand. Write a control sequence for multiplication in this machine.

14.17 One of the character-handling commands in System/360 is TRANSLATE, which functions as follows. The instruction, in the *SS* format, specifies two addresses. The first address specifies an operand ranging from 1 to 256 bytes in length. The second address specifies the origin of a function table of bytes defining the desired translation. In execution, each byte of the argument, scanning from left to right, is in turn replaced by a function byte from the table. The location of the function byte is obtained by adding the argument byte to the table origin. Write a control sequence for executing the TRANSLATE instruction in the configuration of Example 14.3.

REFERENCES

1. Flores, Ivan, *Computer Organization*, Prentice-Hall, Englewood Cliffs, N.J., 1969.
2. Hellerman, H., *Digital System Principles*, McGraw-Hill, New York, 1967.
3. Murphy, J. O., and Wade, R. M., "The IBM 360/195 in a World of Mixed Jobstreams," *Datamation*, April 1970, p. 72.
4. Thorton, J. E., *Design of a Computer*, *The CDC 6600*, Scott-Foresman and Company, 1970.
5. Chen, T. C., "Parallelism, Pipelining and Computer Efficiency," *Computer Design*, Jan. 1971, p. 69.
6. Meade, R. M., "Design Approaches for Cache Memory Control," *Computer Design*, Jan 1971, p. 87.
7. Jones, R. M., "Factors Affecting the Efficiency of a Virtual Memory," *IEEE Trans. Computers*, Nov. 1969, p. 1004.
8. "Control Data 7600 Computer System," *Reference Manual*, Publication No. 60258200.
9. *A Guide to the IBM System/370 Model 165*, GC20-1730-0
10. "Control Data 6400/6500/6600 Computer System," *Reference Manual*, Publication No. 60100000

15

Special-Purpose Systems and Special-Purpose Computers

15.1. INTRODUCTION

Our point of view in this chapter will differ somewhat from that of Chapter 14. In that chapter we attempted to discuss most of the important features which have been utilized to increase the speed of large machines. As we turn our attention to special-purpose systems, the field of view becomes much broader, far too broad for an exhaustive treatment. Here our purpose will be to convey a design philosophy by considering only a sampling of design examples. The techniques illustrated will be applicable to a much broader class of problems.

Many *special-purpose vector-handling digital systems* are not in themselves computers. Some systems, such as I/O and display devices, may be parts of computing facilities. Other systems, such as the digital filter, are intended to function as stand-alone units. The first few sections will illustrate the use of AHPL in a variety of designs. Each example is interesting in its own right, and each is related to a different discipline.

Beginning with Section 15.5 we turn our attention to special-purpose computers. Most of the designs in these later sections will not be carried through to control sequence form. Typically we shall be concerned with the layout and definition of the system at the beginning of the design process. Of particular interest is Section 15.7, which establishes design parameters for the *master computer* of a time-sharing system. In that section a simple cost/performance analysis of time-sharing systems is made. It is illustrative of similar analyses which might be used to determine a first approximation of cost-effectiveness of other systems.

It is the authors' feeling that the availability of MSI logic and LSI memories and ROM's will greatly simplify the design of special-purpose systems and lead to the development of many more such machines. Most special-purpose machines will be microprogrammed. To use microprogramming in subsequent sections of this chapter would have lengthened the discussions considerably. We assume that the reader could easily devise microinstruction formats and translate the AHPL sequences into a microassembly language.

15.2. PUSH-DOWN STORAGE

A very useful special-purpose feature which might be included in a processor is a *push-down storage unit*, sometimes called an *LIFO* (last-in-first-out) list, or a *stack*. No attempt will be made to design a complete special-purpose processor. Only the stack mechanism, which could be included in any machine, will be discussed.

Only three special registers are required in one simple implementation of a stack. Two of these registers, ***R1*** and ***R2***, are the same length as words in the random access memory, **M**. The other register, ***STA***, must store a memory address. Each word entered in the stack is placed in ***R1***. At the same time the word already in ***R1*** is pushed down to ***R2***, and the word in ***R2*** is placed at the top of a list in the RAM. The address of the top word in the list is stored in ***STA***. It is assumed that additional memory space is available at the top of the list. When a word is retrieved from the top of the stack, the rest of the stack moves up one position.

A slightly improved stack control sequence is listed in Fig. 15.1. The new feature is that the register ***R1*** is kept empty so that a new word can be placed on the top of the stack in a single clock period. The main control sequence can thus continue with other activities while the stack is pushed down one

1. $R1, sr \leftarrow AC, 0$
2. $STA \leftarrow \text{INC}(STA)$
3. $M^{\perp STA} \leftarrow R2$
4. $R2 \leftarrow R1$
5. $sr \leftarrow 1$

(a) Push stack down

1. $AC, sr \leftarrow R2, 0$
2. $R2 \leftarrow M^{\perp STA}$
3. $STA \leftarrow \text{DEC}(STA)$
4. $sr \leftarrow 1$

(b) Fetch from stack

FIGURE 15.1. Stack control.

position. A flip-flop, ***sr***, indicates whether or not the stack is ready. A word is taken from or deposited on the stack only if $sr = 1$.

Notice, in the stack fetch sequence of Fig. 15.1b, that the top word is taken immediately from ***R2*** in one clock period. Then the first word of the stack in memory is placed in ***R2***, and ***STA*** is decremented at step 3. The effect of the control sequence in Fig. 15.1 is a stack which can respond much more rapidly than the machine's RAM. This is accomplished using little extra hardware.

15.3. A DISPLAY PROCESSOR

In the last several years the use of computers to control the display on cathode ray tubes has become common. Such systems are often called *graphics terminals*. In this section a simple special-purpose processor will be designed for this function. Whether or not it is a computer is arguable. To permit a single section discussion, the system has been kept as simple as possible. Still, many of the pertinent considerations are introduced, and some interesting design approaches are illustrated.

Our system will provide the display of a picture consisting of alphanumeric characters and interconnected line segments. This picture may be modified by the user sitting in front of the tube. To be of value, the system must have the capability of permanently storing or outputting a data description of the picture to other systems. Although not discussed, we presume this capability to be present. One application example would be the construction of a diffusion mask for an LSI circuit on a graphics terminal. When completed, the data description would be fed to a controller for an automatic drafting machine to initiate the mask-making process.

User control of the system will be effected by typing commands on a keyboard or by operating what has become known as a *joy stick*. The joy stick is simply a lever, movable in two dimensions, which positions a small cross (+) on the tube. This cross indicates the starting point for the next line segment to be placed on the display. If a character is entered, the lower left

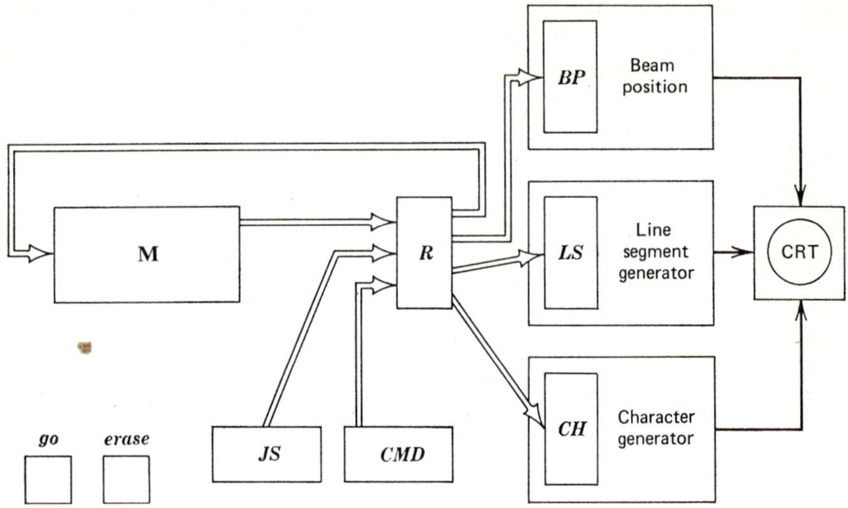

FIGURE 15.2. Display processor hardware.

corner of the character will rest on the center of the cross. For simplicity, the keyboard will include a separate key for each command in addition to the alphanumeric keys. In more complex systems, commands are typed in. This, of course, implies software for compiling the commands.

A skeleton hardware configuration is depicted in Fig. 15.2. The memory **M** is not random access. Only the word in $\mathbf{M}^0$ can be read out at any given time. The same pulse which will cause $\mathbf{M}^0$ to be placed in the register ***R*** will rotate the remaining rows up one position and place the contents of ***R*** in the last location of **M**. Very likely **M** will be constructed using inexpensive MOS shift registers.

Three units, which we shall not design in detail, actually control the movement of the beam on the CRT (cathode ray tube). A control pulse to the *beam position* unit will cause the beam to be blanked while it is moved to the (x, y) position specified by the two 9-bit segments of the 18-bit register, ***BP***. This unit must convert the two numbers in ***BP*** to analog form and take control of the beam from the other two units. A control pulse to the *line segment* generator will cause the beam to trace a line on the scope from its current position on the CRT to the position specified by the coordinates stored in ***LS***. A pulse to the *character* generator will cause two characters to be written on the CRT.

In the absence of inputs from the user, information specifying commands to the three activity units are continuously circulated in **M**. Each time a display command emerges from **M**, the corresponding line or character is

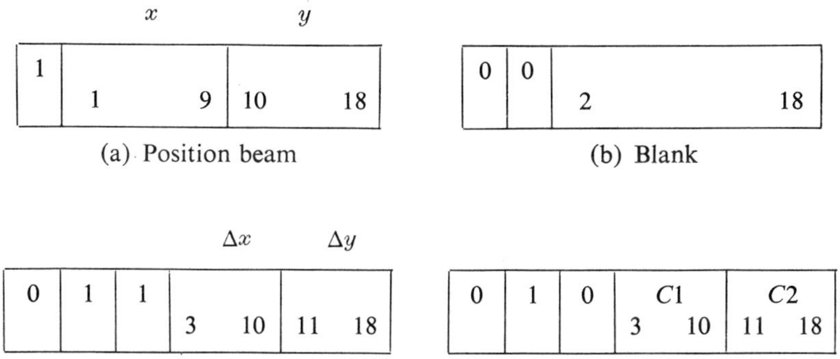

(a) Position beam

(b) Blank

(c) Display line segment

(d) Display 2 characters

FIGURE 15.3. Display commands.

refreshed on the CRT. The formats of the display commands are given in Fig. 15.3. All commands contain 19 bits, so the word length of **M** is 19 bits. A 1 in the left-most bit position indicates a command to reposition the beam. Nine bits indicate the new x coordinate and 9 bits the new y coordinate. If the left-most two bits are both 0, the word is blank and available for storing a new user command. The format of Fig. 15.3c specifies tracing a line segment of length and direction given by $(\Delta x, \Delta y)$. Sign bits are included. The last command specifies the tracing of two alphanumeric characters.

How often must a character or line be retraced on the scope in order that the user will not notice a flicker? This will depend on many factors, an excellent discussion of which may be found in Reference [10]. For the more commonly used CRT phosphors, a repetition rate of between 35 and 50 Hz is recommended. The times required for positioning and line and character drawing vary widely in existing systems. Let's assume the relatively fast positioning time of 20 μsec, a two-character writing time of 20 μsec, and a line-tracing time of 20 μsec. Input command processing and other operations will require neglible time by comparison. We assume that each command must be retraced 40 times in a second. Therefore, each command in **M** will occupy the processor 800 μsec out of each second; and **M** should be constructed to store less than $10^6/800 = 1250$ words.

User inputs to the system are accomplished through registers ***JS*** and ***CMD***, as illustrated in Fig. 15.2. The 18-bit register, ***JS***, which is formatted according to the right-most 18 bits of Fig. 15.3a, instantaneously reflects the position of the joy stick. The format of ***CMD*** reflects the format of the right-most 18 bits in Figs. 15.3c,d. Data and commands are entered into this register from the keyboard. The considerable combinational logic between the keyboard and ***CMD*** will not be detailed.

The registers ***JS*** and ***CMD*** will have no effect unless the user causes one of the flip-flops, ***go*** or ***erase***, to be set to 1. If ***go*** = 1, a new command is to be displayed and stored in **M**. If ***erase*** = 1, control searches for any positioning command with coordinates equal to the present contents of ***JS***. All such commands and the corresponding display commands are eliminated by changing the left-most two bits to 0, indicating blanks.

The first step of the control sequence for the display processor rotates a new command out of memory into ***R*** and moves the just-executed command from the principal register ***R*** to the last row of memory. Step 2 causes a branch back to step 1 and another rotation of **M** if the command in ***R*** was not a positioning command. Rotations continue until a positioning command is found. Since the commands are treated in pairs, the above feature will serve to keep the system synchronized. The reader may observe that the memory will continue to rotate indefinitely if it is initially empty. We sidestep this problem by assuming that a START pulse will effect the storage of a reference dot in **M**. The sequence separates at step 3, depending on the existence of an ***erase***. In the absence of a user input, the current command in ***R*** is executed. This command will be a positioning command. To simplify our notation, we let $n = \rho_2\mathbf{M}$.

1. $\boldsymbol{\alpha}^{n-1}//\mathbf{M} \leftarrow \boldsymbol{\alpha}^{n-1}//\Uparrow\mathbf{M}$; $\boldsymbol{R} \leftarrow \mathbf{M}^0$; $\mathbf{M}^{n-1} \leftarrow \boldsymbol{R}$
2. $\rightarrow (\boldsymbol{R}_0 \times 3 + \overline{\boldsymbol{R}_0} \times 1)$
3. $\rightarrow (\boldsymbol{erase} \times 12 + \overline{\boldsymbol{erase}} \times 4)$
4. $\boldsymbol{BP} \leftarrow \boldsymbol{\omega}^{18}/\boldsymbol{R}$
5. line ***pu*** ← PULSE, WAIT
6. $\boldsymbol{\alpha}^{n-1}//\mathbf{M} \leftarrow \boldsymbol{\alpha}^{n-1}//\Uparrow\mathbf{M}$; $\boldsymbol{R} \leftarrow \mathbf{M}^0$; $\mathbf{M}^{n-1} \leftarrow \boldsymbol{R}$

Steps 4 and 5 execute the positioning command. Line ***pu*** is the control line to the positioning unit. After a memory rotation at step 6, step 7 causes a branch back to step 1 to prevent the writing of garbage on the screen by a blank command. Steps 9 and 11 cause the appropriate display commands to be executed:

7. $\rightarrow (\boldsymbol{R}_1 \times 8 + \overline{\boldsymbol{R}_1} \times 1)$
8. $\rightarrow (\boldsymbol{R}_2 \times 9 + \overline{\boldsymbol{R}_2} \times 11)$
9. $\boldsymbol{LS} \leftarrow \boldsymbol{\omega}^{16}/\boldsymbol{R}$; line ***lsg*** ← PULSE, WAIT
10. $\rightarrow (16)$
11. $\mathbf{CH} \leftarrow \boldsymbol{\omega}^{16}/\boldsymbol{R}$; line ***cg*** ← PULSE, WAIT, $\rightarrow (16)$

Lines ***lsg*** and ***cg*** are the control lines to the line segment and character generation units, respectively. Following the display, control branches to step 16 to handle a possible ***go*** signal.

Execution of an erase request begins at step 12. If the left-most 18 bits of

R match the bits of ***JS***, zeros are placed in $\boldsymbol{R}_0$ and $\boldsymbol{R}_1$, and in these positions in the next command in sequence as well. If the bits of ***R*** and ***JS*** do not match, control returns to step 4 to permit a display operation.

12. $\rightarrow (\vee/(\boldsymbol{JS} \oplus \boldsymbol{\omega}^{18}/\boldsymbol{R}) \times 4) + (\overline{\vee/(\boldsymbol{JS} \oplus \boldsymbol{\omega}^{18}/\boldsymbol{R})} \times 13)$
13. $\boldsymbol{R}_0, \boldsymbol{R}_1 \leftarrow 0{,}0$
14. $\boldsymbol{\alpha}^{n-1}//\mathbf{M} \leftarrow \boldsymbol{\alpha}^{n-1}//\Uparrow\mathbf{M};\ \boldsymbol{R} \leftarrow \mathbf{M}^0;\ \mathbf{M}^{n-1} \leftarrow \boldsymbol{R}$
15. $\boldsymbol{R}_0, \boldsymbol{R}_1 \leftarrow 0, 0;\ \rightarrow (1)$

The control sequence for inserting a new display function in the circulating sequence of commands is equally simple. After a memory rotation, step 17 checks for a blank. If one is not found, control is returned to step 2 to check for a positioning command. When a blank is found, step 18 enters the contents of register ***JS*** as a positioning command. At step 20, the desired display command is entered in the next memory space. Control then returns to step 1

16. $\boldsymbol{\alpha}^{n-1}//\mathbf{M} \leftarrow \boldsymbol{\alpha}^{n-1}//\Uparrow\mathbf{M};\ \boldsymbol{R} \leftarrow \mathbf{M}^0;\ \mathbf{M}^{n-1} \leftarrow \boldsymbol{R}$
17. $\rightarrow ((\boldsymbol{go} \wedge \overline{\boldsymbol{R}_0} \wedge \overline{\boldsymbol{R}_1}) \times 18) + ((\overline{\boldsymbol{go}} \vee \boldsymbol{R}_0 \vee \boldsymbol{R}_1) \times 2)$
18. $\boldsymbol{R} \leftarrow 1, \boldsymbol{JS}$
19. $\boldsymbol{\alpha}^{n-1}//\mathbf{M} \leftarrow \boldsymbol{\alpha}^{n-1}//\Uparrow\mathbf{M};\ \boldsymbol{R} \leftarrow \mathbf{M}^0;\ \mathbf{M}^{n-1} \leftarrow \boldsymbol{R}$
20. $\boldsymbol{R} \leftarrow 0, \boldsymbol{CMD}$
21. $\boldsymbol{go} \leftarrow 0, \rightarrow (1)$

for another pass through the sequence, after a 0 is placed in ***go***. The reader will note that ***erase*** was not similarly reset after step 15. In that case, the control sequencer must continue the search for other line segments, beginning at the same position. After the desired erasure has been performed, the user must reset ***erase*** manually.

15.4. DIGITAL FILTERS

Electrical filter networks have many applications in communications, control, and other signal processing systems. Digital filtering involves substitution of a digital computer for the analog filtering network. The advantage of a digital filter is increased accuracy and flexibility in the realization of the more complex filter transfer functions. Also important are the better stability and reliability of the digital filter.

A simplified block diagram of a system employing an example digital filter is shown in Fig. 15.4. The signals at various points in the system are shown for a typical input signal. The input signal is sampled every T seconds (typically, $10^{-4} < T < 0.1$). These samples are then converted to digital form by the box labeled A/D (analog-to-digital converter). From this sequence of input numbers, the digital filter computes a sequence of output numbers.

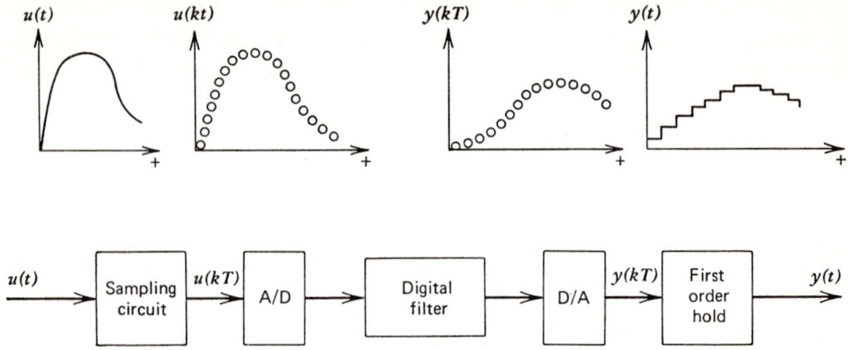

FIGURE 15.4. Block diagram of digital filter.

After conversion back to analog form, the output sequence is shown as $y(kT)$. A satisfactory approximation of the desired continuous output signal is obtained using a first-order hold circuit. As may be inferred from the figure, the hold circuit merely maintains an output corresponding to one sample until the next sample arrives.

It should be clear from the above discussion that digital filtering is restricted to low-frequency applications. Shannon's well-known sampling theorem states that $1/2T$ must be greater than the highest frequency component of interest in the input signal. T is the amount of time available to the digital filter to complete its computation on a single input sample. In addition, the time required to compute each output value represents a delay introduced by the digital computer. For a sampling rate near the minimum permitted by the sampling theorem, this delay could become intolerable.

The computation performed by the digital filter is merely a realization of the difference equation given by Eq. 15.1. Notice that the current value of the

$$y(n) = \sum_{j=0}^{m} a_j \cdot u(n-j) - \sum_{i=1}^{k} b_i \cdot y(n-i) \tag{15.1}$$

output is a function of the previous m input samples and the previous k output samples. The particular coefficients a_j and b_i depend on the transfer function to be realized by the digital filter. The z-transform of the difference equation (Eq. 15.2) is helpful in the determination of the coefficients. There are a number of approaches to the design process for a digital filter. These are beyond the scope of this book [see Reference 2]. Our point of view will be that of implementing the digital filter once the coefficients a_j and b_i have been determined.

$$\frac{Y(z)}{U(z)} = H(z) = \frac{a_0 + a_1 z^{-1} + \cdots + a_m z^{-m}}{1 + b_1 z^{-1} + \cdots + b_k z^{-k}} \tag{15.2}$$

The reader will note that the difference equation 15.1 can represent the transfer function of any electrical circuit. Particular sets of coefficients $\{a_i\}$ and $\{b_i\}$ will make the device a digital filter. In that case, it will behave in just the same manner as an analog filter. It will filter out certain frequency components and allow others to pass. Once again, the particular pass-bands and stop-bands will depend on the coefficients.

The digital filter to be implemented will allow for variable coefficients. That is, the user may determine different sets of coefficients which may be entered via switches on the panel. If necessary, a similar mechanism can be provided for specifying initial conditions for u and y. This is the only control the user will have over the digital filter, other than attaching the input and turning the filter on and off and scaling. When turned on, the filter will perform the computation specified by Eq. 15.1 repeatedly, once each sampling period.

From Eq. 15.1 we see that each calculation will involve $k + m + 1$ multiplications and an equal number of additions. Since the filter is necessarily a dedicated system (very likely destined for a low-budget laboratory application), the cost of combinational logic for the multiplier must be limited. A reasonable compromise between speed and cost is a signed two's-complement carry-save multiplier, as discussed in Chapter 12. We assume that 16-bit accuracy will be sufficient. We also assume the carry propagation in the synchronous adder will require three clock periods. Thus, 19 clock periods will be required for each multiplication; and the time for $k + m + 1$ additions and multiplications is given by Eq. 15.3:

$$\text{Addition and multiplication time} = 22(k + m + 1)10^{-7} \tag{15.3}$$

This assumes a fairly short clock period of 100 nsec.

Let us assume that the digital filter is intended for some such application as speech analysis, so that it must be capable of responding over the range of audio-frequencies. An audio range of 10 kHz requires a sampling rate of at least 20 kHz; so $T \leq 0.5 \times 10^{-4}$. The total computation time for each sample must be less than T. Since the combined addition and multiplication time is approximately the computation time, we have Eq. 15.4:

$$22(k + m + 1)10^{-7} < 0.5 \times 10^{-4} \tag{15.4}$$

For symmetry, we assume that $m + 1 = k$. Thus Eq. 15.5 represents a bound on k:

$$k < \frac{0.5(10^{-4})}{44(10^{-7})} = 11.4 \tag{15.5}$$

If more than eleven coefficients are required to provide sufficient accuracy, some modification must be made in the previously mentioned design assumptions. To allow time for shifting and bookkeeping operations and for convenience of implementation, we assume that $k = 8$ will provide enough accuracy.

As in most special-purpose computers, control would probably consist of microinstructions stored in an ROM. Busing would likely be used to provide the data paths for most register transfers. To shorten the discussion, we omit both of these features. Once a complete control sequence has been developed, the reader should have no trouble planning a busing configuration from a list of required data paths, laying out the format of a microinstruction, and translating the control sequence to a microassembly language.

Other than the ROM, the only memory consists of four semiconductor matrices, each containing eight 16-bit words. These matrices are included in Fig. 15.5. Since no instructions are stored in a writeable memory, the digital filter cannot really be called a computer. It is merely a vector-handling digital system. It is worth considering, however, as a fairly sophisticated example of special-purpose design.

The coefficient a_0 is stored in $\mathbf{A}^0$, a_1 in $\mathbf{A}^1$, and so on. One-origin indexing is used for the coefficients; b_1 is stored in $\mathbf{B}^0$, b_2 in $\mathbf{B}^1$, etc. The most recent eight inputs are stored in $\mathbf{U}$: $u(n)$ in $\mathbf{U}^0$, $u(n-1)$ in $\mathbf{U}^1$, and so on. The most recent eight outputs are stored in $\mathbf{Y}$: $y(n)$ in $\mathbf{Y}^0$, $y(n-1)$ in $\mathbf{Y}^1$, etc. *AC*, ***MQ***, ***MD***, are 16-bit registers which perform their usual functions as arguments in arithmetic operations. ***SAMP***, ***SUM***, and ***OUT*** are also 16-bit registers. Input samples are placed in ***SAMP*** by the A/D converter. Since *AC* is required

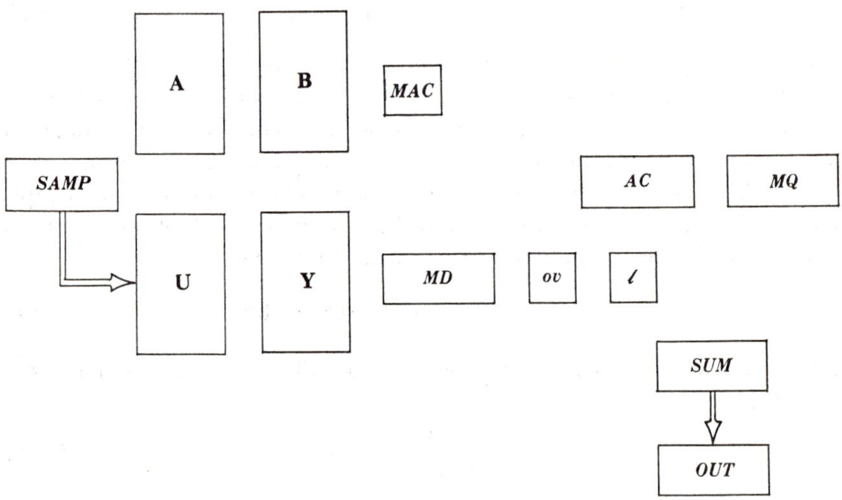

FIGURE 15.5. Registers in digital filter.

in multiplication, the sum, $y(n)$, is formed in another register ***SUM***. Once a computation is complete, the result is placed in the register, ***OUT***, of the D/A converter, and computation begins on the next sample. ***MAC*** is a 3-bit counter which serves as the address register for all four matrices. ***MC*** is the multiplication counter.

If overflow occurs during addition, the flip-flop ***ov*** will be set to 1, lighting a lamp on the panel. Switches are available on both the A/D and D/A converters with which the user can adjust scaling in the event of overflow. Overflow determination is made by a combinational logic function associated with the subroutine ADD and will not appear in the control sequence.

Computation for a given sample begins with a pulse sent to the sampling unit requesting that a sample be placed in ***SAMP***. Three operations take place during the wait for the sample to become available. Step 2 shifts down the rows of **Y**. Recall that ***SUM*** was the output value computed for the previous sample.

1. *sampling unit* ← PULSE
2. $\boldsymbol{\omega}^7//\mathbf{Y} \leftarrow \boldsymbol{\omega}^7//\Downarrow\mathbf{Y};\ \mathbf{Y}^0 \leftarrow \boldsymbol{SUM}$
3. $\boldsymbol{SUM} \leftarrow \overline{\boldsymbol{\epsilon}(16)}$
4. $\boldsymbol{MAC} \leftarrow \overline{\boldsymbol{\epsilon}(3)}$, WAIT for ***sampav*** PULSE

A pulse on the line ***sampav*** indicates that a new input sample is available. Thus at step 5, the matrix of past input values may be shifted down. The computation begins at step 6. Steps 6 and 7 place the multiplier and multiplicand in ***MQ*** and ***MD*** to prepare for the MULTIPLY sequence. Details of

5. $\boldsymbol{\omega}^7//\mathbf{U} \leftarrow \boldsymbol{\omega}^7//\Downarrow\mathbf{U};\ \mathbf{U}^0 \leftarrow \boldsymbol{SAMP}$)
6. $\boldsymbol{MQ} \leftarrow \mathbf{A}^{\perp \boldsymbol{MAC}}$
7. $\boldsymbol{MD} \leftarrow \mathbf{U}^{\perp \boldsymbol{MAC}}$
8. → (MULTIPLY SEQUENCE), WAIT
9. $\ell,\ \boldsymbol{SUM} \leftarrow$ ADD ($\boldsymbol{MQ}$, $\boldsymbol{SUM}$)

the carry-save multiplication will not be presented. The reader should have no trouble in constructing this sequence in light of the discussion in Chapter 12.

We must necessarily use integer arithmetic; so the result of interest is the least-significant 16 bits of the product found in ***MQ***. If the product bits in ***AC*** are non-zero, overflow has occurred. The number in ***MQ*** is then added to the partial sum already in ***SUM***, at step 9. All arithmetic is assumed two's-complement, so no attention is paid to signs. The negative signs appearing in Eq. 15.1 are assumed to be stored with the coefficients in **B**.

Because the number of bits is doubled by the multiplication process, only eight significant bits are actually allowed for the arguments. A better approach would use double-precision addition at step 9. The negative signs in

Eq. 15.1 could result in a final output $y(n)$ of 16 significant bits, even though the inputs and coefficients were also 16 bits. This would be the case in any system with a gain less than 1. The above approach will be left as a problem for the reader.

10. $\rightarrow ((\wedge/\boldsymbol{MAC}) \times 12) + ((\overline{\wedge/\boldsymbol{MAC}}) \times 11)$
11. $\boldsymbol{MAC} \leftarrow \mathrm{INC}(\boldsymbol{MAC}), \rightarrow (6)$
12. $\boldsymbol{MAC} \leftarrow \overline{\boldsymbol{\epsilon}(3)}$

After the eight products of inputs times coefficients have been added to ***SUM***, the process is repeated for the eight previous outputs beginning at step 13. Notice that ***MAC*** serves as a multiplication counter as well as an address register. After eight passes through the loop involving steps 13–16,

13. $\boldsymbol{MQ} \leftarrow \mathbf{B}^{\perp \boldsymbol{MAC}}$
14. $\boldsymbol{MD} \leftarrow \mathbf{Y}^{\perp \boldsymbol{MAC}}$
15. $\rightarrow$ (MULTIPLY SEQUENCE), WAIT
16. $\ell, \boldsymbol{SUM} \leftarrow \mathrm{ADD}(\boldsymbol{MQ}, \boldsymbol{SUM})$
17. $\rightarrow ((\wedge/\boldsymbol{MAC}) \times 19 + (\overline{\wedge/\boldsymbol{MAC}} \times 18)$
18. $\boldsymbol{MAC} \leftarrow \mathrm{INC}(\boldsymbol{MAC}), \rightarrow (13)$
19. $\boldsymbol{OUT} \leftarrow \boldsymbol{SUM}$
20. $D/A\ unit \leftarrow \mathrm{PULSE}, \rightarrow (1)$

the new sample output is placed in ***OUT***, to be converted to analog form. Control returns immediately to step 1 to begin computations for the next sample.

15.5. SPECIAL-PURPOSE COMPUTERS

When one speaks of a *special-purpose computer*, it is usually understood that he means to contrast this machine with a general-purpose computer. Neither of these terms is very well defined, but both satisfy the definition of a computer set forth in Chapter 1. In theory, any calculation which can be done on one computer can be done by any other (within the limits of its memory). However, a given computer might not necessarily work efficiently on a particular class of problems. Similarly, a given computer might not be set up to accept input or provide output in the manner required by a certain application. For our purpose we shall find it sufficient to describe a general-purpose computer in the way it is most commonly understood. From there it will not be difficult to define a special-purpose machine.

A general-purpose computer must be able to handle the most important classes of problems, from business to scientific, with reasonable efficiency. A general-purpose machine can be expected to receive input in the form of

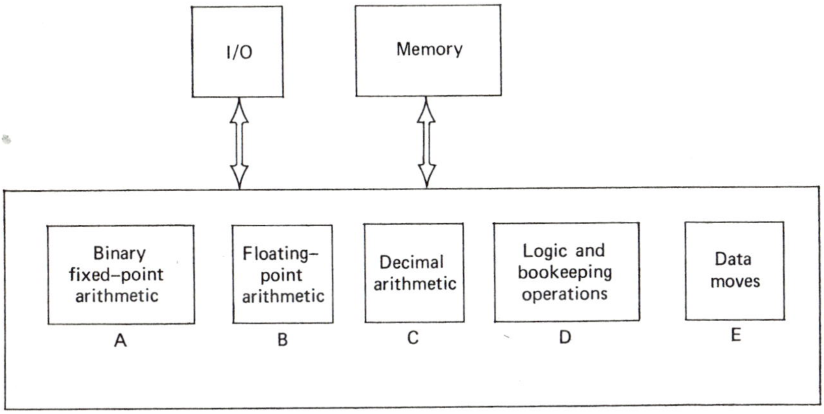

FIGURE 15.6. Typical general-purpose processing capability.

punched cards (in a few cases, paper tape) or from magnetic tape or from time-sharing terminals. Output is usually in the form of printed copy or magnetic tape. The processing capability of a typical general-purpose machine might be as shown in Fig. 15.6. Clearly, not all general-purpose machines have all of the processing capability given in Fig. 15.6. A general-purpose minicomputer may contain only blocks *A* and *D*. Machines whose primary use will not be in business applications, often do not include special hardware for decimal arithmetic or data moves. Still, they are labeled general-purpose computers. Clearly, a certain amount of flexibility must be permitted within the concept of a general-purpose computer.

At the other extreme, a computer miniaturized and mounted in a missile may have most of the features described by Fig. 15.6. Still most would label this machine special-purpose.

Perhaps the easy way out is to accept the word of the designer or manufacturer. If he says the machine is general-purpose, fine. *If the designer has a specific application in mind at the beginning of the design process and creates a machine which satisfies all requirements of the application at minimum component cost, the result is a special-purpose machine.* This point of view may not be helpful to the customer, who must somehow choose from a vast array of alternatives (with a considerable number of dollars riding on the correct choice) the general-purpose machine best suited to his application. Looking through the eyes of the designer, we will find it a convenient concept.

Closely related and somewhat helpful, is the concept of a *special-purpose facility*. Often one or more general-purpose machines, together with a particular set of input/output devices and memory units, can be configured to perform very efficiently on particular classes of jobs. Such special-purpose facilities are more common than the special-purpose CPU because of the considerably lower development cost peculiar to the individual installation.

In the past, the special-purpose computer has been mostly restricted to military and space applications. More recently, special-purpose computers have been used in manufacturing process control applications and in medical and other laboratory applications which require a dedicated machine. Often, in these cases, a choice exists between adapting a general-purpose mini-computer and designing a special-purpose machine. The decision will vary from case to case, depending on how well the capability of the mini-computer coincides with the requirements of the application.

The question might be asked why special-purpose computers aren't designed for major computational tasks as well as smaller peripheral tasks. Why not dedicate and optimize the design of a machine for the solution of partial differential equations, for example. A variety of problems involving partial differential equations is a big user of time at many installations.

The reason that processors have not been designed around specific problems is that most installations must necessarily handle a variety of problems. Only a few facilities are large enough that a large-scale CPU could be permanently assigned to a specific task. As conventional computer organizations are pushed to their limit, interest in special-purpose architectures for important problems is likely to increase. Two machines, ILLIAC IV and the CDC STAR, which fit into this class have already been placed in operation. These machines will be discussed in Section 15.9.

The other three special-purpose computers to be discussed in the next three sections include the master computer of a time-sharing facility, a process controller, and a sort processor for business data processing. We have deliberately chosen examples with widely differing applications.

15.6. SORT PROCESSOR

One of the most time-consuming activities in business data processing is the sorting, ordering, or alphabetizing of lists of data. This process can be made much more efficient through the use of special-purpose hardware. In this section the implementation of specific instructions intended to perform operations related to the sorting problem will be considered. A complete design of the computer will not be presented.

The computer under consideration has a memory of 2^{16}, or 64k, words of 24 bits each. As this computer is to be dedicated to a particular inventory control application, the memory is permanently allocated as shown in Fig. 15.7a. The last half of the memory consists of a set of data files which require frequent updating and resorting. All of the remaining storage, except for the

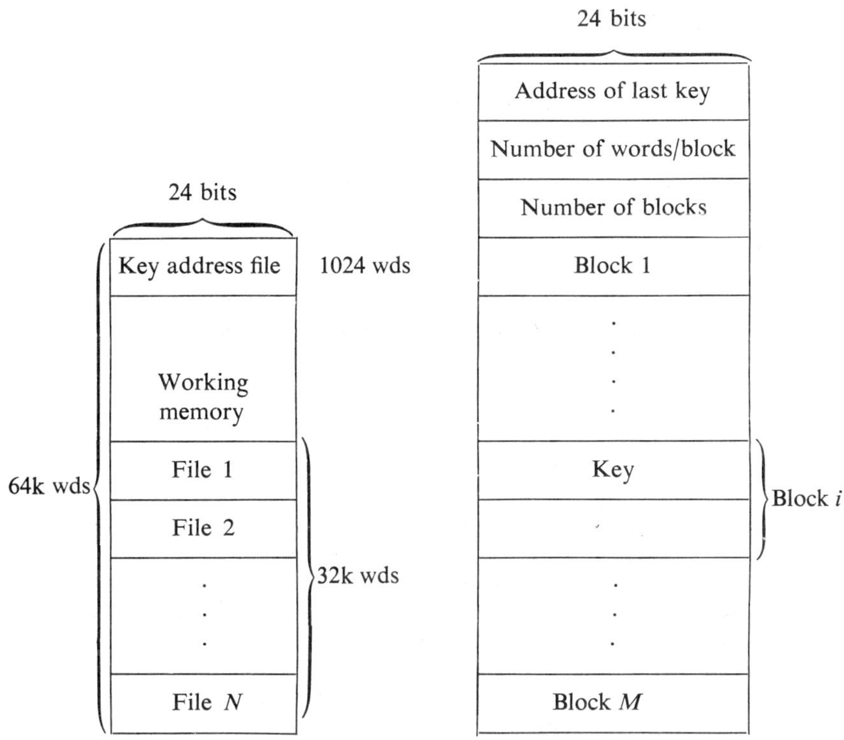

(a) Memory allocation (b) File organization

FIGURE 15.7. Sort processor memory.

first 1024 words, are allocated to program and working storage. The first 1024 words are a working key file. This section of memory may be accessed through a separate address pointer and data register as well as through the usual ***MA*** and ***MD***. This is possible since the entire memory may be assumed to be implemented using semiconductors.

Each file in the 32k file area is divided into a set of file blocks, as illustrated in Fig. 15.8b. The first word in each block is an identifying number called a *key*. No two blocks in the same file will have the same key. The first word in each file contains the address of the last key in the file. The second word in the file contains the number of words per block, which is the same for all blocks in a file. The third word contains the number of blocks.

Several instruction formats are permitted. Only two formats will concern us. One of these is the single-word format of Fig. 15.8a. As with all instructions for this machine, the op code consists of 6 bits. Bits 6 and 7 allow for specification of indexing or indirect addressing, or both, depending on the op

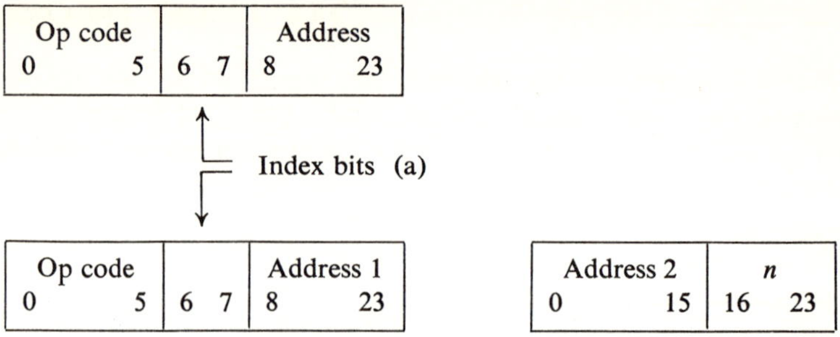

(b)

FIGURE 15.8. Two instruction formats.

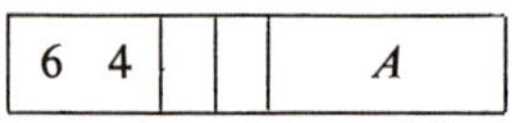

specifies sorting the file whose first word is located at address A (indexed if specified). Sorting consists of placing the addresses of the keys (for the various blocks) in descending order of key magnitude in the first several locations in memory. That is, the address of the largest key is placed in location 0.

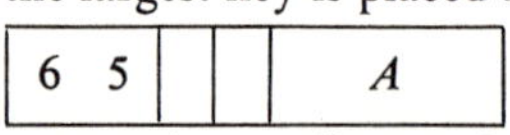

is the same except that the addresses are arranged according to the ascending order of key magnitude.

FIGURE 15.9. Sorting instructions.

Register	Number of bits	Description
AC	24	Accumulator
NBLKS	8	Number of blocks in file
LKA	16	Address of key to last block in file
IR1	24	Instruction register
KEYAD	16	Address of key under consideration
NWDS	8	Number of words per block
MA	16	Memory address register
MD	24	Memory data register
MAC1	10	Counting address register for first 1024 addresses
MAC2	10	Counting address register for first 1024 addresses
POINT	8	Address of selected key

FIGURE 15.10. Register used in sort instruction.

code. The last 16 bits are the address. The first word of the two-word instruction in Fig. 15.8b is interpreted just like a one-word instruction. The second word contains a second address in the left-most 16 bits. The right-most 8 bits contain a constant, n, which may be used in various ways. Indirect addressing is not permitted by either of these two instruction formats. It may be employed by other formats, however.

Let us suppose that op codes 64 and 65 (octal) specify two special sort instructions, as described in Fig. 15.9.

The registers directly involved in the sort instrutions are listed in Fig. 15.10. The use of these registers will become clear with the presentation of the control sequence. The listed sequence begins following the fetch cycle and separation of control from other instructions. We assume that indexing has been completed with the indexed address remaining in ***IR1***.

1. $\boldsymbol{MA} \leftarrow \omega^{16}/\boldsymbol{IR}1$
2. $\boldsymbol{MD} \leftarrow \mathrm{M}^{\perp \boldsymbol{MA}}$
3. $\boldsymbol{LKA} \leftarrow \omega^{10}/\boldsymbol{MD};\ \boldsymbol{MA} \leftarrow \mathrm{INC}(\boldsymbol{MA})$
4. $\boldsymbol{MD} \leftarrow \mathrm{M}^{\perp \boldsymbol{MA}}$
5. $\boldsymbol{NWDS} \leftarrow \omega^{8}/\boldsymbol{MD};\ \boldsymbol{MA} \leftarrow \mathrm{INC}(\boldsymbol{MA})$
6. $\boldsymbol{MD} \leftarrow \mathrm{M}^{\perp \boldsymbol{MA}}$
7. $\boldsymbol{MAC}1 \leftarrow \epsilon^{3}(10);\ \boldsymbol{NBLKS} \leftarrow \omega^{8}/\boldsymbol{MD}$
8. $\boldsymbol{MA} \leftarrow \mathrm{INC}(\boldsymbol{MA})$

The first seven steps obtain the address of the last key in the file, the number of words per block, and the number of blocks, and place this information in the registers provided for this purpose, ***LKA***, ***NWDS***, and ***NBLKS***. Step 7 initializes two counters. The special counters ***MAC***1 and ***MAC***2 serve as separate memory address registers for the first 1024 locations in memory. The addressing networks associated with these registers are completely separate from the ***MA*** network. The memory address register, ***MD***, is used in conjunction with any of the three address registers.

Steps 8–13 obtain the key numbers and place them in a separate list beginning at memory location 100 (octal). The process of comparing key

9. $\boldsymbol{MD} \leftarrow \mathrm{M}^{\perp \boldsymbol{MA}}$
10. $\mathrm{M}^{\perp \boldsymbol{MAC1}} \leftarrow \boldsymbol{MD};$
11. $\rightarrow (\vee/(\boldsymbol{MA} \oplus \boldsymbol{LKA}) \times 12) + (\overline{\vee/(\boldsymbol{MA} \oplus \boldsymbol{LKA})} \times 14)$
12. $\boldsymbol{MA} \leftarrow \omega^{16}/\mathrm{ADD}(\boldsymbol{MA}, \boldsymbol{NWDS})$
13. $\boldsymbol{MAC1} \leftarrow \mathrm{INC}(\boldsymbol{MAC1}),\ \rightarrow (9)$
14. $\boldsymbol{MAC2} \leftarrow \overline{\epsilon}(10);\ \boldsymbol{IR}1 \leftarrow \boldsymbol{INC}(\boldsymbol{IR1})$
15. $\boldsymbol{IR}1 \leftarrow \mathrm{INC}(\boldsymbol{IR1})$
16. $\boldsymbol{IR}1 \leftarrow \mathrm{INC}(\boldsymbol{IR1})$

magnitudes begins at step 17, following the reinitializing of the address registers. The memory address register, *MA*, is used to keep track of the key under consideration.

17. $MA \leftarrow \omega^{16}/IR1;\ MAC1 \leftarrow \epsilon^{3}(10)$
18. $MD \leftarrow MA$
19. $\mathbf{M}^{\perp MAC2} \leftarrow MD$
20. $MD \leftarrow \mathbf{M}^{\perp MAC1}$
21. $AC \leftarrow MD$
22. $MA \leftarrow \mathrm{ADD}(MA,\ NWDS)$
23. $MAC1 \leftarrow \mathrm{INC}(MAC1)$
24. $MD \leftarrow \mathbf{M}^{\perp MAC1}$
25. $\rightarrow (\mathrm{LARGER}(MD,AC) \times 26) + (\overline{\mathrm{LARGER}(MD,AC)} \times 28)$
26. $AC \leftarrow MD;\ MD \leftarrow MA;\ POINT \leftarrow MAC1$
27. $\mathbf{M}^{\perp MAC2} \leftarrow MD$
28. $\rightarrow (\vee/(MA \oplus LKA) \times 29) + (\overline{\vee/(MA \oplus LKA)} \times 23)$
29. $MAC2 \leftarrow \mathrm{INC}(MAC2)$
30. $\rightarrow (\vee/(MAC2 \oplus NBLKS) \times 31) + (\overline{\vee/(MAC2 \oplus NBLKS)} \times 33)$
31. $MAC1 \leftarrow POINT;\ MD \leftarrow \overline{\epsilon(24)}$
32. $\mathbf{M}^{\perp MAC1} \leftarrow MD,\ \rightarrow (17)$
33. EXIT

Each pass through the inner loop, beginning at step 23, represents a pass through the list of keys to find the largest key remaining in the list. The address (in the original file) of the largest key is placed in $\mathbf{M}^0$ on the first pass. The address of the second largest key is placed in $\mathbf{M}^1$ on the second pass, and so on. Once an address corresponding to a key is entered in the list, that key is replaced by zero so that it will not be entered in the list twice. We assume that all keys are greater than zero. At the beginning of each pass, the first key is placed in *AC*. This key is compared to subsequent keys. When a larger one is found, it replaces the original key in *AC*. *MAC1* is used to count through the list of keys in the inner loop. With each step, the number of words per block is added to *MA*; thus *MA* stores the file address of each key, which is compared to *AC*.

MAC2 contains the address of the location in the list where the next key address is to be placed. The contents of *MAC2* are updated each pass through the outer loop. Also, the address in *POINT* is used to replace the selected key by zero each pass through the outer loop.

The major operation is the combinational logic subroutine LARGER(*MD*, *AC*), which is used to control a branch at step 25. The output of the logic unit will be 1 if the first argument, ***MD***, is larger in magnitude than the second argument, ***AC***. The output is 0 otherwise. The writing of this subroutine will be left to the reader. The subroutine LARGER causes the keys to be arranged in descending order to execute the single-address instruction 64. The execution of instruction 65 requires only a slight modification of the routine LARGER.

No software sorting routine will be written to verify the saving which can be provided by the above special-purpose processor. However, the savings should be considerable. In a software version, each AHPL step in the routine listed above would be replaced by at least one fetch and execution memory cycle. Merely avoiding the fetch cycle will result in nearly a 50% saving. Many of the bookkeeping steps which are accomplished above in single register transfers will require a sequence of two or three instructions to accomplish by software. Overall, one can be confident of achieving at least a 3-to-1 speed improvement by using a hardware sorter. This is achieved at the expense of adding several hardware registers and a number of special data paths. Some of the registers can be used by other instructions. In any case, the sorting instruction could be justified only in situations where it is used frequently.

In addition to sorting files, it is likely that the same processor will be called upon to rearrange the blocks in the file. The storage of key addresses in the first few words of memory can only be temporary. The MOVE instruction shown in Fig. 15.11 may be used in the rearrangement of data. If the first three bits of the op code are octal 5, then the instruction is recognized as a two-address instruction and the next word in the instruction sequence is placed in the supplementary instruction register, ***IR2***. Op code 57 indicates an instruction which will move a block of words from one section of memory to another. Address 1 specifies the address of the first word in the block to be moved. Address 2 specifies the new location of the first word in the block. The number of words in the block to be moved is given by the 8-bit binary number, n.

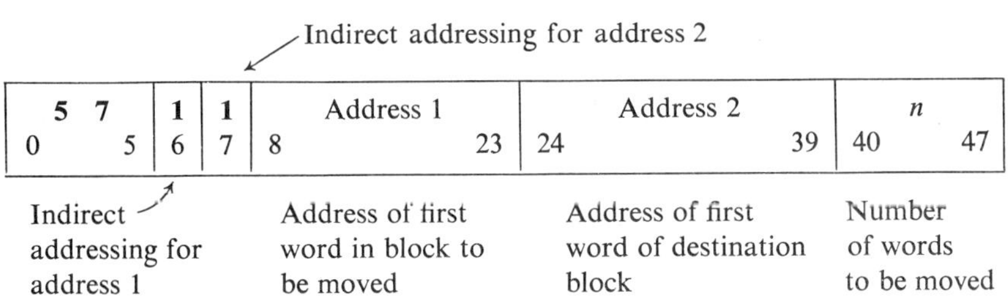

FIGURE 15.11. A MOVE instruction.

15.7. TIME-SHARING

Time-sharing as a medium for executing programs is not special purpose. Most any program which can be executed by a batch processing facility can also be executed by a time-sharing system. The need for special-purpose hardware, except for the input/output terminals, is not apparent either. Many functioning time-sharing systems consist of a general-purpose computer connected through its normal I/O channels to remote time-sharing terminals. Only the software operating system is special purpose.

It is the authors' contention that time-sharing using general-purpose hardware uses this hardware less efficiently than a time-sharing system with hardware particularly adapted to this task. In this section we shall discuss the general functioning of a time-sharing system, pointing out where special-purpose hardware might effectively be used. AHPL sequences describing the system will not be presented. The overall system is far too complex to permit detailing the design in a single section.

A block diagram of one approach to time-sharing is shown in Fig. 15.12. Two processors are used. One processor, the *master*, controls the overall function of the system and assembles information from the user terminals. The larger *slave* computer does nothing but compile and execute user programs. The slave computer may be a large general-purpose computer. The only saving to be made by tailoring the design of the slave would lie in

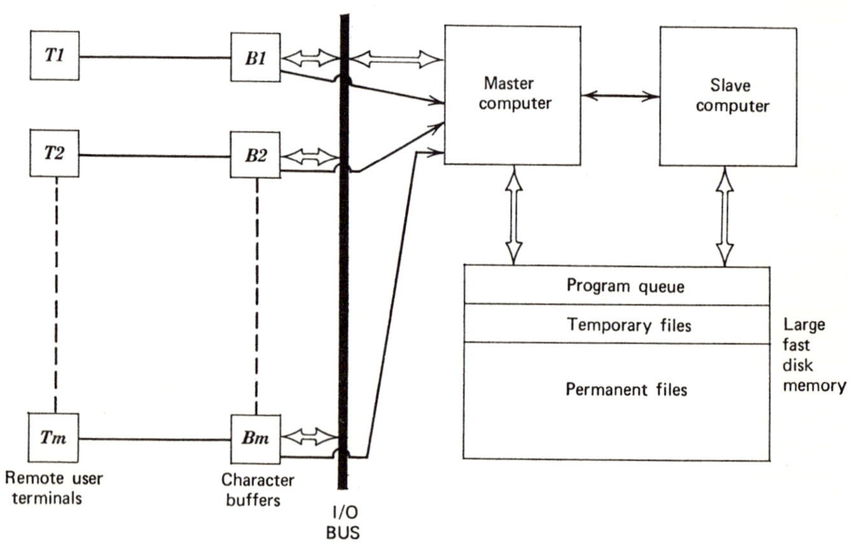

FIGURE 15.12. Block diagram of time-sharing system.

simplifying its I/O handling capability, since it only need communicate with the master computer, the disc memory, and a control console (not shown). The hardware included in the master computer will be most efficiently utilized if this machine is designed as a special-purpose computer.

The master computer is the less expensive machine and must never be the limiting factor in system performance. The goal is to match the computing capability of the slave computer to a planned customer load. That is, the computer must be able to compile and execute programs submitted by the customers with satisfactory promptness, at a time when an expected maximum portion of the terminals are in operation. In order that a long program not tie up the slave and exclude other users, execution of a program is carried on for a maximum of t_r seconds. At the end of this time, another program from a queue of programs stored in the disk memory is loaded into the slave computer for execution. If execution of the first program was not completed, this program is restored in the disk memory at the bottom of the queue. Execution is continued with each "turn" in the central processor, until completed. It is the responsibility of the master computer to enter programs in the queue as requested by the user terminals, and to transmit output information from the disk file to the terminals. The slave relates only to the program queue, except that program *swaps* are made on command from the master and data may be obtained from other files in the disk memory.

The time required to swap programs in the slave computer will be denoted t_s. The number of terminals connected to the system is m. The expected maximum number of programs in the queue (on a typical day) is n. The maximum time a program must wait for a turn in the slave is given by Eq. 15.6.

$$\text{Wait time} = n(t_r + t_s) \qquad (15.6)$$

The worst case ratio of expected computation time for one terminal to real time is given by Eq. 15.7. This expression assumes that a program requested by the terminal is reentered in the queue each time it is swapped out of the slave.

$$\text{Terminal computation time ratio} = \frac{t_r}{n(t_r + t_s)} \qquad (15.7)$$

The above expressions are plotted in Fig. 15.13 for various values of n. An optimistic swap time of $t_s = 20$ msec was assumed. This is slightly more than the time required for one rotation of a disk rotating at 3600 rpm. To achieve this swap time, a separate read-write head would be required for each track on the disc. A longer swap time would significantly degrade the potential performance plotted in Fig. 15.13. The following example illustrates how data of the form given in Fig. 15.13 might be used in planning a time-sharing system.

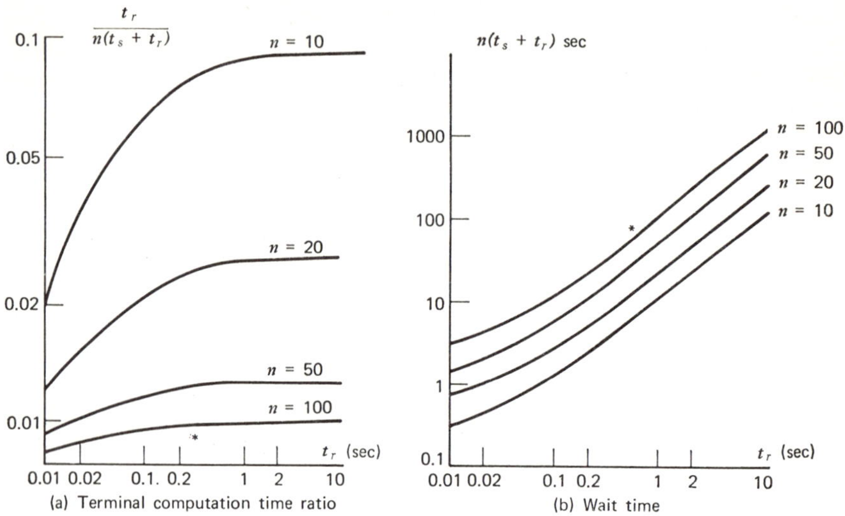

FIGURE 15.13. Time utilization ($t_s = 20$ ms).

Example 15.1

A time-sharing system is to be planned for a particular set of customers. It has been determined that the average program likely to be submitted to the system could be compiled in less than 0.5 sec. Similarly the execution time of an average program for the system is envisioned as 3 sec. These figures, of course, assume a particular slave processor selected for use in the system. It has also been estimated that 50% of all terminals will have a program in the queue at a time of maximum activity. The maximum number of terminals, m, which can be connected to the system is to be determined.

Solution. Assuming all of the rather uncertain assumptions made in the above paragraph, the determination of m remains in part subjective. A critical question is, "How poor a level of service will the customers tolerate during hours of peak activity?" It may be advantageous to overload the system to insure efficient use of the slave at other than peak periods.* Let us assume that a competitive time-sharing service is available; so the customer must be kept happy.

Typical time-sharing users debug their programs on-line by alternately compiling and editing their programs. We assume that users irritation increases rapidly if required to wait longer than 60 sec for compilation of a simple program. We, therefore, let $t_r = 0.5$ and specify a run wait time less than 60 sec. For these figures Eq. 15.6 yields $n = 120$. This point is denoted by an asterisk in Fig. 15.13b.

* In many systems efficiency is maintained by running large batch processing jobs during slack periods.

The user will usually tolerate a longer wait during execution of a program. Let us assume that a 15-min execution time (which could coincide with a coffee break) will be tolerated for a 3-sec program. This implies a terminal computation time ratio of $3/900 = 0.0033$. A point corresponding to this value and $t_r = 0.5$ is denoted by an asterisk in Fig. 13.5a. For $t_r = 0.5$, $1/n$ 0.033, so $n = 300$.

From Fig. 15.13b we see that a tolerable wait time is more difficult to achieve. We therefore conclude that $n = 120$ will satisfy both the wait and the execution time requirements. Therefore, $m = 240$ becomes a design parameter for the system. As we shall see, this number is important in the design of the master processor. ∎

The value of t_r chosen in the above example will result in fairly efficient utilization of the slave. The ratio of computation time to real time $t_r/(t_s + t_r)$ is a measure of efficiency. For $t_r = 0.5$ this ratio is 0.96 (for the assumed very short swap time of 20 msec). This measure of efficiency drops to 0.5 for $t_r =$ 20 msec. This relatively inefficient mode of operation could result if the system were connected to a very large number of terminals for the execution of very short programs. A similarly low efficiency would result from use of a slower disc memory, employing movable read-write heads. The impact of swap time on system efficiency can be lessened significantly by providing for the storage of two programs in the random access memory of the slave processor. In this way one program can be executed while a new program is simultaneously read from the disk to replace the program just executed. Most existing time-sharing systems possess this capability, which is a form of multiprogramming, as mentioned in Section 14.8. We leave the analysis of this technique as a problem for the reader.

The number of terminals, m, is the key parameter in the design of the master processor. This unit must be able to accept a steady stream of characters from all m terminals and to respond to all system commands. From the previous discussion we conclude that service would be very poor if all terminals were in use. Such a situation will be self-limiting in that users would give up if told to wait or if programs took an excessively long time to execute. In any case, the user would be aware of the overload condition. Failure of the system to accept an input character is a much graver sin, a hardware failure. Under certain conditions, chaos could be the result.

Standard telecommunications allows eleven bits (eight information bits, a parity bit, and two bits marking the beginning and ending of a character) per character. These bits are transmitted serially. They are received and stored in an 11-bit buffer, as illustrated in Fig. 15.12. When a complete character is present in the buffer, an interrupt is transmitted to the master. In the absolute worst case, interrupts could issue from all m buffers simultaneously. The master must respond to all of these interrupts by accepting all m characters, before another bit arrives. For a character rate, r (typically between 10 and 20 characters per second), the interval between bits will be $1/11r$.

Since the processor must respond to m interrupts $1/11rm$ sec are available for the processing of a single interrupt. For $r = 20$ and $m = 240$, 19 μsec are available to service each buffer. This is ample time for servicing an interrupt by a hardware control sequence. It would very likely not be sufficient time to service an interrupt via software.

Let us assume that $t_c \leq 1/11rm$ sec are used to input or output each character. If all m processors are in constant communication at the rate of r characters per second, the portion of master processing time devoted to input/output is $t_c rm \leq 1/11$. The remainder of the master time is devoted to other tasks. A very general list of the functions which must be accomplished by the master and the attached buffers are listed in Fig. 15.14.

Characters taken from the character buffers are stored in a line buffer. A line buffer, consisting of between 70 and 200 characters, must be provided for each terminal connected to the system. The line buffers may consist of sections of the master processor RAM. Where speed is crucial, special hardware line buffers may be provided. Just as the master must respond to interrupts from full character buffers, it must check for end-of-line characters in the line buffer. A completed line in the line buffer may be a systems command, or it may be a line to be stored in a file. In many systems these two types of lines are easily distinguished by the presence or absence of a line number. If a line number is present, the line must be removed from the line buffer and placed in what we shall define as a *temporary file*. If $r = 10$ characters/sec, this operation must be accomplished within 0.1 sec.

A temporary file must be provided corresponding to each terminal which is connected. As many as 256 lines are allowed for a temporary file. For illustration, consider a system with 128 characters per line, 128 lines per temporary file, and four characters per word in the master RAM. This implies 4k words per temporary file. For large m it may not be practical to store complete temporary files in the master RAM. If not, a special parallel control sequence must be provided to transfer groups of temporary file lines from RAM to

Activity	Special Hardware
Storage of incoming bits in character buffers	Yes
Filling of line buffers	Possibly
Maintain temporary files	Possibly
Respond to user commands	
Control program queue and slave operation	
Handle output	

FIGURE 15.14. Master activities.

disc while other activities are in progress. This implies cycle stealing or multiple memory banks.

The order of lines in the temporary files is immaterial. This format is convenient for implementing the various EDIT commands by which the user can alter or replace lines in the temporary file. Editing is accomplished by the master. The command SAVE causes lines from the temporary file to be inserted in the permanent file. Lines in the permanent file are in numerical order. A line from the temporary file is inserted in the permanent file between permanent lines with the next higher and next lower line numbers. Where line numbers are identical, the line from the temporary file replaces the line in the permanent file.

Other commands which must be processed by the master are tabulated in Fig. 15.15. Some response must be made to each command in not much more than one second. In some cases the immediate response will consist of printing the word WAIT, indicating that a period of time is required before execution of the command is complete. In other cases the master may respond to a command with a question. In response to the command OLD, for example, the master will ask for the name of the permanent file with which the user wishes to work.

The master must output various sorts of information, including responses to commands, results of programs, and listings. The procedures for each case are somewhat different. All output procedures are approximately the reverse of the input procedure already discussed in detail. We shall omit further discussion of output.

As the reader has observed, the master computer is required to perform a great variety of tasks. The timing of these tasks is not completely under control of this computer. To make possible timely response to all outside demands, the master operating system must be very carefully written to interlace the various activities. Large systems will tend to impose difficult-to-meet performance specifications on the master. Such circumstances suggest

NEW	Calls for a new file to be established
OLD	Requests retrieval of an old file
LIST	Calls for teletype listing of file
SAVE	Temporary file inserted in permanent file
UNSAVE	Eliminate permanent file
COMPILE (FILE NAME)	Compile permanent file and store as named file
RUN	Execute file (compile if needed)
EDIT	Miscellaneous text editing commands available
BYE	Disconnects terminal

FIGURE 15.15. Minimal set of time-sharing commands.

the design of a special-purpose processor, with a control sequencer providing a maximum of concurrent activity.

The commands in Fig. 15.15 suggest a very simple time-sharing system. More commands could be added to permit more flexible utilization of the slave computer. Commands requesting access to magnetic tape files, operation in the remote batch mode, or paper tape input are possibilities.

15.8. PROCESS CONTROL COMPUTER

Process control is perhaps the most important current application of special-purpose hardware. Two elementary process controllers were designed in Chapters 5 and 9. Both of these were intended for essentially *open loop* operation. The only feedback into the controller was provided by the human operator as he manipulated switches on the panel. Open and closed loop process control computer applications are illustrated in Fig. 15.16.

In the closed-loop system of Fig. 15.16b, measurements or state variables from the process are fed back and treated as inputs by the process control computer. Computations on these state variables determine the sequence of control vectors supplied to the system. It should be taken for granted that A/D and D/A converters are involved in the input and output of data to and from the computer.

The specific computations performed on the state variables will vary with the application and are, in general, beyond the scope of this book. In chemical processes, for example, control adjustments may be required by fluctuating

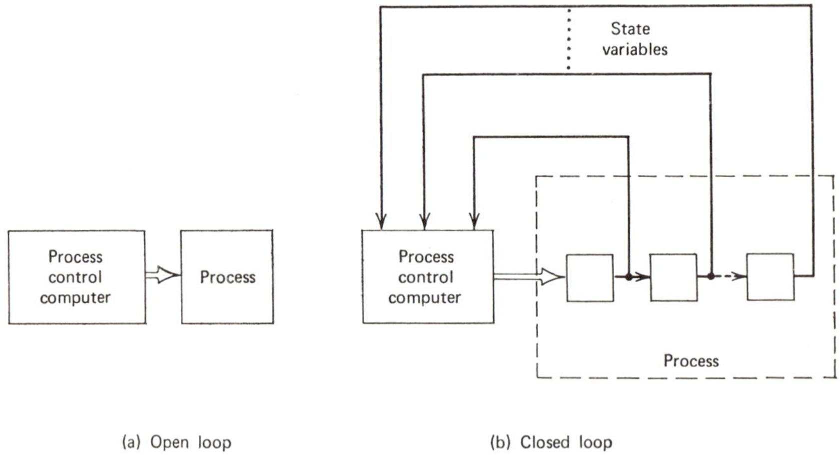

FIGURE 15.16. Process control configurations.

flow rates, impurity levels, or coarseness of materials. Similar parameters influence control for machine tools, mining operations, steel mills, diffusion furnaces for integrated circuits, garment cutting machines, etc.

The process control computer possesses all essential characteristics of a general-purpose computer. In fact, many general-purpose machines have been adapted for process control applications. Since a process control machine is permanently dedicated to one specific application, it may be accepted as a postulate that the component cost of a special-purpose machine will be lower. As mentioned before, component costs are not the only costs involved. The design costs of a small computer for a single application may far exceed the component costs. Thus, general-purpose minicomputers are often adapted to process control applications.

Sometimes the differences between computers required for a group of process control applications are small. Often a special-purpose machine can be designed to handle any of a group of jobs. The machines can be further tailored for the individual applications by slight modifications in their microprograms. Such modifications are inexpensive. The situation is still fluid. The choice of a computer for a particular application, general-purpose or special-purpose, depends on the ingenuity of the designer and salesman.

15.9. LARGE, SPECIAL-PURPOSE MACHINES

Although not installed or constructed on campus, ILLIAC IV, is the fourth of a series of computers developed at the University of Illinois. Most of the special-purpose machines discussed so far in this chapter have been small machines dedicated to one specific task. ILLIAC IV is a very large multi-special-purpose machine. That is, it is intended for use for a variety of problems which consume extremely large amounts of time on ordinary computers. Not all programs can be run efficiently on ILLIAC IV, however.

A simplified hardware layout of one of four identical quadrants of ILLIAC IV is shown in Fig. 15.17. The disc memory and the Burroughs 6500 computer used for I/O communications are actually shared by all four quadrants. The quadrants can work independently or they can be joined together in a single array for large problems.

The 64 processing elements are actually independent arithmetic units. The basic clock period is 80 nsec. The use of emitter-coupled logic permits addition to be accomplished in three clock periods. The carry-save multiplication requires five clock periods. These figures are for 64-bit operations within each individual processing element (P.E.). The processing element memories are constructed using thin film technology to permit an access time of 120 nsec. The reader will note the close match achieved between the addition time and the memory access time.

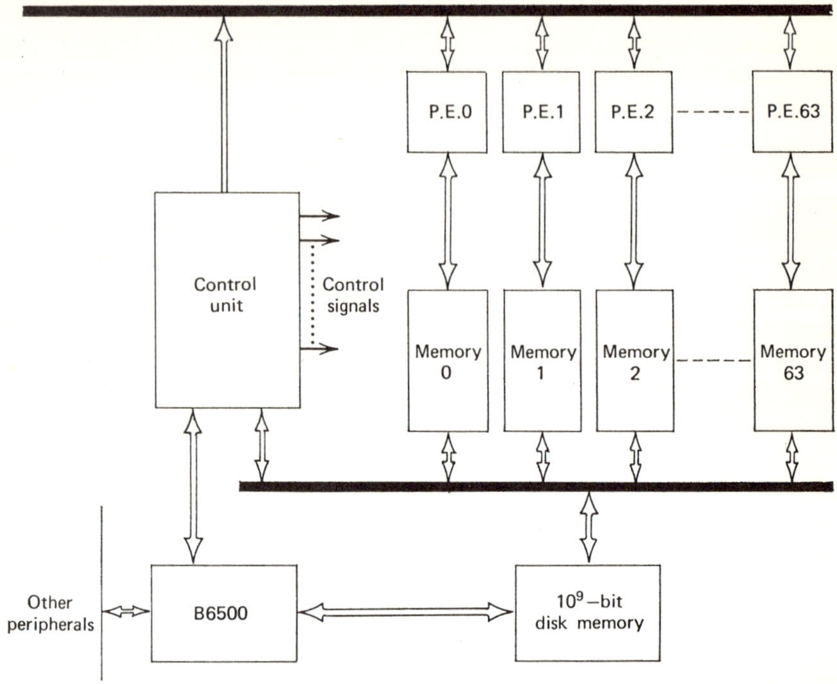

FIGURE 15.17. One quadrant of ILLIAC IV.

The distinguishing feature of the ILLIAC IV organization is that the 64 processing elements do not possess individual control units. All P.E.'s are under control of the single control unit shown. This feature constrains their operations such that all P.E.'s must simultaneously execute the same operation on different data. The only local control available to the individual P.E.'s is an 8-bit register, *RGM*, which stores the results of tests and specifies whether the P.E. will actually execute or will ignore an instruction issued by the control unit. The control unit depicted in Fig. 15.17 includes arithmetic and indexing capability, two 64-word buffer memories for accepting blocks of instructions from the P.E. memories, and broadcast registers to supply identical data items to all processing elements.

A principal advantage of the ILLIAC IV organization is necessarily the economy achieved in the sharing of a single control unit by 64 processing elements. An additional advantage in some applications is the fast transfer of information between operating registers in individual P.E.'s. Interconnections between the P.E.'s are provided so that they may be arranged in a two-dimensional (8 × 8) array or a 64-element linear array. Actual realization of these advantages depends on keeping the processing elements busy. If control signals are disabled by all but a few processors, most of the time, then ILLIAC IV is operating very inefficiently indeed. Achieving a high-P.E. utilization rate requires careful choice of problems and careful programming. Among the problems which seem suited to ILLIAC IV are matrix algebra, partial differential equations including hydrodynamic flow and weather modeling, linear programming, multiple target tracking, and logic simulation for test sequence generation in LSI circuits.

The above discussion has necessarily been brief. For details the reader is referred to References [6] and [7]. The notion of an array of processing elements under control of a single control unit is interesting and worth including. It is the view of the authors that the usefulness of this concept is not limited to huge machines like ILLIAC IV. A smaller array of processors might be efficiently dedicated to any of a variety of special-purpose applications.

Another class of large special-purpose computer seems to be suited to the same set of applications as is ILLIAC IV. These are super-pipeline machines. The CDC STAR is the first of these machines to become operational. The pipeline processor, illustrated figuratively in Fig. 15.18, gains its advantage by starting the retrieval of subsequent sets of operands, each located in memory adjacent to the first, before the first result has been returned to memory. To take maximum advantage of the pipeline concept, data on which similar operations are to be performed must be arranged in adjacent locations in memory. Thus, such sets of identical operations must actually exist in the application algorithm, as they will, to a sufficient extent, in those applications pointed out in the above discussion of ILLIAC IV.

The arithmetic unit of Fig. 15.18 is arranged to perform arithmetic in pipeline form (see Section 14.8). In the special-purpose pipeline processor, the memory read and write operations are also overlapped in pipeline form.

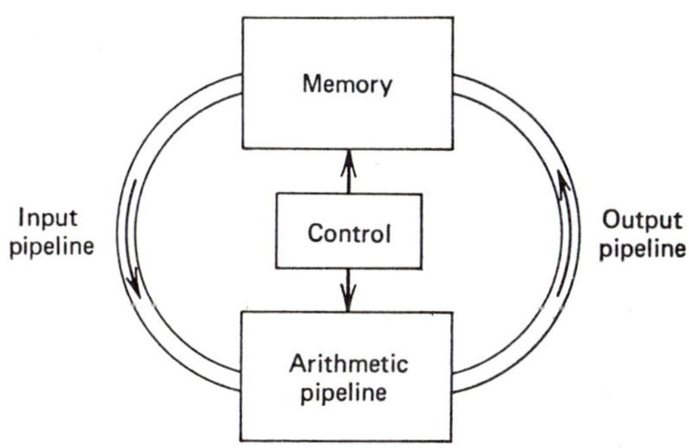

FIGURE 15.18. Pipeline processor.

Thus retrieval, arithmetic, and storage operations are performed in step as data move around the loop in Fig. 15.18. In most cases, all data in the pipeline must be subject to the same arithmetic operation. As an exception, the CDC STAR can perform the inner or dot product of two vectors as their elements pass through the pipeline in pairs.

Reference [8] attempts to compare ILLIAC IV and the CDC STAR with each other and with a more conventional large machine. The issue is left somewhat in doubt. Final verdict must await extended operation of the two machines in a production environment. Much will depend on software development and the skill at efficient use of the machines eventually achieved by programmers.

PROBLEMS

15.1 Write control sequences for execution of the following two additional commands which could be included in the display processor of Section 15.3. Assume separate flip-flops for these commands similar to ***go*** and ***erase***.

a) Erase one line of characters.

b) Erase entire screen.

15.2 Modify the control sequence of the display processor so that it is not necessary to reset the ***erase*** flip-flop manually. Allow for one pass through the memory in search of lines and characters beginning at the specified point.

15.3 (For electrical engineers.) Design the line segment generator used in the display processor. Use gates, flip-flops, operational amplifiers, and FET analog switches. Your outputs should be the inputs of the vertical and horizontal deflection amplifiers and the beam emission control. (Assume typical signal levels.)

15.4 Suppose that 32-bit accuracy is required in a particular digital filter application, so that fifty 100-nsec clock periods are required to accomplish one addition and one multiplication. Suppose that the same accuracy requirement dictates the inclusion of 15 numerator and 15 denominator coefficients. Suppose a 100-nsec clock period special-purpose digital filter is designed to meet these specifications. What will be the maximum allowable input frequency?

15.5 Suppose that it is desired that the coefficients, b_i, in the digital filter of Section 15.4 be entered as positive numbers rather than in two's-complement $(2^{16} - x)$. Modify individual steps in the control sequence to permit this user convenience.

15.6 Modify the control sequence of the digital filter so that additions and subtractions are done double precision, using the full 32-bit products. Noting that all arithmetic is done in integer format, what is the advantage of this approach? Define registers as required.

15.7 Redesign the digital filter of Section 15.4, eliminating the memory address counter ***MAC***. Rather than addressing the memory matrices, obtain the proper arguments by shifting rows. A 3-bit counter, ***MC***, will be required to count the number of multiplications.

15.8 Assume that the key for the first block of a file as described in Fig. 15.7 sometimes serves as an overall key for the file. Write the control sequence for an instruction which will arrange the addresses of these file keys in the first several memory locations in descending order of key magnitude. Is an address required for this instruction? If not, suggest ways in which the address bits might be used to specify variations of the basic instruction.

15.9 Write a subroutine in SIC assembly language which will accomplish the sort function described in Section 15.6. Merely lengthen the SIC word length to 21 bits so that 16 bits can be used to address a 64k memory. Assume that the basic clock rates and memory access times are the same for SIC and the sort processor. Compare the actual times required to accomplish the sort operation by the two methods.

15.10 Write the combinational logic subroutine LARGER used in Section 15.6. Arrange the logic network so that most of it is also applicable to instruction 65 (octal).

15.11 Suppose the slave processor in the time-sharing system of Fig. 15.12 is organized so that two user programs can be stored in memory at one time. While one of the programs is being executed, the other may be replaced by a new program from the queue in the disk memory. Assume that a special DMA control sequencer is included in the slave for this purpose. Suppose a more economical disk memory system, requiring some head movement, is used so that the average swap time, t_s, is 100 msec. Replot Fig. 15.13a and b taking these changes into consideration.

Would it be advantageous to include a larger RAM in the slave so that up to five user programs could be stored at once? Why? Under what circumstances? How would this affect Fig. 15.13?

15.12 Assume an average compilation time of 0.5 sec and an execution time of 3 sec. How many terminals may be handled by the modified version of Fig. 15.12 discussed in problem 15.11, if a 15-min wait for a run would be tolerated and 50% of the terminals are active in peak periods?

15.13 Write the portion of the control sequencer for the master computer in Fig. 15.12 which assembles lines of characters in a temporary file in disk storage. A special character is supplied by the teletype to indicate the end of a line. Define registers, buses, and buffer storage as needed. The configuration should be economically reasonable. (Hint: The only character whose contents is of any interest to this sequencer is the end-of-line character (carriage return).) The sequencer must keep track of the number of lines in each file so that users can be warned when approaching file limits.

Software in the master will accomplish editing and issue warnings. Suggest an approach for integrating the above control sequencer with the primary sequencer for executing instructions.

15.14 Lay out a minicomputer version of ILLIAC IV. Assume that a single control unit will control eight processors, each processing the approximate capability of SIC. Status flip-flops and a routing network must be included. Assume the processors to be arranged in a line.

Specify all registers required in the processors and the controller. Define a complete list of commands for the system. Include commands for routing data between the control memory and the individual processor memories. Also include commands providing for the testing and setting of status bits.

REFERENCES

1. Watson, R. W., et al., "A Design of a Display Processor," *Proceedings AFIPS Fall Joint Computer Conference*, 1969, p. 209.

2. Wait, J. V., "Digital Filters," Chapter 5 of *Active Filters Lumped, Distributed, Integrated Digital* and *Parametric*, by L. P. Huelsman, McGraw-Hill, New York, 1970.

3. Barsamian, H., "Firmware Sort Processor with LSI Components," *Proceedings AFIPS Spring Joint Computer Conference*, 1970, p. 183.

4. Heath, J. R., and Carroll, C. C., "Special-Purpose Computer Organization for Double-Precision Realization of Digital Filters," *IEEE Trans. Computers*, Dec. 1970, p. 1146.

5. Reiner, R. E., *The Design of a Time Sharing Computer System Using Iverson Notation*, M.S. Thesis, University of Arizona, 1970.

6. Barnes, G. H., et al., "The ILLIAC IV Computer," *IEEE Trans. Computers*, August 1968, p. 746.

7. McIntyre, D. E., "An Introduction to the ILLIAC IV Computer," *Datamation*, April 1970.
8. Graham, W. R., "The Parallel and the Pipeline Computers," *Datamation*, April 1970, p. 68.
9. Brooks, F. E., "A Versatile Controller for Data Communications," *Computer Design*, February 1970, p. 67.
10. Machover, Carl, "Graphic CRT Terminals—characteristics of commercially available equipment," *Proceedings AFIPS Fall Joint Computer Conference*, 1967, p. 149.

APPENDIX

Sophistications in Control Unit Hardware

Throughout the body of the book we have consistently assumed an easily-understood pulse-oriented control unit. Our goal was to present an accurate and complete, although perhaps inefficient, physical picture. It was freely admitted that refinements might be required to permit the most economical control delay implementation in terms of a given family of logic components. If small-scale bipolar IC's are used, one would very likely use clocked flip-flops throughout the system. The use of clocked flip-flops necessitates some form of level-oriented control unit, as discussed in Section 7.10.

In Section 7.10 we observed a second advantage of a level-oriented control unit in addition to compatibility with clocked flip-flops; it is possible to use classical sequential circuit techniques to minimize and possibly reduce the cost of sections of this type of control unit. A third very important advantage of level control is flexibility in establishing bus connections. *No separate bus control flip-flops are necessary.* The level outputs from the control sequencer may be used directly to switch inputs onto the ***ABUS***, for example. A version of Fig. 6.13 revised according to this assumption is given in Fig. A.1. To simplify the illustration, D-type flip-flops are shown in the hypothetical control unit.

It is possible to connect fewer than the maximum number of bits to a bus.

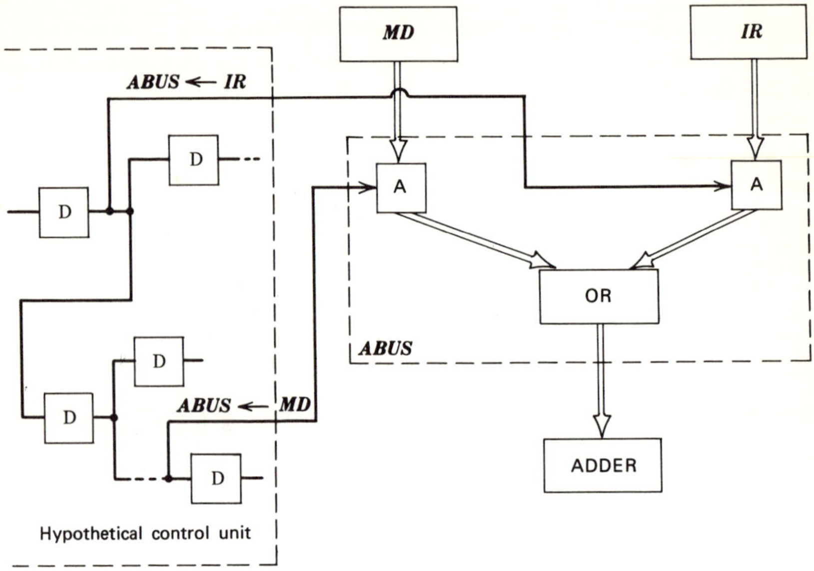

FIGURE A.1. Direct control of busing.

For example, one might use

$$ABUS_0 \leftarrow 1$$

as a step preliminary to setting the sign bit in a register to 1. If a 5-bit argument is to be transferred through the bus to a register such as *MC*, one could use

$$\omega^5/ABUS \leftarrow \overline{\epsilon(5)}$$

to cause connections to be made to the last five bits of the ***ABUS*** only. Notice that there is no overlap between the bus bits involved in the above two statements. In combination they add no more than one to the fan-in of any gate. Bits in the center of the bus can even be used to effect special connections between short registers without affecting the fan-in of gates at either end of the bus. With direct connections to the control sequencer, subsets of bits may be assigned connections to the bus at will throughout the design process. It is necessary only to assure that the fan-in limitation of no single gate on the bus is exceeded. It is *not* necessary to make a list of all bus input vectors at the beginning of the design process to permit set up of a bus control register and decoder.

It is interesting to note that the discussion in the above paragraph does not apply to microprogrammed control units. We recall from Chapter 8 that all bus connections must be tabulated in advance so that certain sets of bits in the microinstruction may be assigned to specify connections to the various buses. This usually has the effect of limiting the variety of bus transfers which can be employed.

If we permit some additional refinements in the level-oriented control unit, it is possible to achieve a hardware saving and an apparent speed improvement over the simple pulse-oriented control unit discussed in Chapter 7. A two-step segment of a modified level control unit is illustrated in Fig. A.2a. The level signal at the output of flip-flop 1 is used to gate the instruction

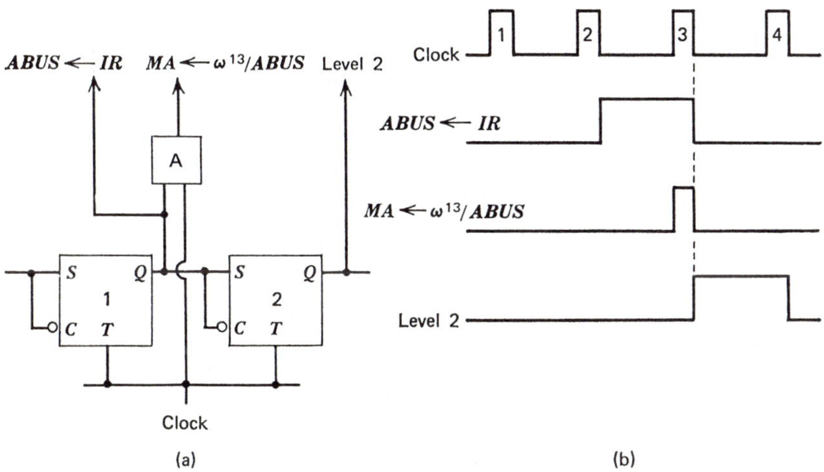

FIGURE A.2. Level-pulse control unit.

register onto the ***ABUS***. As shown in Fig. A.2b this level develops immediately following the trailing edge of clock pulse 2. It remains 1 for one clock period. At the end of the clock period, the level is ANDed with clock pulse 3 to generate the pulse labeled $MA \leftarrow \omega^{13}/ABUS$. It is this pulse which effects the specified transfer of data from the ***ABUS*** to ***MA***. Notice that a data word is switched onto the bus and into the destination register all in one clock period. Apparently this represents a 50% savings in time over the two-step process described for the pulse-oriented control unit. Actually this time saving is something of an illusion. The same saving can be achieved in pulse-oriented systems by carefully overlapping each bus setup operation with the previous transfer into a register.

A very real hardware saving can be achieved in certain cases by using clocked (pulsed) register flip-flops in conjunction with control units such as Fig. A.2a. Suppose the only data input to register ***MA*** is from the ***ABUS***. The familiar configurations using flip-flops without separate clock or pulse

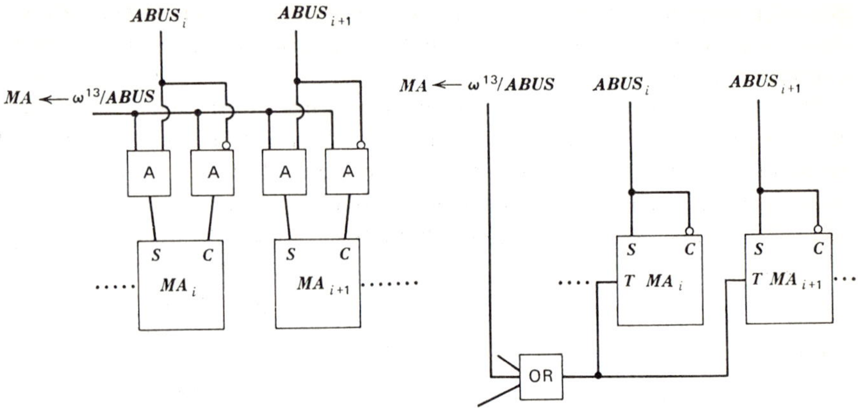

(a) Non-pulsed flip-flops (b) Pulsed flip-flops

FIGURE A.3

inputs is given in Fig. A.3a. The pulsed flip-flops in Fig. A.3b will accomplish exactly the same function. The array of AND gates is not needed in the latter case. In effect, the ANDing of the pulse is internal to the flip-flops. If implementation is in terms of LSI, there may be little difference in the two configurations. If implementation is in terms of SSI (individually packaged IC gates and flip-flops), a reduced package count is achieved by realizing Fig. A.3b. Where inputs must be switched into a register from more than one origin, the AND gates are necessary anyway; and no saving is derived from the use of clocked flip-flops.

A clock pulse must pass through two or more levels of gating before it arrives at the pulse input of a register flip-flop. In some cases, where the

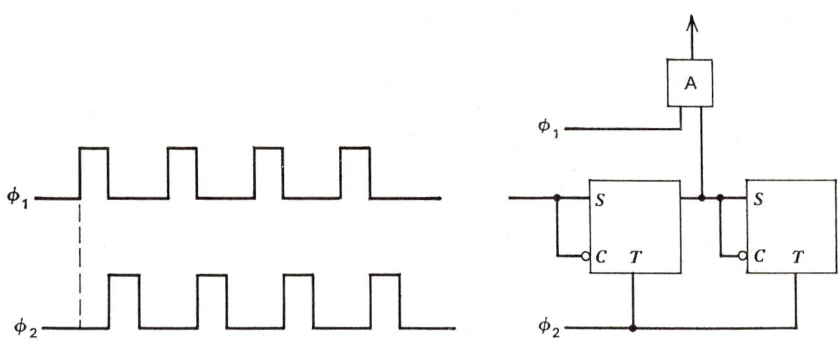

(a) (b)

FIGURE A.4. Two-phase clocking.

statistical variation in gate delays is unfavorable, input values may begin to change before the transfer pulse arrives at a register flip-flop. We see that this is possible by observing that clock pulse 3 also causes the control level, ***ABUS* ← *IR***, to return to zero. The problem is easily avoided by using a form of a two-phase clock, as illustrated in Fig. A.4. Clock phase ϕ_1 goes to 1 slightly ahead of clock phase ϕ_2. Phase ϕ_1 triggers information from a bus into a register. Since ϕ_2 is delayed, the transfer will occur before ϕ_2 causes the control level to advance in the control unit. The delay, Δ, associated with ϕ_2 may be set so that the register transfer always occurs before the control level is advanced. Phase ϕ_2 can be generated from ϕ_1 by simple gate delays. The total amount of wiring is essentially not increased by including ϕ_2. Finally, the overall lengthening of the clock period and slowing of the clock rate caused by adding the second clock phase could be kept very small.

Index